Ecumenical Encounters
with Desmond Mpilo Tutu

REGNUM STUDIES IN MISSION

Series Preface

Regnum Studies in Mission are born from the lived experience of Christians and Christian communities in mission, especially but not solely in the fast growing churches among the poor of the world. These churches have more to tell than stories of growth. They are making significant impacts on their cultures in the cause of Christ. They are producing 'cultural products' which express the reality of Christian faith, hope and love in their societies.

Regnum Studies in Mission are the fruit often of rigorous research to the highest international standards and always of authentic Christian engagement in the transformation of people and societies. And these are for the world. The formation of Christian theology, missiology and practice in the twenty-first century will depend to a great extent on the active participation of growing churches contributing biblical and culturally appropriate expressions of Christian practice to inform World Christianity.

Cover Design

The imagery of the book cover design is inspired by three key elements in Archbishop Tutu's life: his faith, social justice and his sense of humour. His faith is captured by the symbols of his priestly collar and a purposefully rugged cross, to indicate a shared cross of suffering.

Silhouetted by people with raised hands of worship, as well as raised fists in protest against injustice, the imagery acknowledges his role as prophet and priest.

His warm, inviting smile with a twinkle in his eyes captures a hallmark of his character: his disarming humour, which offers the gift of peace in tense situations, and the dignity that is derived from an ethic of Ubuntu.

The intentional use of the colour purple is because it is derived from the serene tranquillity of blue, and the spirited, feisty energies of red, thus representing the dual commitment of the Arch to both peace and justice.

The Dollie House | Visual Anthropology | www.dolliehouse.com

REGNUM STUDIES IN MISSION

Ecumenical Encounters
with Desmond Mpilo Tutu

Visions for Justice, Dignity and Peace

Sarojini Nadar, Tinyiko Maluleke, Dietrich Werner,
Vicentia Kgabe, Rudolf Hinz (Editors)

Foreword by Piyushi Kotecha

First published 2021 by Regnum Books International
Co-published with UWC Press

Regnum is an imprint of the Oxford Centre for Mission Studies
St. Philip and St. James Church
Woodstock Road
Oxford OX2 6HR, UK
https://www.regnumbooks.net/

09 08 07 06 05 04 03 8 7 6 5 4 3 2 1

The rights of Sarojini Nadar, Tinyiko Maluleke, Dietrich Werner, Vicentia Kgabe and Rudolf Hinz to be
identified as the Editors of this Work have been asserted by them in accordance with the Copyright,
Designs and Patents Act 1988.

Copyright © Regnum Books 2021

Produced in partnership with
The Desmond Tutu Centre for Religion and Social Justice, University of the Western Cape and
Bread for the World

British Library Cataloguing in Publication Data
A catalogue record for this book is available from the British Library

ISBN 978-1-5064-8896-7

ISBN 978-1-990995-06-4 UWC Press
ISBN 978-1-990995-07-1 E-version
https://doi.org/10.52779/9781990995071

Typeset by Words by Design Ltd
www.wordsbydesign.co.uk

Cover design by The Dollie House, Visual Anthropology

Distributed by 1517 Media in the US, Canada, India, and Brazil

CONTENTS

PART III: PEACE

3.1. Prayer and Politics

3.2. Reconciliation and Resistance

3.3. Religious Diversity and Plural Spirituality

ACKNOWLEDGEMENTS

We are grateful to Rev. Edwin Arrison of the Desmond and Leah Tutu Legacy Foundation (DLTLF), who first responded positively to the initiative to publish a book honouring Archbishop Desmond Tutu on his ninetieth birthday on 7th October 2021 and also initially suggested several authors.

We are deeply thankful to Piyushi Kotecha, the CEO of the DLTLF for her great support and encouragement.

Our authors hail from many countries reflecting the world-wide ecumenical community Desmond Tutu enjoyed and nurtured: South Africa, Kenya, Malawi, Switzerland, Germany, Denmark, Sweden, Norway, New Zealand, the United Kingdom and the USA.

The collection of voices included in this volume was due to suggestions by several friends who proposed names of additional persons who had been in contact with Desmond Tutu and/or were touched by his witness and work: Brian Brown suggested authors from the UK, USA and New Zealand, Hans Engdahl for Scandinavia, Ulrich Duchrow for the German scene of anti-apartheid activists and Dietrich Werner for the worldwide Oikumene.

We also express our gratitude for financial support and encouragement by certain institutions without which this publication would not have been possible, such as the University of Western Cape (UWC), South Africa, especially the Desmond Tutu Centre for Religion and Social Justice; Bread for the World, development and relief agency of the Protestant churches in Germany, Berlin; the Association of Protestant Churches and Missions in Germany (EMW), Hamburg; and friends in our churches who supported us with considerable donations, but wanted to remain anonymous.

The opinions articulated in this volume express the voices of individual authors in their articles, not necessarily in each detail the opinions of the funding partners or publishers.

We express our gratitude particularly to individual staff from supporting institutions who assisted us administratively in the editorial work and financial facilitation for this volume: Ferial Marlie (UWC), Daniel Kinigopoulos, Janna Lang and Martina Grassmel (Bread for the World), Lucy Howe Lopez and Obiora Ike (providing technical support via Globethics.net).

Rhine Phillip Tsobotsi Koloti, a Master's student working at the Desmond Tutu Centre for Religion and Social Justice, provided diligent, meticulous and constant assistance with the management of different versions of texts, communication with authors and overall technical assistance with a manuscript this large. We are deeply indebted to him for his tireless dedication and commitment.

We sincerely thank Mrs Cynthia Lies, and Mr Mark Shortland for their excellent voluntary support in translating several texts from German to English.

We also express our sincere gratitude to both of our publishers Wikus van Zyl (UWC Press, South Africa) and Tony Gray and Paul Bendor-Samuel (Regnum Books, UK) who accepted our book project and agreed to make this volume available in time for the celebrations planned for 7th October 2021, the birthday of Desmond Tutu. In addition to supporting our own editing, they provided expert peer reviewers and language editors who ensured that the manuscript met rigorous scholarly standards.

This project has enjoyed support and encouragement from various church leaders and ecumenical representatives:

Archbishop of the Anglican Church of Southern Africa, Thabo Makgoba;

Assistant General Secretary of the World Council of Churches, Geneva, Dr Isabel Phiri;

General Secretary of the South African Council of Churches, Johannesburg, Bishop Malusi Mpumlwana;

General Secretary of the All Africa Council of Churches, Nairobi, Dr Fidon Mwombeki.

Last, but not least, we express our gratitude to all the authors, some of whom have been lifetime friends of Desmond Tutu, for their remarkable contributions that honour the living legacy of a person whose lifetime commitment to justice, dignity and peace, deserves to be memorialised.

Thank You! Enkosi Kakhulu! Vielen Dank!

The editors

Sarojini Nadar, Editor, with 'The Arch'

Tinyiko Maluleke, Editor   *Dietrich Werner, Editor*

Vicentia Kgabe,   *Rudolf Hinz,*   *Rhine Phillip Tsobotsi Koloti*
Editor   *Editor*   *Admin research assistant*

FOREWORD
A TEXTURED TAPESTRY OF HOPE AND LEARNING WORLDWIDE

Piyushi Kotecha[1]

In his foreword to Michael Battle's most recent book on Desmond Tutu as South Africa's spiritual confessor, the Dalai Lama congratulates the author and expresses the wish that Battle's book will "encourage further endeavours to know more about spiritual leaders who impact the world with joy, and who aim to bring about genuine and lasting peace in our world."[2] Indeed, this present book represents one of those "further endeavours" which the Dalai Lama expresses a longing for. It is my joy, therefore, to recommend this inspiring collection of contributions from around the world, just in time to form part of the celebrations that we have planned for Archbishop Tutu's 90th birthday.

The chief goal of the Desmond and Leah Tutu Legacy Foundation (DLTLF) is to safeguard and promote the living legacy of Archbishop Emeritus Desmond Tutu and Mrs Leah Tutu for posterity. It is our determination to ensure that this legacy should be galvanised in a rich, powerful, textured tapestry of hope and learning worldwide.

This book, in many ways, represents some of the most significant strands of that textured tapestry, especially from the rich and precious archives that document the time that the Arch spent working in various ecumenical settings, including the South African Council of Churches, the All Africa Conference of Churches and the World Council of Churches in the late 70s and early 80s. This was a profoundly formative period in his life, and the sincere and heart-warming ecumenical recollections of this era, from his counterparts internationally, continentally and locally, is certainly a timely addition to the wealth of publications which depict the remarkable legacy of the Arch. We are proud to be associated with this initiative, as it aligns harmoniously with the Foundation's "knowledge legacy programme."

That being said, there is another reason to commend this book, and that is the intentional effort of the editors to include a younger and more diverse group of contributors, who may have not had personal encounters with Tutu, but whose work and witness are powerfully impacted by him. These diverse contributions represent the Arch's commitment to generous and generative inclusion, and indeed his staunch devotion to new and critical voices. Their inclusion means that this collection presents a bridge between past and present struggles for justice, peace and dignity, struggles which unfortunately did not disappear with the demise of apartheid, nor with the conclusion of the Truth and Reconciliation Commission that was so ably led by the Archbishop.

I therefore warmly commend this book for its rich, distinctive and persuasive accounts of encounters with the Archbishop that transformed individuals' personal and public faith, their social lives and their political and scholarly commitments. It certainly enriches the remarkable legacy of an outstanding human being, imbued with an undoubtedly exceptional range of unique and powerful characteristics and embraced and respected capaciously on global and national stages.

---

[1] Piyushi Kotecha is the CEO of the Desmond and Leah Tutu Legacy Foundation.
[2] His Holiness the 14th Dalai Lama of Tibet. Foreword in Michael Battle, *Desmond Tutu: A Spiritual Biography of South Africa's Confessor* (Westminster, John Knox Press, 2021), p. vii.

INTRODUCTION
A MORAL CONSTITUTION FOR JUSTICE, DIGNITY AND PEACE

Sarojini Nadar[1]

An occasion to honour "the Arch"

Archbishop Emeritus Desmond Mpilo Tutu, "the Arch" as he is fondly known in South Africa, ordained as an Anglican priest in 1960, and a global icon who has worked tirelessly in the pursuit of justice, peace and dignity, is turning ninety on 7 October 2021. Our aim, in this book, is to capture what his life and witness signify in a world still clinging to, and longing for, visions for justice, dignity and peace.

We are convinced that the visions for South Africa and for humanity which Archbishop Desmond Tutu embodied in his life and witness are of ongoing relevance and contextual significance today – particularly in a context in which key elements of this vision currently seem to be betrayed and not fully lived out. Honouring "the Arch" therefore is not just a gesture of deep respect and gratitude to him, it is at the same time a spiritual and political public act of hope that his visions will be remembered in future generations and that his faith will inspire leaders in churches, civil society and political organisations for a future in justice, peace and dignity in South Africa and beyond.

The current social and political context

This book is conceived and compiled during a global pandemic that brought the entire world to its knees. Many scholars[2] have noted that the COVID-19 pandemic did not create inequities and iniquities, as much as it simply revealed and perhaps exacerbated existing injustices, causing some to declare that "we need a moral constitution for our planet's health."[3] At the time of writing, South Africa has less than 5% of its population vaccinated due to the limitation of vaccines, while in many so-called first world countries which have over-stocked on vaccines, citizens still debate the efficacy of the vaccines, and invoke their rights not to get vaccinated. The pandemic indeed invites us to consider how we advocate for access to healthcare as a moral imperative.

While the pandemic rages on in South Africa, we also experienced shadow pandemics of gender-based violence as well as political violence. On 17 June 2020, the state president of South Africa, Cyril Ramaphosa, made one of his regular COVID-19 addresses to the nation. We had come to expect these addresses to be sombre in detailing the scale of the escalating pandemic in the country. This address was even more grave because, added to his regular updates on the pandemic, the president called on the nation to acknowledge gender-based violence as a second pandemic in the country – one as serious, or if not more serious, than the coronavirus. Adopting a tone even more grave than his usual pandemic address tone, he stated: "It is with the heaviest of hearts that I stand

---

[1] This introduction was written by Sarojini Nadar, on behalf of all the editors. The editing of the entire book was a collective effort by all the editors. Sarojini Nadar is the director of the Desmond Tutu Centre for Religion and Social Justice at the University of the Western Cape, where she also holds a research chair and professorship.
[2] See for examples: Ferdinand C. Mukumbang, Anthony N. Ambe and Babatope O. Adebiyi. "Unspoken Inequality: How COVID-19 Has Exacerbated Existing Vulnerabilities of Asylum-Seekers, Refugees, and Undocumented Migrants in South Africa". *International Journal for Equity in Health* 19, no. 1 (2020): 1-7; Jaime A. Teixeira da Silva. "Stigmatization, Discrimination, Racism, Injustice, and Inequalities in the COVID-19 Era". *International Journal of Health Policy and Management* 9, no. 11 (2020): 484.
[3] Jennifer Prah Ruger. "The Injustice of COVID-19: We Need a Moral Constitution for Our Planet's Health". *The Lancet Planetary Health* 4, no. 7 (2020): e264-e265.

before the women and girls of South Africa this evening to talk about another pandemic that is raging in our country – the killing of women and children by the men of our country … At a time when the pandemic has left us all feeling vulnerable and uncertain, violence is being unleashed on women and children with a brutality that defies comprehension."[4]

Almost a year after his address on gender-based violence, the president again made a special address to the country on 12 July 2021, on the violent insurrection that resulted in unrest and looting in KwaZulu-Natal and Gauteng. Several commentators noted that the unrest and looting that was initiated by the arrest of former president Jacob Zuma on failing to appear in court on corruption charges was actually pointing to a larger problem beyond support for the former president. The pandemic amplified the growing economic inequities and unemployment which disproportionately affect the poor and black people, and are directly related to the failure of the democratic state to provide basic health, education and employment for the majority of its citizens. Instead, as Ronnie Kasrils observed: "immense wealth remained with a few white capitalists, and a new, super-rich class of black tycoons."

Political analyst Eusebius McKaiser sums it up well: "Thus, the immediate spark for this instability might have been Zuma's imprisonment. But Zuma is ultimately a spent political force. There is a more human factor at play here. Millions of black South Africans living under conditions of poverty do not have a stake in Nelson Mandela's nominally free South Africa. They have no reason to be excited about waking up tomorrow. They have dim prospects of self-actualization. They do not stand to lose reputations or careers if they are found guilty of public violence and theft, because you can only lose that which you have. They lack hope and confidence in the government, because the political investment in the ANC since 1994 has not delivered on its much-touted political slogan of 'A Better Life for All.'"[5]

The fight against injustice and oppression as a moral and religious imperative

Collecting the narratives of ecumenical encounters with Desmond Tutu in the shadow of a global health crisis, gender-based violence, increased racism, black poverty and political instability seems ironic because, while many of the recollections in this book hearken to decades before democracy, the current situation in South Africa reveals that we are certainly nowhere close to the rainbow utopia envisioned by Desmond Tutu. The fight against injustice and oppression must continue as a profoundly religious and moral imperative because, as the Arch himself says: "To oppose injustice and oppression is not something that is merely political. No, it is profoundly religious. Can you imagine what that Gospel means to people whose dignity is trodden underfoot every day of their life, to those who have had their noses rubbed in the dust as if they didn't count? Can you think of anything more subversive of a situation of injustice and oppression? Why should you need Marxist ideology or whatever? The Bible is dynamite in such a situation. In South Africa, when they banned books, we told the government the book they should have banned long ago was the Bible, for nothing could be more radical, more revolutionary as we faced up to the awfulness of injustice, oppression and racism."[6]

This powerful statement by the Archbishop is a haunting reminder of the work that remains to be done. In this book, his significant contributions in the areas of theology, ethics, politics and African and global ecumenism are celebrated and commemorated through Archbishop Tutu's involvement with the World Council of Churches, the All Africa Conference of Churches, the South African Council of Churches and many other ecumenical bodies.

---

[4] Address by President Cyril Ramaphosa on South Africa's response to the Coronavirus Pandemic, 17 June 2020. The Presidency, Available at: https://www.gov.za/speeches/president-cyril-ramaphosa-south-africa%E2%80%99s-response-covid-19-coronavirus-pandemic-17-jun-2020 (accessed 14 September 2021).

[5] Eusebius McKaiser, "Don't Overlook the Deeper Roots Behind the Violence and Looting in South Africa" in the *Washington Post,* 14 July 2021.

[6] Desmond Tutu. *The Essential Desmond Tutu*. No. 85. New Africa Books (1997), 9.

The background of this volume

This collection of essays and other creative self-expressions to honour the life and work of Tutu emerged from an initiative of two German theologians, Rudolf Hinz and Dietrich Werner, who planned to celebrate and commemorate the 90th birthday of the Archbishop by gathering narratives of ecumenical and engaged encounters in the pursuit of justice and peace, in Europe and beyond. They approached a few South African scholars, Sarojini Nadar, Tinyiko Maluleke and Vicentia Kgabe, who had already been working on similar projects within their own spheres of work, to collaborate on the project. The end result of this cooperation is this inspiring collection of critical and creative contributions honouring the life and work of Desmond Mpilo Tutu. Each editor worked exceptionally hard (within tight deadlines demanded by the complexities of the COVID pandemic) to shape and mould the contributions to fit into the overall thrust of the book. We were proficiently assisted by Rhine Phillip Tsobotsi Koloti, our administrative research assistant, to whom we owe a great deal of gratitude.

The South African editors joined the collaboration with the understanding that the editorial relationship will be characterised by principles of mutuality and reciprocity, and a deep respect for an intersectional, decolonial framing. As such, it was important to the editorial collective to emphasise a diversity of voices, regions and thematic content. We were determined to include a range of younger and more diverse voices whose lives have been impacted by Desmond Tutu. As a result, the voices of many other folk who have also had significant encounters with the Arch could not be included due also to the limitations of space. Their encounters certainly bear telling, and we know that those important narratives will find a home in other similar collections. We are confident that our decision to intentionally include newer and more diverse voices is in line with the Arch's lifelong commitment to not just make more space at the table, but to graciously extend, and thereby courageously transform the shape of the table. Many of these younger contributors have never met Desmond Tutu in person, but their work for justice, and their scholarship and witness have been inspired by him and his work. While we consciously and conscientiously invited newer voices to the table, we also balanced this with the remarkable recollections of colleagues who are themselves in the seventh, eighth and ninth decades of their lives. We are particularly pleased, therefore, that we have been able to compile the narratives of those who have personally met and interacted with the Arch through "ecumenical encounters" and those who have had "engaging encounters" with his work and witness, and have been inspired by it.

Bringing together wider ecumenical perspectives

Our call for contributions was intentionally framed with a view to sourcing imaginative and creative self-expressions from people who have encountered the Arch's work and life in ecumenical settings. We intentionally conceptualised the construct of "ecumenism" beyond the unity of churches, to also broadly include a unity of multiple faith traditions towards the shared goals of peace and justice. Desmond Tutu's life and work has shaped not just the contours of ecumenical encounters between churches, but also created an ethical landscape of multiple faith traditions. His book *God is not a Christian and other Provocations*[7] bears testament to his commitment to collegial collaboration and deeply engaged and robust engagement with various faith traditions. He has influenced generations of theologians, scholars, people of all faiths and people with no faith. Our best efforts notwithstanding, we did not succeed in compiling and showcasing a comprehensive repertoire of the Arch's encounters with multiple faith traditions in the limited timeframe available. This constitutes a certain limitation in this book, and a reminder that this work remains to be done. Beyond constituting a limitation, it is also an important reminder for those of us who work within ecumenical paradigms to be aware of the ways in which the goal of the "unity of the churches" might unintentionally reinscribe Christian-normative ways of being that can sometimes lead to at best, a lack of respect for

---

[7] Desmond Tutu. *God is Not a Christian: and Other Provocations.* San Francisco: Harper Collins (2011).

religious diversity and at worst, outright violence.[8] Lee Scharnick-Udemans' essay in this book explores such religious privilege and calls our attention to the ways in which Christianity is rendered normative through seemingly innocuous concepts like the "rainbow". Her comparison between white privilege and religious privilege and the case studies of prejudices in France and South Africa regarding the choice of women to wear headscarves, is an important prompt to "check our religious privilege" especially the ways in which our engagements might reinscribe normativities. Charles Villa-Vicencio's essay, despite observing the tyranny of Christian theocracy, notes the Arch's ability to drink from his own wells while advocating for theological and religious plurality and ultimately recognising the mystery and unknowability of God.

Another limitation of this book, perhaps, is that we did not manage to depict "herstory" as well as we could have. Mpho Tutu van Furth's short, but hauntingly beautiful, photo-essay draws our attention to the deeply fundamental and central role that her mother played in the Tutu story. In this unusual photo taken at Mpho's marriage ceremony, it is Ma Leah who is foregrounded. Both Nyambura Njoroge and Mpho Tutu van Furth remind us about the neglect of herstory. Njoroge notes that Tutu "…made 48 visits to 25 countries within 3 years. I could not help but wonder what his beloved Leah and children felt and said to him when he showed up at the door. I would love to hear the Herstory of Leah Tutu." Indeed, this herstory bears telling and is important legacy work that remains to be done.

Combining oral history and written history, real-life stories and theological reflection

Despite the aforementioned limitations, we are still pleased to offer here the perspectives and stories of those whose personal and academic encounters with "the Arch" have shaped their ongoing faith-based, activist and academic pursuits for justice and peace. The book is meant to be a memorial recollection of encounters with the Arch, rather than an academic *festschrift*. Hence our call for contributions included, but was not restricted to, the format of a typical academic essay. Anyone familiar with his outstanding contributions to the promotion of justice, dignity and peace, will know that a hallmark of Desmond Tutu's celebrated style is his use of narrative and real-life stories. In honour of his unique and remarkable example, the contributions in this book combine oral history and written history paradigms, as well as sociological, philosophical and theological approaches, all inspired by the style of the Arch. Many of the contributions follow in the style and methodology of writing that Gottfried Kraatz describes in his contribution to this book as follows: "I dive into my memory, not into files or books that were written then or later about this particular time of Bishop Desmond Tutu. I call up a recollection, very subjective and certainly flawed, but most importantly authentic from me." Likewise, in this book, you will find an abundant array of contributions which are at once narrative, creative, artistic, imaginative, innovative, inspiring and scholarly, but most importantly – they are authentic encounters.

A thematic survey

It was difficult to divide the book into thematic focus areas because each of the contributions overlap in multiple ways. This too is testament of the far-reaching and wide-ranging commitments that the Arch has held close to his heart over the years. The poems offered by Betty Govinden and Wilma Jakobsen deftly depict the web of connections between the myriad struggles for social justice that the Arch concerned himself with. That being said, we can broadly categorise the contributions into the three visions we have chosen for the book: justice, dignity and peace. What emerges from almost every single one of the seventy-one contributions which draw on an encounter with Tutu and his

---

[8] See also, the essay by Fulata Moyo and Sarojini Nadar. "Editorial: Gendered Perspectives on the Busan 10th Assembly Theme on Justice and Peace", *Ecumenical Review* 64, no.3 (2012): 233-240. In their essay they argue that the singular goal of church unity within ecumenical settings often leads to the promotion of social injustices.

work is that his visions for justice, dignity and peace are present not *in spite* of his deep spirituality and sense of prayer, but *because* of it. This element of spirituality is therefore the sacred thread that weaves each of the pieces of this tapestry of the Arch's life together.

Justice, liberation, transformation

The vision for justice that derives from a strong theological and faith perspective is best described by Wilma Jakobsen, in the conclusion to her essay in this book. She states: "Desmond Tutu has always and is still always unequivocally clear about faith and justice and equality and inclusion – that God is not a man, God is not homophobic, God is not a Christian, and all human beings, all people – all, all, all, are made in the image of God." Her salient assessment of Tutu's vision for justice is at once startling as it is simple: Indeed, God is not a man, not homophobic and not Christian. The various narratives presented in this book about the struggle for racial justice during apartheid invite a small addition to these observations – "God is not a *white* man." This particular appendage is significant, not least of all because the struggle to overcome racism and white supremacy is at the heart of many of the recollections and ideas in this book. While it might be tempting to think that the struggle is over, at the time of writing this introduction, the South African Human Rights Commission reported that up to 90% of complaints it receives annually are about racism.[9] Michael Battle reflects in his essay that: "There is a subtle force to racism that often renders the church inept and on the wrong side of history." This is a strong reminder that the struggle is far from over, even as we recall the important solidarities that developed during the struggle.

For example, several contributors reflect on the transnational solidarity that developed from the Programme to Combat Racism within the World Council of Churches in 1969. Volker Faigle, in his essay, notes: "The All Africa Conference of Churches played a significant role in the dismantling of apartheid in South Africa. It was especially supportive of the 'Programme to Combat Racism' (PCR) which was launched by the Geneva-based World Council of Churches (WCC)." Sebastian Justke, Hildegard Thevs and Gerhard Küsel all relate narratives of their own as well as others' involvement in the anti-apartheid struggle that was made possible via such programmes.

Petra Bosse-Huber also notes how the churches in Germany were galvanised by the PCR to boycott products from South Africa as a means of economic sanctions against racism. Similarly, in a very moving personal account, Nele Trautwein captures how her grandmother, Ursula Trautwein, spurred into action by the banning of the black Women's Federation in South Africa, and her encounters with Desmond Tutu, founded the "Women against Apartheid" group in Frankfurt am Main. She describes how her "grandmother and her sisters from the 'Evangelical Women's Work' began to call for the boycott of fruits from South Africa, in solidarity with the women on site. The 'Boycott Women' group began holding vigils every week on Thursday in front of the South African Consulate."

In more recent years, South Africa recognised and acknowledged the role of the PCR in its anti-apartheid struggles, and particularly the role of Baldwin Sjollema. Sjollema, who was the first director of the PCR, received the Oliver Tambo Order on 16 June 2004 from Thabo Mbeki, South African president at the time. The award, named after African National Congress (ANC) president from 1967 to 1991, is one of the highest forms of recognition that South Africa can bestow on foreigners. The ANC received much of its funding to support its programmes in the 1970s and 1980s from PCR. Reminiscing on their friendship in the WCC in the 70s, Baldwin Sjolemma, in his short essay in this book, recalls Tutu's transformation: "Back in the 1970s Desmond and I were colleagues at the WCC. He was working for the Theological Education Fund (TEF), based in London, while I was working in the controversial Programme to Combat Racism (PCR) in Geneva which supported

---

[9] Alex Mitchley. "Up to 90% of Complaints SAHRC Receives Are About Racism – Commission Hosts Key Conference". News24, 22 June 2021, https://www.news24.com/news24/southafrica/news/up-to-90-of-complaints-sahrc-receives-are-about-racism-commission-hosts-key-conference-20210622 (accessed 10 September 2021).

the liberation movement. We were not always on the same wavelength. At that time Desmond had to be careful not to be too outspoken against the Pretoria regime in order not to burn his bridges at home. But his attitude changed radically after his return to South Africa." Indeed the role of the PCR in helping to support the anti-racism struggle cannot be under-estimated, especially through the financial support it gave to southern Africa.

These public displays of transnational solidarity against racism did not happen in a vacuum. They happened as a result of deep and considered attention to the ways in which the theological frameworks that uphold injustices needed to change. Hence, a key area for transformation and justice was in the area of theological education. Many of the essays in this book point to the critical role that Desmond Tutu played in theological education in the 20th century, especially in his position as associate director of the Theological Education Fund (TEF) between 1972 and 1975. Several authors note that his desire to transform theological education towards a more critical and justice-oriented paradigm was borne out of his extensive travels through almost all the countries in Africa as well as his sojourns to Latin America, where he encountered liberation theology. In many ways, these encounters led to his own transformation too. As Kuzipa Nalwamba notes: "His tours to African countries became a journey of learning and unlearning, and represented a theological turn in his life. That theological turn entailed walking a tightrope as he pursued a theological vision that sought to bring liberation theology and black theology together." Dietrich Werner, too, notes in his essay that Tutu was deeply dedicated and unwavering in his commitment to create a holistic theological education that developed the student not just spiritually but also critically. Werner cites from one of Tutu's travel reports in May 1975 to demonstrate the kind of student that Tutu sought to develop through a critical theological education: "'Our theological education must set out before it is too late to develop the whole personality of the theological student and especially his [sic] critical awareness which has a passion and a reverence for truth and will not be cajoled or threatened to believe something to be true unless it recommends itself as the reasonable thing to conclude on the basis of the available evidence. It will make them ask awkward questions and not be merely conforming and only thus can they ever hope to be creative. Only those ready to challenge the existing orthodoxies have ever advanced men's [sic] knowledge. Only those who have developed a passion for truth can ultimately be expected to become prophetic leaders to speak out against unrighteousness and injustice and oppression without fear and favour.'" Christine Lienemann-Perrin is therefore accurate in her assessment that: "In the early 1970s, the TEF provided the decisive impulse for the development of theology 'in context'. Its funding programmes can be described as the birth of contextual theology, which has since spread worldwide."

Kuzipa Nalwamba sums up the source of a justice-oriented theological education that was a hallmark of Tutu's work well. She says: "The contextuality of reflections gathered from Tutu's work travel underline his aversion towards universalising discourses. It is a thread that runs through his work and one that is especially evident in accounts of how he grappled with black theology and liberation theology against the backdrop of western theologies. Evidently, to him, to know the specificity of a locality or a person is to accord them dignity by naming them with reference to their reality and locating theological reflection within that reality."

Theo Sundermeier also astutely observes in his essay that the value of developing contextuality as a focus in theological education was that it prevented the proliferation of abstract ideas in situations that called for concrete action. He notes: "In this tense situation, Tutu was the one who emphatically warned against following an abstract concept of freedom. This would lead to a functional narrowing of the concept. He preferred to speak of liberation – in Old Testament terms. Freedom is a communal concept, because freedom is indivisible. Black theology not only serves the liberation of black people, but also reveals the lack of freedom of the white oppressors and serves their liberation as well." Reflecting on the development and relevance of liberation theologies and black theologies in democratic societies, Heinrich Bedford-Strohm claims in his essay that: "public theology is liberation theology for a democratic society." Baloyi Tlharihani offers a counter-view in his essay.[10] He concludes that: "for as long as the black experience involves pain and suffering, as it does in South Africa today, Tutu's theology remains relevant in the struggle for dignity and well-being."

Tlharihani's reminder to remain present in the struggle and not to jump too quickly to the proverbial "pat on the back" in light of seeming victories over injustices, is echoed by Traci West, and is a sobering caution to us, as we reflect with gratitude the role that the Arch played in developing and nurturing conscientisation against injustice. West maintains: "Such expressions of gratitude can be too easily reduced to something perfunctory and narrowly dutiful. They can seem like the delivery of a public thank you note that satisfyingly provides an obligatory acknowledgement of a past gift. The ongoing, renewing, dynamic impact of the Archbishop's leadership is lost in this kind of gratitude … It is as if the accomplishments are commodities being recreationally served up to social justice tourists. This type of gratitude fails to nurture the kind of thoughtful birthing of communal right relation that most authentically reflects the Archbishop's change-making leadership …"

David Haslam reminds us in his essay that this justice-seeking, change-making and communal right relation needs to be consistently nurtured, as he reflects on the crucial role of economic justice in the Kingdom of God, drawing important parallels between the economic sanctions against the South African apartheid state and economic sanctions needed today against the state of Israel occupying the Palestinian territories. Ulrich Duchrow also draws lessons from this case study of resistance in South Africa for the current settler—colonialist occupation and land justice question in Palestine. Brian Brown reminds us in his essay that: "Few church leaders outside of Palestine have made themselves as conversant with these developments as the Arch. Few have told the dual narratives of Palestinian dispossession and Israeli domination so compellingly and so authentically. Few have suffered as he has the charges of anti-Semitism that invariably follow. And few have dared to share his pained shout, on observing a people under ethnic-inspired occupation and dispossession for more than fifty years: 'This is apartheid!'" While Tutu's call for sanctions as a non-violent means of political action was praised when it related to the matter of apartheid, it often attracts charges of anti-Semitism when it relates to the issues of justice regarding Palestine. As with Michael Battle's observation about the church being on the wrong side of history when it comes to racism, this may unfortunately also very well be the case with the matter of injustice in the "Holy Land". It is a pity that we are not inspired to speak truth to power in the same way that Konrad Raiser's recollections about Tutu reflect. Focusing on the Eloff Commission, which was set up to investigate the finances of the SACC, Raiser notes Tutu's declaration: "I want the government to know now and always that I do not fear them. They are trying to defend the utterly indefensible. Apartheid is an evil and as vicious as Nazism and Communism and the government will fail completely because it is ranging itself on the side of evil, injustice and oppression. The government is not God, they are just ordinary human beings who very soon, like other tyrants before them, will bite the dust."

The Arch's recognition of the intersectionality of injustices was clearly evident long before the theory of intersectionality or decoloniality became popular scholarly vernacular. Michael Lapsley observes that: "Archbishop Tutu could have gained a proud place in history as a champion of the rights of black people to a place in the sun. However, the way he embraced and championed other struggles illustrates that he was not just a black man fighting for his people, as important as that was. Archbishop Desmond has championed the rights of all oppressed people regardless of whether it is a popular or unpopular struggle … Demonstrably, he lived out his own famous quote: 'If you are neutral in situations of injustice, you have chosen the side of the oppressor.'"

Vicentia Kgabe also notes his commitment to intersectional struggles for justice: "When he was elected as the first black Metropolitan of the Anglican Church of Southern Africa and Archbishop of Cape Town, on his enthronement Desmond Tutu set the tone for his Arch-Episcopacy, at the

---

[10] See also, Tinyiko Maluleke. "Why I Am Not a Public Theologian", *The Ecumenical Review* 73, no.2 (2021): 297-315.

occasion of his enthronement, by identifying three pressing issues that had his attention for his tenure. He identified these as firstly, ending apartheid, secondly the ordination of women and thirdly the full inclusion of LGBTQIA+ people in the church." Undergirding these goals for his tenure was precisely the recognition of how injustices intersect. Notwithstanding that the last of his goals remain unrealised, several contributors to this volume note his commitment to gender justice and sexual diversity justice. Adriaan van Klinken and Ezra Chitando, as well as Megan Robertson and Traci West, remind us of the integral role that Tutu has played in sexual diversity rights. Van Klinken, Chitando and Robertson have great appreciation for the ways in which Tutu draws on *Ubuntu* and black and African theologies to advance the cause of sexual diversity rights, despite their reservations about his essentialist claims that those who identify as LGBTIQ+ are simply "born this way". They all recognise the importance of Tutu's "strategic essentialism".[11] Traci West takes it a step further in her essay when she asserts that: "gratefulness for this gift means claiming African heritage as a resource for defining the power of black church tradition in terms of its welcoming embrace of black LGBTQ Christians."

As with sexual diversity rights, the Arch's commitment to gender equity is most visibly discernible in his support for the ordination of women priests. In all of the pertinent and personal accounts presented by Vicentia Kgabe, Eliza Getman, René August and Wilma Jakobsen we see the formative role that the Arch played in each of their discernments to their vocation and calling as women priests in a patriarchal church.

Eliza Getman movingly writes: "Arch Tutu helped me to accept myself and unwittingly commissioned me and countless others to work tirelessly for the *kin-dom* of God on Earth (as it is in heaven). He barely knows who I am, but he turned my life upside down and I am an Anglican priest thanks to his role modelling and influence." Vicentia Kgabe also notes: "Discerning a vocation as a woman, when there are no other women priests to reference within one's immediate context can be daunting, to say the least. Yet we drew our hope from ecclesiastical leaders in the calibre of the Arch and others who were standing on the truth that all who are called to serve, regardless of race, class, gender and/or ethnicity should be discerned and given a chance to live out their vocation. This stand was not only heart-warming but also inviting, inclusive and affirming." Even in this process, strategy was key, and Jakobsen draws attention to the ways in which she and the Arch disagreed on the best approach to protest the injustice inherent in the exclusion of women from the priesthood. Vicentia Kgabe also calls attention to the realities of persistent patriarchy despite the success of the struggle for women's ordination. She reminds us that the Arch and all those who were struggling "were not ignorant to the fact that whatever they were advocating for will not make all things bright, beautiful and accepted overnight. Those who were in the opposition were not going to stop being in opposition just because things have changed, regardless of how democratic or prayerful the process was." So, the central question in *The Book of Joy*,' containing deep reflections by the Dalai Lama and Desmond Tutu about joy in the midst of struggle and injustice, is a question worthwhile reflecting on in this book too: "Is it really possible to be joyful even in the face of our daily troubles?"[12] The answer to this question lies somewhere in how we frame our vision for dignity, and this is intricately tied to the themes of hope and joy, as the second section in this book reveals.

---

[11] See also, Elisabeth Eide. "Strategic Essentialism", in *The Wiley Blackwell Encyclopaedia of Gender and Sexuality Studies* (2016): 1-2. Elizabeth Eide notes that the term "strategic essentialism", which is originally attributed to Gayatri Spivak, can be seen as "a political strategy whereby differences (within a group) are temporarily downplayed and unity assumed for the sake of achieving political goals. In political practice, its usage in opposing and fighting against gender oppression is recommended, be it for judicial or social rights ..." but she cautions that "essentialism may be used to subjugate or liberate, but strategic essentialism ought to be seen as a temporary political strategy and not as a universalizing theory or as a universal way of conducting political struggle."

[12] Dalai Lama, Desmond Tutu and Douglas Carlton Abrams. *The Book of Joy: Lasting Happiness in a Changing World*. London: Penguin Books (2016), 4.

Dignity, hope, joy, resilience

An exceptional number of contributions to this book focus on the concept of dignity, in particular as it relates to what Michael Battle has conceptualised as Tutu's "*Ubuntu* theology". At the heart of Tutu's *Ubuntu* theology is the notion of dignity, as Nontombi Tutu, his daughter, reminds us. *Ubuntu* and *Imago Dei* are mirror concepts of each other. "… it is these two cultural and theological frameworks and the ideas, thoughts and principles that undergird them … that to me exemplify what my father tried to teach me about life, faith and the best ways of living", she maintains. "It is in these two concepts that my father's Christian faith and African identity are most clearly seen. I cannot start to describe how often we heard as children the call to be people with *Ubuntu*. Or how often my dad reminded us that each person we encountered was the image of God and was worthy of respect and dignity for that very fact alone", Nontombi notes, as she recalls the ways in which her father practised what he preached about dignity. Christo Lombard and Hans Engdahl also refer to the concept of dignity being the driving force behind Tutu's visionary ethical leadership style.

The importance of understanding dignity beyond its human rights framing is fittingly described by Baloyi Tlharihani: "… beyond the judicial connection with the notion of 'human rights', lies a moral responsibility to be '… my brother's [and sister's] keeper.' This shows the broadness that comes with the notion of human dignity which also possesses a concern beyond oneself. This concern should enable us to ask about the well-being of others both in our neighbourhood and afar. It should be a concern about their well-being in totality."

The concern for the well-being of others is also expressed in the Arch's *Ubuntu* hospitality, as explained by Ingrid le Roux, Tutu's long-standing physician, in her chapter. She relates a delightful story of how her family were visiting from Sweden, and at a Christmas Eve Mass, the Arch invited all ten of them for lunch at his home the next day! With such an expanded guest list, one would hope that the Arch himself was actually the one preparing the lunch! This notwithstanding, his generosity of spirit in offering hospitality and care to visitors is a remarkable trait.

This notion of dignity and care for the other, even within contexts of endless despair, can arguably only find expression in hope. In his essay, Allan Boesak brings Miguel de la Torre and Desmond Tutu into conversation with each other and the two of them do not agree! While de la Torre invites us to reside in hopelessness and to embrace that space as productive for the inspiration to fight against injustice, Boesak reminds us that Tutu was known to turn his face to the rising sun, for looking beyond a place of hopelessness. Boesak concludes on the value of a theology of hope, even amidst the failures of the post-apartheid state: "So, despite the present darkness of this age of re-embraced and reinforced apartheid, the betrayals and the corruption, the greed and hunger for power, the empty grandiosity, the privileges and entitlement that mark our political aristocracy; despite the disappointments and disillusionments, the deceit and broken promises and yet another loss of innocence; despite the fears and uncertainties because of this devastating pandemic and the darkening shadows of our valleys of death, I think of Jesus and the women and Thomas. I remember the youth and our revolution, and like Desmond Tutu, through the pain, the cries and the bewilderments I, too, see Sunday happen, and I will turn my face to the rising sun."

This is not a passive hope, as Musimbi Kanyoro reminds us in her essay. She conceptualises hope as resistance "that perceived reality can be changed for the better … Hope therefore is resistance. It actively resists the void of hopelessness by working for alternatives. Thus, hope is not merely an intellectual frame of mind. Hope is to be lived out. To hope for justice and peace is to work for elimination of injustice and to be a peacemaker. To hope for democracy means to practise being democratic in our personal relationships. To hope for wholeness means to face our own lack of wholeness with courage and to be prepared to go through the pain of self-examination, which leads to change."

Also contemplating the utility of hope (and joy), Roger Williamson in his letter to the Archbishop recalls: "I remember watching as you danced down the aisle in the not-so-formal clerical line-up, which led me to coin the technical ecclesiastical term 'episco-disco' to commemorate your processing style. Where does this irrepressible hope and exuberant joy come from? Not because your life was easy – I think those of us not living under a repressive regime can hardly begin to imagine what it is like to live with such constant tension and danger." Rolf Koppe calls attention to not only the fact that Tutu possessed this irrepressible hope and joy, but that he inspired acts of hopefulness and joy in other people too. Koppe recalls how at the German Expo 2000 "Desmond Tutu turned the attention of his listeners to the situation in South Africa where many people have not enough to eat, not enough space in their houses and not enough jobs for many young men and women to earn their living. But still one could observe in South African churches: in worship services people are filled with joy, clapping their hands and listening to the word of God attentively. The same seemed to be happening right here in Hanover during this sermon at Pentecost, during the Expo."

The conundrum that Williamson raises regarding humour in the face of suffering and pain is a question raised by many of the contributors to this volume too. Tinyiko Maluleke asks the question most candidly in his essay: "How can the oppressed laugh?" In questions that almost leap up off the page and tug at one's heartstrings, Maluleke stirringly asks: "Surely, in such dry places, there are no wells of laughter from which the non-persons can draw? Ordinarily, one would not think that the poor and the marginalised have a need to cultivate and treasure a sense of humour. Of what use is a sense of humour for a people who walk daily in the valley of the shadow of death? Surely, humour and laughter are wasted on the 'wretched of the earth'! Surely those who travel up and down life's Jericho Road in places where 'things constantly fall apart' have no time for humour! Surely, laughter should not be found in destitute villages and impoverished black townships! Surely, those reduced to mere worms, by the apartheid system, had no right to laughter! Not in the midst of all that squalor, poverty, violence and repression! To put it differently, for a people under siege and a people under the yoke of oppression, humour and laughter seem such a wasteful luxury to cultivate and nurture."

Yet without exaggeration, the most commonly described and praised attribute of the Arch, appearing in almost every single essay, is his sense of inexplicable humour. Some ascribe his humour to a means of defusing tension, while others see it as a more deliberate strategy to deal with social injustices, and at the same time provide a means to humanise relationships.

Angela Mai recalls Tutu's ability to use humour in tense situations. Mai recollects the tense situation prevailing at a mass funeral that Archbishop Tutu was conducting. When the police helicopter arrived and hovered over the funeral, she says, he waves and greets them with "Hallo Police." And then at the end of the funeral he asks people to pick up the debris of the food that they had brought. René August also recalls a similar story: "It was in the dark days of apartheid, under the state of emergency all mass gatherings (groups larger than four) were illegal and punishable by up to six months of detention without trial. We would gather in churches, at evening services and funerals. The Archbishop would walk up to the microphone, "Welcome! Welcome to this service of worship. Welcome if you have come from far away, welcome if you have come from Caledon Square (the police headquarters in the city). Welcome to those of you who have come to spy on us, welcome to the security police in plain clothing, welcome to all of you in the South African Defence Force. You are always welcome to join us. We are on God's side, we are on the winning side. All God's children are welcome here."

The Archbishop himself offers an explanation for his humour, that leans on the side of the twin purpose of defusing tension and inspiring a sense of self-worth that was consistently destroyed by the appalling circumstances of one's daily existence. He says: "We tend to want to blow ourselves up, inflate ourselves because most of us have tended to have poor self-image. When you're in a situation such as the one in South Africa where you were discriminated against, it was very easy to lose your sense of self, and humour seems to do something for people. Humour certainly did one good thing: it deflated, defused a particularly tense situation."[13]

Trond Bakkevig and Fernando Enns also capture the Arch's ability to encourage people not to take themselves too seriously, whether they were in church or in a solemn doctoral graduation ceremony. Regarding the latter, Fernando Enns describes a situation that could form material for

---

[13] Dalai Lama, Tutu and Abrams. *The Book of Joy,* 218.

stand-up comedy! Amidst a very sombre and solemn public doctoral defence and graduation ceremony in Amsterdam, a formal procession led by Archbishop Tutu and the dean in full silence was interrupted by very loud laughter by the Archbishop with words akin to: "'I like this', 'You are really serious about this, aren't you!?'" Enns describes the shocked silence for several moments before everyone burst out in laughter. He offers an explanation: "My interpretation is that Tutu was very much aware of what he was doing. I believe that he had been waiting for a moment to express some humanity in the middle of the whole stiff setting, to wink an eye in order to relativise the importance of traditional protocol that seems to illustrate hierarchy, privilege and the self-celebration of academic supremacy. He needed to comment! But how? It is his well-known, brilliant humour that allowed him to question – not what we were doing here, but how we did it. The bursting laughter was a risky, ironic move, which broke the ice and allowed all of us to laugh about ourselves. I have experienced this as very liberating, becoming aware of the fact that, even if we follow tradition closely, we need to allow ourselves to show vulnerability, insecurity, excitement, joy, satisfaction – to be human, after all."

What is most fascinating and noteworthy about all the observations offered by authors in this book regarding Tutu's humour is that the purpose of the humour was never to humiliate, only to humanise. In their essays focusing more directly, rather than in passing, on how the Arch used humour in his struggles for social justice, Fulata Moyo and Tinyiko Maluleke contemplate the utility, the effectiveness and the downright irreverence of the Arch's humour.

Fulata Moyo convincingly contends that "humour not only creates an atmosphere for laughter and joy amidst otherwise gloomy and seemingly hopeless realities, it is also a necessary twist to turn the otherwise difficult conversation into a witty, thought-provoking one that can lead to praxis for social justice." Maluleke befittingly conceptualises this as the wit and grit of the Arch with "the intention to humanise both the victims and the perpetrators of oppression." In his essay, Maluleke convincingly demonstrates that "both the freedom 'walk' of Nelson Mandela as well as the mental and psychological emancipation project of Steve Biko were similar in objective to that of Desmond Tutu, namely, the aim of humanising. However, Tutu stands somewhat apart from Mandela, Biko and other freedom fighters in his deliberate choice, and repeated and structured use, of humour as a humanising tool. In this sense, for Tutu therefore, the motto is not only the famous, 'I belong therefore I am'. He would add, 'I laugh, therefore I am'."

His deep spirituality, his wicked sense of humour and his commitment to *Ubuntu* can be said to be the building blocks of Archbishop Tutu's staunch devotion to the process of peace. We risk a fundamental misunderstanding of the Arch's conceptions of peace, however, if we only frame it within narrow ideas of non-violent passive resistance, as opposed to active agitation and advocacy for justice that promotes social and systemic change, as we will observe in the final section of the book.

Peace, prayer, reconciliation

In his message to Johan Galtung, in the book commemorating Galtung's 80th birthday, Archbishop Desmond Tutu says:

> In South Africa we have come to cherish peace as something much deeper and more meaningful than absence of gunshots or marching soldiers. It is also the absence of threats, of suppression, of structures that keep people in despair, poverty and indignity. What an enormous task, being a peacemaker![14]

What an enormous task indeed it is to be a peacemaker. Raymond van Diemel maintains that the 1984 Nobel Peace Prize "undoubtedly affirmed Tutu's international standing as a peace builder. It captured the world's attention and gave South Africans a sense of hope … There are many

---

[14] Desmond Tutu. "To Professor Johan Galtung on his 80th anniversary", in *Experiments with Peace: Celebrating Peace on Johan Galtung's 80th Birthday*, eds Jorgen Johansen and John Y. Jones. Oxford: Pambazuka Press (2011), 10.

indications that Tutu's Peace Prize forced more countries to take note of the devastating effect of apartheid. His speech paved the way for a policy of stricter sanctions against South Africa in the 1980s."

A great deal of the contributions in this book suggest that the path to peace and the strength needed for that journey were derived from a deep sense of spirituality and prayer. In fact, several contributions from Scandinavia and Europe, for example, talk about how, before starting any meeting, even in predominantly secular settings, the Archbishop's invitation to prayer both surprises those present but also sets the tone for the terms of engagement. Many contributors such as Christian Balslev-Olesen and Gerhard Rein, for example, illustrate such encounters in their reflections, where they recall this invitation to prayer in both a government setting as well as a media briefing.

As Paul Oestreicher asks: "From what does Desmond draw his strength? I have no doubt: from a disciplined life of prayer. He often surprises others by spontaneously turning to prayer, with and for them, sometimes joyfully, at others tearfully." What is crucial for us to note is that this disciplined life of prayer and spirituality did not inspire a passive, contemplative life that was free of the moral imperative to fight injustices.[15] On the contrary, as noted by Archbishop Thabo Makgoba: "Archbishop Desmond Tutu used to say that an effective prayer life would never allow you to remain on your knees. No, it would compel you to get up and go out into the world to bring good news to the oppressed, to bind up the broken-hearted, to proclaim liberty to the captives, release to the prisoners and to proclaim the year of the Lord's favour." Similarly, Atle Sommerfeldt describes being invited to the hotel room of Desmond and Leah Tutu in Norway, to share in the sacraments, and proceeding with an ordinary liturgy instead of one inspired by social action. He notes: "As the invisible God becomes visible in the elements of bread and wine, the invisible life of the sacred is intimately linked with ordinary life, including struggle to change injustice and oppression."

This dual obligation of proclamation and action is inspired by Tutu's deep *Ubuntu* spirituality, as the prayer penned by Edwin Arrison, and cleverly titled "An *UbunTutu* Eucharistic Prayer", reflects. Similarly, Rachele Vernon O'Brien's powerful poem "My Son is Not a Hero" bridges two millennia between the actions of Simon of Cyrene, who picks up the Cross of Jesus when he falls, and Mbuyisa Makhubu, who carries the dying Hector Pieterson after he is shot in the Soweto uprising of 1976. Vernon draws our gaze to Nombulelo Makhubu, Mbuyisa's mother, whose words from the Truth and Reconciliation Commission are etched on the memorial at the Hector Pieterson Museum: "' … according to my culture Mbuyisa is not a hero, he just did what was natural because we are our brother's keepers, according to our culture. He just saw Hector falling down. It would have been a scandal for nobody to pick Hector Petersen up from the ground. As far as we are concerned he was never a hero for picking up Hector Petersen.'" The poignancy of the narratives that are connected across space and time reveal that actions for justice are connected to *Ubuntu* spirituality – we are simply the keepers of our siblings. Peter Lodberg's essay also provides important reflections on the links between prayer and acts for justice when he tells the story of how Desmond Tutu opened an important government meeting with the Minister of Foreign Affairs in Denmark, in prayer. He aptly titled his essay: "When Prayer Meets Politics."

Apart from acts for justice, Archbishop Tutu is also known for speaking out quite strongly and sometimes with all the courage he could muster from his deep wells of righteous anger when encountering injustice. While the phrase "unmute yourself" is arguably the most popular refrain characterising a COVID-19 world, the Archbishop was certainly not afraid to unmute himself during the heydays of the struggles against apartheid. Numerous contributions reveal that the Arch's sharp tongue matched his sharp humour and wit.

The Eloff Commission, which was set up to investigate the finances of the SACC in the 80s, loosened this sharp tongue, as quite a few contributions reveal. Martin Kruse gets to the heart of the

---

[15] See the book by Susan Rakoczy on the relationship between a life of contemplation and social justice. Susan Rakoczy, IHM. *Great Mystics and Social Justice: Walking on the Two Feet of Love*. Mahwah: Paulist Press (2006).

charge against the SACC and ultimately the Evangelical Churches in Germany (EKD). As he describes it: "In a sense then, the EKD was in the dock. The allegation was: You stand up for non-violence in word, but in reality you promote political actions for subversion with your financial means." Werner von Hoerschelmann describes the Arch's anger directed at the EKD's request to vet the SACC's finances, during his tenure as general secretary of the SACC. Von Hoerschelmann recalls: "I knew Desmond Tutu before. But I had never seen him as enraged as he was that day. The EKD's request to vet the SACC's finances, in total disregard of all conventions and subtleties of ecumenical partnership, and of the trust already built up and of the autonomy of the SACC, made his blood boil. With curt and harsh words, he dismissed this imposition."

That was not the last time von Hoerschelmann would witness the Arch's righteous anger. He describes Tutu's response to a propaganda trip by EKD Council members to South Africa (either innocently or led by a pro-apartheid bias), paid for by the South African apartheid state and arranged by the travel agent Hennenhofer in Germany. "I received a call from Desmond Tutu in which he read to me the riot act: what is actually gospel with you people in the EKD? The speech given by Hild? The supportive words of Claß? The partnership agreement between the EKD and SACC signed in 1982?" Von Hoerschelmann concludes his experience of the audibly shaken Tutu in slightly amusing terms: "Never had I received such a verbal slap in the face over the phone!"

Sometimes, the verbal slap happened in quieter ways. Fernando Enns describes a slightly tense situation at the German Protestant *Kirchentag*, in 2007 in Cologne. Enns was part of a commission whose responsibility was to organise "a real prophet of peace and justice to lead us into this day", Desmond Tutu. It was the responsibility of Enns "to be in touch with him, to instruct him, to guide him", which Enns describes as an impossible task because he did not get responses to his emails or phone-calls. "The day in Cologne came, everything was accurately planned – in a very 'German' way. Every single minute of the whole day was scheduled in our script. The hall was packed with 5,000 people. We were all quite nervous. The program started with music, and then – at the last minute – Desmond Tutu arrived, quite relaxed. On top, a huge choir from South Africa flocked in and occupied the front seats of the auditorium. Where did they come from? Well, time for improvisation. Tutu was placed at my side – after all, everyone thought that I had 'instructed' him. He greeted me in the best spirit, providing a feeling of longstanding friendship. As the choir from South Africa started to sing for the Bishop (which was not part of our script), Tutu leaned towards me, whispering: 'What am I going to speak about today?' At this moment, I really became nervous. So, carefully yet insistently I tried to provide some general ideas, about the WCC, the Decade to Overcome Violence, suggesting that he should speak about the truth and reconciliation process in South Africa, maybe combined with some biblical wisdom, and so on. After a few minutes of listening, he gently touched my arm to interrupt me, looked into my eyes with a gracious smile on his face, asking: 'Are you trying to tell me what to say, young man?'" Dan Vaughan illustrates a similar story when he accompanied the Arch on a visit to Germany in the 70s. As Vaughan puts it:

As I learned to my cost one evening in Stuttgart, Tutu did not appreciate unsolicited advice – especially in matters which touched a strongly-held conviction.

We had arrived in Germany after a series of meetings in Scandinavia and the Netherlands in 1979. On this trip, his outspoken criticism of the apartheid government and boldness in calling for sanctions had attracted healthy attendances at the press conferences in each centre. Especially headline-catching was his comparison of the evil of apartheid to the holocaust of Hitler's Germany. Now he was to face his first press conference of this trip in Germany. Over-sensitive to the feelings of our German hosts toward him, I cringed at the thought of Tutu presenting that comparison here in Germany ... I suggested, "Perhaps you should not mention the holocaust here in Germany."

There was dead silence for a full minute as we walked steadily on. Then he abruptly turned on me angrily: 'I will say what I like. No one, no one, will ever tell me what to say.'

Why relate these narratives about the Arch's ability to both quietly and loudly deliver a "verbal slap in the face"? Nico Koopman provides an answer in the conclusion of his essay where he laments the fact that, increasingly, Tutu's forgiving and reconciling approach is not accepted by a young generation of black public intellectuals, one of them being Rekgotsofetse Chikane, son of church leader and prominent anti-apartheid struggle activist Frank Chikane. Koopman argues that "the fact that forgiveness is not accompanied by restitution is the reason for this suspicion of mainly black youngsters against Tutu and against his emphasis on forgiveness and reconciliation." Koopman continues: "Allan Boesak rightly warns against this development where white people embrace Tutu just like white Americans cherished Martin Luther King Jr. The emphasis on forgiveness and reconciliation was misused to only focus on forgiveness, rainbow unity and reconciliation, and to neglect restitution. In the process Tutu is domesticated by white people and used as a buffer between restitution and the perpetuation of white privilege and intergenerational racism and inequality. Boesak rightly pleads for the re-radicalisation of Desmond Tutu." Koopman's assessment is echoed by Rhine Phillip Tsobotsi Koloti, where he makes a case for the importance of restorative justice in cases of gender-based violence in the church as opposed to the "cheap reconciliation" that Boesak speaks of.

The idea of "cheap reconciliation" is countered by Tutu himself, as Heike Spiegelberg shows in reflecting on the sermon that Archbishop Tutu preached at the Boipatong massacre funeral. Both she and Heinz Joachim Held (from his travel diary) describe the sermon as a masterpiece, and as poetic, vacillating between anger and reconciliation: "Archbishop Tutu's description of his understanding of reconciliation was received with visible and audible consent and loud laughter: if you stole somebody's pen, a very nice and useful pen, it will not be enough to apologise and to say, when it comes out, that you are sorry. Of course you also have to give back the pen! ... The mood in the fully packed stadium, among those many hurt and angry people, changed into a liberating laughter. Amid the mourning and wailing, the harsh realities of politics and the gloomy atmosphere, reconciliation became a tangible vision", Spiegelberg concludes.

The tension between restorative justice and reconciliation is also explored in the essay by Demaine Solomons, where he describes the goal of reconciliation as an absurdity, drawing on the image of Sisyphus, "a figure of Greek mythology who is condemned to repeat the same arduous task of pushing a boulder up a mountain, only to see it roll back down again once the summit is reached." Solomons continues: "Driven by the desire for meaning amid meaninglessness, South Africans embarked on a journey of reconciliation, a romantic pursuit for a new way of being in the aftermath of the absurdity of apartheid."

Solomons' essay on the absurdity of reconciliation amidst the absurdity of apartheid reminded me of a poignant, deeply moving, satirical poem I was introduced to in my African literature and poetry class in 1995. The poem is by Christopher van Wyk in his 1979 collection, and is about the bizarre explanations offered by the apartheid police when political prisoners were killed in their custody:

In detention

He fell from the ninth floor
He hanged himself
He slipped on a piece of soap while washing
He hanged himself
He slipped on a piece of soap while washing
He fell from the ninth floor
He hanged himself while washing
He slipped from the ninth floor
He hung from the ninth floor
He slipped on the ninth floor while washing
He fell from a piece of soap while slipping

He hung from the ninth floor
He washed from the ninth floor while slipping
He hung from a piece of soap while washing.[16]

Indeed, reconciliation amidst the absurdity of not just apartheid, but the continuing social upheaval and trauma three decades after this poem was published, seems bizarre. Solomons' appeal in his conclusion, therefore, is apt: "some difficulties are worth enduring in a world that is as precarious and unsettling as ours. This diagnosis is not a fatality. The absurdity of the situation is our reality, but love saves us from it. The paradoxical presence of meaning amid meaninglessness. Perhaps this is the one thing we should learn from the life and work of our beloved Arch", he concludes.

What does it take to embrace this absurdity?

Anne Jaborg, a German pastor, suggests "walking over to each other". Recalling the Arch's ability to defuse tension, she remembers how "he had invited South African faith communities to Stellenbosch to attend a meeting called 'Revisiting the Truth and Reconciliation's Faith Community Hearing'." In this room, set up in the same way that the TRC was, a "tall sturdy white man collapsed and broke into tears" as he confessed the role of the Dutch Reformed Church (DRC) in apartheid. Tutu walks over and hugs him. "This incident with Bishop Tutu left a deep and lasting impression on my mind. It seems that almost everything is possible when people get up and walk over towards each other", she says. In her musical tribute contribution, Gertrud Tönsing also reflects on how she was inspired by Archbishop Tutu in the 80s as a young white South African. She notes how he was able to speak prophetically to the powers that be – whether these were white media, or those within his own political camp.

While we all breathed that collective sigh of relief that Rudolf Hinz describes, which came with the relatively peaceful elections on 27 April 1994, partly due to the National Peace accord brokered by Tutu, as Liz Carmichael recollects in her essay, and, while it might be tempting to use these examples of racial unity as an indicator of a reconciliation that is achieved, John Allen, Tutu's authorised biographer, reminds us in his essay that "in the 21st century, the "rainbow-ism" which Mandela and Tutu are purported to have advocated has fallen on hard times. In the media and public debate, Madiba's rainbow nation is supposed by its critics to have been something he declared as already in existence, brought into being by the magic wand of the 1994 vote. Just as the church in South Africa in the 1970s and 1980s repudiated the idea of 'cheap reconciliation', the people of South Africa justifiably reject any suggestion that inequality has been overcome, that we have liberated our economy and that people's dignity is adequately respected. The current portrayal of the vision which our elders held out is a caricature which distorts what they were saying. In Madiba's case, he presented the idea of a rainbow nation as an ideal to which to aspire, as a society which still needed – and still needs – to be built. Any South African who tries to sell us the idea that what we have now already constituted the ideal that he held out is, as the biblical expression has it, trying to sell us a mess of pottage."

John Allen's sharp observation is stridently instructive to anyone who would want to claim that we are a racially reconciled South Africa. Indeed, we cannot buy that "mess of pottage". There is still much work to be done – work that goes beyond charity to a radical embrace and promotion of justice. Here, the essay by Christian Balslev-Olesen provides a helpful signpost of the essential distinction between charity and justice, where he describes Tutu's "surprise" call for boycotts on Danish national television in the 70s, calling Danish coal imports from apartheid South Africa "disgraceful". Interestingly Klaus Nürnberger, in his letter to Cilliers Breytenbach in 1993, also questioned the wisdom of the economic boycott, though he conceded that "at the time the state unscrupulously

---

[16] Christopher van Wyk. "In Detention", in *It Is Time To Go Home*, ed. Adriaan Donker. Johannesburg: AD Donker Publishers (1979), 45.

deployed much heavier weaponry against the Blacks and that it was the only weapon available to them that had any hope of making an impact. Tutu repeatedly argued that it was also the only non-violent weapon, and that doing nothing would only drive the people towards uncontrollable violence." Balslev-Olesen asserts that in doing so Tutu was alerting the DCA (Danish Church Aid) to the discrepancies within their conceptualisation of "aid". On the one hand, the DCA contributed to long-term poverty-alleviation development work in the black townships, probably saving lives. On the other hand, they provided this aid without questioning the system that supported the poverty – namely, Denmark's purchase of cheap coal from South African mines, because these mines depended on cheap black labour. Tutu was clear that emergency aid for poverty alleviation, in the absence of a genuine questioning of the systems that supported the poverty, was not enough." Likewise, Miranda Pillay too, in her sermon inspired by Tutu and Trevor Huddleston, asserts: "Discriminatory laws, and religious and cultural practices privilege some while they exclude and silence others. This systemic nature of discrimination calls for compassion and solidarity from those who benefit from such laws and practices."

What this section on peace in this book reveals is that the Arch's spirituality, prayer and his yearning for peace were always accompanied by acts for justice that focused on systemic change. To him, the separation between spirituality and social justice was a false binary. It is therefore only fitting that we ended the book with a reflection and beautiful Muslim prayer offered by Sa'diyya Shaikh. She remarks that she is "a Muslim neighbour, or perhaps a kindred traveller wandering through the shared gardens and valleys of our world. When the terrain is particularly bleak and treacherous, turning my existential gaze to such resplendent souls is a source of renewal and hope. Archbishop Desmond Tutu has been one such glimmering beacon, embodying the best of religion, showing how people of spiritual fortitude are able to transform the world. Keenly observing Desmond Tutu for many decades, I recognise a living, loving "Arch-way", exemplifying some of the most capacious ways to be human. I celebrate him as a universal teacher, a holy friend and a discerning guide, who, drinking from the sacred centre, quenches the thirst of others, serving humanity as we yearn and work for a world of love, justice and dignity of all living beings."

Conclusion

To continue the sacred thread of spirituality that runs through all the contributions to this book, I would like to end this introduction with a prayer that I wrote for the opening of the 7th Annual Desmond Tutu Peace Lecture on 7 October 2017:

As we honour the legacy of our revered Archbishop
We also honour his commitment to prayers that are not independent of; but that are accompanied by concrete actions for justice.
It is in this spirit, through this peace lecture, that we recognise that thoughts and prayers ring hollow, in the absence of action for justice

Let us pray ...

God most compassionate, God most merciful
We recognise the futility of lighting candles for the victims of Marikana
When the blood of the dead protestors stain the pages of the report which lies yet unattended
We recognise the hypocrisy of offering thoughts and prayers for the so-called conflict in Israel and Palestine
While keeping our beliefs about divine access to land "in check"
We recognise the futility of offering thoughts and prayers for those affected by natural disasters
And yet we continue to propagate religious beliefs which suggest we have dominion over the earth, instead of stewardship over it
We recognise the futility of offering food parcels for the poor during the holidays,
When we support structural systems that prescribe unjust minimum wages

Which can barely sustain a family on cheap genetically modified foods
We recognise the futility of praying about state capture
While the resources of the country remain firmly captured in past economic injustices
We recognise the futility of offering thoughts and prayers
In the aftermath of the rapes and murders of lesbians in this country
When we judge, based on our sacred texts, and cultural beliefs
same love to be unnatural,
instead of recognising that love is kind and patient and knows not judgement;
Love is indeed divine
We recognise the futility of building shelters for battered women
While we still preach that the man is the head of the home
We recognise the futility of prayers for reconciliation
when there is little action for reparation

Indeed, we recognise God most compassionate, that there is little use for thoughts and prayers when death
and destruction are already before us
Help us therefore, dear God, to concern ourselves more with life before death,
than with worry about life after death

Give us the courage, dear creator,
to supplement, strengthen and sustain our thoughts and prayers with policy and change;
With active agitation for a world of equity, dignity and truth;
And a yearning for peace that's not simply the absence of war, but the presence of justice.

Om Shanti Shanti Shanti …

LIST OF CONTRIBUTORS

A
John Allen
John Allen is the author of *Rabble-Rouser for Peace: A Biography of Desmond Tutu,* and the editor of three collections of Tutu sermons, speeches, writings and sayings. He has served as executive editor of the African news website, allAfrica.com, as communications director of Trinity Church Wall Street in New York, as a spokesperson for the South African Truth and Reconciliation Commission, and as media secretary to Desmond Tutu while he was Archbishop of Cape Town.

Edwin Arrison
Edwin Arrison met then Bishop Tutu in 1985 at the SACC conference and was ordained by Archbishop Tutu in December 1992 after being selected by him to study theology in 1987. During his seminary studies at Grahamstown, he was offered a one-year scholarship to read theology at Wycliffe Hall in Oxford from 1989 to 1990. He worked closely with the Archbishop after ordination often acting as assistant chaplain. He is the General-Secretary of Kairos Southern Africa, serves on the leadership of the South African Christian Leaders' Initiative (SACLI) and is founder and director of the Volmoed Youth Leadership Training Programme, of which the Archbishop is a patron. During the Covid period he was partly responsible for caring for the Tutu's during their stay in Hermanus. He now works as the Development Officer of the Desmond and Leah Tutu Legacy Foundation.

René August
René August is a self-supporting priest in the Cape Town Diocese. She has been a distant disciple of Archbishop Tutu for most of her life. When she worked in the city from 1993 to 1998, she used to attend the Friday morning eucharist at St George's Cathedral. In 2010, she was able to return to that Friday morning service, and as the Arch got older, she used to help with taking photos after the service and sitting with him at the coffee shop, where they were sometimes joined by visitors from out of town. She got to eavesdrop on conversations with hundreds of people from all walks of life and almost every country in the world, and has had the joy of being invited to share meals with the family in their homes and restaurants over a number of years.

B
Trond Bakkevig
Trond Bakkevig is a Pastor in the Church of Norway and holds a Doctorate in Theology from the University of Oslo. He was an Honorary Canon at the Cathedral of the Holy Cross, Gaborone, Botswana and General Secretary of the Church of Norway Council on Ecumenical and International Relations from 1984 to 1993, with leave of absence from 1987 to 1988 to be Personal Adviser to the Minister of Foreign Affairs. He was deeply involved in support for the struggle against apartheid. He also moderated several commissions leading up to the separation between church and state, and facilitated dialogue between religious leaders in the Holy Land. He is the author of several books, and popular as well as academic articles.

Christian Balslev-Olesen
Christian Balslev-Olesen, is a theologian, who currently chairs DIGNITY (Danish Institute against Torture). He was Secretary of the Ecumenical Council in Denmark (1980-85), Programme Officer DanChurchAid (DCA) (1985-2001) Regional Representative in Zimbabwe (1989-1991), General Secretary (1992-2001). He also served the UN and UNICEF as Representative, in Eritrea and Somalia (2002-2009). In addition to being a consultant for the UN, the World Bank and Danida in i.a. Yemen, Libya, Sudan, and Tanzania (2009-2012), he was also the Director of the Danish House in Ramallah in Palestine (2012-2013), and Country Director for DCA in Malawi and Zimbabwe (2013-2016). Christian Balslev-Olesen has worked with Desmond Tutu as staff and general secretary of DCA since the beginning of the 80s and has had the privilege of accompanying and hosting Desmond Tutu when visiting Denmark.

Michael Battle
Michael Battle is currently appointed as Herbert Thompson Professor of Church and Society and Director of the Desmond Tutu Center at General Theological Seminary in New York. He lived in residence with Archbishop Tutu in 1993 and 1994 and was ordained a priest by Tutu in 1993. In 2010, Battle was given one of the highest Anglican Church distinctions as 'Six Preacher', by the Archbishop of Canterbury, Rowan Williams – a distinction given to only a few who demonstrate great dedication to the church that goes back to 16th century England and Thomas Cranmer. Battle has published eleven books, including his new release *Desmond Tutu: A Spiritual Biography of South Africa's Confessor*. He is affiliated to the Desmond Tutu Centre for Religion and Social Justice at the at the University of the Western Cape. Battle and his wife, Raquel, were married by Tutu in Atlanta, Georgia and are parents to two daughters, Sage and Bliss, and a son, Zion – all of whom were baptized by Tutu as well.

Heinrich Bedford-Strohm
Heinrich Bedford-Strohm is Bishop of the Lutheran Church in Bavaria and Chairperson of the Council of the Protestant Church in Germany (EKD). He is Extraordinary Professor at the Theological Faculty in Stellenbosch/South Africa and Honorary Professor at the University of Bamberg/Germany where he was founding director of the Dietrich Bonhoeffer Research Center for Public Theology.

Allan Boesak
Allan Aubrey Boesak is Professor of Black Liberation Theology and Ethics, University of Pretoria. He worked closely with Archbishop Tutu from the time of his leadership of the South African Council of Churches as Senior Vice President, and then throughout the years of the struggle against apartheid after he became Archbishop of Cape Town. During the intensification of the international boycott, divestment, and sanctions campaign against the apartheid regime, their relationship grew. He is privileged to call Desmond Tutu a close friend.

Petra Bosse-Huber
Bishop Petra Bosse-Huber is Head of the Division for Ecumenism and Global Ministries, and Vice-President of the Church Office of the Protestant Church in Germany (EKD).

Brian Brown
While a presbyter of the Methodist Church in South Africa, Brian Brown joined the staff of the Christian Institute (CI) led by Afrikaner dissident Beyers Naudé. Beyers and the Archbishop were soul mates and formidable opponents of apartheid. Brian enjoyed 'reflected glory' moments when working with two icons of prophetic ministry. Following banning and the CI's closure by the regime in 1977, he sought sanctuary and worked in the British Council of Churches (BCC). This allowed re-engaging with the Archbishop during many European visits and a sharing in diverse endeavours to assist apartheid's demise.

C

Ezra Chitando
Ezra Chitando is Professor of History and Phenomenology of Religion at the University of Zimbabwe and Theology Consultant on HIV, World Council of Churches. He writes here in his personal capacity. He is affiliated to the Desmond Tutu Centre for Religion and Social Justice at the at the University of the Western Cape. His research interests include religion and sexuality, human security, climate change, development, politics, gender, masculinities, peace building and others. Although he has not met Tutu in person, he has encountered him in his many writings.

Liz Carmichael
Liz Carmichael MBE is an Emeritus Research Fellow at St John's College, Oxford. She got to know Desmond Tutu in 1975 when he became Dean at St Mary's Cathedral, Johannesburg. She is British but had just started work as a doctor at Baragwanath Hospital. She recalls with fondness how Desmond Tutu was strikingly friendly and direct in his questions to her: "Was she thinking of getting married?" "Would she like to be ordained?" Soon afterwards she married Canon Michael Carmichael, whom Desmond admired (and it was mutual!). They hoped Desmond would not go to Lesotho. Desmond told her that after he accepted to go, he spent that night on a plane to London, jerking awake and thinking: "What have I done? I wanted to be a Bishop – but not like that." But it was good he had that status of Bishop when heading the SACC. Archbishop Desmond Tutu later ensured that she returned, having studied theology, to be ordained in Johannesburg.

D

Raymond van Diemel
Raymond van Diemel is a military university educator at the South African Military Academy. He is the Coordinator of Telematic (Online) Education, Faculty of Military Science, Stellenbosch University. He holds degrees from the universities of the Western Cape (UWC) and the University of South Africa (UNISA). He completed a PhD in Historical Studies from UWC in 1997. His admiration for the former Archbishop Desmond Tutu as a "warrior for peace and justice" dates back to the late 1970s when he witnessed the protest marches to the Parliament led by Desmond Tutu. Tutu's adage "If you are neutral in situations of injustice, you have chosen the side of the oppressor" is engraved in his consciousness. He was privileged to be commissioned by the Cape Peninsula University of Technology (CPUT) to film the Annual Desmond Tutu Peace Lecture held on 7 October 2008.

Ulrich Duchrow
Ulrich Duchrow is Professor of Systematic Theology at Heidelberg University, Germany, specializing in ecumenical theology, interreligious theology and economic issues. He is co-founder and honorary chair of Kairos Europa, an ecumenical grassroots network striving for justice. Kairos Europa also coordinates the Kairos Palestine Solidarity Network in Germany. He is a member of the Academic Council of ATTAC Germany, a movement that is critical of capitalist globalization. The movement is co-founded by Kairos Europa, WEED

(World Economy, Ecology & Development) and Pax Christi founded. Duchrow has worked in various capacities with the World Council of Churches (including guest professor at the Ecumenical Institute in Bossey, 1977-1978), the Lutheran World Federation and the World Alliance/World Communion of Reformed Churches.

E
Hans Engdahl
Hans Engdahl served as an extraordinary professor at the University of the Western Cape (UWC) between 2005 and 2016. During this time, he was part of the initiative that worked towards the establishment of a Desmond Tutu Research Chair at UWC, to which the Archbishop agreed at his 75th birthday in 2006. He has known the Tutus since the late 1980s, when he worked as mission secretary for the Church of Sweden.
Fernando Enns
Fernando Enns was born in 1964 in Curitiba/Brazil. He is Professor for Peace, Theology and Ethics at Vrije Universiteit Amsterdam (The Netherlands), Director of the Amsterdam Center for Religion and Peace & Justice Studies, Professor at the Protestant Faculty of the University of Hamburg (Germany) and Director of the Center for Peace-Church Theology. He is member of the Central Committee of the World Council of Churches and Co-Moderator of the International Reference Group on the ecumenical 'Pilgrimage of Justice and Peace'. He is also Vice-Chair of the Association of Mennonite Congregations in Germany.

F
Mpho Tutu van Furth
Rev. Canon Mpho Tutu van Furth is the youngest of her parents' four children. She has worked with her father as co-author on two books, *Made for Goodness* and *The Book of Forgiving*. She was Director of the Bishop Desmond Tutu Southern African Refugee Scholarship Fund in New York in the 1980s and later founding Executive Director of the Desmond & Leah Tutu Legacy Foundation.
Volker Faigle
Volker Faigle is a German Lutheran Theologian, living in Berlin. He was Parish Pastor in Bavaria/Germany (1978-1984), Ecumenical Co-Worker in Nairobi – Kenya Evangelical Lutheran Church (1984-1990), Head of the Africa Desk of the Protestant Church in Germany (EKD) (1990-2003), Church Diplomat in the Office of the Plenipotentiary of the EKD to the German Government and the EU (2003-2013) and Chair of the Council of the Berlin Cathedral (2013-2019). He served for many years as Special Envoy of the EKD to the Sudan and South Sudan. He was awarded an honorary doctorate in Theology from the University of the Western Cape (2001).

G
Eliza Getman
Eliza Getman is currently the Chaplain at Taunton School in Somerset, UK. She was born in the United States, raised in the Episcopal Church, ordained in the Anglican Church of Southern Africa and is now licenced as a priest in the Church of England. She is married to a South African and has four South African sons. She met the Archbishop through her parents in 1984 when she was a teenager. Her MA was in the area of Religion in Public Life and her PhD focused on motherhood and ministry. She worked as a postdoctoral research fellow, under the auspices of the Desmond Tutu Chair in Religion and Social Justice, supported by the National Research Foundation of South Africa.
Betty Govinden
Devarakshanam [Betty] Govinden has published in literature and literary criticism, education, history, and feminist theology, among other disciplinary fields. She was a founding member of the Circle of Concerned African Women Theologians, and was a lay representative from the Anglican Church in South Africa [ACSA] to the Anglican Consultative Council [ACC], the ACC Standing Committee, and the 1988 Lambeth Conference, held in Canterbury, England. This participation in the wider Anglican Communion, and on provincial structures, was during the episcopacy of Archbishop Desmond Tutu. One of the highlights, during attendance at the 1988 Lambeth Conference, was her joining a small group of South Africans, led by Archbishop Tutu, to attend the celebration of Nelson Mandela's 70th Birthday, held at Wembley Stadium, London, on 11 June 1988. Over 70, 000 people attended this grand anti-apartheid concert, which was broadcast to 67 countries, and an audience of 600 million. Archbishop Tutu addressed the gathering. Betty Govinden is a lay minister at St Aidan's Anglican Church, in Durban.
John de Gruchy
John de Gruchy is emeritus professor of Christian Studies at the University of Cape Town, and an extraordinary professor of theology at Stellenbosch University. Since his retirement in 2003 he and his wife, Isobel have lived at the Volmoed Christian Retreat Centre near Hermanus. He first met Desmond Tutu during 1965 when he was teaching at the Federal Theological Seminary in Alice. In one way or the other that relationship has developed over subsequent years when their paths crossed and their involvements brought them together.

H
David Haslam
David Haslam is a Methodist minister who has entered the age of choice from the age of necessity (i.e. retired), but who continues to campaign for Tax Justice, a Free Palestine and Dalit Rights, along with local work on the environment, refugee support, anti-racism and justice issues in the local churches. He continues to be inspired by 'Justice Heroes' such as Pope Francis, Nelson Mandela, Dorothy Day, Bhimrao Ambedkar and Desmond Tutu.

Heinz Joachim Held
Heinz Joachim Held is a German theologian, Bishop, and pastor of the Evangelical Church in Rhineland. He holds a Doctorate in New Testament studies and was professor of theology at the Lutheran Seminary near Buenos Aires. He was also President of the Rio de la Plata Church in Argentina, President of the Foreign Office of the Protestant Church in Germany (EKD) and Moderator of the Central Committee of the World Council of Churches.

Rudolf Hinz
Rudolf Hinz is a pastor and holds an Honorary Doctorate in Theology. He served as Secretary for Africa in the Foreign Office of the Evangelical Church in Germany (EKD), Director of the Department for World Service of the Lutheran World Federation (LWF), Geneva and Lecturer for Intercultural Theology and Ecumenism at the Theological Faculty of the University of Kiel. He is married to Sabine Hinz-Wegner and has three daughters: Catherina, Dorothea and Veronika.

Werner Konstantin von Hoerschelmann
Werner Konstantin von Hoerschelmann holds a Doctorate in Theology, and from 1967 to 1969 served as Assistant in the Department of Theological Education in the Lutheran Church of Schleswig-Holstein, Germany. From 1969 to 1974 he served as Chaplain for German speaking Protestants in South India and Lecturer at United Theological College (UTC), Bangalore. Between 1974 and 1982 he was also Head of the Africa Department in the EKD Office for Foreign Relations, Frankfurt/Main. Between 1982 and 1997 he was Dean of St.Peter's Cathedral and Provost of Hamburg's ,City circuit, Lutheran Church and also Lecturer at Hamburg University and Member of EKD Synod. He also served as chairperson of the Association of Christian Churches in Hamburg (ACK-H). In 1994 he was an Election Observer in South Africa, and from 1997 to 2003 was Chairperson of 'Kindernothilfe' (KNH), Duisburg (caring for ca. 2 million Children in need in 36 countries)

J
Anne Jaborg
Anne Jaborg is a Pastor of the Evangelical Lutheran Church of Oldenburg, Germany. For 30 years she has been working as a parish pastor and prison chaplain. At Deutscher Evangelischer Kirchentag (Protestant Church Congress) in Cologne, 2007, she met the Nobel Peace Prize Laureate for the first time. Since then, she has been fascinated by his charisma and, in particular, by his statements on the subject of reconciliation. Her contribution is based on her personal diary entry during her sabbatical in Stellenbosch in 2014.

Wilma Jakobsen
Wilma Jakobsen was the first Anglican woman ordained by Archbishop Desmond Tutu, as deacon, 1988, and priest, 1992. She became his chaplain in 1995, until he retired as Archbishop of Cape Town in 1996. She served fifteen years in the Diocese of Cape Town, and seventeen years in the Episcopal Church in California, USA. In 2020 she returned to South Africa to serve as coordinator of the ecumenical Volmoed Youth Leadership Training Program of which Desmond Tutu is the patron. She is also the chaplain at Volmoed Retreat Centre, Hermanus, Western Cape.

Sebastian Justke
Sebastian Justke is a historian and research assistant at the Research Centre for Contemporary History in Hamburg. His doctoral thesis focused on West German Protestant pastors who had been sent by their church to South Africa and Namibia during the apartheid era. He is co-editor of *Apartheid and Anti-Apartheid in Western Europe* (Cambridge Imperial and Post-Colonial Studies), Cham 2021.

K
Musimbi Kanyoro
Musimbi Kanyoro is an accomplished leader with extensive experience in international non-governmental organisations, global multilateral organisations and ecumenical agencies. She is currently a member of the Council of London School of Economics and a Board member of CARE International, UN Global Compact. She also serves as the Senior Advisor to Together for Gender Equality, a program of UN Global Compact and a consultant on Faith and Gender for UN Women. Kanyoro is the immediate past President and CEO of the Global Fund for Women. She holds a PhD in Linguistics from the University of Texas in Austin and a Doctor of Ministry from San Francisco Theological Seminary. She was a visiting Scholar of Hebrew and Old Testament Studies at Harvard Divinity School. She has received numerous awards and recognitions internationally. She has

served in an advisory role on Gender issues with World Bank, UN Women, UNAIDS and various other organisations and initiatives. She currently chairs two international boards: the Women's Learning Partnerships and the United World Colleges.

Vicentia Kgabe

Vicentia Kgabe holds a PhD from the University of Pretoria, and is an ordained Anglican priest who currently serves as the Rector and Principal of College of Transfiguration NPC – Grahamstown, South Africa. The College of Transfiguration is an amalgamation of the previous three theological colleges that were in existence in the Anglican Church of Southern Africa, and was formed in 1993, when Archbishop Desmond Tutu was Metropolitan of the church. He was the first Chairperson of the newly constituted College of Transfiguration Council (Board of Directors).

Adriaan van Klinken

Adriaan van Klinken is Professor of Religion and African Studies at the University of Leeds (UK), and Extraordinary Professor in the Desmond Tutu Centre for Religion and Social Justice at the University of the Western Cape (South Africa). His research focuses on Christianity, gender and sexuality in contemporary Africa. His latest book is *Kenyan, Christian, Queer: Religion, LGBT Activism, and Arts of Resistance in Africa* (Penn State University Press, 2019). He has never had the privilege to meet Archbishop Tutu, but is still hoping for that dream to come true (if not on earth, then in a – hopefully not homophobic – heaven).

Rhine Phillip Tsobotsi Koloti

Rhine Phillip Tsobotsi Koloti is a Master's student working in the Desmond Tutu Centre for Religion and Social Justice, at the University of the Western Cape. He also works as a research assistant and as a tutor. As an activist and an aspiring academic, he works with the United Society Partners in the Gospel and recently participated in the United Nations Commission on the Status of Women. He is also a member of the Association of Practical Theology. His most fond memory of Desmond Tutu goes back to 2008 when he was an altar boy holding the Archbishop's mitre during the Holy Eucharist Service at St Peter's Chains Anglican Church in Katlehong.

Nico Koopman

Nico Koopman is professor of Systematic Theology (Public Theology and Ethics), and Deputy Vice-Chancellor for Social Impact, Transformation and Personnel at Stellenbosch University. He has engaged with the person and work of Archbishop Emeritus Desmond Tutu since his student days at the University of the Western Cape during the 1980s. As pastor and university chaplain, and later as Vice-Rector of Huguenot College, Director of the Beyers Naudé Centre for Public Theology and Dean of the Faculty of Theology at Stellenbosch University, and in his current position in executive university leadership, he cooperated with Archbishop Tutu in church and academic contexts.

Rolf Koppe

Rolf Koppe was born in 1941 in Mahlum, a village in Lower Saxony, Germany. After the study of protestant theology in Heidelberg, Vienna and Göttingen he was a research assistant of the Lutheran World Federation in Geneva, ordained as a pastor of the Lutheran Church of Hanover, and worked as a press and information officer of the EKD. After 5 years as regional Bishop of the district of Göttingen he became the Bishop for ecumenical and foreign relations of the EKD. Up to 2006 – the year of his retirement – he was a member of the Central and the Executive Committee of the WCC and from 1999 to 2002 the protestant co-moderator of the 'special commission' of the WCC. In 1996 he was awarded an honorary doctorate at the University of Klausenburg/Cluij-Napoca, Romania. He is a father of two girls and lives with his wife, Ilse in Göttingen.

Piyushi Kotecha

Piyushi Kotecha is the CEO of the Desmond and Leah Tutu Legacy Foundation. Piyushi's professional career in the higher education sector and civil society spans across key policy-development, transformation processes and institutional building and advocacy processes in the pre-apartheid period and post-apartheid period. Her wealth of experience was gained at the interface of strategic, political, academic, inter-disciplinary, governmental, and civil society.

Gottfried Kraatz

Gottfried Kraatz served as parish Pastor and Dean in West-Berlin and in South Africa (Mitchells Plain 1981-1986), Mission Director of the Gossner Mission with partners in Zambia, Zimbabwe, India, Nepal, Soviet Union and Germany (1986-2002). He is a member of the WCC's Ecumenical Accompaniment Programme for Palestine and Israel (EAPPI) and chair of the German network of EAPPI up to date. Mitchells Plain, where Gottfried Kraatz served as a pastor, is a township in the Western Cape, about 28 km from the city of Cape Town. It is one of South Africa's largest residential areas and originally built during the 1970s to provide housing for 'Coloured' victims of forced removal due to the implementation of the Group Areas Act. It was once a major stronghold of the United Democratic Front, the broad-based ANC-sponsored anti-apartheid body.

Martin Kruse

Martin Kruse holds a Doctorate in theology, and since 1977 has served as Bishop of the Evangelical Church Berlin-Brandenburg, and since the reunification of West and East Germany in 1991, of the Evangelical Church in the greater region of Berlin-Brandenburg-Silesian Upper Lusatia. Since 1983 he was a member of the Central Committee of the World Council of Churches (WCC) and also a member of the Council of the Evangelical Church in Germany (EKD) 1979-1991, and from 1985-1991 served as its Chairman.

Gerhard Küsel

Gerhard Küsel was born in 1946 in Northern Natal, where he studied first at the University of Natal in Pietermaritzburg, then in Oberursel, Göttingen and Berlin before taking up a ministry in the Swazi Diocese of the Evangelical-Lutheran Church of South Africa (1975 to 1978). From there he went to Schortens, Germany, after which he was pastor of the German-speaking Evangelical Lutheran Church in Kenya from 1983 to 1988 before returning to Schortens. Today he lives as a retired pastor in Aurich.

L

Michael Lapsley

Michael Lapsley is a member of the Anglican religious order: The Society of the Sacred Mission. He is the Canon for Healing and Reconciliation at St George's Cathedral in Cape Town, and at All Saints Cathedral in Edmonton in Canada. He is the Founder of the Institute for Healing of Memories of which Archbishop Tutu is the Patron.

Christine Lienemann-Perrin

Christine Lienemann-Perrin is Professor Emeritus of missiology and ecumenical studies at the Faculty of Theology, University of Basel. Born in Switzerland 1946, she studied theology in Bern, Montpellier, France, and Heidelberg, Germany. From 1977 to 1985 she was an academic staff member of the Protestant Institute for Interdisciplinary Research, Heidelberg. Research work and lectures brought her to Congo/Kinshasa, South Africa, South Korea, Brazil, Japan and USA. Her publications are focused on mission and inter-religious dialogue, feminist missiology, ecumenical political ethics, and religious conversion in diverse contexts and World Christianity.

Peter Lodberg

Peter Lodberg is Professor of Systematic Theology, Aarhus University, Denmark. He was the former General Secretary of DanChurchAid and member of the Central Committee of the World Council of Churches.

Christo Lombard

Christo Lombard was born in South Africa but had his schooling and half of his professional life in Namibia (at UNAM). He studied Philosophy/Psychology and Theology at Stellenbosch (1966-1974), but did his post-graduate studies in Utrecht and Basel, and at UWC, where he taught as a lecturer (1975-1983) and as professor (2005-2013). He met Desmond Tutu in Windhoek in 1984, when he persuaded the SACC General Secretary to speak to his students. He had the privilege to help establish the Desmond Tutu Chair/Centre at UWC (2013-2016) after his retirement.

M

Angela Mai

Angela Mai was born in England in 1938 to parents from Durban. She attended school in KwaZulu-Natal, studied drama in London, married a German and had three children. She also spent seven years in Kenya where she built up a toy-making income earning project in a slum. Later in Germany she worked for the Anti-Apartheid Movement, visiting South Africa frequently. From October 1990 to June 1991, she worked with Beyers Naude at Ecumenical Advice Bureau, and met Archbishop Tutu on several occasions. She returned home and worked on a film about the struggle against Apartheid *Memories of Rain*, which went to many festivals and won a prize.

Thabo Makgoba

Thabo Makgoba is the Anglican Archbishop of Cape Town and was accepted for ordination training by Desmond Tutu when the latter was Bishop of Johannesburg. Makgoba was elected Bishop Suffragan of Grahamstown in 2002, Bishop of Grahamstown in 2004 and Archbishop in Cape Town in 2008. He holds a BSc degree, a BA (Honours) in Applied Psychology and an MEd in Educational Psychology from the University of the Witwatersrand, and a PhD from the University of Cape Town. He has honorary degrees from Canada, South Africa and the United States. He serves as Chancellor of the University of the Western Cape.

Tinyiko Maluleke

Tinyiko Maluleke is Senior Research Fellow and Deputy Director of the University of Pretoria Centre for the Advancement of Scholarship. Tinyiko Maluleke is a theologian by training. He has also been part of university executive management at UNISA, UJ and UP serving in various roles including Deputy Vice Chancellor, Executive Director for Research and Advisor to the Principal and Vice Chancellor. Between 2007 and 2009 Maluleke served as President of the South African Council of Churches. In that period Maluleke held several consultations and conversations with Archbishop Tutu.

Fulata Moyo

Fulata Lusungu Moyo believes in the life-changing power of humour in social (gender) justice activism. She is a founder of STREAM (Sex-Trafficking Responses through Educational research, Accompaniment and Mentorship) and a vice-President for AfriAus iLEAC (African Australians, Inspire, Lead, Educate for Change). She holds a PhD in Human Sciences from UKZN, South Africa. She met and spent time with Archbishop and Madame Tutu in Geneva, Switzerland.

N

Sarojini Nadar

Sarojini Nadar holds the Desmond Tutu South African Research Chair (SARChI) in Religion and Social Justice at the University of the Western Cape. She is also the Director of the Desmond Tutu Research Centre, which develops and promotes transdisciplinary advanced research that focuses on the critical intersections between religion and social justice. Her numerous publications span diverse topics of research at the intersections of gender studies and religion, including gender-based violence, HIV, masculinity studies and most recently gender in higher education. She sits on five international journal editorial boards including the Journal of Feminist Studies in Religion, and she is also the editor-in-chief of the African Journal of Gender and Religion. As an activist-academic she is committed to authentic and intersectional socially engaged scholarship

Kuzipa Nalwamba

Kuzipa Nalwamba is a staff member of the World Council of Churches (WCC), serving in a dual role as Ecumenical Social Ethics lecturer at Bossey Ecumenical Institute and Programme Executive for Ecumenical Theological Education (ETE). She is a retired ordained minister of the United Church of Zambia.

Nyambura Njoroge

Nyambura J. Njoroge is a Kenyan ecumenical church leader, theologian and advocate for justice and human dignity. She is Programme Executive for World Council of Churches' Ecumenical HIV and AIDS Initiatives and Advocacy. Nyambura received her first degree at St. Paul's University, Limuru, Kenya, and a Master's degree from Louisville Presbyterian Theological Seminary, Louisville, Kentucky and a Ph.D. in Christian Social Ethics from Princeton Theological Seminary, Princeton, New Jersey, USA. She is a founding member of the Circle of Concerned African Women Theologians. She is the author of *Kiama Kia Ngo: An African Christian Feminist Ethic of Resistance and Transformation*, Legon Theological Studies Series, Legon, Ghana, 2000.

Klaus Nürnberger

Klaus Nürnberger served as an ordained pastor of the Evangelical Lutheran Church in Southern Africa from 1968 to 1979. From 1971-1979 he was a lecturer in Systematic Theology and Theological Ethics at the Lutheran Theological College, Maphumulo, Natal. From 1980 to 1989 he was professor of Theological Ethics at the University of South Africa (Unisa). From 1989 until his retirement in 1998 he was professor of Systematic Theology and Theological Ethics at the University of Natal (now University of KwaZulu-Natal) in Pietermaritzburg, South Africa.

O

Paul Oestreicher

Paul Oestreicher, fled with his parents from Nazi Germany to New Zealand in 1939. An Anglican priest and Quaker, he studied political science and German literature, and he holds a Doctor of Divinity. Living in England and Germany and working for peace and human rights, he was primarily committed to the churches in Communist Eastern Europe and Apartheid South Africa. Desmond Tutu wrote the foreword to his German language pastoral reflections *Auf's Kreuz Gelegt*.

Rachele Vernon O'Brien

Rachele Vernon O'Brien is an Anglican deacon and activist, Jamaican by birth, British by naturalisation, and holds a Doctorate qualification. She first laid eyes on Bishop Tutu, as he was then, at the WCC Central Committee meeting held in Kingston in 1979. The theological students were privileged to serve as stewards for the meeting, looked on with awe at this man who was such a potent symbol that the church was on the right side of the struggle for justice and truth. When she despairs, as she does sometimes, that the church appears to have lost focus, she remembers that Archbishop Desmond has continued to be faithful and courageous, and she realises that he is the representative of what this Jesus movement is all about really. And her faith is renewed.

P

Miranda Pillay

Miranda Pillay is a research fellow at the University of the Western Cape, where she was a senior lecturer in New Testament Studies and Ethics before her retirement. As a lay leader in the Anglican Church, she advocates for gender-justice and continues to draw inspiration from Desmond Tutu's theology of inclusivity and inter-connectedness. For Pillay, Tutu's relational agency is particularly evident in a (1976) letter written to then Prime

Minister BJ Vorster in which Tutu appeals to the common humanity of the apartheid leader. He writes to Vorster as "one human person to another human person"; as "one Christian to another Christian" united through Jesus Christ "who has broken down all that separates us – such as race, sex, culture, status, etc."

R
Konrad Raiser
Konrad Raiser is a German protestant theologian, born in 1938 in Magdeburg. He was Executive Staff in the World Council of Churches from 1969-1983, General Secretary of the World Council of Churches from 1993 until 2002 and professor of theology and ecumenics at the Ruhr University of Bochum, Germany (1983-1993). His recent publications: Religion-Macht-Politik, Frankfurt 2010; Ökumene unterwegs zwischen Kirche und Welt, Münster 2013; 50 Jahre Reformation – weltweit, Bielefeld 2016.

Gerhard Rein
Gerhard Rein is a German journalist, now living in Berlin. He was a youth delegate at the World Council of Churches conference in New Delhi/ India in 1961. Since then the ecumenical movement became his place, his 'Heimat'. From 1992-1997 he was the foreign correspondent of the German public-radio network (ARD) in Southern Africa. During that time, he had close contact to Beyers-Naude, Wolfram Kistner and to the Archbishop.

Megan Robertson
Megan Robertson is a postdoctoral fellow under the auspices of the Desmond Tutu SARChI (The South African Research Chairs Initiative) Chair in Religion and Social Justice. She has worked for three institutions where the Tutu name has served as a compass for its work including the Institute for Justice and Reconciliation, the South African Faith and Family Institute and, now, is a lecturer in the Desmond Tutu Centre for Religion and Social Justice. Her work with people and organisations that carry his name reflects the ways in which his ethics and politics have guided her approach and commitment to social justice work.

Ingrid le Roux
Ingrid le Roux was born in Avesta, Sweden and grew up in Stockholm. She graduated as a medical doctor from the Karolinska Institute in Stockholm 1973. She married Pieter le Roux and settled in Cape Town in 1978.
In 1979 Ingrid, together with women from the "illegal" squatter community Crossroads outside Cape Town, founded the Philani Maternal, Child Health and Nutrition Trust and built the trust's first clinic in Crossroads in early 1980. This was followed by the building of another five clinics in Philippi and Khajelitsha townships during the eighties. During the nineties, the Philani concept expanded and further components like preschools and income generating programmes were added to Philani's activities. The Philani headquarters were built and opened by Philani Patron Archbishop Tutu. Ingrid's academic career began with a Med Kand and Med Lic degree from the Karolinska Institute in Sweden. In addition, she obtained a Master's Degree in Public Policy from Princeton University, USA, as well as diplomas in Maternal, Child Health and Nutrition from Uppsala University, Sweden, and the University of Chile. Ingrid was admitted to the order of Simon of Cyrene by Archbishop Tutu and received the Stefan's Medal from Archbishop Gunnar Weman in 1989. In 2018, Ingrid was awarded an Honorary Doctorate by the Karolinska Institute and a Lifetime Achievement Award at the Hero Gala of Aftonbladet, one of the largest daily newspapers in the Nordic countries. Ingrid lives in Cape Town with her husband Pieter. She has three sons and six grandchildren. She is also Desmond Tutus medical physician.

S
Lee Scharnick-Udemans
Lee Scharnick-Udemans is a senior researcher in the Desmond Tutu Centre for Religion and Social Justice at the University of the Western Cape. She has never met the Archbishop, but his rainbow nation formulation has been a source of inspiration (and frustration) in both her life and her work. As a South African woman of colour, various renditions of violence and exclusion have conditioned her epistemological orientation and it is sometimes challenging to hold out hope for a truly free and equal South Africa. But, when her adorable half-naked four years old son Khalil Hani sings "if you're happy and you know it, Allahu Akbar", with the random abandon of a being that has only ever known radical acceptance and appreciation, she knows that Tutu's vision of the rainbow nation is always worth striving for.

Sa'diyya Shaikh
Sa'diyya Shaikh is Associate Professor in the Department for the Study of Religions at the University of Cape Town. Her research is situated at the intersection of Islamic Studies and Gender Studies, with a special interest in Sufism. Her study of Islam began with an abiding interest in existential questions as well as a commitment to social justice – much of her work is animated by a curiosity about the relationship between the realms of spiritual and the political. Her book *Sufi Narratives of Intimacy: Ibn Arabi, Gender and Sexuality* (UNC Press, 2012) engaged with these formative concerns that still propel much of her work. She has a co-edited book together with Dr Fatima Seedat entitled *The Women's Khutbah Book: Contemporary Sermons on Spirituality*

and Justice from around the World, with Yale University Press (forthcoming in Spring 2022). She is mother to Nuriyya, a feisty, opinionated 18-year-old woman, and Ismael an impish entertaining 13 year old, and wife to Ashraf Kagee, academic, novelist and fun life partner.

Heike Spiegelberg

Heike Spiegelberg is a recently retired minister of the Evangelical Lutheran Church in Germany. At the beginning of the nineties she served as an assistant to Wolfram Kistner and Beyers Naudé at the Ecumenical Advice Office (EAB) in Johannesburg, and later at the Methodist Church of Southern Africa. The EAB and its staff assisted peace activists and survivors in violence afflicted communities. Heike Spiegelberg is married to Samson Mhlambi of Thokoza. For the couple, Archbishop Desmond Tutu is one of the icons of the struggle who even today safeguards the ideas of the Freedom Charter.

Baldwin Sjollema

Baldwin (Boudewijn) Sjollema was born in Rotterdam (The Netherlands), 1927 and obtained a Masters Degree in Sociology at the State University of Utrecht. He worked for nearly 30 years in the Ecumenical Movement: first in Utrecht (Dutch Inter-Church Aid (1953-56), among refugees from Indonesia after its independence; from 1956-57, director of the WCC Refugee Office in Vienna after the Hungarian Revolution; from 1958-69 in charge of WCC Migration Office in Geneva; from 1969-81, first director of the WCC Programme to Combat Racism (PCR), Geneva; from 1982-87 he was in charge of the Anti-Apartheid Programme of the International Labour Office (ILO), Geneva. He is married to Henriette van Sandick and they have five children: Suzanne (died), Inge, Anne Marie, Emilie and Frederik.

Demaine Solomons

Demaine Solomons is a Mandela Rhodes Scholar, lecturer/researcher of systematic theology and social ethics in the Department of Religion and Theology at the University of the Western Cape. He is a recipient of numerous academic awards, including the Desmond Tutu Doctoral Fellowship, through which he was able to complete his doctoral studies at the Vrije Universiteit Amsterdam and the University of the Western Cape. Personal narrative "I remember this quite vividly. My first encounter with Archbishop Tutu was when I was about five years old when he came to our church, St Joseph the Worker Anglican Church in Bishop Lavis. I was with my late grandmother, sitting in the front pew, her usual spot. It was a weekday morning, so the church was not particularly full. At the start of the service procession, the Arch passed my grandmother and I. Looking at me, smiling, he stopped for a second, caressing my face and continued. Of course, like most kids at that age I did not think much of it. However, almost forty years later, I cannot help but appreciate the significance of my first encounter with the Arch. He probably does not remember, but I do!"

Atle Sommerfeldt

Atle Sommerfeldt is a Norwegian prelate currently serving as the Bishop of Borg. Prior to becoming a bishop, he was Assistant General Secretary of the Botswana Christian Council from 1998 to 1993 and Secretary General of the Norwegian Church Aid from 1994 to 2012.

Theo Sundermeier

Theo Sundermeier was born in 1935 in Bünde Westfalen /Germany. He was promoted at the University of Heidelberg, Germany, in 1960. From 1964 to 1975 he served as a Lecturer at the Lutheran Theological Seminary in Otjimbingue/Namibia and from 1971 at the Lutheran Theological College in Umphumulo South Africa. Between 1975 and 1983 he was a Professor of Theology of Religions at the University of Bochum, and from 1983 to 2000 he was a Professor of Missiology and History of Religions at the University of Heidelberg. His numerous publications engage with African Cultures and Religions and Christian Art in Asia, Palestine and Germany.

T

Hildegard Thevs

Hildegard Thev was born in 1940 in Hamburg, and from 1960 to 1967, studied at the universities of Hamburg and Tübingen. Thev holds Master's degrees in Theology, Geography and Biology, was a teacher 1968-1971 in Hamburg, 1971-1974 in Zambia, 1975-2000 in Hamburg; ecumenical studies 1974/1975 at the Bossey Ecumenical Institute, Switzerland, and since then is engaged in voluntary activities in the Ecumenical Conciliar Process.

Baloyi Tlharihani

Baloyi Gift Tlharihani is an Associate Professor of Practical Theology in the Department of Philosophy, Practical & Systematic Theology at the University of South Africa (UNISA). His areas of specialisation are the intersection of Pastoral Care/Counselling and African indigenous therapy, gender studies in African culture and the question of human rights and religion. Although he has not met Desmond Tutu in person, his work (from his postgraduate studies) has had a tremendous influence on his theological life in response to the question of human rights and dignity.

Gertrud Tönsing
J Gertrud Tönsing is a Lutheran Pastor working in the city centre of Pretoria in the congregation St. Peter. She was involved in student organisations such as the National Union of South African Students, the Students' Union for Christian Action and Earthlife Africa. She has ministered in Hillbrow and at the Lutheran Theological Institute in Pietermaritzburg.

Nontombi Tutu
Nontombi Naomi Tutu is Associate Rector All Saints Episcopal Church, Beverly Hills. Her origin story is that her Daddy was at seminary when she was born. A family friend, Valerie Leslie, actually got to see her before he did and her report was, "We just need to put glasses and a cassock on this one and she is you." She has grown up being that girl who looks so (sometimes it felt like too) much like her father. Her parents tried to instill in their children a pride in who they are and in their cultural identity, with Ubuntu being their guiding philosophy.

Nele Trautwein and Ursula Trautwein
The paths of her grandmother Ursula Trautwein crossed repeatedly with Desmond Tutu in the context of her commitment against apartheid. Ursula Trautwein co-founded the 'Women against Apartheid' in Frankfurt am Main, Germany, and was an election observer in Namibia and South Africa. Nele Trautwein who interviewed her grandmother is her proud granddaughter and otherwise active in urban transformation and development.

V
Dan Vaughan
Dan Vaughan worked with Desmond Tutu at the SACC between 1978 up until he took up a new position as Anglican Bishop of Johannesburg in 1985. Vaughan has a long history of working at the SACC before, during, and after Tutu's time at the organisation. He again joined Tutu in 2004 at the Mpilo Trust where he saw to the administration of the office and later accompanied him as his aide in overseas travels until Tutu's retirement in 2011. He has recently written his unpublished memoir reflecting on his journey with Tutu and the profound impact he has had on his life particularly as a white man working and living in apartheid and post-apartheid South Africa.

Charles Villa-Vicencio
Charles Villa-Vicencio is Emeritus Professor at the University of Cape Town; Visiting Professor at Georgetown University, Washington DC; and Former National Research Director of the SA Truth and Reconciliation Commission.

W
Dietrich Werner
Dietrich Werner is an ordained Pastor in Evangelical-Lutheran Church in Northern Germany; Senior Theological Advisor for Bread for the World, Berlin; former Director of Ecumenical Theological Education Program in WCC; former Director of Studies in Missionsacademy at the University of Hamburg and Executive Secretary in the Northelbian Centre for World Mission, Hamburg/Christian Jensen Kolleg, Breklum. He holds a PhD in Theology and is Honorary Professor for Intercultural Theology and Development Ethics at University of Applied Science for Intercultural Theology in Hermannsburg and former Junior Lecturer at the Ecumenical Institute of the Protestant Theological Faculty, Bochum University.

Traci West
Traci C West, is Professor of Christian Ethics and African American Studies at Drew University Theological School, New Jersey, United States. She received her BA from Yale University (New Haven, CT), her MDiv. from Pacific School of Religion (Berkeley, CA), and her PhD from Union Theological Seminary (New York, NY).
She has been inspired by the leadership and life of Archbishop Tutu in countless ways throughout her life, starting from when she was a 1970s college student activist protesting for her university's anti-apartheid corporate divestment to her current invocation of his work in her gender violence activism and scholarship, including her most recent book, *Solidarity and Defiant Spirituality: Africana Lessons on Religion, Racism, and Ending Gender Violence.*

Roger Williamson
Roger Williamson worked with the British Council of Churches (1978-86), was Director, then Research Director of the Life & Peace Institute, Uppsala (1986-92). He worked for the Church of England Board for Social Responsibility and Christian Aid in the 1990s. From 1999-2010, he organized nearly 70 international conferences for the UK Foreign and Commonwealth Office through Wilton Park. After formal retirement, he was a Visiting Fellow at the Institute of Development Studies at the University of Sussex and UNU-WIDER, Helsinki. He was active in UK efforts to help establish the Tutu Professorship at the University of the Western Cape.

PART I
JUSTICE

1.1 Racism and Resistance against Apartheid

1. "I Turn My Face to the Rising Sun": Hope, Hopelessness and the Inspiration for Struggle

Allan Aubrey Boesak[1]

Our cries and our joys and our bewilderments – all of those are taken up in this tremendous offering of our Lord and Saviour Jesus Christ … Nothing can be more hopeless than Good Friday; but then Sunday happens.

Desmond Mpilo Tutu[2]

Desmond Tutu, the man, his theology, his ministry, his life's work – all are almost synonymous with the word "hope". Throughout the many years we have worked together in the church *and* in the struggle for freedom, in the church and in the struggle, this is the one thing he tenaciously clung to, tirelessly preached and unerringly symbolised. It made him more than the proverbial "beacon of hope". He was its very embodiment. So when I read Miguel De La Torre on the subject of hope, I react as one who has seen Desmond Tutu, and therefore seen hope at work.

Miguel De La Torre is a Cuban American liberation theologian from whose writings on liberation theology, ethics and reconciliation I have learned much. In an engaging essay he struggles with the issue of hope and its meaning for people living under the violent heel of American Empire.[3] "In a very real sense", he says to Latinx persons living "on the margins of empire", "the situation seems hopeless".[4] But unlike most theologians and politicians, and against the grain of what most of us dearly want to believe, De La Torre urges us not to rush to "hope". In fact, he summons us to abandon hope and embrace hopelessness. De La Torre does not want us "to keep hope alive". He wants us to grasp the truth that hopelessness is the normal situation of the marginalised. That is what oppression does. It breeds hopelessness.

But for De La Torre, that is not a bad thing. We should, he argues, use this situation for mobilisation. Hopelessness, he argues, is *not* disabling, but instead a spur toward action. The more hopeless we realise the situation really is, the more we understand the brutality of the oppressive systems that rob us of real hope. The more we understand this as a systemic challenge, the more we are likely, and able, to act. "Hope" is what keeps us from seeing this reality for what it truly is, and is therefore "disabling". Hopelessness, and our embrace of it, is not only realistic, it is enabling and empowering. "The hopelessness I advocate", De La Torre writes:

---

[1] Allan Aubrey Boesak is professor of black liberation theology and ethics, University of Pretoria. I worked closely with Archbishop Tutu from the time of his leadership of the South African Council of Churches as senior vice president, and then throughout the years of the struggle against apartheid after he became Archbishop of Cape Town. During the intensification of the international boycott, divestment and sanctions campaign against the apartheid regime, our relationship grew. I am privileged to also call Desmond Tutu a close friend.

[2] Desmond Tutu, interview in Jim Wallis and Joyce Holliday (eds), *Crucible of Fire: The Church Confronts Apartheid,* Maryknoll, NY: Orbis, 1989, 69.

[3] See Miguel De La Torre, "Doing Latina/o Ethics from the Margins of Empire: Liberating the Colonized Mind", *Journal of the Society of Christian Ethics* 33, 1 (2013), 3-20.

[4] De La Torre, "Doing Latina/o Ethics", 9.

rejects quick and easy fixes that may temporarily soothe one's conscience but are no substitute for bringing about a more just social structure that is not based on the disenfranchisement of Hispanics … It is not disabling; rather, it is a methodology that propels toward praxis.[5]

This is about as opposite to the faith and theology of Desmond Tutu as one could get. And where Tutu clings to the Passion and Easter Sunday to deepen and strengthen our hope, De La Torre goes there to wean us from hope. To convince us to embrace hopelessness as inspiration for resistance against empire, De La Torre reaches for Jesus' Passion as described in the Gospels, reminding us of one the most hideous acts of imperial punishment for those who dared to resist. "Hispanics occupy the space of Holy Saturday – the day after Friday's crucifixion – and the not-yet Easter Sunday of resurrection."[6] This is a space of only "some faint anticipation", for the good news of Sunday's Resurrection is "easily drowned out" by the reality and consequences of Friday's violence and brutality.[7] It is the space where "hopelessness becomes the companion of used and abused Latina/o's".[8] For Latina/o's, Good Friday is always too close and Easter Sunday is always too far away. Saturday is always a space of painful in-betweenness.

Among liberation theologians, De La Torre is not the first to reach for the Passion and Easter as metaphor for the situations of the suffering of oppressed people. Two friends and colleagues here in South Africa made that link quite early on. Manas Buthelezi, writing in the seventies, spoke of black people's lives under apartheid as "one long Good Friday",[9] and Takatso Mofokeng, who referred to Christ as "the Crucified among the cross-bearers", i.e. Black people, and made it both the title and theme of his book,[10] muses that for black oppressed people, Easter Sunday was something of a mirage. The most immediate pain of Good Friday, the brutality, the violence, the sense of God-forsakenness, for black people caught up in that in-between state of "faint anticipation" is just too overwhelming. "To sit in the reality of Saturday", De La Torre continues, is to discover that "the semblance of hope becomes an obstacle when it serves as a mechanism that maintains rather than challenges the prevailing social structures".[11] Here De La Torre seems to concede that genuine hope – not the "semblance of hope" – can indeed "challenge prevailing structures" of injustice and oppression. In any case, De La Torre has no intention to encourage passivity, with or without hope. "It may be Saturday, but that is no justification to passively wait for Sunday."[12]

But who says we have to "passively wait" until "Sunday rolls along"?" Certainly not the Gospels, and certainly not the women, who are the most courageous, most persistently faithful, most adamantly risk-taking characters in the Passion story. For while the male disciples were in hiding all weekend, "out of fear" for the Jerusalem elites who have made common cause with the Romans to have Jesus crucified, the women disciples, last at the cross on Friday and first at the grave on Sunday, were very active indeed. They observed the Sabbath, we read in Luke, but not "passively". Their minds were not idle. Their minds were on what they should be doing next, how they can serve God's will, to be done "on earth as in heaven". So "as soon as the Sabbath was over", Mark 16:1 tells us, that is, *on Saturday just after sunset,* "Mary Magdalene, and Mary, the mother of James, and Salome bought spices, so that they might go and anoint him".

Apparently, according to Matthew (27:62-66), "the chief priests and the Pharisees" were busy too, petitioning Pontius Pilate to put a guard of Roman soldiers around Jesus' grave, ostensibly to prevent Jesus' disciples from spreading lies about a resurrection. But while their busyness was aimed against

---

[5] De La Torre, "Doing Latina/o Ethics", 10.

[6] De La Torre, "Doing Latina/o Ethics", 9.

[7] De La Torre, "Doing Latina/o Ethics", 9.

[8] De La Torre, "Doing Latina/o Ethics", 9.

[9] See Manas Buthelezi, "Violence and the Cross in South Africa Today", *Journal of Theology for South Africa,* December 1979, 53.

[10] See Takatso Mofokeng, *The Crucified Among the Cross-bearers: Towards a Black Christology,* Kampen: Kok, 1983.

[11] De La Torre, "Doing Latina/o Ethics", 10.

[12] De La Torre, "Doing Latina/o Ethics", 10.

the Resurrection, the women's busyness was to work towards the Resurrection. The point here, I think, is not that they prepared the spices and ointments to anoint the body of a dead Jesus, but rather that they were meant to be present early on Sunday morning, to become the first witnesses of the Resurrection, of the body and presence of a living Jesus.

From Jesus' birth, throughout his life, at his cross, at the grave, and now at the moment of Resurrection, the women, always on the margins, pushed and held there by the men, placed themselves resolutely in the centre. And that was God's plan all along. So if we blindly follow the patriarchal thread through the Gospels, we do indeed end up with an ambivalent Holy Saturday of complicity and politicking by men, and the fearful passivity of men hiding in the upper room. But if we follow the women, we discover the Saturday filled with holy busyness, sacred impatience and consecrated activism. While the men were staring at the semi-darkness of the upper room and the mesmerising gloom of Saturday, the women were already turning their faces to the rising sun of Resurrection Sunday.

But now that De La Torre has opened the door to the Passion and Easter story, we may discover yet another dimension. Enter Thomas, the one who became notorious among Christians and non-Christians alike as the personification of doubt. Thomas, as in "doubting Thomas", has been cemented in our world of everyday language as a saying, and all this based on what the Gospel of John tells us in chapter 20:24-29. Thomas was not present when Jesus first appeared to the disciples hiding in that room and, when later told about the appearance, Thomas was blunt: "Unless I see the mark of the nails in his hands, and put my finger in the mark of the nails and my hand in his side, I will not believe." The next time Jesus appeared, Thomas was present, and Jesus invited him to touch the wounds. "Don't doubt, but believe," Jesus says. Hence our "doubting Thomas". I think that we are doing Thomas, and ourselves, a grave disservice.

First of all, we act as if Thomas was the only one doubting that Jesus rose from the grave. *All* the male disciples, every single one of them, did the same. They flatly refused to believe the women who came to tell them on Resurrection Morning that Jesus had risen, and why? *Because they were women.* The disciples, Luke writes, thought what the women said was "an idle tale" (24:11). The word Luke actually uses, is *lyros,* idle gossip, idiotic babble, women's talk. That was not only doubt. That was deeply sexist, for behind that dismissal was the question "Why on earth would, if such a thing really even have happened, Jesus appear to women at all, not to mention *first*?" Besides, what would happen to their fragile manhood if they actually conceded that the women were out there, braving the risks of being seen at the grave of this township terrorist by Roman soldiers or the informants of the ruling elites, while they were cowering in some room? While the women found renewed, revolutionary love in the risen Jesus, the men were, as the song says, "looking for love in all the wrong places". No, they were all guilty of that charge.

Second, the "doubting Thomas" angle makes us feel good. Thomas will only believe *after* he has seen and touched. But Jesus says "Blessed are those who have not seen and yet have come to believe". Jesus is talking about *us!* With that holy feather in our cap we look down on Thomas, and all his kind today. So our one-upmanship of Thomas predisposes us to rush to judgement on Thomas, and it's a sin we don't have to repent of, because Thomas deserved it. Perhaps we place too much emphasis on the miraculous, hopeful moment ("My Lord and my God"), and not enough on the revelational moment, "And Thomas, one of the twelve, was not there."

Third, we read as if John's report begins at verse 25. But verse 24 prompts the vital question: so where was Thomas during all this? Thomas was, like the women, and unlike his male colleagues, "out there", roaming the streets, thinking about all that had happened. Unlike his fellows, Thomas was not afraid. We know this by going back to John 11. There Jesus, like always, it seems, is on the road. He did not stay in one place, because the Jerusalem authorities, like always, were after him. I am not disputing that Jesus was, as scholarly consensus dictates, an "itinerant preacher and healer". However, that was not all he was. Much like the struggle activists of our times, Jesus was a political nomad, going from place to place, finding a home to rest his weary body wherever he could, usually in the homes of those sympathetic to the cause of the Messiah. Now he gets a message from Bethany, the home of those two remarkable sisters Martha and Mary, and their ailing brother, Lazarus. They, much like the mothers in our communities who opened their homes as places of refuge to struggle activists on the run from the Security Police, they also opened their homes to Jesus. Lazarus had died, is their message.

Jesus was ready: "Let us go to Judea again", he tells them. All the disciples urge him not to go, because the authorities were after him, just having tried to stone him, "and are you going there again?" (11:7). What they really mean is "Are you really going, *and taking us with you*, into that minefield of danger and death?" They were, as my former comrades would say, "weighing the balance of forces". But in reality, they were afraid for their lives, trying to hide that fear behind their political "realism" and their "concern" for Jesus. The revolutionary Jesus was losing his timing. Now was not the time for that certain confrontation with death. They were not ready for that.

Thomas, however, was of a different mind and spirit. "Thomas, who was called the Twin, said to his fellow disciples, '"Let us also go, *that we may die with him*'" (7:16). These words inspired a flood of commentary from learned scholars. Thomas is "impetuous", they say. "Over-zealous", John Calvin called him. He is the "pessimist" among the disciples. His is the "gloomy" vision of Jesus' mission. But I propose that we look deeper. Thomas understands the difference between glorification of the revolution and commitment to the revolution. He understands the consequences of revolution: those in power will always seek to destroy you, and that by any means necessary, because you threaten their power. If you are for real, and they are serious about their power, they have to. In that sense, Thomas, here accused not of doubt, but of "impetuousness" and "pessimism", was the most realistic of all. But here is the difference: they all knew what might happen, but only Thomas was ready. Thomas was not afraid then, and he was not afraid now.

I think Thomas is not gripped by fear or gloom, but by hopelessness, making him, on that first "Holy Saturday", the perfect example of De La Torre's "Holy Saturday" helpless in-betweenness. But again we should ask "Why"? Here is what I think. Thomas was a disciple with Jesus right from the start. There are some scholars who argue that his persistent designation in the Gospel of John, "The Twin" (*Didymus* in Greek), does not mean that he literally was Jesus' twin brother as some others have posited, but that his mind was so closely aligned with Jesus' thinking that he may as well have been a twin. That is hugely complimentary and says much more of Thomas than we give him credit for. For me that means that for Thomas, the revolution that Jesus brought was not conceptual or ideological, it was real, personified in the words *and* actions of Jesus. Here was somebody who, unlike other revolutionaries of his time – Jesus Barabbas for example, who was jailed and sentenced to death for his violent acts of resistance against the powers that be – engaged in revolution *with authority*, that authority that rhymes with authenticity, a characteristic that so irked the Jerusalem elites, because it was immediately and unfailingly recognised by the people. It was the *authenticity* of his revolutionary presence and activism that really frustrated and frightened the enemies of Jesus, and caused them to ask each time: "Where does this man get his authority from?"

Thomas was with Jesus and he heard and saw Jesus in action. For three years he witnessed what Jesus meant by his revolution: challenging the powers that be at every turn, healing, restoring and casting out demons, making clear that what he was casting out was the evil and polluting presence of Roman imperialism, occupation and exploitation; the greed, the hunger for power and the moral cowardice that collaborated with imperialism. All the while Jesus was uplifting the poor, the meek and the lowly. With every word, every deed, Jesus restored dignity to the people. He saw Jesus cross boundaries – of territory, tradition, race and perceived religious supremacy, as with the Canaanite woman, and the sister from Sychar in Samaria. He saw Jesus in the Temple, overturning the tables of profiteering while overturning the rules of religious propriety and customs that served only the powerful and the privileged, demythologising the myths of sacralised patriarchy, demystifying the powers of privilege, wealth and status, ripping the religious mask off the love of money and the worship of Mammon parading as the worship of God. Thomas saw, and stood in awe of, Jesus' revolutionary irreverence toward the political powers that be ("Go tell that fox [Herod]"), and toward the Jerusalem elites, heard the seven-fold "Woe to you!" against those "hypocrites", "blind fools", "white-washed tombs", who are "full of hypocrisy and lawlessness".

Thomas heard him defy Pontius Pilate, humiliating that powerful hegemon in front of the crowd and his puppets; saw Jesus defy the High Priest by refusing even to speak to him at trials that were a travesty of both the justice the Romans were so proud of, and the justice demanded by Yahweh. Thomas saw, experienced and knew Jesus to be the truth of God's reign personified as Jesus fulfilled before their very eyes what was only fulfilled "in their ears" in that manifesto-sermon in the synagogue in Nazareth that day: "The Spirit of the Lord is upon me, and I have come …" The poor, the captives, the oppressed, the broken-hearted, the destitute, the widows and the orphans, the women without patriarchal protection, the street children who were the prey of a heartless society – that litany of wretchedness turned into a liturgy of revolutionary redemption, all knew it and believed it. And Thomas knew and believed: the reign of God had come in all its indivisible, radical, compassionate justice, solidarity, equality and love. This was a revolution, and he wanted to be part of it, was ready to lay down his life for it, just like the prophet standing before him.

Thomas knew and understood something else. The world of power and might, the imperial throne, the governor's mansion, the palace and the Temple could never accept this. But Thomas also saw the reaction of the people in the synagogue in Nazareth that day, who first rejoiced when Jesus brought good news for them, but then turned viciously on Jesus when that good news included those they saw as enemies, as outside their own closely guarded circle, as the irredeemable, unacceptable, unloveable Other, unworthy of the love, mercy and justice of God they claimed for themselves only, and wanted to throw him off a cliff. Thomas was there, only a few days ago, with the crowd, all those people Jesus served with so much love and compassion, for whose liberation Jesus had put himself in harm's way, was willing to sacrifice his life for. Thomas watched as his people, and Jesus' people, the colonised, their land, also his, and Jesus', colonised and occupied by the Roman Empire, turned on Jesus and shouted to the representative of that same imperialistic power: "Crucify him!" That may have been the last straw.

Malcolm X tells us how, as he discovered more and more about his country and the plight of black people "in the wilderness of North America", he used to walk around all night long, thinking about what that meant for his people, for himself and for the future. His voice, immortalised on YouTube, still urges his people: "Think about it, brothers and sisters! *Think about it!*" Similarly, Thomas, walking the streets, is thinking about it: if this world, and these people, our *oppressed and colonised* people, cannot and will not accept this Jesus, reject him and his revolution, thereby rejecting their own freedom, dignity and choices for life, what hope is there? Why would Jesus, having been disavowed by such people, his own disciples having denied and betrayed him, and forsaken even by God, having died in vain for such people, rise up from the dead and return, all for the sake of these people and such a world, asks Thomas? That is not just doubt. That is the epitome of senselessness and hopelessness. It is De La Torre's Holy Saturday of dreams deferred and betrayed, of hope denied and decayed. The hopeful message of the women, placed against the backdrop of these realities, and the belated excitement of other doubters, sounded too much like the fanciful flights of frightened imaginations needful of divine assurances.

So when Jesus comes a second time, especially for Thomas, a few things become clear. First, the word the New Testament uses for "resurrection" is *apanastasia.* That means "rebellion" or "revolution." The Resurrection of Jesus is God's rebellion against that world that so dispirited Thomas. Thomas was there, ready for that revolution, and as far as the world was concerned the crucifixion put an end to that. Now Jesus is saying, Thomas, my revolution comes in phases. It is an open-ended work. The phase that ended with my crucifixion is only the first phase. There will be a second phase, and a third, and more, for as long as this world is held captive by those evil forces you saw me fight against, as long as imperial lusts prevail, for as long as God's people are not completely and joyfully free, the revolution is not complete. My Resurrection, Jesus is saying here, says that my death is not the end of the revolution. As long as there are believers, like the women, the revolution will continue. And in these struggles they will not be left on their own, for "I will be with you always, until the end of the age", Matthew records Jesus as saying (Matt. 28:20).

Martin Luther King Jr understood that when he wrote in *Chaos or Community* that black people in America should get ready for the second phase of their revolution, and that it would be much harder because white racism is everywhere, and deeply entrenched, and the demands of the ongoing revolution would be for much more than just integration. It would be something America was far from ready for: a deeply systemic and structural challenge to society, and to American Empire.[13] And even if you are not at the grave on Sunday morning, Jesus assures Thomas, Sunday is not yet over. There is hope, not just for the revolution, but also for you.

And here is the second reason Jesus comes. Not to convince Thomas that the danger is over, and that the followers of Jesus would be safe. The Romans are still in control and the sell-outs are still running rampant. Jesus knows better. He came, rather, to convince Thomas that hope does not die. Not even on a cross. If Jesus could, he would have shown Thomas the future: believers and followers who did not give up, and who kept the fires of revolution burning. From those Christians who defied the Roman Empire in those first three centuries with their non-conformism and militant non-violence, to the Christians who remained faithful when the Roman Empire finally colonised and domesticised the church. Those among later colonised peoples who held onto Jesus the revolutionary prophet of occupied Galilee despite slavery, racism and white supremacy. Despite oppression, genocide and cultural destruction. Despite patriarchal, heteronormative hegemony and capitalist exploitation. They understood the audacious hope Jesus invites Thomas to accept, and with the audacity *to* hope, rejoin that revolution, at the same time joining the women who have taken the lead.

The third reason lies in the way Jesus shows his disciples the meaning of the difference between love for the revolution and revolutionary love. Love for the revolution knows no compassion or understanding. It knows only undiluted and uncompromised love for the cause. For such people, love and compassion are weaknesses that sap the strength of revolutionary fervour. But it is the open door to hard-heartedness, to passion without soul. So they rear up in self-righteous, ideologised indignation, and defend their version of the revolution with passion, but without pathos for the people of the revolution. Jesus did not allow the revolution to stand in the way of love for Thomas. It is something revolutionaries are yet to learn, or to re-learn if they have forgotten. When Jesus comes for Thomas, he comes not because he was angered at Thomas's doubt in the Resurrection. For Jesus honest questions and reflection on the path and validity of the revolution are not an unforgivable sin. It did not put Thomas beyond the pale.

Jesus did not forget the Thomas of John 11 who, standing up against the self-interest of his brothers, did not flinch when the call for sacrifice came. Thomas questioned the path of the revolution, but he never sold out. Jesus comes not in wrath and retribution towards the Thomas losing hope in the future of the revolution, but in loving remembrance of the Thomas who understood the heart of the revolution better than his peers. *That* Thomas, Jesus knew, did not disappear under the onslaught of hopelessness brought about by what Thomas had seen throughout Jesus' life and ministry and especially in the week of the Passion: the vicious, ruthless power of the ruling elites, and the damaging, hurtful, forgetful powerlessness of the people. So now Jesus came to call upon the Thomas who in his hopelessness had thought the revolution was going to be for naught, but still deep in his heart believed, otherwise Thomas would not have come to that upper room that Sunday evening. That is truly amazing.

But finally is that indescribably wonderful moment when Jesus invites Thomas to reach out and touch the wound in his hands, his feet and in his side. This is not to invoke any kind of sentimentality whatsoever. Jesus is not a self-enchanted, self-indulgent narcissist who likes to call attention to his own martyrdom. Neither is it a kind of underhanded, covered-up reprimand to shame Thomas into confession. No, Jesus comes to remind Thomas of what, in his moments of disillusionment, he might

---

[13] Martin Luther King Jr, *Where Do We Go from Here: Chaos or Community?* (The King Legacy), Boston: Beacon, 1967, 3.

have forgotten, even though he reminded others of it. In a revolution, Jesus is saying, one must be ready to be wounded. The revolution is not only about lofty ideals and catchy slogans, it is about the willingness to step into the breach, here and now, for those upon whom wounds are inflicted on a daily basis: the poor, women, LGBTQI persons, the children, our vulnerable, exhausted Mother Earth. In that struggle for life the wounds intended for them will also be inflicted upon those who stand with them. There is no revolution, no freedom, without wounds. It is only when Thomas understands this, that he can say "My Lord and my God". Despite the gathering night, Thomas has seen the light of the rising sun.

In Alan Paton's *Ah, But Your Land is Beautiful,* he tells the story of the Soweto principal who defended his joining the 1976 revolution of the children to his white friends. "One day", he explained, "I will have to stand before the Great Judge in heaven. And the Judge will ask me, 'Where are your wounds?' And if I say, 'I don't have any,' the Judge will ask, "Was there then nothing to fight for?'" Think about that for a while. Think also about this, if you are a Christian. The One asking Thomas, and who will surely ask us one day, will be the One with the wounds in his hands, feet and side.

Hope is not passively waiting, nor is it deceitfully pontificating, pulling the wool over the eyes of a people desperate for change. It is stepping into the breach, into the heat of struggle, despite the wounds I know are coming, because it is worth it. It is what people, in the grip of integrity, honesty and decency, do.

De La Torre writes: "The disenfranchised have no options but to struggle for justice regardless of the odds against them. If not for themselves, then for their progeny."[14] He is correct. But, I would argue, they do this precisely out of a sense of invigorating, inspirational, life-giving hope, never out of hopelessness. One does not struggle because one has no options. One struggles because hope allows us to create options where there seem to be none. Hopelessness is just not able to inspire a person to lay down one's life for someone else, for a generation one does not know, or knowing not what that generation will understand of, or do with one's sacrifices.

I say this because I have seen, felt and lived it. This willingness to sacrifice for an unknown progeny, is exactly what has surprised, encouraged and inspired me so much about the generation of the revolutions of 1976 and the 1980s which Desmond Tutu and I were privileged to share in. Those were all young people, high school, college and university students, some only fifteen, sixteen and seventeen years old. What was it, I still reflect, with a sense of wonder, that made them do what they did? Conceive of a dream of justice, freedom and dignity, start or join a revolution against a vicious system designated as "a crime against humanity", against the mightiest military power on the African continent? Against a people all the more unforgiving of rebellion because of their jealously guarded power, their racism, white supremacist entitlement and the rightness of their religious fervour? From their religious point of view, as F.W. de Klerk, leading millions of others, protests to this very day, they were good people, fulfilling the will of God, and without fail their churches told them so. A bad person is a bad person, someone once said. But it takes religion to turn a good person into a truly evil person. Indeed.

But these young people nonetheless rose up, and stood their ground, and that quite magnificently. They set aside their own dreams and hopes and aspirations for their own future, for the sake of this struggle. They accepted persecution, imprisonment and torture. They were willing to be wounded, scarred for life and traumatised, laying their own lives on the line every time they stepped into the streets of protest, not ever having any guarantee that they themselves would see freedom and have peace and justice in their lifetime. But they did it anyway, not for themselves, but so that the next generation would enjoy the full humanity that apartheid had denied them. Never for themselves, always for others. That, I posit strongly, hopelessness can never do. That is only possible if one embraces Augustine's hope: a mother with two daughters, called Anger and Courage.

---

[14] De La Torre, "Doing Latina/o Ethics", 10.

So when I read De La Torre, I understand fully what he is trying to say. But I remember our students and our youth and how they, despite the darkness of apartheid, the not knowing what would come, and the possibilities of betrayal, yet turned their faces to the rising sun, never mistaking that for the false dawns of duplicitousness. That was their secret. That is their legacy. And it is unforgettable, irrevocable and irreplaceable. So, despite the present darkness of this age of re-embraced and reinforced apartheid, the betrayals and the corruption, the greed and hunger for power, the empty grandiosity, the privileges and entitlement that mark our political aristocracy; despite the disappointments and disillusionments, the deceit and broken promises and yet another loss of innocence; despite the fears and uncertainties because of this devastating pandemic and the darkening shadows of our valleys of death, I think of Jesus and the women and Thomas. I remember the youth and our revolution and, like Desmond Tutu, through the pain, the cries and the bewilderments I, too, see Sunday happen, and I will turn my face to the rising sun.

2. "My Goodness, I Am Happy that I Am Not Your Enemy": The Frankfurt Women against Apartheid

Nele Trautwein and Ursula Trautwein[1]

What I describe in this article I heard from my grandmother, Ursula Trautwein, and found it in the biography of my grandfather, Dieter Trautwein.

In my family we have been repeating for decades the story that when Desmond Tutu visited my grandparents' house and listened to my grandmother's story of actions against apartheid right in the centre of Frankfurt he said to her: "My goodness, I am happy that I am not your enemy." We all tell this story with the secret pride that the great Bishop Desmond Tutu visited my grandparents and paid respect to their commitment against the apartheid regime.

I am writing here about the memories of my grandmother Ursula Trautwein, co-founder of the Frankfurt Women Against Apartheid, who were driven by the conviction that international ecumenism could support each other across borders.

She was born in 1932 in the south of India and raised in the south of Germany. Her father was a pastor of the Protestant Church and so she grew up with her eight siblings in a parsonage. After the war my grandmother decided to train to be a parish worker in a small town called Bad Nauheim. There she met my grandfather, Dieter Trautwein, who was in his early years pastor, and became Provost of Frankfurt am Main many years later. My grandfather passed away in 2002, but left us his memoirs, so I can include his perspective next to my grandmother's in this review about the years between 1960 and 1994.

A provost is, in short, the elected representative of the Protestant Church for Frankfurt in this case – let's call it a regional bishop. Accordingly, the ministry was closely linked to political developments. Indeed, my grandfather was very much involved in the political developments of his time. International ecumenical cooperation was an important focus point in his work. Despite this, it was especially my grandmother who stood out for her (church) political commitment. My grandmother was and is an activist who takes the potential impact of each person very seriously, and who has spent her life fighting with impressive patience and assertiveness against what she could not bear to see. Accordingly, Tutu's phrase "I am happy not to be your enemy" so perfectly describes the nature of my grandmother that this quote will definitely not be forgotten.

In the 1960s my grandparents were starting to follow the political developments in South Africa. They had met young pastors who, as missionaries, had come into conflict with their Lutheran Church in South Africa. This was because the latter had adapted to the system of "'separate development'" of whites and blacks and supported Bantu education. From 1967 onwards, they repeatedly received direct information about the true situation of developments in South Africa. In his memoirs, my grandfather describes how Dr Beyers Naudé's visit to Frankfurt finally and forever opened their eyes. Dr Beyers Naudé spoke as a Boer in the Dominican monastery in Frankfurt and told of his conversion, as a former member of the Broederbond, who now saw that the black brothers and sisters of Jesus were suffering the worst injustices. As a result of his actions, Naudé lost all his ecclesiastical positions and was banned by the government in 1977.[2]

In the same year, the Black Women's Federation was also banned. In response, my grandmother and her sisters from the "Evangelical Women's Work" began to call for the boycott of fruits from

---

[1] The paths of my grandmother Ursula Trautwein crossed again and again with those of Desmond Tutu in the context of her commitment against apartheid. She co-founded "Women Against Apartheid" in Frankfurt am Main and was an election observer in Namibia and South Africa. I, Nele Trautwein, am in this context mainly her proud granddaughter and otherwise active in urban transformation and development.

[2] Here I refer to the book of my grandfather Dieter Trautwein, *"Komm Herr segne uns!" Lebensfelder im 20. Jahrhundert,* Frankfurt am Main: Verlag Otto Lembeck (2003), 305-330.

South Africa, in solidarity with the women on site. The "Boycott Women" began holding vigils every week on Thursday in front of the South African Consulate in the centre of Frankfurt. A travel agency housed in the same building advertised above their heads "Discover South Africa" and the women stood below replying "Discover a different South Africa".

They were insulted and spat at by passers-by, not least because they stood on the street as women who expressed themselves politically; still a very unusual sight at that time.

Many passers-by shouted at them that they should rather do something for the people in the communist East. The women had blank placards with them and asked the troublemakers to write down their personal request and stand with them. Of course, no one did this – because that was not the point.

The anger at the protest and commitment against apartheid was not just shown by the passers-by but was a widespread attitude. It was difficult for my grandfather to get the president of the 1979 German Evangelical Church Assembly in Nuremberg to distribute 20,000 postcards on which my grandmother and the other women demanded that Pastor Dr Beyers Naudé, Dr Mamphela Ramphele and Prof. Fatima Meer be released from the ban that had been imposed on them.[3] The German Evangelical Church Assembly (*Deutscher Evangelischer Kirchentag*/DEKT) take place every two years over a few days, spread out like huge fairs over the respective host city. Those congresses are an important platform where (church) political discourse is of great importance. So it was a significant sign that the apartheid regime became a topic at this church congress. The postcard campaign was connected with the hope to create a solidarity movement in the different communities. And indeed, the ecumenical commitment against apartheid grew. My grandparents became part of a large network and the rectory where they lived in Frankfurt was always full of visitors, hosting many guests from South Africa and other countries of the world. And because of the international airport in Frankfurt, the city was often on the way. As described at the beginning, Desmond Tutu was also a guest of my grandparents. They had met him in Ghana in 1974 and crossed paths again and again.

A few years later, in 1984, Desmond Tutu, as secretary general of the South African Council of Churches, invited my grandparents to South Africa. My grandfather followed the invitation, but my grandmother was denied a visa. As a member of "Women Against Apartheid" she was not allowed to enter.

Fortunately, my grandmother was allowed to visit as an "ordinary" tourist, a little while later, when the visa requirement for Germans was lifted, as South Africa was considered a popular vacation destination.

Nevertheless, she did not fly via Johannesburg, since she had to assume that she would be on the appropriate lists to be sent back. And besides, she had some money with her that was destined for black oppressed groups.

Somehow she managed to visit political prisoners in the state prison near Pretoria, some of whom were threatened with the death penalty for "high treason". Among them were Patrick Lekota and Popo Molefe, who later held high positions in the government of the new South Africa.[4]

My grandmother often told me about this visit to the state prison when I asked about her impressions of that time. She always described how deeply impressed she was by the moment when one of the prisoners held his hand against the glass separating them, while she did the same on the other side, and asked her not to forget their names. The international attention, the knowledge and exposure of the individual determinants was their only hope. And that's what the Boycott Women stood for in the streets every Thursday, holding up pictures with faces and names: "I stand here for …"

We all don't know exactly how it came about, moreover, that my grandmother was given a Bible by Winnie Mandela, who had received it as a death threat – carved into the pages of the Bible was the

---

[3] Trautwein, *"Komm Herr segne uns!"*, 305-330.
[4] Trautwein, *"Komm Herr segne uns!"*, 305-330. Popo Molefe after 1994 became prime minister of the North West Province of South Africa.

shape of a pistol. When my grandmother met Winnie Mandela in person some time later, she asked her if she wanted the Bible back. Since this was not the case, my grandmother gave it to the Bible Museum in Frankfurt am Main.

Later, through the Council of Churches, my grandmother was an election observer at the first democratic election in South Africa. There she met Tutu again, at one of the polling stations.

All in all, the biographies of my grandparents, especially in terms of their commitment against apartheid, stand in the context and great sign of international *Oikumene* and mutual support across borders.

Both had grown up at the time of fascism in Germany and had developed an awareness that never again should people put themselves above others. This time had probably also strengthened both of them in the belief that the actions of each individual have an influence and that international understanding and joint action can bring about great things. An awareness that we want to carry forward.

3. I AM ANGLICAN WHEN I PUT "TU" AND "TU" TOGETHER: REFLECTIONS ON RACE AND RELIGION

Michael Battle[1]

Introduction

When I, an African American, lived with Archbishop Desmond Tutu in 1993, I often walked into town to buy groceries. On one particular day doing so I read the following graffiti on the wall outside of Tutu's residence: "I was an Anglican until I put 'tu' and 'tu' together". There is a subtle force to racism that often renders the church inept and on the wrong side of history. We need only look at the complicity of the church with the North Atlantic slave trade. The subtlety is in how "church decline" in the Global North points to how the church's entropy is not by accident. Each generation that tries to learn from history (as well as make the same mistakes from history) seems to grow less interested in a church often on the wrong side of history. Desmond Tutu, however, is a chemical accelerator causing a different reaction in the world. When his history is written and his legacy thoroughly engaged, many will be able to embrace a relevant and vibrant church that is overtly part of solutions rather than problems.

There is also an overt force to racism. It can be felt in the "normal" ways we define each other. For there is a tendency in each of us to single out those who are somehow less than us, so that we can feel less insecure in comparison to the one we claim authority to define. Yes, even black folks do this, especially many successful black folks. Tutu's spiritual genius is in how he pays attention to both overt and subtle forms of racism that affect the legitimate recipient of racism to mimic its effects. Tutu resists this mimicry and instead offers vision to see what our most important identity looks like. Of all institutions, one would think that the church would share in Tutu's vision; however, when it comes to how racism performs in the world, the church has often been the last to resist such performance.

Often when we bring religious identity into play with racial identity, we lose motivation to bring both identities together in a healthy way. It is sobering to realise that Jesus instructs the disciples how to pray by helping them deal with the question of motivation. Jesus states:

> When you are praying, do not heap up empty phrases as the Gentiles do; for they think that they will be heard because of their many words. Do not be like them, for your Father knows what you need before you ask him. (Matthew 6:7-8)

To use good things to our own end is always the sign of false religion. How easy it is to take something even like prayer and make it a means to an evil end and even try to use it to get God to do what we want. All of this applies tragically to the church.

George Bragg, a biographer of Absalom Jones (a black pioneer in the Episcopal Church), illustrates how that which is good has gone completely awry. Bragg describes this in the pivotal moment in the life of Absalom Jones. Bragg writes:

---

[1] Currently appointed as Herbert Thompson Professor of Church and Society and director of the Desmond Tutu Center at General Theological Seminary in New York, Michael Battle lived in residence with Archbishop Tutu in 1993 and 1994 and was ordained a priest by Tutu in 1993. In 2010, Battle was given one of the highest Anglican Church distinctions as "Six Preacher" by the Archbishop of Canterbury, Rowan Williams, a distinction given to only a few who demonstrate great dedication to the church that goes back to 16th-century England and Thomas Cranmer. Battle has published eleven books, including his new release *Desmond Tutu: A Spiritual Biography of South Africa's Confessor*. Battle and his wife, Raquel, were married by Tutu in Atlanta, Georgia, and are parents to two daughters, Sage and Bliss, and a son, Zion, all of whom were baptised by Tutu as well.

The Negroes were moved from place to place, as the exigencies seemed to demand. Thus, on one Sunday morning, during the year 1787, just as divine services began, a very unpleasant scene was enacted. While at prayer, Absalom Jones, the leader of the Negro group, was pulled from his knees, and he and the others ordered some distance in the rear. Whereupon the entire group of colored worshippers arose and walked out of the Church. They never returned. They were persecuted, harassed and threatened; but they never more returned. This unpleasant and unchristian episode was the occasion which called into being the very organization among "free Negroes" of which we have any record.[2]

So, the subtlety of racism performs even in prayer and uses such prayer against a person's identity. Tutu's life witness invites the break of both subtle and overt forces of racism in our lives. His prowess of prayer and Christian spirituality paid attention to even the smallest bad tendencies toward power and control over someone else. He understands that unless we break free of all kinds of racism we inevitably are bound to repeat all kinds of racism. Tutu helps us see that without deeper forms of spirituality, we easily allow nonessentials to take precedence in our lives; and even worse, we allow evil to be in control. How quickly we crave things we do not need until we are enslaved by them. The apostle Paul warns us: "All things are lawful for me, but I will not be enslaved by anything" (1 Cor. 6:12).

Dialectic: Black and Anglican

The difference between prayer and human equality has been a perennial source of confusion. The dialectical tension in the Anglican church of "tu" plus "tu" in South Africa is just as real among Anglican Episcopalians in the United States. There were the same traditional Anglican establishmentarian ideas of racism in the US. Episcopalians in the early 20th century assumed the unification of American society to be largely constitutive of white people. Of course, there were white clergy and lay people who worked hard for the full inclusion of black people. Some, as in the case of Episcopal seminarian Jonathan Daniels, even gave their life for such inclusion. But despite such heroism, the fact that many Episcopalians remained Anglican until putting "tu" and "tu" together.

Only recently has the Episcopal Church moved from being the church of the establishment to being a church of advocacy. A serious time lag existed in the Episcopal Church, from Absalom Jones being yanked from his knees in 1787 to the Episcopal Church in 2015 finally sanctioning the gravitas of a black presiding bishop (equivalent of an archbishop in the Anglican Communion) – the Most Rev. Michael Curry. So far, most of the history of being Anglican in the United States promoted the invisibility of black people, to use Ralph Ellison's famous metaphor. This was true especially within the authoritative structures of the church; black folks were invisible. This begs the question of why black people held on for so long to the Anglican Church; after all, black Episcopalians were looked upon with great suspicion by other black folks. For example, African American educator Booker T. Washington provided a scathing critique of black clergy as unfit to be the leaders in America. Such clergy were seen by Washington as out of touch and uneducated. In his speech in 1895, he was no doubt accommodated by conservative whites as Washington assured them that most black people were not trying to be their social equals and just wanted to develop the practical skills needed to make a successful living.[3]

Even more critical was the African American intellectual, W.E.B. Du Bois. Du Bois grew up in the Episcopal Church – his grandfather even served as a parish treasurer for one of the most famous black Episcopalians, Alexander Crummell.[4] Du Bois, however, grew up to be a sharp critic of the

---

[2] George F. Bragg, *The Story of the First Blacks, the Pathfinder Absalom Jones 1746-1818* (Baltimore), 1929.
[3] Booker T. Washington, "The Colored Ministry: Its Defects and Needs", in Louis R. Harlan et. al., eds, *The Booker T. Washington Papers* (Urbana: University of Illinois Press), 1972; Booker T. Washington, *Up from Slavery: An Autobiography* (Garden City, N.Y: Doubleday), 1901.
[4] A tragic history of General Theological Seminary where I teach is that Crummell was denied admission in 1839.

Episcopal Church, even going so far to say that the Episcopal Church has "probably done less for black people than any other aggregation of Christians". Du Bois found it hard to imagine how a church could take so long to recognise human and Christian equality for black people. In light of the time lag, the Episcopal Church's "shameful" record on race would be hard to overcome. Du Bois concludes: "the southern branch of the Church is amoral dead weight, and the northern branch of the Church never has had the moral courage to stand against it, and I doubt if it has now".[5]

And so, it was not only white South Africans abandoning the Anglican church when they put "tu" and "tu" together, thousands of black folk also abandoned their membership in the Episcopal Church and other white-controlled denominations, between 1865 and1870. The black churches that grew were the African Methodist Episcopal Church (AME), the African Methodist Episcopal Zion Church (AMEZ) and black Baptist churches. For these black folks, these churches represented the ability to achieve freedom from the institution of slavery. No longer would black folk sit in the back and balconies of churches and be treated as voyeurs of worship. They sought escape from a slave religion. Against this backdrop of church decline in the Episcopal Church, the major task developed in the General Conventions of the Episcopal Church to figure out how to heal black and white divisions that occurred during the Civil War. According to historians, however, this was a tall task since Episcopalians were generally unmoved by the abolitionist movement – unlike the massive divisions among Presbyterians, Methodists and Baptists. The Episcopal Church oddly maintained unity during the controversy and tragedy of slavery. One such historian, Gardiner Shattuck, states: "Abhorring ecclesiastical schism more than the suffering people held in bondage, white Episcopalians had argued that slavery was a purely political question and, as such, beyond the church's concern."[6]

Synthesis

In essence, this essay in honour of Tutu has a different calculation of a church in decline when I put "tu" and "tu" together.[7] Indeed, there must be a decline of power which seeks to usurp our primary identity as a child of God. In Christian spirituality, we do this first in baptism, in which persons come to know that our essential identity is in God who alone knows how to define the other. Tutu writes:

> I am now convinced that the black consciousness movement did not accomplish its work completely. Too many of us still have a sense of self-loathing to the extent of our being capable of doing things that no self-respecting African would be capable of. This self-loathing is then projected onto other people. We show it in so many ways. We behave on the roads as if we have contempt for one another. We also show it by the way we treat the areas in which we live. Our homes are spotless and our people are tidy, but we tolerate litter and filth around them. We don't respect ourselves and we show it by being disrespectful to other people and often kow-towing to white people … We must address all the causes of violence if we are to bring it to an end …[8]

Instead of the primacy of race, Christian baptism informs us that the spiritual is central to earthly life, thereby allowing transformation of all human realms, including that which is political, biological and social. Folk who pray no longer have the justification to manipulate persons on the basis of European anthropological constructs of racial development. Such constructs embedded and leveraged European colonialism's pursuit to divide and conquer the world. Practising the presence of God, however, embeds and leverages God's interdependent image in creation to resist the evil of racism

---

[5] W.E.B. Du Bois, ed., *The Negro Church* (Atlanta: Atlanta University Press), 1903, p. 139.

[6] Gardiner H. Shattuck Jr, *Episcopalians and Race: Civil War to Civil Rights* (Lexington: The University Press of Kentucky), 2000, p.9.

[7] Michael Battle, *Desmond Tutu: A Spiritual Biography of South Africa's Confesso*r (Louisville: Westminster John Knox), 2021.

[8] Desmond Tutu, "Stop the Rot Everybody", *City Press*, 14 March 1993.

infecting the church. When material and social resources are scarce, the transformation of human realms made in God's image resists any reversion back to subtle and overt forms of racism.

In order to think beyond racial conflict, our primary identity must be seen through the image of God, which I have argued looks like the lens of *Ubuntu*, an African concept which means: "We can be human only in fellowship, in community, in *koinonia*, in peace."[9] In other words, you are a person through other persons. You don't know that you're beautiful, unless there is another person to help you see and understand that there is such a thing as beauty. You don't know that your jokes are not funny, unless another person is there to help you understand this by not laughing. All of us are inextricably linked together. Furthermore, in Christian baptismal identity, the only way to be a person through other persons is to be a person through the greatest other person, God, who paradoxically, Tutu states, "... knows [suffering] from the inside and has overcome it not by waving a magic wand, but by going through the annihilation, the destruction, the pain, the anguish of a death as excruciating as the crucifixion. That seems to be the pattern of true greatness – that we have to undergo to be truly creative."[10]

When the rubber hits the road for Tutu, "Christian faith is determined by what you do with suffering, yours and that of others".[11] Faith in the Christian God who entered suffering takes all human life seriously. And the church practises this claim through ordinary, mundane, material things such as bread, water, wine and oil in order that the material universe may not be "recalcitrant and alien to the spiritual, and that it will all be transfigured to share in the glory of the kingdom, where all things will have been made new, including human relationships [chief among them the relationships between black and white people]."[12]

This God, revealed in Jesus, helps persons determine their identity apart from being strangers and oppressors and helps them to understand God's reality in their very encounter of each other. This is why we pray, namely, to practice the presence of being true persons in relation to God. In so doing, personhood is discovered even more, then instead of becoming chains and threads, racial differences provide the means of how one comes to appreciate how God creates by relating to difference. The ultimate example of this is creation *ex nihilo* – the way God creates out of nothing. Tutu shows how we are to appreciate such a God:

> If religion is seeking to worship and praise God, then it is trying to be present, in awe, wanting to remain in a wordless, imageless experience. Perhaps, this will help us understand what Thomas Merton meant when he said, "The Contemplative is simply he who has risked his mind in the desert beyond language and beyond ideas in order no longer to clench his mind in a cramp upon itself, as if thinking made us exist." It is to let God empty us of ourselves and to fill us with God's fullness, so that we become more and more Godlike, more and more Christlike, that we should live and, yet, it should not be we who live but Christ living in us. Then we shall be holy even as the Lord God is holy, a holiness that is not static or to do with ritual purity, but a holiness that must express itself in ethical, political, economic and social responsibility for our neighbor, for the widow, for the orphan and the alien in our midst ... He became what we are so that we could become what he is.[13]

---

[9] See Michael Battle, *Reconciliation: The Ubuntu Theology of Desmond Tutu* (Cleveland: Pilgrim Press), 2009. Also see Tutu, "Nobel Lecture, December 11, 1984", p. 246.

[10] "The Archbishop, the Church and the Nation", in *Monitor: The Journal of the Human Rights Trust*, June 1991, p. 7.

[11] Desmond Tutu, handwritten address, "God Who is There", National Christian Youth Convention, Australia, 1987.

[12] Desmond Tutu, "The Theologian and the Gospel of Freedom", in *The Trial of Faith: Theology and the Church Today* (West Sussex: England Churchman Publishing, 1988), p.65.

[13] Desmond Tutu, address, "Where is Now Thy God?" Trinity Institute, New York, 8 January 1989.

Conclusion

All accounts of racism make persons valuable in the sight of God on the basis of political and biological attributes, and only by this criteria can it ultimately describe God's faithful remnant. However, "if your value depends on something like [racial difference], it means that not everybody can have the same value. That is contrary — totally contrary – to the Scriptures, which say our value is because we are created in the image of God".[14] Tutu used Christian spirituality as a means to break the restraints which keep us from being our true individual selves and our true community called the church. John of the Cross, a Christian mystic who found God in the dark night of his soul, said that it doesn't matter whether the sparrow is held by a chain or a thread. Both restraints will keep it from flying. Prayer is a means to discover the restraints which keep us from being our true selves; and prayer is a means to discover the restraints which keep us from being our true community called the church. We will need to be our true selves in order to survive in a world such as this.

In a *News and Observer* article I read a while back, I saw an example of restraint of those who are meant to fly. The article is entitled "Pigeons killed in peanut race":

A homeless man who was scrambling to eat peanuts thrown to pigeons near the state Capitol Sunday evening killed seven of the birds before passers-by asked a police officer to stop him, police said.

About 7:30 p.m. Sunday, people throwing peanuts to the pigeons at the Capitol Square entrance to Fayetteville Street Mall complained that a man was killing any bird that reached a nut before he did.

"If a pigeon got to a nut first, he would grab the bird and wring its neck", said Lt. R.C. Friese of the Raleigh police.

The officer cited Eladio Castillo, 65, for violating a city ordinance that makes it illegal to "trap, hunt or otherwise kill ... starlings or similar birds or fowl" in an area declared a bird sanctuary by the city, he said.[15]

Unfortunately for us, we live in such a world where downtrodden people who are meant to live fully as God's children end up trapping and restraining birds from flying ... end up competing with animals for the scraps and nuts which fall to the ground. The appetites of the animal and that of the homeless take on the same desperation. But prayer in some inexplicable way allows us to experience the deepest appetites we have, without those appetites consuming us (appetites of power, prestige, fame). Prayer allows us to become more aware of the false gods we substitute for the Living God.

This is what was happening with Jesus in the wilderness: he was being tempted to be less than his true nature. Satan wanted to see the use of power to dazzle the crowd ... wanted to see Jesus operate within an acceptable new world order in which some were at the top and some were on the bottom. Jesus refused. There was something in Jesus that kept him aware that "it doesn't matter whether the sparrow is held by a chain or a thread". This something in Jesus I call prayer. Jesus prayed a lot because he knew how easy it is to be held by idols of God. When we contemplate the saintly lives of people like Desmond Tutu, we want to put "tu" and "tu" together. Tutu's life makes us aware of the tragedy that we live in such a world, which creates a homeless man who entraps birds and steals their nuts. Tutu's genius was in how he knew how easy it is to ignore our capacity for God to live within us; and his strength was in his ebullient encouragement for us to live in God's image.

---

[14] Jim Wallis, interview with Desmond Tutu in Jim Wallis, ed., *The Rise of Christian Conscience: The Emergence of a Dramatic Renewal Movement in the Church Today* (San Francisco: Harper & Row), 1987, p.58.
[15] *News and Observer* (Raleigh, North Carolina), August 14, 1989. See: https://www.newspapers.com/browse/us/north-carolina/raleigh/the-news-and-observer_3272/1989/08/14/.

4. ARCHBISHOP DESMOND TUTU: SYMBOL OF THE CHURCH INVOLVED IN THE FREEDOM STRUGGLE AGAINST APARTHEID

Gottfried Kraatz[1]

Bishop Tutu – an icon

Anyone who has heard of Bishop Desmond Tutu will always recognise him. His voice, his way of speaking and his rational thinking have given him a very exceptional profile.

A particularly beautiful scene with Tutu can still be found on the Internet:[2] Pieter-Dirk Uys, a South African satirist, is doing an impression of Tutu. Tutu himself is sitting in the first row of the audience, listening attentively. During the short speech that Uys gives, imitating Tutu with a bishop's cap, one actually believes that one is looking at Tutu. His voice, the stretched syllables with which he sets his accent, the hands that hold the words and the listener together, and the favourite topics that are played in – they are unmistakably Tutu's. And then, like the seal under the unforgettable Desmond Tutu, instead of the liturgical "Amen" at the end, with a raised fist, he cries "Amaaaaaandla!!!" The scene is so memorable because you watch the real Tutu, clearly amused and delighted about the true-to-life impression.

Together with the camera, the viewer changes between the talking bishop wearing a burlesque version of a mitre on his head and the listening Desmond Tutu. The viewer has to change quickly between their own laughter about the rhetorically versed, light-mannered orator and the laughing listener Tutu, both with Tutu's distinctive large glasses. In the end there are two men – the friendly caricaturing actor and the laughing real Desmond Tutu, not the least bit unnerved by the satire – embracing each other.

The lingering memory of the devoted laugh of Bishop Desmond Tutu stays with one, after watching this video. Tutu as a bishop and politician remains authentic – always human.

Bishop Tutu – and the grassroots of resistance

Desmond Tutu – the name already had a positive ring to it before we met him personally. By "we" I mean the pastors in the township of Mitchells Plain near Cape Town. Further, I speak about a young generation who started to organise the political resistance against the apartheid regime in South Africa, to broaden and to anchor it deeply in civil society. I talk from the base and the years 1981 through 1986. I dive into my memory, not into files or books that were written then or later about this particular time of Bishop Desmond Tutu. I call up a recollection, very subjective and certainly flawed, but most importantly authentic from me.

It is important to ensure that in looking back it is not just one person who is getting glorified and made the bearer of a social process who was "only" part of this process. Instead, it is precisely these

---

[1] Pastor Gottfried Kraatz served as parish pastor and dean in West Berlin and in South Africa (Mitchells Plain 1981–1986), mission director of the Gossner Mission with partners in Zambia, Zimbabwe, India, Nepal, Soviet Union and Germany (1986–2002), member of the WCC's Ecumenical Accompaniment Programme for Palestine and Israel (EAPPI) and chair of the German network of EAPPI up to date. Mitchells Plain, where Gottfried Kraatz served as a pastor, is a township in the Western Cape, about 28 km from the city of Cape Town. It is one of South Africa's largest residential areas and was originally built during the 1970s to provide housing for coloured victims of forced removal due to the implementation of the Group Areas Act. It was once a major stronghold of the United Democratic Front, the broad-based ANC-sponsored anti-apartheid body.

[2] Pieter-Dirk Uys & Desmond Tutu in a cabaret show, by Marcel Harmsen: https://www.youtube.com/watch?v=AMtPIXflGWw (28.5.2013) De fantastische Pieter-Dirk Uys met een schaterende Desmond Tutu. www.cabaretblog.nl.

many people in the townships, congregations, new organisations of resistance which played a major role in the social process, but which are often forgotten.

The resistance against apartheid did not grow at the desk of a bishop or in the cell of a prisoner, but in society at large. This specific growth, courage of resistance and the increase from passive resistance to active struggle happened at the base and were first carried into the public of the white society of South Africa and then out into the world by many men and women. Personalities like Tutu proved to be loyal, well connected to the grassroots, self-sacrificing, often selfless and with a good understanding of the potential of their position. This movement revealed many very gifted and talented leaders. Some of them have become international icons of resistance in this very specific struggle for freedom. Bishop Desmond Tutu is one of them. Bishop Tutu was such an icon of a committed church when I immersed myself in the life of black South Africa in 1981. The order is important to me: the dynamic came from the black base, where courage, imagination and ultimately political strategic thinking had grown, which gave cohesion and direction to the resistance of the people. It just came from below and was picked up above by people like Desmond Tutu. We were grateful for these people in top positions, especially within churches, where, as with us at the base, a greater sense of independence from the state could develop. And even more: Tutu in particular was not only respected, he was popular. He was naturally close to the grassroots people, both in the community and growing political scene. Not only did he speak a simple language, he also spoke the township dialect (as can also be heard in the scene with Pieter-Dirk Uys). In short: he was a black among the blacks in South Africa.

Tutu as a Bishop carrying out the missing political mandate for the oppressed

Generally speaking, Tutu was known as Bishop of Johannesburg and the general secretary of the South African Council of Churches (SACC). However, for us pastors, Tutu had gained prominence because he represented the resistance internationally. We learned of conversations the Bishop had with other church leaders outside of South Africa. Furthermore, he was known from funerals of prominent dissidents who had been killed by the security forces of the apartheid regime.

Tutu was a voice of black people who were not represented in parliament, government, or administration. He clearly addressed the fact that the vast majority in the country had no political or administrative representation whatsoever. Tutu called the atrocities of apartheid by name.

We knew that Tutu identified himself with our specific commitment. Moreover, he represented our position that the church had a political function in this situation. Tutu's voice was heard in white South Africa, and while his voice provoked rejection and contempt, it could no longer be silenced.

Obviously, Tutu had to enforce his aspiration to have a political mandate for the deprived people on the national level. The same was needed at the grassroots. In South Africa, ecumenism was a gathering of the committed churches in the SACC as well as in the Western Province Council of Churches (WPCC) and on parish level. We established a committee and gave us a platform and thus we were a political church that explicitly advocated non-violent resistance and fight for freedom.

In order to understand what is meant by "we", I have to explain more about the base. In the years 1981 through 1986, I was a pastor in the newly built and largest township in Cape Town, Mitchells Plain. Having been "lent" from the Berlin Mission to the Evangelical Lutheran Church in Southern Africa (ELCSA) it was my job to gather and build up the Lutheran congregation in the new township. During my first weeks, I got involved in the ecumenical cooperation with colleagues from the many denominations in the township. As the Ecumenical Pastors Convention we took on the role of representatives in the community and campaigned for the interest of the residents: against expulsion of families who were unable to make their payments due to unemployment; for providing a nearby cemetery for the township of approximately 100,000 people; for calmer traffic in small streets where children played and were at great risk. After all, there was simply no black or 'coloured' mayor or any other representative, only the white administration. Therefore, we were the church on site and church for the underprivileged. Amongst us pastors particularly with the evangelicals we had a heated theological discussion about how far we as Christians and representatives of the church should exercise this political mandate.

This is the background of my picture of Desmond Tutu, who as bishop of the great Anglican Church and general secretary of the SACC perceived this missing political mandate for the oppressed in a prominent way. Even inside our churches we sometimes were reminded that with our political activity we were a minority: we were at the grassroots level like our leaders in the SACC.

In 1983, we continued our political role in the struggle for freedom. For instance, we made some of the church buildings available for political meetings that otherwise could not have taken place anywhere else. I remember vividly the year 1983, for me the year of the 500th anniversary of Martin Luther's birthday. The founding event of the Mitchells Plain branch of the United Democratic Front (UDF) took place in one of the Anglican churches. I had to throw on my robe and simulate a service because a warning of a police operation had come to our attention and to my delight, "the congregation" was very attentive to what I "preached" about the political dimension of the Reformation.

Let me emphasise the relevance of the UDF for our struggle. In 1983, as the ecumenical representatives of the Churches of Mitchells Plain, we naturally sent a representative to the founding event of the United Democratic Front (UDF), to express our support on behalf of the churches in this township. Hence, we were part of the political level that had formed during these years. "The Church" that we represented had integrated into the political scene. We were part of the resistance. It was known of Bishop Tutu that he had been asked whether he wanted to be the chairperson of the newly founded UDF, which he refused. Tutu wanted to remain impartial and did not want to dissociate himself from the other groups of the black resistance. It was important for us as the ecumenical community of Mitchells Plain to show our full support for the UDF. I would like to describe my personal role there. The suggestion to send a spokesperson for the Churches of Mitchells Plain to this great national founding event had come from me. After a short discussion, a large majority agreed. However, when asked who should go, nobody volunteered and the assignment was passed on to me. I refused, pointing out that the only white pastor of Mitchells Plain should not be sent there. They did not accept that and said: "You are not our White, but our Lutheran".

The importance which personalities like Tutu had for all of us was that he belonged to the first generation of black bishops and church leaders who were particularly charismatic. Churches grew out of the missionary tradition and colonial history, and emancipated themselves from their prehistory. Tutu was the first black general secretary of the SACC and he was the first black bishop in Lesotho, in Johannesburg and finally in Cape Town. This brought a new situation into the respective churches, where the black members would identify more and more with their church leadership. In the case of Tutu and many of his black bishop colleagues, there was also the fact that their white church members had to learn that black people also had a high level of education and the competence for leadership, a trust in leadership that they had never granted them before.

Bishop Tutu – our voice into the white public of South Africa

In addition to the church scene, there was also the political one, equally important to me.

Shortly after arriving in the Cape I was engaged in the "squatter crisis". Squatters were black families who emerged from the small courtyards and annexes of the black townships to enforce their right to live in Cape Town. The new concept of apartheid actually had defined the whole Cape Province as restricted to white and coloured people only. When after 1949 this concept was implemented, the families were defined "coloured" or "black" and the existing townships were separated into "coloured" and exclusively "black" (Langa, Gugulethu and Nyanga). These black people were exempt from the basic law and regarded "legal". But in the course of time more black people mainly from the Eastern Cape had infiltrated and secretly settled in the backyards and tiny extensions inside these black townships. They were living "illegally" in the Cape.

Now in 1981, they stepped out of their hiding places and provocatively squatted in front of the administration building outside Gugulethu, demanding legalisation. With branches and black plastic sheeting, they built small dwellings, camping between bushes and sand dunes. The police used to destroy those dwellings and deport the people forcibly with trucks to the Eastern Cape homelands, Ciskei and Transkei. But some courageous whites (clergy from the Anglican Church) brought them back the same way to the squatter camp in Cape Town.

Therefore, during the nights we stayed in the centre of the squatter camp praying and singing under a huge wooden cross, with a group of clergy, while the police watched from outside waiting for us to leave and start again their forced eviction of the squatters to the Ciskei.

Shortly after, I was asked to join an organisation for "urban planning", which was a code word for building up a resisting civic society (Churches' Urban Planning Commission, CUPC). This organisation became more and more important for activists in the resistance, even in the illegal underground. These types of organisations needed people like me, in order to be recognised by the city administration and state agencies, because all foundations and organisations needed an executive body with a majority of white members. Ultimately, I dove more and more into the political scene and got to know it well. But whatever I did I was seen and respected as a pastor and part of the anti-apartheid clergy.

"We" were the many young leaders of the newly emerging illegal trade unions, the organisers of the consumer boycott and of the election boycott in the coloured townships of the House of Representatives, a "chamber" of the white parliament for the coloureds; and finally the cadres who worked underground. They were the new political elite which grew out of the existing and the newly formed organisations. All these people had a clear feeling for the broader spectrum of resistance and respected us, the representatives of the churches, for contributing non-violent action. Tutu was one of the very prominent supporters of this non-violent struggle.

"We" were the many young people and students, e.g. from the Moravian Theological Seminary and from my confirmation class. They had grown up in this struggle for freedom. One student told me how she saw her own mother coming out of the supermarket during the consumer boycott. The adults shouldn't actually shop in the white-owned supermarkets and the group of adolescents wanted to make this clear. My student hid quickly, but someone else poured washing powder on her mother's vegetables, making her "blackleg" (items bought against the boycott) shopping items entirely useless. The young people deliberately rebelled against their own parents, accusing them of obediently and cowardly allowing that they be declassified into slaves of the whites.

At the end of my time in South Africa, after I was released from prison and lived underground, our Lutheran adolescents put up posters in the townships which announced a great church service to which their pastor would emerge from the underground and preach. The police chased these teenagers and some of them were caught and beaten. They were proud because at last a Lutheran pastor had the fame of a prominent freedom fighter and publicly challenged the government – like Tutu.[3]

This was part of the context in which Tutu was considered the great prophet of the freedom struggle.

Tutu as a part and icon of the freedom struggle

Without a doubt Tutu was an important figure. He was privy to the main developments and an important supporter of the non-violent resistance. Tutu was not directly involved in any political organisations. Unlike Allan Boesak, Tutu was neither a member nor in the leadership of the large mass organisation the United Democratic Front (UDF). Tutu did not want to be partially involved.

---

[3] In October 1985 with the state of emergency I was arrested and kept in Pollsmoor Prison as "No 2 Awaiting trial" in December '85. After seven weeks I was released and put under banning orders; in February 1986 I got the expulsion order, but decided to defy the government and stay in the country illegally. In March '86 I finally left the country.

Instead he remained open to support and criticism of the various and sometimes divided black resistance organisations. But Tutu appeared, for example, as host for a great guest from the USA: Edward Kennedy. This was early in 1985 and a huge event because this prominent US politician was not a guest of the government but of the resistance movement. The leaders organised a big event in a stadium. Here, the banned ANC appeared as a vital organisation: the stewards appeared in khaki uniforms, obviously as fighters of the Umkhonto we Sizwe (MK), i.e. the ANC's armed wing. ANC flags were waving in the stadium. Kennedy's security guards had negotiated with the UDF and the MK and agreed to work together while the government's security and protocol chiefs were not involved. The white administration had to accept this arrangement: the guest from the USA was simply too prominent to rule differently. In the stadium an introductory message was read out coming from the general secretary of the SACC, Bishop Desmond Tutu. So, for us he was present, although not in person.

"Tutu" was an icon for the nationwide resistance and a thorn in the flesh of the regime. For example, a good friend came to visit us right after one of his many arrests and told us the following: a dozen arrested men were ordered to line up and to march into the courthouse. The prison guards ordered the men to walk in a disciplined manner in a row of two. In their harsh English the guards shouted "Two-two, two-two"! Our friend commented this loud enough for his fellow inmates and, much to their amusement but incomprehensible to the guards, said that he was so pleased to hear that Bishop Tutu was enjoying such high appreciation in this place.

Before Kennedy's visit, there had been occasions when Tutu appeared as Bishop of Johannesburg or as general secretary of the SACC in Cape Town. Twice I saw him in St George's Cathedral. Once, it was on the occasion when squatters had found refuge inside St George's Cathedral. There was a major service that was to have national impact, and the secretary general of the SACC, Desmond Tutu, came from Johannesburg to attend. In my memory it was here, where Tutu appeared entirely as a bishop and performed the service in the high church liturgical order. He wanted to present himself as a spiritual leader. In his sermon he accentuated the message that the church had to be a prophetic one for the poor and oppressed.

The second occasion I remember was the "End Conscription Campaign" in early 1985 when one of the three prominent conscientious objectors conducted his three-week fast with supporters at St George's Cathedral. The three objectors were sons of generals or politicians, who for their part stood for white dominance and the absolute superiority of the South African military. Their public action intended to use their fathers' prominence to give more weight to the white anti-apartheid resistance. The End Conscription Campaign was a response to the crumbling myth of the unconvinced South African Defence Forces. Tutu, when preaching, stressed the exegetical endeavour to interpret war and readiness for war as incompatible with Jesus' Sermon on the Mount. He urged us as well to "fight the war nonviolently". There would be no other way to act according to the Sermon on the Mount.

There were other big appearances of Tutu throughout the country, and we were familiar with them. For instance, some comrades had come back from the Eastern Cape in winter 1985 where they had attended the big funeral of the "Craddock Four". Their detailed reports were complemented by "our" newspapers (*Grassroots* and *South*). The Craddock Four were four prominent activists of the UDF, and were cruelly murdered. Their mutilated corpses were thrown into a rubbish dump. Bishop Tutu, Allan Boesak, "Oom Bey" (Beyers Naudé) and Victoria Mxenge spoke there and thus represented the mourning and defiant black South African society. The funeral became an event of high national prominence and it was of no surprise that shortly after, President P.W. Botha announced the state of emergency for the Province of the Eastern Cape.

Once we had a rally in a big hall. The rows were filled up to the last seat. We waited quite a while for the main speaker, Tutu, when suddenly, the backdoor opened and Bishop Desmond Tutu stormed down the aisle. The Bishop with a red waving cape strode full of energy along the rows and jumped onto the stage. He immediately began his speech, sometimes in quick staccato and sometimes in long meaningful sentences. He dominated the audience. And he ended his speech, which he had delivered breathlessly, with the inevitable shout: "Amaaaandla!" And the big hall replied loudly and in a deep bass: "Awethu!" (All power – to the people!), followed by "Mayibuye" by Tutu and the hall's response: "I Africa!" (Come back – Africa!).

The audience had its idol and Tutu had his audience.

Those were our mental highlights in the "struggle" while usually it was strenuous legwork. The internationally renowned Bishop Tutu – he proved to be one of us. This was my feeling whenever his name was mentioned or a picture was shown in a newspaper.

Archbishop Desmond Tutu – the Nobel laureate

Years later, in 1993 and 1994, as the Archbishop of Cape Town and the Primate of the Anglican Church of Southern Africa I got to see him again, even though from a distance. My role as an election and peace observer as part of the Ecumenical Monitoring Programme in South Africa of the World Council of Churches (WCC) had brought me back to South Africa.

At that time, Tutu was chair of the Truth and Reconciliation Committee (TRC) whose meetings were aired on TV. Sitting with some congregants in a local parsonage I watched one of the hearings. We got to hear the many stories of mothers who accused officers of having maltreated their sons and husbands and hastily burying their bodies in the middle of nowhere. In one case, one officer confessed in detail. The meeting hall fell completely silent and only the weeping of the mothers, of the audience and of Tutu himself could be heard. Tutu respected this moment of grief and pain and eventually ended the silence with a prayer. I understood that we were observing a momentum of the change from enmity and struggle to healing and reconciliation of a nation.

Lastly, I'd like to point out one totally unexpected reunion. I was part of the WCC's Ecumenical Accompaniment Programme in Palestine and Israel (EAPPI). One day in 2008 two of us walked along the high wall in Bethlehem: my partner Justice, a black pastor from Soweto, and I, the pastor from Mitchells Plain, when suddenly we stood before a graffito of the Archbishop's face and a quotation of Tutu saying that the occupation of Palestine had to end like apartheid in South Africa.

We both felt encouraged by this echo of our non-violent struggle against apartheid in Mitchells Plain and Soweto. We felt content with the face of our comrade, the Archbishop and the quote on the wall announcing the eventual end of occupation in Bethlehem and Jerusalem and of the siege in Gaza.

Thank you, comrade Archbishop!

5. DESMOND TUTU'S FAME AND HIS ECUMENICAL NETWORKS: A PART OF THE GLOBAL HISTORY OF APARTHEID AND ANTI-APARTHEID

Sebastian Justke[1]

Without doubt, Desmond Tutu is one of the world's most famous religious personalities, often mentioned in the same breath as Mother Teresa and the Dalai Lama. In his time as general secretary of the South African Council of Churches (SACC) and later Archbishop of the Church of the Province of Southern Africa, Tutu symbolised the Christian resistance to apartheid more than anyone else.

In this essay, I examine the relationship between Tutu's fame and the struggle of Christian churches against apartheid and argue that his fame was an integral part of the history of apartheid and the global anti-apartheid struggle.[2] I begin with Tutu's first appearance on British television in 1968, and I present a graph of the course of his fame since then. Then, I describe Tutu's transnational church networks through which he made his anti-apartheid message heard outside South Africa. Finally, I detail the global scope of Tutu's media presence and the honours that he has received.

Desmond Tutu in *The Heart of Apartheid*

On the evening of 10 September 1968, the BBC broadcast a 50-minute television documentary on South Africa entitled *The Heart of Apartheid*. The producer and director was Hugh Burnett, a British filmmaker who would produce other documentaries about apartheid and South Africa in the following years.[3] At one point in the film, a black man suddenly appeared on the screen with no introduction or caption from the narrator.

Gazing into the camera, he seemed to be looking directly at that evening's audience. He talked about what it meant to be a black person in South Africa:

> I went with my wife to a large city, and about lunchtime we wanted food. And in the city there was no restaurant for Africans and, so, what did we do? We did what most Africans had to do in this kind of situation, go and buy a packet of fish and chips and sit by the pavement and eat out of the packet with people passing you by. It is being looked at in a particular kind of way as some squirmy bit of organism that hits at your vitals. It's the kind of thing that happens when you go into a shop. Almost invariably,

---

[1] Dr Sebastian Justke is a historian and research assistant at the Research Centre for Contemporary History in Hamburg. His doctoral thesis focused on West German Protestant pastors who had been sent by their church to South Africa and Namibia during the apartheid era. He is co-editor of Knud Andresen, Sebastian Justke, Detlef Siegfried (eds). *Apartheid and Anti-Apartheid in Western Europe* (Cambridge Imperial and Post-Colonial Studies) (London: Palgrave Macmillan: 1st ed. 2021).
This essay is based on my paper presented at the conference "Celebrity and Protest in Africa and in the Anti-Apartheid Struggle", Copenhagen, 10 October 2018.
[2] The connections between celebrity and the struggle against apartheid is a topic of more recent research. As Louise Bethlehem and Tal Zalmanovich point out, "opponents of apartheid, both in South Africa and outside the country, were cognisant of the importance of cultivating ties with local and global media, as well as with individuals who enjoyed easy access to the media as a consequence of their fame as writers, musicians, intellectuals or high-profile clergymen. Activists were alive, in other words, to the power of 'celebrity capital'." Louise Bethlehem and Tal Zalmanovich, "Celebrity and Protest in the Anti-Apartheid Movement", *Critical Arts* 34, no.1 (2020), 3.
[3] *The Heart of Apartheid* (1968), BBC Tuesday Documentary, first broadcast 10 September 1968, produced and directed by Hugh Burnett. The documentary was a sequel to his successful *White Africa*, which aired in January 1968. As the title suggests, it focused on the perspective of "white" South Africans. See Gavin Schaffer, "The Limits of the 'Liberal Imagination': Britain, Broadcasting and Apartheid South Africa, 1948-1994", *Past and Present* no. 240 (2018), 255.

whether you came first or whenever you came, you will be served generally after the white customer. And often, a mere slip of a girl behind the counter, because she is white, can say to your father, who maybe is sixty or thereabout, as my own father is, a former headmaster of a primary school, she can say to him "yes boy, what do you want?" And this gives you a pain in the heart that you can't describe.[4]

Figure 1: Screenshot from The Heart of Apartheid *(1968)*

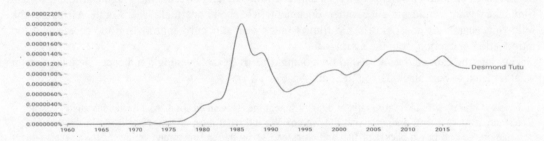

Figure 2: Ngram visualisation of "Desmond Tutu", 1960–2019. The y-axis shows the frequency with which "Desmond Tutu" appears throughout the Google Books corpus "English 2019".[5]

This man was Desmond Tutu, then in his mid-thirties. At the time, he was a tutor at the Federal Theological Seminary and a chaplain at the University of Fort Hare, both in the town of Alice in South Africa's Cape Province.[6] As his name was not mentioned, he was an anonymous black South African man to the audience, who, because he was dressed casually, could not even tell that he was clergy. Despite being a black South African impressively recounting his experiences of being marginalised in everyday life by white people under the apartheid system, one wonders retrospectively why Burnett chose Tutu, who was then unknown, for his film. As figure 2 shows, he became world famous only after the late 1970s.

---

[4] Own transcription from the film *The Heart of Apartheid*.
[5] Google Books Ngram Viewer, "Desmond Tutu",
https://books.google.com/ngrams/graph?content=Desmond+Tutu&year_start=1960&year_end=2019&corpus=2
6&smoothing=0&direct_url=t1%3B%2CDesmond%20Tutu%3B%2Cc0#t1%3B%2CDesmond%20Tutu%3B%2
Cc0.
[6] See Charles Villa-Vicencio, *The Spirit of Freedom: South African Leaders on Religion and Politics*. Berkeley, Los Angeles, London: University of California Press (1996), 284.

This graph was created by the Google Books Ngram Viewer and shows how frequently "Desmond Tutu" occurred in print, primarily in English, throughout the world. It quantifies interest in Tutu over time. Attention begins to accelerate around 1978 and reaches its peak in the mid-1980s. These two points correspond to important events that increased Tutu's fame. The first was his being elected general secretary of the SACC in March 1978. The second was when he was awarded the Nobel Peace Prize in October 1984. Both were milestones on Tutu's path to becoming one of the most prominent clerics in the 20th century.

Returning to the question, why did Tutu appear in a British television documentary in 1968 when, as the graph shows, he was unknown? The reason is that he was well connected. Earlier, Burnett had received funding for his documentary *White Africa*, which aired in January 1968, from the South Africa Foundation, a South African business lobby group with links to the apartheid regime. But because he interviewed South Africans belonging to the oppressed majority, most of whom opposed the regime, for *The Heart of Apartheid*, Burnett had to rely on other networks. The British anti-apartheid movement was well connected with the South African opposition. One of its best-known activists was the Anglican Bishop Trevor Huddleston, who was Tutu's mentor and friend.[7] They had met in the 1940s, when Tutu was in high school.[8] Huddleston's biographer Shirley du Boulay states that he was "the greatest single influence" on Tutu, and the two clergymen remained in close contact over the intervening decades.[9] Furthermore, Tutu, who had studied at King's College at the University of London from 1962 to 1965,[10] had friends in the city. Burnett probably met Tutu through Huddleston and Tutu's London contacts.

From the start, these kinds of international contacts and networks, which Tutu had maintained since his youth, drove his career.

Ecumenical networks

In 1972, four years after his appearance on British television, Tutu moved back to London with his family to work as an associate director of the Theological Education Fund (TEF), which had financed his university study. Founded by the International Missionary Council (IMC) in 1958, the TEF joined the World Council of Churches (WCC) in 1961, when the IMC was incorporated in the WCC at its 3rd Assembly in New Delhi.[11] The TEF's mission was to improve theological education in seminaries of the Global South and thereby make the so-called "young churches" of the Global South, which had emerged during decolonisation, more independent of churches in Europe and North America.[12] Its founding reflected the changes in Protestant churches worldwide that were taking place as a result of decolonisation, changes that constituted Protestantism's second phase of internationalisation.[13]

---

[7] On Trevor Huddleston's own celebrity and the networks he built between politicians, journalists, businessmen, church representatives, artists, writers and musicians since the late 1940s for the struggle against apartheid, see Tal Zalmanovich, "Trevor is 'News": Celebrity as Protest in the Early Anti-Apartheid Struggle, 1948–1960", *Critical Arts* 34, no. 1 (2020), 25-40.

[8] See Tinyiko Maluleke, "Desmond Tutu's Earliest Notions and Visions of Church, Humanity, and Society", *The Ecumenical Review* 67, no. 4 (2015), 577.

[9] Shirley Du Boulay, *Tutu: Voice of the Voiceless.* London: Hodder and Stoughton (1988), 31.

[10] See Steven D. Gish, *Desmond Tutu: A Biography.* London: Greenwood Press (2004), 31.

[11] See Dietrich Werner, "Theological Education in the Changing Context of World Christianity: An Unfinished Agenda", *International Bulletin of Missionary Research* 35, no. 2 (2011), 93.

[12] See Katharina Kunter, "Introduction", in *Changing Relations Between Churches in Europe and Africa: The Internationalization of Christianity and Politics in the 20th Century,* eds Katharina Kunter and Jens Holger. Sjörring,Wiesbaden: Harrassowitz (2008), 5.

[13] The first phase of internationalisation had been Protestant missionary work in Europe's colonies throughout the long 19th century, which saw the rise of the so-called age of Protestant world mission. See Hartmann Tyrell, "Weltgesellschaft, Weltmission und religiöse Organisationen", in *Weltmission und religiöse Organisationen. Protestantische Missionsgesellschaften im 19. und 20. Jahrhundert,* eds. Artur Bogner, Bernd Holtwick and Hartmann Tyrell.Würzburg: Ergon Verlag (2004), 14.

The World Missionary Conference in Edinburgh in 1910, which initiated the Christian ecumenical movement, was only the first step of the "second major transformation process of World Christianity".[14] A particularly important step, which began with decolonisation in the 1960s, was the former colonies' mission churches declaring their independence from the European mother churches. When they became members of the WCC they changed the WCC and its institutions from a western and white organisation to a really worldwide and all-churches-encompassing ecumenical body.[15]

Tutu found himself in the middle of this transformation. His job as an associate director of the TEF from 1972 to 1975 was to raise money for seminaries in Africa. So, he had to build international networks, and in the early 1970s that meant extensive travel. Tutu spent almost half of his time travelling through the world, particularly the Third World.[16]

The TEF was a crossroad of international theological ideas, and Tutu's tenure there changed his theology and understanding of faith. His colleagues in the organisation's headquarters came from across the Global South. Shoki Coe from Taiwan was responsible for Northeast Asia; Aharon Sapsezian from Brazil was in charge of Latin America; Ivy Chou from Malaysia administered Southeast Asia; and the US-American Jim Bergquist managed Oceania.[17] Concerned with the new role of the independent churches emerging from decolonisation, these theologians discussed the new "Contextual Theology". Coe had coined the term to express opposition to the Eurocentrism of traditional theology. According to contextual theology, a Christian's practice of faith should reflect the socio-cultural conditions in which people live. In light of decolonisation and the contemporary North–South conflict, this understanding of Christian faith implied a fundamental commitment to emancipation. Thus, contextual theology was intricately linked to liberation theology and black theology and their deeply socio-political understanding of faith and church.[18] Tutu first encountered Latin American liberation theology at the TEF, which since the early 1970s had promoted a global community, materially and spiritually, of churches. What he learned there would help him in his career and his struggle against apartheid. He became more political and learned techniques, most importantly international networking, to publicise his political goals.[19]

In March 1978, Tutu took up the position of general secretary of the South African Council of Churches, an umbrella organisation representing more than 12 million Christians, most of them black South Africans, through its member churches.[20] The SACC was then in a special position. Five months earlier, on 19 October 1977, the apartheid regime, having already outlawed most opposition groups, had banned many of the organisations in the Black Consciousness Movement and the Christian Institute, whose head, Beyers Naudé, had made it a significant force in the opposition. So, the SACC was one of the few organisations that could legally advocate for South Africa's oppressed majority.[21] Consequently, the regime went to great lengths to discredit the SACC and its general secretary.

---

[14] Dietrich Werner, "Theological Education in the Changing Context of World Christianity: An Unfinished Task. Translatability of the Gospel and Ecumenicity of the Church as Imperatives for the Future", Lecture for the Overseas Ministries Study Center (OMSC) Mission Leadership Forum, New Haven CT, 28 April 2012, 4.

[15] See Katharina Kunter and Annegreth Schilling, "'Der Christ fürchtet den Umbruch nicht': Der Ökumenische Rat der Kirchen im Spannungsfeld von Dekolonisierung, Entwestlichung und Politisierung" in *Globalisierung der Kirchen: Der Ökumenische Rat der Kirchen und die Entdeckung der Dritten Welt in den 1960er und 1970er Jahren* eds Katharina Kunter and Annegreth Schilling. Göttingen: Vandenhoeck & Ruprecht (2014), 30.

[16] See Gish, *Desmond Tutu*, 53.

[17] See Du Boulay, *Tutu*, 89.

[18] See John W. de Gruchy, "The Church and the Struggle for South Africa", *Theology Today* 43 (1986), 233.

[19] Non-religious ideas such as Pan-Africanism and Black Consciousness also influenced Tutu. See Maluleke, "Desmond Tutu's Earliest Notions", 587.

[20] See Bernard Spong, with Cedric Mayson, *Come Celebrate! Twenty-Five Years of Work and Witness of the South African Council of Churches*. Johannesburg: Communications Department of The South African Council of Churches (1993), 73.

[21] See John W. de Gruchy and Steve de Gruchy, *The Church Struggle in South Africa*. Minneapolis: Fortress Press (2005), 109.

Media attention and honours

But this campaign had the opposite effect, as a portrait of Tutu in the *New York Times Magazine* in March 1982 suggested:

> His prominence in religious circles did not automatically bring him a following among blacks. But once pro-Government commentators and politicians started to assail him for his role at the Council of Churches and his calls for economic pressure on the white regime, he emerged quickly as a leader, as if the hostility of the white authorities is part of what is needed now to validate a black as a spokesman for his people.[22]

The article is typical of how the Western European and North American media reported on Tutu. As the SACC's general secretary, he was the subject of increasing coverage. And unlike his appearance in Burnett's *The Heart of Apartheid* in 1968, he was now mentioned by name and recognised by media consumers. Since the late 1970s, newspaper articles about South Africa and apartheid often referred to Tutu. Western media and audiences had come to see him as a symbol of the South African anti-apartheid struggle.

What were the reasons for this attention? The shock of Soweto in 1976 had ended the heyday of apartheid and stimulated domestic violent resistance. Most of the opposition's leaders were in exile, imprisoned or, like Steve Biko, had been murdered.[23] In this circumstance, the general secretary of the SACC was, as a *New York Times* journalist characterised him in 1980, "the most influential black leader in South Africa outside prison."[24] And as a Christian, Tutu was seen as embodying the hope that apartheid would not end in a cataclysm of violence but through peaceful negotiations.[25] Western observers believed that a peaceful transition was essential for African stability, South Africa's continuing relations with the West and, not least, maintaining the Cold War balance of power.

However, the attention that Tutu enjoyed was not due solely to the power vacuum in the South African opposition. Another reason was his international campaign against apartheid. As head of the SACC, fundraising for its projects, particularly from international sources, dominated Tutu's time; as at the TEF, he had to network and, so, to travel.[26] But he now had the attention of politicians and media from Western Europe and North America. He gave many newspapers and television interviews to maximise attention to his concerns. For example, in an interview for Danish television in autumn 1979, Tutu said that it would be "rather disgraceful" for Denmark to buy South African coal.[27] And he regularly called for sanctions and boycotts, arguing that international economic pressure was needed to force the South African government to abandon apartheid.

The third source of his fame was the numerous honours and prizes awarded to him, especially in Western countries.[28] The first to award Tutu an honorary doctorate was King's College London in 1978, followed by Kent University in the same year. Many other awards followed, including the Nobel Peace Prize in 1984. As figure 2 shows, his popularity increased immensely since then. The honours raised public attention worldwide, which Tutu saw as a means to convince the world to abolish apartheid.[29]

---

[22] Joseph Lelyveld, "South Africa's Bishop Tutu", *New York Times Magazine,* 14 March 1982, 23.

[23] See Leonard Thompson, *A History of South Africa.* New Haven, London: Yale University Press (2001), 239.

[24] Barbara Slavin and Milt Freudenheim, "Botha Abandons Black Council", *New York Times*, 10 August 1980, Section T, 3.

[25] See Rob Skinner, *Modern South Africa in World History: Beyond Imperialism.* London, New York: Bloomsbury Publishing (2017), 125.

[26] See Hugh Murray, "Interview: Bishop Desmond Tutu", *Leadership*, First Quarter (1985), 62; Gish, *Tutu*, 73.

[27] Gish, *Tutu*, 77.

[28] See Du Boulay, *Tutu*, 265.

[29] See Murray, "Interview: Bishop Desmond Tutu", 67. One of the reasons given by the Nobel Committee for awarding the Nobel Peace Prize was that it wished "to direct attention to the nonviolent struggle for liberation to which Desmond Tutu belongs, a struggle in which black and white South Africans unite to bring their country out of conflict and crisis." "Text of Nobel Announcement", *New York Times*, 17 October 1984, Section A, 14.

Tutu became one of the world's most famous clerics as a result of the internationalisation of the (non-Roman Catholic) Christian churches in the 1960s in the course of decolonisation, a process that was particularly visible in the ecumenical movement. Tutu both benefited from and contributed to these changes, which took place at different levels. First, new institutions were founded and existing ones, like the TEF, transformed. Second, new church actors from the Global South reshaped the ecumenical movement. Third, new theologies emerged and transformed the understanding that many Christians worldwide had of their faith. These changes positively impacted on the development of church institutions in the Global South, for example, seminary education. Furthermore, the ecumenical movement was focused on the subject of apartheid from the 1960s until the end of the regime, and it paid special attention to Tutu as a South African theologian in the anti-apartheid movement. The story of Desmond Tutu's celebrity status therefore must be understood as an integral part of the global history of apartheid and anti-apartheid.

6. "PASTOR OF THE NATION" – A TRIBUTE TO DESMOND TUTU

Baldwin Sjollema[1]

Desmond Mpilo Tutu is a unique and humble character. His contagious sense of humour and laughter have helped to resolve many critical situations in South Africa's political and church life. He is able to break almost any deadlock, sharing with us the laughter and grace of God.

Back in the 1970s Desmond and I were colleagues at the WCC. He was working for the Theological Education Fund (TEF) based in London while I was working in the controversial Programme to Combat Racism (PCR) in Geneva which supported the liberation movement. We were not always on the same wavelength. At that time Desmond had to be careful not to be too outspoken against the Pretoria regime in order not to burn his bridges at home. But his attitude changed radically after his return to South Africa when he was appointed Dean of Johannesburg in 1975 and one year later Anglican Bishop of Lesotho, then general secretary of the South African Council of Churches (SACC) and finally the first black Archbishop of Cape Town (1987).

On the WCC's Programme to Combat Racism (PCR) he commented: "It is obviously an understatement to say that the PCR and its grants put the cat among the pigeons."[2] Our two largely white gatherings were making the standard with condemnatory statements and were ready to pass appropriate resolutions in line with their sentiments about so-called terrorists when some of us asked on whose behalf the church was speaking. In the past I would not have wanted to ruffle any feathers but the TEF (Theological Education Fund) had helped to train me in England and I had come to accept that personal integrity sometimes demanded uncomfortable things. PCR has proved to be a very crucial element in the WCC's witness and has helped many to discover a credibility for the churches and for the gospel of our Lord and Saviour which it was losing rapidly among the marginalised, the wretched of the earth. Sadly, its work, while concentrating on Southern Africa, does not seem to be going to end in a hurry.[3]

In the 1980s, when the struggle against apartheid reached its peak, Desmond was fearless in predicting black rule: "We need Nelson Mandela", he said in April 1980, "because he is almost certainly going to be that first black prime minister." At the end of the 1980s President Botha imposed a nationwide state of emergency, giving the police drastically more powers. Black leadership was either in hiding or in jail. The only gatherings permitted were those in churches. At that time Tutu as the Bishop of Johannesburg preached a militant sermon in the cathedral, asking with his arms outstretched: "Why are we allowing this country to be destroyed?"

His great courage and moral authority were recognised by the international community when he was awarded the Nobel Peace Prize in 1984.

Together with many other church leaders in South Africa, Desmond was in the forefront of the struggle, providing leadership at both local and national levels. Churches became meeting places and centres of information. Desmond was not frightened to speak the truth to those that were in power: straightforward and with humour. He was irrepressible.

When liberation finally came and a democratically elected parliament started its work, he exclaimed: "I love this dream. You sit in the balcony and look down and count all the terrorists. They

---

[1]Baldwin (Boudewijn) Sjollema was born in Rotterdam (The Netherlands), 1927 and obtained a Master's degree in sociology at the State University of Utrecht. He worked for nearly thirty years in the ecumenical movement: first in Utrecht (Dutch Inter-Church Aid,1953–56), among refugees from Indonesia after its independence; from 1956 to1957 was director of the WCC Refugee Office in Vienna after the Hungarian Revolution; from 1958 to1969 was in charge of WCC Migration Office in Geneva; from 1969 to1981, was first director of the WCC Programme to Combat Racism (PCR), Geneva; from 1982 to1987 he was in charge of the Anti-Apartheid Programme of the International Labour Office (ILO), Geneva.

[2] This and the following quotations below are given from oral memory of the author.

[3] "40 years of the WCC", *The Ecumenical Review*, July/Oct 1988, p. 436.

are all sitting there passing laws. It is incredible!" Unabated he continued speaking out against injustice, corruption and the abuse of power. When MPs came under fire accepting big salaries, Tutu commented: "The Government stopped the gravy train long enough to get on it." This and many other pronouncements earned him much criticism from the new government.

I remember watching his emotions when, as chairperson of South Africa's Truth and Reconciliation Commission (TRC), during hours, weeks and months he listened intensely to the cries and sorrows of thousands of black victims of apartheid. At that moment he became the pastor of the nation. Nelson Mandela had appointed him to the daunting task in 1994. At the opening session Tutu spoke with untypical brevity: "For once", he said, "the Archbishop does not have many words, thank goodness."

Desmond has been instrumental in developing the notion of *Ubuntu*: a person is a person because of other people; it implies mutual responsibility and compassion. It became the guiding principle of the TRC and has been written into the South African Constitution. Tutu stressed time and again the TRC's central role of forgiveness. He emphasised that there was no future without forgiveness. "You can only be human in a humane society. If you live with hatred in your heart, you dehumanize not only yourself, but your community". But his vision – and that of Mandela – was not shared by all. Others would say that it was too big a demand to make on anybody, especially people who had suffered and were abused. More modestly, they argued that learning to live together and respect one another is all one could ask.

Desmond Tutu foremost is a friend and colleague who reminds us time and again that instead of racism, disunity, enmity and alienation, "God has intended us for fellowship, for *koinonia*, for togetherness, without destroying our distinctiveness, our cultural identity".

I pray that Desmond's laughter and humour will continue for years to come!

7. DESMOND TUTU: AN ICON OF JUSTICE AND RECONCILIATION – AND A BEACON FOR DANCHURCHAID (DCA) AND DENMARK

Christian Balslev-Olesen[1]

"I find it disgraceful that Denmark buys South African coal and thus increases its dependence on South Africa" said Desmond Tutu, in a primetime TV news interview in September 1979.

In the TV studio, Max Kruse, who had recently been appointed staff of DCA, stood with a cold sweat. He had been given the task of accompanying Desmond Tutu, the newly elected general secretary of the South African Council of Churches (SACC), on his first visit to Denmark and DCA.

While walking around Copenhagen, Max Kruse told an interested Desmond Tutu about the Danish campaign against apartheid, which among other things focused on a boycott of coal and fruit from South Africa.

"I remember that we discussed in detail the Churches' Programme to Combat Racism campaign against South African goods in Danish shops and an impending arrival of a coal ship from South Africa in Denmark. But it was never the intention that Tutu should use what I told, because it had nothing to do with DCA's work", says Max Kruse.

Max Kruse was concerned that he had led Desmond Tutu a little astray in relation to what he really had to do, namely, to talk about South Africa and the work of the South African Council of Churches. The first interview had to be repeated for technical reasons, and Max Kruse used the break to caution Tutu that it might not be wise to include the Danish boycott initiatives in the discussion. Tutu disagreed, and the journalist was eager to include the boycott angle in the interview. So, in the next interview, Tutu underlined his message and came up with his famous statement that Danish coal imports from South Africa were "disgraceful".

The statements attracted enormous attention both at home and abroad, and already the same evening, the Danish Broadcasting Corporation (DR) was contacted by the South African Consulate General, who wanted a copy and a transcript of the interview.

It was neither planned nor agreed upon that Tutu would come up with a call for a boycott of South African goods. The announcement also prompted the South African government to revoke his passport when back home. And the SACC's leadership afterwards accepted that Tutu had expressed his own views and not SACC's position in Denmark on a boycott as an effective non-violence strategy.

At DCA, Tutu's clear message had far-reaching consequences. Until 1979, DCA had provided financial support for some humanitarian and development work in South Africa. After Desmond Tutu's visit, the Board had to decide whether it was enough.

They considered Tutu's message carefully. He was alerting the DCA to the discrepancies within their conceptualisation of "aid". On the one hand, the DCA contributed to long-term poverty-alleviation development work in the black townships, probably saving lives. On the other hand, they provided this aid without questioning the system that supported the poverty – namely Denmark's purchase of cheap coal from South African mines, because these mines depended on cheap black

---

[1] Christian Balslev-Olesen (b. 1947), Cand.theol., currently chair of DIGNITY Danish Institute against Torture. Secretary of the Ecumenical Council in Denmark, DanChurchAid (DCA) in 1985 and regional representative in Zimbabwe in 1989, general secretary of DCA 1992. The UN and UNICEF in 2002 as representative, in Eritrea and Somalia. Worked from 2009 as a consultant for the UN, the World Bank and Danida in Yemen, Libya, Sudan and Tanzania. In 2012, director of the Danish House in Ramallah in Palestine, and in DCA 2013–2016 as country director in Malawi and Zimbabwe. Christian Balslev-Olesen is a pastor in a local congregation since 1983. Christian Balslev-Olesen has worked with Desmond Tutu as staff and general secretary of DCA since the beginning of the 80s and has had the privilege of accompanying and hosting Desmond Tutu when visiting Denmark.

labour. Tutu was clear that emergency aid for poverty alleviation, in the absence of a genuine questioning of the systems that supported the poverty, was not enough. Following Desmond Tutu's visit, DCA increased its support for the South African Church Council work. Funds went to programmes that supported political prisoners and their families, provided legal aid in political cases and scholarships to apartheid opponents on the run.

But more fundamentally, Tutu's call for DCA led to an understanding that it was not enough to help needy and oppressed people – one must also ask questions about the causes of the need and the oppression, and be willing to intervene as well.

The realisation was so deep that it had to be written into DCA's statutes in line with emergency relief and development work.

It became a longer process where DCA also had to take on a responsibility for both helping and acting. It initially became an issue of more information and more educational material. Later it became what we today call advocacy programmes. Today, the essential task of advocacy is built into the work of all who work with emergency and development aid. This is also now an integral part of DCAs vision: "... to inform about the causes of distress and inequality and mobilize popular and political action to change these conditions".[2]

The fact that advocacy today is an essential and legitimate part of not just DCA's work but for most civil societies is to some extent thanks to Desmond Tutu's statement in 1979. Tutu has helped to define a language and a space apart from a technical humanitarian and political language. He has helped to define and consolidate an ethical or moral foundation for the fight against racism and for global solidarity that did not exist before.

For Desmond Tutu, the fight against apartheid was not just a matter of politics but what it means to be human, created by God and embraced by the love of God.

And Desmond Tutu has kept reminding us that the Church of God must say that, despite all the signs of the opposite, this is the world of God. God cares that in God's universe there is ultimately a difference between what is good and evil, and that the Resurrection of Christ proclaims that good is for victory.

The life and witness of Desmond Tutu reminded both the church in South Africa and Denmark that it must be a prophetic church that shouts from the rooftops "thus saith the Lord". It must put an end to injustice and violence, oppression and exploitation, any humiliation of God's children that prevents life in its fullest expression. Many listened – others accused Tutu and DCA of politicising.

Desmond Tutu's critics both inside and outside South Africa claimed that he politicised the gospel and mixed Christianity with the political freedom struggle. But for Desmond Tutu, the confrontation with apartheid was not a matter of politics, but of what it means to be human, and how human beings preserve their humanity and human dignity when experiencing war, famine and injustice.

Or as he has himself said: "I am an ordinary pastor who is merely passionate about justice, peace and reconciliation – in that order."[3]

Tutu is a man of prayer – he combines a rare combination of radical political engagement with a sincere piety. "Not praying is like forgetting to brush your teeth", says Tutu.

This was something new for many within the churches in Denmark. The Danish Evangelical Lutheran Church has a long and solid theological tradition of separating church and society, pretending that it is not politicising.

But for many Danes Desmond Tutu became instrumental in mobilising the Danes like no one else before, because he succeeded in lifting the fight against apartheid beyond the political realm. The anti-apartheid campaigns were not any longer an issue for left-wing activists only.

Denmark is changing course.

---

[2] DCA statures and related Danish texts – English version provided by the author, internal policy paper, unpublished.

[3] Erik Bjerager, 'Vi skal være stille for Gud' (English: 'We must be quiet before God'), *Kristeligt Dagblad*, August 3, 2001. See https://www.kristeligt-dagblad.dk/kirke-tro/desmond-tutu-til-danske-kirkedage.

Desmond Tutu's statements on TV laid the groundwork for Denmark being the first country to apply a boycott of all South African goods and take the lead in supporting the fight against apartheid.

From being a mobilising call for youth activists and the left, the idea of a boycott suddenly became acceptable to majority political parties and to most Danes.

Desmond Tutu and later his successors, like Beyers Naudé, Frank Chikane and Allan Boesak, as church leaders visited Denmark again and again and spoke and advised the government and members of parliament and briefed the press and the public on the situation in South Africa.

Desmond Tutu and the South African church leaders became some of the most influential advisers to the Danish government.

In 1985, the parliament decided to stop the extensive import of coal from South Africa. Many other trade connections were also shut down, e.g. the Scandinavian airliner SAS closed the direct flight connection between Copenhagen and Johannesburg.

Uffe Ellemann-Jensen, the then minister of foreign affairs, explained when Desmond Tutu was awarded the Nobel Peace Prize in 1984: "In more than one sense, Bishop Tutu follows in Martin Luther King's footsteps, as Tutu's arguments are also based upon Christianity in his fight for the rights of blacks. Tirelessly and fearlessly, he speaks the cause of his oppressed people.

When I met him, I especially felt struck by his tireless energy and strong will to reconcile with his opponents despite repeated humiliation."[4]

Ole Bertelsen, the then Bishop of the Evangelical Lutheran Church in Copenhagen explained it so: "Desmond Tutu is a necessary and gifted beacon for us today. Bold, mature, and solid. He speaks so radically about the present reality because he is rooted in the gospel of the crucified and risen Lord."[5]

Desmond Tutu has become one of the most influential theologians within the Danish churches during the past thirty to forty years. Tutu has told and taught Danish pastors and theologians again and again that "we inhabit a moral universe where goodness, and justice, truth, and freedom will ultimately always defeat their horrible contradictions".[6]

Desmond Tutu has challenged our self-understanding and laid the foundation for us as Danes to understand that giving is not enough. We must also act. He has succeeded to such an extent in his call and today has become an icon of justice and reconciliation to all Danes. This icon status is also in no small way due to his ability to express the deepest seriousness in the highest humour.

Many have asked how Desmond Tutu, as the newly elected secretary general, found the courage to speak so clearly and uncompromisingly on Danish television during his first visit to Denmark in 1979.

The Danish journalist Jesper Strudsholm asked him about this in an interview in the Danish newspaper *Politiken* in 2001.[7] And with the humour that Tutu is so famous for – and which has undoubtedly been one of the reasons why he has survived his fierce struggle against the apartheid regime and its generous distribution of death threats – he replied:

> In a way, I was seduced. The TV journalist Ms Karen Lis Svarre was very pretty. The responsibility was, of course, mine. But as I sat looking at this beautiful creature, I may not have been quite as aware of what I was saying as I should have been.

Desmond Tutu has been to Denmark on several occasions and provided moral answers in major globally important cases – poverty, debt, climate, education and torture. And he said yes, every time. He has been tireless in the fight for a more just world.

---

[4] Flemming Behrendt: "Nobels fredspris 1984 Desmond Tutu Skabt i Guds billed", *DanChurchAid, The Ecumenical Council and The Churches Program to Combat Racism* (Copenhagen 1984), 6.

[5] Behrendt: "Nobels fredspris 1984", 4.

[6] Kjeld Holm: "Vores provinsielle folkekirke kan lære meget af modige biskop Tutu", *Politiken*, 16 December 2012.

[7] Jesper Strudsholm: "Den politiske præstekjole", *Politiken*, 29 July 2001.

No other person has meant as much to DCA as Desmond Tutu. He is an icon for everything that DCA has done and wanted to achieve since 1979.

For that DanChurchAid is privileged and we are grateful to Desmond Tutu.

8. As I Experienced It:
Desmond Tutu at the Boipatong Massacre Funeral, 1992

Heinz Joachim Held[1]

Note by the editors: *The Boipatong massacre took place on the night of 17 June 1992 in the township of Boipatong, South Africa. The attack on township residents was carried out by armed men from the steelworkers' residence KwaMadala Hostel, which is located about 1 km from the township. Approximately forty-five people died. The attackers were widely believed to be supporters of the Inkatha Freedom Party (IFP). At the time, the South African government and several other political groups were negotiating in the Convention for a Democratic South Africa (CODESA) talks. Shortly after the massacre, it was claimed by many members of the community and several eyewitnesses that the South African police force had accompanied and supported the killers. A criminal trial held later in 1993, which included testimony of 120 Boipatong residents, convicted some IFP supporters of crimes in the massacre, but ruled that the police had played no part in it.*

The following contribution is from the travel diary of Bishop Joachim Held, after the mass burial of the victims of the massacre. Cynthia Lies, Husum, translated this text.

On the morning, Monday 29th June, we set off early from our hotel together with Wolfram Kistner to go to the offices of the South African Church Council (SACC), where the participants were gathering to go together to the funeral in Boipatong.

There we met Dr Beyers Naudé and Professor Johan Heyns, the moderator of the NGK, and the new ecumenical commissioner Professor Meiring. They had known one another for a long time, but for years had not really had anything more to do with each other and, separated both politically and church-wise, had become "enemies". And now they greeted one another warmly and began a deep, warm and friendly conversation, as though there had been no problem, or so it seemed: the dissident from among the NGK and the two officials of the Dutch Reformed Church in South Africa (NGK) met each other – until very recently decidedly in opposition to each other, and perhaps still the case. It moved me to see this, a scene full of symbolism and hope. And then we drove together in a car to Boipatong. As the promised bus did not come, we all had to travel in a long line of cars through the big city and the width of the land in the South with its industrial manufacturing plants, black settlements and rubbish tips. Then on good motorways and asphalt roads. And we got there on time through dust and sunshine, and gathered together in a small church near to the stadium in Boipatong, where the funeral was to take place and where thousands of people were already there.

In Boipatong, a township some 45 km south of Johannesburg, in the night of 17th June 1992 houses and families had been attacked and then the people cruelly murdered by gangs of thugs from a nearby migrant workers' hostel: on the face of it, people believed to be ANC sympathisers were killed by people believed to be Inkatha supporters. However, many members of the community believed that the killers were accompanied, encouraged and assisted by members of the white police force. These seemed like political murders. With altogether more than fifty fatalities: women, men, children and old people, with no consideration at all, brutal, dreadful! There was of course huge indignation, and tension remained, both at that place and on that date.

On the day of the funeral, the Boipatong sports stadium was full with up to 35,000 people – many also sitting in droves on the low walls surrounding it. Thirty-seven coffins containing victims of the massacre were placed at the front. I was invited to go onto the improvised VIP make-shift stage,

---

[1] Bishop Heinz Joachim Held is a German theologian, pastor of the Evangelical Church in Rhineland, and doctor in New Testament studies. He was a parish pastor, professor of theology at the Lutheran Seminar near Buenos Aires, president of the Rio de la Plata Church in Argentina, president of the Foreign Office of the EKD churches and moderator of the Central Committee of the World Council of Churches.

where it was almost impossible to find a place and where it almost caved in under the weight. Seated there were representatives of the ANC, the PAC, the Communist Party and the Trade Unions, ambassadors, Church people such as Dr Frank Chikane, Bishop Desmond Tutu, Beyers Naudé, Johan [sic] Heyns, the Lutheran Bishop Serote and the Anglican Bishop David as well as Archbishop Trevor Huddleston, as representative of the Archbishop of Canterbury. I was named among the first three Guests of Honour as Representative of the Evangelical Church in Germany (EKD) and former moderator of the World Council of Churches (WCC). There were many other guests from near and far.

The funeral service lasted from roughly nine o'clock in the morning until around three o'clock in the afternoon, much longer than was planned. The sun rose up high and it became hotter and hotter. There was no shelter from its [sic] burning sun.

The SACC directed the programme and controlled the proceedings. No one was meant to gain political capital from this, although that was really what they all had in mind.

Dr Frank Chikane, General Secretary of the SACC, held the reins in his hands, and made use of all his gentle charm and authority in order to keep the masses under control. Everyone was under pressure to ensure that there should be no unrest and most certainly no panic should occur. Again and again he and Archbishop Desmond Tutu called upon those attending the funeral to keep calm and to show dignity and to show those "up there" that black people are not chaotic. "Up there" were the police helicopters circling over the area; and of course there was also the government, de Klerk, the President himself, whose resignation was constantly called for by political speakers in heated demands and slogans:

De Klerk must go!

Down with the government!

Viva ANC!! Viva PAC!!

There was a sinister atmosphere and it wasn't at all clear whether in this atmosphere of excitement and tension there would be no incidents. It worked – through the goodness of God and probably also through the authority of the SACC and the Churches, who here once again had to take on a political role. There was no other institution that had the proper authority to act. It was inevitable for the Church to become political and it was a stroke of luck – for what happened here and in other parts of the country.

The following people and organisations spoke at the funeral:

- The Boipatong Black Citizens Council which encompassed local administration and a citizens' initiative.
- An eyewitness of the massacre, who survived and said quite clearly that in the second line behind the murderers he had recognised the white police.
- The political parties PAC, ANC and SACP, as well as the trade unions COSATU and NACTU.

The celebrated Bishop Trevor Huddleston, formerly in South Africa, then expelled, now over 80 and retired in England: a very emotional speech, not always with full concentration but received with enthusiasm.

The political speakers fought hard, called out for opposition and the PAC and SACP almost made a call to take up weapons to overthrow the government. No one had any doubt that the Government was behind this. They all expressed their sorrow and their indignation, again and again, and made vehement attacks against the government demanding:

- the takeover of power
- a transitional Government
- a legislative Assembly
- elections based on "*one man, one vote*"
- all of this to take place in this year.

Self-critical voices were also clearly heard:
- a call for the unity of Black People and among the opposition movements
- acknowledgement of their own weakness and fragmentation caused by stubbornness

There was a call that the ANC was not to be left alone in its dealings with the Government, or even treated with hostility, but rather to be encouraged to apply more pressure in its negotiations.

The ANC itself announced its further willingness to negotiate with the Government, but no longer under the present conditions. The President now had to move, had to make firm commitments and take steps to create new and unambiguous conditions for a transition. It depended on him; it was his turn now. Then there will be further negotiations. It was clear: the ANC was the only political movement that proved to have a feeling for political realism and a statesman-like stature at this funeral.

Bishop Desmond Tutu in his sermon that I regard as a masterpiece, had prepared it in writing, had the small pages in his hands and looked through them once more while it was the previous speaker's turn. As I sat quite close to him, I was able to observe him. But he soon put his concept papers aside and preached freely and for a long time.

He was the pastor and shepherd of the masses, who used his gift of speech, his charisma to the full: positively, liberatingly, constructively, with wit and humour. He even in this oppressive powerless situation made the people smile, even laugh. He did not hide anything, nor did he gloss over anything: neither the sharp criticism of the government nor the firm condemnation of the riots, not only here and now, but always and everywhere in South Africa. But he also spoke of the signs of hope: the recognition of the ANC, the new approach to dialogue, the small progress, and of the certainty that all suffering and pain will come to an end; that the false rulers will step down, because God reigns and wants justice for all, for all in South Africa. And that we in South Africa must not let ourselves be divided from each other: the blacks, the whites and the coloureds. Tutu said: We are the rainbow people of God! If you take away even one colour, you destroy the rainbow. We do not want that! We don't do that! Do we?"

In this way the preacher made the people think things over, come to their senses and understand. He provided an outlet for the accumulated tension and bitterness. He asked:

Where are they now, the former masters?! The President and the police minister of a few years ago? They are gone!!

How foolish they were, who wanted to make skin colour a criterion for being human and for humanity! Just imagine that someone would come up with the strange idea of making a long nose the characteristic of true humanity. And then: This entrance, these toilets, this bank and this university only for long noses, and who has none, must come to the Ministry for Long Noses for an exceptional permission. How funny! How nonsensical!! But that's how it is with apartheid, just unreasonable, nonsensical, foolish, ridiculous.

And the people really had to laugh. They were amused. And he asked them all to repeat after him: "We are very special people!" "VIP!" "Black and White!", "I am VIP!" "You are VIP!"
He went on to say with great urgency:

We represent a noble cause, a noble cause, a cause of nobility and dignity! Let us also pursue it with nobility and dignity! Not like those others who champion their cause with bad, unworthy means, with murder and manslaughter, with burning and robbing. Let us punish the lies that deny us our dignity! Let us show what we want to achieve and enforce our good cause in a good way – and that we are able to do so: Human dignity in a humane way, justice by right means, freedom for all by freedom for all!! And when President De [sic] Klerk comes and says: Brothers, we have wronged you, we want to change, we ask for your forgiveness – how I wait for this moment! What will we do then?! We will forgive him, as the Lord commanded us and because we are Christians and want to follow Jesus. But forgiveness is based on the recognition of guilt, and this requires repentance, and repentance in turn requires remorse. This is the good way.

Let us be sure that God is with us, as God was with the people of Israel on their way out of bondage in Egypt to freedom. But let us also make sure that we are with God! God's people in God's ways – that was the tenor of this remarkable sermon in an extraordinary situation.

Never before have I witnessed such pastoral care, such comforting of a crowd by a preacher. It seemed to me that by God's grace this was a special hour.

To keep the people on the path of moderation and humanity, in all their sorrow and bitterness, with all their impatience and indignation – a masterstroke, and a blessing.

To be sure, Archbishop Desmond Tutu was also clearly political. He reiterated the demands that the SACC had made, and had them endorsed almost plebiscite-style by the masses in the stadium:

1. hold the guilty to account
2. hold an investigation into the violence in South Africa – with international participation
3. disarm the illegal police units (Koevoet and Battalion 32 [sic])
4. withdraw South Africa from the Olympic Games.

It was incredible and great, breath-taking and yet calming, both pastoral and political at the same time. And the people there remained peaceful and disciplined, leaving the stadium quickly at the end in an orderly way under the admonishing words of Frank Chikane: "Let us keep order and keep calm! Take care of each other so that no one gets hurt! Don't push anyone into the barbed wire on that side! Go out of the stadium on the other side. Let us calmly disappoint those who do not trust us to behave with dignity and keep calm."

Our throats had become warm and dry from the sun and the dust, from the tension and the experience. But it was absolutely important for us to be there in Boipatong. It simply had to be, for the sake of the sign of our empathy that we wanted to set for ourselves, for the EKD and for the WCC, but above all for the sake of this special experience! We were deeply touched, enriched and blessed.

9. HOPE WITHIN US – GIVING EVIDENCE TO THE ELOFF COMMISSION

Martin Kruse[1]

Together with our warmest wishes for blessings on your special birthday, we dedicate to you, dear Arch, several sections of Martin's memoirs. They are taken from the chapter "For Overcoming Apartheid in South Africa".[2]

Our relationship to you and the South African Christians stems from two sources: a common history and a long spiritual community with the Evangelical Lutheran Church in Southern Africa. The Berlin Mission, which grew out of our Berlin church, also played a role in its coming into being. In the same way the ecumenical community spirit between the South African Council of Churches (SACC) and the Protestant Church in Germany are part of it.

First remembering our meeting in August 1983 during the World Council of Churches' Assembly in Vancouver, the larger section deals with the Eloff Commission, with its dreadful inquiries and "hearing". In the early 1980s the apartheid government had sought for a pretext to ban the SACC, and at the same time to get rid of the strong ecumenical network against racism. But they did not succeed. Thanks to the unshakeable trust in faith of the SACC and also the ecumenical network, and with God's help, hope maintained the upper hand.

With thankful memories of friendly encounters and in brotherly and sisterly solidarity

Marianne and Martin Kruse, Berlin

I remember Desmond Tutu's speech before the WCC Assembly in Vancouver in August 1983. He had arrived late, was greeted stormily and immediately asked to greet the Assembly. He had the undivided attention of the delegates and guests as he always did when he took the floor anywhere. He used his greeting – probably to everyone's surprise – to make a passionate appeal: "You must not hate the white brothers and sisters in South Africa, you must love them, only through the love of Christ will they be freed from their blindness."

Desmond Tutu was an unusual figure, small in stature, articulate, mercurial, always ready for a joke or an ironic remark, but never shallow, and filled with a deep seriousness; he was at home in the Bible, an inspiring, charismatic preacher, full of infectious confidence and an unwavering trust in God.

On 3 November November 1981, the South African government had set up a commission of inquiry (called the Eloff Commission after its chairman) to find out whether the SACC had misused church donations from abroad for political purposes. Obvious weaknesses in the SACC's financial management provided the government with a welcome excuse for this decision. A considerable part of the donations came from the Evangelical Church in Germany (EKD) and its member churches and from independent initiatives. In a sense then, the EKD was in the dock. The allegation was: You stand up for non-violence in word, but in reality you promote political actions for subversion with your financial means.

---

[1] Martin Kruse, Doctor of theology, since 1977 Bishop of the Evangelical Church Berlin-Brandenburg and since 1991 (reunification of West and East Germany) of the Evangelical Church in the greater region of Berlin – Brandenburg – Silesian Upper Lusatia. Since 1983 member of the Central Committee of the World Council of Churches (WCC), member of the Council of the Evangelical Church in Germany (EKD) 1979-1991, from 1985-1991 its Chairman.

[2] Martin Kruse, *Es kam immer anders: Erinnerungen eines Bischofs*. Freiburg: Herder (2009), 273 and 278-283, with kind permission of Herder GmbH Publishing House. Cynthia Lies, Husum/Germany, translated these pages.

On 11 March 1982, the Council of the EKD issued a detailed statement on the partnership between the SACC and the EKD. It reads: "The EKD supports the SACC in its efforts to reduce the effects of discrimination and injustice by non-violent means. It recognises the numerous activities of the SACC in the charitable field and in the field of socio-ethical reflections, as a genuine Christian commitment for justice and reconciliation." Written agreements had been reached on the use of funds in each individual case.

The investigations dragged on for months. In February 1983, the (secret) police submitted its report on the work of the SACC. It recommended that the SACC be "banned", that it be declared an "affected organisation", that is, that it be prohibited from having any connections with foreign donors. The goal of the SACC's work was not spiritual but secular, the overthrow of political conditions in South Africa, i.e. revolution. The "ban" was intended to paralyse the SACC and render it unable to act.

Under this threat, Bishop Tutu, the general secretary of the SACC, called the ecumenical partners from Europe and the USA, i.e. also the EKD, and asked them urgently to be prepared to appear as witnesses before the Eloff Commission.[3]

Three of us then set out in 1983: Bishop Heinz Joachim Held, head of the EKD's Foreign Office, Oberkirchenrat Rev. Warner Conring, in charge of the "Church Development Service" in the EKD's Church Office, and me as chairperson of the EKD's Evangelical Commission for Southern Africa (EKSA). Again there were difficulties with getting a visa. It came "at the last minute" and contained the handwritten note "for the sole purpose of giving evidence to the Eloff Commission". This was to exclude any travel or visiting in the country, but it did not prevent me from accepting a long-standing invitation to Vendaland to visit the Venda – Chief Mphephu. A small mission plane took me safely and unnoticed to the north and back to Pretoria.

During this week, Danish, Dutch and American representatives and we three Germans from the EKD were called to the witness stand one after the other. The schedule shifted. The commission, above all the Chairperson, was visibly anxious to observe the rules of a fair trial. The atmosphere was almost friendly and objective. The judges were obviously impressed by the fact that a small ecumenical group had come together rather spontaneously to assist the SACC. The statements of the EKD representatives carried particular weight for two reasons; first, because the majority of the foreign funds were contributed by the EKD, but also because the EKD was considered thoughtful and "conservative" because of its critical inquiries into the special fund of the WCC's Programme to Combat Racism (PCR).

The floor was essentially taken by the prosecutor, a public prosecutor of German origin, Dr von Lieren [sic] und Wilkau. He spoke fluent German, but only during the breaks. The defence counsel for the SACC, Mr Unterhalter, of Galician–Jewish descent, was quite a match for him in his eloquence and power of argument. Mr Unterhalter took pure delight in the thorough preparation of the three Germans. Warner Conring knew his way around all the programs of the SACC which received support from the EKD, he had all the figures in his head and did not owe an answer to any question of the prosecution. Heinz Joachim Held drew a wide arc from the insights of the Confessing Church in Germany during the Hitler era, to the experience of ecumenical love and solidarity by Christians all over the world in the post-war period and to the legitimacy of the partnership between the SACC and the German churches. It is in line with the biblical message and the teachings of the Church "when the South African Council of Churches advocates for the rights of those suffering under the current situation of apartheid, and when it emphasizes the need for fundamental change that will lead to real justice."

When I was called to the stand to be sworn in, I objected that I was a bishop and committed to the truth. I know that I am bound by the words of Scripture: "Always be ready to answer to anyone who

---

[3] Bishop Desmond Tutu (general secretary of the SACC 1978–1984) also himself had to provide witness before the Eloff Commission later: the text of his remarkable witness and contribution is made available under: https://disa.ukzn.ac.za/tra19821104026019.

asks you to give an account of the hope that is in you" (1 Peter 3:15). I was therefore reluctant to be sworn in before a foreign court. The meeting was briefly interrupted, and the Chairperson then announced that the Commission had granted my request. I then gave information about my life in the church, about the structure and working methods of the EKD, about the partnerships with the now independent churches in South Africa that had arisen from the missionary work, and about the objectives of the Evangelical Commission for Southern Africa. I was aware that the accuser would argue that there was no unified opinion in the EKD on the situation in South Africa. I could refer to the fact that the allocation of funds in all regional churches and in the EKD was discussed and decided in detail and in public by synods.

Of course, Desmond Tutu, Wolfram Kistner and other SACC staff members followed the process with close attention, since the very existence of the SACC was at stake. Members of the press were also present; some newspapers reported on the course of the hearings, but refrained from commenting. I had expected to find among those attending the hearing members of the German-speaking white churches as observers, which were after all contractually connected with the EKD; this was – at least that week – not the case. The Eloff Commission negotiations dragged on for months.

The SACC emerged from this stress test rather strengthened. It was forced to reflect comprehensively on its work, it was able to give an account before the public and to profess the necessity of fundamental change, and it also experienced the solidarity of its ecumenical partners – all this made it difficult to "ban" it, and thus to push it underground. So the SACC was allowed to continue its work without significant restrictions, still strongly supported by its ecumenical partners.

Unrest in the country grew. The youth were radicalised, no longer willing to be "put off". In 1990, a few months after the fall of the Berlin Wall, I was in southern Tanzania on a partnership visit. Even in far-off villages people expressed hope that the apartheid wall in South Africa will soon fall. It surprised me at first. What do the developments in Europe have to do with the developments in southern Africa? Africans saw an immediate connection: if the white government in South Africa can no longer use "communist world domination" as an enemy, then the apartheid system will also fall.

After twenty-seven years in prison, Nelson Mandela, who had long since become a symbol of the anti-apartheid struggle throughout the world, was released without any conditions on 11 February 1990. It was a miracle with what wisdom and willingness to reconcile that Nelson Mandela went to work to prepare the way for a South Africa that had emerged from free elections. In May 1994, he was elected South Africa's first black president. Incidentally, he spent his first night of freedom in Bishop's Court in Cape Town as guest of Archbishop Desmond Tutu. In his autobiography *Long Walk to Freedom*, Mandela describes Tutu as "this man who had inspired an entire nation with his words and his courage, who had revived the people's hope during the darkest of times".[4]

---

[4] Nelson Mandela, *Long Walk to Freedom*. Boston, New York, Toronto, London: Little, Brown and Company Publishers (1994). Quoted from the German translation: Nelson Mandela, *Der lange Weg zur Freiheit*, Frankfurt – Main: S. Fischer (1994), 757.

10. WHEN DESMOND TUTU DID NOT MAKE A SPEECH

Hildegard Thevs[1]

23 July 1989 marked a double anniversary in Soweto: the 10th anniversary of John Edward Matthews' release from prison and the 25th anniversary of the "Little Rivonia Trial".

It was a Sunday with typical winter weather. After a cold night, it became pleasantly sunny and warm around midday. A total state of emergency had been in force in South Africa for three years.

My Johannesburg host, Rev. Bernard Spong, was one of the liberal whites in the South African Council of Churches (SACC). "Keeping a low profile", he ran a programme to train black people in media technology and its application, the Interchurch Media Programme (IMP), which was also supported by the Evangelisches Missionswerk (EMW) in Hamburg. The studio had its premises at the headquarters of the South African Council of Churches, first in Diakonia House, and from 1981 in Khotso House, where Rev. Spong also served as house chaplain. Every morning there was a prayer service in the chapel for all those working in the building. The spirit of the house was set by Desmond Tutu, the first black general secretary of the SACC in 1978. His inspiration, his spirituality, his orientation towards the Bible, his attitude to prayer and the Eucharist shaped the community as faithful Christians in the face of the fundamental evil of apartheid. The award of the Nobel Peace Prize in 1984 made him known worldwide as a non-violent resistance fighter.

A year before the anniversary meeting, on 31 August 1988, a bomb attack had devastated Khotso House and the chapel. The then general secretary of the SACC, Frank Chikane, was attacked twice in April and May 1989 by poisoning his clothes. He was the successor to Desmond Tutu who, in the meantime, had become Archbishop of the Anglican Church in Cape Town. Now, as I write this, Alexei Navalny was to be poisoned in the same way in Russia.

As a clergyman, the colour barrier did not apply to Bernard Spong, which is why he was able to take me as his guest to the Soweto township. I did not know what to expect. We entered the courtyard at the side of one of the typical small houses with a garage, which was full of people. They stood close together, talking animatedly to each other, as is customary at such receptions. There may have been about fifty people, including only a few whites. The feast was steaming in large pots: maize "pap" (porridge) and gravy, while the goat meat was simmering, vigorously stirred by the women.

John Matthews was one of the five accused in the "Little Rivonia Trial" which followed the High Treason Trial in Rivonia (9 October 1963–12 June 1964) in November/December 1964. A sixth perpetrator turned himself in as a state witness and thus escaped prosecution. The charges were sabotage, in particular the destruction of power lines, which carried sentences ranging from twelve years to life in prison.

All six belonged to the Umkhonto we Sizwe (MK), the armed wing of the ANC. It was formed in 1961 after non-violent liberation movements – ANC and PAC – were declared illegal.

John Matthews, like his co-accused Dave Kitson, both white, Laloo Chiba and Mac Maharaj, both Indian, were communist. Wilton Mkwayi, the only black person among them, was a trade unionist. He was the only one sentenced to life imprisonment.

John Matthews received a prison sentence of fifteen years, Dave Kitson one of twenty years. They were both imprisoned in Pretoria Central Prison, where Denis Goldberg, the only white man in the Rivonia treason trial, was also held. The other three were taken to Robben Island, where they had to do hard labour in the quarry, together with Nelson Mandela and the other "comrades".

---

[1] Hildegard Thevs, born 15 September 1940 in Hamburg, 1960–1967 universities of Hamburg and Tübingen, Master's degrees in theology, geography and biology, teacher 1968–1971 Hamburg, 1971–1974 Zambia, 1975–2000 Hamburg; ecumenical studies 1974–1975 at the WCC in Geneva, since then voluntary activities in the ecumenical conciliar process.

Except for Wilton Mkwayi, all the co-accused were released from prison on time and could have attended the ceremony. However, Dave Kitson had moved to London after his release. Whether the other two attended the celebration, I do not know. Wilton Mkwayi's widow Irene had died of cancer in December 1988. When they became engaged to each other, Wilton was living underground, so they could not marry. This only became possible in 1987 when, like Nelson Mandela, he had already been moved from Robben Island to Pollsmoor Maximum Security Prison. Wilton had not been allowed to attend his wife's funeral. Archbishop Tutu delivered the funeral sermon. The funeral became a demonstration by hundreds of ANC supporters, led by clergy, surrounded by police. Tensions were high, but did not erupt into violence.

The political situation, which had been explosive for years, reached its peak in 1989 when State President P.W. (Pieter Willem) Botha resigned from office in the first half of the year for health reasons. "The Great Crocodile", as he was called, had carried out economic reforms on the one hand, expanded the security apparatus on the other, and in 1983 carried out a constitutional reform that was intended to strengthen and consolidate the apartheid system and the power of the state president. A tricameral system of parliament was newly established, representing whites, coloureds and Indians and excluding blacks from national parliamentary participation. Their rights were supposed to be represented in their homelands. This system provoked the formation of the United Democratic Front (UDF) as an extra-parliamentary opposition in which initially 400, later 700, civil organisations formed a loose alliance from which boycotts, protest actions and illegal strikes (stay-aways) were organised and carried out. It also had its office in Khotso House. Archbishop Tutu was a member.

Then the UDF was administratively strangled. Financial and other outside support became illegal and its protagonists were banned – a speciality of the South African repressive apparatus, which sentenced people to house arrest and banned contacts. From the UDF and the then powerful trade union federation COSATU (Congress of South African Trade Unions) evolved the Mass Democratic Movement, MDM, which took the place of the UDF. Its loose structure made its banning as an organisation impossible.

In July 1989, the successor to P.W. Botha had not yet been decided. Who among the contenders to succeed P.W. Botha would be able to pacify the situation? Would it be the equally conservative F.W. (Frederik Willem) de Klerk, who had succeeded him as leader of the National Party after P.W. Botha's stroke in February and who, like him, was an advocate of apartheid? Would he, according to Botha's will, become his successor as president after the parliamentary elections in September 1989? During these months, there were rallies outside Parliament House in Cape Town and acts of civil disobedience in the surrounding area which Archbishop Tutu participated in or led. Developments were drifting towards a confrontation.

Those present at the anniversary gathering were aware that Nelson Mandela had already been transferred from Robben Island to Pollsmoor Maximum Security Prison in 1982, but did they know that he was already one step closer to his release and was being prepared for his life of freedom in Victor Verster Prison? Did any of those present know that he had been invited to tea by P.W. Botha at his official residence earlier that month? Who knew that Nelson Mandela's release was conditional on the ANC renouncing violence? Who knew about mediation attempts by various governments, organisations and individuals and the secret talks between representatives of the South African government and representatives of the liberation movements that began in 1987? In retrospect, it has become much clearer to me how tense the situation was at the time of the above-mentioned anniversary.

Who were the people present, whom did they consider themselves to be? Those released from prison were still considered terrorists though they had served their sentence. The laws according to which every man and woman could be imprisoned without trial still applied. In addition to the general uncertainty about the future, there was also uncertainty about the reliability of those invited. It had become habitual to take the presence of the secret service into consideration directly or indirectly. Was there a guarantee of safety for the participants in this jubilee? If so then it lay in the presence of the Nobel Peace Prize winner and Archbishop of the Anglican Church of Cape Town, Desmond Tutu. What would he say in this situation?

Archbishop Tutu appeared with his wife, Leah. They came directly from Cape Town; perhaps it was just part of an overall important journey. With their arrival, those present turned to Archbishop Tutu expectantly. Would he make a speech?

He mingled with the people, engrossed in conversation until the meal began. It was natural that Desmond and Leah Tutu should be invited to the head of the only table. It was half in front and half in the garage. The other guests held their plates in their hands. It was equally natural for African hospitality that I was seated next to them as an ecumenical guest. There were no table speeches, no table talks. Was that "custom", or was it due to the situation?

Looking back on this banquet, I wonder about the Sunday mood of those present, while it was seething everywhere. That Archbishop Tutu did not give a speech in this semi-public situation, I understand only in retrospect. But he had come, he was there, he was with the people.

Sources

In those days, it was not opportune to leave any material traces. I have described this memorable feast day from my memories, which I have checked against contemporary sources. Inevitably, errors and gaps have remained.

I used Nelson Mandela, *Long Walk to Freedom*, London 1994; Bernard Spong, *Sticking Around*, Pietermaritzburg 2006; Desmond M.H. Tutu, *Reconciliation is Indivisible*, Wuppertal 1977; Ruth Weiss, *Analysis of the Zimbabwe Institute for Southern Africa (ZISA) Project 1987-1993*, Berlin, 2010.

1.2. Liberation Theology and Theological Education

11. VISIONS ON A TIGHTROPE: TUTU'S SOJOURN AS AFRICA ASSOCIATE DIRECTOR OF THE THEOLOGICAL EDUCATION FUND (1972–1975)

Kuzipa Nalwamba[1]

Desmond Tutu served as Africa Associate Director of the Theological Education Fund (TEF) at the World Council of Churches (WCC) from 1972 to 1975. Relocating from South Africa to London in order to work at the WCC was fraught with tension. At the time, WCC had taken a decisive position against the racism of the apartheid regime. His tours to African countries became a journey of learning and unlearning, and they represented a theological turn in his life. That theological turn entailed walking a tightrope as he pursued a theological vision that sought to bring black theology, African theology and liberation theology together. This contribution offers an assessment of Tutu's tenure at the WCC, through the lens of the tensions that ensued from the social, political and theological tightropes Tutu trod, which encapsulate his visions of justice, dignity and peace.

Background

My motivation to reflect on Bishop Desmond Tutu's work at the WCC arises from my position in my current role as an employee of the WCC. Part of my dual role in the organisation includes serving as programme executive for Ecumenical Theological Education (ETE), whose antecedent, the Theological Education Fund (TEF), is the programme the "Arch" served in as associate director for Africa. I value the association, however remote. I consider the tightropes he navigated against the background of his life in South Africa and his TEF work of stimulating theological education on the African continent.

The WCC launched the TEF in the late 1950s in order to help establish theological educational institutions and programmes in the Global South. The goal was to make theological programmes financially viable. The TEF operated a fund for theological training for people from the Two-Thirds World. Many Global South theological institutions and programmes benefited from the initiative. Tutu himself was a beneficiary when he obtained a scholarship to study in England and returned to teach at the legendary Federal Theological Seminary (FEDSEM) in South Africa, which was a creation of, and beneficiary of, WCC TEF grants.

TEF evolved through several phases of promoting contextually based theological education in the Global South and eventually that TEF mandate came to an end and was replaced by the current programme, ETE, from 1993. The focus has shifted from financial viability to the viability of theological formation itself. While financial viability remains a concern, it was subsumed within a broader context and debate of methodologies, substance and aims of theological education.

South Africa to London – circumventing powerlessness

Tutu's job as TEF director for Africa required that he relocate to London against the background of rising tensions between the South African apartheid government and student protest movements. Tutu was initially refused permission to leave by the South African authorities due to his

---

[1] Kuzipa Nalwamba is a staff member of the World Council of Churches (WCC), serving in a dual role as ecumenical social ethics lecturer at Bossey Ecumenical Institute and programme executive for Ecumenical Theological Education (ETE). She is a retired ordained minister of the United Church of Zambia.

involvement in the Fort Hare student protests when he served there as a member of the chaplaincy. This act of solidarity with students is illustrative of the commitment he had to the quest for justice and resistance against white oppression in his own country.

Tutu was leaving South Africa to join WCC, an organisation that had irked the apartheid administration by taking a decisive stance against apartheid and declaring the Christian ideology that justified it as un-Christian. In this moment, Tutu straddled two seemingly irreconcilable situations. His South African citizenship and prospective employment seemed irreconcilably polarised. Tutu negotiated that tightrope by contending to the authorities that taking up the WCC position would earn South Africa good publicity and the government yielded. Even in a society where white domination was already a fixture, he whose quest was for justice and equal dignity would find a way.

The South African situation of those years is summed up in the words of Njabulo Ndebele's foreword to the 40th anniversary edition of Steve Biko's *I Write What I Like*, when he observes that, according to the architects of the apartheid system, "whiteness would always precede 'blackness' because 'whiteness' as power created 'blackness' to be its powerless opposite".[2]

Three years after the union between Britons and Boers, in 1913, the British-government-sanctioned whites-only agreement came into effect. Novelist Sol Plaatje surmises that after that "the South African Native found himself [sic], not actually a slave, but a pariah in the land of his [sic] own birth".[3] This was the context in which Tutu negotiated with his government to let him go and work at the WCC. In March 1972, Tutu and his family moved to the United Kingdom and lived in Bromley where the TEF's headquarters were located. In addition to his WCC role, Tutu served as honorary curate of St Augustine's Anglican Church.[4]

Despite being categorically powerless, given the absolute power of the state, Tutu negotiated his way through. Did growing up in Klerksdorp, that crucible of power contestation between the Boers and Britons, implant in him tact and elasticity that made him dare to straddle seemingly irreconcilable polarities?

A sojourn in Africa – learning and unlearning

Tutu's work as the Theological Education Fund (TEF) associate director for Africa from 1972–1975. The work of assessing grants made to theological training institutions and students suitable for TEF grants brought Tutu into more intimate contact with the African continent in ways that signalled a turn in his theological orientation. Tutu's tours of Africa in the early 1970s account for a significant contribution to, and reflection on, theology and theological education on the continent at the time. Granted, though, he is most renowned for his role in the struggle for peace and justice as general secretary of the South African Council of Churches (SACC), the work that also won him the Nobel Peace Prize.

His accounts of socio-political and cultural contextual realities are instructive and speak of a theological reckoning that was not confined to religious themes. He wrestled with sights of corruption, poverty and ethnic tensions. Allen's biography aptly captures how Mobutu's military regime in Zaire (present day DRC), interfaith relations between Muslims and Christians in Nigeria, ethnic conflicts in Nigeria post-Biafra war and Idi Amin's expulsion of Asians from Uganda all had an impression on Tutu and would significantly impact his worldview and theology, including his own inert biases.[5]

The contextuality of reflections gathered from Tutu's work travel underline his aversion towards universalising discourses. It is a thread that runs through his work and one that is especially evident

---

[2] Steve Biko, *I Write What I Like, Steve Biko: A Selection of His Writings* (Johannesburg: Picardo Press, 2017): xi.

[3] Sol Plaatje, *Native Life in South Africa Before and Since the European War and the Boer Rebellion* (1916) (Johannesburg: Raven's Press, 1982): 21.

[4] Steven D. Gish, *Desmond Tutu: A Biography* (Westport, Connecticut and London: Greenwood Press, 2004).

[5] John Allen, *Rabble-Rouser for Peace: The Authorised Biography of Desmond Tutu* (London: Rider, 2006).

in accounts of how he grappled with black theology and liberation theology against the backdrop of western theologies. Evidently, to him, to know the specificity of a locality or a person is to accord them dignity by naming them with reference to their reality and locating theological reflection (read: education) within that reality.

African theology or black theology?

Tutu's theological turn was owed to experiences during his tour of duty on the African continent, his preceding knowledge and attraction to black theology and discovery of liberation theology through his TEF Latin American counterpart, Aharon Sapsezian. All informed and shaped his theology in remarkable ways, and influenced the work he did regarding theological education on the continent. Combining the various strands of these theologies was not without inherent tensions.

James Cone, the father of black theology, speaks of it as a coherent study of God's being in the world with reference to the existential condition of oppressed communities and connecting of liberation to the crux of the gospel of Jesus Christ. By the time Tutu joined the WCC, he had embraced the liberative motif in black theology. Black theology arrived in Southern Africa in the early 1970s through Basil Moore, a Methodist theologian. It gave rise to, and developed in tandem with, the black consciousness movement that influenced the freedom struggle against apartheid in South Africa and Namibia.[6] The black consciousness movement also prepared the ground for the 1986 Kairos Document.[7]

While giving a lecture at Union Theological Seminary in New York in 1973, Tutu stated that black theology is "an engaged, not an academic, detached theology. It is a gut level theology, relating to the real concerns, the life and death issues of the black man [sic] … a straightforward, perhaps shrill, statement about an existent. Black theology is. No permission is being requested for it to come into being …"[8] His assertion is a direct challenge to absolutist white (men's) theologies that underpinned (and still do to a great extent, even though a turn seems imminent) the political, social, economic and religious structures of oppression of non-white people.

Although Tutu was attracted to Black theology, he is not named among the black theologians of his time in South Africa. Yet, his participation in student protests when he served at Fort Hare illustrates his commitment and support for the black consciousness closely associated with black theology. In a survey of Christianity in South Africa, black theology proponent Tinyiko Maluleke names fellow South African black theologians in one section. In another section he names old mainline church leaders, among whom is Tutu. While the author does not list Tutu among black theologians, he associates him with Steve Biko and the black consciousness movement. If mentioning the latter in the same sentence counts, it is clear that Maluleke approximates Tutu to the black consciousness movement.[9]

Another black writer, Njabulo Ndebele, in his foreword to Steve Biko's *I Write What I Like*, lauds the moving foreword that Tutu penned for the same book's 2000 Raven Press edition.[10] Tutu is at once associated with and dissociated from black theology. Shirley du Boulay notes that Tutu became one of the most eloquent black theology proponents through sermons and addresses.[11]

---

[6] Mokgethi Motlhabi, "The History of Black Theology in South Africa" in Dwight N. Hopkins, Edward P. (eds). *The Cambridge Companion to Black Theology* (Cambridge, England: Cambridge University Press, 2012): 221-233.

[7] Vuyani S. Vellem, "Prophetic Theology in Black Theology, with Special Reference to the *Kairos Document*", *HTS Teologiese Studies / Theological Studies* 66, no.1 (2010): doi:10.4102/hts.v66i1.800.

[8] Allen, *Rabble-Rouser*, 138-139.

[9] Tinyiko Maluleke, "South Africa" in Kenneth R. Ross, J. Kwabena Asamoah-Gyadu, and Todd M. Johnson (eds) *Christianity in Sub-Saharan Africa* (Edinburgh: Edinburgh Press, 2017): 43-54.

[10] Biko, *I Write What*, viii.

[11] Shirley Du Boulay, *Tutu: Voice of the Voiceless* (London: Hodder and Stoughton, 1988).

Tutu did not dedicate himself to producing systematic academic treatises on the subject; rather, he situated his theology in the lived experience of Africans, something he thought African theology could learn from black theology. In the conference paper presented at the Union Theological Seminary in 1973 he stated what he saw as the shared experience of black people:

> Black theology seeks to make sense of the life experience of the black man, which is largely black suffering at the hands of rampant white racism, and to understand this in the light of what God has said about (God)self, about (wo)man, and about the world in his very definite Word ... Black theology has to do with whether it is possible to be black and continue to be Christian; it is to ask on whose side is God; it is to be concerned about the humanisation of man, because those who ravage our humanity dehumanise themselves in the process; [it says] that the liberation of the black man is the other side of the liberation of the white man – so it is concerned with human liberation.[12]

Consequently, Tutu sought to bring black theology and African theology together. African theologians like John Mbiti regarded black theology as irrelevant to African realities because it was an import from America and reflected the life of black Americans.

The condition of non-white South Africans during that period motivated Tutu's approval of black theology. By placing an accent on the shared experience between the African and black theologies,[13] Tutu not only responded to Mbiti's critique, he thereby alluded to reconciliation, a theological theme that would become the hallmark of his legacy as it would later find expression in the Truth and Reconciliation Commission work he did in post-apartheid South Africa.

TEF Legacy on the future of theological education in Africa

In the WCC and the ecumenical movement at large, theological education is a strategy for the renewal of the vision to witness the Good News of Jesus Christ. The TEF contributed to that vision through providing funding to individuals and institutions. Desmond Tutu's contribution to the work of the TEF was profoundly influenced by the lived experiences of the local contexts he visited. The WCC have made those reports available in the archives. They provide a repository for research and evaluation that could inform future work.

Today some of the institutions, like FEDSEM, that were funded by TEF have collapsed or are struggling to survive. They produced some of the best theological minds and served as incubators for African theology in their time. What can we learn from this trajectory? Were the methods and institutional capacities inadequate? If the brief reflection on Tutu's method should serve as an object lesson, it cannot be either/or. We need to attempt to bring methodological and structural strands into a conversation.

Recalling another birthday

On 7 October 2006, the then WCC general secretary, Samuel Kobia, wrote to congratulate Archbishop Desmond Tutu on his 75th birthday. I would like to end this tribute on that note:

> The World Council of Churches and the ecumenical movement as a whole are deeply indebted to you. From the days in the early seventies when you served as a staff member of the WCC until today, you have challenged and pushed us never to adjust to the powers that are, but always to discern the signs of God's coming kingdom and to act accordingly ...

---

[12] Allen, *Rabble-Rouser*, 138-39.
[13] Du Boulay, *Tutu*, 447.

Dear brother Desmond, let me express our deep gratitude to God who entrusted you with incredible faith and hope, humour and vitality. We ask God to continue His [sic] rich blessings toward you, your wife Leah and your whole family, and toward all who sustained you and helped you.[14]

From Tutu to WCC-ETE

ETE, as a professional descendant of the TEF programme that Tutu served, certainly picks a leaf from the Arch's tightrope walking and his hopeful rejoinder that "Evil, injustice, oppression, all of those awful things, they are not going to have the last word. Goodness, laughter, joy, caring, compassion, the things that you do and you help others do, those are going to prevail."[15]

---

[14] Letter of WCC General Secretary Sam Kobia tio Archbishop Desmond Tutu at the occasion of his 75th birthday; in: https://www.oikoumene.org/resources/documents/archbishop-desmond-tutu.

[15] Address of Archbishop Desmond Tutu to officers at the ecumenical Center in Geneva at the occasion of the World Health Assembly 20 May 2008, in: https://www.oikoumene.org/news/desmond-tutu-caring-and-compassion-will-prevail-over-evil-and-injustice (accessed 3 June 2021).

12. CONTEXTUALISATION AND SPIRITUAL TRANSFORMATION IN THEOLOGICAL EDUCATION IN AFRICA – VISIONS INSPIRED BY DESMOND TUTU[1]

Dietrich Werner[2]

The critical role of theological education for the future of African Christianity

There can be no doubt that theological education plays a crucial role for the future, the integrity and the social shape of African Christianity. Prominent voices underline this conviction: John Pobee once argued: "Because Christianity is growing faster in Africa than in any other continent, the future of world Christianity may well depend on how African Christianity develops".[3] John Baur, author of *2000 years of Christianity in Africa*, on the other hand, has argued: "The picture of the church in Africa after thirty years of ecumenical history is disappointing. What has been achieved is a general peaceful co-existence, but little cooperation and much less congruence. Almost nobody feels the urgency to go further, and it would be difficult to distribute the blame for this lethargy."[4]

Both statements point to the strategic importance of theological education for the future of African Christianity. Without ecumenical theological education, fragmentation and both confessional and religious disunity will increase in African Christianity. Without theological education African Christianity cannot play the vital role it should play for world Christianity. It is not very well known that in the 20th century Desmond Tutu played a major role in enhancing theological education on the African continent and raising critical questions on its contextuality and ecumenicity.

The founding of TEF as an instrument for enhancing theological education on African soil: Ghana 1958

It was the missionary movement that first established most of the theological colleges in churches and countries of the South; humble beginnings of an educational revolution, without which much of what happened afterwards in terms of decolonialisation, nation-building, liberation and return to indigenous traditions would have been unthinkable.[5] Following some crucial recommendations of Tambaram mission conference in 1938 for the improvement of theological education in the Younger Churches, a series of detailed studies on the needs and challenges for theological education in Asia and in Africa was developed in the years between 1941 and 1957, one of which was called "Surveys

---

[1] Part of the reflections of this article in the first two sections come from an earlier article of the author. Dietrich Werner, "Viability and Ecumenical Perspectives for Theological Education in Africa: Legacy and New Beginnings in WCC and AACC", in D. Werner, *Theological Education in World Christianity, Ecumenical Perspectives and Future Priorities*, PTCA Kolkata, 2011, pp. 89-104.

[2] Werner, Dietrich, Rev. Prof., PhD (Germany), ordained pastor in Evangelical Lutheran Church in Northern Germany; senior theological advisor for Bread for the World, Berlin.

[3] John Pobee, "Africa" in Lossky, Nicholas; Miguez, Jose; Bonino, Jose Miguez; Pobee, John; Stransky, Tom; Wainwright, Geoffrey; Webb, Pauline (eds), *Dictionary of the Ecumenical Movement* (Geneva: WCC, 1997), p.7.

[4] John Baur, *2000 years of Christianity in Africa*, p. 476, quoted in John Briggs, Mercy Amba Oduyoye and George Tsetsis (eds), *History of the Ecumenical Movement* Vol 3, WCC Geneva, 2004, p. 478.

[5] See on this complex history amongst others:Dietrich Werner (ed), *World Study Report on the Future of Theological Education in the 21st Century 2009*, p. 8ff, WCC Geneva. The thesis held here is aware of the two-sided face and role of Christian mission history in Africa as there are other examples also where Christian education had strengthened and reinforced colonial oppression. See also: David Esterline, "From Western Church to World Christianity: Developments in Theological Education on the Ecumenical Movement" in Dietrich Werner, Namsoon Kang (eds and others), *Handbook of Theological Education in World Christianity*, Regnum Books, Oxford, 2013, p. 13ff.

of the Training of the Ministry in Africa and Madagascar" (between 1950 and 1957) in which among others Stephen Neill, Christian Baëta and Bernd Sundkler were involved.[6] It was the International Missionary Council (IMC) which drew some strategic consequences for action out of these study surveys and took the step to structure the concern for theological education programmatically.

The Ghana Assembly of IMC in 1958 received these series of critical surveys on theological education in Asia and Africa which were started by Charles Ranson (general secretary of IMC at that time). As a consequence, an action plan was formulated to create the Theological Education Fund (TEF) as the first institutionalised attempt to promote theological education with a major global fund. The major goal of TEF was to promote creative indigenous leadership in the churches of the South and to support "theological excellence" (which at this time certainly was still understood primarily in terms of copying western standards). It was through a major grant of J.D. Rockefeller – the same man who had donated for the founding of the Ecumenical Institute in Bossey, Geneva – that the creation of TEF was achieved. His sizeable donation of USD 2 million was given on condition that mission societies would raise a similar amount sparked off a remarkable history of solidarity in global theological education which lasted for some fifty years. The three distinctive dimensions or concerns in the understanding of the overarching goals of TEF's work were:

- *Quality* of theological education combining intellectual rigour, spiritual maturity and commitment
- *Authenticity* involving critical encounter with each cultural context in the design, purpose and shape of theological education
- *Creativity* of theological education, understood as promoting new approaches of the churches obedience in mission.[7]

Already in the TEF committee meeting in 1960 in Edinburgh a "Special Programme for Theological Education in Africa" was launched which focused on: "1) strengthening a limited number of theological schools, 2) assisting many theological school libraries, and 3) developing theological literature and aiding the 'increased use of Africans as faculty members of theological schools'."[8]

In its three mandate periods the Theological Education Fund has promoted different strategic objectives all of which related to the major aim of an indigenous or contextualised theological education in the churches of the South. It might be helpful just briefly to recall the key phases which all had their own characteristic emphasis:

- *First mandate period* 1958–1965: emphasis on indigenous and interdenominational places and institutions for theological education in the South
- *Second mandate period* 1965–1970: emphasis on new curricula developments for the churches of the South and new teaching materials written by leading theologians from the South
- *Third mandate period* 1970–1977: critique over and against western concepts of theological education and major calls for contextualisation of both forms of ministry and forms of theological education in the South.[9]

The key role of Desmond Tutu in the third mandate period in TEF, 1972–1976

Before joining the Theological Education Fund in London, Bromley, as Africa secretary, Desmond Tutu had already developed a deep passion for theological education. He had lived with his family in London between 1962 and 1966 in order to pursue his Bachelor's and his Master's degree in

---

[6] Christine Lienemann-Perrin, *Training for a Relevant Ministry: A Study of the Contribution of the Theological Education Fund*, WCC, Geneva 1981, p. 9ff; part of the reports of IMC from the 1950s are indexed in the *Index Theologicus*, see: https://ixtheo.de/Record/1135235627 (accessed 23 June 2021).

[7] C. Lienemann-Perrin, *Training for a Relevant Ministry*, pp. 33-122 (First Mandate Period); Charles W. Ranson, "The Theological Education Fund", *International Review of Mission* 47, no. 4 (1958), pp. 432-438.

[8] TEF Committee Minutes, Edinburgh 1960, p. 30, to be found in WCC Archives, Ecumenical Centre Geneva.

[9] C. Lienemann-Perrin, *Training for a Relevant Ministry*, p. 33ff.

theology at King's College London. He had also served as a university chaplain at University College of Fort Hare in South Africa and as one of six lecturers in the neighbouring Federal Theological Seminary. In the years between 1972 and 1976, when he received the crucial invitation to serve as the Africa Secretary of the Theological Education Fund in London, Bromley, where he returned with his family, he joined and inspired one of the most creative and even revolutionary periods of the TEF which focused on contextualisation.[10] The TEF – an instrument of the IMC – was a unique hub of creative thinkers and innovative theologians from the South: Aharon Sapsezian, the South American associate director of the TEF, introduced concepts of liberation theology, inspired by Gustavo Gutiérrez from Peru. Shoki Coe, the Asia director from Taiwan, coined the term "contextualisation of theological education", by which not only cultural adaptation was referred to, but critical socio-political awareness-building and the relevance of public theology for the political context. All of the key publications and studies that emerged from this last phase of the TEF programme (and later the first phase of the PTE programme in WCC) centred around various aspects of "contextualisation in theological education" (like "Ministry in Context", "Learning in Context", "Viability in Context", also including the birth of the new concept for "theological education by extension" (TEE), non-residential forms first practised in Guatemala, then also implanted in some African contexts by the TEF colleague Ross Kinsler[11]). Desmond Tutu's key role was to prepare grant applications for theological education projects on the African continent. These grants provided opportunities for extended travel and familiarisation with the challenges of post-colonial processes of liberation and self-determination in Africa. The fascinating history of the TEF[12] in laying the ground for strengthening and profiling the first pioneering centres of theological education on the African continent remains to be told through the wealth of archival resources that are contained in the TEF archives, now held in WCC. The important contribution of Desmond Tutu and the significant history of his work at the TEF remains to be told. In the next section I aim to tell one small part of the remarkable contribution.

The visionary legacy of Desmond Tutu at the end of his period with TEF

Amongst the hundreds of letters, reports and notices which bear witness to Desmond Tutu's work for theological education in Africa, one document stands out for its personal style and conceptual approach, which is a final report of Tutu after his last trip for TEF in May 1975 where he critically looks back at his own work and thatof TEF in Africa. In his typical manner of understatement, humour and play with words he begins: "This is my last trip as TEF director and it tugs at my heartstrings. I am grateful for the privilege of growing by trying to serve in some small way the cause of theological education in Africa. I have gained a large fund of friends. I have been received most warmly and treated with fervent hospitality almost everywhere I went. It has been truly humbling in every way."[13] But then he continues in quite an un-diplomatic and straightforward way to note some self-critical points of observation for TEF. He points to the issues of contextualisation and the unequal division of power in the area of the grant business at that time. "We often give the impression that we are sort of imperialists by appearing to boss people around once they apply for grants. We ask far too many questions in their view or force people to put their requests in a particular way to suit our ideological stance. We do not seem to respect their integrity and however much we speak of contextuality it often appears to be our understanding of what their contextuality ought to be."

---

[10] As one of the prominent publications of that period see Shoki Coe (ed), *Learning in Context: The Search for Innovative Patterns in Theological Education*, TEF Publication, Bromley, London, 1973.

[11] See Ross Kinsler's publication on *Diversified Theological Education,* which was published 2007 with William Carey International University Press.

[12] C. Lienemann-Perrin, *Training for a Relevant Ministry*.

[13] WCC archives, Theological Education Fund, travel reports, Desmond Tutu (unprocessed material), simply titled "Reflections" (May 1975), p. 1.

But apart from a quite self-critical assessment of the work of TEF, Desmond Tutu even goes to the core of developing a new contextualised and politically conscious form of Christianity in Africa. While holding an appreciation of past missionary achievements he also highlights the demand for a more critical Africanisation of Christian faith and theological education in a way that appears to set the tone for the visionary formulation of the struggles in decades to follow. In the same concluding report of Tutu from 1975 it is stated in very sharp formulations:

> As for myself, looking at Africa, I think that in many ways the quiet vilified expatriate missionary has really done a splendid job of work. Hospitals, schools, theological colleges, agricultural education, technical education – many of these in most countries owe much to their efforts. And it would be churlish and indeed unchristian not to acknowledge this in deep and fervid gratitude to God and to them. Many of us are converts today due to their efforts and we should not allow the many faults in a great deal of what they did to blind us to the extraordinary results of their work. Most of the political leaders in Africa are Christians or obtained most of their training in Christian schools, and, interestingly, many leaders of the liberation movement are, indeed, ordained men (Rhodesia). They must have caught the vision of something most worthwhile from somewhere. Of course now in Africa we are calling for a Christianity which is authentically African in contra-distinction to one which remained basically alien and imported. (There is a sense in which the Gospel remains alien to any context, but this is not the sense I mean here). There is also the continued struggle for liberation. These two are almost all-consuming interests and concerns in Africa today.[14]

Spiritual transformation and critical awareness as essential components in theological education

Desmond Tutu closes his reflections about TEF's work in summarising his recommendations for a still outstanding reform of theological education in Africa with two key criteria which indicate much of what he himself has embodied in his life's ministry and work in later decades:

> Our seminary graduates tend far too often for comfort, to be elitist, uncritical, conforming and authoritarian. I fear that it seems to me our theological educational system needs a major overhaul if its products seem to be so unsatisfactory, and this in particular is in two areas as I see it:

> 1. Spirituality: This refers to the development of a living and deep personal relationship with God the father, the Son and the Holy Spirit and is characterised in all respects by having the mind of Christ formed within us. It means like Him, becoming first and foremost a man of God; theocentric in order then to become a man of God for others. It means having the true humility of Christ who emptied himself. It means to be marked with a mark of servanthood after the pattern of him who came to serve and not to be served; who girded his loins and washed his disciples' feet; it is to be the good shepherd, to be concerned especially for the stray, knowing your sheep by name, and it is to become the sort of minister for whom persons matter enormously; ultimately it means to be ready to lay down your life for your flock entrusted to your care and in the present situation in Africa this can mean a real share in Christ's suffering through harassment, detention, banning, imprisonment and perhaps death, because you have dared to face the wolf who sought to scatter and devour your flock.

> 2. Critical awareness: Our theological education must set out before it is too late to develop the whole personality of the theological student and especially his [sic] critical awareness which has a passion and a reverence for truth and will not be cajoled or threatened to believe something to be true unless it recommends itself as the reasonable thing to conclude on the basis of the available evidence. It will make them ask awkward questions and not be merely conforming and only thus can they ever hope to be

---

[14] WCC archives, Theological Education Fund, travel reports, Desmond Tutu (unprocessed material), simply titled "Reflections" (May 1975), p. 2.

creative. Only those ready to challenge the existing orthodoxes have ever advanced men's [sic] knowledge. Only those who have developed a passion for truth can ultimately be expected to become prophetic leaders to speak out against unrighteousness and injustice and oppression without fear and favor.[15]

Isabel Apawo Phiri and Dietrich Werner, co-editors of the African Handbook on Theological Education *with Archbishop Desmond Tutu during the AACC Theological Symposium, Nairobi, Kenya, December 2012. Archbishop Tutu was the Africa secretary and associate director of the Theological Education Fund (TEF) of the International Missionary Council (IMC) in London, Bromley (predecessor organisation of WCC-ETE) between 1972 and 1975, which had launched the first "Special Programme for Theological Education in Africa" already in 1960.*

The unfinished journey and mandates for transforming theological education in Africa

These visionary imperatives for the future of African theological education are not only worth being recalled today, but they have also left their mark in the years of further ecumenical enhancement of theological education which followed his period in TEF.

In 1976, one year after Desmond Tutu left the TEF in London, the fifth Assembly of WCC was held in Nairobi, the first WCC assembly on African soil. It focused on the liberative and uniting dimension of the work of Jesus Christ ("Jesus Christ frees and unites"). The emergence of contextual theologies from the South was in the air, the revolution in education and pedagogy was debated. A whole section dealt with "education and renewal in search of true community". The Theological Education Fund (TEF) by this time had become an integral part of WCC, particularly the Commission of World Mission and Evangelism (CWME) which, since the integration of IMC and WCC in 1961, was carrying on the tasks of the global missionary movement within WCC.[16]

---

[15] WCC archives, Theological Education Fund, travel reports, Desmond Tutu (unprocessed material), simply titled "Reflections" (May 1975), p. 3.
[16] John Pobee, "Some Forty years of Ecumenical Formation" in *Ministerial Formation* 38, July 1997, p. 25ff; also: Dietrich Werner (ed.), Jubilee Issue of *Ministerial Formation* 110, April 2008, with key articles from the fifty years of history of WCC's involvement in ecumenical theological education; from earlier publications see: Samuel Amirtham and John Pobee (eds), *Theology by the People: Reflections on Doing Theology in Community*, WCC, 1986; Samuel Amirtham and Wesley Ariarajah (eds), *Ministerial Formation in a Multifaith Milieu: Implications of Interfaith Dialogue for Theological Education*, WCC, 1986; Ross Kinsler, *Ministry by the People: Theological Education by Extension*, WCC, 1983.

The formulation of the core mandate, in 1977, of the Programme on Theological Education (PTE), the successor of TEF, reflected some of the spirit and passion for a liberative and contextual approach in theology and pedagogy which Desmond Tutu had stood for. PTE at that time was asked to give attention to three matters: firstly "the influence of the context and culture of theology and ministerial training and practices" was to be considered. Secondly, "the need to liberate theological education and ministerial formation and practices from bondages which hamper faithfulness in their life and witness" was highlighted. Thirdly, "cross-cultural discussion of key aspects of theological education was encouraged".[17] The following thirty-year history of *Ministerial Formation*, the journal of the WCC Programme on Theological Education (PTE) which was started in 1976 by Ross Kinsler, can be seen as a continued reflection and unfolding of the heritage and legacy of Desmond Tutu for contextualisation of theological education in Africa and beyond.

It would be an interesting question to further discuss[18] whether churches in Africa and the global ecumenical movement – around 110 years after Edinburgh 1910 and around 60 years after the first "Special Programme for Theological education in Africa" (1960) – took up the visions of Desmond Tutu. He was concerned about a spiritually engaged and critical and contextualised theological education in Africa. Should his visions be seen as already implemented, as still delayed in realisation or rather as betrayed by the ecumenical movement?[19] While the ecumenical commitment for theological education seems to be dwindling on global ecumenical levels, evangelical circles have taken up some of the passion for theological education in their own ways.

---

[17] John Pobee, "Education" in Lossky, Nicholas; Miguez, Jose; Bonino, Jose Miguez; Pobee, John; Stransky, Tom; Wainwright, Geoffrey; Webb, Pauline (eds), *Dictionary of the Ecumenical Movement* (Geneva: WCC, 1997), p. 387.

[18] See on the broader ecumenical debate of this question: D. Werner, *Theological Education in World Christianity*.

[19] See for further African debates and trends: Isabel Apawo Phiri and Dietrich Werner (eds), *Handbook of Theological Education in Africa*, Regnum Books, Oxford, 2013.

13. Faith with Feet: Reflections on Contextual and Embodied Theologies

Eliza Getman[1]

Dear Arch Desmond

Most years on your birthday I send you short emails – and you have graciously responded on several occasions. I usually say the same thing – that I am so grateful for your life and witness; and that I am an Anglican priest because of you. Because of you I wanted to come and live in South Africa. Because of you Christianity started to make real and practical sense to me.

There is a larger backstory that those emails reflect. You know my parents (Tom and Karen Getman) who are American social justice activists. You know they raised me right. But until I met you and others in the movement committed to the struggle for liberation in South Africa, I didn't understand the transformative power of faith. You set me on a faith journey beyond my wildest imaginings. You showed me how faith could have feet. Your feet of faith have given wings to so many of us who have followed in your footsteps. You never sought fame or glory but have always pointed to the One we all follow on the way. Like the current primate of the Episcopal Church of the United States, Bishop Michael Curry, you invite us to join the Jesus movement. As you say, "Come on over to the winning side!" This has never been about conversion to a particular religion or denomination. It has always been about a *metanoia* of the heart towards justice. Your call to practise *Ubuntu* ("I am because we are") has been heard by millions of people. You say: "Do your little bit of good where you are. It's those little bits of good put together that overwhelm the world." Your life and witness have helped to inspire a movement of people to be more aware, alert and alive. We – alongside the cloud of witnesses – are busy practising overwhelming the world with love.

So in celebration of your 90th birthday, here is the full story of how you have inspired me.

Introduction

Church events very often begin with a moment of pause for quiet reflection. This moment invites scripture and prayer to open us to the movement of the Holy Spirit. One of the passages that speaks to Arch Tutu's courage and commitment to embodied theology most clearly for me is the story of the raising of Lazarus from the dead in the Gospel of John 11:33-39 (NRSV):

> [33]When Jesus saw her weeping, and the Jews who came with her also weeping, he was greatly disturbed in spirit and deeply moved. [34]He said, "Where have you laid him?" They said to him, "Lord, come and see." [35]Jesus began to weep. [36]So the Jews said, "See how he loved him!" [37]But some of them said, "Could not he who opened the eyes of the blind man have kept this man from dying?"

> [38] Then Jesus, again greatly disturbed, came to the tomb. It was a cave, and a stone was lying against it. [39]Jesus said, "Take away the stone."

[1] Rev. Dr Eliza Getman is currently the chaplain at Taunton School in Somerset, UK. She was born in the United States, raised in the Episcopal Church, ordained in the Anglican Church of Southern Africa and is now licensed as a priest in the Church of England. She is married to a South African and has four South African sons. She met the Arch through her parents in 1984 when she was a teenager. Her MA was in the area of Religion in Public Life and her PhD focused on motherhood and ministry through the University of KwaZulu Natal. She completed a postdoc under the auspices of the Desmond Tutu Chair in Religion and Social Justice [Grant Number: 118854], supported by the National Research Foundation of South Africa. The opinions, findings and conclusions or recommendations expressed in the research are those of the author alone; the NRF accepts no liability in this regard.

Jesus "was greatly disturbed in spirit and deeply moved" in his body. There is an acknowledgment of suffering, compassionate witness and a clear call for practical engagement. Archbishop Desmond Mpilo Tutu answered the call to "come and see" and then he extended that invitation to others. It's heavy work that echoes Jesus' command to "Take away the stone". This work of the people can only be accomplished together, and this collective power is affirmed in the Arch's words of prayer:

> Goodness is stronger that evil;
> Love is stronger than hate;
> Light is stronger than darkness;
> Life is stronger than death;
> Victory is ours through Him who loves us. Amen.[2]

Much has been made of Archbishop Emeritus Desmond Mpilo Tutu's hands. I want to draw attention to his feet. Fourth century North African Bishop Augustine of Hippo is sometimes credited with saying, "solvitur ambulando". This Latin phrase simply means, "it is solved by walking" and it goes a long way to explain what the Arch's practical, pastoral and embodied theology looks like. He walked alongside people in the movement for liberation in South Africa. Protestors sang as they walked the long hard road. He walked with them and prayed with them and sang with them: *Siyahamba ekukhanyeni kweNkosi* ("We are marching in the light of God") and *Hamba nathi mkhululu wethu* ("God, walk with us" – for the journey is long). Singing good theology is both unifying and powerful. But protest action for the Arch and Mama Leah Tutu was more than marching and singing. It also involved writing and speaking and the exhausting work of travelling the globe to raise awareness. As they travelled, they found more people to join them in the marching and educating and the taking away of the stone of apartheid. They provided "a lever and a place to stand".[3] This quote by Archimedes is an excellent metaphor for the way the joined-up contemplation and action can change the world. The contemplative stance is the same one used by the best cricketers: calm, centred, alert and deeply rooted.

We need this same rootedness as we read and interpret Scripture. The Arch helped to make the Bible come alive for me. He said:

> The Bible is not some dry and dusty list of rules. It is the story of how we are created good in God's eyes, how that goodness was damaged, and how wholeness is ours with God. Depravity came into the world through individual choices, drip by drip. The Bible is an invitation to wholeness instead of brokenness. We can choose wholeness and a life of beauty. We can choose to work for peace in the small choices that face us each day. Each of us has the dignity of these choices, whether we are rich or poor, from the global North or South, in prison or not. The Bible shows us how. It is about peace and reconciliation. It is about social justice in your neighbourhood. It is about joy and laughter.[4]

It is a serious responsibility sharing that invitation with others joyfully. As the chaplain at Taunton School in Somerset, UK (and previously at Durban Girls' College), I use some of the gifts that the Arch has provided, including the *Children of God Storybook Bible* retold in his strong, accessible voice that goes straight to the heart of the gospel. This treasure of a book is illustrated by talented artists from all over the world. In the introduction, Tutu speaks directly to each of us, reminding us that God loves us, and wants us to experience and practise love:

---

[2] Desmond Tutu, *An African Prayer Book*. New York: Doubleday (1995), 80. And set to music by John Bell, GIA © 1996 Iona Community.

[3] Richard Rohr of the Center for Action and Contemplation wrote a book called *A Lever and A Place to Stan: The Contemplative Stance, the Active Prayer* (Hidden Spring, 2011).

[4] Desmond Tutu, "Foreword," in *Fresh from the Word: A Bible for a Change*, ed. Nathan Eddy, vii, IBRA (International Bible Reading Association), https://shop.christianeducation.org.uk/pdfs/9781905893614.pdf (accessed 23 June 2021).

Jesus says we should love God, love other people, and love ourselves.
How do we do this?
By doing three important things:
Do what is RIGHT, be KIND TO ONE ANOTHER,
and be FRIENDS WITH GOD.[5]

This resonates with the reassuring words pronounced prior to confession in the *Scottish Episcopal Church 1982 Liturgy* (based on 1 John 4:16-19):

God is love and we are God's children. There is no room for fear in love. We love because he first loved us.

We long to hear these words of love and acceptance. We need to be reminded on a regular basis that we are beloved. One of Desmond Tutu's greatest gifts has been knowing his own belovedness and practising loving God and his neighbours (all of them) as himself. In Tutu's own words:

Some of us may look like an accident, [...] but none of us is an accident. God wanted me. God loved me. God loves me. God loves me forever and forever and forever. I know that we will be free, not because we are good, not because we deserve it, but because God is God.[6]

Arch Tutu helped me to accept myself and unwittingly commissioned me and countless others to work tirelessly for the *kin-dom* of God on Earth (as it is in heaven). He barely knows who I am, but he turned my life upside down and I am an Anglican priest thanks to his role modelling and influence. As a deeply prayerful person, he exudes a tap-rooted presence, praxis and power. He is like a great baobab tree. And once you have seen a baobab, you see the world differently. My dad often used the expression "being bitten by the Africa bug", meaning that it is a continent that gets under one's skin and lodges in one's heart. Despite our estranged and prodigal whiteness, my family found our common humanity and origins in South Africa. It was here that a "rainbow people of God" and a "rainbow nation" offered an invitation to return home. As Ghanaian President Osagyefo Kwame Nkrumah said, "I am not African because I was born in Africa but because Africa was born in me."[7] I was not South African born, but I became South African nevertheless. Tutu welcomed me home.

This story begins with my dad's friendship with the Arch before he became the Arch. Tom Getman remembers it like this:

In 1979 the General Secretary of the South African Council of Churches showed up unannounced without an appointment at Senator Hatfield's office (where I was the director of legislative affairs). He was still relatively unknown – I'd certainly never heard of him. But Tutu had heard that Hatfield was sympathetic to issues of social justice and he wanted a briefing on what the Senate was doing in regard to "African Issues" – and more specifically where the United States government stood in terms of apartheid. Initially, I wasn't very welcoming as I was busy, but quickly realised that this kind and patient (and forgiving) man with an endearing laugh, was deserving of the most high level attention. Senator Hatfield met with him and we arranged for him to meet more senators the next day in the Foreign Relations Committee rooms in the Capitol.

As a result Tutu offered to host several senators in Johannesburg so that they could understand what was happening on the ground. Tutu was actively promoting an international economic boycott

---

[5] Desmond Tutu, *Children of God: Storybook Bible.* Wellington (SA): Lux Verbi (2010), 5. (Capitalised in the original).

[6] Pete Early, "Desmond Tutu," https://www.washingtonpost.com/archive/lifestyle/magazine/1986/02/16/desmond-tutu/3fc3da7f-4926-44cf-896a-5d1bf7f00206/ (accessed 23 June 2021).

[7] Afua Hirsch, "What Does it Mean to be an African?" in *New Daughters of Africa: An International Anthology of Writing by Women of African Descent*, ed. Margaret Busby. Oxford: Myriad Editions (2019), 685.

of South African goods. In 1981, three senators (including Hatfield) and their entourage (including me) flew to South Africa. Here we met many grassroots anti-apartheid activists and we would return to Washington, DC to draft and implement the sanction legislation. During the visit, Tutu encouraged me to come back with my family to meet him again – along with other members of the South African Council of Churches and the banned United Democratic Front. This inspired a Getman family sojourn in 1984. We showed up in Johannesburg at the time of Thandeka Tutu's wedding. Her father was officiating and the whole Getman family was invited at the last minute and we were given front row seats on the floor. The rest is history.

> During the heady days of liberation, Tutu invited me and a couple of friends to go to Cape Town for the last of the False Bay "free the beaches" campaigns. He joyfully thanked us for coming, and for the anti-apartheid legislation, but then said to me, "if you want to prove your bona fides commitment to human rights, you are excused from here and now you must turn your eyes to the Palestinians". We heeded his directive and ten years later when he came on another visit to Jerusalem, my wife and I were on his host committee. At a private lunch Karen said, "You have to be careful what you say to people because they will do what you suggest. And you are the reason we are here!" As I recall, he laughed exuberantly – very pleased with himself.

> Every year in every place we have lived, we have had the delight of personal fellowship time with him and Leah. We have joined them at church services big and small and private breakfasts and at some of the big events like his retirement party after his time as the Archbishop – and the celebrations of Madiba's democratic election. His friendship has been one of the greatest blessings of our lives – and he certainly set a course for us from that "chance meeting" in 1979![8]

The Arch broadened the Getman family's collective worldview and theology. In the same time frame in which my father was first making his acquaintance, Tutu concluded "Black Theology – a book Review" (written in 1980) thus:

> In a world that groans under much oppression, injustice and exploitation and the results of Western imperialism even in theological thinking, it is good to be reminded that a biblical or divine concern is for liberation, the setting free of God's children to enjoy the glorious freedom He has in store for them, so that they can become more fully human with a humanity measured by nothing less than the full humanity of Himself. It is salutary to be reminded yet again that all Theology is provisional, contextual and particular. That is why we need one another in a pluralistic world for none can ever be self sufficient. We are interdependent or we must perish.[9]

Even as early as 1973, Tutu knew in his bones that theology had to be embodied:

> Black theology is an engaged, not an academic, detached theology. It is a gut level theology, relating to the real concerns, the life and death issues of the black man[10] [sic] ... Black theology seeks to make sense of the life experience of the black human, which is largely black suffering at the hands of rampant white racism, and to understand this in the light of what God has said about himself, about humans, and about the world in his ... Word. Black theology has to do with whether it is possible to be black and continue to be Christian; it is to ask on whose side is God; it is to be concerned about the humanization of humans, because those who ravage our humanity dehumanize themselves in the process; it says that the liberation of the black human is the other side of the coin of the liberation of the white human – so it is concerned with human liberation. It is a clarion call for humans to align themselves with the God who is the God of

---

[8] Private email correspondence with my father, Tom Getman, 7 March 2021.
[9] Desmond Mpilo Tutu, *Hope and Suffering: Sermons and Speeches.* Johannesburg: Skotaville Publishers (1983), 37.
[10] In keeping with Tutu's commitment to the use of gender inclusive language, I have changed the original rendering of "man" to "human" throughout the rest of the citation.

the Exodus, God the liberator, who leads his people, all his people, out of all kinds of bondage – political, economic, cultural, the bondage of sin and disease, into the glorious liberty of the sons of God.[11]

Five years after my father first met the Arch, my parents put a second mortgage on their fixer-upper townhouse in Washington, DC and took their three children on a madcap seven-week sojourn through South Africa. It was 1984 and I was a self-conscious and self-centred thirteen-year-old who had never had a passport. It was a whirlwind of a horizon-expanding tour of a select few European and African countries. South Africa was the central destination.

I will never forget attending the Tutu family wedding of Thandeka Tutu and Mthunzi Gxashe in Soweto with Tata Desmond officiating. He wore vestments in the Anglo-Catholic tradition and the music was rich with harmonies. At the very beginning, he stopped the singing and made the congregation start again as he said they didn't sound joyful enough. "This isn't a funeral!" he said. I'd never met a priest like him – reverent and irreverent – intense yet effervescent. We received the Eucharist from his hands that day. I can't remember whether he used the invitation to communion that I attribute to him and use whenever possible now: "Behold what we are. May we become what we receive". Nevertheless, Desmond Tutu changed how I see the world and myself and the responsibility I have to make a difference.

We travelled from there in a budget rental car crammed full of long-legged, bad-tempered children and huge mesh nets of oranges and paper packets of biltong and Zulu baskets and wooden carvings and the smell of wood fires and veld fires and dust and sweat and sea salt. We drove across the entire country, staying in peoples' homes and in cheap hotels and at mission stations. We went to nature reserves and pristine beaches. We picked up ticks from the safari walks. We visited squatter camps that were at risk of being bulldozed. We met activists and church leaders and ordinary grassroots citizens. I met local teenagers – three of whom would become lifelong friends: two became pen pals and one I later married.

That trip was my Damascus Road and "Through the Looking Glass" experience all rolled up in one. It was a minefield that blew my mind. Once you see certain things, you can't unsee them. I tried to project all my anxiety. I accused white South African teenagers of racism only to be told to examine myself and the racist ideology and policies of my own country. I believed that I could be a white saviour. But I learned that the story wasn't actually about me or my guilt or shock and need for acceptance/absolution. And yet here I was welcomed and invited into the conversation. This experience was such a formative part of my education in global outlook and faith and politics. It was a glaring example of how (as Palestinian Lutheran priest Mitri Raheb explains) "Empires create their own theologies to justify their occupation".[12]

South Africa was where I learned that faith can be more than just formative or fostering of social cohesion: it can be politically galvanising and energising – especially when linked to social justice activism. Desmond Tutu helps us to make good sense of Christianity. He is a man of deep faith twinned with an impressive intellect, not to mention a mischievous sense of humour. He recognises the importance of aligning strong heads with loving hearts and clear principles. He practices an engaged theology of the gut. He embodies contextual theology. He saw the suffering of his people. He named it, and called for accountability and a change of heart and behaviour. But he didn't demonise the oppressors. And he didn't practise exclusion. In fact, he made clear that all were welcome in the joyful experience of liberation. He said clearly:

Often and often our people are filled with despair and they wonder, what have we done to deserve all this suffering? It is important for the Church of God to tell the people of God, "Hey, hey, hey! our God sees. Our God hears. Our God knows and our God will come down and deliver us." And we say it. We say it –

---

[11] John Allen, *Rabble-Rouser for Peace: The Authorised Biography of Desmond Tutu*. London: Rider Publishers (2007), 139.
[12] Mitri Raheb, *Faith in the Face of Empire: The Bible Through Palestinian Eyes*. New York: Orbis Books (2014), 5.

in South Africa – we say to them: "Hey! Hey! Hey! We are going to be free. We are not asking permission from the rulers of our land. We know we are going to be free." And we say to our oppressors, we say to them, "Do you know what? We are being nice to you. We are inviting you to join the winning side. Come and join the winning side because you have already lost."[13]

After meeting Desmond Tutu and experiencing the transformative power of black liberation theology, my life's trajectory fixated on returning to South Africa. I wanted to be part of building a new society. It provided common cause and practical purpose and a clear sense of destination and identity. I had grown up in inner city, predominantly African-American schools and, from the time I was eleven, I had wanted to be black. Even today, I wear my white "Americanness" with some degree of stigma and shame. The day I was naturalised South African was one of the proudest moments of my life. I could finally declare myself "South African/American"! I could finally vote in the South African democratic elections. Being part of the Rainbow Nation was the realisation of a dream. I align myself with the winning side and invested my energy into rolling away the stone.

It was a long and circuitous journey back after that initial visit with my family that turned my world upside down. John Reid (former vice chancellor) of the University of Cape Town (who was another family friend) had suggested that maybe I should consider coming back to study there. This idea became an obsession. But I was far too young at that point and the state of emergency made it impossibly dangerous. But my parents did agree to let me go to Paris as a high school exchange student. Then when I started university at McGill in Montreal, it became clear that priesthood was the only vocation that made any sense for me. I studied French literature and theology and continued to correspond with (and receive visits from) my pen pals in Pietermaritzburg and Cape Town.

And then there were the heady days of liberation. Nelson Mandela came to Washington, DC on his international speaking tour and the queue to see him at the convention centre went all the way around the block. It was a celebration that heightened my longing to return.

After finishing my undergraduate degree, I returned to Washington, DC where I started work as the youth director at my local Episcopal church. And then I received my call up for a Peace Corps placement in Mali, West Africa. After orientation and training outside of Bamako (attending mass at the Catholic seminary), I was sent to a small Christian village on the border of Burkina Faso. With barely any medical training, I was expected to support the village midwives. The book *Where There Is No Doctor* by David Werner was of limited help when it came to complex births, especially without electricity or running water. Between my unqualified naiveté, and other dangers such as poisonous snakes, scorpions and Anopheles mosquitoes, it was a miracle I lasted a year. It was a wilderness experience in which I made lovely friends – and a few powerful enemies. I got caught up in village politics between rival families and have never been quite so out of my depth in terms of cross-cultural misunderstanding. Once a small child in a remote village I passed through on my bicycle ran screaming at the sight of me as they'd never seen a white person before and thought I was a ghost. Others chanted "toubabou" when they saw me. It was a confusing and challenging and humbling time. My white skin had never been more obviously a privilege and a curse.

For Christmas break, I flew from Bamako to Cape Town, where my father (who was back in South Africa for work) met me off the plane. After waiting so many years (and especially coming straight from the intensity of life in Mali) South Africa felt like the Promised Land. Within days my dad had organised an early morning meeting with Rev. Wilma Jakobsen, Archbishop Tutu's chaplain at Bishopscourt, who escorted us into the chapel to join the Arch at Morning Prayer. I was struck by his stillness. He was unperturbed by the arrival of people who loved and admired him. It was clear that he was doing the important work of being present and open to God.

In a 1986 *Washington Post* article, Pete Early wrote about the Arch's prayerfulness:

---

[13] Desmond Tutu and John Allen, *The Rainbow People of God: South Africa's Victory over Apartheid.* London: Bantam Books (1995), 160.

For more than 30 years, the Anglican clergyman has prayed each morning for the 23 million disenfranchised blacks in South Africa. He also has prayed for the 4.5 million whites who dominate them. Often, the prayers for the whites have not come easily.

"Sometimes I get angry," Tutu explains later. "Sometimes that feeling of anger is so intense that I have to ask myself if it isn't, you know, bordering on hatred."

Still, Desmond Tutu, the first black bishop of Johannesburg, prays – earnestly, unrelentingly.

"I pray for the government by name every day," he says. "You see, if you take theology seriously, whether you like it or not, we are all members of a family – God's family. They are my brothers and my sisters too. I might not feel well disposed toward them, but I have to pray that God's spirit will move them."[14]

This was what I witnessed that morning. My father says that Tutu spoke to me about the possibility of ordination in South Africa, but I cannot remember a word of what he said that day – partly I was in awe and partly the words didn't matter. His presence and action and attention spoke volumes. His silence was golden. When it comes to prayerfulness, the Arch is the real deal.

My father took me to Sunday Eucharist at St George's Cathedral where Dean Colin Jones told me that he was about to lead a pre-ordination retreat – and that he would consider it a success if he managed to put even one candidate off going forward with ordination. He warned me that it is a thankless vocation and that the institutional church chews priests up and spits them out. But I remained resolute.

I travelled onward to Durban with my father who reintroduced me to my future husband, Jonathan Burns. Our family had visited his family in 1984 and later we wrote each other real paper and ink letters in the days before email. It turned out Desmond Tutu had stayed briefly in his family home. And Jonathan and his mother had first sampled rum and coke during his visit.

Less than a year later, Jonathan and I were married and had taken up residence in Cape Town. The deal clincher had been when he said he would support my vocation – and that he supported me keeping my own name.

I started a Master's degree in the Department of Religious Studies at the University of Cape Town, fulfilling a lifelong dream. I also started working for RICSA (the Research Institute of Christianity in South Africa). Wilma Jakobsen started to mentor me and taught me to preach "low, slow and with the flow" at St Paul's Anglican Church in Rondebosch. She also invited me to join the local chapter of the Circle of Concerned African Women Theologians (founded by Mercy Amba Oduyoye) which met at Denise Ackermann's home in the shadow of Table Mountain. My Master's thesis was on religion in public life entitled "Analysing transition narratives: Christian leaders in public life in post-apartheid South Africa". I had hoped to interview Tutu for this project, but when I made the request via Wilma, he left no room to argue with his response. He told her to tell me "that he'd learned a new word in the English language: No".

Of course, I was disappointed – yet had nothing but more respect for this man who established and maintained healthy boundaries. The other narrative interviews with the individuals who agreed to be subjected to my barrage of questions about their journeys of life and faith were nothing short of inspirational. As always, Tutu had removed himself away from the centre of attention to make room for others to shine. And what is more, I understood that I had already received a large portion of the blessing from his hands.

Many years later, after my ordination in KwaZulu-Natal, my friend René August took me back to St George's Cathedral for the midweek Eucharist. During the service Tutu made a plea for contributions towards the roof repair fund – and said he'd be happy to offer selfies in return for cheques! There were many American and other visitors in the congregation who swarmed around to meet him after the service. I greeted him respectfully – but I had no money to offer and still felt embarrassed by my American accent. Claiming a closer connection would have felt like a pushy

---

[14] Early, "Desmond Tutu".

imposition when so many in his fan club wanted a piece of him. I could barely imagine how exhausting it must have been for him to engage so patiently with each of his hero worshippers. He reprimanded me later via my father for not introducing myself properly. But I genuinely felt I'd already received more than my fair share.

Then, during another Cape Town visit, I attended a Women's Day conference at which he was speaking. I was accompanied by my breastfeeding baby, Samuel Thomas. Sam started crying during the talk. So I took him out a side door to change his nappy. I was racing to get back in, but as I finished I heard the audience applauding. Suddenly the doors burst open and there was the Arch with Mthunzi his son-in-law. I seized the moment and thrust my baby in front of him, blurting out, "I'm Tom Getman's daughter. This is his grandson. Please, will you bless my baby?" He said a prayer that began "Baba Wethu somandla…" and moments later he was bustled away again. Sam is so lucky to have received a blessing from Archbishop Emeritus Desmond Tutu.[15]

Whenever I have the privilege of celebrating at any altar and whenever I have the privilege of sitting in any pew, I replace the word "many" in the Eucharist liturgy with the word "all" because Desmond Tutu's invitation rings in my ears: "Jesus did not say, 'I if I be lifted up I will draw some'," Tutu said, preaching in two morning festival services in Pasadena, California. "Jesus said, 'If I be lifted up I will draw all, all, all, all, all. Black, white, yellow, rich, poor, clever, not so clever, beautiful, not so beautiful. It's one of the most radical things. All, all, all, all, all, all, all, all. All belong. Gay, lesbian, so-called straight. All, all are meant to be held in this incredible embrace that will not let us go. All."

And as often as possible, I use the invitation to communion that I have heard him use:

Behold what we are – may we become what we receive.

This is a variation on the invitation, "Holy things for holy people" and goes back to Saint Augustine's theology and practiSe. *Solvitur ambulando*. We walk forward. We open our hearts in prayer, our hands to receive communion, our lives to receive a blessing that changes everything.

The Arch paved the way for the ordination of women in the Anglican Church in Southern Africa. He modelled speaking truth to power even after liberation. In a podcast interview with Krista Tippett called "A God of Surprises" (recorded on 23 September 2019), Tutu said:

We didn't struggle in order just to change the complexion of those who sit in the Union Building […] It was to change the quality of our community/society. We wanted to see a society that was a compassionate society – a caring society.[16]

He also makes abundantly clear that the work is never done. The work is in our hands now, too. He said, "The worst thing we could do in our country is to become sycophantic lickspittles. True patriots will know that the price of freedom is eternal vigilance."[17]

This call to action has been taken up by many, including South African women theologians who are now holding the Anglican Church to account for the gender-based violence that is perpetuated in patriarchal institutions.[18] We have been empowered to talk back. And the courageous conversations must continue.

---

[15] That little blonde South African boy also received a blessing from the late Bishop Barbara Harris at a conference celebrating the 20th anniversary of the ordination of women priests in South Africa.

[16] The On Being Project, "In the Room with Desmond Tutu and Krista Tippett", https://youtu.be/INN7kSuQaFE (34.35 minute mark) (accessed 23 June 2021).

[17] Tutu and Allen, *The Rainbow People of God*, 265.

[18] Volmoed Youth, "Gatvol Yet Hopeful! Women Call the Anglican Church of Southern Africa to Action", https://volmoedyouth.org.za/gatvol-yet-hopeful-women-call-the-anglican-church-of-southern-africa-to-action/ and "Gatvol! ACSA Women in Conversation with The Most Revd Dr Thabo Makgoba", https://youtu.be/k4LIOOVkhSI (accessed 23 June 2021).

A working group of contemporary African women theologians have adapted Trevor Huddleston's blessing (the original that is still used in many Anglican churches in Southern Africa can be found in *An African Prayer Book* (p. 79) – to make it less infantilised and more inclusive and empowered:

God bless Africa
Protect our children.
Transform our leaders.
Heal our communities.
Restore our dignity.
And give us peace.
For Jesus Christ's sake. Amen.

In closing, I give thanks for Archbishop Desmond Mpilo Tutu and his encouragement to us all to come over to the winning side, and to follow Jesus not only with our lips, but with our feet – so that we collectively continue to roll away the stones that bury so many alive. *A Black Rock Prayer Book* (from Burning Man) has a blessing that I think the Arch would appreciate:

The world is now too dangerous
and too beautiful for anything but love.
May your eyes be so blessed you see God in everyone.
Your ears, so you hear the cry of the poor.
May your hands be so blessed
that everything you touch is a sacrament.
Your lips, so you speak nothing but the truth with love.
May your feet be so blessed you
run to those who need you.
And may your heart be so opened,
so set on fire, that your love,
your love, changes everything.[19]

The last word should go to our beloved Arch who reminds us through his own life and witness that we are called to love and to be loved. He invites us to participate in the flow of love:

At the centre of this existence is a heart beating with love. You know, that you and I and all of us are incredible – I mean, we really are remarkable things! We are, as a matter of fact, made for goodness.[20]

Go and be who you are.[21]

[19] Religious AF Camp, "A Black Rock Prayer Book: An Offering from Religious AF Camp," 9. http://www.ees1862.org/wp-content/uploads/2019/10/A-Black-Rock-Prayer-Book-2019.pdf (accessed 23 June 2021).
[20] The On Being Project, "In the Room with Desmond Tutu and Krista Tippett" (39.30 minute mark).
[21] Desmond Tutu Peace Foundation, "Ubuntu: A Brief Description", https://youtu.be/wg49mvZ2V5U (1:18 minute mark).

14. ENCOUNTERS WITH DESMOND TUTU: LIBERATION THEOLOGY IN CONTEXTS OF SURVEILLANCE

Theo Sundermeier[1]

When the newly founded university in the Ruhr area in Bochum, Germany, celebrated its twentieth anniversary in 1981, the Faculty of Theology decided to celebrate the anniversary by awarding an honorary doctorate. I suggested Desmond Tutu, whose name, however, most of the faculty members did not know. Theological developments such as "liberation theology" or "black theology" were foreign terms. Only by pointing out that we were dealing with a South African theologian who was constrained by human rights violations, explaining his profession and his "doing theology" was it possible to build a bridge to reality in the Ruhr area. The theological director of the Orthopaedic Institute in Volmarstein, Ruhr, who himself was severely challenged by polio and who had developed a theology relevant for diaconia, was also honoured at this ceremony. When he attended the graduation ceremony he came with a number of people with disabilities from his institute. Together with their teacher, they felt honoured and publicly acknowledged in society.

However, one name needed to be added, that of Desmond Tutu. Despite the intervention of foreign minister H.-D. Genscher and of Johannes Rau, the then prime minister of North-Rhine Westphalia and the later president of the Federal Republic of Germany, the South African government did not grant Tutu permission to leave the country to participate in the ceremony at the Ruhr University, Bochum. Tutu's doctoral lecture had to be delivered on his behalf by a theology student from South Africa, Ben Khumalo. In this speech, Tutu precisely summarised what theologically inspired him under the racist regime in South Africa: it was the situation that became a decisive factor in the interpretation of the biblical message, just as the Bible in turn questioned the given situation.

I had met Desmond Tutu several times at the college in Umphumulo, KwaZulu Natal and also at our house, when the college was in a most difficult situation. Under the influence of James Cone's North American black theology, some of our students were radically questioning traditional theology. On the other hand, other students were equally suffering from the political situation, but held to a rather apolitical, conservative Lutheran theology. In this tense situation, Tutu was the one who emphatically warned against following an abstract concept of freedom. This would lead to a functional narrowing of the concept, he argued. He preferred to speak of liberation in Old Testament terms. Freedom is a communal concept, because freedom is indivisible. Black theology not only serves the liberation of black people, but also reveals the lack of freedom of the white oppressors and serves their liberation as well. Reconciliation is indivisible. This was also the core of Tutu's message in Bochum. It is no coincidence that Tutu was later appointed chairperson of the Truth and Reconciliation Commission set up by the Mandela government.

Ben Khumalo later presented the doctoral certificate to Desmond Tutu in Johannesburg on behalf of the faculty. It was the first honorary doctorate in theology that he received. Several more were to follow.

I met Desmond Tutu again in Johannesburg a few years later. On television, which existed in South Africa by then, a parliamentary session was broadcast live, during which the prime minister called the South African Council of Churches a "murder pit" (Luke 19:40, "den of iniquities") and

---

[1] Prof. Dr Theo Sundermeier DD, born 1935 in Bünde Westf.,Germany. 1960: Promotion at the University of Heidelberg. 1964–1975: Lecturer at the Lutheran Theological Seminary in Otjimbingue, Namibia and from 1971 at the Lutheran Theological College in Umphumulo, South Africa. 1975–1983: Prof. of Theology of Religions at the University of Bochum. 1983–2000: Prof. of Missiology and History of Religions at the University of Heidelberg. Numerous publications on African cultures and religions and Christian art in Asia, Palestine and Germany.

explicitly and harshly criticised two staff members: Wolfram Kistner and Desmond Tutu. As I was staying at Kistner's house as a guest, we watched the programme together. I was surprised at how calmly Kistner watched the programme, shrugging his shoulders. How would Tutu react? I met him the next day in the lift in the SACC building on the way to his office. How did he react to the programme? He smiled: "Already this morning the minister of education came to see me and asked me for advice."

I needed some specific information from Tutu. But in his office, he didn't let me ask my pressing questions. He took out one map after another from a box of postcards of different cities: "Look, I was in Nairobi. Isn't that an interesting city?!" He showed me several postcards and explained them. But then, without comment, he pulled out a white postcard with the inscription: "This room is bugged." I understood and immediately switched to the mode of speaking that we all had long practised in South Africa out of caution. One spoke of harmless things and circled around the topic so that everyone knew exactly what the other was thinking and what the discussion was about. In this way I got the necessary information I had come to see him about.

I enjoy thinking back to the time of such encounters that were characterised by an atmosphere of trust. I congratulate the 90-year-old and wish him God's guidance every day in the years to come. May the peace of God strengthen and surround him.

15. AT THE CROSSROADS OF PUBLIC THEOLOGY AND LIBERATION THEOLOGY: IN HONOUR OF DESMOND TUTU

Heinrich Bedford-Strohm[1]

The dancing David – Desmond Tutu as an inspiring spiritual leader

My first encounter with Desmond Tutu reaches way back into my biography. I was a theology student at the Pacific School of Religion in Berkeley. Engaging in the sanctuary movement, which gave shelter in churches for illegal refugees, and in the Emergency Response Network protesting against the Reagan administration's support of the Contras fighting the Nicaraguan revolution, I became familiar with the non-violent protest and civil disobedience tradition in the USA. Moreover, I participated in demonstrations for the divestment of the University of California's pension funds from companies doing business with the South African apartheid regime. On 9 April 1985, the protest of the Berkeley students began. There were demonstrations, sit-ins and many arrests by the police. "What do you want?" "Divestment!" "When do you want it?" "Now!" I can still hear the chants we shouted in my head. More than one year later, the Regents of the University of California made the decision to divest. A small man from South Africa who had come all the way to Berkeley to speak at one of the rallies played a crucial role for generating public support. Already then, Bishop Desmond Tutu was a legend in his struggle against apartheid. In his speech at the Greek Theatre on the Berkeley campus that spring, he said to us students: "As God looks down on you today, he's saying, hey, hey, have you seen my children in Berkeley? Eh? Don't you think that they're something else?"[2]

Having been involved in the German peace movement in the early 1980s I had heard many speeches at demonstrations before. But Tutu's speech was unique. I had heard passionate pleas for peace and justice from other speakers. But I had never experienced a speaker, who connected a very clear prophetic and political stand in these themes with such humour, joy and even playfulness. Bishop Tutu radiated in his words and habit what we were all struggling for: a life of spiritual abundance, of dignity for all human beings and relationships where peace and justice kiss each other (Ps 85:10).

In my German political and intellectual environment, characterised by seriousness and soberness, the playfulness, which I experienced in this and many other speeches of Desmond Tutu was a true inspiration and made Desmond Tutu something of a role model for me. I think of him every time I read this beautiful passage in II Samuel 6:16, where the respected King David begins to dance with everyone in his joy of bringing home the ark to Jerusalem. His wife Michal, however, raised by her father Saul with the behavioural rules of a king's daughter, is deeply embarrassed by David's authentic expression of joy: "As the ark of the Lord came into the city of David, Michal, daughter of Saul looked out of the window, and saw King David leaping and dancing before the Lord; and she despised him in her heart."

---

[1] Heinrich Bedford-Strohm is presiding bishop of the Lutheran Church in Bavaria and presiding bishop of the Protestant Churches in Germany. He is extraordinary professor at the Theological Faculty in Stellenbosch, South Africa and honorary professor at the University of Bamberg, Germany where he was founding director of the Dietrich-Bonhoeffer Research Centre for Public Theology.

[2] A video with this passage in this speech can be found at: https://vimeo.com/156597542. See also: https://www.universityofcalifornia.edu/news/how-students-helped-end-apartheid. See special website of University of California: 'How students helped to end Apartheid. The UC Berkeley protest that changed the world', in https://www.universityofcalifornia.edu/news/how-students-helped-end-apartheid.

The King's daughter despises the authenticity and liveliness of King David in his joy about the homecoming of the spiritual centre of his people. Her deference to protocol mirrors a sad spiritual emptiness. David's dance has set a different example. Spiritual leaders who show joy of life and gratitude for the daily gifts of God and connect this love of life with a passionate struggle for a life in dignity for all God's children have become a source of inspiration for many. This is what Desmond Tutu stands for. And this is what has continued to inspire me when I met him again personally much later after this first encounter in 1985. It was a joy for me to personally hand over the "Tutzing Lion" to Desmond Tutu on 23 February 2016 in Cape Town, an award of our Protestant Academy in Tutzing honouring public voices for peace, justice and tolerance (photo with the director of the Academy, Udo Hahn).

Desmond Tutu as a church leader at the crossroads of public theology and liberation theology

The legacy of Desmond Tutu is intimately connected with the journey of South Africa from an evil apartheid system, which systemically and systematically ignored human dignity, to a democracy which, as frail as it may be, holds the promise of respecting the dignity of every human person.

In times of apartheid, Desmond Tutu publicly represented a theological position which could be best characterised with the term "liberation theology". Liberation theology is a theological paradigm, originally developed by Latin American theologians in the 1970s and 1980s, which critically analyses systemic socio-economic injustice in societies and reflects upon the biblical narrative of liberation from oppression as a source of political liberation from oppression today. Its crucial biblical themes are the Exodus of the people of Israel from oppression in Egypt into the Promised Land and God's preferential option for the poor, characteristic for many different biblical traditions.[3] More precisely, we have to talk about "liberation theologies", because other contextual theologies have followed, such as black theology, feminist theology, Dalit theology and many more, taking up the same basic theme.

In his own biography Desmond Tutu has experienced the transition from a systemically evil apartheid system into a democracy which has been struggling to fulfill the promise of human dignity for all inscribed in its DNA. In its nature, it is fundamental opposition which characterises the

---

[3] I have largely reflected upon this in my dissertation: *Vorrang für die Armen. Auf dem Weg zu einer theologischen Theorie der Gerechtigkeit* (München: Chr. Kaiser 1993), 2nd edition with a new preface (Leipzig: EVA 2018).

rhetoric of liberation theology. Speaking to power is based on questioning the very legitimacy of this power. Prophetically unmasking the illegitimacy of this power and seeking to overthrow its systemic basis is intrinsic to a liberation theology approach. Resistance to the systemically unjust system is basic for an approach which takes the preferential option for the poor seriously.

The fundamental opposition intrinsic to such a liberation theology approach is, however, not appropriate anymore in or after a transition to democracy. If people have voted for a government in free elections, justice might still be far from being a reality. There might be many reasons to criticise those who have been voted into power. But the way to make progress in achieving such justice is through public debate. A change in policy requires gaining political majorities for it. That is why theology in transforming societies must move towards a public theology, which equips the church with the necessary argumentation power to effectively intervene and participate in the public debate. Public theology is liberation theology for a democratic society.[4]

Thus, it is not surprising that public theology has developed a special dynamic in transformation societies.[5] In countries like South Africa,[6] Brazil,[7] or even Rwanda moving beyond the trauma of genocide,[8] there are, with different intensities, moves towards developing a civil society and overcoming decades of authoritarian or dictatorial regimes. Moreover, the churches have to find their role in such developments. Their moral voice is needed in reconstruction efforts.

Yet, the nurturing of that moral voice needs consideration. The churches need both spiritual authority and competence in politics and economics to contribute to public discourse in their countries in a meaningful and helpful way. Churches need public theology in order to make an impact on politics, contributing moral expertise. In transformation societies, as much as in countries like Germany, the United States of America or Australia, many leading politicians are actually church members and often committed Christians. The churches, therefore, cannot retain an attitude that is fundamentally critical of politics, even though a clear prophetic witness may be important and necessary in certain issues.[9] Rather, the churches need to clarify what advice they can give to people who bear political responsibility and try to act according to their Christian faith in their daily political decisions. Indeed, it would be irresponsible to leave such politicians alone.

Public theology is a clear relative of political theology and liberation theology as it tries, like these other two theological approaches, to bear witness to the liberating power of the gospel in the realm of public policy. Political theology and liberation theology are forbearers of public theology. Liberation theology, with its fundamental critical nature, witnesses of the gospel, especially under the conditions of dictatorship. Where former liberation fighters have entered the presidential offices of government buildings, they need ethical guidance for their difficult decisions in government, inclusive of all the dilemmas. In order to accompany their work critically we need public theology.

While there is also a close kinship to political theology, public theology makes clearer than political theology that the witness of the gospel in the political realm is never to be simply identified with a certain political programme. Even though there are clear ethical guidelines in the biblical

---

[4] I have chosen this characterisation as the title of my collection of essays in public theology: H. Bedford-Strohm, *Liberation Theology for a Democratic Society: Essays in Public Theology* (Wien/Zürich: Lit 2018).
[5] For public theology in transformation societies, see Christine Lienemann-Perrin and Wolfgang Lienemann (eds), *Kirche und Öffentlichkeit in Transformationsgesellschaften* (Stuttgart: Kohlhammer 2006).
[6] For the context of South Africa, see Kathrin Kusmierz, "Theology in Transition: Public Theologies in Post-Apartheid South Africa" (Berlin: Lit 2016).
[7] For the context of Brazil, see Eneida Jacobsen, Rudolf von Sinner, Roberto E. Zwetsch (eds), *Public Theology in Brazil. Social and Cultural Challenges* (Berlin: Lit 2013) and Rudolf von Sinner, *The Churches and Democracy in Brazil: Towards a Public Theology Focused on Citizenship* (Eugene: Wipf & Stock, 2011).
[8] As an example for various conference documentations initiated by the Dietrich-Bonhoeffer Centre for Public Theology in Kigali, Rwanda see: Heinrich Bedford-Strohm, Tharcisse Gatwa, Traugott Jähnichen, Elisée Musemakweli (eds), *African Christian Theologies and the Impact of the Reformation. Symposium PIASS Rwanda February 18-23, 2016* (Wien/Zürich: Lit 2017).
[9] See Heinrich Bedford-Strohm and Etienne de Villiers (eds), *Prophetic Witness: An Appropriate Mode of Public Discourse?* (Berlin: Lit 2011).

material, such as the option for the poor, there must be a continuous and open political discourse about the best ways to translate them into government policies.

Desmond Tutu, in his public theology from the end of apartheid up until now, always remained true to his liberation theology impulses. As chairperson of the Truth and Reconciliation Commission he constructively supported the new government's efforts to create the basis for a new beginning by acknowledging the injustices of the past. While he participated in these efforts of those now in power, he likewise took a clear stand in emphasising the prophetic role of the church. The church must criticise power where necessary, and take sides in political debates as an advocate for the poor and powerless in democratic societies instead of seeing itself only as a neutral moderator in society. Tutu's present successor as Archbishop of Cape Town, Thabo Makgoba, quotes him with a very telling metaphor: "If an elephant has its foot on the tail of a mouse and you say that you are neutral, the mouse will not appreciate your neutrality." And Makgoba continues: "We need to rise up, to stand up and speak up for our rights, our children's rights, our grandchildren's rights."[10]

With his political interventions against the cancer of corruption and state capture in South Africa but also against LGBTQI+ discrimination Tutu has continuously put these words into practice. His strong role modelling is an important source of inspiration also for his successor Thabo Makgoba who, in his 2017 Christmas sermon in Cape Town, even openly called for the removal of President Jacob Zuma from the presidency.

On 12 June 2009, the University of Vienna awarded Desmond Tutu an honorary doctorate for his role in developing the theological approach of public theology. Tutu, the university emphasised, is one of the most important theologians worldwide. He further developed the classic approach of liberation theology into the internationally established theological paradigm of public theology.[11]

When we founded the Global Network for Public Theology at a conference in 2007 at Princeton, Desmond Tutu was not physically present. His context, his legacy and his spirit was, however, very well represented by the delegation of the Beyers Naudé Centre for Public Theology at the University of Stellenbosch, led by the dean of the Faculty of Theology and present deputy vice chancellor of the university, Nico Koopman.

The life of Desmond Tutu will always be a shining light at the crossroads of public theology and liberation theology.

---

[10] Thabo Makgoba, *Faith and Courage. Praying with Mandela* (Cape Town: Tafelberg 2017), 210.
[11] See press release of university of Vienna: Desmond Tutu erhält Ehrendoktorwürde der Universität Wien, in: https://www.pressebox.de/inaktiv/universitaet-wien/Desmond-Tutu-erhaelt-Ehrendoktorat-der-Universitaet-Wien/boxid/268331.

16. DOING THEOLOGY IN THE STRUGGLE FOR JUSTICE IN THE HERE AND NOW – THE KEY ROLE OF DESMOND MPILO TUTU

Petra Bosse-Huber[1]

Having been installed as the new head of the Division for Ecumenism and Global Ministries in the Church Office of the Evangelical Church in Germany (EKD), one of my first tasks was to participate at a conference in Wuppertal, in March 2014. The conference was about the history of the relations between churches and mission agencies in Germany and in Southern Africa.[2] The results of a second phase of this study process were presented there with academic rigour. The research contributions reviewed their multi-faceted relationships, in particular during the apartheid period. I was familiar with the struggle against apartheid due to my own involvement during my study days; however, my views were predominately based upon the perspective of an individual EKD member church, the Evangelical Church in the Rhineland, with all their frictions and tensions. Now, the German churches collectively came into my view. An initial study process, which had been completed several years beforehand, had looked at the colonial period from an academic angle. However, it was during the conference of 2014 on the "Holy Hill" in Wuppertal that the research findings made it all too obvious to myself how complex and conflict-ridden the churches' relationships had been. What was also profound was to reflect on the process of change which the churches and organisations in their quest for the right attitude towards the South African state and the oppressive apartheid system had undergone.[3]

The discussions within the churches and in the political arena ran deep and frequently touched not only upon the churches in South Africa or Germany, but also society as a whole. In this, the campaign for the World Council of Churches' Programme to Combat Racism or the calls for a boycott of South African products, such as the campaign "Buy No Fruit of Apartheid", co-ordinated by the evangelical women's ministry in Germany, proved to be most effective as publicity, and led to highly emotionally charged discussions. Although there was a general agreement that apartheid was to be condemned, even within the EKD, contentious positions were voiced. One of these issues was the question as to whether, and how unequivocally, the church was to express these opinions in public, or else, how existing relationships with state authorities of South Africa were to be addressed, and in which ways they should be maintained.[4] First and foremost, however, it was the relationships with the churches in South Africa and Namibia, which had grown out of either mission or German

---

[1] Bishop Petra Bosse-Huber, head of the Division for Ecumenism and Global Ministries. Vice-president of the Churchwide Office of the Protestant Church in Germany (EKD).

[2] See: https://www.harrassowitz-verlag.de/Au%C3%9Fereurop%C3%A4ische%20Geschichte/The_German_Protestant_Church_in_Colonial_Southern_Africa/titel_4216.ahtml and https://www.harrassowitz-verlag.de/Umstrittene_Beziehungen_/_Contested_Relations/titel_1028.ahtml (accessed 23 June 2021). The Evangelical Church in Germany (EKD), the United Evangelical Lutheran Church of Germany (VELKD) and the Reformed Alliance in Germany (RB), together with all member churches of the EKD which are connected with Lutheran and Reformed Churches in South Africa and Namibia and their Mission Works, all Evangelical Lutheran Churches in South Africa and Namibia and two reformed churches in South Africa (URCSA and NGK) commissioned two study processes on the historical links between these churches in Germany and southern Africa during the colonial period in Southern Africa and during the apartheid era in South Africa.

[3] Hanns Lessing, Tilman Dedering, Jürgen Kampmann, Dirk Smit (eds), *Contested Relations: Protestantism between Southern Africa and Germany from the 1930s to the Apartheid Era* (Harrassowitz: Wiesbaden, 2015).

[4] Gunter Hermann, "Hennenhofer PR. On the Attempts to Influence German Politicians and the Leadership of EKD" in *Contested Relations*, eds Hanns Lessing et al., 610-625.

immigration, that were discussed: how these partnerships could be continued and in which ways they should develop further. These were difficult discussions and the relationships were under great strain.

In the academic reappraisal of these debates, the study process revealed in which ways these ecumenical relationships, especially those relating to the churches involved, had changed over the course of time. For the EKD, this is visible in the conceptual orientation of the Global Ministries within the Church Office of the EKD. This orientation – as a consequence of these discussions about South Africa and apartheid – was clearly embedded within ecumenical relations and closely entwined with international ecumenical ministry.[5]

Such learning processes were initiated through the organisations involved, but, first and foremost, through proactive individuals on the German as well as on the South African side. These were people who had taken a clear stance against apartheid and advocated the very same, unambiguously and publicly, and who, on the other hand, had also not broken off discussions with those who were not so decisive.

Amongst these helpful, clear voices was, most importantly, the South African Council of Churches (SACC), with many committed individuals including, in particular, its general secretaries. Desmond Tutu, the later Anglican Archbishop of Cape Town, held this office from 1978 to 1985 and had, whilst in this position, not only succeeded in attracting the attention of the international community to the dramatic situation in South Africa in relation to human rights, but also in urging the churches worldwide to come to a clear decision related to the struggle against the injustice of apartheid. He had challenged the SACC not to engage in "pie-in-the-sky theology" and to focus exclusively on life after death, but instead to prove itself in the struggle for justice in the here and now. The church was to declare its solidarity; it was to be with, and suffer with, the people.[6] Desmond Tutu called for this attitude not only in the SACC, but in the church in general. In his own welcoming and caring, yet also very clear, attitude he provoked those in positions of responsibility within the church to make a decision about the very way to do theology in view of the blatant injustice of apartheid, and which conclusions to draw for themselves, as well as in their ecumenical relations.

The example of Desmond Mpilo Tutu is inviting us today not to spare ourselves from asking the topical question as to how we, as churches today who are living in the here and now, in spite of our inhibitions and constraints, are willing to perceive injustices in all their poignancy, clearly calling them by name and confronting them decisively. Thereby, this book wishes to congratulate Desmond Tutu on his 90th birthday, keep his theological legacy alive and thank him for his lifelong commitment with all of our hearts.

[5] Rudolf Hinz, "The Alternative to Apartheid is Essentially No Apartheid: The Realignment of the EKD's Stance on South Africa at the beginning of the 1970s" in *Contested Relations* eds. Hanns Lessing et al., 522–528.
[6] Drea Fröchtling, "'Partners in the Struggle' and 'Midwives to a New Life in Justice': The Role of the South African Council of Churches in the Struggles against Forced Removals and Homeland Consolidation in the 1970s and 1980s – A Community Perspective", in *Contested Relations*, eds Hanns Lessing et al., 449, n. 20.

17. "ARCH ANECDOTES": REFLECTIONS ON THE ESTABLISHMENT OF THE DESMOND TUTU CHAIR AND CENTRE AT THE UNIVERSITY OF THE WESTERN CAPE

Christo Lombard[1]

Meeting Desmond Tutu

My first contact with Archbishop Tutu was when he was on a short ecumenical visit to Namibia in 1984. What an honour it was to persuade the Nobel laureate, then still strongly functioning as the SACC general secretary, to speak to our students at the Academy for Tertiary Education (the forerunner of the University of Namibia). Given the pervasive surveillance of the South African security agents at that stage it was a rather risky thing to do for both of us! Needless to say that on that occasion he inspired a big group of young Namibians to stand firm in the struggle for justice and liberation; many of them stepping forward to strongly resist the South African control of their country and to become leaders of the young nation.

The second contact with Tutu was through a letter to him, again from Namibia. After the elation of independence in 1990, many surviving so-called SWAPO (South West Africa People's Organisation)[2] ex-detainees returned to Namibia, exposing stories of torture and disappearances of comrades in the SWAPO camps in Angola, and eventually forming the "Breaking the Wall of Silence" movement in 1997. This was at the time when Archbishop Tutu was chair of the South African Truth and Reconciliation Committee (TRC). I was then asked, as a founding member of the BWS movement, to again do a risky thing: to write to Tutu to request that the human rights abuses perpetrated by the Namibian liberation movement against many of its own members be included in the work of the TRC. I still treasure the prompt and personal response of the Arch, explaining that the issues we mention are, sadly, known to the TRC, but cannot directly fall under its jurisdiction. Namibia had in the meantime become a sovereign state that had to deal with its own issues of truth and reconciliation. Nonetheless, the Arch graciously wished us courage and fortitude in our efforts in search of truthful reconciliation.

These two early encounters with Desmond Tutu, like the brief ones I had with Beyers Naudé while studying at Stellenbosch, transformed my life and thinking radically, and ever since, they have been my heroes and ethical role models.

Little could I know then that I would one day have the privilege and honour of being instrumental in setting up the Desmond Tutu Chair and the Desmond Tutu Centre at the University of the Western Cape – honouring the fearless ethical leadership of this great and famous son of Africa. It was only years later, when I returned to teach at UWC, that I had the honour of really meeting and getting to know the Arch.

Preparatory work towards the Desmond Tutu Chair and Centre at UWC

In September 2005 I was privileged to be appointed, this time as a senior academic, to the Department of Religion and Theology at UWC, where Desmond Tutu was by then the famous chancellor.[3] While the release of Nelson Mandela, and what followed, signalled wonderful new

---

[1] Christo Lombard was a professor of theology at the University of the Western Cape (2005-2013). He had the privilege to help establish the Desmond Tutu Chair/Center at UWC (2013-2016) after his retirement.
[2] The liberation movement that successfully fought for the independence of Namibia from South African rule and became a political party that has democratically been in control of Namibia since 1990.
[3] I previously did both my Master's and doctorate in theology at UWC under Prof. Jaap du Rand (later also vice-rector at UWC) and taught there for nine years (1975–1983).

opportunities, also for the previously disadvantaged universities in South Africa, the years before and after the birth of the new South Africa were difficult at UWC in terms of finances, morale and leadership. For the relatively small Department of Religion and Theology that remained at UWC after the once-powerful Faculty of Theology moved to Stellenbosch University, these were challenging years. This controversial move, following a decision of the Uniting Reformed Church in Southern Africa (URCSA) to join the Stellenbosch Faculty of Theology, *inter alia* to foster better relations and cooperation between the Dutch Reformed Church (DRC) and URCSA, also positively resulted in a thorough rethinking of offerings in religion, theology and ethics in the UWC Faculty of Arts.

Fortunately, through resolve and restructuring, the new department survived and found a comfortable home in the multi-disciplinary context of the Faculty of Arts. The department developed contextual ecumenical courses for a degree in theology, and within the span of a decade also a strong major in ethics – providing graduate and postgraduate service courses for various professional study directions (for more than a thousand students per annum).

When I started this second teaching spell at UWC, the process of consolidating the new department was already progressing rather well under the leadership of professors Ernst Conradie and Douglas Lawrie. Since Archbishop Desmond Tutu's 25-year-long and longsuffering term as chancellor of the "University of the struggle" was sadly coming to an end, the department started investigating possibilities to honour his legacy through the establishment of an endowed Chair in Ecumenical Theology and Social Transformation. The extraordinary UWC Professor from Sweden, Hans Engdahl, and myself formed a resolute team on behalf of the department to realise this dream of a chair in Tutu's name. During 2013 and 2014 we thus, equipped with promotional brochures, undertook various ecumenical fundraising trips, *inter alia* in England and Europe. In London we visited King's College, the famous institution where Tutu did his Master's degree in theology, and where the larger-than-life picture of its most famous alumnus greets one at the entrance. There we especially talked about the possibilities of cooperation in digitising the Tutu legacy. We also visited the offices of the Archbishop of Canterbury, where we received assistance to organise an information session at the House of Lords, at which many faith-based organisations and former representatives of the strong anti-apartheid movement in Britain supported our efforts. We visited representatives of the Church of Norway and the Church of Sweden, as well as the universities of Uppsala and Lund. At the latter, we had in-depth talks with the Lund Mission Society, which eventually resulted in an endowment of EUR 1 million in support of the Desmond Tutu Chair at UWC. Our trip also included a visit to Geneva where we visited the WCC headquarters and the Ecumenical Institute at Bossey, thus consolidating valuable future ecumenical contacts.

Eventually, after these extensive campaigns, supported by a twenty-page brochure with photos and core information about the life and work of Desmond Tutu and the plans at UWC to honour these, with the blessings of Archbishop Tutu himself, and with the supportive participation of the dean of the Faculty of Arts (Prof. Duncan Brown) and the rector (Prof. Brian O'Connell), the success of raising ZAR 14 million could be announced and celebrated. The Board of the Lund Mission Society, who decided to sponsor the endowed chair, visited the University of the Western Cape, and the formal process of establishing the Desmond Tutu Chair, and advertising the position, was joyfully started.

On 26 March 2014 a crucial meeting took place at the Desmond and Leah Tutu Legacy Foundation in Cape Town, where the UWC Rector Prof. Brian O'Connell (together with the dean of arts, the chair of the Department of Religion and Theology and myself) met with Archbishop Desmond Tutu (together with Rev. Mpho Tutu, director of the Desmond and Leah Tutu Legacy Foundation). At this historic meeting the UWC plans for the chair and the centre in Tutu's name were endorsed and blessed, and close cooperation on this precious legacy was sealed.

*From left to right (Ernst Conradie, Larry Pokpas, Mpho Tutu van Furth, Christo Lombard,
Brian O'Connell, Duncan Brown with Archbishop Tutu – seated)*

Establishing the Desmond Tutu Chair at UWC

During 20102011, the Department of Religion and Theology, in anticipation of the establishment of the Desmond Tutu Chair, started planning and launching a series of academic seminars/conferences under the rubric of "Ecumenical Studies and Social Ethics", that resulted in various publications in ecumenical theology and social transformation between 2012 and 2015.

Some of the themes and titles from these cooperative research efforts, published in cooperation with EFSA (the Ecumenical Foundation for Southern Africa, Stellenbosch) are:

> Reconciliation: A Guiding Vision for South Africa?; Notions and Forms of Ecumenicity; The Quest for Identity in So-Called Mainline Churches; NGOs and FBOs as Dynamos for Social Transformation in the Western Cape; Religion and Moral Transformation Towards Responsible Citizenship; Current Ecclesial Reform and Deform Movements; Pentecostal Movement and the Ecumenical Movement in Africa; Ecclesiology, Ethics and Ecumenism; Desmond Tutu's Ethical Leadership Style.

During the second semester of 2013 the international scholar, Prof. Charles Amjad-Ali from the USA (originally: Pakistan), was appointed as interim Desmond Tutu chair. After his short tenure, I had the privilege to keep this initiative running – during the period 2014–2016 – until Prof. Sarojini Nadar was appointed as the first full-time Desmond Tutu Chair of Ecumenical Theology and Social Transformation, on 1 August 2016.

During my term as Desmond Tutu Chair, the formal aspects of approving a board and a constitution for the proper functioning of the chair and the centre, and the responsible management of the trust fund that was set up, were taken care of within the frameworks of the Faculty of Arts.

The dream of a Desmond Tutu Centre at UWC

After establishing the Chair, another dream, of supplementing the chair with a Desmond Tutu Centre for Spirituality and Society (as it was called initially), linked to the Department of Religion and Theology, was approved in the Faculty of Arts. I had the additional privilege of serving as the founding director of this centre, which was set up as a link between the university and civil society, especially to support and liaise with faith-based organisations (FBOs) on spiritual and ethical issues in society. In fact, the centre initially merely consolidated the already existing cooperation between UWC and FBOs such as SAFFI (South African Faith and Family Institute), IAM (Inclusive and Affirming Ministries), IJR (Institute for Justice and Reconciliation), EFSA (Ecumenical Foundation of Southern Africa), Institute for Healing of Memories (IHOM), etc. – in total almost a dozen such civil society initiatives.

The Desmond Tutu Centre for Spirituality and Society was launched in the presence of Archbishop Desmond Tutu and Ma Leah Tutu, at the University of the Western Cape, on 2 December 2014 with an inaugural lecture that I prepared on the theme "Desmond Tutu's Style of Ethical Leadership". It was published as a brochure of the Desmond Tutu Centre, capturing the essential contribution which Tutu has delivered to the world at large: his style of ethical servant-leadership.

The first big conference, organised by the Desmond Tutu Centre (jointly with the Department of Religion and Theology) at UWC, on Ecclesiology and Ethics: The State of Ecumenical Theology in Africa, was held at UWC, 3–5 June 2015. This was the culmination of the Ecclesiology and Ethics Project which embodied the dream that led to the institution of the chair and centre.

Desmond Tutu's style of ethical leadership

In honouring Desmond Tutu and congratulating him on his 90th birthday, I can think of no better way than to briefly share the story of how various UWC postgraduate groups have benefited from studying his life and work from an ethical perspective. The module "The ethical leadership of Archbishop Desmond Tutu", has become a frequently attended postgraduate study course at UWC, at the time when Tutu was still the leader of The Elders, the famous global ethical watchdog group consisting of retired world leaders of the highest ethical profile and integrity.

As an introduction to the question "Why ethical leadership?", the class read Reuel Khoza's book *Attuned Leadership* (2011).[4] His passionate plea is for a return to *attuned* leadership; leadership that can be trusted and followed; leadership that uses African humanism as a compass, embodying efficacy, ethics, personhood, good governance, responsibility and accountability – nationally, continentally and globally. In his last chapter, on *Ubuntu*, Khoza, however, wrestles with the future of Africa which may unfortunately also devolve into a corrupt and totalitarian scenario. However, Khoza's positive vision still represents a type of Tutu-inspired future, dreaming together a special package: a prophetic vision, of independent, inspiring, servant-leadership by example; a communicative leadership, full of charisma, stewardship, courage; a leadership willing to risk bold changes to empower people; ethical leadership attuned to the needs and aspirations of the small and left-behind people. Reading *South Africa's Nobel Laureates* (Luthuli, Tutu, De Klerk, Mandela),[5] filled our little study community with pride and gratitude for the role of South African leaders towards justice and a better future for all, a view also shared by veteran journalist Allister Sparks, who wrote a sobering trilogy about the road towards liberation and transformation in South Africa.[6]

The relevance of ethical reflection on human activity was strongly underlined at UWC during the vibrant term of Prof. Brian O'Connell as rector, who never tired of reminding us that the whole concept of a university started with philosophers such as Socrates building a community of enquiring students, doing ethical reflection on all aspects of what it means to be human, living on this earth,

---

[4] R.J. Khoza, 2011. *Attuned Leadership: African Humanism as Compass*. Cape Town: Penquin. Also R.J. Khoza, 2006. *Let Africa Lead: African Transformational Leadership for 21ˢᵗ century Business*. Johannesburg: Vezubuntu.

[5] K. Asmal, D. Chidester and W. James (eds), 2004. *South Africa's Nobel Laureates*. Jeppestown: Jonathan Ball, 1-146.

[6] A. Sparks, 1994. *Beyond the Miracle: Inside the New South Africa*. Chicago: University of Chicago Press. In spite of many misgivings, Sparks still ends on a cautiously optimistic note, based on the belief in the possible return to and affirmation of ethical leadership amid disturbing chaos and corruption.

and "to make sense of it all" – the real job of a university! This line of thinking was also taken on board in the inaugural lecture of Archbishop Thabo Makgoba when he became chancellor of UWC in the footsteps of Archbishop Tutu.[7]

Tackling this prime task of a university, via studying the life and example of Desmond Tutu, we agreed to approach Desmond Tutu on ethical theory by asking a simple question: which ethical approach is followed by Desmond Tutu? Is he, for instance, a deontological, utilitarian, contractarian, virtue or feminist ethicist, in his approach to ethical issues? What is his main focus: the *rules* of the Bible (or dogma or reason), the *utility* for all concerned, the *social contract* which makes democracy possible, the emphasis on building *character and virtue* in the individual and from there into society, or a *feminist critique of patriarchy*?

Usually the standard approach to such questions works with an either-or option. In Tutu's case he brings *synergy* where others only see opposition or difference. He also has a gift to cut right through various options, theories and schemes, to the heart of the matter. When that happens, new transcending perspectives open up, a new spirit guides the thinking and the argumentation, and consensus seems much closer, if not the need for some compromise to accommodate the "other".[8]

Where it is widely agreed that *deontological ethics*, in both religious and secular forms, can easily lead to "fundamentalist" certainties and rigid rules for conduct,[9] Tutu lives in God's free moral universe where choices need to be made, given the total picture in a given situation.[10] In Tutu's moral universe, humanity lives in God's "dream", God's "vision of goodness", for which all human beings were created,[11] and where each situation demands creative thinking and creative solutions.[12]

Tutu's clear, decisive response to the "complex" debate on sexual diversity is insightful in this regard,[13] and clearly illustrates how his ethics are clearly anchored in his theology. He is a firm believer in the goodness of God's creation. He captured this theology as follows:

> Goodness changes everything ... if we are fundamentally good, we simply need to rediscover this true nature and act accordingly. This insight into our essential goodness has shifted how I interact with other people, it has even shaken how I read the Bible. Goodness changes the way we see the world, the way we see others, and, most importantly, the way we see ourselves. The way we see ourselves matters. It affects how we treat people. It affects the quality of life for each and all of us. What is the quality of life on our planet? It is nothing more than the sum total of our daily interactions. Each kindness enhances the quality of life. Each cruelty diminishes it ... And we feel different. We are happier, healthier. God is pretty smart.

---

[7] See Thabo Makgoba, *Inauguration as Chancellor of the University of the Western Cape*, 28 February 2012, on the topic: "Moral leadership and the task of education for the 21st century". Cape Town: UWC (printed inauguration text). https://archbishop.anglicanchurchsa.org/2012/02/inauguration-as-chancellor-of.html (accessed 23 June 2021).

[8] See P. Ricoeur, 1992. *Oneself as Another.* Chicago: University of Chicago Press, 22-35.

[9] See Rowan and S. Zinaich (eds), 2003. *Ethics for the Professions.* Belmont, CA: Wadsworth (Thomson Learning), 22-35; L.P. Pojman, 2002. *Ethical Theory: Classic and Contemporary Readings.* Belmont, CA: Wadsworth (Thomson Learning), 251-328.

[10] For our gift, ability and responsibility to "choose", see D. Tutu, 2011. *God is Not a Christian (And Other Provocations).* New York: HarperOne, 10-15; see also D. Tutu, 2010. *Made for Goodness.* London, Sydney, Johannesburg: Rider, 57-82 ("Free to choose").

[11] See D. Tutu, 2004. *God Has a Dream. A Vision of Hope for our Time.* New York/London: Doubleday, 1-42, for the positive dream that God has for each human being: God believes in us, his dream includes everyone, God loves you as you are.

[12] See also for such perspectives, D. Capps, 2014. *Still Growing: The Creative Self in Older Adulthood.* Eugene: Cascade Books.

[13] See S. de Gruchy and P. Germond, 1997. *Aliens in the Household of God.* Claremont: David Philip. In the "Foreword" to this book Tutu easily cuts through six selected homophobic "texts" in the Bible, which seem to override the deep moral intuition that all human beings are created equal and can demand the highest respect for who and what they are. Tutu's mind is clear: if anyone wants to doubt, cancel or question the baptism of a homosexual person because of a specific sexual orientation, Tutu would see that as blasphemy against God!

It feels good to be good. And we know it! When we attend to our deepest yearnings, our very nature, our life, changes forever, and person by person, so does our world.[14]

Tutu's theology, not surprisingly, also carries a deep layer of *virtue ethics* and feminist critique against stubborn patriarchy.[15] His transfigurative view of the world and his truly ecumenical hermeneutic is captured in the telling title of one of his provocative books, *God is not a Christian*. God is not the authoritarian God, dispensing and guarding "Christian" dogmas and principles, like a *pater familias*, and Tutu would not believe in a God that discriminates against people on the basis of any additional factor such as skin colour, race, gender and sexual orientation.[16]

Looking at various factors, which according to the experts (such as Piaget, Kohlberg, Erikson, Freud and Dewey) could have affected Tutu's moral development negatively,[17] the postgraduate class concluded that Tutu's positive development by far outweighed the negative counter-forces.[18] In this assessment we used the comprehensive view of moral formation provided by Van der Ven, including Erikson's moral formation "grid".[19]

From the background sources on Tutu's life and work, one gets a fairly good idea of the dreams, choices, challenges and chances which contributed to his "moral formation".[20] He was destined for leadership *in* the church, but *for* the world, which resulted in his becoming South Africa's major prophet for justice and peace.[21]

We can characterise Tutu's style of leadership in a few key words. His leadership was transformative, it was definitely a form of servant-leadership, it was inclusive and affirming of his co-workers, but it also had a very disciplined side to it, including prayer and meditation and real dedication to the task. He trusted people to do their own thing, he could delegate various tasks, but importantly decided to write his own sermons, speeches and letters. In fact, he spent much time writing to or directly confronting South African leaders and world leaders, whom he approached on the basis of their own faith commitment, bringing in the moral dimension of politics and whatever the issue was. The same treatment was dished out firmly but respectfully: letters to especially P.W. Botha and John Vorster, but also to F.W. de Klerk. During the time of international sanctions against

---

[14] Tutu, *God is Not a Christian*, 7-8.

[15] See for this e.g. Tutu, *God Has a Dream*, 71-112.

[16] See Tutu, *God is Not a Christian*, ad lib; De Gruchy and Germond 1997, Tutu's "Foreword".

[17] The class studied moral formation theories via the detailed analyses of J.A. Van der Ven, 1998. *Formation of the Moral Self*. Grand Rapids, MI: W.B. Eerdmans. See 48-76 for Durkheim on discipline; 85-110 for Berger on socialisation; 182-234 for Piaget and Kohlberg on personality development; 308-318 for Erikson on early childhood development; 318-332 for Freud on shame, guilt, sexuality and love; and 346-357 for Dewey on character and the common good.

[18] Factors such as having an abusive father; coming from a poor background; being a product of second-class "Bantu education"; not being in a position to follow his dream of becoming a doctor; having been an invalid as a child, and many others, can be taken into account. For a detailed chronology and summary of Tutu's life, see www.en.wikipedia.org/wiki/desmond_tutu; also note 19 below.

[19] Van der Ven, *Formation of the Moral Self*, incorporates seven time-tested formative perspectives into a versatile approach to moral formation, distinguishing the *informal* mode of formation, including "discipline" and "socialisation", from the *formal* mode via settings such as school and religious formation institutions. In these formal settings, "transmission of values", "cognitive development", "self-clarification of values" and "emotional development" take place. These six forms of moral development, together, culminate in the seventh, which has been seen as the goal of moral formation since Aristotle: the "formation of character".

[20] See A. Sparks and M. Tutu, 2011. *Tutu Authorized*. New York: HarperOne, 23-52 on his formative years; J. Allan, 2006. *Desmond Tutu. Rabble-Rouser for Peace: The Authorised Biography of Desmond Tutu*. London/Johannesburg: Free Press, 9-26 on Tutu's youth, 41-100 on his studies and formation as leader; see also L. Crawford-Browne and P. Meiring (eds), 2006. *Tutu As I Know Him: On a Personal Note*. Roggebaai: Random House Umuzi, 15-16 for chronology, 24-28 on Tutu as a student at King's College, 35-38 Tutu's time at Fort Hare.

[21] As illustrated through the many different aspects of his prophetic ministry, as reflected upon by admirers and brought together and edited by L. Hulley, L. Kretzschmar and L.L. Pato, 1996. *Archbishop Tutu: Prophetic Witness in South Africa*. Cape Town, Pretoria, Johannesburg: Human and Rousseau.

South Africa he used his Nobel Peace Prize status to influence world leaders such as Ronald Reagan, Margaret Thatcher and Helmut Kohl on moral and Christian grounds.[22] He could be very persistent, making the queen of England, according to an unverified anecdote, ask at one occasion: "Why is this little man so unpleasant?", receiving the answer that this little man was probably angry, and rightfully so!

Tutu's leadership rested on a vision, an understanding of God's dream for humanity; it was anchored not on managerial gimmicks, but in deep spiritual roots, including his belief in the power of the Resurrection (coming from the Community of the Resurrection); it was also fed by his strong belief in what Khoza calls African humanism or *Ubuntu*. He was creative in language and symbolism, theological language which became part of the *lingua franca* of liberation. His oeuvre is saturated by phrases such as "we are prisoners of hope"; "we are the rainbow nation"; "not violence, but the truth will set us free"; "we shall overcome"; "victory is certain"; "apartheid is evil and cannot last"; "we live in a moral universe, where good will always cónquer evil". His humour was always just below the surface, and his dancing was joyful even in difficult times. He had no fear or did not show it. God was always nearby. His courage in dangerous situations was legendary: intervening in angry crowds, telling stories that made people laugh and then he seriously would address the real issues in a better mood. He affirmed people, encouraging them but also sometimes making his critical points very firmly, as even the ANC later had to learn. In short, his leadership was extraordinary, unique, based on more than developmental potential.

A theology of transformation

So, if not via moral development theories, how could we explain Desmond Tutu's very unique personality and brand of leadership? What was his secret? His theology, as reflected in especially *Hope and Suffering:* Sermons and Speeches (1983); *No Future Without Forgiveness* (1999); *God Has a Dream: A Vision of Hope for our Time* (2004); *Made for Goodness* (2010) provide good clues, and are gems of spiritual strength, to be read and internalised over and over again.[23]

He was totally convinced that God had a dream, that God's dream was not a myth but the most real reality, and that we as human beings, as God's children and God's friends, were intricately part of God's dream.

God believes in us, God has a dream that will be fulfilled: goodness will conquer evil, God loves us as we are, we can and must accept ourselves. We are affirmed, God is on our side. However, God also loves our "enemies", God is also on their "side". We need to learn to "see" God's presence and God's work: seeing with the heart. We need to hear God's voice, which only happens in stillness;

---

[22] For Tutu's letters to South African and world leaders, see M. Mutloatse (ed.), 1983. *Hope and Suffering: Sermons and Speeches.* Braamfontein: Skotaville Publishers, 1-9, to Mr John Vorster (May 1976); 91-106 and 119-124, on opposition to Afrikaner politics and the Dutch Reformed church; 137-150, to the Reagan administration. A more recent summary of Tutu's prophetic speeches was collected and summarised in J. Allen, 1994. *The Rainbow People of God.* New York: Doubleday, 3-10, to B.J. Vorster (1976); 41-52, to P.W. Botha (1980); 53-81, witness to the Eloff Commission about the inquiry into the South African Council of Churches (1982); 97-104, to the UN General Assembly; 145-156, again to P.W. Botha (1988); 199-202, to the US Military Academy (1990).

[23] See D. Tutu, 1982. *Crying in the Wilderness: The Struggle for Justice in South Africa.* Grand Rapids: Eerdmans; D. Tutu, *Hope and Suffering*; B. Thlagale and I. Mosala, 1986. *Hammering Swords into Ploughshares. Essays in Honour of Archbishop Mpilo Desmond Tutu.* Braamfontein, Johannesburg: Skotaville publishers; D. Tutu, 1994. *The Rainbow People of God. The Making of a Peaceful Revolution.* New York: Random House; D. Tutu, 1999. *No Future without Forgiveness.* New York: Doubleday (Image Books); D. Tutu, 2004. *God Has a Dream. A Vision of Hope for our Time.* New York/London: Doubleday; D. Tutu, 2006.*An African Prayer Book.* New York: Doubleday; D. Tutu, 2010. *Children of God. Storybook Bible.* Wellington: Lux Verbi BM; D. Tutu and M. Tutu (edited by D.C. Abrams), 2011. *Made for Goodness: And Why This Makes All the Difference.* New York: HarperOne; D. Tutu and M. Tutu (edited by D.C. Abrams), 2014. *The Book of Forgiving: The Fourfold Path for Healing Ourselves and our World.* London: William Collins.

that is why we need to seek God in that stillness, we need discipline, we need prayer. In the fullness of time God will reveal God's dream and make it come true in ways we could never expect.

This then is the secret of Desmond Tutu's leadership. It is ethical not because it follows some or other "theory" about authority, or contracting with the other, or utility to be gained, or even virtue to be practised *per se*. It is following God's way, God's dream, God's gift in Jesus, living to our full potential as God's partners. We can talk with God, we can listen to God, we can share with God. There is a secret here. Ethical leadership is a gift, a precious gift of God to humanity, for humanity.

An eschatological anecdote: two veteran campaigners for good meet again

I have been privileged to be instrumental in driving the famous German theologian, Jürgen Moltmann, to meet the Arch in his retirement home in Hermanus, and to be part of that fantastic conversation – like a fly on the wall. This was one of the last things I did as I was preparing to say farewell to UWC and to take up a retirement job at the United Lutheran Theological Seminary in Windhoek in 2018. Prof. Jim Cochrane of UCT and his wife, Rev. Renate Cochrane (a student of Moltmann), were married by Moltmann, and knowing that Moltmann (at the age of 93) was receiving an honorary degree at the University of Pretoria, organised for him to also come to Cape Town. Yes, Moltmann said, but on one condition: that he meet Desmond Tutu.

Moltmann was one of the critical European theologians who was banned from visiting South Africa during the apartheid era, so it was a very special occasion for these two stalwarts to meet again. The first ten minutes or so were spent on mutual praises and expressions of respect and adoration, and gratitude for the privilege of sharing their thoughts again, looking back on long lives of commitment to the Good News. Eventually, Moltmann had to ask the inevitable question: whether, given the current situation at the time (already under Zuma's state capture and with the ANC in disarray), Tutu had not been deeply disappointed with those developments. Tutu immediately answered: Yes, it has been a big disappointment! "This is not what the struggle was about!" And so they went into various details of the disappointment and the betrayal, only, eventually, to return to the theology of hope which they both shared deeply. Moltmann said: "Let us never forget, that, as Karl Barth also said towards the end of his life: 'Gott ist im Regiment!'" (God is in control!), to which Tutu responded: "Yes, in God's moral universe goodness will always eventually triumph over evil!" For these two friends, the joy of God's reign coming, God's presence of goodness in all circumstances, is greater than all the disappointments.

I could not help imagining the smile on Beyers Naudé's face as he was looking down on this happy meeting, and wondering how the eschatological conversation between these three, maybe one day soon, will unfold …

1.3. Gender Justice and Sexual Diversity

18. "A PICTURE SPEAKS A THOUSAND WORDS": MAKING MA LEAH TUTU VISIBLE

Mpho Tutu van Furth[1]

Below is an image of a painting of my parents. The image was based on photographs taken of my parents at the celebration of my marriage. My father was not well at the time. Whenever my father receives an award or an honour he acknowledges the role my mother has played in his life as advisor, counsellor, friend and challenger as well as being the mother of his children, his wife and lover. What we, as their children, have experienced is that second only to his faith, she is the rock on which he relies. This image captures the strength that she represents. She looks so bright and strong. I feel it makes visible something that is very present but not always visible.

[1] I am the Rev. Canon Mpho Tutu van Furth. I am the youngest of my parents' four children. I have worked with my father as co-author on two books, *Made for Goodness* and *The Book of Forgiving*. I was director of the Bishop Desmond Tutu Southern African Refugee Scholarship Fund in New York in the 1980s and later founding executive director of the Desmond & Leah Tutu Legacy Foundation.

19. GRATITUDE FOR BLACK CHRISTIAN TRANSNATIONAL LGBTQIA EQUALITY ADVOCACY

Traci C. West[1]

So many of us here in the United States have found succour and encouragement in Archbishop Desmond Tutu's words and actions in support of LGBTQIA rights, equality and freedom. The audacious resource of this longstanding, public commitment by Archbishop Tutu has provided particular sustenance for the hungry minds and spirits of US-American black activists facing deep betrayals by our black Christian clergy opponents and others in our community contexts. In the face of their arguments claiming the space of authentic blackness and morally virtuous Christianity as exclusively homophobic and heterosexist, Archbishop Tutu's countering exercise of moral authority grounded in awe-inspiring, anti-apartheid, black African church leadership has been a bulwark of empowerment for us. Gratitude is due for the reliability and strength of the bountiful, transnational, Christian resource of solidarity he has supplied. I want to thank Archbishop Tutu.

But I am very picky about how to do so. Such expressions of gratitude can be too easily reduced to something perfunctory and narrowly dutiful. They can seem like the delivery of a public thank-you note that satisfyingly provides an obligatory acknowledgement of a past gift. The ongoing, renewing, dynamic impact of the Archbishop's leadership is lost in this kind of gratitude. Or sometimes the expression of it can sound too much like calling attention to a diverse menu of his singular accomplishments in South Africa and on the world stage in order to invite my audience to voraciously gobble them up. It is as if the accomplishments are commodities being recreationally served up to social justice tourists. This type of gratitude fails to nurture the kind of thoughtful birthing of communal right-relation that most authentically reflects the Archbishop's change-making leadership for which I am expressing appreciation. And, especially within the Christian religious contexts in which I most often work, I find expressions of gratitude to leaders with the religious stature of Archbishop Tutu can be effusive about theological and spiritual import but frustratingly anaemic and sparse in their attention to political interventions. Without question, the benefits of his leadership have been deeply emotionally and spiritually impactful for me, a black feminist activist member of a predominantly white United Methodist denomination that doggedly touts its heterosexist and transphobic rules. I need those benefits when confronting church leaders' stunning indifference to and sometimes fomenting of gender violence and hate crimes disproportionately targeting black and brown transgender members of our communities. The benefits of Archbishop Tutu's leadership have assuaged the spiritual pain of exclusion experienced by countless religiously persecuted LGBTQIA persons across many faith communities and racial groups here in the United States. But those benefits must not be depoliticised. I believe that the most appropriate expression of gratitude to Archbishop Tutu must explicitly recognise the model of rare political courage *together with* the bolstered, personal faith, hope and spirituality that we have received from him.

Gratitude for the benefits of his political interventions starts with the reality that Archbishop Tutu has provided a transnational resource of knowledge that we desperately need here in the United States. Our steadfastly maintained white supremacist culture and global myth of US moral exceptionalism in support of human rights substantially contribute to our neediness for him. It is, therefore, crucial for US-Americans to openly identify our dependence on the critical moral

---

[1] Rev. Traci C. West, PhD, is professor of Christian ethics and African American studies at Drew University Theological School, New Jersey, United States. She has been inspired by the leadership and life of Archbishop Tutu in countless ways throughout her life, starting from when she was a 1970s college student activist protesting for her university's anti-apartheid corporate divestment to her current invocation of his work in her gender-violence activism and scholarship, including her most recent book, *Solidarity and Defiant Spirituality: Africana Lessons on Religion, Racism, and Ending Gender Violence.*

knowledge of this black African religious leader regarding the collective denial of human worth and dignity in our society. We have required lessons from Archbishop Tutu about the authentic meaning of justice and freedom that remedies systemic harms targeting particular social identities of members of our communities. There are hundreds of references to and citations of Archbishop Tutu by black US-American activists, clergy and political leaders in their writings, speeches, sermons and posts across social media platforms that can illustrate the vastness of our dependence on him for this kind of guidance. But I have selected only a few early 21st-century examples. I focus on the methods and characteristics of our reliance on the moral knowledge Archbishop Tutu has generously shared with us and stress what it means to deploy that knowledge. These examples demonstrate active appreciation that is vivaciously participatory and contextually embedded in public situations of church and community life.

The ongoing, renewing impact of Archbishop Tutu's leadership thrives in specific transformative church practices. Pastor-scholar Antonio LaMar Torrence, a black gay Christian leader, describes his study of the kinds of equality-nurturing strategies utilised in a majority Afro-Caribbean congregation in New York City during the second decade of the 21st century. He charts the ways in which the church's leaders seek to enable the congregation's transformation from predominantly anti-LGBTQIA views to one that offers a welcoming embrace to LGBTQIA Christians.[2] Torrence offers a detailed discussion of the approaches to transformative preaching that they practised to achieve this goal. He explains that Archbishop Tutu was invoked in sermons that provided "excerpts from prominent people of African heritage" and thereby "helped to shape the vision of diversity in worship for the hearers."[3] The renewing impact of instilling the ideas of the Archbishop in this sermon project surges in the development of a black transnational connectedness of African, Afro-Caribbean and black US immigrant Christianity. That is, in the act of appreciatively preaching about Archbishop Tutu within this unique church worship setting, black transnational connectedness fuels the process of transforming church values of exclusion and of attaching stigma to black LGBTQIA Christians and community members. The gift of Archbishop Tutu's witness is experienced as a dynamic resource in this New York City-based project that defies the enduring political imprint of colonialism and transatlantic slavery on black church morality. Gratefulness for this gift means claiming African heritage as a resource for defining the power of black church tradition in terms of its welcoming embrace of black LGBTQIA Christians.

A different example makes clear how the birthing of communal right-relation and justice occurs when accessing specific content in Archbishop Tutu's witness. Black lesbian activist theologian Irene Monroe cites him in her description of the "bittersweet moment" of celebrating the first ordination of an openly gay man in the Presbyterian Church (USA) in 2011. Monroe emphasises the bitter struggle that allowed that celebration to take place and invokes those "who were either defrocked or flatly denied ordination because they were either open about their sexual orientation or their local presbytery suspected they were LGBTQIA."[4] Monroe cites Archbishop Tutu in her naming of the significance of this historic ordination pointing out how "in an 'Open Letter to the Presbyterian Church (USA) from Archbishop Desmond Tutu, he expressed the ultimate reason the church needed to abolish its discriminatory policy: justice!" Monroe then includes a quotation from his letter where he affirms "that in making room in your constitution for gay and lesbian Christians to be ordained as church leaders, you have accomplished an act of justice …"[5]

---

[2] Antonio LaMar Torrence, *R.I.C.H. in Preaching: Transforming Strategic Leaders Within an Afro-Caribbean Congregation to Become Agents of Radical Inclusive Christian Hospitality Towards the LGBTQ Community Through Preaching* (Eugene, OR: Wipf and Stock Publishers, 2020).

[3] Torrence, *R.I.C.H. in Preaching*, 56.

[4] Irene Monroe, "Presbyterian Church's Ordination of Gays Bittersweet", *La Progressive*, https://www.laprogressive.com/presbyterian-ordination-gays/ (accessed 31 May 2021).

[5] Monroe, "Presbyterian Church's Ordination." See also, National LGBTQ Task Force, "Open Letter to the Presbyterian Church (USA) from Archbishop Desmond Tutu," https://www.thetaskforce.org/open-letter-to-the-presbyterian-church-usa-from-archbishop-desmond-tutu/ (accessed 31 May 2021).

For Monroe, Archbishop Tutu teaches US Christians, in this case the Presbyterian Church (USA), about the meaning of institutional transformation focused on the deliberate practices of exclusion and inequality. The moment of celebration of the church's reversal of those practices must be understood in the context of a legacy of struggle, of entering into a space created by others who have borne deeply wounding costs for the sake of equal treatment they would never have the opportunity to receive. Such celebrations ought not, I would add, signify one's newly established acceptance in a private Christian club now bestowing legitimation of one's sexual and gender identity as no longer shameful. Monroe deploys Archbishop Tutu's wisdom as a means of providing guidance on how to recognise such watershed celebrations of equality and inclusion as the righting of deliberately perpetrated institutional wrongdoing and dehumanisation.

In activist efforts to combine anti-racist struggles for justice with LGBTQIA struggles for justice we have sorely needed the distinctive help that Archbishop Tutu's anti-apartheid leadership and transnational black African moral vision provides. In this intersectional justice work, few areas of contestation have produced more sharply divided reactions among US black Christian activists than the legacy of the 1950s and 1960s US civil rights movement. What does that movement have to teach about who truly deserves human freedom and rights in the activist aims of Christian liberation from oppression? In 21st-century US struggles over the enactment of state and federal marriage equality laws, for instance, Rev. William Owens, president and founder of the Coalition of African-American Pastors, organised black clergy opposition. He explained: "I marched in the civil rights movement, and I did not walk a single step for gay marriage when I marched for civil rights."[6] Equality activist Reverend Gilbert Caldwell deployed the wisdom of Archbishop Tutu when he responded to the coalition's efforts with a countering opinion-editorial in the Washington, DC *Blade* newspaper.[7]

Caldwell's response asserted: "I write you as a retired African-American United Methodist Pastor who was a 'foot soldier' in the Civil Rights Movement … As I have read about the coalition and your opposition to President Obama's support for same-sex marriage as well as the support by the board of the NAACP for marriage equality, I was reminded of some words from Archbishop Desmond Tutu …"[8] Caldwell includes a stirring quotation from Archbishop Tutu that names specific racial and ethnic groups interspersed with the identification of targeted sexual minority groups and then urges his US audience to recognise all of them as one family, God's family. Here, Archbishop Tutu populates a Christian liberationist movement vision with a mixed array of historically stigmatised social groups that jointly deserve equality. Caldwell appreciatively participates in Archbishop Tutu's vision by invoking it to assist him in navigating conflicting black activist clergy positions regarding what constitutes worthwhile political goals for their advocacy. He relies upon Archbishop Tutu's articulation to formulate theology for the thoroughly intersectional equality activism necessary in an expansive understanding of freedom from social injustice and the means for achieving it in our civic political life.

Activists' disputes over the combining of black civil rights and LGBTQIA rights among black clergy leaders have also referenced the political meaning of blackness and how it either encompasses or erases LGBTQIA black identity. This idea was raised when the 2012 Jacksonville, Florida, City Council considered expanding an existing human rights ordinance banning discrimination such as racial discrimination by adding sexual orientation and gender identity and expression to the

---

[6] As quoted in 27 February 2013, Catholic News Agency, "Coalition of African-American Pastors joins March for Marriage," https://www.catholicnewsagency.com/news/26665/coalition-of-african-american-pastors-joins-march-for-marriage (accessed 31 May 2021).

[7] See "the oldest LGBTQ newspaper in the US": Washington Blade: America's LGBTQ News Source, https://www.washingtonblade.com/?__cf_chl_jschl_tk__=pmd_7We792xM6wCnUefNlRnC3AgKjA9slLSdILts iIcqk_s-1629925247-0-gqNtZGzNAhCjcnBszQil (accessed 31 May 2021).

[8] Gil Caldwell, "Open letter to Coalition of African-American Pastors," *Washington Blade*, 23 August 2012. Caldwell also mentions that Archbishop Tutu is quoted on the website dedicated to connecting LGBTQIA activism and black civil rights activism. See Reverend Gilbert Caldwell's organising efforts captured in the documentary he co-produced, *From Selma to Stonewall*, https://www.fromselmatostonewall.com/the-film.

ordinance. Several black clergy organised to oppose it. Again, the dispute and, in this case, direct involvement of Archbishop Tutu, can be found in the public discourse of the news media. One of the black pastors who was an opponent reportedly stated: "To say it's the same as black folk, well, to me, it's not the same … It's being made to sound the same, but it isn't. I was born black. This skin isn't coming off. I had no choice."[9]

This pastor was quoted in a *Los Angeles Times* newspaper story with the headline "Archbishop Desmond Tutu to Jacksonville: Be 'open' to gays" that focused on a letter that the Archbishop had written to the City Council. In it, Archbishop Tutu mentioned the brief time that he had spent in that city and his support for the addition of sexual orientation and gender identity and expression in the local human rights ban on discrimination.[10] Archbishop Tutu's political intervention stressed his experience with dismantling apartheid that incorporated a deliberate insistence on including equality for gay, lesbian and bisexual South Africans in their post-apartheid constitution. The *Los Angeles Times* article describes black pastors as cautious about identifying LGBTQIA community struggles as civil rights issues. Specifically, in the opposition expressed by the black Florida pastor quoted in the news in 2012, the meaning of blackness in the struggle for equality is placed at issue. Heterosexual black skin bearing embodiment seems to signify a unique racial entitlement to be protected from being targeted for discrimination and violence. Ultimately the opponents of the expansion of the human rights ordinance succeeded in blocking it in 2012. But I am appreciative of how Archbishop Tutu's actions radically expand our capacity to understand what black African clergy disruption of public discourse sounds like and what form black clergy moral leadership can take that intercedes in the creation of state laws aimed at barring racial and sexual discrimination.

In expressing my gratitude for Archbishop Tutu's leadership, I fervently embrace the transnational, black-affirming space he has opened up for grasping the meaning of human freedom, worth and dignity, and for resilient political disruptiveness of state and church laws that further racist, heteropatriarchal, and transphobic denials of them. When my determination wanes in the face of the relentlessness and adaptability of those denials, I gratefully dance to the rhythms of the emboldening hope Archbishop Tutu has invented that enables continued disruptiveness on behalf of justice and planetary well-being.

---

[9] Matt Pearce, "Archbishop Desmond Tutu to Jacksonville: Be 'open' to gays", *Los Angeles Times*, 25 June 2012.

[10] Pearce, "Archbishop Desmond Tutu to Jacksonville".

20. STRETCHED TOWARDS INCLUSION: TUTU, GENDER AND SEXUALITY

Wilma Jakobsen[1]

Desmond Tutu's support for gender equality and women's ordination in the Anglican Church in Southern Africa was not an integral part of his cultural and church formation. How did his passion for this equality emerge from his patriarchal cultural and church background? I believe it was his years of international exposure and personal experiences with women clergy in the ecumenical and Episcopal/Anglican churches that fostered this passion and commitment.

Over the years he met women clergy and people from the LGBTQIA communities who responded to his inspiring vision and passionate commitment to bring about equality, respect and dignity for all South Africans. They challenged and stretched his own understanding of gender, church and society. His tireless commitment to work for women's ordination, including my own, was stretched and increased to include equality, respect and dignity for all, especially LGBTQIA people. I observed this as his last chaplain before he retired from the Anglican episcopate. He became more vocal towards the end of his Anglican episcopate and after he retired, was unequivocally clear that God is not a man, God is not homophobic, God is not a Christian, and all human beings, all people – all are made in the image of God.

I am beyond grateful for Archbishop Emeritus Desmond Tutu. My first two encounters with him were ecumenical and the third would change my life. In 1981 I was twenty-one years old, getting a lift from Pietermaritzburg to Durban, in the car with him and Michael Cassidy of Africa Enterprise. He was then general secretary of the South African Council of Churches (SACC). They were going to speak at an ecumenical mission at the then University of Natal. I was an intern with the Student Christian Association (SCA). I sat in the back, overawed to be with these famous people as they talked together about their last visits with Prime Minister P.W. Botha. About halfway there he turned to me and said "Now tell me about yourself", to which I stammered a reply about SCA, SUCA (Student Union for Christian Action) and faith-based activism. "No, not what you do, but who you are", he said. My enduring memory of this man is of one who pays as much attention to the "little people" as he does with the highest international leaders, who would interact with you with his full attention.

The lunchtime talk was powerful; I was inspired by his passion and clarity about faith, justice and equality. I was disillusioned by the media reporting that only criticised him in two sentences focusing on his call for economic sanctions against South Africa.

The next encounter was 1984 in Pasadena, California, USA, where he spoke at a "Bread for the World" event. I was by then a new student at Fuller Theological Seminary, preparing to be a university chaplain, as Anglican women priests at that time were not permitted in Southern Africa. I greeted him in the long queue of people, and he remembered me from the car ride.

At the third encounter in 1986, he had just been consecrated as Archbishop of Cape Town, and I met with him in his new Bishopscourt office. In 1985 the Anglican church had decided to ordain women as deacons but not as priests. I was discerning a vocation to priesthood, having experienced a strong sense of call through my interactions at Fuller Seminary with many women preparing for ordination in all denominations. Also, through All Saints Episcopal Church, Pasadena, a courageous, joyful, activist church which he called his church home in the USA, where there were two women

[1] Rev. Wilma Jakobsen was the first Anglican woman ordained by Archbishop Desmond Tutu as deacon, 1988, and priest, 1992. She became his chaplain in 1995, until he retired as Archbishop of Cape Town in 1996. She served fifteen years in the Diocese of Cape Town, and seventeen years in the Episcopal Church in California, USA. In 2020 she returned to South Africa, to serve as coordinator of the ecumenical Volmoed Youth Leadership Training Program www.volmoedyouth.org.za, of which Desmond Tutu is the patron. She is also the chaplain at Volmoed Retreat Centre, Hermanus, Western Cape.

priests on the staff. In faith and trust, I had asked for an appointment with him while I was on a visit back home in South Africa, as it was not clear from the international media at the time if he was supportive of women's ordination to the priesthood. I need not have worried. After opening with a prayer and then saying, "I suppose you want to know if I support women priests!", he was unequivocally positive about women priests' ordination, he supported my process of discernment, but said he could not ordain me as a priest until the Anglican Church in Southern Africa voted in a synod resolution.

Almost two years later on 5 June 1988, in St George's Cathedral, he joyfully ordained me a woman deacon, the first he ordained, in the diocese of Cape Town. Those were turbulent years – I was assigned to Westridge, Mitchells Plain, the only "white" ordained Anglican cleric there, and the only ordained woman in the archdeaconry and the diocese until 1990, when he ordained Margaret Vertue as deacon. My first ordained years were spent in church ministry and activism. Plans to visit parishioners were often interrupted by his call for clergy to join a protest at St George's Cathedral in Cape Town, many of which ended in tear gas and chaos. He led his clergy with courage and clarity, and inspired me with his prayer, prophetic preaching and actions. At least twice, he showed up in Mitchells Plain at ecumenical protests or funerals where I was leading, which I found both supportive and sometimes intimidating, as I was so much "the new white woman on the block".

As supportive as he was about women priests, we also found ourselves disagreeing on the process of how to make it happen in the church. He discouraged protest actions that many young people, students and supportive people wanted to take. It seemed to us inconsistent that he encouraged students and young people to protest in church synods to get more representation and recognition, that anti-apartheid protests and sanctions were strongly part of our existence as church, but we were told not to protest about women's ordination as priests. He explained that he and the other Cape Town bishops already agreed with us about the ordination of women priests so it hurt them when we protested.

It had happened at the first ordination service after the vote failed at the 1989 synod, in a prayerful, peaceful way, as people wore small purple ribbons to express their sadness at the exclusion of women and their prayer for women priests in future. It was painful to receive a card from him that said he was disappointed in the protest at the ordination, mistakenly assuming that I was responsible for it, when I had in fact restrained the students and others from taking stronger action! We talked about it one Friday morning after an early Eucharist. We told each other how we felt. We disagreed. In the end we had to agree "not to hurt each other" in future. I left in tears and had to keep breathing. I think this and other interactions where I was able to be honest about the difficulty of being the only woman deacon in the diocese, how excluding language in liturgy or speech was hurtful, stood me in good stead for my future connections with him.

I used to console myself by reminding myself that he was raised in a patriarchal church and a patriarchal culture. That it was a disagreement of strategy and method, not of principle, and that he was very supportive of women's ordination.

In 1992 his desire for women's ordination was fulfilled, one of two overarching goals for his episcopate. It had failed in 1989 by only thirteen votes and he was devastated, he was tearful. I am told he was sad that he still could not ordain me a priest. He understood the pain of exclusion and was fully supportive of my priestly calling. He was determined to ensure the process of discussion, dialogue and debate continued at all levels of the church so that the vote could pass the next time. He asked every religious community he knew around the world to pray for the next synod of the Anglican church in Southern Africa. With his support there were a number of workshops held in different dioceses to continue the learning, dialogue and discussions, and a large conference where most dioceses were represented. Ultimately all the prayer and hard work made a difference.

Desmond Tutu was a masterful chair of meetings. Never more so than in Waterford Kamhlaba, Swaziland, for what many called the "women's synod". For this synod, many dioceses had elected more women delegates than usual, as it was recognised that this was a watershed moment for the church. Some women had been told by their bishops to vote against it. We had to inform delegates that they were free to vote with their conscience on any resolution. A twenty-four-hour prayer chain of women was set up at the synod. Prayer vigils were taking place around Southern Africa. On the day of the debate the Archbishop collected notifications of those who wanted to speak for and against. Before lunch he asked Bishop John Ruston of St Helena Bay, who was known as a holy, prayerful person, and against women's ordination, to speak. To our surprise, he described himself as having shifted to undecided as he was so moved by listening to the theology of the debate, proposed and seconded by Dean Colin Jones and Ms Maureen Sithole. He implored people if they were unsure, to abstain. For himself, he stated he might even vote for it! A hush came over the synod. It was early for lunch but in a brilliant move, inspired by the Spirit, Archbishop Tutu said, "Let's go to lunch" and we floated out of the synod hall on this note of grace.

By the end of the day, pausing for prayer before voting, grace prevailed, and the synod voted to ordain women priests with an unexpectedly high majority of 79.2%. The Archbishop had requested silence, no clapping or verbal response, whatever the outcome. This restraint was monumentally challenging! He immediately had a resolution ready to say that the church cherished and treasured those who could not agree to the ordination of women priests, which passed. It was his plan to keep the church united and, as difficult as that moment was, it worked.

He walked out of the synod hall, emotionally exhausted. At evening prayers later, he found me and hugged me, not once but four times. He was exhilarated, each time saying "I'm going to ordain you!" It was an unforgettable, joyful moment. The ordination was five and a half weeks later, on 29 September 1992, the feast of St Michael and All Angels. He presided over the joyful, packed-out service, which was a sign of hope in South Africa, during the transition to democracy. He ordained myself and Margaret Vertue, who twenty years later was elected a bishop.

More ordination of women priests took place in the following years but his commitment to gender equality and justice was also about the broader leadership of women in the church. Women were encouraged to become synod delegates, to take up leadership positions. There was a groundswell that made a difference in the 1990s, as diocese after diocese ordained their first women priests. It was exciting. At the same time, South Africa moved towards independence and democracy, and women took up leadership positions at high levels in government and society. It was inspiring.

In 1995 in the middle of an ordination service when I was greeting him at the peace, he asked me to be his chaplain, which left me speechless. It is a job that includes saying morning and evening prayers with him, driving him to events, organising the chapel and his trips within South Africa, liaising with diocesan clergy and a host of other tasks as needed. Later I said yes. It was the first time a woman had ever been an archbishop's chaplain, and it was enormously challenging, stretching and rewarding. It was such a privilege to work closely with this giant spiritual leader, this holy, wise, global elder, who inspired me and prayed for me. I experienced at first hand the depth of his spirituality and prayer life, the core of the source of his never-ending energy for justice, faith, equality and love, along with his sense of humour and signature chuckle.

I have often wondered how Desmond Tutu became so passionately supportive of women's ordination, given that this was not an integral part of his African cultural or Anglican church formation. In part, it was the logical extension of his passionately held theology of justice, equality and inclusion, that every person is made in the image of God. Differences like race, gender, sexuality, are not reasons for discrimination. He was positive towards women's ordination for many years before the debate became more public. I wonder if it was because of his experiences in the years of ecumenical work and ministry with the Theological Education Fund, as general secretary of the SACC, and all the experiences as a global spokesperson in the anti-apartheid movement and in ecumenical churches abroad. He met many women clergy, women leaders, of all denominations, all races, in many countries, who were strong leaders, outspoken about gender and women's rights. He also knew strong women in South Africa in the SACC and other ecumenical organisations, where women loudly proclaimed that no one is free until women are free.

These women were not afraid to challenge him. I remember him telling me a story of how a woman priest overseas took him to task for having told a sexist joke in his sermon. It was a joke he

told often in SA – a joke about heaven. The encounter with her made him think, and I did not hear
him tell that joke again. I believe that international, ecumenical women clergy and women leaders
fostered this passion and commitment. Though he remained always an Anglican bishop, archbishop,
and therefore an inextricable part of the male hierarchy that still dominates the Anglican church.

Desmond Tutu's passion for equality and justice went beyond women's ordination as priests and
women's leadership. According to his biographer John Allen: "In the 1970s he had been tolerant of
gays but mentioned them along with drug addicts and the poor." However, he began to accept that
sexuality, like race or gender, was probably not a choice. His earliest public comments on this were
in 1990. Towards the end of his episcopate when I was his chaplain, I noticed that he started to speak
more boldly and publicly on this issue when he was overseas. For him the principles of justice and
equality meant that the conclusion was inevitable: discrimination against gays and lesbians was as
wrong as that against blacks and women.[2]

I remember having to reply to a letter he received from a senior priest in the diocese. Like a few
others who wrote, he was a hundred percent affirming of the Archbishop's opposition and actions to
end apartheid, as well as supportive of his move to ordain women priests. This priest then wrote: "I
have the utmost respect for you Archbishop, but on this issue you are wrong." I was sad that there
was not even a hint that perhaps given the Archbishop's intellect, ministry, morality, principles,
leadership, wisdom, experience, there might be a willingness to think and pray and consider that
Desmond Tutu might also be right about this. I had to receive on his behalf the phone calls from
people who wanted to tell him how wrong he was to think that gay and lesbian people were welcome
in the church. It was challenging.

One of the wonderful memories about this issue as a chaplain was the process to make a
submission to Section 9 of the new South African constitution, on equality. The great debate was
whether sexual orientation would be included in a non-discrimination clause, alongside race, gender,
religion and other characteristics. This was groundbreaking and we knew the Archbishop needed to
make a submission. I was asked by friends in the gay and lesbian activist community for my help. I
did this by keeping the issue near the top of his list of ongoing tasks. There was a deadline, and he
was about to leave the country and the timing was tight. There was a process of writing, and he asked
me to work on it, which I did with the help of my gay and lesbian activist friends. Once finished, he
worked on it again, then gave it to me just a short while before he was leaving for the airport. With
only a few minutes to go, the whole of Bishopscourt staff rallied around. We printed out the
submission, photocopied the pages, collated the document and the signature pages, with agonising
slowness given the rush. I literally ran at full speed from the office to the car outside where he was
waiting to leave. I put the pages and the pen in his hand, and he signed. We breathed a sigh of relief,
it was submitted in time and in 1996 the new constitution made history. The South African
constitution prohibits discrimination on the basis of sexual orientation, making it one of the most
progressive constitutions in the world. Desmond Tutu's submission was a significant voice and,
together with the staff, I was a part of making history. What a privilege.

Desmond Tutu continued to speak out about injustice to the LGBTQIA community. He became
one of the foremost religious leaders to speak out on this in the world. By this stage I was working
for All Saints Church, Pasadena, California, where same-gender marriage was accepted and
practised. There were many members of the LGBTQIA community there, and around the world in
churches of all kinds, who have been inspired by him, reminded through his statements and his
sermons that they are equally human, equally made in the image of God, equally loved by God.
Perhaps over the years they were also an inspiration to him.

In 2020 I returned to South Africa from the USA, after seventeen years as an Episcopal priest in
California. I came to be the chaplain at Volmoed Retreat Centre, in Hermanus, near where the Tutus
lived. I was asked to help him with some paperwork once a week. When Covid-19 and lockdown
began, the job changed. I was asked to celebrate Eucharist three times a week with him and Mam'

---

[2] John Allen, *Rabble-Rouser for Peace,* Free Press, 2006, p. 372.

Leah. I shared in prayer, song and Eucharist, and helped them during lockdown. We joked that it was like being his chaplain again. It was a joy to bring him his morning hot chocolate after the services. It was a joy to talk about those days of women's ordination, or of equality, and current affairs in the world and the church.

I remain inspired by this most wonderful person in my life and am so grateful for his influence and impact on my life. Without him I would not be who I am. I am eternally grateful for all the years of ministry, connection, service and challenge.

Desmond Tutu has always and is still always unequivocally clear about faith and justice and equality and inclusion – that God is not a man, God is not homophobic, God is not a Christian, and all human beings, all people – all, all, all, are made in the image of God.

May we follow his inspiring example.

Haikus in honour of Desmond Mpilo Tutu

Ninetieth birthday
Desmond Mpilo Tutu
Celebrate his life

Giant of justice
Prophetic priest and pastor
Spoke courageous truth

Apartheid prophet
Unafraid to speak his mind
Heart worn on his sleeve

Preached with clarity
All are made in God's image
Equal and Beloved

Preached with energy
Everyone, All, are welcome!
Arms stretched wide open

Stories and jokes told
Often with sting in the tail
Twinkle in his eyes

Champion of women
Listened to marginalised
Ordained women priests

Moral leadership
Global Statesman and Elder
Standing for the truth

Prayerful at all times
Leading by his example
Tata we love you

21. TUTU'S VISIONARY INCLUSIVE LEADERSHIP WITH REGARD TO WOMEN'S ORDINATION TO THE PRIESTHOOD

Vicentia Kgabe[1]

Many of us have been blessed to come to ministry or discern a vocation to the ordained ministry during the time and leadership of Desmond Tutu, "the Arch". Discerning a vocation as a woman, when there are no other women priests to reference within one's immediate context can be daunting, to say the least. Yet we drew our hope from ecclesiastical leaders in the calibre of the Arch and others who were standing on the truth that all who are called to serve, regardless of race, class, gender and/or ethnicity should be discerned and given a chance to live out their vocation. This stand was not only heart-warming but also inviting, inclusive and affirming. The Arch and all who believed in this truth were not ignorant to the fact that whatever they were advocating for will not make all things bright, beautiful and accepted overnight. Those who were in opposition were not going to stop being in opposition just because things have changed, regardless of how democratic or prayerful the process was.

When he was elected as the first black Metropolitan of the Anglican Church of Southern Africa and Archbishop of Cape Town, Desmond Tutu set the tone for his Arch-Episcopacy, at the occasion of his enthronement, by identifying three pressing issues that had his attention for his tenure. He identified these as firstly, to end apartheid, secondly to have the ordination of women become a reality and thirdly for the full inclusion of LGBTQIA people in the church. These three priorities set him apart and indeed put him on a collision course with many both in and outside the church. For him to fulfil and achieve these tasks he knew he could not do this all by himself, he needed willing, available and dedicated fellow leaders, members and masses with faith as little as a mustard seed. In this essay, I will focus on his leadership and vision of an inclusive church specifically on having the ordination of women become a reality in the Anglican Church of Southern Africa.

As a sixteen-year-old girl growing up in Soweto, the 14th August 1992 will remain etched in my memory for a lifetime. It was on this day that the Anglican Church of Southern Africa meeting in eSwatini (formerly Swaziland) for their Triennial Provincial Synod voted in favour of women being ordained to the priesthood. At that time women were only allowed to be deacons and could not be ordained as priests. Women's ordination to the priesthood depended on a change in legislation or the canons, which in turn required a motion to serve at the supreme legislative authority within the church – the Provincial Synod. In the Provincial Synod the delegates had to debate the motion and then vote on it. The motion to ordain women was one of the motions that fell under the category of "measure" because it dealt with a change to the canon. It was not a "procedural motion" or "motions of greetings". The "measure" had to pass three stages before it could finally be approved and become law.

The president of the synod was Archbishop Desmond Tutu in his capacity as the Metropolitan of the Anglican Church of Southern Africa, known as the Church of the Province of Southern Africa (CPSA) at that time. This "measure" had been tabled before at the previous synod of 1989 meeting in Durban, and after a lengthy debate the vote was called, and the results were recorded as 121 votes against ordaining women and 79 in favour of the ordination of women.

---

[1] The Revd Canon Dr Vicentia Kgabe (PhD) is an ordained Anglican priest and currently serves as the rector and principal of the College of Transfiguration NPC – Grahamstown, South Africa. The College of Transfiguration was born out of the amalgamation of the then three theological colleges that were in existence in the Anglican Church of Southern Africa. And this happened in 1993 during Archbishop Desmond Tutu's time as the metropolitan of our church. And he was the first chairperson of the newly constituted College of Transfiguration Council (Board of Directors).

Leading the way in women's ordination

In his Charge to the Provincial Synod of 1992 meeting in eSwatini, he said amongst other things: "The Bible is quite clear that the divine image is constitutive of humanity irrespective of gender. I cannot have struggled against an injustice that penalises people for something they can do nothing about, their race, and then accept with equanimity the gross injustice of penalising others for something they can do nothing about, their gender. We have heard some say that the ordaining of women would go counter to African culture. Fortunately, that has been proved untrue … women have played and are playing leading roles in African traditional society as leaders, prophets, and rulers."

In the account provided below of what transpired before, during and after the vote on the "measure" of the Ordination of Women to the Priesthood, it is clear that Archbishop Tutu demonstrated leadership that held the church together when it could have experienced schism because of divergent views and standpoints. This is the kind of leadership that needs to be celebrated and emulated.

Before the debate Archbishop Desmond Tutu had declared his support for ordaining women saying:

> We have had a wonderful opportunity to demonstrate this acceptance of one another despite all kinds of differences especially in the matter of the ordination of women. Since 1989 the Synod of Bishops, following the request of the Provincial Synod, has kept the issue under review. The Synod of Bishops made funds available so that two conferences in 1991 and 1992 could be held, one on the Ministry of Women in general, and the second on the Ordination of Women to the Priesthood. I am proud of the fact that discussions of these issues have been thorough but without bitterness or acrimony. I hope that at this Synod we will continue that good tone and spirit. We must show the world that it is possible to hold differing views and express them vehemently but in a spirit of Christian charity and affability. We must not be obnoxious or acrimonious, making personal attacks. We must play the ball, not the man or the woman. The resolution that will come before the Synod was crafted by a group of Bishops representing both sides of the debate which just shows how far we have moved. A substantial majority of the Synod of Bishops is now in favour of the ordination of women to the priesthood with some quite significant converts to this position. We must remain in communion with one another and continue to respect one another's right to our point of view and not to pillory those of an opposite viewpoint. I am more convinced than ever before that theologically, biblically, socially, ecumenically, it is right to ordain women to the priesthood. The most radical act that can happen to any human being is to become a member of the body of Christ. If gender cannot be a bar to baptism, which makes us all representatives of Christ and partakers of the only priesthood there is, His royal priesthood, then gender cannot be a bar to ordination.[2]

Wrap-up on women's ordination for extra-provincial readers of Bishopscourt update, regarding views of Archbishop Desmond Tutu – August 28, 1992

The Anglican Church of Southern Africa has voted by an overwhelming majority to ordain women as priests. At the end of a four-hour debate on August 14, the church's Provincial Synod passed a resolution saying, "it gives its approval to the ordination of women as priests."

The historic decision followed a strong plea in support of the ordination of women by Archbishop Desmond Tutu in his opening charge to the meeting. The majority was 79%. Archbishop Desmond, the President of the Synod, had declared the issue to be "controversial", meaning that it needed a two-thirds majority to be approved. In 1989 the proposal to ordain women failed to secure the two-thirds majority by a narrow margin.

The Synod also asked the Synod of Bishops to draw up guidelines "to meet the needs of those who have difficulties of conscience" with the decision. However, it rejected a suggestion that no women

---

[2] Anglican Church of Southern Africa Archives, *Provincial Synod daily bulletin: Measure on ordination of women to priesthood.* Johannesburg: Wits University Archives (1992).

should be ordained before the next Provincial Synod had approved "protective legislation" for those opposed to the move.

Bishops, clergy, and lay representatives voted separately on the resolution, which was proposed by Dean Colin Jones of Cape Town and seconded by Ms Maureen Sithole of the Diocese of South-Eastern Transvaal (now called Diocese of the Highveld).

In the House of Bishops, the vote in favour was 21 to 6. In the House of Clergy, it was 70 to 25 and in the House of Laity, it was 75 to 14. The total votes were 166 in favour and 45 against.

At the start of the debate, the Archbishop reminded the Synod that this was a particularly divisive issue. "Wouldn't it be wonderful if especially South Africa could see that we disagree and disagree vehemently, and yet remain friends?" he asked. He also stressed that members were free to say just what they believed and to vote accordingly. "We need, under the Holy Spirit's guidance, to be open to one another, to hear what God is saying to us through one another. And every one of us must be free to express exactly what they feel, what they believe, what the Holy Spirit of God has convicted them to say."

The Archbishop took no part in the debate itself. But after the result had been announced and he had led the synod in prayer, he commented: "I think that having expressed the concern [in the prayer] that we do have for those for whom this is a painful decision, we also have to give thanks for the joy in the hearts of many who over such a long time have felt hurt in the church. "It is important for me to stress that no Bishop is compelled [to ordain women]. The Bishop ordains those they believe are called and ready to be ordained. This decision cannot compel any Bishop to ordain those they would not wish to be ordained. And that is important to know. But much more is the fact that we hold together, and as Bishop Michael Nuttall was saying, we are on a pilgrimage. In 1989, when the result was announced, I said, perhaps God is saying, Wait – that we should be able to move together. And I praise God that we today can say we are moving together in this fellowship, that is not a fellowship of uniformity, but unity."

Overcome with emotion, the Archbishop left the Synod meeting hall after saying: "I don't know where you are. Emotionally I am unable to continue ..." And the following day he addressed the Synod and said, "I could not sleep last night, bearing in mind the desolation of the many who would have found the decision yesterday painful and unacceptable, yet also thinking of the joy and thankfulness of those such as Wilma Jakobsen in my diocese." He paid tribute to all women deacons for "their quiet dignity" and "how they have borne the pain".

He and Bishop Nuttall, Dean of the Province, then moved to retain the church's unity. They proposed a resolution assuring those opposed to the decision "that there is a cherished place for them in (our Lord's) church, which would be impoverished without them."

It went on to say; "this synod salutes with deep appreciation and gratitude the theological integrity and the devotion to, and love for, our Lord as well as the dedication to Catholic truth, belief, tradition and spirituality of those in the church who oppose the ordination of women to the priesthood."

The Revd David Wells SSM, of the Diocese of Lesotho, responded to the resolution by thanking Archbishop Tutu for the "sensitive way" in which he handled debate on the issue. The synod gave the Archbishop a standing ovation. Later he led the synod in an ovation for Bishop Nuttall.

Conclusion

The above narrative shows that what the Arch was proposing and willing to lead on was not cosmetic change but an attempt and commitment to change the ingrained cultural, religious and societal norms. I would argue that his faith emboldened his leadership. His leadership was derived from his beliefs, his discipline of worship and prayer to a God who has lovingly created all of us and fashioned us in

God's likeness, a God who is love. The Arch is quoted saying "do your little bit of good where you are; it's those little bits of good put together that overwhelm the world."[3]

The Arch could vision a church and society that could not comprise only of black and white or only male and female. He saw the rainbow children of God. He coined the term "rainbow people of God". John Allen notes that this phrase was used in numerous meetings, but the most notable occasion was 13 September 1989 outside Cape Town City Hall when the Arch addressed the masses with these words "… they tried to make us one colour: purple. We say we are the rainbow people! We are the new people of the new South Africa!"

The first time I heard the phrase was in February 1990 at a stadium outside Johannesburg on the occasion of Nelson Mandela's release. In his own words, the Arch described the rainbow "as depicted in the Bible as a sign of peace. The sign of prosperity." He went on to say, "we want peace, prosperity and justice and we can have it when all people of God, the rainbow people of God, work together." He cared about the greater good and well-being of all, not only those who agreed with him but also those in opposition to his opinions and what he stands for. He brought his full humanity into his leadership roles inspired or fortified by his strong spirituality and the discipline he learned at seminary (St Peter's, Rosettenville) of doing daily morning and evening prayers. And this was evident in the full display of his emotions: he was moved to tears, he laughed, he made others laugh and accepted when he was wrong and when he did not have answers. He is a gift, and we thank God for giving her world and her church a leader like Desmond Mpilo Tutu.

Postscript

While I have celebrated the victory of women's ordination and the role of the Archbishop in helping us achieve this, there is still much work to be done, in transforming our theologies that support gender-based violence, both structural and physical. The sharp increase in gender-based violence during the COVID pandemic brought to public attention the seriousness of gender-based violence in the country. Even the president of South Africa, in one of his addresses to the nation during his COVID-19 updates, acknowledged that GBV had reached pandemic proportions. A group of Anglican women clergy and theological scholars drafted a statement regarding gender-based violence that was presented to Archbishop Thabo Makgoba, in a Facebook live public engagement, on 22 July 2020. The event inspired a number of practical commitments, including the possibility of a Master's scholarship at UWC that will enable research on church policies with regard to GBV. I also believe that it is worthwhile replicating the "call to action" that we constructed, in its entirety below, to highlight that, while we may have achieved a small victory with the struggle for women's ordination, the larger struggle for women in the Anglican Church continues.

Gatvol Yet Hopeful!
Women Call the Anglican Church of Southern Africa to Action[4]

Preamble

Women are gatvol yet hopeful! Southern African, ordained and lay Anglican women and scholars of religion met to summon the Church to action. The descriptive Afrikaans word "Gatvol" means "completely fed up and upset". "Gatvol" sums up the fatigue, despair, anger, anguish and pain we continue to experience physically, emotionally, psychologically and spiritually as women. But we are

---

[3] Desmond Tutu Peace Foundation, "10 Pieces of Wisdom from Desmond Tutu on his birthday," http://www.tutufoundationusa.org/2015/10/07/10-pieces-of-wisdom-from-desmond-tutu-on-his-birthday/ (accessed 03 May 2021).
[4] Rene August, "Gatvol! ACSA Women in conversation with The Most Revered Dr Thabo Makgoba," YouTube, May 30, 2021, 0:00 to 1:10:16, http://www.tutufoundationusa.org/2015/10/07/10-pieces-of-wisdom-from-desmond-tutu-on-his-birthday/ (accessed 10 June 2021).

here – again – because the unstoppable love of God, the witness of Jesus the Christ who treated women as equals, the empowering force of the Holy Spirit, give us courage and compel us onward. Because of this we have hope, we have agency, we have resilience.

We gathered to "consider, take counsel and speak out" (the closing words of the gruesome biblical narrative of Judges 19, the story of a woman who was gang raped) against gender-based violence, yet again. We lament that we have to do so, yet again.

We acknowledge that there has been "speaking out" in the past, but we wish to interrogate why this "speaking out" has not been enough to curb the pandemic of violence against those gendered as women, by those gendered as men. The 2017 Mothers' Union Diocese of Cape Town protest march, included a request for action, "We have marched and prayed but we need something more tangible than symbolic marches" the women said. On 3 June 2017 twelve representatives of different women's groups met with the Archbishop of Cape Town and appealed to him, "You declared apartheid evil and a sin, please declare gender-based violence to be evil and a sin as well." Today we declare that patriarchy is not just a sin, but a heresy.

The purpose of this statement is to call for a deeper consideration by the Church of the insidious links between gendered belief systems and violence; of the violence of patriarchy reflected in the absence, ignoring or minimising of women's voices in leadership, in promises made in synodical or other resolutions not followed up or not resulting in action, or broken promises.

The source of all gender-based violence is patriarchy. Patriarchy prevents us from seeing a faithful picture of who God is, in God's identity and in God's compassion. In the gender binaries the dominance of masculine language and masculine images of God, priest and church, renders theology and society poverty stricken. We yearn and strive for the kin-dom of God, where justice for women is restored! A new, beloved community where all humans are affirmed as image bearers of the living God.

We call the Church to condemn its death-dealing beliefs, doctrines, and practices

While there have been prior resolutions and strong statements issued by the Church in the past against GBV and the violence of patriarchy, these strong statements have sought to locate the problem outside of the Church's doctrines, teachings, beliefs and most importantly, practices.

There is substantial research and evidence to suggest that religious belief systems play a leading role in perpetuating dangerous conditions for women. We therefore call on the Church to speak out against these death-dealing beliefs and doctrines. We ask the Church to condemn all of its own teachings and practices that are less than life-giving for women. The following is not an exhaustive list, but some of the major areas which need challenge and redress:

1. Male Headship – We call on the Church to denounce theologies of headship and "natural order" which suggest that men are by nature to have dominion and power over women. Male authority must be dismantled in all spheres – from the family to the pulpit. Therefore the Church must avoid language like calling male priests "Father" as it reflects a male clericalism which renders women priests "invisible" in the presence of male colleagues who close ranks and insist on addressing one another as "father". Liturgical language that reflects the images of God as gender-neutral should be encouraged and practiced.

2. Female submission – We call on the Church to denounce theologies of submission, which require women to be submissive to men, to their husbands, and by extension other forms of male authority. The Church must intentionally address the transformation of previously male dominated ecclesial spaces by authorising and using teachings, liturgies and practices that are life-giving for women. The Church cannot continue to ordain women and expect them to practice "business as usual" as if they were men. Women are tired – no gatvol – of conforming to patriarchal theologies and ecclesiastical practices and liturgies. Those who do confront these, often exit to follow their calling elsewhere, outside the "institutional" church. Those who remain struggle to find ways to navigate their ministry within patriarchal norms and practices. Women need to be represented in all

levels of church leadership, for effective action and transformation to curb the pandemic of GBV and the violence of patriarchy.

3. Family Values – We call on the Church to denounce the recent call to return to "traditional family values" where power differentials are not acknowledged, and where the sanctity of family takes precedence over the sanctity of the lives of women and those who identify as LGBTQIA.

4. Codes of Purity – We call on the Church to dismantle codes of purity. Teachings about modesty and purity which young women are expected to adhere to, promote rape culture and apportion blame to women for violence against their bodies. We condemn the ongoing practice of sanctions against women for "sexual impurity" while the men who are directly involved continue to enjoy pastoral care and impunity.

5. Discourses of Powerlessness – We call on the Church to stop peddling discourses of powerlessness and vulnerability about women. Women are not naturally powerless and vulnerable – they are rendered powerless and vulnerable through the harmful and toxic theologies of the Church. We call on the Church to refrain from grouping women with children as a category. We recognise that the abuse of children is an important matter to address, but the continuous grouping of women with children reinforces the idea that women are minors.

6. Discourses of Protection – Women do not need to be protected. They need equal access to power; then they would not need protection from those who are given more power than them. The church needs to model equal access to power, material resources (including theological education and formation) and structural representation for women through the way in which it engages with women clergy and leaders. Since 1992 only two women have been consecrated to the Episcopate and that took twenty years after women's ordination; only four as Dean, Provost or Senior Priest. The number of women delegates at Provincial Synod has decreased since the Synods of 1992, 1996, 2002 and 2005. There were more women participating and leading in those synods because intentional steps were taken by the Church leadership. While representation does not necessarily result in transformation, representation must remain a key commitment of the Church. Without women in leadership in the Church, without the perspective of women in decision making about the Church, theology is insipid and fails to speak life and truth and value to women who are victims of toxic violent patriarchy in every form.

7. Discourses of Pity – We call on the Church to stop perpetuating a discourse of pity and charity surrounding our women. When men speak of our women they perpetuate the idea of ownership of women and their bodies – this is at the heart of the problem of gender-based violence. Responding to gender based violence is an issue of justice, not of charity.

Conclusion

In summary, beyond issuing statements of condemnation against GBV, or lack of women's leadership, the Church needs to acknowledge its complicity in, and repent of, its own role in perpetuating gender-based violence. Our hope is in the Church of God that fully reflects the wondrous beauty and diversity of God who is beyond all genders and loves all creation fiercely.

Consider this, take counsel, speak out and act!
SINETHEMBA!

Rev. René August
Rev. Wilma Jakobsen
Rev. Canon Dr Vicentia Kgabe
Canon Delene Mark
Prof. Sarojini Nadar
Dr Miranda Pillay
Rev. Natalie Simons-Arendse
Ms Pumla Titus

22. RACE AND SEXUALITY IN DESMOND TUTU'S THEOLOGY OF *UBUNTU*[1]

Adriaan van Klinken[2] and Ezra Chitando[3]

Archbishop Desmond Mpilo Tutu is mostly known to the world for his highly prominent role in the campaigning against apartheid in South Africa (the institutionalised system of racial segregation in the period 1948–94). As general secretary of the South African Council of Churches (SACC) (1978–85), Tutu transformed the SACC into a Christian organisation that was highly vocal on the question of race, speaking out against the white Afrikaner nationalist government and its apartheid policies, calling for non-violent protest and for international economic pressure. He continued this very public leadership after he made history by becoming the first black African to serve as Bishop of Johannesburg (1985–86) and then as Archbishop of Cape Town (1986–96) in the Anglican Church of Southern Africa. Tutu's role in the struggle against apartheid was internationally recognised by the award of the 1984 Nobel Peace Prize. After the democratic transition in South Africa in 1994, he played a high-profile role as chair of the Truth and Reconciliation Commission, the public hearings of which were widely reported in the national and international media.

In more recent years, Tutu, who retired as archbishop in 1996 and who announced his retirement from public life in 2010, has become known for his strong advocacy on issues of sexuality, in particular the rights of lesbian and gay people. Indeed, his biographer John Allen concludes that "nothing kept Tutu's name in the public eye after his retirement as archbishop more than his attitude toward homosexuality".[4] For instance, in 2013, he made global headlines with the clear and succinct statement, in typical Tutu fashion, that he would rather go to hell than to a homophobic heaven.[5] Being by far the most high-profile African religious leader to support gay rights has added to his international reputation as a progressive thinker and activist, especially in the Western world, but was met with suspicion on the continent itself. A fellow Anglican bishop, Emmanuel Chukwuma from Nigeria, even declared him to be "spiritually dead".[6] Similarly, Robert Mugabe, former president of Zimbabwe, retorted Tutu's criticism of his leadership by saying that Tutu himself should step down because his pro-gay stance was a "disgrace".[7] Yet Tutu's unquestionable moral authority and his firm

---

[1] This is a slightly edited version of a chapter that was originally published as "Race and Sexuality in a Theology of Ubuntu: Desmond Tutu", in Adriaan van Klinken and Ezra Chitando, *Reimagining Christianity and Sexual Diversity in Africa* (African Arguments series) (London: Hurst & Co, 2021), 23-38. We are grateful to Hurst Publishers for granting permission for this republication.

[2] Adriaan van Klinken is professor of religion and African studies at the University of Leeds (UK), and extraordinary professor in the Desmond Tutu Centre for Religion and Social Justice at the University of the Western Cape (South Africa). Adriaan's research focuses on Christianity, gender and sexuality in contemporary Africa. His latest book is *Kenyan, Christian, Queer: Religion, LGBT Activism, and Arts of Resistance in Africa* (Penn State University Press, 2019). He has never had the privilege to meet Archbishop Tutu, but is still hoping for that dream to come true (if not on earth, then in a – hopefully not homophobic – heaven).
[3] Ezra Chitando is professor of history and phenomenology of religion at the University of Zimbabwe and theology consultant on HIV, World Council of Churches. He writes here in his personal capacity. His research interests include religion and sexuality, human security, climate change, development, politics, gender, masculinities, peace building and others. Although he has not met Tutu in person, he has encountered him in his many writings.

[4] John Allen, *Rabble-Rouser for Peace: The Authorised Biography of Desmond Tutu* (New York: Free Press, 2006), 372.
[5] BBC, "Archbishop Tutu 'would not worship a homophobic God'", 26 July 2013, https://www.bbc.co.uk/news/world-africa-23464694 (accessed 22 January 2020).
[6] Christopher Craig Brittain, and Andrew McKinnon, *The Anglican Communion at a Crossroads: The Crises of a Global Church*. University Park: Penn State University Press (2018), 2.
[7] News24, "Mugabe attacks 'gay-supporting Archbishop' Desmond Tutu", 28 July 2013. https://www.news24.com/Archives/City-Press/Mugabe-attacks-gay-supporting-Archbishop-Desmond-Tutu-20150429 (accessed 24 March 2020).

rootedness in traditions of African theology and spirituality mean that his voice cannot be ignored. Indeed, his thinking on matters of sexuality is an essential stepping stone for the constructive reimagination of sexuality and Christianity in Africa. Such a reimagination is particularly important in light of the recent politicisation of homosexuality in many parts of the continent, with popular forms of Christianity perpetuating a discourse of postcolonial amnesia in which African histories of sexuality are problematically reconfigured through the prism of colonial and neo-colonial Christian moral agendas.[8] Against this background, Tutu has made a significant contribution to the process of "Africanising the discourse on homosexuality" – a contribution that reflects and extends the progressive traditions of black and African theologies of inculturation and liberation that have shaped his thinking.[9] Tutu has also sought to address and intervene in the crisis over homosexuality that, since the 1998 Lambeth Conference, has escalated in his own ecclesial family, the Anglican Communion.[10]

This chapter offers a critical reconstruction of Tutu's thinking about same-sex relationships and the rights and dignity of gay and lesbian people, and discusses how it is connected to Tutu's longstanding concern with race, and is inspired by his broader theology of *Ubuntu*. Although we do recognise some limitations of Tutu's thinking about this subject, especially in the contemporary context, the chapter overall seeks to acknowledge Tutu's visionary progressive leadership in the area of Christianity and sexual diversity in Africa and beyond.

Sexual politics in church and state

As Archbishop of Cape Town, Tutu was also the primate (most senior clergy) of the Anglican Church in Southern Africa. In that role he led the process for the church to open up ordination into the priesthood to women (in 1992), a cause he was deeply committed to. At the end of his term in office, he also initiated a review of the official church policy on gay and lesbian clergy, which required celibacy of clergy of homosexual orientation. Although Tutu had thus far defended this policy publicly, according to Allen he had "privately acknowledged that it was not logically sustainable" and was a form of "discrimination based on an attribute people could not change".[11] In fact, already in 1997, Tutu had strongly denounced this policy, describing it as "illogical, irrational

---

[8] See Ezra Chitando and Adriaan van Klinken (eds), *Christianity and Controversies over Homosexuality in Contemporary Africa* (London and New York: Routledge, 2016); Ezra Chitando and Lovemore Togarasei, "'Beyond the Bible': Critical Reflections on the Contributions of Cultural and Postcolonial Studies on Same-Sex Relationships in Africa", *Journal of Gender and Religion in Africa* 17, no. 2 (2011), 109-125; Marc Epprecht, *Heterosexual Africa? The History of an Idea from the Age of Exploration to the Age of AIDS* (Athens: Ohio University Press, 2008); Neville W. Hoad, *African Intimacies: Race, Homosexuality, and Globalization* (Minneapolis: University of Minnesota Press, 2007); Kapya Kaoma, *Christianity, Globalization, and Protective Homophobia: Democratic Contestation of Sexuality in Sub-Saharan Africa* (New York: Palgrave Macmillan, 2018); Adriaan van Klinken and Ezra Chitando (eds), *Public Religion and the Politics of Homosexuality in Africa* (London and New York: Routledge, 2016).

[9] See Ezra Chitando and Pauline Mateveke, "Africanizing the Discourse on Homosexuality: Challenges and Prospects", *Critical African Studies* 9, no.1 (2017), 124-40. For an overview of debates on sexual diversity in contemporary African Christian theology, see Masiiwa R. Gunda, "African Christian Theology and Sexuality: Some Considerations", in Elias K. Bongmba (ed.), *The Routledge Handbook of African Theology* (London and New York: Routledge, 2020), 367-80; Adriaan van Klinken and Masiiwa R. Gunda, "Taking Up the Cudgels Against Gay Rights? Trends and Trajectories in African Christian Theologies on Homosexuality", *Journal of Homosexuality* 59, no.1 (2012), 114-38.

[10] For instance, see Miranda K. Hassett, *Anglican Communion in Crisis: How Episcopal Dissidents and Their African Allies Are Reshaping Anglicanism* (Princeton, NJ: Princeton University Press, 2007); Hoad, *African Intimacies*; William L. Sachs, *Homosexuality and the Crisis of Anglicanism* (Cambridge: Cambridge University Press, 2009).

[11] Allen, *Rabble-Rouser for Peace*, 281.

and frankly un-Christlike, totally untenable".[12] He considered it illogical and irrational for the church to teach that celibacy is a vocation while at the same time making it mandatory for gay and lesbian people. He considered it un-Christlike because the policy denied gay and lesbian people the possibility of expressing their sexuality in ways that allow them to become "more considerate of each other, more gentle, more compassionate, more ready to engage in self-giving, and so to become more and more like God".[13] In spite of his strong feelings, Tutu was unsuccessful in changing the church policy on this issue, which remains in place to date. His own daughter, Mpho Tutu, who was an ordained priest, became the victim of this policy when she married her female partner in 2015 and was subsequently pressured to give up her priestly licence.

It has been described as a tragedy that Tutu's Anglican Church and many other South African churches which fought successfully against apartheid have failed to overcome "another fundamental and equally oppressive division: one that divides straight people from gay and lesbian people" after liberation in the 1990s.[14] In South Africa at large, this division had been addressed more adequately, at least legally speaking. The country's new 1996 constitution was historic for many reasons, including the fact that it explicitly included sexual orientation into the non-discrimination clause. Tutu had actively advocated for this, arguing:

> It would be a sad day for South Africa if any individual or group of law-abiding citizens in South Africa were to find that the Final Constitution did not guarantee their fundamental human right to a sexual life, whether heterosexual or homosexual. I would strongly urge you to include the sexual orientation clause in the Final Constitution.[15]

The inclusion was recognition of the fact that several gay people, such as the first openly gay black anti-apartheid activist Simon Nkoli, had actively participated in the liberation movement, and had successfully "insisted upon the inseparability of the struggles against apartheid and homophobia".[16] Tutu had embraced this notion, stressing that apartheid had not only denied blacks, but also gay and lesbian people, of "their basic human rights and reduced them to social outcasts and criminals in their land of birth". He had urged the writers of the constitution "to include gay and lesbian people in the 'Rainbow People' of South Africa".[17] Indeed, the new constitution reflected the strong commitment of the country's political and judicial elites to building a legal safety net remedying past injustices by guaranteeing equal protection and rights to all citizens of the "new" South Africa. Arguably, these legal provisions did not automatically translate into a change of social attitudes towards lesbian and gay people at a grassroots level, and homophobia remains widespread in South African society up to date. Yet on the basis of the progressive constitution, the country's Constitutional Court in 2005 ruled that the common-law definition of marriage should be opened up to same-sex couples, making South Africa in 2006 the first (and so far, only) country on the African continent to legalise same-sex marriage. Tutu himself was supportive of the campaign towards this move, and also approved of church blessings for same-sex relationships, although he preferred the term "union" over "marriage" in order to prevent "a lot of hassles", which illustrates that, as a man of principle, he could also be pragmatic.[18]

The hassles concerned may have to do with the crisis around issues of homosexuality – in particular, the blessing of same-sex relationships and the ordination of gay and lesbian clergy – that

---

[12] Desmond Tutu, "Foreword", in Paul Germond and Steve de Gruchy (eds), *Aliens in the Household of God: Homosexuality and Christian Faith in South Africa* (Cape Town: David Philip, 1997), x.

[13] Tutu, "Foreword", x.

[14] Germond and de Gruchy, *Aliens in the Household of God*, 2.

[15] Quoted in Mark F. Massoud, "The Evolution of Gay Rights in South Africa", *Peace Review* 5, no. 3 (2003), 303.

[16] Ryan Richard Thoreson, "Somewhere over the Rainbow Nation: Gay, Lesbian and Bisexual Activism in South Africa", *Journal of Southern African Studies* 34, no. 3 (2008), 680.

[17] Thoreson, "Somewhere over the Rainbow Nation", 687.

[18] Allen, *Rabble-Rouser for Peace*, 373.

had escalated in the worldwide Anglican Church since the 1998 Lambeth Conference of Anglican bishops.[19] Conservative African bishops, such as Peter Akinola from Nigeria, played a prominent role in protesting against the, in their opinion, too-liberal attitudes of American, European and South African Anglican churches, and the conference passed a resolution stating that same-sexual relationships are "incompatible with Scripture". Tutu, as a retired bishop, did not attend the 1998 and 2008 Lambeth conferences where the controversy around homosexuality caused deep divisions.

However, in spite of his initial decision not to interfere in these debates publicly, he could not keep quiet for long and "began to include, in speeches and sermons, careful remarks which made his position clear".[20] In 2001, he wrote a letter in support of Bishop Christopher Senyonjo, who had been expelled by his church, the Anglican Church of Uganda, for his pro-gay stance.[21] A few years later, in 2004, he preached at Southwark Cathedral in London, shortly after the openly gay canon of the cathedral, Jeffrey John, had been forced to withdraw his acceptance of a nomination to become bishop. In his sermon, Tutu saluted John for acting "with so much dignity and selfless *generosity*", and stated that "the Jesus I worship is not likely to collaborate with those who vilify and persecute an already oppressed minority".[22] Tutu's interventions, to his great frustration, appear to have had little effect in moving the Anglican Communion to a more accepting and affirming position on issues of sexuality. He reportedly wrote to George Carey, the then Archbishop of Canterbury, that he felt ashamed to be an Anglican. Nonetheless, his public speaking out on those issues has allowed him to become "perhaps the world's most prominent religious leader advocating gay and lesbian rights".[23] Consequently, it is important to understand the theological basis of his activism in support of the rights of lesbian and gay people in Africa and other parts of the world.

Homophobia, like apartheid, is a heresy

For distant observers, Tutu's gay rights advocacy might appear to be a recent phenomenon. For his critics, it might be another illustration of how Tutu has become a "sell out", striving to be the darling of white liberal audiences in the Western world. However, Tutu's commitment to defending gay rights is far from a recent development. As early as the 1970s, he took a relatively "tolerant" stance on gay issues, a stance that gradually evolved in the following decades towards full acceptance and affirmation.[24] Admittedly, he was operating in a very complex field, as became evident when, as Bishop of Johannesburg, Tutu forced the dean of the cathedral, Mervyn Castle, to resign after the police had ensnared him in a trap and charged him for homosexuality, which at that time was legally banned. The decision reportedly "haunted Tutu for years" and he later tried to make up for it by appointing Castle as his personal chaplain, and by consecrating him as Bishop of False Bay in 1994.[25]

Tutu has repeatedly made it clear that for him, the struggle for gay rights is very much in continuity with his long-standing resistance against apartheid and his relentless defence of black civil rights in South Africa. At the heart of both struggles is Tutu's strong moral and political commitment to defending the human dignity and rights of all people, and his deep theological conviction that every human being is created in the image of God and therefore is worthy of respect.

[19] Hassett, *Anglican Communion in Crisis*.
[20] Allen, *Rabble-Rouser for Peace*, 373.
[21] Christopher Senyonjo, *In Defense of All God's Children: The Life and Ministry of Bishop Christopher Senyonjo* (New York: Morehouse Publishing, 2016), 86. For a discussion of Senyonjo's remarkable ministry, see Adriaan van Klinken, "Changing the Narrative of Sexuality in African Christianity: Bishop Christopher Senyonjo's LGBT Advocacy", *Theology and Sexuality* 26, no. 1 (2020), 1-6.
[22] Desmond Tutu, "Sermon by Archbishop Desmond Tutu at Southwark Cathedral", 1 February 2004, https://www.anglicannews.org/news/2004/02/sermon-by-archbishop-desmond-McCartutu-at-southwark-cathedral.aspx (accessed 21 January 2020).
[23] Allen, *Rabble-Rouser for Peace*, 372.
[24] Allen, *Rabble-Rouser for Peace*, 372.
[25] Allen, *Rabble-Rouser for Peace*, 223.

Tutu uses the strongest possible theological terminology to reject homophobia and heterosexism, when he writes: "The church has joined the world in committing what I consider to be the ultimate blasphemy – making the children of God doubt that they are children of God. Lesbians and gays have been made to reject God and, in their rejection of the church, they have been made to question why God created them as they were".[26] The use of the term "blasphemy" is particularly significant in the South African context. Ten years prior to making the just-quoted statement, Tutu had used exactly the same word to theologically condemn apartheid: "Its most blasphemous aspect is … that it can make a child of God doubt that he [sic] is a child of God. For that reason alone, it deserves to be condemned as a heresy".[27] He made this statement in his contribution to a book entitled *Apartheid Is a Heresy*, a title inspired by the prophetic declaration with which the World Alliance of Reformed Churches in 1982 categorically rejected the theological justification of apartheid as developed by the South African Dutch Reformed Church.

Although the terms blasphemy and heresy have slightly different meanings, in the South African theological debate about apartheid they were used somewhat interchangeably. As early as 1956, the Johannesburg-based Anglican missionary priest and anti-apartheid activist Trevor Huddleston (who later became a close friend and ally of Tutu) had used both words in his anti-apartheid book *Naught for your Comfort*.[28] Apartheid was seen as a heresy because it was considered to go against fundamental Christian beliefs, in particular the belief in the equality of all human beings on the basis of humankind being created in the image of God. Exactly because of this doctrine of the *imago Dei*, the failure to recognise human equality and instead treat people as inferior on the basis of race (or any other trait) was also seen as blasphemy, that is, an insult of God-self.

The echo of this prophetic language that dominated Christian anti-apartheid discourse in the 1980s can be heard in Tutu's above-quoted statement about "ultimate blasphemy". In the same way that apartheid, and its false theological justification, wanted black people to believe that they do not fully bear God's image and are less valuable children of God, homophobic and heterosexist theologies make gay and lesbian people believe they are inferior in the eyes of God. Both theologies, Tutu suggests, are fundamentally un-Christian. It is for that reason that shortly after the end of apartheid, Tutu declared:

> If the church, after the victory over apartheid, is looking for a worthy moral crusade, then this is it: the fight against homophobia and heterosexism. I pray that we will engage in it with the same dedication and fervour which we showed against the injustice of racism, so that we may rehabilitate the gospel of Jesus Christ in the eyes of many who have been deeply hurt.[29]

Tutu firmly believes that opposing any form of discrimination and injustice, and defending the full humanity and dignity of all human persons, is at the heart of Christian witness. Hence he criticises the church for "instead of being hospitable to all, it has made many of God's children outcasts and pariahs on the basis of something which, like race or gender, they could do nothing about – their sexual orientation".[30]

Black African theology

Tutu is a theologian deeply grounded in the tradition of South African black theology which emerged in the 1970s as a contextual theology of liberation, prophetically denouncing the injustices of

[26] Tutu, "Foreword", x.
[27] Desmond Tutu, "Apartheid and Christianity", in John W. de Gruchy and Charles Villa-Vicencio (eds), *Apartheid is a Heresy* (Grand Rapids: Eerdmans, 1983), 46-7.
[28] See R. G. Clarke, "Apartheid is a Heresy", *Reality* 16, no 2 (1984), 7.
[29] Tutu, "Foreword", x.
[30] Desmond Tutu, "Afterword", in Michael G. Long, *Martin Luther King Jr., Homosexuality, and the Early Gay Rights Movement: Keeping the Dream Straight?* (New York: Palgrave Macmillan, 2012), 150.

apartheid while constructively affirming black dignity, solidarity and freedom.[31] This theology was inspired by and indebted to the Black Consciousness movement spearheaded by anti-apartheid activist and student leader, Steve Biko; by American black theology as developed by James H. Cone whose book *Black Theology and Black Power* was published in 1969; and by African theology as developed by scholars such as John Mbiti from Kenya and Bolaji Idowu from Nigeria. Because of these various sources of inspiration, South African black theology had to negotiate the relationship between blackness as a political category and Africanness as a cultural category, and had to reflect on the problems both these categories posed in light of the history and contemporary experience of Christianity in the South African context. For Tutu, however, there was not so much a conflict between black and African theology, stating: "I myself believe I am an exponent of Black Theology coming as I do from South Africa. I believe I am also an exponent of African Theology coming as I do from Africa".[32] Indeed, his theological thinking, including about the question of sexuality, reflects both traditions.

In the tradition of black and other liberation theologies, God, for Tutu, is the God of the Bible book of Exodus, "choosing to side with a rabble of slaves, a God who is always concerned with the plight of the widow, the orphan, the alien".[33] Jesus, for him, reflects the same "bias" as God, as he was "firmly on the side of those who had been pushed aside – the hungry, the homeless, the poor".[34] In the days of apartheid, this belief drove his commitment to denounce racial injustice and to radically affirm the dignity of black people. Yet after political liberation in 1994, the same belief inspired his continued struggle against homophobia and his affirmation of the dignity of gay and lesbian people who, in his perception, simply were the next group of oppressed people in need of liberation. "The Jesus I worship is a Jesus who was forever on the side of those who were being clobbered, and today it's the gays and lesbians who are being clobbered".[35]

Emphasising the radically inclusive character of Jesus' ministry, Tutu states that this is what inspired him in the struggle against apartheid, and what now inspires him in the struggle against homophobia. Clearly, Tutu is a liberation theologian for whom the question of race and the question of sexuality are part of the same spectrum. Indeed, he has referenced Martin Luther King Jr as a source of inspiration, not only for his fight against apartheid, but also for his current commitment to the fight for gay and lesbian human rights. "He [King] encouraged me to see each person as made in the image of God, as someone God loves deeply, and as my own brother or sister in God's colourful family".[36] According to Tutu, it is time to return to, and reinvigorate the dream of Martin Luther King Jr: "A world of peace, a world of justice, a world of love without discrimination – this is the dream of Martin Luther King Jr. It should also be the dream of all of God's people. So let us return to the dream!"[37]

Tutu powerfully captured his own dream for South Africa in the metaphor of the rainbow, which he first used in 1989 when he addressed the thousands of protesters (from diverse racial backgrounds) participating in an anti-apartheid demonstration as "the rainbow people of God".[38] Nelson Mandela later incorporated this notion in the inaugural address after his election as president, referring to South Africa as a rainbow nation. The rainbow metaphor was intended to capture the coming together of people from diverse backgrounds, racially, culturally, linguistically, and it conveyed the belief that the beauty of these groups together, in their differences, exceeded the sum of its parts. It symbolises unity in diversity. Of course, for Tutu the rainbow also has a biblical connotation. In the

---

[31] Mokgethi Motlhabi, *African Theology/Black Theology in South Africa: Looking Back, Moving On* (Pretoria: UNISA Press, 2008).

[32] Quoted in Motlhabi, *African Theology/Black Theology*, 46-7.

[33] Tutu, "Foreword", ix.

[34] Tutu, "Foreword", ix.

[35] Tutu, "Afterword", 150.

[36] Tutu, "Afterword", 149.

[37] Tutu, "Afterword", 150.

[38] Allen, *Rabble-Rouser for Peace*, 391.

Old Testament story of Noah and the Flood, the rainbow is a sign of God's covenant with humankind, symbolising the divine promise that never again will the waters destroy all life (Gen. 9). Likewise, Tutu's metaphor suggests that under God's covenant with the people of South Africa, all human life is sacred and will not be destroyed by the evils of apartheid, racism and other forms of discrimination. Critics have been sceptical about "rainbowism", describing it as naïve and sentimental, and as covering up the ever-existing racial and economic inequalities in post-apartheid South Africa. Tutu might agree that it is idealistic indeed, yet for him the ideal is rooted in his understanding of *Ubuntu*.

Ubuntu

Tutu's thinking has been aptly described as "*Ubuntu* theology".[39] The engagement with the indigenous Southern African concept of *Ubuntu* qualifies his theology as a form of African theology, firmly grounded in African cultural concepts and worldviews. *Ubuntu* is an isiXhosa and isiZulu word, and it has been widely adopted in African philosophy as a concept of human existence in community. It is often translated as "I am because you are" or "A person is a person through other people".[40] Tutu, who popularised the word, associates it with values such as generosity, hospitality, care, compassion, openness towards and affirmation of others in recognition of their full humanity, and a celebration of diversity.

For Tutu, *Ubuntu* is a theological concept because it is closely connected to his understanding of creation. It provides a correction to a Western theology of salvation, which is traditionally concerned with the individual, and instead it allows for an "emphasis on the integrity of creation and the habitual recalling of our image of God (*imago Dei*) in the midst of human conflict".[41] To put it simply, from the perspective of *Ubuntu*, human beings collectively (rather than individually) present the image of God. The traditional Christian doctrine of the Trinity further enlightens this because, according to this doctrine, God exists in three persons – Father, Son and Holy Spirit – and each of these persons is defined in their relation to the others. Thus, as the Trinity is internally relational and interdependent, so is humankind. It is in our relationality, interdependence and vulnerability – that is, in expressing *Ubuntu* – that human beings reflect the image of God.[42]

For Tutu, the implication of *Ubuntu* is that "what dehumanises you, inexorably dehumanises me".[43] Applying this to the context of apartheid, he argues that those who supported apartheid and perpetrated violence and injustice under this system towards fellow human beings were themselves also victims, as their own humanity was damaged while they inflicted harm on others. This inspired his vision for the Truth and Reconciliation Commission after the end of apartheid, as he believed that the idea of *Ubuntu* "equips you to look at your torturers, to realize that they need your help and to stand ready to enable them to regain their humanity".[44]

Although Tutu has not systematically reflected on questions of sexuality from the perspective of his theology of *Ubuntu*, it is obvious that it shapes his thinking about sexuality considerably. First, *Ubuntu* for him is closely connected to the celebration of human diversity, for it is through the complementarity of our differences that we together grow in humanity, affirm one another, and reflect collectively the image of God. This applies to sexual diversity as much as it does to racial diversity. Thanks to his *Ubuntu* theology, Tutu could radically imagine society as "the rainbow people of God". Second, Tutu insists that *Ubuntu* calls us to always first and foremost recognise the humanity of the other. This implies, in particular, an affirmation of those human lives that are

---

[39] Michael Battle, *Reconciliation: The Ubuntu Theology of Desmond Tutu* (Cleveland, OH: The Pilgrim Press, 1997).

[40] Allen, *Rabble-Rouser for Peace*, 347.

[41] Battle, *Reconciliation*, 5.

[42] Battle, *Reconciliation*, 46.

[43] Desmond Tutu, *No Future Without Forgiveness* (New York: Doubleday, 1999), 35.

[44] Allen, *Rabble-Rouser for Peace*, 396.

marginalised on the basis of societal and cultural norms, and indeed it puts such norms under critique. In the words of Aloo Mojola:

> The *ubuntu* perspective demands a human and compassionate treatment of and respect for all humans, especially those on the edges and the margins. This necessarily includes those whose lifestyles are considered deviant, unconventional and non-traditional including those espousing alternative sexualities, masculinities and femininities.[45]

Ubuntu makes us attentive to the authentic experiences of people who live on the margins, thus reminding us that "sexual politics is about people – it carries the human face".[46] Third, in the same way as the perpetrators of apartheid, according to Tutu, were dehumanised by their own deeds, one could argue that those who endorse homophobia and heterosexism are also damaged in their own humanity. This awareness calls for an attitude of ongoing dialogue with, and respect towards those who fail to recognise the humanity of lesbian and gay people.

Further extrapolating Tutu's thought, one could argue that *Ubuntu*, as a philosophy of community, might offer a starting point for an indigenous African philosophy that affirms sexual diversity, as an alternative to Western, highly individualised accounts of LGBT rights. It has been suggested that *Ubuntu* can, in fact, have a negative effect on the debate about homosexuality in African contexts, because of its possible coercive aspects, suppressing individual preferences and freedoms to the interests and needs of the community.[47] Tutu's conception of *Ubuntu*, however, appears to be more liberationist, as *Ubuntu* for him requires the flourishing of all, and thus the interrogation of any societal norms that marginalise and oppress certain members of the community. From that perspective, if lesbian and gay people are ostracised because of heteronormative norms that prevail in a certain community, this not only restricts the flourishing of these individuals but subsequently also of the community to which they belong as a whole.[48] Tutu's conception of *Ubuntu* also appears to be more liberal, as he does seem to privilege individual autonomy and freedom, stating that "to be human is to be free".[49] However, for him this freedom is not for self-centred purposes, but allows people to contribute to the community in the spirit of *Ubuntu*: "We are created to exist in a delicate network of interdependence with fellow human beings and the rest of God's creation".[50] While traditional African ways of dealing with sexuality and relationships have often been concerned with the value of biological reproduction, *Ubuntu*, as Tutu understands it, calls for a broader understanding of human flourishing. In the words of Ghanaian theologian Mercy Oduyoye, such an understanding acknowledges alternative ways of being fruitful.[51]

---

[45] Aloo Osotsi Mojola, "The African Bantu Concept of Ubuntu in the Theology and Practice of Desmond Tutu and its Implications for African Biblical Hermeneutics", in Madipoane Masenya (Ngwan'a Mphahlele) and Kenneth N. Ngwa (eds), *Navigating African Biblical Hermeneutics: Trends and Themes from our Pots and our Calabashes* (Newcastle: Cambridge Scholars, 2018), 66.

[46] Kaoma, *Christianity, Globalization and Protective Homophobia*, 178.

[47] Jones Hamburu Mawerenga, *The Homosexuality Debate in Malawi* (Mzuzu: Mzuni Press, 2018), 173-4.

[48] Also see Elias K. Bongmba, "Homosexuality, Ubuntu, and Otherness in the African Church", *Journal of Religion and Violence* 4, no. 1 (2016), 15-37.

[49] Desmond Tutu, "The First Word: To Be Human Is To Be Free," *Journal of Law and Religion* 30, no. 3 (2015), 386-90.

[50] Tutu, "The First Word", 388.

[51] Mercy A. Oduyoye, "A Coming Home to Myself: The Childless Woman in the West African Space", in Margaret A. Farley and Serene Jones (eds), *Liberating Eschatology: Essays in Honor of Letty M. Russell* (Louisville: Westminster John Knox Press, 1999), 105-22. For a discussion of Oduyoye's contribution to thinking about Christianity and sexual diversity, see Van Klinken and Chitando, *Reimagining Christianity and Sexual Diversity*, chapter 2.

Limitations?

It has become clear that Tutu's advocacy for gay and lesbian human rights is shaped by his longstanding commitment to social justice, in particular his struggle against apartheid. His approach to gay rights advocacy reflects a specifically South African narrative in which sexuality is equated to race. This narrative emerged during apartheid, when activists like Simon Nkoli had drawn a strong connection between the struggles against racism and homophobia, and it continued to be powerful and effective after liberation. As Ryan Thoreson points out, the considerable legal and political successes that the gay and lesbian movement achieved in post-apartheid South Africa were made possible by the discursive strategy that the movement employed:

> From the outset, GLB activists framed their agenda in terms of identity politics: everyone, they insisted, has a sexual orientation, whether gay, lesbian, bisexual, or heterosexual. Instead of referring to choice ("sexual preference") or practice ("sexuality"), activists insisted upon the terminology of a concrete, immutable identity – "sexual orientation", which was cognate to racial categorisation – and strategically dropped the "language of fluidity and contingency of sexuality" … Their strategy enabled activists to link their cause to forms of gender and race-based discrimination that the post-apartheid government had vowed to eradicate, making it more difficult for religious groups and conservative political parties to argue that public morality and tradition justified discrimination on the basis of sexual orientation.[52]

Tutu's stance on gay issues reflects this approach, as for him sexual orientation, just like race and gender, is not something a person can do anything about. It is innate and, theologically speaking, part of how God created us. This approach can be characterised as both biologically and theologically essentialist. "We do not choose our sexuality any more than we choose our race or ethnicity. As God has made me black, so has God made some of us gay. And how incredibly wonderful it is that God has created each of us to be who we are. That's reason for celebration".[53] This essentialist approach offers a strong basis to oppose discrimination. In Tutu's own words, it is "always wrong to discriminate against people because of the way God has made us (black or white, male or female, gay or straight)".[54]

There are some possible limitations to this approach, however. First, although it may be a powerful strategy in South Africa with its history of apartheid, it may not necessarily be equally effective in other parts of the continent where the language of culture or "Africanness" appears to be more prominent than the language of race or "blackness". Second, Thoreson suggests that in South Africa itself, the essentialist emphasis on sexual orientation may be the reason why, in spite of the successes in securing lesbian and gay rights, "bisexuality has been scarcely visible and the transgender movement has struggled to secure legal protections".[55] Indeed, this blind spot can also be observed in Tutu's case, as his interventions make little or no explicit reference to bisexual and transgender people (although there is no reason to assume that he would not recognise them as bearers of the *imago Dei*). Third, one may wonder how long this narrative will continue to appeal to younger generations in South Africa, growing up more than 25 years after the end of apartheid. This question is particularly salient because, with the emergence of queer studies, the language and understanding of sexuality has generally shifted away from biological essentialism to concepts that underscore the fluidity, ambiguity and performativity of gender and sexuality (and perhaps also of race), thus opening up new possibilities for sexual politics.[56]

---

[52] Thoreson, "Somewhere over the Rainbow Nation", 681.

[53] Tutu, "Afterword", 149.

[54] Tutu, "Afterword", 149-50.

[55] Thoreson, "Somewhere over the Rainbow Nation", 681.

[56] E.g. see Zethu Matebeni, *Reclaiming Afrikan: Queer Perspectives on Sexual and Gender Identities* (Athlone: Modjaji Books, 2014); James W. McCarty III, "A Paradoxical Theology of Biology: Desmond Tutu's Social Ethics in Light of His Sermon at Southwark Cathedral", *Theology and Sexuality* 19, no. 1 (2013), 89-97.

Conclusion

Regardless of the above-mentioned limitations, Tutu's contribution to the debate about sexual diversity in contemporary Africa is a major one. He has emerged as one of the most influential faith leaders, in Africa and globally, unequivocally advocating for the human dignity and rights of sexual minorities, and campaigning for the destigmatisation and decriminalisation of same-sex relationships.[57] Tutu yearns for "resurrection, new life, new beginning, new hope".[58] His prophetic commitment to defending human dignity, equality and justice continues to inspire and set an example to many people across the world. Although other parts of Africa have not had the experience of apartheid, they have experienced colonialism and the systematic racism inherent in it, thus making Tutu's equation of racism and homophobia powerful across the continent. Furthermore, with his theology of *Ubuntu* he allows for a conceptualisation of sexual diversity that is meaningful in African contexts and that enhances the human flourishing of gay and lesbian people as part of their communities. *Ubuntu* is clearly based on values such as hospitality and generosity, and built on the foundation of solidarity and shared humanity. Therefore, anything that threatens the health and well-being of even one member of the community (for example, through ostracism, stigma and violence) is contrary to the spirit of *Ubuntu* that Tutu extolls. One can only hope for his prophetic voice on this subject to shape and reshape attitudes towards sexual diversity in African and Christian circles, and in the world at large.

---

[57] Ezra Chitando and Tapiwa P. Mapuranga, "Unlikely Allies? Lesbian, Gay, Bisexual, Transgender and Intersex (LGBTI) Activists and Church Leaders in Africa", in Ezra Chitando and Adriaan van Klinken (eds), *Christianity and Controversies over Homosexuality in Contemporary Africa* (London and New York: Routledge, 2016), 171-83.

[58] Tutu, *No Future without Forgiveness*, 258.

23. TUTU THE ALLY:
LESSONS FROM ARCHBISHOP DESMOND TUTU'S QUEER ADVOCACY

Megan Robertson[1]

Introduction

Witty quips and compelling soundbites are a distinguishing marker of Archbishop Desmond Tutu's legacy. Over the last two decades a number of these soundbites have been directed at LGBTIQ+ rights and freedoms. However, it would be remiss to dismiss these merely as memorable one-liners. While Tutu has not developed a substantive queer[2] theology, his statements are compelling, partly because they are underwritten by the history of his fortitudinous fight for civil rights and particularly black freedoms in South Africa. In addition, his *Ubuntu* theology,[3] rainbowism and social justice ideology is the thread which ties his LGBTIQ+ advocacy to his anti-apartheid activism and, thus, lends it political and theoretical weight.[4] His advocacy has not, however, bypassed critique, both from conservative African Christian leaders who believe he has "sold-out" to the views of the colonial west[5] and queer theologians who argue that his sermons and statements rely too heavily on biological essentialism in ways that continue to limit the attainment of LGBTIQ+ rights and freedoms.[6] Yet, Tutu remains one of the few church leaders in South Africa and Africa more broadly to strongly and consistently advocate for the rights and dignity of LGBTIQ+ persons and to position himself as an ally to the fight for queer liberation both within and outside the church. In this essay I use some of Tutu's "soundbites" in relation to LGBTIQ+ issues to reflect on how his advocacy challenges and directs queer allies.

Lesson 1: Use your privilege to critique heteronormative power

In South Africa, Tutu's statements as a church leader are significant as he stands in contrast to many other religious leaders who, while vehemently fighting for black liberation, continue to remain silent on LGBTIQ+ issues. At the time of writing, over the course of the first few months of 2021, a spate of killings of LGBTIQ+ people in South Africa had been reported. In response, Rev. Teboho Klaas, Fr Thabang Nkadimeng, Mrs Thabisile Msezane and Rev. Ecclesia de Lange released an open letter

---

[1] Dr Megan Robertson is a postdoctoral fellow under the auspices of the Desmond Tutu SARCHI Chair in Religion and Social Justice (Grant No. 118854). She has worked for three institutions where the Tutu name has served as a compass for its work including the Institute for Justice and Reconciliation, the South African Faith and Family Institute and the Desmond Tutu Centre for Religion and Social Justice, where she is now a lecturer. Her work with people and organisations that carry his name reflects the ways in which his ethics and politics have guided her approach and commitment to social justice work.

[2] Noting the politics, particularly in Africa, around the use of the term "queer", in this paper I use "LGBTIQ+" in reference to non-normative sexualities and gender non-conforming people and "queer" in reference to broader theories and politics.

[3] Michael Battle, *Reconciliation: The Ubuntu Theology of Desmond Tutu* (Cleveland, Ohio: Pilgrim Press, 1997).

[4] While Tutu has not theorised his own theology in relation to LGBTIQ+ issues, as Adriaan van Klinken points out, "Tutu's commitment to defending gay rights is far from a new development" and is fundamentally attached to his *Ubuntu* and liberation theologies.

[5] Adriaan van Klinken and Ezra Chitando, eds, "Race and Sexuality in a Theology of Ubuntu: Desmond Tutu", in *Reimagining Christianity and Sexual Diversity in Africa* (London: Hurst & Company, forthcoming): 28.

[6] Van Klinken and Chitando, "Race and Sexuality"; James W. McCarty III, "A Paradoxical Theology of Biology: Desmond Tutu's Social Ethics in Light of His Sermon at Southwark Cathedral," *Theology & Sexuality* 19, no.1 (2013): 89-97.

to church leaders titled "'You are muted, unmute yourself': An open letter to South African church leaders on the plight of the LGBTIQ+ people."[7] This letter encourages religious leaders to acknowledge the churches' complicity in the violence meted out against LGBTIQ+ people and urges them to add their voices to promote transformed and more affirming attitudes and beliefs. Unsurprisingly this letter has not received many responses. Some of the responses it has provoked are defensive cries from selected church leaders who felt it was unfair to "accuse them" and that it was unproductive to be "pointing fingers" at church leaders. This response came despite the fact that those who had written the letter were themselves church leaders. Research shows that particularly in relation to LGBTIQ+ issues, churches take defensive and ambiguous stances largely due to the looming threat a division in church membership poses, and the accompanying possibility of a loss of political and moral clout.[8] This has meant that church leaders have often placed the reputation and unity of the church above speaking out against queerphobia.

In contrast, Tutu's statements on the issue do not shy away from critiquing and holding the church to account for the injustices it has committed to, and beliefs it has perpetuated about, LGBTIQ+ people. Perhaps Tutu's most well-known call to action in relation to LGBTIQ+ rights is in his foreword to Paul Germond and Steve de Gruchy's book in 1997 *Aliens in the Household of God: Homosexuality and Christian Faith in South Africa* where he writes, "If the church … is looking for a worthy moral crusade, then this is it: the fight against homophobia and heterosexism".[9] At various times Tutu has admitted that he has been ashamed at his church's attitude towards LGBTIQ+ people. During a visit to the University of North Florida in 2005 in response to debates about the first openly gay Episcopal bishop, the Rt Rev. Gene Robinson, Tutu spared no hesitation in saying that, "God must look on and God must weep."[10] Tutu's willingness to call the church to account for its role in perpetuating queerphobia, and his encouragement of the church to act, remains a rarity amongst religious leaders.

Critiquing his own church is of course not without its difficulties. In an interview with the *Washington Post* in 2013 in relation to speaking up about LGBTIQ+ rights, he said, "It's the kind of thing you heard the prophet Jeremiah complain of where he says, 'You know God, I didn't want to be a prophet and you made me speak words of condemnation against a people I love deeply. Your word is like a fire burning in my breast.'"[11] The people whom he loves and to whom he is referring in this quote seems to be the church, both the institution and its leadership. Despite the difficulties associated with critiquing his own church, "the fire burning in [his] breast" also speaks to the inescapable responsibility required of an ally. As a well-loved and respected political and religious figure, as well as a heterosexual, cis-gender man, Tutu is afforded a certain amount of protection and privilege to be able to call out his own church. For allies who are afforded similar protection and privileges, perhaps in ways which LGBTIQ+ persons are not, Tutu upholds an ethic of responsibility to call out the very systems of power which grant his protection and privilege. This is a simple yet important lesson for religious leaders and those who are allied to the cause.

[7] An updated version of this letter was again sent out with additional signatories after only one religious leader responded to the original letter.

[8] Megan Robertson, Sarojini Nadar and Johnathan Jodamus, "Antagonism, Ambivalence and Affirmation: Exploring Ecclesial Paradigms for Queering the Church in South Africa", *NCC Review* 138, no. 6 (2018): 356-366.

[9] Desmond Tutu, "Foreword", in *Aliens in the Household of God: Homosexuality and Christian Faith in South Africa*, eds Paul Germond and Steve de Gruchy (Cape Town, South Africa: David Philip, 1997): ix–x.

[10] 2005, "Tutu calls on Anglicans to accept gay bishop", *Spero News*. URL no longer available.

[11] S. Bailey, 2013, "Interview: Desmond Tutu on gay rights, the Middle East and Pope Francis", *The Washington Post.* Available: https://www.washingtonpost.com/national/on-faith/interview-desmond-tutu-on-gay-rights-the-middle-east-and-pope-francis/2013/09/13/1875eff2-1c9d-11e3-80ac-96205cacb45a_story.html (accessed 13 May 2021).

Lesson 2: Your liberation is bound up with mine

While Tutu himself has not theoretically linked his *Ubuntu* theology to his advocacy of LGBTIQ+ rights in church and society, other scholars have. In their forthcoming book chapter for example, Adriaan van Klinken and Ezra Chitando illustrate how *Ubuntu*'s celebration of human diversity and its emphasis on the liberation of the collective provides a framing "for an indigenous African philosophy … that affirms sexual diversity …"[12] I would further this by arguing that Tutu's *Ubuntu* theology also provides a helpful direction for allyship. In a quote associated with Lilla Watson and the Aboriginal activists group Queensland in the 1970s, they direct allies by saying, "If you have come here to help me, you are wasting your time. But if you have come because your liberation is bound up with mine, then let us work together." Tutu has used a similar directive to motivate for the liberation of LGBTIQ+ people, particularly in South Africa.

Tutu has on multiple occasions made connections between the anti-apartheid struggle and the fight for queer liberation. In 2013 at the United Nations' launch of its gay rights programme Tutu said, "I would not worship a God who is homophobic and that is how deeply I feel about this. I would refuse to go to a homophobic heaven. No, I would say sorry, I mean I would much rather go to the other place. I am as passionate about this campaign as I ever was about apartheid. For me, it is at the same level."[13] As van Klinken and Chitando[14] point out, Tutu has on different occasions labelled both racism and homophobia blasphemous, thus denouncing both as inherently un-Christian. By connecting his own positionality as a black person fighting racism in apartheid South Africa to various forms of unjust inequality and discrimination including homophobia and heterosexism, Tutu positions himself not as an outsider "helping" LGBTIQ+ people but rather as someone whose liberation is indivisible from the freedom of others. This could perhaps be framed as an *Ubuntu* activism or *Ubuntu* allyship – one which is informed by a recognition that social justice and liberation must involve the subversion and transformation of various and interconnected systems of power.

Lesson 3: Transformation might not always be theoretically sound

For queer and gender studies scholars, it might make us cringe to read a quote in which Tutu says, "… Sexual orientation is not something that you choose, it's a gift"[15] or "as God has made me black, so God has made some of us gay. And how incredibly wonderful is it that God has created each of us to be who we are."[16] Essentialising race and sexuality in this way is contrary to queer theories that argue gender and sex are not something which people are born with but, rather, something people construct through repetitive performativities. However, as Ryan Thoreson points out, it has historically been a strategically effective queer activist strategy in South Africa.[17] This is because of the fertile ground apartheid liberation strategies had created for an essentialist identity politics in which race, gender and sex all become unchangeable identities which should not be treated indiscriminately because essentially these characteristics are inherent and outside of one's control. Thoreson goes on to argue that this strategy was particularly effective against religious homophobia:

---

[12] Van Klinken and Chitando, "Race and sexuality", 33.

[13] Yasmine Hafiz, 2013. "Desmond Tutu Would Prefer Hell Over A Homophobic Heaven", *The Huffington Post*. Available: https://www.huffpost.com/entry/desmond-tutu-hell-homophobia_n_3661120 (accessed 13 May 2021).

[14] Van Klinken and Chitando, "Race and Sexuality", 29.

[15] Mihlali Ntsabo, 2018, "Desmond Tutu says that sexuality is not a choice", *Mamba Online*. Available: https://www.mambaonline.com/2018/06/05/desmond-tutu-says-that-sexuality-is-not-a-choice/ (accessed 13 May 2021).

[16] Desmond Tutu, "Afterword", in *Martin Luther King Jr., Homosexuality, and the Early Gay Rights Movement: Keeping the Dream Straight?*, eds. Michael Long and Desmond Tutu (New York: Palgrave Macmillan, 2012): 149.

[17] Ryan Thoreson, "Somewhere Over the Rainbow Nation: Gay, Lesbian and Bisexual Activism in South Africa", *Journal of Southern African Studies* 34, no. 3 (2008): 679-697.

Their strategy enabled activists to link their cause to forms of gender and race-based discrimination that the post-apartheid government had vowed to eradicate, making it more difficult for religious groups and conservative political parties to argue that public morality and tradition justified discrimination on the basis of sexual orientation.[18]

Tutu's essentialism is perhaps as a result of a similar political strategy. James McCarty II posits that Tutu consistently argued in his anti-apartheid rhetoric that "race, does not matter in questions of justice because all persons, regardless of biological differences, are created in the image of God."[19] Thus he was able to refute apartheid's biological arguments that black people were somehow naturally inferior to white people. However, in relation to LGBTIQ+ issues Tutu has argued that, "Human bodies in their particularity — black or white, male or female or intersex, tall or short, able or disabled, homosexual or heterosexual — are creatures who are recipients and carriers of God's love."[20] Thus, as McCarty argues, Tutu has put forward both that biology matters, in so far as we should not discriminate against a person because of an essentialist quality, and also that it does not matter, in so far as people are created in the image of God and thus should be loved and revered. These somewhat contrasting positions on biological identity can be understood as a result of Tutu juggling between a prophetic and pastoral voice.[21] While his inconsistency here partly reflects that he has not framed his discourses within queer theology and theory, McCarty makes an important point in illustrating that Tutu's discourse around identity is strategically situated in relation to either the political or church context. Indeed, in the current church context in South Africa it remains popular to claim an essentialist argument which relies on ideas that all people are God-created and that God has not erred in creating LGBTIQ+ persons. The limits of his strategic balance of the prophetic and pastoral domains are evident in the fact that such balance has not provided sufficient recognition and protections for bisexual and transpersons in South Africa.[22] However, as McCarty reflects, "This impulse to marry the prophetic and the pastoral is one worthy of imitation. And it must be said that balancing the prophetic and the pastoral is no easy task."[23] Perhaps as allies this is something that ought to be learned.

In my own experience of doing research with LGBTIQ+ clergy in the Methodist Church of Southern Africa (MCSA) and in trying to incorporate an "ethic of solidarity" into my work, I have also engaged in a balancing act, albeit between the academic and the activist rather than prophetic and pastoral. While I do not subscribe to ideas that the academic and activist are disconnected, translating an academic project into a useful tool within the context and politics of the church is not an uncomplicated task. Once my official research project was "completed" I remained in contact with a few key participants who wanted to create platforms and strategies which would challenge the MCSA to become more affirming of its LGBTIQ+ members and leadership. In my brief involvement thus far I have often found that LGBTIQ+ clergy and activists in the church can as easily invoke Foucault and Butler as they can use essentialist discourses around gender and sex in order to push policy decision or to discuss their experiences with the church. I have also found that while I, in my writing, have critiqued attempts at transformation which focus on the single-issue matter of same-sex marriages, LGBTIQ+ clergy and members (even those who had told me they would never want to be married) have restricted their fight to this issue in order to attempt to create space for incremental change. As an ally, what I have learned from the various ways in which Tutu, LGBTIQ+ clergy and church members balance their political and pastoral commitments is that transformation within the context of church politics sometimes means letting go of particular theoretical nuances in aid of the cause. I do not want to dismiss altogether the usefulness of scholarship which imagines queer futures

---

[18] Thoreson, "Somewhere Over the Rainbow Nation", 681.
[19] J. McCarty III, "A Paradoxical Theology", 92.
[20] McCarty III, "A Paradoxical Theology", 93.
[21] McCarty III, "A Paradoxical Theology", 95.
[22] Thoreson, "Somewhere Over the Rainbow Nation", 681.
[23] McCarty III, "A Paradoxical Theology", 95.

and which critiques the trade-offs that are sometimes made in achieving a fraction of that future. Indeed, imagining a queer future for churches is, I think, integral to the academic project lest we settle for superficial inclusion rather than transformation. However, I think it is important that when translating this into activism we engage with the reality of church politics and this is sometimes perhaps not as theoretically neat as we might imagine.

What can Tutu the ally teach us?

As a heterosexual ally (with all its problematics) doing research at the intersections of religion and queer sexuality has meant that I have devoted a significant amount of time to reading and writing on what it means to be an academic ally and activist. By far one of the most well-known religious allies LGBTIQ+ people have had in South Africa is Desmond Tutu. While he has not written theoretically nuanced and lengthy academic papers on the matter, he has offered politically and culturally astute sermons, quotations and soundbites which have captured the public's attention and served (often alone) as a religious voice that has challenged queerphobia and heterosexism. Tutu has used his privilege and position in ways which other religious leaders and allies in the church have been reticent to do. He has come to the cause not merely as a sympathetic outsider, but as a social justice advocate who acknowledges the intersectionality of various systems of power which have diminished the rights and humanity of various people. In this way he has challenged the very systems and institutions that have afforded him a particular position of privilege. He has also shown that allyship in church sometimes involves negotiation of the politics with which it engages. This serves as a strategic lesson in how to meet the church where it is at but also encourages us to find new strategies through a combination of theorising and practicing which is able to both consider the performativity, fluidity and materiality of sex, gender and sexuality while leveraging it in a way that speaks to the politics of church. As a church leader and ally, Tutu's advocacy of LGBTIQ+ rights in Africa carries with it lessons for other allies, activists and advocates.

24. REBUKE, REPAIR, RECONCILE: STRETCHING TUTU'S RESTORATIVE JUSTICE FOR CONTEXTS OF SEXUAL VIOLENCE

Rhine Phillip Tsobotsi Koloti[1]

This essay offers a critical analysis of reconciliation within the context of sexual abuse, with a view to suggesting an alternative feminist theological agenda for further reflection. The essay is divided into three sections. The first offers a brief overview of the role, importance and critique of reconciliation as a guiding principle towards healing in South Africa. In the second section, a critical survey of feminist theological commentary on reconciliation and forgiveness within the context of sexual abuse is offered. The final section explores a possible victim-centred theological approach to gender-based violence for further reflection. The main focus of this essay is on reconciliation within the context of sexual abuse.

In the month of August two significant historical events are commemorated, namely, the anti-apartheid women's march which happened on 9 August 1956, and the recent killings of Uyinene Mrwetyana and Jesse Hess on the 18 and 30 August 2019. These two events are a painful reminder of how "economies of violence have [sic] and continue to sustain the indignity and poverty that women in South Africa experience".[2] These events will coincide with a variety of good wishes before the Archbishop's 90th birthday. Speeches, letters, poems and articles will be written to celebrate his generous heart and forgiving spirit. As popular media has had it in the past, he will most likely be described as a proponent of reconciliation and "unconditional forgiveness".[3] But this snapshot, though arguably accurate, betrays a lack of appreciation for who Archbishop Desmond Tutu was and for what we can learn from his theology and teachings about reconciliation and justice within the context of sexual abuse.

Reconciliation and gender justice in South Africa

Addressing gender-based violence requires a critical focus on reconciliation. In South Africa, the colonial lineage and its subsequent legacy of racism, sexism and exclusivism have created and continue to exacerbate personal, systemic and structural violence against black people, women in particular. Due to this, black women and girls are disproportionately affected by sexual abuse in South Africa. While I concede that sexual abuse affects both men and women regardless of their race,

---

[1] Rhine Phillip Tsobotsi Koloti is a Master's student working in the Desmond Tutu Centre for Religion and Social Justice at the University of the Western Cape. He also works as a research assistant and as a tutor. As an activist and an aspiring academic, he works with the United Society Partners in the Gospel and recently participated in the United Nations Commission on the Status of Women. He's also a member of the Association of Practical Theology. His most fond memory of Desmond Tutu goes back to 2008 when he was an altar boy holding the Arch's mitre during the Holy Eucharist Service at St Peter's Chains Anglican Church in Katlehong. This work is based on research supported by the National Research Foundation of South Africa under the auspices of the Desmond Tutu Chair in Religion and Social Justice [Grant Number: 118854]. The opinions, findings and conclusions or recommendations expressed in the research are those of the author alone; the NRF accepts no liability in this regard.

[2] Desmond Tutu Centre for Religion and Social Justice Annual Report, 2019, page 11 https://desmondtutucentre-rsj.uwc.ac.za/wp-content/uploads/2021/05/FINAL-Annual-Report-2019.pdf (accessed 22 May 2021).

[3] Daily Good, "Desmond Tutu: On Why We Forgive," https://www.dailygood.org/story/688/desmond-tutu-on-why-we-forgive/ (accessed 22 May 2021).

religion, ethnicity and class, statistics show that poor black women represent a significant majority of those killed and raped in South Africa.[4]

Gender-based violence is an umbrella term used to refer to harmful acts perpetrated against a person's will based on socially ascribed (i.e. gender) differences between males and females.[5] These acts include sexual abuse, emotional abuse and intimate partner violence *inter alia*. In her book *Sexual Violence: The Sin Revisited*,[6] Marie Fortune poses a challenge to the church[7] by describing sexual violence as a sin – thus implying that we ought to address it theologically, ethically and pastorally. She draws on the narratives of the rape of Dinah (Gen. 34), the incest of Tamar (2 Sam. 13) and the vulnerability of Bathsheba (2 Sam. 11-12) to remind us of how deeply rooted the issue of sexual violence is in our religious spaces and sacred texts.

Scholarship on GBV supports Fortune's assertions that religion is one of the most detrimental enablers of violence against women.[8] It is thus unwise to ignore religion when addressing issues of GBV. In considering sexual violence as a pastorally and ethically sinful act, we must equally start thinking of pastoral care responses to it. Religious discourses, teachings and doctrines are often used as sources of theological and pastoral care responses to GBV, notably the doctrine of reconciliation and teachings on forgiveness.[9]

Reconciliation, race and the rainbow

Reconciliation is a globally lauded concept that often finds itself in the political rhetoric and public policy of many post-conflict countries aiming towards nation-building. As a concept for unifying a nation, it was blindly applied in South Africa post-1994 as a guiding symbol to harness reconciliation between black people and white people. In assessing the effectiveness of reconciliation as a guiding principle towards healing, we must, as highlighted by Boesak and DeYoung, consider the vast and continuing scepticism among many South Africans over the impact of the proceedings of the TRC. 25 years later the "impulse for retribution is still stronger than the impulse for reconciliation".[10]

Black theologians such as Maluleke express an almost similar impulse for retribution by arguing that the primary need for reconciliation in South Africa should not be between white people and black people but instead a reconciliation between black people and their fundamental means of livelihood such as land, cattle, dignity.[11] For Maluleke, this socio-economic approach to reconciliation must come first. Similarly, Lee Scharnick-Udemans blames the "rainbow", the globally renowned symbol of reconciliation, for the permeating socio-economic lacuna evident in the "gross economic disparity, widespread poverty, rampant political corruption and the tragically femicidal character of South Africa."[12]

---

[4] Stats, SA, "Crime against Women in South Africa," https://www.statssa.gov.za/publications/Report-03-40-05/Report-03-40-05June2018.pdf (2018) (accessed 22 May 2021).

[5] GBV Guidelines, "Guidelines for Integrating Gender-Based Violence Interventions in Humanitarian Action: Reducing Risk, promoting resilience and aiding recovery," https://gbvguidelines.org/en/ (accessed 22 May 2021).

[6] Marie M. Fortune, *Sexual Violence: The Sin Revisited.* Cleveland: The Pilgrim Press (2005).

[7] Throughout this study, I use capitalised "Church" to refer to the specific denomination of the ACSA and lowercase "church" to refer to the broader idea of the Christian church.

[8] Tinyiko Sam Maluleke and Sarojini Nadar, "Breaking the Covenant of Violence against Women", *Journal of Theology for Southern Africa* 114 (2002): 5-17.

[9] Denise J.J. Dijk, "Reconciliation: A Real Possibility for Survivors of Sexual Abuse in Pastoral Relationships?" *Liturgy* 23, no. 4 (2008): 11-18.

[10] Allan Boesak and Curtiss DeYoung, *Radical Reconciliation: Beyond Political Pietism and Christian Quietism.* Maryknoll: Orbis Books (2012), 106.

[11] Tinyiko Sam Maluleke, "The Truth and Reconciliation Discourse: A Black Theological Evaluation" in: James Cochrane, John W. de Gruchy and Stephen Martin (eds): *Facing the Truth: South African Faith Communities and the Truth and Reconciliation Commission.* Cape Town: David Phillip (1999), 101-113.

[12] Lee-Shae Scharnick-Udemans, "Decolonizing Religious Studies in South Africa: Reflections on the Field 26 years after democracy", *Religion Compass* 15 (2021). DOI: https://doi.org/10.1111/rec3.12393.

Both Maluleke and Scharnick-Udemans are critical of the application of racial reconciliation as the first step to healing. Drawing from Fortune's discussion on reconciliation and restitution, I agree that within the context of sexual abuse, reconciliation should not be applied as the first measure. In this context, reconciliation may only be possible, not guaranteed, once restitution has happened. This implies that the offender ought to first show remorse, through various tangible acts, as an indication that the plea for reconciliation is an honest plea to heal the estranged relationship. These acts may vary from case to case and may include, but are not limited to, payment for medical and therapeutic costs incurred by the victim. Although such acts will not undo the damage caused by the sexual violation, they have the potential to enhance the likelihood of reconciliation between the victim and the offender.[13]

Given these limitations to the application of reconciliation, one wonders if it can serve as a vehicle to harness the healing and effective pastoral care to victims and survivors of GBV in the church? Why do victims and survivors of GBV feel pressured by the church to forgive and reconcile with their perpetrators?[14] How does Tutu's understanding of forgiveness encourage churches to promote unconditional forgiveness?[15] Ultimately, I wonder if Archbishop Desmond Tutu's theology of reconciliation and restorative justice perpetuates GBV or does it offer the church a better opportunity to "tend" to its "flock"? The answers to these direct yet challenging questions represent the thesis of this essay.

Reconciliation in the church

Some religious institutions, including a few churches, perceive elements of their faith such as doctrines, liturgies, sacred texts, and religious discourses as infallible.[16] The importance of reconciliation for Christians finds expression in all these elements. Biblically, the *Missio Dei,* translated as the mission of God, is best understood in Jesus Christ's purpose on earth as expressed in Paul's Second Epistle to the Corinthians (5:19 [NRSV]): "God was in Christ, reconciling the world to himself, no longer counting people's sins against them", therefore Jesus' mission was and is to reconcile humanity with God. From an intercultural pastoral care approach, reconciliation is listed as one of the main functions of pastoral care. Lartey describes it as the one function responsible for the restoration of fellowship and harmony between previously estranged parties.[17]

As part of the Anglican liturgy, the Anglican Prayer Book (APB)[18] celebrates the Holy Eucharist with the presiding priest proclaiming the following words to the congregants: "Drink of it all of you; for this is my blood of the new covenant, which is shed for you and for many for the forgiveness of sins; whenever you drink it, do this in remembrance of me." Elsewhere in the same prayer book, just before the priest can consecrate the bread and the wine into the body and blood of Christ, the presiding priest shares the peace with the congregation saying: "If when you are bringing your gift to the altar, you remember that someone has a grievance against you, leave your gift where it is before

---

[13] Fortune, *Sexual Violence: The Sin Revisited,* 168-170.
[14] Pamela Cooper-White, *The Cry of Tamar Violence Against Women and The Church's Response.* Minneapolis, Minnesota, USA Fortress Press (1995), 252.
[15] In 1990, the Dutch Reformed Church, through Willie Jonker, sought forgiveness for its theological support of the apartheid regime. In response Tutu's recorded saying, "When that confession is made, then those of us who have been wronged must say, 'We forgive you,' and together we must move to the reconstruction of our land," Afrikaner Cleric Asks Blacks to Forgive, *Willie Jonker Digitale Argief,* https://williejonker.co.za/rustenburg_koerantberig_buiteland_new-york-times_19901108/ (accessed 22 May 2021).
[16] For example, in the Roman Catholic Church, when the Pope speaks *ex cathedra,* defining a doctrine concerning faith or morality, he possesses the infallibility that Christ willed for the church. See, Gerald Kelly, "The Roman Catholic Doctrine of Papal Infallibility: A Response to Mark Powell" *Theological Studies,* no. 74 (2013): 129-137.
[17] Emmanuel Lartey, *In Living Color: Intercultural Approach to Pastoral Care and Counselling.* London: Jessica Kingsley Publishers (2003), 65.
[18] *An Anglican Prayer Book.* Jeppestown: HarperCollins Publishers (1989), 118.

the altar. Go, make peace, and only then come and offer your gift."[19] When congregants hear these words, one wonders if they perceive their inability or unwillingness to forgive as an act that will exclude them from God's grace? This call to forgive one another which is taught biblically and liturgically creates an obligation on the part of the victims to forgive their offenders immediately which only "serves to heal the wound lightly".[20]

Based on these liturgies, one may deduce that the Holy Eucharist celebration depicts the sacramental table as a place of reconciliation, unity and forgiveness. A place where those who participate in it receive a closer communion with God and with each other. This is well expressed through this isiXhosa chant, during the Holy Eucharist: "*Thina sibaninzi nje simzimba mnye ngokuba sonke siyamkela isonka sine*"[21] meaning, we who are many are one body for we all partake in the one bread. This idea of unification through the Eucharist is not exclusively Anglican as it has been referenced before by 13th-century "church father'" Thomas Aquinas.

According to Gilles, Aquinas derived his understanding of Eucharist as a unifying sacrament from Augustine's development of the *Didache*[22] which stated that: "Our Lord has proffered his Body and his Blood in those things which, from a multitude, are reduced to unity, since the bread is one single reality made of many grains; while the wine is one single [drink] made of many grapes".[23]

In contrast, scholars such as Grundy have challenged the view that considers the celebration of the Holy Eucharist as a unifying tool. According to Grundy, the celebration of the Holy Eucharist has certain attributes which reveal what he calls "traces of the liturgical abuse of power, the liturgical coercion of unity, and a presumptive enactment of forgiveness that smoothes the need for just relationships and actually discourages deeper reconciliation."[24] Much like Grundy I am critical of the "liturgical coercion of unity" and the "presumptive enactment of forgiveness" present in the liturgy of the church. From a feminist perspective, I am suspicious of the overemphasis on unity and unlimited forgiveness present in the celebration of the Holy Eucharist whilst an emphasis on offender rebuke and repentance is seldom referenced. From a GBV activist perspective, I worry about the implications of hearing such liturgies as a victim of sexual abuse, much worse if the liturgy is being said by my perpetrator, as is the case with clergy sexual abuse.[25]

In my critique I am not totally against reconciliation or forgiveness; however, I hold the view inspired by Marie Fortune and others who argue that forgiveness should always be viewed from the experience of the victim and not the perpetrator.[26] Forgiveness has a role to play as a pastoral resource to achieve wholeness and restoration for the victim. This view is inspired by Archbishop Desmond Tutu's theology of reconciliation where he argues that when one forgives, one does not serve the interests of the offender; instead, one frees oneself from the chains of being consumed by hate and revenge. This is particularly evident in one of his speeches to the international community about the TRC, where he said: "Forgiveness is not pretending that things are other than they really are – forgiveness can be confrontational, telling it as it is, looking the beast in the eye. Forgiveness is letting go of your right to retaliation."[27] Liturgies about forgiveness ought to reflect this, instead of coercing members to forgive and forget.

---

[19] *An Anglican Prayer Book*, 142.

[20] Marie Fortune, "Sexual Abuse by Religious Leaders", in Valli Boobal Batchelor (ed): *When Pastors Prey*. Geneva: WCC Publications (2013): 14-21.

[21] *Incwadi Yomthandazo Yase Tshethsi*. Jeppestown: HarperCollins Publishers (1989), 127.

[22] The *Didache* is a short Christian manual that was created to focus on memory whilst offering training in "The Way" of the Lord, the practices of the Church as well as the hope for the future for the community of Israelites.

[23] Giles Emery, "The Ecclesial Fruit of the Eucharist in St. Thomas Aquinas", *Nova et Vetera* 2, no. 1 (2004): 43-60.

[24] Christopher Grundy, "A Table in the Midst of My Enemies? Power,
Abuse, and the Possibilities for Reconciliation in Holy Communion", *Liturgy* 23, no. 4 (2008): 27-34, DOI: 10.1080/04580630802205512

[25] Thomas Aquinas, *Summa Theologiae*. New York: McGraw-Hill (1965), 58.

[26] Fortune, *Sexual Violence: The Sin Revisited*, 163-170.

[27] Desmond Tutu, "Speech: No Future Without Forgiveness", *Archbishop Desmond Tutu Collection Textual* 15,

On forgiveness

A common problem identified by womanist and feminist theologians researching in the area of sexual abuse is that forgiveness is often romanticised by the canonisation of "forgive and forget" discourse. For example, in cases of clergy sexual abuse, the victim is often encouraged to forgive the "man of God" through an institutional protection agenda that uses liturgical coercion and language to protect the priest and the church from scandal: for example, "Judge not that you not be judged."[28]

Scholars such as Pamela Cooper-White are critical of the notion of instant forgiveness within the context of sexual abuse where she claims that victims of sexual abuse are often encouraged by family, religious leaders, friends and society to forgive and forget.[29] According to Cooper-White, one of the ways in which this is done is by reminding victims that they must forgive just as Jesus forgave his prosecutors from the cross (Luke 23:34).

However, victims can never forget, they know very well that reciting liturgies of forgiveness can never erase the trauma they went through, they know nothing has changed for them. Once an expectation to react, to forgive and forget, is put on the victim and taken away from the offender, the offender is never held accountable. Fortune contends that forgiveness can still assist the victim if it is on her terms. For example, she writes: "Forgiving means letting go and putting the rape experience in perspective: I can never forget what happened. But I choose to put it here and leave it behind. If I ever need to recall it, I know where it is. But I refuse to carry the pain any longer".[30]

There is no justice in forgetting. For example, the current situation in South Africa where the poor have remained poor and the white have remained wealthy is argued to be as a result of restorative justice that encouraged forgiveness at the expense of restitutive justice which encourages reparations. By emphasising forgiveness, Tutu's theology of reconciliation and restorative justice during the TRC is described by many as a tool that allowed perpetrators to get away too easily without any justice.

Some detractors of the TRC criticised its application of forgiveness and restorative justice as pioneered by Archbishop Tutu, with Lyn Graybill, who has written extensively on the TRC, describing it as an "imposition of a Christian morality of forgiveness" on people who did not adhere to Christian values and morals. To this she cites an extract from a letter written to the weekly *Mail & Guardian* where a complainant says about the TRC: "I understand how Desmond Tutu identifies reconciliation with forgiveness. I don't, because I'm not Christian and I think it grossly immoral to forgive that which is unforgivable."[31]

Within the context of sexual abuse, I believe that restoration and forgiveness should be the last steps in the process of healing. Prior steps should be taken before that in order for the victim to feel the need to forgive. As mentioned earlier black people must first be reconciled with their livelihoods before reconciling with their oppressors.[32] In the same way, I believe victims of sexual abuse must be reconciled first with their dignity which has been stripped off by the oppressor before they can be expected to forgive the perpetrator. In the synoptic Gospel of Luke, Jesus rebukes the passive religious discourse of "forgive and forget" which skips retribution, reparation, restitution and jumps to restoration:

> Take heed to yourselves; if your brother sins, rebuke him, and if he repents, forgive him; and if he sins against you several times in the day, and turns to you seven times, and says, "I repent," you must forgive him. (Luke 17:3-4, [NRSV])

---

no. 2 (2003): 1-8.

https://digitalcommons.unf.edu/archbishoptutupapers/15?utm_source=digitalcommons.unf.edu%2Farchbishoptutupapers%2F15&utm_medium=PDF&utm_campaign=PDFCoverPages (accessed 22 May 2021).

[28] Fortune, "Sexual Abuse by Religious Leaders", 14-21.

[29] Cooper-White, *The Cry of Tamar*, 251-252.

[30] Fortune, *Sexual Violence: The Sin Revisited*, 165.

[31] Lyn Graybill, "South Africa's Truth and Reconciliation Commission: Ethical and Theological Perspectives", *Ethics & International Affairs* 12 (1998): 43-62. DOI:10.1111/j.1747-7093.1998.tb00037.x.

[32] Maluleke, "The Truth and Reconciliation Discourse", 101-113.

This Scripture indicates that before forgiveness can be achieved there are key steps that must be adhered to. Whereas the aforementioned scripture makes reference to rebuking and repenting as the conditions for forgiveness, Burton expands in detail steps that can be followed by the church in responding to sexual abuse, specifically when the church leader is the perpetrator. These steps can be seen as elements of justice.

An alternative feminist "Tutu" theological agenda

Archbishop Desmond Tutu's approach to national reconciliation, through the TRC, recognised the role of confession and forgiveness as vehicles to harness healing. According to his understanding, South Africans have "no future without forgiveness".[33] I do not wish to discount or reject the role and emphasis on forgiveness embedded in Tutu's theology of reconciliation in responding to conflict or estrangement. On the contrary, I recognise that a process of forgiveness and reconciliation may be spiritually beneficial for both the victim and the perpetrator. However, I suggest that, because of the pervasive nature of sexual abuse, unconditional restorative forgiveness is not morally or even theologically appropriate. Following Marie Fortune, I argue that, because of the gruesome nature of sexual abuse and the long-term effects of the trauma on victims, restoration and forgiveness should not be the first, let alone the only, step through which the church responds. In line with Luke's gospel, elements such as "rebuking", restitution and reparation should be explored first in the best interest of the victims. Only then can spiritual healing through forgiveness and restoration be explored. I agree that the value of forgiveness is conditioned by "vindication of the victim/survivor experienced through justice".[34]

When applied without careful consideration for the victim and her subsequent physical, emotional and spiritual damage, restorative justice runs the risk of revictimisation. Due to the power disparity between the offender and the victim, a blanket approach to restorative justice will not serve any justice except to exonerate the offender. If the church fails to "rebuke" the offender, then it might jeopardie the safety of the victim and future potential victims. Scholars such as March and Wagner argue that, in cases where there is a continuation of a relationship between the offender and the victim, such as clergy sexual abuse and incest, restorative justice might perpetuate further abuse.[35]

As mentioned in the previous section, Burton explores several steps that ought to be taken by churches in responding to the phenomenon of clergy sexual abuse; however, due to the limitations of this paper I will only highlight two. First, Burton argues that churches need to stop protecting priests who sexually violate congregants. Instead, the church ought to "rebuke" what she describes as errant priests by removing them from their roles as religious leaders. This removal does not mean that they are not recipients of God's redeeming love and forgiveness. They can still receive God's forgiveness even when removed from office. Rebuking is not mutually exclusive to forgiveness but instead one of the elements of justice, such as reparations and restitution, that are part of the healing and reconciliation.[36] Second, Burton is aware of the pervasive nature of sexual abuse within the church and notes that removal is not the only solution as clergy sexual abuse can also be systemic and thus will need the church to confront its sexist, ageist and racist character.

In expressing my critique of Archbishop Tutu's theology of reconciliation and restorative justice within the context of sexual abuse, I fervently embrace his lifelong dedication to promoting peace and healing through forgiveness. I am sure that he will agree with Allan Boesak that reconciliation is a painful journey with steps that must still be climbed and felt in order to avoid burying our wounds in shallow graves in pursuit of cheap reconciliation where "instead of offering genuine repentance and remorse, instead of coming with contrition to ask for forgiveness and to make amends with the

---

[33] Desmond Mpilo Tutu, *No Future Without Forgiveness.* London/Johannesburg: Rider (1999), 220.

[34] Fortune, *Sexual Violence: The Sin Revisited*, 164.

[35] Francesca Marsh, Nadia M. Wager, "Restorative Justice in Cases of Sexual Violence: Exploring the Views of the Public and Survivors", *Probation Journal* 62, no. 4 (2015): 336-356.

[36] Garlinda Burton, "Protecting the Vulnerable" in Batchelor (ed.) *When Pastors Prey*, 14-21.

undoing of justice and the doing of justice. Instead of breaking down the walls of separation and the fortresses of white supremacy, racism, homophobia, transphobia and gender injustice ... looking for cheap reconciliation [is]– avoiding the costly path of reparation and restoration, hoping that the crumbs falling from the empire's table will satisfy the hunger and thirst of these masses for justice and righteousness."[37]

---

[37] Allan Boesak, "Race, Reparations and Reconciliation", https://www.presbyterianmission.org/story/race-reparations-and-reconciliation-webinar/ (accessed 22 May 2021).

25. The Man in the "Red Dress":[1] Transformative Tutu

Nyambura J. Njoroge[2]

I dream of the day when every 13-year-old African child will read the authorised biography[3] of the man captured in a "Red Dress", a cross, his mouth wide open in front of a mic and a Bible in his right hand with his left hand pointing out to the audience. Mention the name Desmond Tutu. This image of that book cover pops up in my mind.

Just before starting to write this piece, I went home for lunch from the office. As I opened the door, our daughter Njeri called for what has become a traditional lunch conversation during these COVID-19 days. The speaker was on and after I said grace aloud, I soon found myself completely lost in my own world. My husband Njoroge and Njeri kept talking. "By the way, did you know I did not hear a word you both said? I am lost in the world of Desmond Tutu. I was supposed to write something for his 90th birthday in October. I completely forgot. Today I got one of those WhatsApp reminders," I said to them.

"You mean he is one of those hitting the 90s" the question came over the phone from Njeri. "Is there anything wrong that man has ever done?" she asked. "How would I know? I have only met him a few times," I answered.

Njoroge remembered when we first met him in the home of the late John Samuel Pobee in the 1990s here in Geneva. Njeri too remembered the occasion. "Wow, he has done so much for justice and peace," we all agreed. We reflected on how he was not only an icon during the struggle against apartheid; but he has also spoken up against discrimination of LGBTI individuals, not a small thing in Africa. Lunch was over but we were not done. We wondered, with human beings like Tutu, why have many African countries continued to choose violence? Africa, embrace justice and peace!

Truthfully, I wrote back to the WhatsApp sender to say, "I am not in the mood of writing yet again about a creature with a '…' because we have heard enough about his-story. My mind is carried away by herstory. I related how I was occupied with researching women who literally head and lead many homes and who put tithes on offertory plates to support the clergy who remain predominantly men." The WhatsApp sender persisted, "Why not write about that? Tutu was always one to call out injustice, especially gender injustice, wherever he saw it." I gave in.

I am in the practice of looking for trailblazers to learn how they did it. In the World Council of Churches (WCC), my employer since March 1999, Desmond Tutu was a pioneer among Africans to hold a position in Theological Education Fund (TEF) with its head office in Bromley, Kent, in Britain. TEF was the predecessor program of WCC-Ecumenical Theological Education (ETE), the position I held 27 years after Tutu, albeit in Geneva, Switzerland. There is much more to Tutu and the World Council of Churches but the three years he served in TEF speaks volumes about the man in the "Red Dress": Transformative Tutu.

---

[1] Despite the clerical colour of bishops being purple, it has always fascinated me that on the cover of John Allen's biography the cassock that Tutu is wearing is red! This image is so poignant because it speaks of life and transformation, hence my reference to the red dress.

[2] The Reverend Dr Nyambura J. Njoroge is Kenyan ecumenical church leader, theologian and advocate for justice and human dignity. She is programme executive for the World Council of Churches' Ecumenical HIV and AIDS Initiatives and Advocacy. Nyambura received her first degree at St. Paul's University, Limuru, Kenya, and Master's degree from Louisville Presbyterian Theological Seminary, Louisville, Kentucky and a PhD in Christian social ethics from Princeton Theological Seminary, Princeton, New Jersey, USA. She is a founding member of the Circle of Concerned African Women Theologians. She is the author of *Kiama Kia Ngo: An African Christian Feminist Ethic of Resistance and Transformation*. Legon Theological Studies Series, Legon, Ghana, 2000.

[3] John Allen, *Rabble-Rouser for Peace: The Authorised Biography of Desmond Tutu*. Random House Publishers, 2006.

John Allen captures Tutu criss-crossing African countries,[4] in the chapter titled "Transformation" in his biography. Interestingly, the transformation that Allen seems to allude to is not on the quality of theological education that was offered in theological institutions in Africa, south of the Sahara. John Allen seems to rather focus on Tutu's transformation as a result of his travels. Tutu took extensive notes on the social, political and economic realities of the countries he visited. Literally, it feels like Tutu was describing these countries to his fellow women and men in South Africa who were blocked away from the rest of the continent. No doubt, these visits and the insights he gained prepared him well for the pastoral ministry, advocacy for justice, peace and ecclesiastical leadership that awaited him in Southern Africa. He learned first-hand the challenges, successes, failures and complexities of newly independent countries. Not surprising the chapter concludes with his first visit to the United States of America for a conference on African and black theology at Union Theological Seminary in New York in 1973. All these experiences transformed Tutu's theology as well as his extensive dialogue with his counterpart Aharon Sapsezian, TEF associate director for Latin America, who introduced him to liberation theology. It is therefore no wonder that John Allen names this chapter "Transformation".

In my research for my "Herstory – Women in Ordained Ministry of Word and Sacrament in Africa", I will be seeking to discover how these three theologies – African, black and liberation – informed the man in the "Red Dress", the "Transformative Tutu", in his dialogue with women in the church of Southern Africa in their struggle for ordination.[5] I am hoping to discover to what extent Tutu can be considered a feminist.

Papa, God willing I will honour your once-upon-a-time invitation to visit you and your beloved Leah in your home in South Africa. For now, may you continue to enjoy God's gifts of peace, grace, humour and humility!

Blessed and Adventurous Birthday@90

---

[4] He made 48 visits to 25 countries within 3 years. I could not help but wonder what his beloved Leah and children felt and said to him when he showed up at the door. I would love to hear the herstory of Leah Tutu.
[5] Denise Ackermann, Jonathan A. Draper and Emma Mashinini, eds. *Women Hold up Half the Sky: Women in the Church in Southern Africa.* Cluster Publications, 1991.

26. "Do You See This Woman?": A Sermon Inspired by Desmond Tutu

Miranda N. Pillay[1]

Background

This sermon that I offer as a tribute to Desmond Tutu was inspired by a critical formative incident from his early life that shaped his commitment to social justice. I preached this sermon on Sunday 12 August 2018 in Cape Town at St Margaret's Church, Parow. National Women's Day is commemorated in South Africa on 9 August – remembering the agency of the women who protested against apartheid Pass Laws on 9 August 1956.

Readings: Galatians 3:17-29; Luke 7:36-50

National Women's Day in South Africa has now evolved to Women's Month – much to the delight of shops and beauty salons offering this or that "special" for women. These "Women's Month Specials" range from advertising washing powder to dishwashers; from pampering treats to weekend holiday-breaks.

So, it is good for us to pause, as we are doing today, to remember the year 1956, when on 9 August, over 20,000 women of all ages and races from across South Africa marched towards the Union Buildings in Pretoria.[2]

When those women marched to protest against the Pass Laws, designed to control the movement of black people, it was a call to resist the exploitation and oppression of both men and women in apartheid South Africa.[3] Here I'm reminded of Desmond Tutu who said that freedom from apartheid is not only meaningful for people of colour – but it also means freedom for white people – from their claims to superiority.

While we remember the names of those women who led the protest march on 9 August 1956, Helen Joseph, Rahima Moosa, Sophy Williams-De Bruyn and Lilian Ngoyi, we should remember that it was the collective attitude of all the women on that day – black, coloured, Indian and white – that made it one of the largest protests against discrimination in our country's history. Thus, Women's Day should not only be seen as a "pampering day" offering this or that special treat – lest we forget what that historic day on 9 August was really about![4]

---

[1] Miranda Pillay is a research fellow at the University of the Western Cape, where she was a senior lecturer in New Testament studies and ethics before her retirement. As a lay leader in the Anglican Church, she advocates for gender justice and continues to draw inspiration from Desmond Tutu's theology of inclusivity and inter-connectedness. For Pillay, Tutu's relational agency is particularly evident in a (1976) letter written to then prime minister B.J. Vorster in which Tutu appeals to the common humanity of the apartheid leader. He writes to Vorster as "one human person to another human person"; as "one Christian to another Christian" united through Jesus Christ "who has broken down all that separates us – such as race, sex, culture, status, etc." (See "A Growing Nightmarish Fear: An Open Letter to Prime Minister B.J. Vorster (1976)", in Desmond Tutu: *The Rainbow People of God – South Africa's Victory over Apartheid,* ed. John Allen (Toronto: Bantam Books, 1995), 3-14.

[2] South African History Online, "The 1956 Women's March, Pretoria, 9 August," https://www.sahistory.org.za/article/1956-womens-march-pretoria-9-august (accessed 11 August 2018).

[3] National Library of South Africa, "Generation Equality: Realising Women's Rights for an Equal Future: #IAmGenerationEquality," https://www.nlsa.ac.za/womensmonth/ (accessed 11 August 2018).

[4] See Sarojini Nadar, "I dream of the freedom to use the F words", *Sunday Tribune*, News and Views, 17 August 2014, 20.

August is also marked as the month of "compassion" on the calendar of many churches. On the one hand it gives us the time and space to lament the lack of opportunity for women to flourish and acknowledge the need to transform leadership styles, organisational structures and ecclesial spaces; while on the other hand it also creates the space to celebrate the leadership integrity of women as we commemorate and give thanks for the prophetic impulses of freedom initiated by those women in 1956.

And so, during the month of August (and beyond) we want to say that celebrating Women's Day is much more than showing "appreciation" for women's beauty or women's useful, caring ways. It's also a day for men and women to acknowledge the integrity of women leaders. This is why we have to be intentional about addressing popular, cultural and religious attitudes, beliefs and practices that justify the inferior "nature" of women.

Now, you ask why all this talk about whites and blacks; men and women? After all, we come to church to hear God's word! Besides, it's very simple! We heard the reading from Paul's letter to the Galatians 3 which clearly states that, "We are all one in Christ"!

Well, perhaps it is not all that simple and clear. The question is, "How do we live out Paul's claim that there is neither Jew nor Greek, nor Slave nor free, nor male nor female, today?"

Maybe you've already heard Archbishop Desmond Tutu tell the story of his first encounter with the white priest, Trevor Huddleston? But I'll share it here, anyway.

In his usual delightful tone our beloved Arch tells the story of the day he (then nine years old) and his mother were walking down the street when a tall white man dressed in a black suit came towards them. In those days (of apartheid) a black person was expected to step off the sidewalk (into the street) to allow the white person to pass first.

It was also expected that the black person nod his/her head as a gesture of respect and honour towards the white person. But on that day, before young Desmond and his mother could step off the sidewalk, the white man stepped into the gutter and, says the Arch, "as my mother and I passed, the man tipped his hat in a gesture of respect to her!"[5]

That man was, of course, Trevor Huddleston, an Anglican priest who was critical of the apartheid laws that discriminated against people of colour. He regarded it as anti-gospel and anti-Christian. So he was *intentional* about breaking the law. Now, *that* was certainly not "good behaviour" according to the law of apartheid. But Trevor Huddleston saw two people. He did not see a black woman and a black child whose primary purpose was to serve and respect him – a white man.

When young Desmond asked his mother why that man stepped aside for them to pass, his mother said it's because "he is a man of God". A person who "sees" that a law which privileges him and belittles others not only diminishes the dignity of others, but also diminishes his own dignity. And, as a person who believes that in Christ there is no discrimination on the bases of race, class or gender (Gal. 3:28), he was intentional about acting differently.

Now we should consider that, at the time Paul was writing, and also in our own not so distant past, only sons (the eldest) were seen as heir to (the father's) land and the owners of property. So there was much prestige and status in being an eldest son and heir – and certainly no daughter was even considered to be an heir. So the question would be "is Paul challenging this law that discriminated on the basis of gender when he says: "If you [men and women] belong to Christ then you are Abraham's seed and heirs according to God's promise" (Gal. 3:29)?[6]

Or, is Paul addressing men only? And, if Paul is only addressing men in his letter to the Galatians, what should we make of his argument that they are "[neither] male nor female"? Is he talking about gender-neutral spiritual beings as we so often make it out to be? It is with this question in mind that I now turn to the gospel reading, Luke 7:36-50. "Do you see this woman?" Jesus asks his dinner host, Simon.

---

[5] Pete Earley, "Desmond Tutu," *Washington Post*, February 16, 1986, https://www.washingtonpost.com/archive/lifestyle/magazine/1986/02/16/desmond-tutu/3fc3da7f-4926-44cf-896a-5d1bf7f00206/ (accessed 11 August 2018).
[6] Also see Romans 4:13; 8:16-17; 9:8.

The art of "seeing" – of recognising, of being aware and the act of behaving differently are important facets of Luke's gospel. And, throughout the gospel we "see" the affirmation of people's bodies and dignity when Jesus challenges those who use their cultural and religious status to claim God's favour – particularly rich over poor, but also Jews over Samaritans (Luke 10); eldest son (heirs) over younger sons (Luke 15).

Throughout Luke's gospel there are also parallel references to men and women. For example, there is mention of the "priestly line" of Zechariah and Elizabeth (Luke 1); there's Simeon and Anna (Luke 2) who both prophesy into Jesus' future; Jesus raises the widow's son (Luke 7) and Jarius' daughter (Luke 8).

In a sense Luke presents Jesus as someone who challenges the way cultural and religious laws were used to determine one's social standing and status in order to set certain people apart from others.

In the gospel reading, Jesus is having dinner at the home of Simon, the Pharisee, who may have invited Jesus to confirm for himself whether Jesus was "the one". If Jesus were a prophet, he would bring honour and status to his host, Simon. But when Jesus "accepts" the actions of a woman who was shamelessly caressing his feet with her hair (both of which have sexual connotations) Jesus was bringing shame upon himself and, according to Simon's reasoning, could therefore not be a prophet.

Ironically though, Jesus, aware of what Simon is thinking, fulfils precisely Simon's understanding of prophetic awareness, because Jesus even "knows" what Simon is thinking! Now, Simon is the shameful one and the woman's actions are seen as honourable.

Thus, we also see reversal of the roles (and status) of Simon, the Pharisee, and the nameless woman. In the beginning, the Pharisee is the host and the woman is considered "a sinner". He has honour (the host of a banquet), she is shameful – making a public spectacle of herself, Jesus and the dinner host.

As the story develops, the woman's actions are seen to be hospitable while Simon (the host) fails to show any special kindness towards Jesus, his dinner guest. The (unnamed) woman understands Jesus to be a prophet; Simon rejects Jesus' prophetic character. She now has honour; Simon is shamed. Her sins are forgiven, and Simon? "Do *you see* this woman?" Jesus asks him. What is Simon's sin? Is it being short-sighted?

Of course, Simon did see the woman because he says: "If this man were a prophet, he would know who is touching him and what kind of a woman she is …"

But Simon sees the woman through cultural/religious lenses that view an autonomous woman who acted independently (and who was not under the control of her father or husband) as sexually deviant. But Jesus turned towards the woman (7:44) and said to Simon, "Do you see this woman?"

The woman's presence and actions allow Jesus to re-focus what Simon ought to see: that the woman provided that which he, as a host, failed to provide; and that the woman "knew" what he (Simon) did not know!

Unlike Simon, the nameless woman knows and believes that Jesus is more than a prophet; that he has healed many and that he even forgives sins. And perhaps by her weeping, she mourns Simon's sin of ignorance and lack of care towards Jesus – and not because she is "repenting" of a sin society has labelled her with. The reason why I say this is because this woman is bold in her actions. We read at the beginning of this chapter, Luke 7, about Jesus' care, concern and compassion for those cast out as *sinners*. This may have given this (unnamed) woman the confidence to be bold and intentional.

Jesus applauds the woman's actions of boldness. Her actions challenged the cultural and religious laws that would otherwise require her to remain in the background; and in doing so, Jesus challenges the laws that require a "holy man" to know that being touched by such a woman would render him impure/ unholy – not worthy to be a prophet!

Let's turn the spotlight back to young Desmond Tutu, Mrs Tutu and Revd Huddleson. What I see is an example of a person challenging his own privileged position. Trevor Huddleston saw that his white privilege dehumanises others. I also see that he may have risked his own "status" because back then he would have been labelled a "*k****r-boetie*" when, in fact, his actions reflected compassion towards, and solidarity with those who suffered because they were labelled racially inferior.

Revd Huddleson's actions say to Desmond Tutu and his mother "You are not inferior to me. We are one in Christ". Thus he embodies and lives out Galatians 3:28.

Discriminatory laws and religious and cultural practices privilege some while they exclude and silence others. This systemic nature of discrimination calls for compassion and solidarity from those who benefit from such laws and practices.

It is also the case that those discriminated against sometimes internalise the negative views imposed on them by the socially powerful to the extent that they defend the system that excludes and exploits them. This is especially the case when the Bible is used to justify the superiority of one group over another – be it by virtue of race, class or gender. In this case those who benefit from the exclusion and exploitation of others see their position as "God-ordained".

Back to the dinner party. What does Jesus want Simon to see? Does he want him to see past his own prejudices and privilege of class and gender? As a Pharisee, Simon "knew" the laws and social codes needed to be apart from those labelled "sinners".

The good news, according to Luke (7:36-50) is that Jesus turns Simon's gaze, and ours. To see "others" as part of who (and whose) we are. Today, Jesus calls us (like he called Simon) "to see" that while labelling/stereotyping others (on the basis of race, class or gender) may seem right; it certainly also makes us guilty of not seeing that, through Christ, we are all equal heirs as sons and daughters in God's kin-dom (family).

Finally, Jesus addresses the unnamed woman (Luke 7:50) and says, "Go in peace …" This was a common greeting in Judaism. In Luke 7:50 and Luke 8:48 "Go in peace" includes the absence of strife and discord but it also takes on the deeper significance of *shalom* which means safety, wholeness, welfare and solidarity in community.

Therefore I'd like to end this special Women's Day sermon with the words of Denise Ackermann, whom Desmond Tutu sees as a woman who wants to come to terms with the privileges that "came just because of her ethnicity and her skin colour".[7] She believes that:

> No man can be liberated as long as women are not. Just as some whites joined the struggle for liberation from racist oppression, men must join women in the struggle against discrimination, abuse and violation. It is about their humanity as much as it is about ours. Solidarity is what we ask.[8]

This we ask in the name of Jesus Christ who teaches and shows us that everyone is a part of the other.

AMEN.

---

[7] Desmond Tutu, "Foreword," in *After the Locusts: Letters from a Landscape of Faith*, ed. Denise Ackerman (Cape Town: David Phillip, 2003):8.

[8] Michael W Klein, "Work and Play: International Evidence of Gender Equality in Employment and Sports," *Journal of Sports Economics* 5, no. 3 (2004): 42. See also: Sarojini Nadar, "Palatable Patriarchy and Violence against Women in South Africa – Angus Buchan's Mighty Men's conference as a case study of Masculism," *Scriptura: Journal for Biblical, Theological and Contextual Hermeneutics* 102 (2009): 154.

PART II
DIGNITY

2.1. Humour and Humanity

27. THE LIBERATING HUMOUR OF DESMOND TUTU

Tinyiko Maluleke[1]

(How) Can the oppressed laugh?

If there was a prize for the cultivation of self-pity, then hymn number 203 in the hymnary of the Evangelical Presbyterian Church in South Africa[2] would take the prize any time. But before we blame the hymn and its composers, let us hasten to add that the lyrics of this hymn are based on the debilitating words of Psalm 22 set against the hymnological traditions of Europe in the late 19th and early 20th centuries. Psalm 22 opens up with a cry of anguish that has come to signify the ultimate sense of aloneness and abandonment, that is, abandonment by God: "My God, my God, why have you forsaken me?" The same cry which Jesus issued while hanging on the cross. In the Evangelical Presbyterian Church hymnary, verse 6 of the Psalm 22 is devastatingly translated into "*ndzi fana na xo xivungu, a ndzi munhu wa nchumu*", literally, "I am just (like) a worm, I am a good-for-nothing person of no consequence". It is one thing for certain people to be condemned by others as unimportant people of no consequence, but it is quite devastating when the condemnation appears to be self-inflicted.

The space of abandonment where "good-for-nothing persons of no consequence" live is precisely that place which has been identified by black and African theologies as the habitat of the black, the poor and the oppressed. It is the place where the crucified lives among the cross bearers,[3] the home of the non-persons.[4] In such places of abandonment, there is little to no infrastructure, food and hope are equally in short supply, disease is widespread, death comes early, often, and violently.

Surely, in such dry places, there are no wells[5] of laughter from which the non-persons can draw? Ordinarily, one would not think that the poor and the marginalised have a need to cultivate and treasure a sense of humour. Of what use is a sense of humour for a people who walk daily in the valley of the shadow of death? Surely, humour and laughter are wasted on the "wretched of the earth"![6] Surely those who travel up and down life's Jericho Road[7] in places where "things constantly fall apart"[8] have no time for humour! Surely, laughter should not be found in destitute villages and impoverished black townships! Surely, those reduced to mere worms, by the apartheid system, had no right to laughter! Not in the midst of all that squalor, poverty, violence and repression! To put it

---

[1] Senior research fellow and deputy director of the University of Pretoria Centre for the Advancement of Scholarship, Tinyiko Maluleke is a theologian by training. He has also been part of university executive management at Unisa, UJ and UP, serving in various roles including deputy vice chancellor, executive director for research and advisor to the principal and vice chancellor. Between 2007 and 2009 Maluleke served as president of the South African Council of Churches. In that period Maluleke held several consultations and conversations with Archbishop Tutu.

[2] "We, Yehovha, Hosi yanga", Hymn No 203. *Tinsimu ta Vakriste*. Braamfontein: Sasavona, 2016.

[3] Takatso Mofokeng, *The Crucified Among the Crossbearers: Towards a Black Christology*. Kampen: J.H. Kok (1983).

[4] Gustavo Gutiérrez, *A Theology of Liberation*. London: SCM (1974).

[5] Gustavo Gutiérezz, *We Drink from Our Own Wells: The Spiritual Journey of a People*. New York: Orbis (1985).

[6] Frantz Fanon, *The Wretched of the Earth*. London: Penguin (1961).

[7] Martin Luther King Jr., *Strength to Love*. Philadelphia: Fortress (1981), pp.30-38.

[8] Chinua Achebe, *Things Fall Apart*. London: Heinemann (1958).

differently, for a people under siege and a people under the yoke of oppression, humour and laughter seem such a wasteful luxury to cultivate and nurture.

Liberation humour: The cases of Mandela and Biko

Both Steve Biko and Nelson Mandela, each in his own way, believed that under apartheid black people had lost their humanity and that an essential aim of the struggle of freedom was the restoration of the humanity of black people[9] and that in the process the restoration of the humanity of white people would also occur.

Mandela and humour

For Mandela, the reality of the sense of black exclusion from humanity hit home at his homecoming ceremony upon his return from the initiation school. On that occasion, one of the chiefs gave a rousing rhetorical speech in which he confessed, on behalf of "the Xhosa nation", that the returning initiates had been lied to when they were told initiation school would make men out of them. According to the chief, after circumcision school, the boys had not and could not become men because "all black South Africans are a conquered people".[10] For this reason, Mandela recognised that whatever the significance of the circumcision ritual and its homecoming ceremonies, he did not become "a man (human being) that day and would not truly become one for many years". Hence his later decision to join the struggle for freedom, which was, according to him, the only way black people could have their humanity and their dignity restored.

In a few of his speeches, especially the impromptu ones, Mandela showed clear awareness of the power of humour and laughter. The CNN's Robyn Curnow marvelled at Nelson Mandela's "sense of humor, his dry wit and his remarkable ability to render someone speechless with a well-placed one-liner".[11] She also noted how Mandela would often poke fun at himself[12] as an old man and how he recalled instances when children had been unflattering in their opinion of him. There is an often repeated, and self-effacing[13] Mandela anecdote with a five-year-old who enquired after his age:

> Mandela replied, "I can't remember, but I was born long, long ago." She then asked him why he went to jail. Mandela replied, "I didn't go there because I liked it. Some people sent me there." She asked how long he had been in jail. Mandela again replied, "I can't remember, but it was a long, long time." Mandela then relays to his audience that after a thoughtful pause the little girl said, "You are a stupid old man, aren't you?"

On stage during a live interview, in the middle of an impromptu speech or in those moments when Mandela intuitively mounted the stage to dance alongside the singers and the artists, we have seen him put his tremendous emotional intelligence to good use; we have seen him deploy a wicked sense

---

[9] Unfortunately, both men tended to use the sexist language "black men" instead of "black people" who had lost their "manhood" instead of "humanity" as was vogue in their times.

[10] Nelson Mandela, *Long Walk to Freedom*. London: Little Brown and Company (1994), p.34.

[11] Curnow, Robyn. 2013. "Nelson Mandela used humor to charm and cajole." *CNN*. Turner Broadcasting System. December 5 (accessed 29 May 2021); http://www.cnn.com/2013/12/05/world/africa/nelson-mandela-humor/.

[12] Tinyiko Maluleke, "The Search for a More Human Face for Nelson Mandela: An Urgent Task", *HTS Teologiese Studies/Theological Studies* 71(3) (2015), p.4-7. https://hts.org.za/index.php/hts/article/view/2941/6141.

[13] Tinyiko Maluleke, "Beyond a Giant, Saintly Mandela". *Sunday Independent* (5 July 2015). https://www.pressreader.com/south-africa/the-sunday-independent/20150705/282059095663042.

of humour. However, in the vast majority of Mandela's formal and written speeches, both before and after 1994, humour is not a frequently invoked tool.[14]

Biko and humour

For Steve Biko it was painfully clear that "all in all the black man (human being) has become a shell, a shadow of a man, completely defeated, drowning in his own misery, a slave, an ox bearing the yoke of oppression with sheepish timidity".[15] With the problem defined in those drastic terms, according to Biko, the only way to make the "black man' to "come to himself"[16] was through the adoption of Black Consciousness in order "… to pump life back into his empty shell; to infuse him with pride and dignity …"[17]

It would neither be fair nor reasonable to expect much humour in the writings of Steve Biko. Unlike Mandela, he did not live to see the fruit of his labour. His only glory was that of struggle. His mission was specific; and now with the benefit of hindsight, we know that his time was rather limited. From the few recorded interviews and the collection of essays he bequeathed us, it seems that the chief Biko strategy was that of combining crystal clear socio-political analysis with vivid pictures of "the shell", the "shadow of a man", the "complete defeated" black person who the oppressed were turning into. Biko has left us several witty one-liners and memorable passages which reveal an amazing intellect and a very sharp if also a downplayed sense of humour. One can imagine a smirk on Biko's face as he wrote to fellow students, saying, "it seems sometimes that it is a crime for the non-white students to think for themselves".[18] Surely Biko must have been chortling albeit with some irritation when he wrote about the repressed and misdirected anger of the black man who:

> … in the privacy of his toilet his face twists in silent condemnation of white society but brightens up in sheepish obedience as he comes out hurrying in response to his master's impatient call. In the home-bound bus or train he joins the chorus that roundly condemns the white man but is first to praise the government in the presence of the police or his employers.[19]

As he offered a piece of advice to a bunch of ministers in Pietermaritzburg, the young Biko must have chuckled when he concluded, saying: "Finally, I would like to remind the black ministry, and indeed all black people that God is not in the habit of coming down from heaven to solve people's problems on earth".[20] Nor could Biko avoid a naughty cackle as he unmasks the motives of white liberals, saying: "Not only have they kicked the black but they have also told him how to react to the kick. For a long time, the black has been listening with patience to the advice he has been receiving on how best to respond to the kick".[21]

Sometimes Biko dished more anger than humour: "They tell us that the situation is a class struggle rather than a racial one. Let them go to van Tonder in the Free State and tell him this. We believe we know what the problem is, and we will stick by our findings".[22]

Perhaps Biko's sharp wit and blinding sense of humour manifested most when he, for four and half days, was a witness during the 1976 BPC–SASO trial.[23] Occurring within a month of the Soweto student uprising of 1976 Biko's testimony was probably inspirational to the students. Sadly that

---

[14] Kader Asmal, David Chidester and Wilmot James (eds), *Nelson Mandela: From Freedom to the Future: Tributes and Speeches*. Johannesburg: Jonathan Ball (2003).

[15] Steve Biko, *I Write What I Like*. London: Bowerdean Press (1978), p.31.

[16] Biko, *I Write*, p.31.

[17] Biko, *I Write*, p.31.

[18] Biko, *I Write*, p.4.

[19] Biko, *I Write*, pp.30-31.

[20] Biko, *I Write*, p.65.

[21] Biko, *I Write*, p.72.

[22] Biko, *I Write*, p.99.

[23] Millard Arnold (ed.), *The Testimony of Steve Biko*. Johannesburg: Picador Africa (1978), p. 9.

BPC–SASO trial was to be the last public appearance of Biko as he was found dead in a police cell, in Pretoria, fifteen months later.

When Judge Boshoff asked Biko as to "why do you refer to you people as blacks? Why not brown people? I mean you people are more brown than black", Biko said in response, "in the same way as I think white people are more pink and yellow and pale than white".[24] But perhaps one of the funniest moments in the trial came when Judge Boshoff kept making factual mistakes about the politicians and the political parties in Kenya, only to receive a history lesson from Biko. At one stage, Judge Boshoff asked a rhetorical question as to whether a Kenyan politician Josiah Mwangi Kariuki had survived the violent party politics in Kenya, to which Biko answered: "Oh well, My Lord, several politicians don't survive it seems; like Verwoerd didn't survive".[25]

Although Biko was fiercely focused on the decolonisation of the mind of the oppressed,[26] much wit and humour attend to several of his interventions in pursuit of the goal of mental emancipation. Similarly, although Mandela thought the best way to restore black humanity was through the struggle for freedom, including the armed struggle, he was not completely oblivious to the role of humour, wit and performance as tools to reach out to friend and foe.

The humanising humour of Desmond Tutu

If ever someone tries always to reach out to the human core inside both the perpetrator and the victim, the insider and the outsider, men and women, black and white, gay and straight, Palestinian and Jew – that person is Tutu. His brilliant story-telling techniques and his legendary sense of humour are part of his relentless pursuit of the human core. All his jokes and all his stories have the proverbial sting in the tail designed either to offend or to humour people into action. Indeed, many of the jokes are about Tutu himself – his height, his size and his big nose. Behind Tutu the apparent jester is a radical ethicist and an engaging social theoretician.[27]

In his life, Desmond Tutu has proven that, alongside righteous anger, bravery and grit, humour is an important tool for the humanisation of both the oppressed and the oppressor in the struggle for justice. This character trait sets him apart from many of his fellow freedom fighters. Again and again, in rhetorical anecdotes, speeches, sermons, song and dance, Tutu has employed and deployed humour to great effect. However, as I tried to argue in the passage quoted above, Desmond Tutu is no Trevor Noah. The aim of his humour is not merely to entertain but to humanise. In this regard, the humour of Desmond Tutu is a dimension of his philosophy of *Ubuntu*,[28] that is, the ability to reach out to one another through laughter and humour is part of what makes us human.[29] But for humour to be truly attuned to *Ubuntu*, we have to move beyond the state of either *laughing at* or *being laughed at*[30] even as we move towards the state of *laughing with* and *laughing together*. Basically, each time Tutu tells a joke; makes or suggests a funny gesture, he is reaching out to the innermost human core – the *Ubuntu* dimension – of his fellow human beings.

His spirituality notwithstanding,[31] we have noted that Mandela was largely persuaded that the committed and selfless execution of the freedom struggle would lead to the humanisation of both the

---

[24] Biko, *I Write*, p.115.

[25] Biko, *I Write*, p.141.

[26] Ngũgĩ wa Thiong'o, *Decolonising the Mind*. Nairobi: East African Educational Publishers, 1986.

[27] Tinyiko Maluleke, "Desmond Tutu, Archbishop of the World". *Mail and Guardian* (August 2015). https://mg.co.za/article/2015-08-27-desmond-tutu-archbishop-of-the-world/ (accessed 29 May 2021).

[28] Michael Battle, *Reconciliation: The Ubuntu Theology of Desmond Tutu*. Ohio: The Pilgrim Press (1997).

[29] James Ogude (ed.), *Ubuntu and Personhood*. New Jersey: Africa World Press (2018).

[30] Thabo Mbeki, "Stop the Laughter", in Thabo Mbeki, *Africa: The Time has Come: Selected Speeches*. Cape Town: Tafelberg (1998), pp.289-295.

[31] Dennis Cruywagen, *The Spiritual Mandela. Faith and Religion in the Life of South Africa's Great Statesman*, Cape Town: Penguin (2016).

freedom fighter and the oppressed. His entire biography[32] is framed much like a story of the journey – the long walk – of a freedom fighter. Humour, jest and laughter are conceived of as much smaller dimensions of the "long walk" necessary for the restoration of humanity and the dignity of Africans.

Similarly, we have noted that for Biko, the most crucial step in the journey towards the restoration of the humanity of Africans is mental and psychological emancipation, hence the need for Black Consciousness. So intense and so short is his life that Biko had to prioritise mental and psychological emancipation above all else. It is not as if Biko was unaware of the spiritual, the cultural and the humorous in the restoration of the humanity of oppressed black people – if anything, Biko must be counted among the first generation of black theologians.

Understandably, it is the confessor, priest and archbishop Desmond Tutu who manages to bring together the struggle dimensions found in Mandela's walk to freedom, Biko's quest for psychological emancipation and the role of humour in the humanisation of the oppressed.

Although focused on his role as the confessor of the nation – thanks to his role as chairperson of the Truth and Reconciliation Commission – Tutu biographer Michael Battle makes a profound side remark about the impact of Tutu's humour:

> I grieve not being able to write a complete work just on Tutu's sense of humor and profound contagious laughter, both of which contributed to his lectures being anything but dry. In many ways I think his sense of humor was Tutu's greatest God-given weapon as a confessor, because humor disarms pretension and deceit.[33]

It is nothing short of amazing that humour should be an important weapon in the arsenal of a leader whose tenure traversed the gloomiest and the bloodiest period in the history of South Africa. In 1955 he taught at Johannesburg Bantu High School. He was ordained as a priest[34] in the Anglican church in 1961. In 1996 he retired as the Anglican Archbishop of Cape Town. But it was only in 2010 when he retired from public life.[35]

> Tutu's personality and character were fashioned by a spirituality forged at the intersection of the beliefs of the African Independent churches, mainline Christianity, the simple faith of Mavoertsek (his mother), the work ethic of his father, the African philosophy of Ubuntu and the lived experience of apartheid brutality. His overall style and mannerisms bear the influence of the "happy" music of Sophiatown. It is astounding that one whose ministry coincided with so dark a period in the history of South Africa and the world would also be renowned for his love and advocacy of laughter.[36]

As an adult, Tutu lived through the destruction of Sophiatown,[37] the Sharpeville massacre,[38] the declaration of the South African republic, the jailing of the Rivonia trialists, the banning of political movements, the flowering of the Black Consciousness movement,[39] the reconstitution of the Christian Council of South Africa into the South African Council of Churches, the Soweto 1976 student protests, the killing of Steve Biko, the ungovernable 1980s and the precarious 1990s. And yet in spite of having been through all of that, Tutu still managed to reach out to people "through the

---

[32] Mandela, *Long Walk*.

[33] Michael Battle, *A Spiritual Biography of South Africa's Confessor*. Louisville: John Knox Press (2021), p.3.

[34] Buti Tlhagale and Itumeleng Mosala (eds), *Hammering Swords into Ploughshares: Essays in Honour of Archbishop Mpilo Desmond Tutu*. Grand Rapids: Eerdmans (1986), p.5.

[35] Battle, *A Spiritual Biography*, p.4.

[36] Maluleke, T. (Sep 27. 2015). "The making of Desmond Tutu. Sunday Independent". Retrieved from https://www.iol.co.za/sundayindependent/the-making-of-desmond-tutu-1921480 (accessed 29 May 2021).

[37] Don Mattera, *Memory is the Weapon*. Grant Park: African Perspectives (2009).

[38] Tom Lodge, *Sharpeville: An Apartheid Massacre and its Consequences*. Oxford: University Press (2011).

[39] Ian Macqueen, *Black Consciousness and Progressive Movements Under Apartheid*. Pietermaritzburg: UKZN Press (2018).

paradox of his sincerity and his sense of humour. For Tutu … making people laugh is part of his character".[40]

A tentative categorisation

The humour of gesture, movement and sound

The first category of the humour of Desmond Tutu is neither text nor speech.[41] It occurs when Tutu comes dancing onto the stage as a prelude to his speech or when he shuffles his feet as he walks off the stage at the end of a speech. Or when he attempts to teach the Dalai Lama to dance to the jazz of Sophiatown. It also occurs when he paces up and down the stage, stopping here and there to mimic a dance or whatever action he may be speaking about. Sometimes it comes through exaggerated hand and facial gestures as Tutu makes important points – in joy, amazement or anger – during a speech.

As noted elsewhere, "his sermons are a total performance, not an academic reading of a speech".[42] Sometimes the humour comes in the manner in which Tutu is dressed, such as when he was dressed completely in the colours of the South African football team, from head to toe, when he addressed a stadium full of people during the FIFA World Cup hosted by South Africa in 2010. Sometimes the humour is in his voice and in his high-pitched and infectious laughter. When Tutu is in his element, he does not need to say anything in order for audiences to connect with him through laughter.

Tutu's storytelling humour

The second category of Tutu humour comes through his tremendous story-telling. Tutu has a bag full of short anecdotal stories which, in terms of literature, sit somewhere between fiction and non-fiction, and between Bible stories and folklore. Most of the stories are too good to be (literally) true, but they are good all the same.

Humour in the biblical hermeneutics of Desmond Tutu

These anecdotal stories may be further subdivided, first into those that take off from stories or passages in the Bible but often do so humorously and irreverently. In the process Tutu has invented what I have chosen to name *Ubuntu* biblical hermeneutics. Here is an excellent example:

> You know the story of Adam and Eve. Adam lived in a garden and he was happy. In the garden everything was just lovely. The animals loved each other and they were friendly. The lion played with the lamb. There was no fighting, there was no bloodshed. They were all vegetarians in the garden. Did we say everything was alright in the garden? No, not quite, because God – who was friendly with Adam and used to visit him – said, "It is not good for man to be alone." So God asked Adam to choose a mate from the animals passing in procession before him. "What about this one?" God asks. "Nope," says Adam. "Well how about this one?" "Aikona!" "And this one?" "Not on your life." And so God put Adam to sleep, took his rib and formed that lovely, delectable creature, Eve. When Adam awoke and saw Eve, he said "Wow! This is just what the doctor ordered!"[43]

Again and again, Tutu deploys this kind of comic but captivating re-telling of biblical stories to great effect. Here is another example of *Ubuntu* biblical hermeneutics at work:

> God wanted his people, the children of Israel, to be freed from bondage in Egypt. He could have done it on his own, but he wanted a human partner. So he went to Moses. "Hi Moses." "Hi, God." "I want you to go to the Pharaoh and tell him: "Let my people go." Moses was thoroughly flabbergasted: "What? Me?

---

[40] Battle, *A Spiritual Biography*, p.152.

[41] Desmond Tutu, *The Rainbow People of God: The Making of a Peaceful Revolution*. New York: Bantam Doubleday (1994).

[42] Maluleke, "The Making of Desmond Tutu".

[43] Tutu (and Allen), *The Essential Desmond Tutu*, p.3.

What have I done now? Go to Pharaoh? Please, God, no! You can't be serious!" Forgetting that God knew everything, Moses pleaded: "God, you know I stammer. How can I address Pharaoh?" Mercifully, God did not accept Moses' first negative reactions. If he had, in a real sense the children of Israel would still be in Egypt in bondage. The God we worship is the Exodus God, the great liberator God who leads us out of all kinds of bondage.[44]

One of the effects of Tutu's *Ubuntu* hermeneutical moves is to "humanise" both God and biblical characters who have become part of the mythical history of the world. In the process, the biblical characters feel like the people we know and God becomes accessible.

Humour in the race hermeneutics of Desmond Tutu

The second sub-category of Tutu's anecdotal stories could be titled, race hermeneutics. Tutu has an assemblage of stories, fables and anecdotes that speak to the relationship between black people and white people. While Tutu invents a few stories of his own, probably based on his own experiences, it seems that Tutu gleans many of these stories from contemporary folklore. Here is one such story:

Long ago, when the missionaries first came to Africa, we had the land and they had the Bible, and they said, "Let us pray". We dutifully closed our eyes and at the end they said, "Amen", and when we opened our eyes – Why! the whites had the land and we had the Bible.[45]

Without fail, Tutu always uses this anecdote not to bash and critique the missionaries and the white man. On the contrary, he uses it to show how the Bible was the best deal that Africans could have wished for and that on the basis of his particular reading of the Bible it is possible both for black and white people to reconcile, and for black people to use the Bible to get the land back.[46]

But the *Ubuntu* race hermeneutics are not always smooth and noble – sometimes the white people were at the sharp end of Tutu's jokes. One evening during one of his live performances at the Market Theatre in 2006, Hugh Masekela[47] told an anecdote he once heard from Desmond Tutu. This anecdote would fall into the sub-category of "Van der Merwe jokes" – a widespread South African sub-genre of humour in which white people in general and Afrikaners in particular, become the butt of jokes. This is the joke as told by Tutu himself:

At home they tell stories which feature a character called Van der Merwe, who is not over-endowed with intelligence. He was browned off, so they say, because the Americans and the Russians were getting all the kudos for their space programmes, so he announced that South Africa was to launch a spacecraft to the sun, no less. Knowledgeable people told him, "Van der Merwe, it will be burned to cinders long before it gets anywhere near the sun." Nothing daunted, Van der Merwe retorted: "You don't think we South Africans are stupid. We will launch it at night."[48]

Apparently, while studying theology in London in the sixties, Tutu struck up a great friendship with a white South African, one Brian Oosthuysen.[49] Rightfully, Tutu noted that "Brian and I would not have been in the same tertiary institution in South Africa … That mundane everyday occurrence of students sitting side by side was in fact of monumental significance. It was saying as eloquently as

[44] Tutu (and Allen), *The Essential Desmond Tutu*, p.15.
[45] Desmond Tutu, *In God's Hands: The Archbishop of Canterbury's Lent Book 2015*. London: Continuum (2014), p.9.
[46] Tinyiko Maluleke, "Black and African Theologies in Search of Comprehensive Environmental Justice", *Journal of Theology for Southern Africa,* No. 167 (2020), pp.5-19.
[47] Hugh Masekela (and D. Michael Cheers), *Still Grazing: The Musical Journey of Hugh Masekela*. New York: Random House (2004).
[48] Tutu (and Allen), *The Essential Desmond Tutu*, p.76.
[49] Tinyiko Maluleke, "Forgiveness and Reconciliation in the Life and Work of Desmond Tutu", *International Review of Mission*, Vol 109, No. 2 (2020), pp.210-221.

a massive tome that you were in fact, a human too."[50] This incident, which must have been duplicated many times for Tutu in his various sojourns overseas, seems to have inspired another, not-so-comforting Van der Merwe joke. In several versions of the anecdote shared by Tutu, the two South Africans, Van der Merwe and Dlangamandla, happen to befriend each other while living in the USA, where, at some stage:

> … they got into big trouble and were convicted of a capital offence. They were given the choice of an electric chair or the rope. Van der Merwe went first and chose the electric chair. He was strapped in and they pulled the switch. Nothing happened. This was repeated three times and they decided to reprieve him. As he went out, Dlangamandla was next in the queue [and seeing his "comrade" marching out, he inquired as to what had just happened]. Van der Merwe told him: "The damned thing doesn't work. Choose the rope!"[51]

So much for friendships of convenience! In tapping on the Van der Merwe folk jokes that were in circulation within South African society, Tutu was joining the masses in "hitting back" at the rulers of the land – a choice strategy of many oppressed groups in the world. Above all, Tutu is challenging his audience to imagine a world in which Dlangamandla and Van der Merwe can become human enough to love and respect one another beyond the exploitative and abusive ways in which they tended to relate.

Sometimes Tutu used his humour to critique racist South African politics in relation to fellow African countries, which tended to be looked down upon by the white South African government:

> Once a Zambian and a South African, it is said, were talking. The Zambian boasted about his country's Minister of Naval Affairs. The South African asked, "But you have no navy. Zambia is landlocked with no access to the sea. How can you have a Minister of Naval Affairs?" The Zambian retorted, "Well, in South Africa you have a Minister of Justice, don't you?"[52]

Nor would Tutu spare fellow Africans in the diaspora, including African Americans:

> When the South African government was using its divide and rule tactics, classifying us on the basis of ethnicity, I told an audience in one of my addresses that my father was a Xhosa and my mother was a Tswana. When I asked what that made me, Harry Belafonte called out from the back: "A Zulu!"[53]

With the above joke, Tutu "kills several birds", namely, he exposed the irrationality of the race- and ethnicity-based social engineering by the apartheid state and perhaps also the ignorance of well-meaning Africans in the diaspora about the ethnic details pertaining to South Africans in particular, and Africans in general.

Humour in the spiritual hermeneutics of Desmond Tutu

After Michael Battle's breathtaking book on Tutu as a mystic,[54] it is now perfectly possible to think of the humour in the *spiritual hermeneutics of Desmond Tutu*, as noted by Battle. It is possible to populate the humour of Tutu across the three parts into which Battle's book is divided, namely: purgation, illumination and union. I would further suggest that there are two spiritual notions expounded by Tutu between and from which sprang both his spiritual humour and his spirituality, namely, the idea of "resting in God's presence" and the idea of being under the influence of "God

---

[50] John Allen, *Rabble-Rouser for Peace: The Authorised Biography of Desmond Tutu*. London: Rider (2006), p.86.
[51] Tutu (and Allen), *The Essential Desmond Tutu*, p.76.
[52] Tutu (and Allen), *The Essential Desmond Tutu*, p.64.
[53] Tutu (and Allen), *The Essential Desmond Tutu*, p.60.
[54] Battle, *A Spiritual Biography*.

pressure … a feeling of being compelled to act, even against the voice of reason".[55] Such was Tutu's faith in both prayer and humour that he would jestfully boast that:

> once I met an Anchorite, a person who spends time in solitary prayer. I asked her to tell me about her life and she said, "Well, I live in the woods in California. My day starts at two in the morning and, Bishop Tutu, I pray for you regularly." Then I say, "Hey, here am I being prayed for at two in the morning, in the woods in California. What chance does the South African Government stand?"[56]

Tutu's biographical Humour

The person who is most often the butt of Desmond Tutu's biographical jokes is Desmond Tutu himself, and his big nose is a frequent victim of these:

> I suppose it's been one of those wonderful coincidences, if you like, that I am an African with a fairly easy name: Tutu. If I'd had a more outlandish name, it may have been more difficult to get our cause overseas so easily publicised. I think they've got this guy with a big nose and an easy name, and that helped to give people a picture of South Africa.[57]

In most of them, Tutu is often shown up as erratic and self-conceited:

> Last year my wife and I were in Australia and I was really going great guns in saying to a crowd of young people, 2,000 of them, the trouble with many of us is that we never really celebrate who we are, giving thanks to God for creating us as we are. How about giving yourselves a standing ovation and how about giving God a standing ovation for being such a tremendous God, and they did. They really went to town, brought the roof down, and without thinking at the end of it, I said, "thank you".[58]

The moral of the story is that, between the moment when Tutu asked the people to give a standing ovation and by the time they finished he had quietly and shamelessly moved into the role of "god". In this way Tutu opens up for discussion the human desire to be bigger and better than we are:

> Recently, I was on a flight to Durban, and one of the pretty air hostesses approached me to say: "Excuse me Sir, a group of passengers would like you to autograph a book for them". Well, I thought, there are some nice people about who show they have a good sense of values. They appreciate a good thing when they see it. I was trying to look suitably modest, when she went on to say, "you are bishop Muzorewa, aren't you?"[59]

Now, Bishop Abel Muzorewa was the favourite of white South Africans in the late 70s and early 80s – just when they viewed Tutu most negatively! It is bad enough to be mistaken for someone else but to be mistaken for a person whose views and values are the direct opposite of yours is quite another. In this way Tutu was able to broach a subject that has dogged him for most of the 1980s, that is, the intense dislike and hatred he suffered at the hands of many white South Africans. As a champion of the underdog, Tutu often tells stories of places where and when he was corrected or "put in his place" by the underdogs whom he presumed to represent:

> I remember an instance saying to our youngest, who was then a very chirpy three-year-old, and quite sure that there were very few things she did not know in the world: "Mpho, darling, please keep quiet, you talk

---

[55] Tinyiko Maluleke, "Tutu in Memory, Tutu on Memory", *Missionalia*, 47:2 (2019), pp.177-192 (p. 181).

[56] Tutu (and Allen), *The Essential Desmond Tutu*, p. 74.

[57] Tutu (and Allen), *The Essential Desmond Tutu*, p. 128.

[58] Battle, *A Spiritual Biography,* p.153.

[59] Desmond Tutu, *Crying in the Wilderness: The Struggle for Justice in South Africa*. Grand Rapids: Eerdmans (1982), p.52.

too much!" Do you think she was at all deflated by this rebuke? Not at all – quick as a shot she retorted: "Daddy, you talk a lot too. You talk all by yourself in church!"

Concluding thoughts

Situating the wit and the grit of Desmond Tutu within the framework of a genre I have chosen to name the humour of liberation or liberating humour, I have tried to paint a picture of what such humour looks like in general. More importantly, I have attempted to put the humour of Desmond Tutu, its nature, purpose and impact, within a specific analytical framework – namely the intention to humanise both the victims and the perpetrators of oppression.

By way of contrast, I have suggested that both the freedom "walk" of Nelson Mandela as well as the mental and psychological emancipation project of Steve Biko were similar in objective to that of Desmond Tutu, namely, the aim of humanising. However, Tutu stands somewhat apart from Mandela, Biko and other freedom fighters in his deliberate choice, and repeated and structured use, of humour as a humanising tool. In this sense, for Tutu therefore, the motto is not only the famous "I belong therefore I am". He would add, "I laugh, therefore I am".

I started the essay on a melancholic note, inspired by Psalm 22. The aim was to probe deeply what the place of laughter might be in the lives of the poor and the marginalised. Having done that using the three case studies of Biko, Mandela and Tutu, we can now confirm that laughter has a place in the struggle. We have seen brilliant glimpses of it in the lives and works of Biko, Mandela and especially Tutu.

28. DESMOND TUTU, HUMOUR AND SOCIAL JUSTICE

Fulata L. Moyo[1]

One of the life-changing encounters I had with Archbishop Desmond Mpilo and (Archbishopess) Leah Tutu was in 2011 when I spent some time with them at the Ecumenical Institute of Bossey. After his inspiring presentation at the Ecumenical Center in Geneva, Switzerland, he was asked a few questions. One of the questions was about his becoming a Nobel Peace Prize laureate in 1984. He answered, "Just have a short name (Tutu) and a big nose!" It is widely accepted that Tutu propagated the idea of "the Rainbow Nation."[2] In this essay, I want to argue that, for the Archbishop and all those who have taken up leadership roles in the praxis for justice, humour not only creates an atmosphere for laughter and joy amidst otherwise gloomy and seemingly hopeless realities, it is also a necessary twist to turn the otherwise difficult conversation into a witty, thought-provoking one that can lead to praxis for social justice.

Douglas Abrams sees laughter and a sense of humour as a universal index of spiritual development. He rates Archbishop Tutu (and the Dalai Lama) as being at the top of that index as spiritual leader. "... they skewered humbug, status, injustice, and evil, all with the power of humor ... So often their first response to any subject, no matter how seemingly painful, was to laugh."[3] Nancy Goldman argues that humourists are able to critique the dominant forces in society and ridicule those in power. She gives examples of high-level humourists like the USA president Benjamin Franklin and Mark Twain (she doesn't mention Maya Angelou and James Baldwin, but they too can be counted here):

> Humor is a social corrective ... it can validate experience, help us think more flexibly and reframe situations, illuminate the ways in which we live in the world politically, and be used to critique social injustice. Humor can diffuse tensions around controversial topics ... satire can subvert authority and expose hypocrisy ... [comedians can] obscure the lines between news and comedy ... [some can use their sense of humour and their body] to confront society while making a safe space for people to be open and absorb information.Goldman looks at the relationship between humor and stereotypes and the impact that humor about race and ethnicity plays in society ... [it can] make the invisible visible. Humor engages audience members in thinking, feeling and speaking about ways that we live in the world together, all of which can reform change.[4]

For Goldman, social critique that is communicated using the medium that makes people laugh has more power to sink into the listeners' psyche for behavioral change than polished moral essays or stern words of rebuke. I also want to argue that words of rebuke or moral essays that border on being judgemental or accusatory in their approach tend to either create guilt, fear or shame (for the guilty) or a deceptive feeling of perfection (for those with a sense of righteousness). Both do not have an embedded motivation to inspire lasting transformation. Humour, however, whatever form it takes, has the power to strip us naked of all our self-protective layers that lead to the practice of "Keeping

---

[1] Fulata Lusungu Moyo believes in the life-changing power of humour in social (gender) justice activism. She is a founder of STREAM (Sex-Trafficking Responses through Educational Research, Accompaniment and Mentorship) and a vice-president for AfriAus iLEAC. She holds a PhD in human sciences from UKZN, South Africa. She met and spent time with Archbishop and Madame Tutu in Geneva, Switzerland.

[2] Desmond Tutu. Encyclopedia Britannica. https://www.britannica.com/biography/Desmond-Tutu (accessed 29 May 2021).

[3] His Holiness the Dalai Lama and Archbishop Desmond Tutu with Douglas Abrams, *Lasting Happiness in a Changing World: The Book of Joy* (London: Hutchinson, 2016), 215.

[4] Nancy Goldman, "Comedy and Democracy: The Role of Humour in Social Justice" https://animatingdemocracy.org/resource/comedy-and-democracy-role-humor-social-justice, p1 (accessed 29 May 2021).

Up Appearances"[5] of perfection: we become vulnerably our true selves disrobed of all pretence. Drawing on George Carlin,[6] Goldman suggests that it is when we genuinely laugh that we are more ourselves because then our defences are down. We become open because we are completely our vulnerable selves with the reflections of our life gazing squarely back at us. One can argue, therefore, that humour opens us to a vulnerability that is conducive to a possibility of transformation. Hence humour can arguably entice a daring self-critique, as our guards are lowered enough to be able to laugh at ourselves, when everything else in society urges us to relentlessly be on guard.

In these short reflections, I am exploring humour as a medium for social justice out of my own biased interest. As a Malawian Christian woman who was widowed early in life and had the joy of raising three boys as a single mother, I was often judged sternly for working two jobs to supplement my PhD[7] partial funding. It is humour that helped make sense of the struggles that surrounded my life, the life of rural wo/men I worked with in my PhD research as well as the mainly black wo/men I interacted with in post-apartheid South Africa, and the highly racialised European context where I found and still find myself. For example, when my Christian community expected me to be unsexual as a widow without engaging with me in a conversation about how I was actually coping, I would humorously respond to the "Fulata, how are you doing?" with "I am suffering from SARS" and I would immediately unpack SARS as "Severe Absence of Romance and Sex". Some people regretted ever asking how I was doing, they would make an embarrassed sigh or an embarrassed laugh while urging their feet to take them away from me at a speed of lightning. But some would laugh and in a more relaxed mood, they would engage in a conversation to make sense of my widowhood struggles.

As a Christian I would like to first muse at whether there is some humour in the Christian sacred texts that remain an important source of my spirituality. Recently holding a conversation with one of my best friends, Rev. Nicole Ashwood, she reminded me of the story about King Solomon's method of determining justice – though we had to agree that the story is more on the side of dark humour than the Tutu ones. Here is the story:

> Later, two women who were prostitutes came to the king and stood before him. [17] The one woman said, "Please, my lord, this woman and I live in the same house; and I gave birth while she was in the house. Then on the third day after I gave birth, this woman also gave birth. We were together; there was no one else with us in the house, only the two of us were in the house. Then this woman's son died in the night, because she lay on him. [20] She got up in the middle of the night and took my son from beside me while your servant slept. She laid him at her breast, and laid her dead son at my breast. [21] When I rose in the morning to nurse my son, I saw that he was dead; but when I looked at him closely in the morning, clearly it was not the son I had borne." But the other woman said, "No, the living son is mine, and the dead son is yours." The first said, "No, the dead son is yours, and the living son is mine." So they argued before the king. Then the king said, "The one says, 'This is my son that is alive, and your son is dead'; while the other says, 'Not so! Your son is dead, and my son is the living one.'" So the king said, "Bring me a sword," and they brought a sword before the king. The king said, "Divide the living boy in two; then give

---

[5] Many of us who have enjoyed watching the BBC1 sitcom *Keeping Up Appearances* created by Roy Clarke, which features Patricia Routledge, Clive Swift and Geoffrey Hughes, find ourselves laughing at the high level of self-deception of Hyacinth (Patricia Routledge) in her attempt to prove her social superiority. Much of the humour of this sitcom comes from the clear conflict between Hyacinth's imagination of herself and her family with the actual reality of her lower class. By the time you finish watching an episode, you laugh at the clear stupidity of her futile attempts to be what she is not. As the laughter sinks in, it illuminates for the viewer their own moments of trying to be what they are not, instead of seeking the joy of being who you really are even as you envision a better life. https://en.wikipedia.org/wiki/Keeping_Up_Appearances (accessed 29 May 2021).
[6] Goldman, "Comedy and Democracy", p2.
[7] It is understandable that in a world where the stupidity of the hierarchy of knowledge has been endorsed, those holding a PhD (Doctor of Philosophy) are viewed as having the last word on their areas of expertise. Unfortunately, in our world marked with unequal power relations, it seems to matter where one's PhD is harvested from. I often laugh at the irony of how having a PhD often translates into "Permanent Head Damage" because of the high level of specialisation that, the older I grow, the more I find myself less competent to venture in areas of knowledge that are outside my own specialisation, however interested I might find myself.

half to the one, and half to the other." But the woman whose son was alive said to the king – because compassion for her son burned within her – "Please, my lord, give her the living boy; certainly do not kill him!" The other said, "It shall be neither mine nor yours; divide it." Then the king responded: "Give the first woman the living boy; do not kill him. She is his mother." All Israel heard of the judgment that the king had rendered; and they stood in awe of the king, because they perceived that the wisdom of God was in him, to execute justice. (1 Kings 3:16-28).[8]

According to Musa Gotom,[9] Solomon might have applied a principle remembered from the ancient Israelite law dealing with a situation where two owners are claiming one live ox after one dies. In such cases the living ox was equally shared between the contending owners (Exodus 21:35). The idea behind the king's theatrical performance, asking that his court servant use his sword, was based on the expectation that the true mother had too much compassion to bear the thought of her own child being cut into two – murdered. The dark humour comes in when you picture the assigned servant holding the sword raised high, pretending to be ready to cut the living child while waiting in anticipation that the right mother will come forward and sacrificially plead that the child be given to the other woman. Where would that sword end up cutting if both women continue in their competitive spirit arguing: "No, the living son is mine, and the dead son is yours" rather than the graciousness of: "Give the first woman the living boy; do not kill him. She is his mother"? Solomon's manifestation of God's wisdom in this drama depends on the feminist ethical commitment of one of the women.

What would his wisdom have led him to do if, for example, after trying to encourage three times to spur the right mother to a more life-giving redemptive decision, none of them gave in to the above graciousness? It would have become a captivating suspense knowing that, while in the case of a divided ox both owners benefit, in the case of a child the cutting into two is not close to an anticipated result of a king who still worshipped a God of justice that did not delight in human sacrifice. It is humorous as long as the suspense leads to the right mother being a moral agent, so that the raised sword is dropped back to where it belongs without cutting short any life.

The story of King Solomon's decision-making process regarding the determination of maternity of the child in the case of the two contending mothers after one of the two suffocated her own child might seem odd to contemporary sensibilities. It can, however, only make sense as humour if the interpreter understands the laws regarding an ox, but even more significantly (and ironically) if the person sharing knows the pain of losing a child, is a trusted as a caring person for the struggles of the community and is able to share from her/his own vulnerability to the issues s/he is addressing.

For this essay that is in honour of Archbishop Tutu's Nonagintennial Jubilee, this story reminds us of his role as chair of the Truth and Reconciliation Commission. The many times when there was suspense as to how the people would react to the stories narrated. The times when the response from the narrators and respondents caused him and others to shed tears with those expressing their pain. He gave into forgiveness and reconciliation rather than to vengeance and calls for retribution. He made a choice to exercise compassion; to forgive the perpetrators of apartheid, the settlers who successfully contended for and owned what otherwise belonged to him as an indigenous South African. It is a manifestation of the gracious choices to forgive and forego one's rights, instead of using one's rights as a sword that with vengeance cuts to pieces those who have caused so much racial pain and loss of life. Like the real mother of the living child that chooses to give away her right to motherhood in the biblical narrative above, Tutu's commitment to forgiveness is a decision to share his rights with others who otherwise would not be deserving. Like humour, forgiveness unveils pretence so that we face up to the ugliness of our fallenness with the hope for transformation.

---

[8] National Council of Churches of Christ in the United States of America, *The Holy Bible, NRSV* (Nashville: Thomas Nelson Publishers, 1989), 306.

[9] Musa Gotom, "1 and 2 Kings", in *Africa Bible Commentary: A One-Volume Commentary Written by 70 African Scholars*, ed. Tokunboh Adeyemo (Grand Rapids: WordAlive (Zondervan), 2006), 420, 409-466.

We found that one of the best ways of helping our people direct their energies in positive directions was laughter. Telling jokes, even at our expense, was such a wonderful flip to our morale. Of course some of the things that happened were so horrendous. Like I was saying yesterday, about Chris Hani, humor helped to defuse a very, very tense situation, telling stories that made people laugh and especially to laugh at themselves … My weaponry, if you can call it that, was almost always to use humor, specially self-denigrating humor, where you are laughing at yourself.[10]

What makes something funny? It is important to acknowledge the significance of contextuality in determining the relevance and effectiveness of humour. According to Julian Rosenblum,[11] there is no full consensus as to whether something is humorous or not. Neither can the impact of what is considered funny be measured before the response of the audience is experienced. Rosenblum gives an example of a comedian to emphasise the point that, while one can determine how to deliver a joke, no one can determine how the audience will receive the comedy; and that while comedy often makes sense, it does not always do that. All these are valid observations about humour especially as expressed through comedy. Like Rosenblum, I want to argue that what makes humour appreciated and well received, with a possibility of being a medium for transformation, is mainly when the audience feels a certain amount of safety.

Therefore, I would like to contend that firstly, when the humourist uses her/his own story, it creates an atmosphere of safety for the audience. This is because s/he is actually stripping self-naked of any pretence and is presenting oneself vulnerably as a human being with similar human struggles, rather than a perfect being that is there to judge or accuse. Secondly, I would also insist that the humourist's character of trustworthiness, dependability and commitment to social justice provides a more needed, conducive atmosphere especially in contexts where one uses dark humour – more as a coping mechanism. Otherwise, if there are no other premises of assuring safety of listeners, such humour would end up hurting some of the listeners because of the context of their life's realities that sometimes might not be known to the humourist. Thirdly, I would assert that knowledge and acknowledgement of the context of the audience is crucial for determining the relevance of the humour. This provides a better chance of eliciting a more positive response. In the words of Julian Rosenblum:

> Broadly speaking, a *context* for a joke consists of the comedian, the audience, the comedian's public beliefs, the audience's beliefs, and the audience's perceived beliefs of everyone else. In order to make this more useful, we must also define the *funniness* of a joke in a context, which can be broken down into two components: *humor value* and *externality*. Humor value is straightforward and can be basically measured by amount of laughter. Externality refers to the perceived effect of the joke in the context on the world at large.[12]

In my view all the above components of what makes humour funny have been present in the Archbishop's own use of humour in his praxis of justice and practice of forgiveness.

At one of those apartheid-connected funerals at Ciskei homeland the Archbishop, hearing Chris Hani belting out six verses of a Xhosa song from memory, could humorously say to him: "Aren't you a godless Communist? … I think the newspaper called you the AntiChrist. You are not living up to your billing!"[13] In the midst of pain and loss caused by an unjust and violent system that both Tutu and Hani were actively resisting and calling for change, his humour was funny and therapeutic, and a

---

[10] His Holiness the Dalai Lama and Archbishop Desmond Tutu with Douglas Abrams, *Lasting Happiness in a Changing World,* 217.

[11] Julian Rosenblum, "Humor, Social Justice and a Little Math", https://julianrosenblum.medium.com/humor-social-justice-and-a-little-math-a5a4ec33bea4 (accessed 29 May 2021).

[12] Julian Rosenblum, "Humor, Social Justice and a Little Math", https://julianrosenblum.medium.com/humorsocial-justice-and-a-little-math-a5a4ec33bea4 (accessed 29 May 2021).

[13] Desmond Tutu and Mpho Tutu, *Made for Goodness: And Why this Makes All the Difference.* (London/Sydney/Auckland/Johannesburg: Rider, 2010), 57-58.

booster to their transformative work together. For me, it is his wit for the right kind of humour at each point of his praxis for justice that I have admired most about him, and I am celebrating. Viva, Archbishop, viva your sense of humour even as *aluta continua* for social justice!

29. DEFEATING APARTHEID WITH FAITH AND HUMOUR

Trond Bakkevig[1]

"Can I touch the Royal Palace? In South Africa we cannot touch such buildings," Desmond Tutu asked. It was an early morning springtime, 1984 in Oslo, Norway. Bishop Tutu, Dan Vaughan and I passed the Royal Palace on our way between the hotel and the Ministry of Foreign Affairs. Not even the palace guards raised an eyebrow when he touched the southeast corner of the building. "Next time you come, you will be inside the Palace," I said – hoping that in December he would receive the Nobel Peace Prize and have an audience with King Olav V. "Tutu, who?" the police sounded like question marks through the telephone line when I called them and asked if they had thought about his security in the hotel.

10 December 1984, in front of the "rising sun" painted by Edvard Munch, the moderator of the Nobel Committee, Egil Aarvik, in the rostrum, King Olav sat between the aisles, in the middle of the Grand Aula of the University in Oslo. A policeman came in from behind, whispered something to the King who shook his head, obviously disagreeing. The policeman, however, moved on, said something to Mr Aarvik, took the microphone and said: "We have had a bomb threat. Please leave the room immediately. Don't pick up your clothes or anything else." The King left, we left – and the orchestra with all their instruments.

Outside, it was freezing cold, minus 10 centigrade. We waited in the university plaza, in front of the Aula, hoping the ceremony could proceed, if not inside, then on the steps outside. Just around the corner, the King waited in his car. I felt vindicated for my earlier contact with the police. Half an hour later we could return to the Aula. No bomb was found, but there was no orchestra on the podium. Bishop Tutu, who was about to speak, commandeered all South Africans up there. The Khotso House trio sang. When they sang "Nkosi Sikelel' iAfrika", we all, including the King, stood up and joined the choir – many with raised fists.

Terror, yes. Threats, yes. But Munch's "rising sun" shone on the Nobel Prize laureate with his compatriots and supporters. The day ended with a gala dinner, where the Bishop took control, almost as a master of ceremonies. He distributed thanks: to the King, the Nobel Committee, the government, the church with its trade union (to the astonishment of the National Trade Union!) and all supporters of the struggle against the apartheid regime. We enjoyed ourselves and thought that no regime can survive an opposition which uses the force of humour.

However, other means were also necessary!

Discussions in the Ministry of Foreign Affairs circled to a large degree around financial support for the various activities of the South African Council of Churches (SACC). The ministry was generous and channelled funds through the Church of Norway Council on Ecumenical and International Relations. Meetings in the ministry also gave room for orientations about the current situation in South Africa and how this should be handled by the international community. One of the crucial issues was sanctions: should sanctions be implemented? Would they work? And what about the Norwegian shipping of oil to the apartheid state – oil used by the South African Army for oppression of the majority population and for wars elsewhere in Africa? The Norwegian government of 1984 was against sanctions. Tutu responded with a glimmer in his eye: "So, the idea is: if I don't steal that car, somebody else will steal it!" He could not say much more since the apartheid state followed him everywhere. In 1979 he heard that Denmark imported coal from South Africa. He recommended an end to this and did not give in to pressure to retract the recommendation. Consequently, he lost his passport and for some years could not travel.

---

[1] Trond Bakkevig is a Pastor in the Church of Norway, and holds a Doctorate in Theology from the University of Oslo.

When I today read his Nobel lecture from 1984, it strikes me how relevant it still is: "In pursuance of apartheid's ideological racist dream, over 3 million of God's children have been uprooted from their homes, which have been demolished, whilst they have then been dumped in the bantustan homeland resettlement camps."[2] It is unavoidable not to associate what he said with stories about the Rohingyas being driven out of Myanmar, or Palestinians being evicted from their family homes in Sheikh Jarrah and Silwan in Jerusalem. There may be reasons not to label systems in other parts of the world as "apartheid" since they do not share the idea that some races or persons have more worth and should have more rights than others. Practices may, however, resemble what we witnessed in South Africa: people are driven into refugee camps or just dumped on the street with all their furniture. People are treated as "things" just because they are Rohingyas or Palestinians, and "not as of infinite value as being created in the image of God".[3]

Tutu continues by listing how such a system keeps control of the black majority population:

- Pass Laws (or walls?) prohibit families to follow a breadwinner closer to the workplace
- laws require people to be registered (and hence classified) by their ethnic (racial) background
- security laws are used to keep people in indefinite detention

Such mechanisms for oppression are easily recognised. They are universal in nature and are used – especially when ethnic minorities or majorities are being suppressed.

Towards the end of his lecture, Bishop Tutu dealt with the fact that people choose different means in the struggle against the apartheid state. He acknowledged that there is a wider front combatting the apartheid system when he lends a hand to freedom fighters, often called terrorists. Violence did not start with them: "The South African situation is violent already, and the primary violence is that of apartheid, the violence of forced population removals, of inferior education, of detention without trial, of the migratory labor system, etc."[4] Such words should always be kept in mind when an oppressive system labels opponents as "terrorists".

As much as he spoke clearly about the need to confront oppressors, he always underlined that apartheid and all kinds of injustice dehumanises both the oppressor and the oppressed, yes, perhaps the oppressors mostly because they allow themselves to dehumanise others – treat them as "things" – not as humans created in the image of God. Therefore, the oppressor and the oppressed need each other to become free, to become human: "We can be human only in fellowship, in koinonia, in peace."[5] The content is there, but this time, he did not use the word "*Ubuntu*". He linked this with repeating God's call to us that we become fellow workers in the Kingdom which is characterised not only by justice and peace, but also by caring and laughter.

"What a wonderful God this one is", is a typical Tutu expression. Often, he would continue by describing how God listens, sees, knows and acts, leading to these Tutu sentences about a God which combines that which is very down to earth and the heavenly: "God does not fold God's hands and look on."[6] So, what does God do? Well, God wants to see the good ruler in place, who rules with justice, defends the poorest, saves children in need – and crushes the oppressor. His way of closing in on political realities without speaking politics had a deeper impact than a direct political statement. In a sermon he gave on a visit to Panama when General Noriega still was the ruler, he repeated what he said to oppressors everywhere: "You are not God. You are just an ordinary human being. Maybe you have a lot of power now. Ah, ah, but watch it! Watch it! Watch it!" Then he listed tyrants who lost their power and were gone, and mentioned the actual dictator in Nicaragua, Somoza. The audience laughed and waited for a name closer to home, but Tutu said: "I'm going to Africa."[7]

---

[2] Desmond Tutu, *The Rainbow People of God: South Africa's Victory Over Apartheid*. London: Transworld Publishers LTD (1994), 86.

[3] Tutu, *The Rainbow People*, 86.

[4] Tutu, *The Rainbow People*, 90.

[5] Tutu, *The Rainbow People*, 92.

[6] Tutu, *The Rainbow People*, 157.

[7] Tutu, *The Rainbow People*, 160-161.

When the Nobel festivities were over, he toured Norway. Everywhere he linked his message to words like "God is wonderful"[8] and continued by how gracious God is. To believe in God means that we have to mirror God's grace, God's sense of humour, and the God who does not fold the hands, but participates in the struggle for justice. He said all of this and accompanied it with invitations to laugh, clap hands, respond loudly to what he said. He made us participate in his sermons. No other preacher has brought so much humour and joy to Norwegian pulpits. In the far north, in the Arctic Cathedral in Tromsø, he got 900 people to stand up in the benches and shout "Hello South Africa. We love you." After the Eucharist, he invited people to dance with him between the aisles. To Norwegian churchgoers in the 1980s this was a new experience. If a Norwegian bishop had done something like this, many eyebrows would have been raised. In our churches the support for the struggle against apartheid was accompanied by happy and rhythmic South African songs and dances. We dared because he made us dare.

He demonstrated this playfulness also when he was interviewed by the panel which would present the shortlist of candidates for the Truth and Reconciliation Commission. One of the panel members asked him whether people could find him intimidating because of his church titles: "Your Highness", "Father" or "Bishop". He responded: "You can call me anything as long as you don't call me 'Your Graciousness'… I hope they think I'm fun." His humour never hits those who struggle. It hits the mighty who tread on people and finds words which we all would wish we could find to enjoy life, smile and feel we are part of a happy, fighting crowd. His sense of humour is witness to his closeness to people's daily life, struggles, pain and wounds. When he was asked what kind of people he would like to see on the Truth and Reconciliation Commission he responded: "People who once were victims. The most forgiving people I have ever come across." People who know that to forgive and receive forgiveness is to relate to people, not to avoid it by addressing God. "… if you've had a fight with your wife, it is no use only to ask forgiveness from God".[9] Alex Boraine, deputy moderator of the commission, quoted the poet Antjie Krog when he wrote: "Whatever role others might play, it is Tutu who is the compass. He guides us in several ways, the most important of which is the language … it is this language that drags people along with the process."[10]

This was demonstrated when he spoke at Chris Hani's funeral – a prominent communist and head of ANC's military wing. He had earlier stood beside Chris Hani when they sang the hymn "Fulfil Your Promise, Lord of Truth." Hani knew all the verses by heart and sang "in a wonderful baritone" and just laughed when Tutu asked him how a communist could join in a Christian hymn? Hani just laughed. Without enrolling Hani in the church, Tutu is still able to give a Christian interpretation of the killing of Hani which reflects his faith in a God who includes: "Chris died between Good Friday and Easter Sunday. Let us recall that God extracted out of the death of Jesus Christ a great victory, the victory of life over death, that life is stronger than death, that love is stronger than hate. God is telling us the same message in the horrible death of Chris Hani. His death is not defeat. His death is our victory."[11] Our faith is a lens which we can use to recognise God and God's work where we normally would not look for it.

Faith furnishes us with hope. Defiance is another element in hope – things do not need to be as they are: another world is possible. Hope and faith give the courage to tell the apartheid president, P.W. Botha, that "… we had already won and invited him and other white South Africans to join the winning side. All the 'objective' facts were against us … (but) … God cares about justice and injustice. God is in charge."[12] And if the white South Africans do not want to join right now, Archbishop Desmond is able to convince people that God will deliver his people: "… maybe not

[8] The following short quotes in this paragraph are partly from my own memory and partly told by my friend.
[9] Antjie Krog, *Country of my Skull*. Johannesburg: Random House (1998), 16-17.
[10] Alex Boraine, *A Country Unmasked: Inside South Africa's Truth and Reconciliation Commission*. Cape Town: Oxford University Press (2000), 269. Quoted from Krog, *Country of My Skull*, 152.
[11] Tutu, *The Rainbow People*, 245-246.
[12] Desmond Tutu, *God has a Dream: A Vision of Hope for Our Time*. London: Doubleday (2004), 2.

today. Tomorrow? Maybe not tomorrow. But what can separate us from the love of God? Absolutely nothing … If God be for us, who can be against us!"[13]

In Norway we are reminded of this faith in an inclusive God and an inclusive humanity when watching the Norwegian men's handball team playing. They finish all time-outs by joining hands while saying "*ubuntu*". European teams often have their stars, but stars are always part of a team. They do not win one single match on their own. "*Ubuntu*" is the reminder that you can only win as part of a team. When watching and hearing this word in the middle of an exciting match, some of us are always reminded of our Archbishop.

Archbishop Desmond and Leah from time to time spent some weeks at a farm in Nittedal, a few kilometres north of Oslo. They were there only with themselves, but many were surprised when they met a smiling Nobel Prize winner jogging in the forest around the farm. He calls it "our farm".

Tutu captivates us with his presence, his humour, his language, his spirituality – whether we sit in a church, a big hall or are invited to his hotel room to celebrate a morning Eucharist with him. With him, we are included – not only personally, but a whole humanity under God and by God.

And what have we learned from him? To have faith in God – as part of a team which stretches from Cape Town to the end of the world. To have faith in God, our trustworthy companion in the struggle for peace and justice. To have faith in a God who has an abundant sense of humour.

---

[13] Tutu, *The Rainbow People*, 161.

30. Charismatic, Pious and Humorous for a Just Peace: Inspiring Encounters with Desmond Tutu

Fernando Enns[1]

South Africa has taught me a lot – and continues to do so. It has become part of my theological, political and ecumenical formation for the past thirty-five years. And I will be forever grateful for the many *companions* in the ecumenical movement (the ones with whom you share the bread with on the way) from South Africa. One of them is "the Arch", Desmond Tutu.

It was in my early years of theological training at the University of Heidelberg in Germany, in the mid-1980s, that I heard his name for the first time. We, young students, were shocked by the news about the brutality of the cruel apartheid system on the other side of the globe. We learned about the courageous political witness of the black churches. And we tried to get a hold of theological reflections from that context; listening to Allan Boesak's "Apartheid is a Heresy" at the German *Kirchentag* (nationwide church congress), reading about the need for solidarity and a "confessing church" against the injustice by C.F. Beyers Naudé, meditating on the biblical reflections of *Hope and Suffering* by Desmond Mpilo Tutu. It allowed us to understand that Dietrich Bonhoeffer's call for the church "not merely bandaging those under the wheel, but in attacking the spokes of the wheel itself" was not simply a dictum of a long-gone past, but valid in the "here and now" of that time. Investigating the role of our own context in Germany, and the Global North in general, we started to organise demonstrations on the streets of Heidelberg and approached our own churches to speak up.

For me personally, these events led to a self-critical examination of my own tradition of a "Historic Peace Church" (Mennonites). I had been raised in a Christian faith that is strongly informed by blessings and commandments of the Sermon on the Mount. Essential for following Jesus is a clear and unshakeable position on non-violence, whatever the cost. The witness of many martyrs in our tradition had been communicated well. Yet, confronted with the screaming injustice in South Africa, I began to question who has the right to ask for absolute non-violent actions to stop the injustice. Ever since, I have continued to reflect theologically, ethically and ecumenically on these questions; the responsibility of the global Body of Christ and a credible witness to peace *and* justice in situations of oppression, discrimination and suffering. Without the companionship of friends from South Africa, I would not be who I am today, as a theologian, as a human being. And here, the personal encounters with Desmond Tutu are clearly outstanding. Let me share three examples.

A charismatic prophet

It was the German Protestant *Kirchentag*, 2007 in Cologne. I was part of a commission whose responsibility was to organise a whole day on "Overcoming Violence". The World Council of Churches had announced the years of 2001–2010 as a "Decade to Overcome Violence: Churches seeking Reconciliation and Peace", and the churches in Germany had become quite active players in it, locally as well as globally. Every day at a *Kirchentag* opened with one hour of Bible study, and we wanted to invite a real prophet of peace and justice to lead us into this day. It did not take long to agree on the name of Desmond Tutu. We were thrilled when we heard that he had accepted our invitation. It was my role to be in touch with him, to instruct him, to guide him – which turned out to

---

[1] Rev. Dr Fernando Enns was born in 1964 in Curitiba, Brazil. Professor for (peace-) theology and ethics at Vrije Universiteit Amsterdam (The Netherlands) and director of the Amsterdam Centre for Religion and Peace & Justice Studies; and professor at the Protestant Faculty of the University of Hamburg (Germany) and director of the Center for Peace-Church Theology. Member of the Central Committee of the World Council of Churches, co-moderator of the International Reference Group on the ecumenical "Pilgrimage of Justice and Peace". Vice-chair of the Association of Mennonite Congregations in Germany.

be an impossible task. I did not get responses to my emails, nor did I ever get him on the phone. Yet, his secretary assured me that Tutu would be present. That was all I could rely on.

The day in Cologne came, everything was accurately planned – in a very "German" way. Every single minute of the whole day was scheduled in our script. The hall was packed with 5,000 people. We were all quite nervous. The program started with music, and then – at the last minute – Desmond Tutu arrived, quite relaxed. On top, a huge choir from South Africa flocked in and occupied the front seats of the auditorium. Where did they come from? Well, time for improvisation. Tutu was placed at my side – after all, everyone thought that I had "instructed" him. He greeted me in the best spirit, providing a feeling of longstanding friendship. As the choir from South Africa started to sing for the Bishop (which was not part of our script), Tutu leaned towards me, whispering: "What am I going to speak about today?" At this moment, I really became nervous. So, carefully yet insistently I tried to provide some general ideas, about the WCC, the Decade to Overcome Violence, suggesting that he should speak about the truth and reconciliation process in South Africa, maybe combined with some biblical wisdom, and so on. After a few minutes of listening, he gently touched my arm to interrupt me, looked into my eyes with a gracious smile on his face, asking: "Are you trying to tell me what to say, young man?" – I was lost for words.

Tutu approached the stage; he did not need any further introduction. Those 5,000 people were here to listen to this "prophet". And then he gave the most inspiring speech, theologically sound, including political analysis, interpreting Scripture, and empowering in every regard to stand up against injustice and violence, wherever it may occur. Since he would illustrate all that wisdom by sharing stories of personal experience, the hour went by too quickly. When he was about to leave the stage, everyone was on their feet, cheering, blessing each other, and the choir was praising God. With a great brotherly hug and a trusting look in his eyes, we departed. No further words needed to be exchanged. The charismatic spirit stayed with us during the entire day, and beyond.

Authentic piety

December came, in that same year in 2007. In a Hamburg newspaper, I read about some award that Desmond Tutu was about to receive in the city where I now lived. What an opportunity, I thought, so I got on the phone to South Africa in order to see if Tutu was willing to accept an invitation to speak at the Hamburg University – since he would be in town anyway. I also got in touch with our friends, the Potters, who lived in Lübeck at the time (some 50 km from Hamburg). I knew that Bishop Bärbel Wartenberg-Potter was always ready to organise some meaningful ecumenical encounters at short notice. Again, long-distance communication to South Africa was not easy, but when I mentioned the possibility of organising a personal meeting with former WCC general secretary Philip Potter (1972–1984), Tutu came back with a clear proposal: "Please, no public event. Yet, it would be wonderful if we could meet privately, just to talk, the Potters, you and me" – not exactly what I had hoped for initially, but what a great opportunity!

Together with the Potters and my wife Renate, we arrived at Tutu's hotel in Hamburg. Somehow, the press had taken notice of the private meeting. So, the first thing to do was to shoot some pictures as we were welcomed in his hotel room. After a few minutes, Tutu basically told the press to leave, and we sat down at the table. Tea was prepared. I felt so honoured to have the privilege to be present as these ecumenical giants were meeting privately, eager to listen to what they would share. To my surprise, the first thing Tutu did was invite us to a prayer. A long, calm and thankful prayer followed, creating a spiritual space and a sense of the special gift that we could meet here and now.

After that, Desmond and Philip shared some analysis of the current political situation in different parts of the world, every now and then recalling some common struggles of the past. Tears were shared, incredible loud laughter was heard. To this day, I feel so blessed that I was privileged to sit at their feet and listen. I had not imagined the pain these two black leaders of the global church had shared in the past, I had not been aware of their intelligence in shared political strategy, driven by theological, ethical reflection. Some of it might never be told in public. Here, I realised new dimensions of ecumenical companionship.

When the hour came, Tutu invited us to pray again. His words were full of trust in God, full of faith in the power of the Holy Spirit, full of hope in the church, full of thanks for friendship. After the prayer, not many words were left to say. Hugging, deep looks into each other's eyes, mutual blessings. The presence of Christ was felt in this very moment.

Ever since this impressive encounter, I have felt the courage to open and close meetings with prayer myself. One has to understand that in Western Europe's secularised settings, this is not self-given at all. And sometimes, people seem to be too shy to pray. It simply seems "inappropriate". Yet, here I witnessed the very authentic, natural and self-evident framing of a personal encounter with prayer, and how it affected all present; turning together to God, for thanksgiving as well as for guidance.

Critical humour

An encounter some ten years later at the Vrije Universiteit Amsterdam, in the Netherlands. Having become a professor at the wonderfully diverse Faculty of Religion and Theology, I was invited to be one of the opponents during a PhD-defence ceremony. My colleague, Eddy van der Borght – holding the "Desmond Tutu Chair" at our faculty – had managed to get Desmond Tutu to be part of the ceremony, since the PhD candidate was a scholar from South Africa himself, promoted by the close relationship to South African universities. We were all thrilled that Tutu would be with us this morning.

As it is the usual practice, the public defence of a PhD is a very festive moment in the life of our university, following a strict traditional protocol – to a degree you would not expect in this mainly "casual" culture. The professors meet in a specially designated room in full gowns and barrets to get prepared. We are introduced to each other, get further instructions of how to behave during the upcoming "liturgy" in the huge Aula, and we read a passage from Scripture. After that we proceed two by two down the centre aisle, this day led by Archbishop Tutu and our Dean – in full silence, while the audience rises respectfully. During the hour of defence, various scripted phrases need to be spoken and heard. The cloud of professors then retires for deliberations, only to appear again in full glory in the Aula to announce the results – it is quite theatrical, entertaining, stiff and tense.

Tutu was following the protocol step by step, until the moment came that we professors would exit the centre aisle for the last time. I could not help but get the impression all the way through that he did not feel comfortable in this liturgical corset, which basically leaves no room for improvising. As we proceeded, suddenly, there was very loud laughter from the Bishop. I hear him saying something like "I like this", "You are really serious about this, aren't you!?" I do not remember the exact words, but I do remember that there was a moment of shocked silence among everyone present, then looking at each other. The audience, the cohort of professors and the PhD candidate all burst into laughter. And that laughter became more and more joyful as we were leaving the Aula.

What happened? My interpretation is that Tutu was very much aware of what he was doing. I believe that he had been waiting for a moment to express some humanity in the middle of the whole stiff setting, to wink an eye in order to relativise the importance of traditional protocol that seems to illustrate hierarchy, privilege and the self-celebration of academic supremacy. He needed to comment! But how? It is his well-known, brilliant humour that allowed him to question – not what we were doing here, but *how* we did it. The bursting laughter was a risky, ironic move, which broke the ice and allowed all of us to laugh about ourselves. I have experienced this as very liberating, becoming aware of the fact that, even if we follow tradition closely, we need to allow ourselves to show vulnerability, insecurity, excitement, joy, satisfaction – to be human, after all.

I believe that Desmond Tutu is one of the few people on this planet who has mastered the art of critical humour in a way that no one feels offended, yet we all become aware of who we are after all: vulnerable human beings in search of some acknowledgement.

I will be ever grateful for these and more encounters with Desmond Tutu. I feel privileged to have witnessed his charisma, his authentic piety and his splendid humour. Putting these personal experiences next to the enormous political and ecumenical achievements for building peace with justice, far beyond South Africa, I bow my head before this man, ever thankful for the many gifts God has granted to this companion in faith – to serve in so many regards.

Philip Potter, Bärbel Wartenberg-Potter, Desmond Tutu –
in a hotel room in Hamburg, Germany, December 2007.

31. HUMOUR IN TIMES OF DANGER:
A SHORT REFLECTION ON TUTU AND DEFUSED TENSIONS

Angela Mai[1]

Between October 1990 and July 1991, I was working with Beyers Naudé in Johannesburg. On 26 January 1991 I accompanied him to a mass funeral in Sebokeng. Archbishop Tutu spoke at this funeral.

Thirty-nine people were to be buried. They were all victims of an attack on a night vigil some weeks before. The vigil had been for a young ANC activist, Chris Nangalembe, who was to have been buried the next day.

The background to this terrible tragedy lay in the chaos, confusion and violence that reigned in the township. A criminal gang had been active in Boipatong for some time, and the ANC-aligned youth had decided to try and curb their activities. This resulted in the gang approaching young people thought to be close to Inkatha, the rival group to the ANC, secretly supported by the apartheid government. Although some alliances were clear, often suspicion, hearsay and fear reigned and resulted in senseless bloodshed.

There were witnesses to Chris Nangalembe having been forced by a group of men into their car and driven away. These men were known to be aligned to the criminal gang or to Inkatha. Nangalembe's body was found the next morning at a rubbish dump. He had been throttled.

His funeral was planned for 13 January and the traditional vigil was planned for the night before. As the date drew near there were more and more rumours that the vigil would be attacked. Nangalembe's brother therefore went to the police and asked for protection to be given to the mourners. This was promised but the next evening when the wake was attacked by men in cars who shot indiscriminately into the group and threw hand grenades into the house, the police were nowhere to be seen. 39 people, men, women and children, were killed.

When we arrived at the cemetery there was a massive crowd assembled. Our car drove at walking pace through the people to the platform where a seat was reserved for Beyers. From there we had a view over the vast assembly and behind them, standing at regular intervals, their guns slung over their shoulders and held at the ready, a large police force.

The crowd was restless, but when Tutu started to speak there was silence, his statements only punctuated by affirmative exclamations. And then we heard a drone in the air and every head turned upwards and watched the approach of a police helicopter.

It flew low over the crowd, and I held my breath, feeling "This is too much. It is a provocation." A rumble ran through the crowd, a kind of muted growl. The appearance of the power which enabled, even stimulated and benefited from the violence in the townships, hovering threateningly above the people mourning the victims seemed a cold-blooded demonstration of their dominance and threatened to unleash an uncontrollable fury. A cold shudder ran through me.

And then I saw Tutu throw his arms into the air and start waving to the pilot of the helicopter. "Ah", he called through the microphone, "there are our friends, the police. Let us wave to them! Hallo, police, hallo, hallo!" For a long moment it was still and then laughter broke out which became a crescendo roar of mockery, as the crowd raised their arms and waved to the pilot.

Tutu had turned the collective fury into collective derision. The rejection of the state and its servants was stated, resistance confirmed, but violence had been avoided and the mourners protected from further calamity. The helicopter turned and flew off, Tutu lowered his voice, I think he started to pray, and he finished his speech in a calm and collected atmosphere.

---

[1] Angela Mai lives in Bavaria, where she uses her range of experiences from South Africa, in her work engagements with refugees.

Postskriptum

At the end of the ceremony, Tutu again took the microphone. The ceremony had been long; many people had brought drinks or food with them. The ground lay littered with discarded tins and wrappings. In his same easy, authoritative but humorous style he called on everyone to take their rubbish with them. I do not remember his exact words, but the gist was: "Let us leave everything tidy. We don't want people thinking we don't know how to behave." And everyone bent down and picked up what lay on the ground.

32. "That Cheeky Boy" –
Personal Reflections on the Arch, Peacebuilding and Reconciliation

Paul Oestreicher[1]

No Englishman has done more for the liberation of South Africa than Trevor Huddleston. Without Father Huddleston's profound influence on young Desmond, he might never have made his way to the priesthood. Never to be forgotten was this white priest raising his hat to Desmond's mother. Apartheid be damned, was the revolutionary message of this simple act of respect. When young Mpilo, that's what his aunt called him, was ill with TB, Father Trevor came to visit him.

It was Father Trevor who, around 1971, suggested I should visit a South African priest and his family living near me in South London. So, I went to see the Tutus. It was a refreshing experience. Desmond and Leah's children were about the same age as ours. While we talked, the children played together. Since the Sharpeville massacre in 1960 and reading Father Trevor's *Naught for your Comfort*, I had been committed to the anti-apartheid cause. I was therefore full of questions for Mpilo. I still had a lot more to learn.

There was, however, not much time to deepen our friendship. Desmond was mostly away travelling in his role as the Africa secretary of the World Council of Churches' Theological Education Fund. This was his ideal introduction to the African continent, long before he could see himself as president of the All Africa Conference of Churches. Nor did I foresee in this evidently bright fellow priest the Tutu that the world now reveres.

Soon after that first meeting, John V. Taylor, general secretary of the Church Mission Society and one of the very few prophetic 20th-century theologians of the Church of England, was to be made Bishop of Winchester. He and his family lived in my parish. We were good friends. At his consecration in Westminster Abbey, John Taylor had chosen Desmond to be the preacher. On that day, I woke up to the fact that it takes a prophet to know a prophet.

Here, I encountered Desmond as an evangelist and theologian at the very heart of the Anglican establishment. I began to see in my new friend a truly remarkable personality. He was rather solemn on that day, with his exuberant charisma kept in reserve. Westminster Abbey can do that to people, even to Mpilo.

I had been working for the British Council of Churches' Division of International Affairs, and also chairing Amnesty International UK. Visits to South Africa were therefore inescapable, even though the Bureau of State Security (BOSS) tried, but failed, to stop me. Desmond's paths and mine inevitably crossed, though we seldom met in person. However, on one human rights mission, Desmond and Leah were kind enough to invite me to stay over at their home in Orlando. Those two days still feel to me like yesterday; life with the Tutus on their home ground. Mpilo was up at five, pounding the neighbourhood roads to keep fit. There followed the essential priest, breaking bread, on that day as every day, celebrating the Eucharist, but without the ecclesiastical trappings. The liturgy had long been internalised, moving swiftly, almost silently until the form gave way to spontaneity, to intercession, to prayer for a suffering world to be loved. That took a lot of time, moving from the local and personal to the global and universal, taking to God everything that mattered on that day. I was sharing an intimate conversation around the world that Desmond was serving and would go on serving for as long as God allows. From what does Desmond draw his strength? I have no doubt:

---

[1] Canon Dr Paul Oestreicher, with his parents, fled from Nazi Germany to New Zealand in 1939. An Anglican priest and Quaker, he studied political science and German literature. Living in England and Germany and working for peace and human rights, he was primarily committed to the churches in communist Eastern Europe and apartheid South Africa. Desmond Tutu wrote the foreword to his German-language pastoral reflections *Aufs Kreuz Gelegt*.

from a disciplined life of prayer. He often surprises others by spontaneously turning to prayer, with and for them, sometimes joyfully, at others tearfully.

It was some moons later, just as apartheid was beginning to disintegrate, that I next visited the Archbishop of Cape Town at Bishopscourt, an aftermath of Empire, now living grandly and technically illegally in a white suburb. That "cheeky boy" had broken every barrier. Those who loved him and those who hated him could describe him with opposite intent. He could live with that. Sometimes he signed himself, tongue in cheek and not without pride, simply as "boy". Through generations every black man had been put down as simply that.

In Desmond's study he turned on the television news. Together, we watched the demise of the East German Communist regime. As one system tumbled, another around us was tumbling. Desmond was glad. True, communists had helped the ANC. Tutu respected that, but their vision for the future was not his. Their global propaganda never fooled him.

The path to democracy was not a smooth one. One of the biggest obstacles was the ongoing violent conflict between the ANC and Chief Mangosuthu Gatsha Buthelezi's Inkatha Freedom Party. The Archbishop was doing all in his power to end the conflict. Could Buthelezi be brought in from the cold, to share in the transitional negotiations for a new South Africa?

Tutu had heard that Buthelezi knew and trusted me. I had hosted him, a devout Anglican, at the Southwark Diocesan Retreat House when he came to London to raise money for a Zulu newspaper. Bishop Michael Nuttall invited me and, at the Archbishop's request, asked me to join those trying to persuade the Zulu chief to end the bloody conflict and to participate in the 1994 elections for South Africa's first democratic government. White reactionary forces were at work behind the scenes to prevent that from happening.

In his private plane, I flew twice to the chief's headquarters in Ulundi. It took far more than my long conversations with the Zulu chief to turn the tide, to make him understand that to stand out alone as head of a Zulu state was neither in South Africa's nor in his own interest. The Zulu chief was a complex character, charming, willing to listen and ambitious. Simply to define him as "Margaret Thatcher's favourite black" did him less than justice. Good sense did finally prevail. The prospect of a place at the top table of a united South Africa helped. The last piece in this complex jigsaw was, I believe, put in place by the Nigerian foreign minister. That's a story for historians to get right. Thanks to "the Arch", I was privileged to play a small role in it.

This is no place for me to evaluate the impact of Tutu's ministry in South Africa and worldwide. His progress from celebrity to global icon and into old age as the wisest of the wise, is uniquely well known, as it deserves to be. He believes that of himself, and enjoys his fame unreservedly, with amazing good humour. The interior spiritual price he pays, God alone knows. Disrespect, when he meets it, hurts him deeply. Like being sidelined at the funeral of his friend Mandela. His long struggle with prostate cancer is, like the man himself, public property.

In his global ministry there is, in my view, one insight that is, among Christian leaders, probably unique. He is not afraid – as practically all others are – to speak the truth about the Israeli–Palestinian conflict. Given the shameful Christian anti-Jewish record, culminating in the Holocaust, the fear of being thought anti-Semitic has silenced, indeed gagged, most of world Christendom, and left the oppressed Palestinian people, both Muslim and Christian, without effective spiritual advocates. Tutu has lived and studied in Jerusalem, he has seen the reality and has, as always, spoken out. "I know apartheid when I see it". Who else compares? No churchman, but ex-president of the USA Jimmy Carter.

My last personal meeting with Mpilo was when John Petty, Dean of Coventry Cathedral and I, as Coventry's director of the Centre for International Reconciliation, hosted him. The word reconciliation almost defines him. (Add to that, compassion and forgiveness). This cathedral, unlike Westminster Abbey, brought out the exuberant Tutu that the world has come to celebrate and enjoy. I still see him dancing down the aisle to Sydney Carter's theologically challenging "Lord of the Dance". Briefly, a dancing congregation forgot that they were English. Sadly, Mpilo could no longer hold hands with his like-minded poet and radical fellow Christian, Sydney Carter. Death is no stranger.

On Coventry Cathedral's patronal festival, the Feast of the Archangel Michael, who expelled evil from heaven as Mpilo continues to fight it on earth, I shall, God willing, turn ninety. As will, nine days later, also God willing, Desmond Mpilo Tutu, with his hundred or so well-deserved honorary doctorates. He occasionally called me his elder brother. Older, I cannot deny, but most certainly not wiser.

I am writing these words on Easter Sunday. Mpilo, in Yiddish, a *Mensch*, a true human being, spoke of his people as the rainbow nation, and expressed in himself the boundless joy of the Resurrection of his Jewish friend, Jesus of Nazareth.

33. "Opposing Apartheid and Working for Reconciliation" (A Letter to Archbishop Emeritus Desmond Tutu)

Roger Williamson[1]

Dear Archbishop,

I know your close friends refer to you as "the Arch", but English Anglican deference and British civil service training inhibit me from doing so. Anyway, let's jump straight in with birthday greetings (and thanks to the editors for this invitation to honour you on your 90th birthday).

I first encountered your work when I was doing my PhD on German church reactions to the World Council of Churches' Programme to Combat Racism. You were an early proponent of black theology and African theology. Your letter to Prime Minister John Vorster warning of the danger of violence engulfing the country looked grimly prophetic when the police started killing school children in Soweto in June 1976. I was reminded of that letter when I went to the memorial service at which you spoke in St Martin's-in-the-Fields some years later. The statue depicting Hector Pieterson, the thirteen-year-old who was the first to be killed, was installed in the London church on that occasion. I remember watching as you danced down the aisle in the not-so-formal clerical line-up, which led me to coin the technical ecclesiastical term "episco-disco" to commemorate your processing style. Where does this irrepressible hope and exuberant joy come from? Not because your life was easy – I think those of us not living under a repressive regime can hardly begin to imagine what it is like to live with such constant tension and danger.

In 1978, after a spell as Bishop of Lesotho, you were made general secretary of the South African Council of Churches (SACC). After the banning of the Christian Institute and the Black Consciousness organisations, the SACC increasingly took on, under your leadership, the role of "voice of the voiceless".

From that time, I remember, with gratitude, your kind words to me as a young staff member of the British Council of Churches, affirming the importance of our work against torture. That was in the early 1980s at a meeting which you addressed of the British Council of Churches and we had a private word on the margins. In your address, you told the story of the little girl, displaced in one of the "Homelands" or Bantustans in 1979, who described having to borrow food, or, if there was no food, drink water to suppress her appetite. The human cost of the massive project of displacing more than 3 million people was poignantly illustrated. You used this story with your government, in public addresses at home and abroad, to highlight the inhumanity of the apartheid system.

The SACC had a key role at this time – it had a strong, committed staff and international financial support, so it could support social projects, including families of detainees, as well as engaging in policy debate. It was an inspiration to me to see a sister Council of Churches providing an example of what churches can do to defend the poor.

From the early 1980s onwards, the SACC faced escalating attempts by the government to muzzle its activities, including the Eloff Commission into its finances (1982), the bombing of its headquarters in 1988 and the attempted murder by poisoning of General Secretary Frank Chikane in

[1] Dr Roger Williamson worked with the British Council of Churches (1978–86), was director, then research director of the Life & Peace Institute, Uppsala (1986–92). He worked for the Church of England Board for Social Responsibility and Christian Aid in the 1990s. From 1999–2010, he organised nearly seventy international conferences for the UK Foreign and Commonwealth Office through Wilton Park. After formal retirement, he was a visiting fellow at the Institute of Development Studies at the University of Sussex and UNU-WIDER, Helsinki. He was active in UK efforts to help establish the Tutu Professorship at the University of the Western Cape.

1989.[2] The role of the security forces in the last two incidents was fully brought to light by the Truth and Reconciliation Commission and later, confirming widely held suspicions.

I also remember, from 1983, the expectation and then joy which we felt when you appeared at the midnight prayer vigil during the World Council of Churches' Assembly in Vancouver. Until the last minute it was unclear whether the South African government would let you travel – an anxiety with which you were familiar.

In August 1983, the United Democratic Front was launched – of which you were a patron. To many of us outside the country, the sudden emergence of a coalition of over 600 community groups came as a surprising confirmation of the strength of internal resistance to apartheid.

The award of the Nobel Peace Prize in 1984 was well deserved and the higher international profile probably gave you some measure of protection. It was an indication of the bizarre injustice of apartheid that you were already an archbishop and a Nobel Prize laureate before you could vote in your own country. I think it was both typical and great that you took the opportunity of the Nobel acceptance speech to denounce apartheid as an "evil system".[3]

Similarly, in the second half of the 1980s, you used your access to the United Nations and such world leaders as Ronald Reagan and Margaret Thatcher to call for economic sanctions as the only realistic alternative to prolonged violence and repression.

Thatcher and Reagan resisted your arguments, but international pressure on South Africa was building. From that period also comes your meeting with President Botha (1988) when you were treated to the full finger-wagging, intimidatory and bad-tempered performance with which John Allen begins his authorised biography of you.[4] The churches had engaged in a campaign of civil disobedience, and you provided leadership, along with the mayor and civil society leaders such as Allan Boesak, for the peaceful march through the centre of Cape Town in September 1989.

When F.W. de Klerk took over running the country, no one expected such dramatic change. His announcement of the unbanning of the African National Congress (ANC), Pan Africanist Congress (PAC) and South African Communist Party (SACP), led to the release of Nelson Mandela – who chose to spend his first night of freedom at your residence, Bishopscourt.

I have always been amazed at the way in which you have preached at big political funerals – from that of Steve Biko in 1977 to that of Chris Hani in 1993. At the former, you drew parallels between Biko and Jesus – "We, too, like the disciples of Jesus, have been stunned by the death of another young man in his thirties. A young man completely dedicated to the pursuit of justice and righteousness, of peace and reconciliation."[5]

Hani was a popular ANC military leader, whose funeral drew a huge crowd. You used this occasion to assure people that victory was coming. Your sermon, and then not-yet-president Mandela's calming address on television, helped to ensure that Hani's assassination did not de-rail the delicate pre-election negotiations.[6]

After the ANC's landslide election victory, it was fitting that President Mandela should write the foreword to the collection of your public statements from the 1976–94 period, *The Rainbow People of God.* One can only echo his words: "The negotiations process and South Africa's first democratic

---

[2] Khotso House also housed the offices of the United Democratic Front. On his poisoning, see: Frank Chikane, *The Things that Could Not be Said: From A(IDS) to Z(imbabwe).* Johannesburg: Picador Africa (2013), 178-206.

[3] Desmond Tutu, "'Apartheid's 'Final Solution'; Nobel Lecture (1984)," in: Desmond Tutu, *The Rainbow People of God: South Africa's Victory over Apartheid.* London: Doubleday (1994), 83-92. Quote from 88.

[4] John Allen, *Rabble-Rouser for Peace: The Authorised Biography of Desmond Tutu.* New York: Simon & Schuster (2006), 3-7. This is the single most valuable source for dates and biographical information on the subject.

[5] Desmond Tutu, "Oh God, How Long Can We Go On (1977)", in Tutu, *Rainbow People of God,* 15-21. Quote from 19.

[6] The sermon text can be found as: Desmond Tutu, "His Death is our Victory (1993)", in Tutu, *Rainbow People of God,* 244-248.

elections in April 1994 have vindicated the struggles and sacrifices of peace-loving South Africans, among whom Archbishop Tutu will remain an eminent example."[7]

Having retired as Archbishop of Cape Town, you must have been looking forward to retirement or at least a less pressured context for your life of deep spirituality, but it was not to be.

In the pre-election negotiations, the Afrikaners were concerned about the danger of a witch hunt. Many others were alarmed at the prospect of perpetrators literally "getting away with murder". The deal which was reached between the Nationalist government and the ANC was amnesty in return for full disclosure. In your book on the Truth and Reconciliation Commission (TRC), *No Future without Forgiveness*, you refer to this as steering the difficult path between "Nuremberg or national amnesia".[8]

The scope of the commission was from 1960–94, from the Sharpeville massacre to the election, and the focus was on killing, torture, abduction or severe ill-treatment. Your commission made some important choices – such as holding the hearings in public in different parts of the country and allowing access to the media in different South African languages.

Above all, I think the focus on the victims – and the way in which you set the tone when chairing for the victims and their family members to feel safe enough to recount their experiences – was exemplary. You have consistently reached out to those who suffer and been prepared to "weep with those who weep" (Romans 12:15 [NRSV]). Even reading accounts of the hearings such as your *No Future without Forgiveness* or Martin Meredith's *Coming to Terms* is gruelling enough.[9] To actually hear these accounts of state agents barbecuing victims, of murder on a mass scale, of routine torture and of rape and sexual violence, must have been almost overwhelming for you and your fellow commissioners, and others including the interpreters. The sheer scale – with 21,000 victims who testified (over 2,000 of whom spoke at the hearings) between 1996–8 – gives an idea of the extent of the repression and violence. That so many came forward to testify speaks volumes about the trust accorded to your efforts.

A fundamental choice had already been made in the way that the commission was established; namely, that mass trials of perpetrators would not take place. There were compelling arguments – mass trials would paralyse the legal system, the cost would have been prohibitive, if the mass trials option had been adopted, alleged perpetrators would use every means to avoid disclosure.[10] More importantly, it is quite possible that the elections would not have taken place without the compromise of amnesty for full disclosure.

It seems to me that the strength of the approach taken by the TRC is twofold. It provided a public forum for the victims to be heard and enabled a fuller picture of the major violations of human rights than was ever available before. The picture would have been more complete if the security forces had not destroyed massive quantities of documentation. Even so, the indictment of the apartheid system, and the description of the repressive means used to keep it in place, are damning. Tens of thousands of people were kept under detention without trial. Torture was routine and deaths in detention frequent. The security forces used bombing, abductions and murder to attack the opposition. Much of this was known beforehand; but what is different about the TRC report is that it is also based on testimony from perpetrators as well as victims and it is an official report. Meredith's book, *Coming to Terms*, draws extensively on the TRC report to show how the political decision-making, the security architecture and the operational level of hit squads fitted together in the apartheid system. The key committee was the State Security Council (SSC), chaired by the president, which co-ordinated military and police responses to opposition to apartheid.[11]

---

[7] Nelson Mandela, "Foreword", in Tutu, *Rainbow People of God*, xiii-xiv. Quote from xiv.

[8] Desmond Tutu, *No Future without Forgiveness*. London: Rider (1999), 10-36.

[9] Tutu, *No Future without Forgiveness*; Meredith, *Coming to Terms: South Africa's Search for Truth*. Oxford: Public Affairs (1999). I have drawn on the latter extensively for this piece. The full TRC report can be accessed at: https://www.justice.gov.za/trc/report/ (accessed 20 April 2021).

[10] As the TRC Report argues. See Meredith, *Coming to Terms*, 321-2.

[11] Meredith, *Coming to Terms*. See 173-177 on the SSC.

Under P.W. Botha, South Africa destabilised neighbouring countries such as Mozambique and Angola and attacked ANC bases in the front-line states. Through the TRC, a fuller account emerged of some of the most notorious groups of killers. To give just one example, Eugene de Kock ("Prime Evil") commanded the Vlakplaas farm where many of the killers were stationed and trained. De Kock himself was involved in over seventy killings in South Africa and neighbouring states.[12]

State collusion with the Inkatha Freedom Party in the "Third Force" killings in KwaZulu-Natal was already suspected before the 1994 election. The violence between Inkatha and the ANC–UDF supporters could have derailed the plans for political transition.

What could the report of your commission do to document and clarify the extent of the violations? How far up the chain of command did the orders come from? It is not necessary to rehearse all the findings of the TRC report – Meredith's *Coming to Terms* provides an accessible summary.[13]

One of the most important achievements of the TRC process and report is, in my view, that the apartheid system is officially and comprehensively discredited. As you put it, no one now can plausibly say: "We did not know".[14]

You really went the extra mile to try to get the senior politicians to admit responsibility. Two former presidents adopted different strategies – P.W. Botha refused to cooperate despite the commission's best efforts and was eventually taken to court. F.W. de Klerk blamed subordinates acting out of line, not government policy, for the many gross violations of human rights and murders. The commission report is rightly careful not to go beyond the evidence in allocating blame, particularly in dealing with the state presidents. Certainly a chance was missed by F.W. de Klerk when he first made and then substantially qualified his apology for apartheid – your verdict on him is clear: "He was incapable of seeing apartheid for what it was – intrinsically evil."[15]

There is much more that could be said – on the verdicts on each of the presidents; the confessions by former government ministers; the major share of the blame accorded to the apartheid government's Inkatha allies for the killings in KwaZulu-Natal, but the ANC–UDF also committed gross violations of human rights, according to the TRC report. The report agreed with the United Nations: apartheid was a "crime against humanity". Opposing it was a just cause – but not all actions taken by the ANC were justified. The ANC was criticised in the report for a number of its actions. The PAC was also criticised. It was clear too that the long hearing of Winnie Madikizela-Mandela and the abductions and murders by the Mandela United Football Club was a painful episode for you and the wider black community.

It must have been a huge blow for you and all associated with the commission when, just before the official submission of the 2,700-page, five-volume report, the ANC sought to block publication by going to court.[16] They had previously tried to get the findings of the commission changed and, in a written submission, accused the TRC of "criminalizing" the struggle to defeat apartheid.[17] The bid failed. President Mandela accepted the report. Above all, President Mandela's later verdict is worth citing: "I am President of the country … I have set up the TRC. They have done not a perfect but a remarkable job and I approved everything they did."[18]

For you and your colleagues, it was a marathon of empathy and compassion. A fuller account would have given detailed examples of the searing testimony, the structures of repression, the findings on the former government and the liberation movements.

---

[12] Meredith, *Coming to Terms*, 48. See also 26-54.

[13] Meredith, *Coming to Terms,* 287-307.

[14] Tutu, *No Future without Forgiveness*, 171-205.

[15] Tutu, *No Future without Forgiveness*, 202-3. Quote from 203.

[16] Two further volumes concluding the work were submitted to President Mbeki in 2003.

[17] Meredith, *Coming to Terms*, 302.

[18] As told to his biographer in January 1999. Anthony Sampson, *Mandela: The Authorised Biography.* London: HarperCollins (2011, first published 1999), 532.

However, I will leave your story here, with the presentation of the TRC report in 1998. But as a self-styled deferential Anglican, it feels fitting to leave you the last word. As you said over twenty years ago:

> In South Africa, the whole process of reconciliation has been placed in very considerable jeopardy by the enormous disparities between the rich, mainly the whites, and the poor, mainly the blacks. The huge gap between the haves and the have-nots, which was largely created and maintained by racism and apartheid, poses the greatest threat to reconciliation and stability in our country. The rich provided the class from which the perpetrators and beneficiaries of apartheid came and the poor produced the bulk of the victims. That is why I have exhorted whites to be keen to see transformation taking place in the lot of blacks. For unless houses replace the hovels and shacks in which most blacks live: unless blacks gain access to clean water, affordable health care, decent education, good jobs and a safe environment – all things which the vast majority of whites have taken for granted for so long – we can kiss goodbye to reconciliation.[19]

Of course, this is not your "last word". Since then your "divine discontent" and the gap between your vision of "the Rainbow People of God" and the often tragic reality of our world and your South African home have provoked you into public statements on many issues, including developments in South Africa. A flavour of their diversity and scope is given in the collection *God is Not a Christian*.[20] But that, as they say, is another story – and there are many others better placed to tell it.

You have inspired us with your courage in looking at the dark places of our world and still having hope. I thank you for your challenge, encouragement and testimony, and greet you, Leah and your family on your 90th birthday!

---

[19] Tutu, *No Future without Forgiveness*, 221.
[20] Desmond Tutu, *God is Not a Christian: Speaking Truth in Times of Crisis*. London: Rider (2011).

2.2. *Ubuntu*, African Theology and Leadership

34. *UBUNTU* AND *IMAGO DEI*

Nontombi Tutu[1]

Many years ago I was asked to put together a collection of my father's speeches and sayings for publication as *The Words of Desmond Tutu*. In putting the collection together I was also asked to write a foreword. In that foreword I wrote that it was impossible to understand Desmond Tutu divorced from his Christian faith. What I didn't say then, and I wish I had, is that one could not try and understand Desmond Tutu unless you recognised how fundamental his faith and his African identity are to who he is, and how he has lived. So I am especially thankful for the opportunity to be a part of this volume as it offers me a chance to correct that lapse in my earlier writing.

It was always important for my father that we know that our faith was not something that corrected our Africanness. That is, our being African was not something that needed to be excused by God. It would have been very easy to believe that becoming Christian meant doing away with parts of our African identity because that is what many of the missionaries taught. In order to be good Christians we had to turn our backs on a large part of our culture because, according to the church and the colonial governments, one could not be a good Christian and still hold on to a full African identity. Making this claim, as my father and other Christians on the African continent and the countries of Asia and Latin America did, that God did not need us to try and become Western in order to be fully Christian was a significant contention. This perspective was very important in our faith lessons because of the reality in which Christianity was most often lived in apartheid South Africa. For example we were taught that Christian names had to be European names. Both in church and in school and workplaces we were required to have an official name that could not be African. It was as though God would not be able to recognise us as Her children if we were called Nontombi, Kelebogile, Nomthandazo or any of the other beautiful, meaningful African names!!! Another example is the way in which we were taught to worship, particularly in the Anglican Church. The fact that we were discouraged from singing anything but hymns translated from the English hymnal *Hymns Ancient and Modern*, and that Christian singing had to be derived from European modes of worship, was further evidence of the split between our African and Christian identities. We were even schooled in the idea that instruments that did not have an origin in Europe, like the drums and the marimba, would not make a sound pleasing to the Lord. I remember my father saying words to this effect on many occasions: "They would have us believe that God created this whole continent of Africa then turned around and forgot all about the people and created order here. That not until white people came did we have a relationship with God. This is a lie." He would go on to tell the congregation or gathering that God did not make mistakes, that God made us African because God wanted us to be African, and God desired us to praise God as Africans.

He would even go further in his own life and in our lives as his family. The church frowned on the continuation of African traditional ways of carrying out funerals, weddings and other ceremonies. We would be told in church that to follow these traditions was going against Christian faith because those ceremonies, we were told, were about ancestor worship. We could not therefore carry out traditional ceremonies of mourning etc. and still be good Christians. Yet throughout our lives my father made it

---

[1] Nontombi Naomi Tutu, Associate Rector, All Saints Episcopal Church, Beverly Hills. My origin story is that Daddy was at seminary when I was born. A family friend, Valerie Leslie, actually got to see me before he did and her report was: "We just need to put glasses and a cassock on this one and she is you." I have grown up being that girl who looks so (sometimes it felt like too) much like her father. My parents tried to instil in us a pride in who we are and in our cultural identity, with *Ubuntu* being our guiding philosophy.

clear that the rites of passage that were a part of our culture were an important part of who we were in the world. Indeed, these rites were in fact a way in which our people connected our lives to the larger created order and therefore to God. Rather than being signs of being not fully Christian he taught us that the ways in which our people have historically marked significant life events were what tied us to the stories of our heritage and our faith.

I have titled this essay "*Ubuntu* and *Imago Dei*" because these two cultural and theological frameworks and the ideas, thoughts and principles that undergird them exemplify what my father tried to teach me about life, faith and the best ways of living. It is in these two concepts that my father's Christian faith and African identity are most clearly seen. I cannot start to describe how often we heard as children the call to be people with *Ubuntu*, or how often my dad reminded us that each person we encountered was the image of God and was worthy of respect and dignity for that very fact alone. When one of us would come home after a sports match bragging about how we scored the winning goal, or blocked the other team's attempt to score, he would say to us, "remember *umntu ngumntu ngabantu*". He always tried to make us aware of the fact that we could not have scored or blocked that goal without the other members of our team, that we were indebted to the support and work of the rest of the team for our achievement. When we would argue and fight, as siblings are wont to do, one of his favourite ways of trying to end such strife was to remind us of our actions in church. He would remind us how we would genuflect when the red light was lit in the sanctuary showing that the Blessed Sacrament was in the Tabernacle, and told us that in truth we should also genuflect to our siblings as they too were God bearers! Needless to say we were not convinced that the siblings who got on our nerves were worthy of being genuflected to. So, as you can imagine, there was very little (if any) genuflecting to one another, but the idea that all people were the image of God was central not only to disciplining us but to how he has lived his life.

It was always clear to him that the concept of *Ubuntu* was a companion piece to the centrality of *Imago Dei* in our Christian belief system. So in teaching us about the proper way to be in the world, my mother and father taught us that we are to look for God in all whom we encounter and to live our lives governed by *Ubuntu*. Both ideas teach that our connection to one another as human beings is of utmost importance to our culture on the one hand and our faith on the other. *Ubuntu* teaches us that the person to be most admired is the one who recognises the full humanity of every person with whom they come into contact, and therefore mistreating and demeaning others is actually an assault on your own humanity. In the Xhosa culture we come from and in most of the other Southern African cultures, someone who has *Ubuntu* is a person not only to be emulated and admired, but is also to be recognised as one who is fully human in the best meaning of that term. One cannot be fully human and refuse to acknowledge the humanity of others. So the person who does not have *Ubuntu* is actually to be pitied because they have cut themselves off from some aspect of their own humanity. This is also the measure of a true Christian, one who recognises the fully created image of God in others, and treats them with dignity and respect for that reason if for no other reason. We are all made in God's image and therefore we are all called to see God in each person we encounter, and to treat them accordingly. Clearly then, discrimination against people based on race, ethnicity, sexual orientation and gender identity is not just wrong, it is a sin. It is possibly the very worst sin that we can contemplate, because it is what leads to the abuse of some of God's children. But it is not just the physical violence that comes from discrimination that goes against God's plans for humankind. For my father it is the very act of behaving as though anyone is less than a child of God. That apartheid would make black people feel inferior, that homophobia makes our LGBTQIA sisters and brothers unable to live their full, free lives, that sexism denies women the opportunities to achieve in the way that men do: all of these forms of discrimination finally make children of God question their place in God's creation. That is the true sin, and it is that sin that both *Ubuntu* and the recognition of *Imago Dei* call out.

One of my father's favourite examples of someone who epitomises being truly Christian and one who shows *Ubuntu* in their interactions is the story of Bishop Malusi Mpumlwana. When he was still a young activist, my father spoke of him as one who so clearly lived his faith and Africanness in the most powerful way. In his interactions with fellow activists and other members of the community he was always one who treated others with utmost respect, listening to each person who approached him with full care and attention. Then he was arrested and tortured. When talking about the experience Bishop Mpumlwana speaks of realising that those who were torturing him had lost a sense of their own humanity. He says, "I realised that they needed us to help them reclaim their humanity." I am not sure that most of us would have the ability in that circumstance to be concerned about the humanity of those who are harming us. My father shared Bishop Mpumlwana's story over and over because he said it showed us how compassion for others is the central tenet of an identity that is both African and Christian. This living out a truly African sense of the Christian faith is what my father has always aspired to and, while it has won him accolades, it has also led him to choices that others, including his family, have questioned. I clearly remember many conversations at home regarding his willingness to meet with members of the apartheid government. We would have very heated discussions about why we thought it was a waste of time, and simply a way for the government to show the outside world that it was willing to meet with those critical of it, while doing nothing to end apartheid. His response to us was always that, whether they liked it or not, these were his brothers. They were fellow human beings made in God's image and he had the responsibility as one trying to live a life of faith to continue to reach out to them, in the hopes that their hearts and minds would be changed. We would ask him, how many times are you going to keep holding out hope for this, and put yourself in the way of looking like a fool. He would respond that he could not give up on anyone because he believed in the full humanity of everyone. As irritating as it was for us as young people, angry at the injustice of apartheid to hear his position, it made it clear to us that he did not simply give lip service to the lessons inherent in *Ubuntu* and *Imago Dei*, but that indeed for him what he said was how he tried to live.

Many of those who criticised my father for his actions and words during the anti-apartheid struggle saw him as a politician, pretending to be a priest. The truth is that he was simply trying to live as best he could the lessons he had learned as an African Christian. Those two identities are still the core identities and it is impossible to understand him if you do not acknowledge that. I hope that the lessons he and my mother tried to instil in me and my siblings, about the importance of being true to being Christian and African, are lessons that will guide my life in the way they have guided theirs.

35. HUMAN DIGNITY AND WELL-BEING AS CORNERSTONES OF DESMOND TUTU'S THEOLOGY AND LIFE

Baloyi G. Tlharihani[1]

Introduction

The discussion of human dignity remains essential in the context of South Africa, particularly in the discourse of human rights and well-being. However, the challenges of high levels of poverty, inequality and lack of basic service undermine the realisation of human rights and human dignity. Beyond the judicial connection with the notion of "human rights" lies a moral responsibility to be "... my brother's [sister's] keeper" (Gen. 4:9), which should remain at the centre of Christian ministry. Desmond Tutu, although in some circles referred to as a political "predikant" (political minister/priest) who was accused of bringing politics into the pulpit, embodied this kind of ministry as a priest whose theology was relevant and authentic to the people. The paper argues for the need to emulate Tutu in his prophetic theology alongside the poor and the oppressed for justice and dignity. While it is clear that there are policies and programmes in place to alleviate these challenges, they are not sufficient, especially when implementation is overtaken by corruption. The article concludes that, for as long as black experiences involve pain and suffering, as they do in South Africa today, Tutu's theology remains relevant in the struggle for dignity and well-being.

As one of the world's most known activists and defenders of human rights and well-being, Desmond Tutu played a significant role against apartheid's racial policies which made the existence of black people impossible. Without any doubt, Desmond Tutu's work has had tremendous influence on many people in their socio-political, academic and church or religious life. His concern for justice and peace, together with his ability to interact significantly with conflicting parties, set him apart as an instrument of God's peace in bringing love and justice in a context which is hostile and unjust. His moral integrity compelled him to respond to the struggle for justice in pursuit of peace and dignity. Even though his leadership grew stronger during the apartheid era in South Africa, his approach was very much pastoral in that he did not aim at drawing people to join a particular organisation, but to work for peace and oneness in the country. This kind of leadership can only come from a person who is not self-serving but has an interest in justice for all.

While we celebrate and reflect on the life and work of Tutu, the question of what it means to be human is an important one particularly where human dignity seems to have been removed by existential conditions. In the context of South Africa and many other African countries, corruption has established itself as an institution where ransacking resources that are meant to alleviate poverty is worsening. In such a context, how can human dignity be defined or understood in a situation where hunger, unemployment, poor health and lack of basic services exist? In all of these challenges, the existence of poverty diminishes the rights to dignity to the core. These are vital issues which require a voice on behalf of the voiceless to challenge the unjust system which continues to exploit people and undermine the essence of their being. Even though the evils of apartheid have been defeated, the current condition as faced by poor people is an oppression that tramples on their dignity. It is a system that reduces their being from the zone of human to the zone of non-human. Moreover, it

---

[1] Baloyi Gift Tlharihani is an associate professor of practical theology in the Department of Philosophy, Practical & Systematic Theology at the University of South Africa. His areas of specialisation are the intersection of pastoral care/counselling and African indigenous therapy, gender studies in African culture and the question of human rights and religion. Although he has not met Desmond Tutu in person, his work (from his postgraduate studies) has had a tremendous influence on his theological life in response to the question of human rights and dignity.

makes the poor and oppressed look like *things undeserving* of social and economic liberation. While the chapter reflects on the achievements of Desmond Tutu as clergy, theologian, activist and a spiritual leader, it also looks at Tutu's methods of theologising for justice and dignity as something to be employed for the goal of justice. Throughout the various stages of his leadership, his spirituality was a constant reminder and a guiding tool about who he is in fighting for justice. This is something which many leaders and pastors forget when they are in positions of leadership.

Desmond Tutu as a spiritual leader

Desmond Tutu is a committed pastor and a theologian who discovered in his context of oppression and suffering the liberation of God. Tutu is a man of deep faith in God, a spiritual leader and a man of deep prayer. The combination of theological knowledge and the formation of his spirituality was the greatest motivation for seeking justice for the downtrodden. His theology and pastoral tasks were meaningful and relevant when done from the context of the oppressed and dehumanised. Tutu explains this:

> If we take the incarnation seriously we must be concerned about where people live, how they live, whether they have justice, whether they are uprooted and dumped as rubbish in resettlement camps … whether they have a say in the decisions that affect their lives most deeply …[2]

This kind of thinking can only come from a person who has "... a spirituality that is God-centred and that is rooted in the unshakable truth that God is in control of all life."[3] It can only come from someone who understands the role of being a servant with the need to serve the people of God with passion. It is vital to acknowledge and appreciate this spiritual part of Tutu in order to understand that anything he does is rooted in the cross of Jesus Christ from which comes empathy, loving and caring towards the other.

This is evident in the type of spirituality he lived and professed throughout his life, which was borne out from the fact that humanity is created in the image of God. This means that humans must be treated with dignity no matter their class, race, gender and social status. In the context of South Africa and its racialised history, Tutu's spirituality and theology brought relevance of the church to the situation faced by people. This gave him courage to confront political bullies who wanted to silence the truth even from within his own Anglican church. Even though he was accused of bringing politics into the pulpit, to the point of him being described as "political predikant",[4] his theological reflections are inseparable from the experiences of people on the ground – the experience of black people which became a fundamental starting point for establishing theological truth.

The reference to Tutu as "political predikant" was nothing but a refusal to comprehend the significant link between the church and its people in respect of socio-economic and political injustice. For Tutu, the church had to be the voice of the voiceless in search for justice and restoration of human dignity. Those who described him as "political predikant" failed to see the church as a moral vehicle with obligations to challenge the unjust system against other human beings. They failed to understand that the church does not exist in seclusion and without people. Tutu's persistent participation in the process of liberation of the oppressed blacks, in spite of criticism against him as clergy, displayed a link between Christ's gospel with the marginalised, the oppressed, the bruised, the wounded and the poor.

Therefore, Tutu's theologisation was a demonstration of how theology and the church should be made real and relevant to society. As James Cone contends: "Christian theology begins and ends with

---

[2] Desmond Tutu, *The Rainbow People of God: The Making of a Peaceful Revolution.* New York: Doubleday (1994), 117.

[3] Njongonkulu Ndungane, "UTutu: Ngumtu lowo", in *Archbishop Tutu: Prophetic Witness in South Africa,* eds Leonard Hulley, Louise Kretzsmar and Luke Lungile Pato. Cape Town: Human &Rousseau (1996), 71-92.

[4] *Predikant* is an Afrikaans word meaning priest or minister of religion.

the biblical story of God's liberation of the weak ..."[5] Tutu's methods for dealing with issues of human oppression was to return to the Scripture in search for a liberative approach with the people and for the people. He placed the Bible at the centre of theologisation and black people's struggles. He believed that God is found among the downtrodden and not in the systems that disregard humanity.

The unstoppable Tutu and his thirst for peacebuilding was deeply embedded in the cross of Jesus Christ and in the need to do what is right. His spirituality was not limited within the walls of the church buildings, but it crossed through to broader society. His is a theology, ministry and life in context and in sync with the realities of people.

Human dignity and well-being

Although the discussion on human rights played a crucial role in the popularisation of the notion of human dignity, the two are best understood when read and treated together. In a context where human rights are violated, the dignity of people is likely to fall off. Where people are reduced to a level of non-human or non-person, not only their rights but their dignity are diminished. Tutu's continued emphasis on the need for human rights and dignity is rooted in the fact that humanity is created in God's image. Therefore, beyond the judicial connection with the notion of "human right", lies a moral responsibility to be "... my brother's [and sister's] keeper". This shows the broadness that comes with the notion of human dignity which also possesses a concern beyond oneself. This concern should enable us to ask about the well-being of others both in our neighbourhood and afar. It should be a concern about their well-being in totality. The responsibility entrusted to all believers should be the same as those displayed by Tutu as pastoral leader, an activist for human rights and a peacemaker.

This also demonstrates how broad the ring of responsibility is. This does not necessarily mean only to sympathise with the victims, but to take concrete action to better the situations of other human beings who suffer. The project of human dignity requires us to seriously scrutinise what it means to be human, and to examine our own values and deeds in response to those who suffer.

He did not allow his clerical responsibility to influence or dictate the rights of individuals. While other clergy may argue for the promotion of their religious or Christian laws and church doctrines, Desmond Tutu's approach is purely on the side of human rights and well-being. In other words, the rights of an individual are more fundamental in the pursuit of well-being and dignity than denominational commitments. This remains central and core to Tutu's theologisation. It is not about the doctrine of the church, but the rights of a person first. Human rights laws place humans at the centre and view them as someone with value and not as something valueless. The starting point is always at the rights of people which in the end, protect human rights and defend justice. Religious laws put God in the centre in terms of its doctrines. The challenge with religious law is that it fails to protect the rights of people in a non-discriminatory manner as equality is a fundamental principle of law.

In his chapter in the book, *Christianity and Human Rights*, Desmond Tutu talks about the life of a human person as an inviolable gift from God. Tutu points out that the "creation narratives in Genesis 1-2 assert quite categorically that human beings are the pinnacles, the climax, of the divine creative activity. if not climactic, then central or crucial in the creative activity."[6] This means that to be created in the image of God means to have fullness of life and dignity in that image as created by God and none other. Tutu further states that to be human is to be free which means an unfree human person becomes a contradiction of this creation. "Human beings have an autonomy, an integrity

---

[5] James Cone, *Speaking the Truth: Ecumenism, Liberation, and Black Theology*. Michigan: Grand Rapids (1986), 6.

[6] Desmond Tutu, "The first Word: To Be Human is to Be Free", in *Christianity and Human Rights: An Introduction,* eds John Witte Jr and Frank Alexander. USA: Cambridge University Press (2012), 1-7.

which should not be violated, which should not be subverted". This has implications, which Tutu argues:

> … to treat such persons as if they were less than this, to oppress them, to trample their dignity underfoot, is not just evil as it surely must be; it is not just painful as it frequently must be for the victims of injustice and oppression. It is positively blasphemous, for it is tantamount to spitting in the face of God.[7]

Tutu maintains that no human being exists by accident. He argues "even though some of us might look like accidents [especially in the eye of an oppressor], but none actually is."[8] This is where Tutu places emphasis on the worth of a human person as intrinsic. Tutu argues that "God does not love us because we are lovable. We have said that before and we will repeat it *ad infinitum*: God loved us even before we were created."[9] There is absolutely no need for us to be deceived that we need to impress God in order to receive God's love.

Conclusion

In appreciating and celebrating Desmond Tutu's contributions for peacemaking in South Africa, we see characteristics of leadership that are God-centred. Tutu's leadership was holistic in that it focused on the unity of humankind in all aspects of life such as race relations, gender relations and relations between Christians and non-Christians. Desmond Tutu's theology remains relevant within the South African context for continuous search for justice and peace. It is necessary especially where poverty and suffering have revealed an aspect which has the potential to reduce the dignity and rights of individuals.

Tutu's life, work and writings are reminders about the characteristics of a peacemaking church and leadership we ought to see today in South Africa. His was a God-centred church which was concerned about the well-being of its members in totality. Even though many churches are used as vehicles for self-enrichment and not necessarily as vehicles to address important social challenges that affect people, Tutu's theology should serve as a reminder about the meaning of a church in a society. The church is the church only when it exists for others in society. The most unfortunate is that the gospel is being commercialised even to the detriment of the most vulnerable. In many instances, people who fall prey to these unscrupulous pastors are mostly those who come from the context of poverty in anticipation for a better life through misleading prophecies. This makes the black church manipulative and advantageous to the situation of black people. The role of the church is to be compassionate and liberative to all, especially those in poor conditions.

For Tutu, the church has to lead with its moral voice in the process of liberating its people from any condition that seeks to dehumanise them. For as long as the system continues to take advantage of people and contribute to their miserable conditions, Desmond Tutu's theology will remain an absolute necessity in South Africa. While it is clear that there are policies and programmes in place to alleviate some of the challenges, they are not sufficient, especially when implementation is overtaken by corruption. Tutu's kind of leadership is needed to challenge the authorities and leadership of the world for justice and well-being, hence the imperative to emulate his prophetic theology and activism.

---

[7] Tutu et al. "The First Word", 3.

[8] Desmond Tutu, *In God's Hands: The Archbishop of Canterbury's Lent Book 2015*. London: Bloomsbury (2014), 70.

[9] Tutu, *In God's Hands*, 67.

36. PERSPECTIVES ON TUTU'S LEADERSHIP: A JOURNEY OF STRUGGLE AND HOPE[1]

Dan Vaughan[2]

In May 1976, a deeply disturbed South African clergyman, under a burning compulsion he himself only dimly understood, sat writing a letter to his country's prime minister, John Vorster.

> I am writing to you, Sir, because I have a growing nightmarish fear that unless something drastic is done very soon then bloodshed and violence are going to happen in South Africa almost inevitably. A people can take only so much and no more.[3]

The clergyman was Desmond Tutu. Then Dean of the Cathedral of St Mary's in Johannesburg and relatively unknown, he was soon to attain international fame: first as the indefatigable fighter against apartheid, and later as icon for world peace.

Tutu appealed to Vorster's heart as a "father and husband and doting grandfather". His requests were simple: "Accept us as part of South Africa. Repeal the laws that divide us. Let us work together for the evolution of our country into a non-racial, open and just society". He ended his letter: "Please may God inspire you to hear us before it is too late".

Tutu's plea fell on deaf ears. A bare six weeks later his prophecy of blood and violence was fulfilled: On 16 June 1976 the high school pupils of Soweto, the large black township south of Johannesburg, angered at the ongoing indignities inflicted on their parents, marched in their thousands in protest against yet another dictatorial imposition upon the blacks of South Africa. The police stopped them with bullets. When the country-wide uprising that followed was finally crushed, 600 had been killed and nearly 4,000 injured. Thousands more had fled the country to avoid detention, many joining the mobilising armies of the liberation forces.

The 1976 Soweto uprising was a significant turning point in the struggle against apartheid. In a now free South Africa, Youth Day is celebrated each year on 16 June, the day the youth rose up against apartheid.

I met with Desmond Tutu for the first time two years later. He was then newly installed as general secretary of the South African Council of Churches, where I worked. From that day on he was to exercise a penetrating influence on my life.

My journey to that place had been slow. I too had been one of those who carelessly and unthinkingly accepted apartheid as a "way of life". When my eyes were later opened to the pain that we were inflicting on others, I had to face my own monster, the enigma of my blindness. I had to ask the question, "What is there in me and my kind that has allowed this shameful oppression of my fellow countrymen and women?"

---

[1] This chapter was extracted from a forthcoming unpublished book called "This One Thing: Journeying with Desmond Tutu", a memoir by the author. As the author was ill with COVID in hospital at the time, Megan Robertson, with the help of his granddaughter, Leila Emdon, extracted and edited this essay. This was done with the permission of the author.

[2] Dan Vaughan worked with Desmond Tutu at the SACC between 1978 up until he took up a new position as Anglican Bishop of Johannesburg in 1985. Vaughan has a long history of working at the SACC before, during and after Tutu's time at the organisation. He again joined Tutu in 2004 at the Mpilo Trust where he saw to the administration of the office and later accompanied him as his aide in overseas travels until Tutu's retirement in 2011. He has recently written his unpublished memoir reflecting on his journey with Tutu and the profound impact he has had on his life, particularly as a white man working and living in apartheid and post-apartheid South Africa.

[3] D. Tutu, "A Growing Nightmarish Fear", in J. Allen (ed.), *Desmond Tutu: The Rainbow People of God.* New York, New York: Random House (1976), pp. 6-13 (10).

Something of an answer to that question lies in this memoir, my journey from indifference to the beginning of an understanding that before God all men and women are equal.

Tutu's people

Tutu was appointed general secretary of the South African Council of Churches (SACC) and took office in March 1978. The Bishop of Johannesburg gave him oversight of St Augustine's church in Orlando West, Soweto, and he shared with us about his work there, always with the excitement of a pastor's heart. It was obvious that his calling to the priesthood was never to be displaced by the role he had accepted in leading the SACC. Later, after his enthronement as Archbishop of Cape Town, tales abounded of his close care for the priests in his charge.

Tutu expected loyalty from his staff, and received it. He was deeply hurt, and heavily criticised for at first failing to prosecute, when Bishop Isaac Mokoena, heading the Independent Churches Division, was found to have committed fraud. And Tutu was angered when a secretary, temporarily assigned to work in his office, was found to have stashed heaps of unanswered letters in the bottom drawer of her desk. He would, he said, have preferred that she had just let him know that she was not able to cope.

Tutu may have been accommodating and generous with his staff but he was no pushover as far as discipline was concerned. Always a stickler for time, he was quick to comment when we arrived late for an appointment – or too early, for that matter. We also learned that excuses only hindered our cause when he had occasion to reprimand us for shoddy or incomplete work. More concerned that we move on to rectify matters than explain at length the reasons for our failure, he would say with exasperation, "Man, why are you so defensive?" And when we brought him complaints about fellow staff members his invariable response was to invite us to repeat the complaint in the presence of the other. He did not tolerate tale-telling. He readily invited our opinions in matters that were his to deal with, and he always responded quickly when he was instructed toward a particular course of action by the National Executive Committee. But, as I learned to my cost one evening in Stuttgart, Tutu did not appreciate unsolicited advice – especially in matters which touched a strongly-held conviction.

We had arrived in Germany after a series of meetings in Scandinavia and the Netherlands in 1979. On this trip, his outspoken criticism of the apartheid government and boldness in calling for sanctions had attracted healthy attendances at the press conferences in each centre. Especially headline-catching was his comparison of the evil of apartheid to the holocaust of Hitler's Germany. Now he was to face his first press conference of this trip in Germany. Over-sensitive to the feelings of our German hosts toward him, I cringed at the thought of Tutu presenting that comparison here in Germany.

It was a long walk from the arrivals lounge to the airport press conference. We were alone, apart from the escorting airline official, chatting about matters related to our visit to Stuttgart. This was where the headquarters of the German church's "Bread for the World" organisation, one of our strong supporters, was located. When our talk moved toward the coming press conference, I suggested, "Perhaps you should not mention the holocaust here in Germany."

There was dead silence for a full minute as we walked steadily on. Then he abruptly turned on me angrily: "I will say what I like. No one, no one, will ever tell me what to say." I realised that I had overstepped the line, and cringed, berating myself for my stupidity and insensitivity. "When will I ever learn?" I thought.

We walked on in stony silence, eventually arriving at the press conference. About forty members of the media were waiting for us. We took our places on the podium, I smiled very sheepishly, still smarting from his rebuke. I knew I was forgiven when at some point in the conference he said something like, "My colleague Dan," waving his arm in my direction, "says I should not compare apartheid here in Germany with the holocaust, but I am going to do so all the same." And he proceeded to do so, amid the laughter of the media at my obvious embarrassment.

Tutu believed that it was important that as many of our people as possible should travel abroad. It was essential, he said, that they should also taste the freedom that was the norm in other countries. He used to watch for invitations to international events which allowed a wider range of staff members to represent the SACC abroad. Our donors supported him in this and freely opened their doors, and hearts, to their South African visitors.

He took the concept a step further when in July 1980 he sent a large group of young people, of all races and from every part of South Africa, on a "Pilgrimage of Hope". He told us that the idea had originated when he was on a visit to the Taizé religious community in France, attending what he spoke of as a "hauntingly beautiful" service. "Out of the blue I was struck by the imagery of Revelation 7 of the 144,000, the perfect number of the blessed," he said. Wanting to share the experience with others, he devised the idea of a party of 144 young South Africans travelling together to Europe. On this trip they would learn what it was like to be among people who did not live by the apartheid system that divided us in South Africa. It would be an exercise, as he said, "in anticipation of a non-racial, non-sexist, democratic South Africa," a veritable "Pilgrimage of Hope".

Tutu had wanted to lead this pilgrimage but his passport was withdrawn in March that year. Instead, he asked the well-loved Bishop Bruce Evans to take his place as leader. He commissioned Sol Jacob to organise the event.

The experience for the young people was successful beyond expectation. Travel abroad was a new experience for most of them; there were some who had hardly travelled outside their black home townships into white South Africa. Now, they found themselves in the international world, in ordinary conversation with whites, young person to young person. They soon got to know each other well, despite their diversity of race and background. In the way they knew best, they soon formed a close-knit group.

The trip started with a tour of the Holy Land. After that the group went on to Geneva, visiting the home offices of the World Council of Churches. There they were hosted by the churches of the city. They met church leaders and attended events where they interacted with Swiss youth. In the offices of the World Council of Churches (WCC) they were briefed on the affairs of the world church by members of the organisation's staff.

Taizé in France was their third and final destination, and perhaps, for the young pilgrims, their most significant. Situated in Burgundy, it was – and still is – the home of a Swiss Protestant community. This was a special place of pilgrimage, visited by many thousands of mainly young people each year. They came mainly from Europe, but also from many countries around the world. Here the young South African pilgrims of hope were welcomed by Brother Roger and the other Taizé brothers.

They felt immediately at home. With all the others from many nations, they prayed, attended Bible studies led by the brothers and shared in the communal work. Three times a day they met in the Chapel of Reconciliation, singing together songs in many languages. The South Africans introduced some songs in isiZulu. They stayed there some days, sleeping in tents, and intermingling with others from around the globe.

Tutu's Pilgrimage of Hope met all Tutu's expectations. The exercise had a profound effect on everyone in the group. As one participant put it, it shaped their views about what sort of country they wanted.

Tension increases

By 1980 civil society in the townships was mobilising with increasing efficiency. Protests and disruptions were common, despite the bannings and detentions. Elements of the liberation forces infiltrated the country and attacks against police stations and other government installations increased. The first serious waves of labour unrest appeared. The SACC was now more than ever focused on the struggle. We were engaged in constant activity, as crisis followed crisis. Our field workers and those of the regional councils of churches became more and more deeply involved in the protests. Our Justice and Reconciliation cluster was particularly engaged on every front. The long agendas at our quarterly National Executive meetings were litanies of the woes of the nation, with no signs of a change. Each year, repeatedly, our annual conferences deplored the actions of the state. These issues filled my life, sometimes to overflowing despair. When would apartheid come to an end, I wondered? It seemed at that time that the answer was never.

Inevitably, other complications arose. One was the competing ideologies of the two main South African liberation movements. A significant difference between the African National Congress (ANC) and the Pan Africanist Congress (PAC) was their view of the place of white people in the free South Africa they were looking to. The ANC, established in 1913, held to the Freedom Charter. This was a landmark statement of hope and intent adopted at the Congress of the People, a significant gathering of various groups initiated by the ANC in June 1955. Its preamble stated that "South Africa belongs to all who live in it, black and white". On the other hand, the PAC, formed in 1959 by a breakaway ANC group, rejected the Freedom Charter. Its policy pronounced that "blacks should be in control of their own liberation struggle" and that "whites had too much to lose to be regarded as reliable allies". There were other differences but this one was the most significant at that time. It was in fact to be the cause of my undoing in the end.

These differing sentiments intruded even into the ranks of the clergy, giving rise to off-agenda debates on matters of the definition of blackness and who was in fact black enough to lead the struggle and build the new nation.

In this escalation of tension, Tutu's anchoring maturity was our steadying factor. He never took sides, nor for that matter did he ever indicate where his party loyalty lay. His denunciation of every atrocity may have been angry and immediate, but he never resorted to the posturing of others who used the funerals of prominent activists to denigrate or elevate any particular group or ideology. He spoke as a preacher should – pronouncing the word his listeners needed to hear at that time, pleading for justice, for unity, for the need never to abandon hope, and above all for a righteousness that overcame evil. Writer and editor Allister Sparks tells that in Tutu's eulogy at the funeral of Steve Biko, the Black Consciousness leader who had been tortured and killed by the security police, he had the courage to call on 15,000 angry mourners to pray for white South African leaders and policemen "because they needed to regain their humanity", just as humanity needed to be restored to their victims as well. His message to the government on that occasion was equally powerful. "Please, please for God's sake listen to us while there is just a possibility of reasonably peaceful change."[4]

At one rather tense gathering of the SACC senior staff we were discussing a possible meeting with then prime minister, P. W. Botha. Some were horrified at the thought of asking for a meeting with a man who had done so much to hurt so many. One described the possible meeting as "supping with the devil". Yet Tutu insisted that the prime minister was still a fellow creation of God and that we should not shy away from any opportunity to influence him.

It had in fact been the leaders of the SACC who had requested this meeting with Botha. This was after three very public and closely related events: a protest by Johannesburg clergy at the arrest of one of their number, their subsequent mass arrest and the international uproar that had followed.

John Thorne was the pastor of a Congregational church in Johannesburg, and, as the reader may recall, had briefly served as SACC's general secretary, preceding Tutu. He was a mild man of God, not known as an activist. Thorne was arrested in May 1980 for assisting protesting students. Joe Wing, a leader in his denomination, had called on the clergy of Johannesburg to join him in a protest march to seek his release. They would march from Wing's office to John Vorster Square, the notorious police headquarters on the edge of the city centre, where Thorne was being held. This was in May 1980.

It was to be a clergy-only event. The procession was led by Tutu, Peter Storey (then SACC president) and Wing. Fifty-one church ministers followed them in procession, singing hymns as they

---

[4] Desmond Tutu, "Stephen Bantu Biko", in Jill Werman Harris (ed.), *Remembrances and Celebrations: A Book of Eulogies, Elegies, Letters of Condolence, and Epitaphs*. New York: Pantheon, 1999, p.5.

marched down the long hill toward the city centre. In their clerical robes they made an impressive sight.

The starting point was the Congregational church headquarters, not far from our offices. After Tutu left to join his colleagues, I decided to follow him, in case the trouble I half expected with the police should materialise. I had done this before when he had been involved in a similar event in the city centre.

By the time I caught up with the marchers they were already in downtown Johannesburg. They had been stopped by a large contingent of police. Nearby was a line-up of police trucks and other vehicles ready to take these churchmen to jail. The authorities had clearly gained advance knowledge of the protest – small wonder, it was no secret – and had prepared accordingly.

Of all places, they had chosen to halt the clergy just outside the offices of *The Star*, Johannesburg's foremost afternoon newspaper. Crowding the windows of their offices to see what had caused the hubbub in the street below, the surprised reporters heard a police officer calling out through a loud-hailer in a voice that could have been heard blocks away, "Reverends, you are under arrest." The clergy were standing still, silently facing a large contingent of police with their guns at the ready. With Tutu at the head of the procession it was a ready-made story for the journalists. By then Tutu had gained international reputation as the voice of the oppressed people of South Africa and the reporters hurried back to their desks to tell the world what was happening in the street below.

I walked on the sidewalk alongside the halted procession to its head, to see more clearly what was happening. There I saw Tutu and Storey. I had just turned towards them, to speak with them, when a plain-clothes policeman came up to me.

"Are you with them?" he asked.

"Yes", I replied, "I work for the Council of Churches."

"Come with me," he said, grabbing my arm and pulling me toward one of the police vehicles. I tried to shrug him off.

"You needn't hold my arm," I said. He gestured toward a large police truck nearby. I took it that he wanted me to get into the truck with him to talk with me and started to open the door to climb in the front passenger seat. It was only when he hauled me round to push me in at the back, clanging the door shut after me, that I realised I was under arrest. I sat for about three or four minutes in the locked van wondering what was going to happen to me, when the door opened and Storey and several clergy climbed in after him to sit next to me on the iron benches lining the sides of the vehicle. Storey greeted me with, "You're here as well, Daniel?" and I realised then that the entire procession had been put under arrest and were being taken to police headquarters.

The trucks were driven into an enclosed area, where we stood about for perhaps an hour. Eventually we were separated, blacks and whites, and moved to separate sections where our names were taken and we were fingerprinted. Then they asked for the contents of our pockets and we handed in our keys, cash, wallets and watches, as well as belts, ties and shoelaces – in case we had suicidal tendencies, I suppose. I was placed in a cell with four young ministers. In a twist of irony four of the five of us were past students of the Bible Institute at Kalk Bay, near Cape Town. It is a small and conservative missionary training institution, one least expected to produce alumni who would take part in this kind of protest. It was a long night. We slept on thin sponge mattresses, a perk only the whites could enjoy. I learned later that the black clergy had only blankets between themselves and the concrete floors. Our discomfort was made worse by the police on duty continually waking us for obviously unnecessary roll calls and the clanging of cell gates. They also continually switched the lights on and off.

The next morning we were taken to the magistrate's court. We were packed into small low-roofed "holding cells" and seated on benches that ran around the walls. Our cell held about fifteen of us, including Wing. He was a man whose life commitment was to church unity and he was clearly moved by the support of his fellow clergy. He said a prayer. We sat and waited.

As hour followed hour our jocularity started to wane; the earlier banter about the stories to be told back home faded. With no indication of the charges against us, we shared an unspoken fear of the possibility of a prison sentence or detention without trial. I was sure that my more pragmatic companions were mentally reviewing their appointments and wondering how they could contact their offices. Some were probably casting about in their minds for alternative arrangements for Sunday's sermon. We sat in silence.

When we eventually appeared in court we were questioned one by one. When my turn came, I moved into the small dock. After I had given the magistrate my name, he asked me, "What is your denomination?"

"Baptist," I replied. There was a long silence. I began to wonder whether (as some of my more eloquent companions had done) I should make some kind of protest statement but, to be honest, at the time such heroics were beyond me. Eventually I was told to stand down. "Next," he called. In the end we were each fined for a traffic offence and the contravention of the Riotous Assemblies Act. The SACC paid the fines.

If nothing else, this episode changed my name at the SACC. Tutu was highly amused at the way the police kept pronouncing my name as "*Vau-gan*" – which he promptly morphed into what I took to be a more affectionate form, "Vaughie". So from then on, I was "Vaughie" in the SACC, and still am to Tutu.

Reconnecting with Tutu[5]

After two years (1998–2000) in Atlanta in the United States writing *No Future Without Forgiveness*, while he was visiting professor at Emory University's Candler School of Theology, Tutu returned to South Africa. He set up an office near to his Milnerton home to deal with his correspondence and complex international travel arrangements. He registered the Mpilo Ministries Trust to oversee his office and staff and to ensure transparency in the financial administration of his public life. As Trustees he nominated his wife Leah and himself. He added Keith de Vos, his parish priest, and Colin Moses, an accountant well versed in the management of church finances. For staff he engaged Crawford-Browne as his personal assistant and Lungi Jodwana to assist her in the office.

I started working with Tutu in January 2004 and served him until 2011, when he retired from public life and the Mpilo Trust was wound up. My job was initially administrative. It included the general oversight of Tutu's office and staff, and the financial management of the Trust. Soon after my appointment Tutu asked me also to accompany him as his aide in his overseas travels. I owe that opportunity indirectly to Mandela.

That happened in late April 2004, when Tutu was in the Caribbean, on the island of Granada with Mandela. The South African government had asked their support in South Africa's ultimately successful bid to host the 2010 Soccer World Cup event. Both were Nobel Peace Prize laureates. The government was exploiting this unique feather in South Africa's cap in touting for the votes of officials attending the annual conference of the Confederation of North, Central America and Caribbean Association Football. Voting for the favoured host country was to take place in two weeks' time, on 15 May, and this was their last chance to lobby a vote for South Africa.

It was there, as Tutu describes it, that Mandela discovered that Tutu was travelling alone. They were strolling together toward their parked cars, after a meeting, when Mandela asked, "Where is your driver?" "I don't have one", replied Tutu. "I am on my own." This clearly upset Mandela. He was determined to do something about it. Returning to South Africa he called the CEO of a well-known charitable trust to ask him to provide earmarked funding to the Mpilo Trust to make sure that Tutu had an aide by his side whenever he travelled abroad. The CEO agreed and when Tutu learned of it, he asked me whether I would accompany him in the future on his overseas trips. I was glad to

---

[5] The events detailed here take place in the latter years of the author's working life. By this time Vaughan had resigned from the SACC in March 1986, worked for St John's and rejoined the SACC in 1993 to organise the WCC's 1994 Central Committee meeting in Johannesburg. This turned into a more permanent position before he retired in 1996. He was then called out of retirement by Tutu in 2004.

say yes. Daphne, my wife, was ready to accept that I would be away from home from time to time. There was never a murmur of complaint from her, even in the years that followed when the number of trips increased and I was sometimes away for weeks on end.

When I reported for duty in the Mpilo office in January 2004, I was a little uncertain of myself. Tutu's stature had increased considerably since our time together in the SACC twenty years before. Since then, he had become the highly visible Archbishop of Cape Town and, even more prominent after that, as the chairperson of the TRC. Then there was his time in the United States and the publication of his book. He had become even more of an international figure. I wondered what it would be like to work for him now.

I need not have been concerned. Nothing had changed in our relationship, or in the style of his leadership, for that matter. It was all as it was in the old days, almost as if I had just returned from a lengthy trip abroad.

My first job was an easy introduction to my new environment. Crawford-Browne explained to me how the office filing system worked, pointing out that it needed some attention. So, my first week found me happily digging into the Mpilo files, sorting and splitting the files where required and generally tidying up. Scanning through those piles of papers taught me a great deal about the new world I was about to enter. This new parish of Tutu was a wide world and free from the long shadow of apartheid that had hung over former days when we had worked together. Here also was gone for me the distress I used to feel when those near to me attacked Tutu so viciously. Here was now a world that appreciated Tutu and frequently called for his help. Now he was the encourager, the teacher, the advocate of peace and reconciliation. I was to find this a time of friendship and acceptance. I had started out on what turned out to be the easiest and happiest time of my entire working life.

37. A Musical Tribute to the
Inspirational Leadership of Archbishop Desmond Tutu

J. Gertrud Tönsing[1]

It was only once that I had the opportunity to meet Archbishop Tutu face to face, but his personality was a towering presence in the background of the turbulent years that shaped me as a young white anti-apartheid South African activist. The earliest memories I have of him are of someone demonised by the white media but deeply respected by the white progressive grouping that my parents were involved in. My mother, Monika Wittenberg, worked in the Pietermaritzburg Agency for Christian Social Awareness (PACSA) and remembers how Peter Kerchhoff persuaded the editor of the *Natal Witness* to come to meet the Bishop personally when he came to Pietermaritzburg. Meeting the "Arch" personally deeply impressed the editor and the "Tutu bashing" ceased. He was of course vilified by the establishment for his pro-sanctions stance and his unashamed prophetic voice. I took his stand and his courage as inspiration for my own journey, and was particularly deeply impressed by his brave stance when his own "side" began to perpetrate brutal acts, putting himself in harm's way to speak up against the brutality flowing from anger against informers. Through my friendship with some Anglican women theologians I gained some insight into the painful road taken by the Anglican church towards women's ordination, a journey that the Archbishop was instrumental in leading, until that joyous moment when my fellow female theology students could prepare themselves for ordination. Of course the deepest impression was left by his leading of the Truth and Reconciliation Commission, which opened up many wounds but became a testimony to the world of how a traumatised nation can take steps to healing. My only direct encounter with him at a PACSA function in the Cathedral of the Holy Nativity in Pietermaritzburg leads me to describe him in three words: "Humility, humanity and humour". The tribute below is a song of thanks for all the many prophetic figures who led us, of which he is a particularly inspiring example.

Thank you for the prophets

Tune: Vukani nilalele (Zulu Lutheran Hymnal)

Lord, we thank you for the prophets
who follow when you call,
those who stand against the violence,
who risk their life, their all.
You call people to be faithful,
protect the poor and weak,
to see those who are forgotten,
hear those who never speak.

In all ages, you've called servants
who overcome their fear,
those who speak the truth to power,
expose the lies they hear,
those who break taboos and barriers

[1] J. Gertrud Tönsing is a Lutheran Pastor working in the city centre of Pretoria in the congregation St Peter. She was involved in student organisations such as the National Union of South African Students, the Students' Union for Christian Action and Earthlife Africa. She has ministered in Hillbrow and at the Lutheran Theological Institute in Pietermaritzburg.

with courage from above
and preach reconciliation,
show enemies your love.

You call leaders for your people
who help us find our way,
show us paths of transformation,
help build a brighter day.
They are signs of your good guidance,
Your help for hope's rebirth,
every step they take a signal
you won't forsake the earth.

38. TUTU AND ME: PERSPECTIVES ON BROKENNESS AND WHOLENESS

Michael Lapsley[1]

Desmond Tutu became the Bishop of Lesotho in 1975. In September of 1976 I was expelled from South Africa and, with the agreement of my community, the Society of the Sacred Mission (SSM), I went to live there where SSM had been ministering since 1912. Soon after my arrival I applied to the National University of Lesotho to complete my undergraduate degree in English and sociology. The Bishop used his good offices to facilitate my immediate acceptance. Since I was already a priest when I was studying in South Africa I soon assisted the Lesotho university chaplaincy. This was the situation that led the then Bishop Tutu to refer to me much later as the most obstreperous person he'd ever met! When I heard this I reflected and realised that without excluding ego and other personality traits, the person he met in 1976 had been engaged in fighting on many fronts, not least church hierarchies, and had been traumatised by three years of living in, and resistance to, apartheid South Africa.

Later I told Bishop Tutu that I was considering joining Umkhonto We Sizwe, the military wing of the ANC. He responded that I was in danger of over-identification. His answer confused me. As I saw it, I was simply taking my beliefs to their logical conclusion in the tradition of Latin American revolutionaries like Nestor Paz and Camilo Torres. Theologically, wasn't the Incarnation God's identification with us? Had Jesus over-identified I wondered?

In 1982 the church expelled me from Lesotho after the Maseru massacre of that year "for my own safety and that of others". In 1990, I survived an assassination attempt in the form of a letter bomb in Zimbabwe, with the loss of both hands and an eye.

I went to Australia to receive medical treatment and returned to Zimbabwe the next year. I went to see the bishop with whom I was about to start working at the time of the bombing and he looked surprised to see me. He asked me what I could do since I was now disabled. I replied that I felt that I could be more of a priest with no hands than ever I had been with two; and I could also still drive a car.

I returned to South Africa in 1991 by which time Desmond Tutu was Archbishop of Cape Town and, despite his diminutive stature, was a towering giant on the world stage. Archbishop Tutu hosted me for dinner and invited me to come and work in his diocese. "I have one priest who is blind and now one with no hands. Wow!" Whereas my first bishop saw my disability as a liability and an obstacle to my ministry, the Archbishop saw my disability as an asset. At the time, I was still getting used to my prosthetic hands and managed to spill my coffee over the Archbishop. He asked if I wanted to go home. I replied, "No, let me have another cup of coffee".

Back home in South Africa the following year, I initially started working for an NGO but it did not work out and I went to see Archbishop Tutu for advice. He told me, "If you wake up and dread going to work you should quit".

The stars were aligning and shortly thereafter I was appointed as chaplain, and as one of the first two employees, of the Trauma Centre for Survivors of Violence and Torture. The Trauma Centre was situated at Cowley House in Cape Town, initially an Anglican monastery. It became a half-way house for families from all over Southern Africa to visit their relatives imprisoned on Robben Island.

Around the time of the first democratic elections, the Archbishop made the arbitrary decision that priests could not be members of political parties. Because at that time I was not a South African citizen, my right to return from exile and live in South Africa was derived from my membership of

[1] Rev. Michael Lapsley is a member of the Anglican religious order The Society of the Sacred Mission. He is the Canon for Healing and Reconciliation at St George's Cathedral in Cape Town and at All Saints Cathedral in Edmonton in Canada. He is the founder of the Institute for Healing of Memories of which Archbishop Tutu is the patron.

the ANC. If I resigned from the ANC, I could no longer live in South Africa. The Archbishop looked at me and said there could be no exceptions. We both knew he meant the opposite. The *quid pro quo* was that I kept a low profile.

Whilst I was at the Trauma Centre, with other colleagues, we created an experiential process called the Healing of Memories.

In 1998, we launched the Institute for the Healing of Memories, conceived of as a parallel process to the Truth and Reconciliation Commission.

Archbishop Tutu agreed to be a Patron of the Institute and has remained so to date.

Often on public platforms, he would refer back to those early days in Lesotho and how difficult he found me. It did not sit easily with me when the Archbishop suggested that he was thankful for the transformation brought about in me as a consequence of the bomb and its aftermath. However, it is important to stress that the bombing was not God's will. God helped me to redeem that evil act.

Nevertheless, I can say that I know that I am a better human because of the journey I have travelled.

In 2012 I published my memoir, *Redeeming the Past: My Journey from Freedom Fighter to Healer*[2] with my co-writer Stephen Karakashian. Archbishop Tutu wrote in the Foreword: "... Since his bombing Father Michael has become a marvellous advocate for healing and reconciliation in South Africa and other strife-torn regions of the globe. He has truly become a citizen of the world, and I have watched his work with a growing sense of awe and admiration. Although he was broken physically, he has become the most whole person I know, truly a wounded healer". It was deeply humbling to be described in such glowing terms.

Archbishop Tutu could have gained a proud place in history as a champion of the rights of black people to a place in the sun. However, the way he embraced and championed other struggles illustrates that he was not just a black man fighting for his people, as important as that was. Archbishop Desmond has championed the rights of all oppressed people regardless of whether it is a popular or unpopular struggle. For that he has my deepest admiration. Demonstrably, he lived out his own famous quote:

If you are neutral in situations of injustice, you have chosen the side of the oppressor.

I attended the Provincial Synod of the Anglican Church in (then) Swaziland in August 1992, which was to debate whether to allow women to be ordained to the priesthood. Archbishop Tutu was in the chair but was not neutral. He was known to be strongly in favour. The Archbishop had, in front of him, two piles of paper of those requesting to speak for and against the motion. He was alternating between the two piles. A number of people speaking in support had not always done so but were converted by women with vocations to the priesthood, whom they met. Now I should mention that all of us clergy were dressed in our black cassocks, full-length black dresses one might say. A man stood to oppose the motion. He said it would be wrong for women to be ordained, for that would mean women would be wearing men's clothing. The synod collapsed in laughter. Shortly after, the Archbishop asked us to bow our heads in prayer. Then we voted overwhelmingly in favour. Prayer used very strategically, I thought to myself. Immediately after, the Archbishop asked us to be sensitive to those who had lost the vote and were hurting; promoting and advocating for justice while being pastoral to all.

It was on the rights of same gender-loving persons to an equal place in God's kingdom that the Archbishop was an outspoken advocate. "I would refuse to go to a homophobic heaven. No, I would say sorry, I mean I would much rather go to the other place", Archbishop Tutu said at the launch of

---

[2] Michael Lapsley with Stephen Karakashian, *Redeeming the Past: My Journey from Freedom Fighter to Healer*. New York: Orbis (2012).

the Free and Equal campaign in Cape Town. "I would not worship a God who is homophobic and that is how deeply I feel about this".[3]

On a continent where thirty-eight countries still criminalise homosexuality and many churches are stridently homophobic, the Archbishop's statements were not well received in many quarters. Clearly for Tutu, we are all God's children, all First Class, equally deserving to be treated with dignity with no exceptions.

In the face of growing corruption in South Africa during the democratic era, Desmond Tutu became the embodiment of the conscience of the nation. This brought him the ire of much of the political elite whilst Tutu was cheered on by millions of long-suffering citizens still living in abject poverty.

My final story sums up the tenderness and deep affection which has characterised our relationship over many years.

After F.W. de Klerk denied that apartheid was a crime against humanity early last year, the Groote Kerk, mother church of the Dutch Reformed Church, organised a Day of Lament and invited me to preach the following Sunday. I told the Archbishop about the invitation and said I feared that when I ascended the pulpit the roof would fall in. Tutu responded that the angels would sing. Because of COVID-19, everything was cancelled. In 2021, Dr Riaan de Villiers invited me to preach on Good Friday. I wrote to tell the Archbishop "… With a year's delay because of Covid I finally climbed the steps to the pulpit yesterday …. roof intact and angels everywhere. Now planning a long-term partnership between the Institute and the Kerk …" Tutu responded:

My dear Michael,
How simply wonderful. God has a real sense of humour.
Thank you and God bless you as God uses you as God's wonderful instrument. Yippee!
Much love and Easter blessings,
Arch

---

[3] BBC News, "Archbishop Tutu 'Would not worship a homophobic God'", 26 July 2021. Available from: https://www.bbc.com/news/world-africa-23464694.amp (accessed 10 June 2021).
As is well known, the Archbishop also has a deep personal spirituality that suffuses his whole being. He has a deep appreciation of the role of the religious orders in the church. Sometimes his staff would call asking where our latest intercession list was. It was comforting to know that he was praying for all the brothers of the Society of the Sacred Mission by name. We also witness his embodiment of how worship and justice are two sides of the same coin. As an Institute for Healing of Memories and as a Society of the Sacred Mission, we are inspired by the example and witness of Archbishop Desmond Mpilo Tutu and give thanks for his ninety years of life.

39. A Statement from the Mother of Simon of Cyrene: Reflections on *Ubuntu* Across Millennia

Rachele Vernon O'Brien[1]

In the holy land of Soweto, the nurturing place of many witnesses to freedom, including Desmond and Leah Tutu; Nelson and Winnie Mandela; and my beloved friends George and Gladys Wauchope, stands the Hector Pieterson Museum, a memorial to one of the children and young people shot by the security forces during the Soweto student uprising on 16 June 1976.

The world cannot forget the courage of the young people reflected in Sam Nzima's photograph of three young people, twelve-year-old Hector, his sister, Antoinette Sithole, and Mbuyisa Makhubu, who picked up and carried the dying Hector. This story of Soweto is one that connects to the universal stories of bravery and compassion that call us to be more than we can be.

Mbuyisa's mother, Nombulelo Makhubu, also lost her son on that day. He was not killed that day, but eventually had to take refuge overseas. Nombulelo died in 2004, not knowing where Mbuyisa was. Her words from the Truth and Reconciliation Commission are etched on the memorial at the museum:

> I said according to my culture Mbuyisa is not a hero, he just did what was natural because we are our brother's keepers, according to our culture. He just saw Hector falling down. It would have been a scandal for nobody to pick Hector Pieterson up from the ground. As far as we are concerned he was never a hero for picking up Hector Pieterson.[2]

The gospels name Simon, a man of Cyrene, in what is now Libya, as a passerby compelled to carry Jesus' cross. We know from Mark 15:21 that he had two sons, Rufus and Alexander, presumably known to the Christian community. But he must have had a mother, and her spirit may well have resonated with that of Nombulelo, that other African mother, and with every mother who has lost a child to injustice.

My son is not a hero ...

My son is not a hero.
He saw you fall
And stepped forward.

The soldiers seized upon his pity
"You carry it then,"

---

[1] Revd Dr Rachele Vernon O'Brien. Anglican deacon. Activist. Jamaican by birth, British by naturalisation. I first laid eyes on Bishop Tutu, as he was then, at the WCC Central Committee meeting held in Kingston in 1979. We theological students privileged to serve as stewards for the meeting looked on with awe at this little man who was such a potent symbol that the church was on the right side of the struggle for justice and truth. When I despair, as I do sometimes, that the church appears to have lost focus, I remember that Archbishop Desmond has continued to be faithful and courageous, and I realise that he is the representative of what this Jesus movement is all about really. And my faith is renewed.

[2] Questions and Answers. Date 30 April 1996. Name Nombulelo Elizabeth Makhubu. Case GO/0133 Johannesburg. Day 3. South Africa. 1999. Truth and Reconciliation Commission of South Africa report. Cape Town: The Commission. https://www.justice.gov.za/trc/hrvtrans/methodis/makhubu.htm (accessed 31 May 2021).

He was compelled
Not by their swords
But by
His heart of
Compassion.

From my womb
He had learnt
To reach out
To each one as family.

To ignore your pain
Would have been
The ultimate scandal.

So as your brother,
He carried the cross
On which you would offer up
Your body
Bowed and broken
For us all.

No hero
But an acolyte
In the celebration
Of life.

Beyond the cross.

40. REFLECTIONS ON DESMOND TUTU AND HIS EXERCISE OF LEADERSHIP IN AFRICA

Hans S. A. Engdahl[1]

This essay is a brief reflection on Archbishop Tutu's involvement in Africa, especially during his terms as president of the All Africa Conference of Churches (AACC), 1987–1997.

It is a fond reminiscence of AACC's General Assembly in Addis Ababa in October 1997, Tutu's last meeting as president. We came as a small delegation of three from the Church of Sweden.

It was an unforgettable meeting. The theme was "Troubled but not destroyed", the text was from 2 Corinthians 4:8-9, in condensed form. There were several sub-themes addressed in the meeting, including poverty, leadership crises and political stagnation.

I recall the feminist theologian Mercy Amba Oduyoye entering the podium to give her keynote address: "Whither Africa", she said. "Where are things going to end?"

Her honesty was breathtaking. Her speech became a kind of *kairos* moment which was felt by everyone, for what she said was inclusive. She made everybody feel that all of us, as members of the church, were implicated in what happens in Africa. Through her speech, Oduyoye provided a good illustration of the ecumenical mission paradigm called "the church for others".

In the midst of taking stock of what was deeply troubling on the continent, people trusted that they would not be destroyed, hence the assembly was also a celebration. It was also a moment where Tutu's leadership style was showcased, as the following incident demonstrates.

Following the impending end of his term as AACC president, an election process for the new president of the AACC was initiated and Ghanaian professor of theology, Kwesi Dickson, was elected by majority vote.

After a word of congratulations, Tutu jumped up from his seat on the podium and shouted "Yippie, yippie, I am free, I am free!!", performing what looked like the first steps of a toyi-toyi dance. The newly elected president looked on in disbelief at what was happening.

Later on, quietly and in all seriousness, Tutu and José Chipenda, the outgoing general secretary of the AACC, from Angola, gave their report to the assembly. What stood out from the report were the extensive visits to heads of state all over the continent that Tutu and Chipenda undertook. They had urged the political leaders to work for peaceful solutions and for honouring democratic constitutions and elections. They also reported that often their appeals fell on deaf ears.

On a very sombre note, and this despite some spectacular changes like the South African democratic elections, Tutu did articulate the desperate state of affairs in which the continent found itself, and he stressed that any overcoming of the dire debt crisis must have a move towards democracy as a prerequisite: "True democratisation – when it is clear that the people participate in decision making; human rights are respected; the money saved is used directly for the benefit of the so-called ordinary people; and we demilitarise. If these conditions are met then the debt should be cancelled."[2] Tutu concluded with the following exhortation:

> Let us show the world that Africa is a giant awakening, that Africa is going to have vibrant markets, that it will be the tiger of the future and that those who help us will be doing themselves a great favour. Let us refuse to be divided … Let us show the world that Africa was traditionally a place that allowed for different points of view. The good chief was the one who judged consensus correctly. I have full confidence in the future of Africa because God came to find a refuge in Africa, because civilisation had its cradle in Africa, because God loves Africa. Let us throw out the dictators and bring freedom and justice

---

[1] Hans Engdahl served as an extraordinary professor at the University of the Western Cape (UWC) between 2005 and 2016. During this time, he was part of the initiative that worked towards the establishment of a Desmond Tutu Research Chair at UWC, to which the Archbishop agreed at his 75th birthday in 2006. He has known the Tutus since the late 1980s, when he worked as mission secretary for the Church of Sweden.
[2] 7th AACC Assembly Report. October 1997, Addis Ababa, Ethiopia.

everywhere for our God does not sleep, does not go on holiday. Our God is not deaf, our God sees, our God knows and our God comes down to deliver us. Dictators beware, Africa will be free.

Isaiah 42: 1-3: I behold my servant, whom I uphold, my chosen, in whom my soul delights; I have put my Spirit upon him, he will bring forth justice to the nations.
He will not cry or lift up his voice, or make it heard in the street;
a bruised reed he will not break, and a dimly burning wick he will not quench;
he will faithfully bring forth justice.[3]

The relevance of this text is indeed striking even today.

As it happened Tutu's birthday occurred during the conference (7 October). The large South African delegation and a few Swedes made their way to the hotel rooms where the Tutus resided. It must have been quite agreeable to him that we sang and prayed for him that evening, despite the intrusion.

Fairly soon, however, Tutu announced that the party would now be over. Another day would soon take its toll. But there was hesitancy. Nobody wanted to move. Then Mama Leah said: "The party is still on, but he may go to bed", which Tutu did.

Again, this story also has a more serious side to it. This happened in October 1997. In 1996 Tutu had gone into retirement as Archbishop of Cape Town. Very soon after, in December 1996, he was called by President Nelson Mandela to chair the Truth and Reconciliation Commission (TRC). So much for retirement!

While celebrating his birthday in Addis Ababa, or rather, while deliberating on the plight of Africa, he was in fact still deeply involved in the TRC work and the final report of seven volumes was still in the process of being compiled.

In summary, Archbishop Tutu has held daunting leadership roles. He has had the grace to make them look pleasurable. But duty also has an end. His inner strength, grounded in disciplined prayer and sacramental fellowship, helped him to recognise the end of duty.

I wish that more leaders, having completed their particular task, would imitate Archbishop Tutu: jump up from the chair and shout: "Yippie, yippie, I am free, I am free"!

---

[3] 7th AACC Assembly Report.

41. DESMOND TUTU: AN ICON OF *UBUNTU* HOSPITALITY

Ingrid le Roux[1]

My first contact with the Tutu family was in 1975 in Johannesburg. My husband Pieter and I were running a "Centre of Concern" in our house in Melville. Ma Leah, who was director of that national organisation, frequently visited us and the students attending our literacy, math or English classes. The three of us often had a rushed supper of toast and eggs at the kitchen table before the classes started. It was the beginning of a lifelong friendship.

We had been living in Cape Town a few years when Desmond Tutu was elected Anglican Archbishop in 1986. I was asked if I could be his primary physician once they moved to Cape Town. It has been an easy job with the most exemplary and compliant patient.

In that role I have had the privilege to prescribe periods of rest for him and Ma Leah away from South Africa. It was especially important during the dramatic eighties when he was in the middle of the struggle against apartheid and under great pressure from a violent and intimidating regime. A Christian conference and youth centre – Stiftsgården – in the beautiful village of Rättvik, on the edge of Lake Siljan in central Sweden, hosted the Arch and Ma Leah during these periods of rest. The Arch used to say that God must have been in a very good mood when he created Siljan and the countryside around the lake.

The Arch's mode of transportation during his times in Rättvik was a red "lady's bicycle" on which he explored the surroundings. Many locals were stunned meeting the famous Archbishop cycling around the village. A summer luge track had been built on a steep ski slope outside the village. When he heard my children complaining that they were not allowed to try it, he said it sounded fun and he definitely wanted to. Ma Leah joined him flying down the mountain on a small carrier.

One Friday afternoon the Arch came home puzzled from a visit to the centre of Rättvik. He and Ma Leah were invited to dinner with the director of Stiftsgården and he had wanted to buy a bottle of wine to take along but had not been able to find the bottle store. He did not know that the then state-owned bottle stores in Sweden were often hidden behind curtained windows with posters discouraging people from drinking alcohol. When apologising for coming empty handed to the dinner he was reassured by the director that that was just as well, as Stiftsgården was a so called "dry place" – no alcohol allowed.

He became the instant hero and confidante of a group of young exiled South African men and women studying in the Soviet Union but spending some summer weeks at Stiftsgården. The Swedish youth attending confirmation classes and camps at Stiftsgården were star struck and in awe as they gathered around the fire in the evenings to listen to the Arch who told them never to stop dreaming of and working for a better world.

I have been part of a group of friends who for years have celebrated Eucharist with the Arch at St George's Cathedral in Cape Town on Friday mornings, followed by coffee and amazing conversations at a nearby café. The Arch shared with us his conviction that we live in a righteous universe, we are created for goodness and that no one is beyond redemption – not even apartheid's worst executioners.

---

[1] Ingrid le Roux was born in Avesta, Sweden and grew up in Stockholm. She graduated as a medical doctor from the Karolinska Institute in Stockholm 1973. She married Pieter le Roux and settled in Cape Town in 1978. In 1979 Ingrid, together with women from the 'illegal' squatter community Crossroads outside Cape Town, founded the Philani Maternal, Child Health and Nutrition Trust and built the trust's first clinic in Crossroads in early 1980. This was followed by the building of another five clinics in Philippi and Khayelitsha townships during the eighties. During the nineties, the Philani concept expanded, further components were added. Philani headquarters were built in Site C, Khayelitsha and opened by Philani Patron Archbishop Desmond Tutu.

Word spread among visitors to Cape Town that if you wanted to get a glimpse of the great man you should come to St George's and participate in the Friday morning worship. It often took a long time for the Arch to come to have coffee as the visitors wanted pictures, autographs or a chat. While we "the regulars" felt slightly impatient – this was after all "our" Arch – he patiently engaged with each person, with his complete presence in every meeting making them feel as special and remarkable as he knew they were.

The Arch is not overly respectful of the world's famous and powerful. They are treated as ordinary people, who are served Ma Leah's amazing roast chicken on her beautiful blue china like any other friends. The Arch and Ma Leah entertain with great generosity and warmth.

My extended family has many times been at the receiving end of that generosity and hospitality. One Christmas when my sister and her family visited us in Cape Town we attended midnight mass at St George's Cathedral on Christmas Eve, led by the Arch. As he handed me the bread he said something I did not hear properly. The next morning, he phoned and asked if we were coming for lunch – all ten of us. That is what he had asked me as he served communion. This is probably the best example of "*Ubuntu* hospitality" that one can find.

I spent a few days in Washington, D.C. with the Arch during one of his lecturing tours to Howard and Georgetown universities and attended some lunches and dinners organised in his honour. There were senators and congressmen and women and others from the Washington political elite at those occasions, everyone vying for a seat next to him or a chance for a handshake and a chat. The Arch is honoured and respected in South Africa but here he was worshipped. I have often wondered how someone can cope with so much adoration and keep his perspective and humility intact. He lives close to the cross in prayer and meditation. I believe this is where he finds his power, wisdom, perspective, humility and humour, and it seems God does not let him get away with getting a big head.

On Freedom Day, a year after South Africa's first democratic election, the Arch opened and blessed as its patron the new headquarters of Philani Maternal, Child Health and Nutrition Trust in Khayelitsha. With his usual vision, and long before women and children became top priorities of international aid organisations, the Arch used his own assets, his networks and widespread contacts to mobilise resources for women and children living in deprived circumstances. At every opportunity he gently urged royalty, tycoons, rock stars and billionaires to commit their material wealth and other resources to South Africa's children – and they did this willingly because of who he is. He often came back to the Philani Centre after the opening to visit, reading to the children in the preschools, often having difficulty leaving.

The Arch and Ma Leah recently had their Covid vaccinations at Brooklyn Hospital in Cape Town. They were honoured guests at the launch of the second vaccination phase in Western Cape and it was a great media occasion with a big audience. He was received with warmth, joy and cheers by the crowd. It was a celebration again of who he is and what his presence means to so many. In his presence hope, joy, faith and love become realities. That is his magic.

42. An *UbunTutu* Eucharistic Prayer

Edwin Arrison[1]

The Lord be with you
And also with you
Lift up your hearts
We lift them to the Lord
Let us give thanks to the Lord our God
It is right to give God thanks and praise
Holy Spirit of God, you blow where you will.
You are complete freedom. Space and time cannot contain you.
You are there when we are born, when we shout our first breath.
You are there when we die, when we sigh our last breath.
You are always with us, in us, between us, among us
Even though we may not always be conscious of your Presence.
YES: You are the ever-present YES in all creation.
YES: You were present at the dawn of creation.
YES: You were present with the Khoi and the San people, the indigenous people of the land.
YES: You were present with the lepers and the missionaries
YES: You were present when the humanity of some were questioned.
YES: You were present when that same humanity was affirmed as
Co-equal, interdependent, worthy of being celebrated
YES: You are the presence of our *Ubuntu*, of beloved community
YES: You are the spirit of justice, peace and reconciliation.
And now, with all creation, we sing your unending Praise:
Uyingcwele, uyingcwele, uyingcwele
Holy, Holy, Holy
God of Power and wisdom and might
Heaven and earth are full of your glory
Hosanna in the Highest
Blessed is the one who comes in the Name of the Lord
Hosanna in the Highest
Holy Spirit, you are indeed present. You are indeed a gift.
Jesus is united with you and with his Abba. You are in Jesus and Jesus is in you.
And you are all united with us, affirming not only our humanity but also our divinity.
On the day before Jesus died, he knew that he wanted to be ever-present with us,
Ever in community with us
So that we can always be in community with each other
Knowing that the forces of division would always try to divide us
Jesus wanted to leave us a sign of that community in unity, rooted in the earth and in our memory.
He asked for bread and wine to be gathered and sat down with his small community
Jesus knew their strengths and weaknesses, and yet made them an everlasting part of his community
He took bread, blessed it and said: *Thabathani nidle*, take and eat, *neem en eet*
This is my body that was given for you, do this in memory of me.
After supper, Jesus took the cup of wine, he blessed it and said: This is my blood, *igazi lam, my bloed*

---

[1] Rev. Edwin Arrison met the then Bishop Tutu in 1985 at the SACC conference and was ordained by Archbishop Tutu in December 1992 after being selected by him to study theology in 1987. During his seminary studies at Grahamstown, he was offered a one-year scholarship to read theology at Wycliffe Hall in Oxford from 1989 to 1990. He worked closely with the Arch after ordination, often acting as assistant chaplain. He is the general-secretary of Kairos Southern Africa, serves on the leadership of the South African Christian Leaders' Initiative (SACLI) and is founder and director of the Volmoed Youth Leadership Training Programme, of which the Arch is a patron. During the COVID period he was partly responsible for caring for the Tutus during their stay in Hermanus. He now works as the development officer of the Desmond and Leah Tutu Legacy Foundation.

Wat vir julle uitgestort word. That will be shed for you. Do this, as often as you drink it, in memory of me.
So we confess the mystery of our faith:
The Christ has died
The Christ has risen
The Christ will come again.
Jesus, we are ALL made in your image. Christians, Jews and Muslims, Buddhists and Hindus and even those who claim to have little faith or no faith.
With you, superiority is a lie. Apartheid is a sin. Division is no more. Inequality is evil.
You love us all. Your love is the Alpha and the Omega. You unite where we divide.
You call on us to love our enemies. To create community even with them. To bless those who despise us.
Give us the strength, the will and the grace to do that. Give us the wisdom, the patience and the intellect to tell and live and embody your new story of *Ubuntu*, of the beloved community.
May this bread and wine, your body and blood strengthen and unite us
With you, with one another, with all creation
So that we may truly say: **We who are many are one body, for we all partake of the one bread**
May we mean what we say and say what we mean
And have the courage to heal all that needs to be healed
And live the values of your kin-dom
Both now and forever.
Amen

"Eternity is in the now; redeem the time!"
The largesse of your God
Bursting through the walls dividing us.

You go on a rampage for justice,
Stand in the breech,
Staring into machetes, sticks and petrol bombs,
Prostrate at the altar of forgiveness
For both oppressor and oppressed.

When you finally stop weeping
With the bereft,
Your laughter somehow manages
To fill the wilderness;
Blossoms sprout in the desert.
Your prayers break from the lofty apses
Lifting the yoke of slavery.

Soldier for peace, you rail ever against
The scourge of prejudice, poverty,
HIV/AIDS,
Hunger, wars,
The butchering of the white rhino …

From the Solomon Islands to Darfur
From Guantanamo to Gaza,
Your umbilical cord is buried again and again
Under the baobab, banyan and olive tree.

You are hewn from the Rock,
From which stream
Life-giving waters,
From Abraham to Augustine,
Desert Fathers to the Dalai Lama,
Mother Theresa to Wangari Maathai.

Today, your basket is filled
With liturgies and offerings,
Sunbeams, songs, plaintive roses
And fruits of love.
And children's prayers.

2.3. Transnational Solidarities

44. PROPHET OF CONSISTENCY CONNECTING STRUGGLES FOR JUSTICE IN PALESTINE AND SOUTH AFRICA

Brian Brown[1]

One of many joys in serving the British Council of Churches (BCC) for eleven years from 1979 was helping devise the European travel itinerary of the Arch on his many and significant deputation visits. I recall accompanying him to Lambeth Palace in London to meet fellow Anglican Robert Runcie, then the Archbishop of Canterbury. As they shook hands amidst much palatial splendour Runcie remarked: "Welcome to my humble carpenter's shop". Desmond exploded with glee and mirth as only he can. The bonding was immediate, both of them given to a winsome self-deprecating humour. Runcie's understanding as to the enormity of the crime of apartheid developed, commensurate with their friendship.

I can't think of the Arch without thinking of the Tutu hug. In those healthier times before the coronavirus pandemic, a hug was an expression of love and friendship rather than an invitation to illness. On his farewell to return home after these visits the Tutu hug would be accompanied by the cry: "Next year in Johannesburg!" By virtue of my lengthy banning (similar to house arrest) I was debarred by the apartheid regime from returning to South Africa. Both of us were identifying with the cry long associated with the hope of exiled Jewish people, initially in biblical Babylon and subsequently in the many places where Jews suffered persecution – next year in Jerusalem! Desmond's cry was always louder and more enthusiastic than mine. But then Desmond's capacity to be imprisoned by hope was always much greater than mine.

On looking back, the dire consequences of that freedom cry for the indigenous people of Palestine over the past century are all too apparent. "Next year in Jerusalem'" energised the Zionist vision that established the State of Israel. But what is hugely disturbing is that the cry now furthers Neo-Zionism's hopes of Greater (Eretz) Israel materialising – an extended and expansionist Zionist state from the Mediterranean Sea to the Jordan river and perhaps beyond. Palestinians under Israeli occupation have seen their Gaza Strip territory occupied, blockaded and rendered an open-air prison of about 2 million people; their East Jerusalem, designated as the capital of a Palestinian state, illegally "annexed" by the Israeli government; and their West Bank territory under the ultimate control of Israel's military; all of this achieved in violation of international law and United Nations rulings.

Few church leaders outside of Palestine have made themselves as conversant with these developments as the Arch. Few have told the dual narratives of Palestinian dispossession and Israeli domination so compellingly and so authentically. Few have suffered as he has the charges of anti-Semitism that invariably follow. And few have dared to share his pained shout, on observing a people under ethnic-inspired occupation and dispossession for more than fifty years: "This is apartheid!" Very few in fact have raised their heads above the parapet to say "Amen" to his call for Boycott, Divestment and Sanctions (BDS), so as to focus attention on Israel's emerging apartheid state and address the magnitude of the injustices to be overcome. Never for a moment are these calls made

---

[1] While a presbyter of the Methodist Church in South Africa, Brian joined the staff of the Christian Institute (CI) led by Afrikaner dissident Beyers Naudé. Beyers and the Arch were soul mates and formidable opponents of apartheid. Brian enjoyed "reflected glory" moments when working with two icons of prophetic ministry. Following banning and the CI's closure by the regime in 1977, he sought sanctuary and worked in the British Council of Churches. This allowed re-engaging with the Arch during many European visits and a sharing in diverse endeavours to assist apartheid's demise.

with malicious intent but always as a contribution to the justice that the Arch has long seen as the gateway to a shared peace.

The earlier BDS call of the Arch, in the struggle era of South Africa, provided difficult challenges when engaging with his white parishioners. While his prophetic and courageous spirit required that he promote these non-violent measures for change, his sensitive temperament and need to be loved would have caused him to wince before the verbal assaults and cessation of friendships that followed. In the days before Tutu became a household name and books about him abounded, I collaborated with author Shirley du Boulay and editor John Webster on their Tutu publications. It wasn't by accident that the respective titles were: *Voice of the Voiceless*[2] and *Crying in the Wilderness.*[3] Those were dangerous, wilderness times for Desmond. The relative immunity from the apartheid regime's response that he came to experience, particularly from actions against him outside of the rule of law, was initially in short supply. Growing international acclaim and recognition would come to confer greater protection.

I had the privilege of collaborating with Desmond in calling for BDS to become church policy in Britain. Prime Minister Margaret Thatcher was resisting the entire Commonwealth in refusing to endorse sanctions. A major problem was her insistence that the long-imprisoned Nelson Mandela and his African National Congress (ANC) liberation movement were terrorists. We arranged for Runcie to convene a meeting between the leaders of the member churches of the BCC and Oliver Tambo, head of the movement in exile and close confidant of Mandela. Tambo had been an aspirant Anglican priest before the banning of the ANC sent him into exile to assume his daunting responsibility. He testified for over an hour as to his faith, his beliefs in democracy, equality and inclusivity, the difference between the regime's primary violence and the ANC's counter violence, the crimes of apartheid, the enormity of his people's hurt and his hopes for non-violent BDS measures to facilitate transformation. His audience was spellbound. Having accompanied Tambo out of the building I returned to a room of astonished silence. Runcie broke it: "Thank you Brian for allowing us to meet a remarkable terrorist". The meeting exploded in laughter. All were aware that Runcie had intentionally repudiated Thatcher's absurd assertion of terrorism.[4]

In 1979 I accompanied the Arch on a train journey to the BCC Assembly that followed the momentous meeting with Tambo. Following his presentation, the assembly voted to endorse economic sanctions: It "declared its conviction that progressive disengagement from the economy of South Africa is now the appropriate basic approach for the churches to adopt until such time as it is clear that all the people of South Africa are to be permanently entitled to share equally in the exercise of political power in regard to the whole country".[5] The vote was unanimous.

The day that I felt I had not totally failed my children in their development was when I observed a large poster of Desmond adorning a bedroom wall. Posters in my childhood's bedroom were of a more alluring nature. The poster was not there without reason. Our son Sean was one of twenty-five who in 1988 marched from Glasgow to London. One walker for every year that Mandela had been incarcerated. The long walk to Wembley Stadium culminated in a "Free Mandela" rally. Desmond was the keynote speaker. Introduced to the walkers during the event, the Arch noticed that Sean's trainers were much the worse for wear, though probably a touch less battered than the feet within them. A few weeks later a box and accompanying note of appreciation arrived. The box contained a pair of state-of-the-art Reebok trainers. Thus do the great reveal authentic greatness. Desmond's influence on the family's "old man" has, hopefully, been no less inspirational. A prayer of constant thankfulness is that I engaged with, and hugged, the Arch!

As the Arch witnessed an apartheid state emerging in Israel, he brought the same forthrightness, passion, uncompromised analysis and integrity of presentation as he had portrayed in regard to South

---

[2] Shirley du Boulay, *Tutu: Voice of the Voiceless* (London: Hodder and Stoughton, 1988).

[3] John Webster, *Crying in the Wilderness* (London: Mowbrays, 1982).

[4] Brian Brown, *Born To Be Free: The Indivisibility of Freedom* (The Church in the Market Place Publications, 2015).

[5] Brown, *Born To Be Free*, 244.

Africa. With Mandela, his friend in justice pursuits, he is acutely aware of the indivisibility of freedom. Mandela famously declared: "We know too well that our freedom is incomplete without the freedom of the Palestinians".[6]) Desmond observes how Israel replicates the policies of dispossession of the old South Africa and similarly suggests that the freedoms of Jew and Arab are indissolubly joined. Long before leading human rights bodies within and without Israel came to affirm Israel's apartheid credentials, these two iconic figures united in calling for Palestinians to be granted the same freedoms that they came to experience in South Africa, however belatedly.

In prophetic mode the Arch declared in 2002 as to how he viewed Palestine's enduring occupation and its consequences:

My heart aches. I say, why are memories so short? Have our Jewish sisters and brothers forgotten their humiliation? Have they forgotten the collective punishment, the home demolitions, in their own history so soon? Have they turned their backs on their profound and noble traditions? Have they forgotten that God cares deeply about the downtrodden? Israel will never get true security and safety through oppressing another people. A true peace can ultimately be built only on justice. We condemn the violence of suicide bombers, and we condemn the corruption of young minds taught hatred; but we also condemn the violence of military incursions in the occupied land ... Israel has three options: revert to the previous stalemated position; exterminate all Palestinians; or – I hope – to strive for peace based on justice, based on withdrawal from all the occupied territories side by side with Israel, both with secure borders ... People are scared to say wrong is wrong because the Jewish lobby is powerful – very powerful. Well, so what. For goodness sake this is God's world! We live in a moral universe. The apartheid government was very powerful but today it no longer exists. Injustice and oppression will never prevail. Those who are powerful have to remember the litmus test that God gives to the powerful: What is your treatment of the poor, the hungry and the voiceless? And on the basis of that, God passes judgement'.[7]

The power of this statement is further enhanced when viewed in the context of Desmond's close association with the Jewish community in South Africa. March 2019 witnessed racially motivated attacks on Muslim worshippers in Christchurch, New Zealand, with many deaths. The South African Holocaust and Genocide Foundation, a Jewish organisation dedicated both to Holocaust remembrance and to helping transform society, resolved to send its condolences to the families and communities of the victims. This read in part: "In words of the Foundation's Patron, Archbishop Emeritus Desmond Tutu, speaking at the opening of the Holocaust Centre in Cape Town in 1991: 'We can become more human, more gentle, more caring, more compassionate, valuing every person as being of infinite worth, so precious that we know such atrocities will never happen again and that the world will be a more human place'".[8] This vision by the Arch of a more compassionate world in which all are affirmed as of infinite worth is embraced by Jewish leaders and conveyed to distant sufferers. He inspires something beautiful to happen. Jewish friends of the Holocaust Foundation were using the words of a Christian friend to reach out to Muslim friends across the globe to condemn an Islamophobic attack and to convey condolences.

This incident reveals the nature of the Arch's supportive identification with the Jewish community. Others can be cited. So his condemnation of the ways in which Palestinians suffer domination at the hands of the Israeli state might have surprised many and certainly stretched friendships. But not for those who know the man and that which makes him tick. Here is someone who proudly embraces his roots – poor, black, oppressed and deemed second-class – and yet also lives beyond ethnicity. In terms of his identity, ethnicity is significant but secondary. He has long resolved any identity crisis. His mentor Jesus would have him be all good things to all of humanity. He lives without fear or favour under the tutelage of a friend who has no favourites. The same

[6] *Middle East Eye*, 11/2/2020. Speech by Mandela in 1997.
[7] *The Guardian* newspaper, 29/4/2002.
[8] The South African Holocaust and Genocide Foundation: https://ctholocaust.co.za/, March 2019 (accessed 24 May 2021).

expectation is of course required of all followers of the Way who aspire to faithfulness; Desmond aspires and attains better than most of us.

Much has happened in the two decades since the Arch made his prophetic cry for a justice-based peace, an end to illegal occupation and the recognition of an equitable Palestinian state in the "Holy Land". A trickle of illegal settlements in the West Bank has become a flood and Israeli dispossession of land, nationality and human rights of Palestinians has only intensified. Furthermore, Israel's leadership has declared there will never be a Palestinian state and that Jerusalem, beloved by so many of the region's faithful, is to be the undivided, one and only capital of a Jewish Israel.

When Jesus lamented over a Jerusalem that would shortly be destroyed by its Roman occupiers and before he suffered brutal death at their hands, he offered a prescient prayer for his beloved people. He sensed that his prophetic ministry of living beyond ethnicity, exceptionalism, entitlement and exclusivity would contribute to being "stoned".[9] It's a descriptive word for the occupational hazards that face true prophets. Desmond has been "stoned" as a terrorist, communist and a black hater of whites. More recently "stoned" by jibes of being anti-Semitic and supportive of Palestinian terrorism and hatefulness. Yet I don't believe he has a racist or anti-Semitic bone in his body.

It's difficult to imagine Desmond yielding to the "ecumenical contract" that prevails, at least in current British inter-faith dialogue. The unwritten rules are that Jewish participants will not raise the issue of the contribution of Christians to the Holocaust (and it was huge) and Christians will not raise the issue of Palestine's occupation (and it continues). This is a reason why indigenous Palestinian church leaders are frequently erased from inter-faith dialogue, and Palestine with them. The marginalising of that voice is a reason for this article intentionally recalling the costly interventions of the Arch as a "voice of the voiceless". Not totally alone, but much a wilderness prophet, he raises one of the most neglected issues of injustice in our time.

Among the many factors that make the Arch such a towering figure in the pantheon of moral icons of our age is his consistency. It's no good cosying up to him to be exempt from his prophetic strictures. Or of threatening that stones or words will break bones or spirit. Or of trying to play the ethnic card, or the race one, or the god of favourites one. We will fare best with the God of justice one. Max du Preez, Afrikaner dissident in the apartheid era, reminds us that on his release Mandela chose to stay the night in Tutu's house: "It would have been so easy for Tutu to bask in the admiration of the nation and become just another one of the African National Congress after 1994 (the year of South Africa's democracy). But he felt compelled to speak up against the excesses and failures of the new government".[10] How true. What you see is what you get, be it yesterday, today or tomorrow. In one sense the Arch is almost boring in his consistency!

Consistency is matched by Desmond's persistence. My admiration merges with some annoyance in this regard. He is an enduring embarrassment for those of us seeking to reach for our retirement slippers and a good escapist yarn. His voice haunts us in recalling that we can never be free until those who are unfree attain their freedom. If anyone deserves the pleasures and pampering of retirement, it's the Arch. Why not spend the days hearing ball upon bat at his beloved Newlands cricket ground, or dip toes into waters of the whites-only beaches so long denied him? But Desmond's persistent witness suggests that there is no retirement from the agenda of justice – or of rest for the wicked as my family teasingly say! But would I have it otherwise? To share in some small way in this banquet of life with the prophet Desmond is a reward, beyond deserving.

The prophetic consistency and constancy which Desmond personifies are beyond my descriptive powers. So I'll end on a personal note. On a visit to the BCC offices Desmond asked to meet Cathy, my secretary, now a computer-killed species. In the typist pool it was banter at its best and the warm glow was palpable. Here was a man fresh from being a recipient of the Nobel Peace Prize, returning to who knows what, and yet engrossed with a section of staff for whom such an encounter was probably without precedent. Not too long thereafter my letter to Desmond was brought by Cathy for

---

[9] Gospel of Matthew, Chapter 23 verse 37 (NRSV).
[10] Brown, *Born To Be Free*, 271.

signing. She was about to go on maternity leave and asked to add a personal PS to the Arch, informing him of developments. It could be argued that at the time Desmond was holding in tension the demands of leading both church and civil society in their respective struggles against the apartheid regime.

By return of post his reply arrived, brought triumphantly to my office: "Dear Cathy, I am bereft. Thank you for doing all the hard work in arranging my programmes while Brian derived the glory. What will that man do without you?" Prophets on the cutting edge of momentous issues might be excused sternness of bearing, some self-importance, even indifference towards life's trivialities. But with the Arch the affirming of our humanity, our equality of worth and our development of self-esteem were not things to get in the way of the struggle. They were the reasons for it. I know that Cathy (who had twins by the way) has never forgotten that life-affirming moment. Just a pity though that the Arch made it happen at my expense!

45. "Africa's Most Refreshing Son": Inspiring Solidarity Between the German and African Churches

Volker Faigle[1]

We all have our special memories of Archbishop Desmond Tutu. As Africa Secretary of the Protestant Church in Germany (EKD) I had the privilege of many encounters with this remarkable personality who has led the church during most challenging times in South Africa.

His unforgettable consoling and encouraging "rainbow-sermon" at the funeral service for the victims of the Boipatong massacre, his strong conviction that reconciliation and forgiveness were political necessities after the atrocities of the apartheid system, the deep spiritual moments of the Friday morning prayers at St George's Cathedral in Cape Town or receiving his phone call from South Africa when hospitalised in Germany, are just a few of many lasting memories I treasure.

On the occasion of his farewell as Archbishop of Cape Town a worldwide-operating soft drink company saluted him in newspaper advertisements as "one of South Africa's most refreshing sons". However, in my opinion this holds not only true for South Africa. It should therefore read "Africa's most refreshing son", because Desmond Tutu is not only an icon of church and society in his home country, South Africa. He also played a decisive role in the ecumenical and political context on the entire African continent and beyond.

This leads to Nairobi, the capital of Kenya, where the offices of the All Africa Conference of Churches (AACC) are housed. "Churches in Africa together for life, peace, justice and dignity", describes the mission of this ecumenical institution which accounts for over 140 million Christians across the African continent. For a period of ten years, from 1988 to 1997, Desmond Tutu served this ecumenical organisation as president in close cooperation with the AACC general secretary, Rev. José Chipenda from Angola.

Troubled but not destroyed

When Desmond Tutu took over responsibility as president of the AACC in 1988 he was faced with a major building construction problem. The building along Waiyaki Way in Nairobi was supposed to become a representative conference centre for the AACC. However, due to lack of finances and administrative quarrels the construction came to a standstill for many years. Waiyaki Way is one of the busiest main roads in Nairobi and as time went on, the ugly-looking unfinished building became well known in the city as the "ruin of the Churches". Living in Kenya during this time I myself felt that the state of the construction did not reflect a good reputation of the church in Africa. Especially given that at the top of the building a beautiful cross, a gift by the Ethiopian Orthodox Tewahedo Church, was installed already. In a conversation with the Archbishop Tutu I mentioned that, whenever I passed by this construction site, I felt uncomfortable about this eyesore.

The Archbishop had not forgotten this remark at all. Years later he took me aside, reminding me of the eyesore in Nairobi. He urged me to join hands and to assist in the search for financial aid abroad in order to ease the pain we shared on the unfinished building. In the end, the Nairobi eyesore story turned out to be another healing story. The completion became possible through the assistance of ecumenical partners which the Archbishop so successfully challenged. The inauguration of the

[1] Volker Faigle, German Lutheran theologian, Berlin, parish pastor in Bavaria, Germany (1978–1984), ecumenical co-worker in Nairobi – Kenya Evangelical Lutheran Church – (1984–1990), head of Africa desk of the Evangelische Kirche in Deutschland – EKD – (1990–2003), church diplomat in the Office of the Plenipotentiary of the EKD to the German Government and the EU (2003–2013), chair of the Council of the Berlin Cathedral (2013–2019). Served for many years as special envoy of the EKD to the Sudan and South Sudan. Honorary theological doctorate of the University of the Western Cape (2001).

building took place in 1992. In this way the theme of the 7th AACC general assembly held in Addis Ababa in 1997, "Troubled but not Destroyed" (2 Cor. 4: 8-9) got an additional special meaning. As outgoing AACC president in his address to the general assembly the Archbishop recalled: "When José and I were elected in 1987 at the Lomé Assembly you might say that the AACC was definitely troubled. Deeply troubled, and on the verge of ignominious collapse, somehow reflecting the parlous state of mother Africa, our beloved continent derided by many as the Dark Continent ... And we were on the verge of bankruptcy reflected in the eyesore of the incomplete office block of the circular building in Nairobi."[2]

Due to the special efforts of these two giants of ecumenism in Africa, Desmond Tutu and José Chipenda, the representative office complex serves as the administrative building of the AACC even until now. While this building bears the name of the Lutheran Bishop Josiah Kibira from Tanzania, also a strong advocate for the course of the ecumenical movement in Africa, a recently erected modern and representative guesthouse and conference facilities were dedicated to its former president named "Archbishop Desmond Tutu Ecumenical Centre".

Far distant friends but close at heart

The All Africa Conference of Churches played a significant role in the dismantling of apartheid in South Africa. It was especially supportive of the "Programme to Combat Racism" (PCR) which was launched by the Geneva-based World Council of Churches (WCC).

Already back in 1976 a dispute between the AACC and the church in Germany arose. There was the suspicion that the government of the Federal Republic of Germany was instrumental in providing South Africa with nuclear technology. In a telegram a prominent and powerful member of the AACC hierarchy, Rev. John Gatu, wrote to the chairman of the Council of the EKD: "We therefore earnestly urge that (...) the Protestant Church in Germany will do everything possible to bring pressure upon your government and German industrial firms to desist from enabling the apartheid regime in Pretoria to be in a position to threaten the entire African continent and world peace."[3] John Gatu, who later became moderator of the Presbyterian Church of East Africa (PCEA) was active in support of the WCC Programme to Combat Racism and a fierce advocate for liberation from Western domination. In the opinion of the AACC, the EKD did not handle the issue of the nuclear conspiracy with the expected intensity. As the matter could not be solved by correspondence and telegram, a delegation of the AACC, among them its president, Rev. Adriamanjato and the chair of the General Committee, Rev. Gatu, travelled to Germany in order to meet high-ranking officials of the EKD. As a result of the deliberations it was agreed that the Protestant Church in Germany will do everything possible to defuse the situation in South Africa and bring the expected pressure upon the German government and industry.

Another concern critically questioned by the AACC was the fact that the EKD provided German-speaking Lutheran churches in Southern Africa with pastors from Germany while these churches were not ready to employ pastors from their black Lutheran sister churches. This matter sparked heated discussions within the church in Germany as well. The AACC intervention on this issue was an important ignition for a new secondment policy of the EKD. Years later a "transitional agreement" between the EKD and the German-speaking Lutheran churches in Southern Africa ensured that pastoral assistance from the EKD to South Africa and Namibia step by step needs to be replaced in favour of direct assignments of pastors from sister churches in Africa. This was seen as an important contribution to promote unity under the racially divided Lutheran Church family in Southern Africa. The consultations with the AACC also enhanced considerations by the EKD and its aid organisations

---

[2] All Africa Conference of Churches, *Troubled But Not Destroyed,* AACC General Assembly, Nairobi: October (1997). www.africafocus.org/docs97/tutu9710.php (accessed 30 May 2021).
[3] All Africa Conference of Churches, *The Nuclear Conspiracy*, Nairobi (1977), 55.

to provide significant support for the South African Council of Churches (SACC) in its anti-apartheid struggle.

When almost two decades later in January 1994 an official delegation of the EKD visited the AACC in Nairobi, Desmond Tutu in his capacity as president of the AACC also took part in this meeting. The German church delegation, still having in mind the dispute from previous years, saw in this encounter more than just a courtesy visit. John Gatu, the prominent elder church leader of the AACC recalled the past and expressed the necessity to evaluate how the German church handled the concerns of the AACC. The solidarity of the EKD with the SACC during those darkest days in South Africa's history also played a decisive role in the negotiations. Once again it was Desmond Tutu who paved the way for coming to terms with the past. With his charming but meaningful words, "welcome far distant friends but close at heart", the gates for a reconciled and prosperous future of the ecumenical cooperation between the EKD and the AACC were opened again.

The Archbishop in Germany

On many occasions we had the pleasure of welcoming the Archbishop in Germany. Whenever he visited us, he followed his spiritual habit and routine of beginning the working days with early morning prayers and Holy Communion. So he did several times also in the chapel of a church-affiliated hotel in Berlin dedicated to Martin Luther King Jr, the leader of the American civil rights movement, who also used to pray in this room of silence. Spiritual moments (worship and prayer) were doubtless the source of Desmond Tutu's ministry at home and abroad. He often mentioned that he could not do his work without spending time in prayer.

In Germany his major concern was to alert the church and its institutions, but also politicians and NGOs, about the situation in South Africa and to plead for solidarity in the abolition of the apartheid system by non-violent means.

Discrimination of gay and lesbian people equals the horrors of apartheid in South Africa

The Archbishop also addressed the issue of discrimination on the basis of sexual orientation both in South Africa and elsewhere. His courageous testimony was timely as an evaluation of homosexuality by the Protestant Church in Germany and a long-awaited clarity on this issue was only hesitantly underway. In his book *God Is Not a Christian* he confessed: "I cannot keep quiet while people are being penalised for something about which they can do nothing – their sexuality. To discriminate against our sisters and brothers who are lesbian or gay on grounds of their sexual orientation for me is as totally unacceptable and unjust as apartheid ever was."[4]

Likewise, he raised his voice in defence of gay Christians in other countries, as he did in favour of LGBTIQ+ people in Norway living as registered partners when they were banned from holding positions in the Church of Norway. Impressive was also his demand that the World Council of Churches should take a positive stand on the question of sexual diversity during its forthcoming assembly which was planned to be held in Zimbabwe. The background to this demand was the anti-gay statements by the Zimbabwean president, Robert Mugabe. He also challenged the Anglican Church in Uganda on the issue of sexual diversity. During a conference of African church leaders at the AACC in Nairobi he criticised Uganda's proposed Anti-Homosexuality Bill and asked the churches in Uganda to refrain from supporting this law. He even announced that he was not going to attend the AACC's 50th Jubilee celebrations in the Ugandan capital of Kampala, which was planned for 2013, if the Church of Uganda did not stop supporting legal procedures aiming at discrimination against gay and lesbian people. These were insights that have seldom been expressed so clearly in front of African church leaders. The following days the Archbishop's concern on the Ugandan matter was not reflected in the press coverage of the AACC.

---

[4] Desmond Tutu, "All, All Are God's Children", in *God is not a Christian,* London: Rider (2011), 53-56.

The human partner of the liberator God – on the way in God's world

The issue of sexual diversity serves as one example of how in his sincerity and courage the Archbishop never tired of struggling for justice in an unjust world. This was not always met with approval from his fellow bishops. As relentlessly as he fought against the apartheid regime he continued with his mission for peace and reconciliation beyond the borders of South Africa – whether it was mediating in the conflict in Northern Ireland, or drawing attention to the government of Israel and its controversial policy towards Palestine, which caused him much trouble.

Above all, wherever Desmond Tutu appeared in public people were touched by his humour and great cheerfulness rooted in deep faith, which makes him so loveable and authentic. An example of this authenticity I have found in his own words when he was preaching about God who wanted his people to be freed from the bondage in Egypt. Tutu explained that God could have done the liberation on his own, but he wanted a human partner. He continued the story of God and Moses like this:

> So God went to Moses.
> "Hi Moses."
> "Hi God."
> "I want you to go to the Pharaoh and tell him: 'Let my people go'."
> Moses was thoroughly flabbergasted: "What? Me? What have I done now? Go to Pharaoh? Please, God, no! You can't be serious!"
> Forgetting that God knew everything, Moses pleaded: "God, you know I stammer. How can I address Pharaoh?"
> Mercifully, God did not accept Moses' first negative reactions. If he had, in a real sense the children of Israel would still be in Egypt in bondage. The God we worship is the Exodus God, the great liberator God who leads us out of all kinds of bondage.[5]

This story sums up how I know Desmond Tutu: through his compassionate commitment he became a remarkable human partner of the great liberator God. In many ways Desmond Tutu has had a major impact on my personal theological thinking. I thank him and his wonderful wife Leah wholeheartedly for honouring me with friendship and support for many decades. My great affection, admiration and immeasurable gratitude will always go to the beloved Archbishop, "Africa's most refreshing son".

---

[5] John Allen, *The Essential Desmond Tutu*, Cape Town: David Philip (1997), 11-12.

46. MOGOPA AND THE COVENANT PROJECT WITH COMMUNITIES THREATENED BY FORCED RESETTLEMENT – A LESSON FOR TODAY

Ulrich Duchrow[1]

Dear Desmond,

It is not only a great honour but a great joy to greet you on your 90th birthday with some common memories inspiring present struggles.

The first relates to a famous photo of you speaking to the people of Mogopa.

Desmond Tutu speaking to the people of Mogopa." Photo Credit: Unknown.

For those who do not know the story, let me back up a little. In 1983, about 3 million people had already gone through the ordeal of a forced resettlement. Mogopa, a small village, about two hours' drive south of Johannesburg, was also affected by this process. Bulldozers razed churches, schools and several houses in residential areas – beautiful buildings made of natural stone – to the ground. The date for a military eviction in November 1983 was fixed – until then, 300 families had offered resistance against the resettlement. At that time you were general secretary of the SACC and organised a church service in Mogopa, supervised by night watchmen, in which Wolfram Kistner, then director of the Department for Justice and Reconciliation in the SACC, and Allan Boesak also participated. The picture was taken here. This vigil was the beginning of a remarkable story of resistance. Let me briefly sketch some of it.

---

[1] Ulrich Duchrow is professor of systematic theology at Heidelberg University, Germany, specialising in ecumenical theology and interreligious theology and economic issues. He is co-founder and honorary chair of Kairos Europa, an ecumenical grassroots network striving for justice. Kairos Europa also coordinates the Kairos Palestine Solidarity Network in Germany. He is a member of the Academic Council of ATTAC Germany (the movement critical of capitalist globalisation which Kairos Europa with WEED and Pax Christi founded). Dr Duchrow has worked in various capacities with the World Council of Churches (including guest professor at the Ecumenical Institute in Bossey, 1977–1978), the Lutheran World Federation and the World Alliance/World Communion of Reformed Churches.

On 10 December 1983 – Human Rights Day – Wolfram called me. At Pentecost we had set up the grass roots "Ecumenical Network for Justice, Peace and the Preservation of Creation" in Baden, Southwest Germany (which, by the way, gave the name to the Conciliar Process for Justice, Peace and the Integrity of Creation, launched later that year at the WCC's 6th Assembly in Vancouver[2]). Wolfram explained: "If the government launches a military displacement, the community of Mogopa will refuse to be brought to Pachsdraai, a place the government has intended as provisional accommodation for the community. It will flee to Boputhatswana and settle in with some of their relatives who have been living there for several years. Therefore", he continued, "the community urgently needs 180,000 DM (deutschmarks) to get there. Due to the fact that institutions operate too slowly, we would like to ask whether you can get hold of the money for us from the grassroots groups." My jaw just dropped. The requested sum was huge. In addition, we had always tried to leave money out of our North–South relationships in order to prevent the Germans from taking on a "donor mentality" instead of waking up to the fact that historically they were one of those countries who shared continuing responsibility for poverty and oppression in the Global South. The key word "resistance" helped us out of this dilemma. Showing solidarity combined with resistance included the possibility of opposing the pro-apartheid world of economics and banks, and the manoeuvring of the government and most official churches within Germany. We therefore made an appeal and spread it through the network: "300 families in Mogopa threatened by forced removal request DM 600 each from 300 families in Baden in order to be able to finance their resistance." We explained that families could of course team up with other families to obtain the amount of money. Our appeal was met with an overwhelming response. Within a period of three weeks, we raised DM 100,000 at the grassroots level.

As the first act of resistance, the Mogopa community used some of this money to rebuild the destroyed school in January 1984. On 14 February, armed forces showed up. The community fled in trucks, chartered from the rest of the money. A time of squatting and suffering began – it lasted for seven years, but was not in vain. Several countries increasingly put the South African government under pressure. In Germany, newspapers published detailed reports on the matter. The TV journalist Klaus Figge produced three films for the German nationwide programme ARD, making Mogopa and its fate internationally known. We were able to gain German Foreign Minister Hans-Dietrich Genscher's support for an intervention. Lawyers involved the South African government in several lawsuits. In cooperation with you and Wolfram, in 1985 "Aktion Bundesschluss" (the Covenant Project) was launched at the German Protestant *Kirchentag* (a huge biennial lay-run gathering). Over the following years, twenty-three regional groups in Germany (congregations, districts etc.) formed an alliance of resistance with twenty-three South African communities affected by forced resettlement. The organisation of the Covenant Project was impressive. The key and core were the fact that it was possible to link people to people on the ground in mutual empathy and solidarity. But on that scale (in relation to national and international politics) this was only possible because you and Wolfram offered the framework and communication power.[3] You allowed the SACC field workers to be part of the communication structures. They helped the German facilitators, whom you kindly hosted in the SACC, to move around and visit the communities – the basis for what was then shared with the regional groups in Germany.[4] There was not just one group in each region but, e.g. in the Protestant Church in Baden and also in Württemberg, there were five groups/congregations in five towns. When the partners from South Africa – in this case from Mogopa and Driefontein (linked with

---

[2] Where we also met, when you gave your remarkable speech at the peace rally. Heino Falcke tells me he remembers your first sentences there: "When I just flew in from South Africa, crossing over so many countries, I thought: oh my God, how good that I am not god, responsible for all these countries. Thank you that you are our God."

[3] In the time after liberation Eddie Makue greatly supported the project in various SACC positions.

[4] I thank three of them, Lutz Bauer, Karin Saarmann and Rolf Zwick, for commenting on this article from their experience as facilitators. Lutz Bauer also helped me with documentation, literature and an interview to remember details.

Württemberg) – visited Germany they visited all these places, bringing the reality of South Africa to so many people and generating more political pressure in Germany.

Mogopa was the last operation to resettle communities by the military. Ethnic cleansing of this type came to a standstill. From 1991 onwards, the land in Mogopa was tacitly reoccupied by the people. After the democratisation of South Africa, Mogopa was the first community to get back its land in the liberated nation. The community even managed to regain the land as common property – despite the growing neo-liberal trend of privatisation and individualism. Life in Mogopa began to flourish – although the apartheid government had done everything to split the community into factions, some of which even led to pointless struggles after liberation. After the younger generation, at that time headed by Pule Mohutsiwa, had been elected to govern the village, it – much to our surprise – took the initiative in renewing our Baden/Mogopa alliance. In this case, not only mutual visits and public relations were of interest, but also the reconstruction and the development of the land. We helped to support advisory bodies, especially those concerned with ecological farming, assisting with the manifold forms of new life in Mogopa.

What did we learn in the twenty years of Mogopa's struggle that can help in present and future struggles?

(1) Resistance – Resistance to injustice is necessary, possible, linked to suffering but also full of rich spiritual and human experiences – and may lead to victory. This is the only possible path to the dignified survival of human beings within a system that is hostile to life. For Germans, having had an authoritarian history, this is not everyday knowledge. But the impressive resistance of the Mogopa people, which was connected with suffering and simultaneously creative action, was an emotional breakthrough for many people. They became willing to understand and resist systemic and actual injustice. Another important point: after the fall of the Berlin Wall we linked Mogopa to what we called "Twinning Partnerships", which should have been more appropriately named "Triple Partnerships". Twelve communities in Baden, Poland and South Africa were linked in partnerships in order to understand justice issues in the new situation when imperial capitalism was becoming globalised. One of the instruments was travelling youth workshops. Twelve young people each from Poland and Baden visited twelve communities in South Africa and, vice versa, twelve young people from South Africa visited Baden and Poland. These young people learned to link colonial history (racism, exploitation and slavery) with National Socialism (when in Poland, we always visited Auschwitz) and imperial capitalism, that was taking over Poland and South Africa even after liberation. In this way the experience of Mogopa was situated within even a geopolitical context. We came to understand South Africa as the global system in a nutshell – even as it moved from socially regulated capitalism (in the period of "Reconstruction and Development") to brutal neo-liberal capitalism after liberation.

(2) Global Capitalism – This became crystal clear in 1994. Maybe you remember that you contributed to a hearing in the European Parliament in Brussels, organised by the ecumenical grassroots organisation Kairos Europa on the occasion of the 50th anniversary of the Bretton Woods Institutions, the International Monetary Fund (IMF) and World Bank (WB). I still have a photo showing you as the speaker at the press conference of the hearing with me as moderator (overleaf).

In the same year the IMF and WB became crucial for South Africa. At a conference organised by Beyers Naudé, I heard from one member of the ANC delegation, who had negotiated the democratisation with the representatives of the apartheid government, that in these negotiations the whites posed one absolute condition for arriving at an agreement: that the first finance minister of the new government must be a white person. The goal was clear: to recognise apartheid debt (the repayment of which should have been rejected by a new democratic government) in order to place the new South Africa, through credit from the IMF, under the regime of the global financial capitalist system. Under this regime the new government would be bound to follow the rules of this neo-liberal system and abandon any independent social policies, such as "Reconstruction and Development". This, by the way, was analogous to the neo-liberalisation of European Social Democracy at about the same time (Blair in the UK and later Schröder in Germany).

Picture of Desmond Tutu speaking at a press conference at the European Parliament in Brussels;
Ulrich Duchrow (right) was the moderator. Photo credit: KAIROS EUROPA (ed. Dara Molloy):
Kairos Europa 1990-2002. Action – Solidarity – Resistance. A Commemorative Document.
Bruxelles: Kairos Europa, 2002, Cover Foto.

So the international linkage of people in local struggles via global ecumenical communication can open the eyes for global structures and also mobilise people for global justice campaigns.

(3) Land – What we also learned from Mogopa's suffering and resurrection was the central role of land.[5] Modern capitalism (after early commercial and usury capitalism in the Middle Ages) began with the "enclosure", i.e. privatisation, of land in England, starting at the end of the 14th century.[6] So land was subjected to the logic of private property, measured in money. The philosopher who established the rules of this regime, valid to this day, was John Locke – preceded by Thomas Hobbes, who already made private property and contract the absolute law in the capitalist state/Leviathan. Yet Locke went a step further: he defined the human being as a property owner. This led him to the conclusion that the indigenous people in North America were not human beings, because they did not have private property, and so the British settlers had the right to take the land of the indigenous people. And should they resist the land-grabbing of the settlers the latter had the right to wage a just war against the "non-humans" and kill or enslave them.

In the South African context, although the Mogopa people had title deeds on common land as a community, the apartheid government thought it could handle them as non-humans resisting the white European order, in the tradition of Locke. So the privatisation of land is closely linked with colonial settler policy and its support by the violent capitalist state.

(4) Settler Colonialism – With this background it is not surprising that you, Desmond, again stood up against settler colonialism, land grabbing, ethnic cleansing and violence in all its forms, committed first by the Zionist movement and then by the State of Israel against the Palestinian people, and increasingly leading to a new system of apartheid.[7] So we can learn from your

---

[5] See Adeoye O. Akinola, Irrshad Kaseeram, Nokukhanya N. Jili: *The New Political Economy of Land Reform in South Africa.* Cham: Springer Nature Switzerland AG (2021).

[6] For this and the following, see Ulrich Duchrow, Franz J. Hinkelammert: *Property for People, Not for Profit: Alternatives to the Global Tyranny of Capital.* London and Geneva: Zed Books in association with the Catholic Institute for International Relations and the World Council of Churches (2004).

[7] Cf. Brian Brown, *Apartheid South Africa! Apartheid Israel? Ticking the Boxes of Occupation and Dispossession.* A consideration of how the policies of the State of Israel, in violently dispossessing Palestinians

engagement for Mogopa and the other communities affected by forced removal that we need to be vigilant whenever and wherever systemic injustice of a similar kind violates a people's rights. In the case of Israel this is obvious, but much more difficult to oppose than in South Africa because of the Christian historical guilt of anti-Judaism, the general Western modern anti-Semitism and the unique crime against humanity of Nazi Germany, murdering 6 million Jews on an industrial scale in the Holocaust. Looking at this background, people in the West, and particularly Germans, have a bad conscience, which again allows the State of Israel to claim impunity for its crimes against international law and the human rights of the Palestinians. With your permission, dear Desmond, I quote your letter to the German *Kirchentag* and churches in 2015 concerning their hesitance to clearly stand up for justice in Palestine/Israel:

> As Christians, it is our duty to side with the oppressed, the downtrodden, the poor, the prejudiced and unjustly treated – ALWAYS. There is no place for neutrality, because it favours the oppressors. Always ...

> I implore you to listen carefully to what Kairos is saying. Our Christian sisters and brothers in the Holy Land cannot use balanced synod statements expressing sympathy for oppressor and oppressed alike. They are asking all of our help to win their collective freedom back. Please join the ecumenical Kairos movement and raise your voice in public solidarity to liberate Palestine so that Israel can be free, too.[8]

As you know, in 2020 Kairos Palestine and Global Kairos for Justice followed up the Kairos Document with the "Cry for Hope: A Call to Decisive Action" together with the motto: "We cannot serve God and the Oppression of the Palestinians".[9] The call followed Dietrich Bonhoeffer's principles in relation to the Nazi state's treatment of the Jews. Whenever a state systematically deprives a group of its citizens of their fundamental rights, and also when it intervenes in matters of faith, the church is in a state of confession (*status confessionis*). The "call to decisive action" also reminds us of this same situation with regard to apartheid South Africa, which was particularly recognised by the decisions of the Lutheran World Federation (LWF) in 1977 and 1984 declaring that apartheid constitutes a *status confessionis*, and also by the World Alliance of Reformed Churches (WARC) in 1982, calling apartheid a heresy. The WCC realised this seriousness with the Programme to Combat Racism (PCR). The call to decisive action claims that the deprivation of the rights of the Palestinians and (Christian) Zionism's misuse of the Bible to justify this injustice constitutes the same seriousness for the Christian churches. This is why the document calls upon the churches at all levels to organise processes in order to come to clear decisions and actions, seven of which are already suggested in the call.

But could there still be something learned from the struggles of Mogopa and the Covenant Project? Let me dream. Would it not be possible to again find e.g. 300 families in a region in Germany to link up with 300 families in the West Bank – in this case whose land was stolen by Israeli settler-colonists; whose houses were demolished by Israeli bulldozers as collective punishment for an alleged crime; whose child was detained in a military night raid etc.? In this way the victims could be supported in their resistance again by a people-to-people approach. Could this be multiplied in various regions or even countries and coordinated in Palestine, perhaps again with voluntary facilitators and communicators accompanying the international groups? In this way grassroots people from congregations and groups could be like leaven in the churches (and the general public) from below.

---

of their land, nationality and human rights, replicate policies of South Africa's era of Grand Apartheid (to be published shortly in the UK).

[8] Tutu, Desmond. "Open letter from Archbishop Emeritus Desmond Tutu to Deutscher Evangelischer Kirchentage." *EAPPI Blog,* 05 December 2015, https://blog.eappi.org/2015/05/12/open-letter-from-archbishop-emeritus-desmond-tutu/ (accessed 01 September 2021).

[9] See https://www.cryforhope.org/media/attachments/2020/06/30/cry-for-hope-english.pdf (accessed 07 May 2021).

At the same time in 2022 – as once in relation to the anti-apartheid struggle – the 11th WCC Assembly in Karlsruhe could be moved by the member churches to seriously respond to the "the call to decisive action" by launching a process for the next seven years to come to clear decisions. This would require a budget, at least one staff person and an international advisory group analogous to the Programme to Combat Racism (PCR), perhaps called "Programme to Combat Occupation" (PCO) or "Programme for Holy Land Justice" (PHL Justice). As finances are less available than in 1968 one could think of parts being covered by crowd-funding by the grassroots groups and their congregations working with the Palestinians in the resistance.

(5) Interaction of all social forms of the church – This brings me to my last point about what can be learned from the Mogopa experience: how wonderful the church, the body of Christ, can be, if all members, all social forms of the church, interact and communicate in hands-on discipleship. You and others from the national church level sided in solidarity with the suffering, endangered and resisting people at the local congregational level when you organised the vigil, expecting confrontation with the military power of the unjust system. This is how a real movement started, even inspiring ongoing and future struggles. Wolfram Kistner mobilised another social form of the church, what I call "discipleship groups", when he phoned me to collect the resistance money through our newly founded ecumenical network in Baden. This mobilised again another form, the congregations in our region. And we all acted in the framework of organisations within the universal social form of the church (LWF, WARC and WCC), which had made clear decisions and thus gave a wide ecumenical framework for the local and national levels. So all five social forms of the church interacted.

My hope is that what succeeded in relation to Mogopa and the Covenant Project, together with thousands of joint struggles to liberate South Africa, may also happen with regard to Palestine–Israel. The biggest hindrances in these struggles are institutional leaders who fear the powers-that-be, money and (unjust) state power – and being viciously called "anti-Semitic", when they ask their governments to make their cooperation with the State of Israel dependent on the fulfilment of international law and human rights. You, Desmond, have been so important for so many struggling people around the world because you have shown throughout that someone in your institutional position could, and can, speak truth to power and live out fearless prophetic theology instead of the normal church or state theology.

In the biography of Shirley du Boulay about you, she reports (p.151) the story when in 1979 you met a child from a community affected by forced removal.[10] You asked her: "'Does your mother receive a pension, a grant or something?' 'No' she replied. 'Then what do you do for food?' 'We borrow food', she answered. 'Have you ever returned any of the food you have borrowed?' 'No'. 'What do you do when you can't borrow food?' 'We drink water to fill our stomachs'."

Perhaps children like this moved your heart to courageously keep standing at the side of suffering people, not only in Mogopa and other communities dehumanised by the apartheid government but around the world. Like Archbishop Romero and today Pope Francis you have shown that the church is strongest when the leaders join with the people struggling for justice, peace and the integrity of creation, thus energising the whole church to become a living sign of God's kingdom. Thank you, dear Desmond. And now enjoy the Sabbath of Life, while the Desmond & Leah Tutu Legacy Foundation is continuing your good work.

---

[10] I owe this quote to Rudolf Hinz.

47. THE "ARCH" IN 1993 – A LETTER OF APPRAISAL FROM SOUTH AFRICA TO BERLIN

Klaus Nürnberger[1]

The original letter from 1993:

From Prof. Dr Klaus Nürnberger,
19 Thorpe Lane, Blackridge,
3201 Pietermaritzburg, South Africa

To Prof. Dr Cilliers Breytenbach
Kirchliche Hochschule Berlin
Teltower Damm 12O-122
1000 Berlin 37
Germany
30.3.1993

Dear Cilliers,

In response to your call, I would like to offer the following remarks concerning Archbishop Tutu. Although I consulted with two colleagues who know Tutu very well, this represents my own limited view.

1. Without any doubt, Bishop Tutu will go into history as one of the most prominent church leaders of our century. At a time when most Black leaders either went into exile, were in prison, or fell silent, he represented the cause of the Black majority with singular self-confidence and courage. He could not be intimidated or deterred by the threats and invectives of the state, the security establishment, the business world, and other organisations. He challenged the Apartheid politicians openly and confronted, in his clerical gown and together with like-minded clerics, heavily armed police forces at demonstrations and funerals. Without doubt, his international prominence shielded him against high-handed assaults of state organs, but on such occasions the bullet of a sniper could easily have struck him down.

2. At the time he opted, together with other Black leaders, for sanctions against South Africa. That caused a lot of enmity against him, especially among Whites and in Western countries. I also had strong reservations against this policy because of its incalculable consequences. However, one must realise that at the time the state unscrupulously deployed much heavier weaponry against the Blacks and that it was the only weapon available to them that had any hope of making an impact. Tutu repeatedly argued that it was also the only non-violent weapon, and that doing nothing would only drive the people towards uncontrollable violence. Every weapon is destructive, and in this case, more harm was done to Blacks than to Whites. But Tutu was confident that most Blacks supported him because they would rather suffer even more than to be exposed endlessly to Apartheid. One must at least respect this interpretation of the "lesser evil".

3. In his struggle against injustice and violence, Tutu was consistent and uncompromising. After being chosen president by the All Africa Council of Churches in 1986, he attacked, even in the presence of the heads of state, the despotism, corruption, and inefficiency of African leaders in their home territories.

---

[1] Prof. Dr Klaus Nürnberger served as an ordained pastor of the Evangelical Lutheran Church in Southern Africa from 1968 to 1979. From 1971 to 1979 he was a lecturer in systematic theology and theological ethics at the Lutheran Theological College, Maphumulo, Natal. From 1980 to 1989 he was professor of theological ethics at the University of South Africa (Unisa). From 1989 until his retirement in 1998 he was professor of systematic theology and theological ethics at the University of Natal (now University of KwaZulu-Natal) in Pietermaritzburg, South Africa. See also: https://klaus-nurnberger.com/47-about-klaus/about-klaus/46-meet-klaus.html (accessed 01 May 2021).

4. When President de Klerk lifted the ban on Black liberation movements, Tutu withdrew from politics to a large extent, leaving further steps in the hands of politicians. He also insisted that Anglican priests should not become members of a political party so that they could be preachers and pastors for everybody. He was criticised for this attitude by his own people, but it shows that he was a man of the church and that he was not motivated by political ambitions. It is quite possible that his integrity will again call him into an important public office if the chaos of the current splintering and feuding of Black political forces continue to grow.

5. The significance of Tutu for the Church in this country may lie, more than anything else, in the fact that he rescued the credibility of the Christian faith and the Church in the view of embittered and politically engaged Blacks, especially the youth. There were enough supporters, hangers-on, down-players and silent people among Christians in those times. Even for many critical people the "inner emigration" was more comfortable than a dangerous political profile. Often it seemed as if the Marxists were the only ones left who displayed sacrificial courage and determination in the struggle against injustice. If we Christians today are still allowed to contribute to the future of the country, we must thank this not least to people like Desmond Tutu and Beyers Naudé. In this sense the role of the Confessing Church and people like Dietrich Bonhoeffer at the time of National Socialism in Germany repeated itself.

6. Tutu's significance for the development of theological education in Africa is not immediately clear to me and my colleagues. In South Africa it can hardly be separated from what has been said above. At our own institution we have many Black students of theology who derive their high degree of public involvement from a deep faith. Without doubt the hidden impact of role models such as Tutu is considerable even if it is not immediately apparent.

I hope that these details serve their purpose for the time being. I wish you a good new beginning at the (Humboldt) University. With kind regards, also to the colleagues who still know me,

Yours, Klaus

A few clarifications and remarks in retrospect (2021)

This letter was written in 1993 in response to a request by Cilliers Breytenbach, a South African professor of New Testament Studies in Berlin.[2] I cannot recall the motive for his request. I guess that the faculty may have been considering an award to Desmond Tutu.

It was a time of explosive tensions in South Africa. The unbanned liberation movements were convinced that only an escalation of the struggle would lead to a breakthrough towards a new dispensation. A "third force" committed brutal atrocities such as "necklace" murders and throwing commuters out of moving trains. South Africa hovered on the brink of social chaos and civil war.

Apart from the globally celebrated attitude of Nelson Mandela, one can hardly overestimate the significance of Roelf Meyer on the government side and Cyril Ramaphosa – the current president of the country – on the side of the liberation movements, who negotiated a constitution of South Africa that is widely acknowledged as being exemplary for many "Third World" countries, especially in Africa, and which imposed the rule of law on a population with widely disparate interests, loyalties and backgrounds.

However, the change of attitudes was just as important. My intuition that "the Arch", as he was affectionately called, would again play an important public role materialised when Nelson Mandela appointed him as the head of the Truth and Reconciliation Commission. Though its shortcomings are

---

[2] Prof. Cilliers Breytenbach, born 1954 in Lydenburg (South Africa) was associate professor for New Testament studies at the University of South Africa (UNISA) from 1985 to 1988, professor for New Testament studies at the University of Pretoria from 1990 to 1997. From 1990 to 1993 he was professor for New Testament studies and director of the Institute for Ancient Christianity and Antiquities at Church University in Berlin Zehlendorf, as well as professor for New Testament with emphasis on literature, religions and contexts of ancient Christianity (1993–2019) at Humboldt University Berlin. From 2003 to 2020 he served as professor for New Testament studies and ancient studies at Stellenbosch University, South Africa.

often highlighted, this Commission was critically important in defusing the pent-up anger and bitterness among the victims of apartheid as well as the fear of many whites that they would be overwhelmed, disempowered and impoverished. A common humanity and empathy began to surface in the painful proceedings and disclosures of the various sessions.

My own hesitancy concerning economic sanctions was partly based on a study that I had just published on *The Scourge of Unemployment in South Africa* (1990). I had realised that sanctions would worsen the situation to an inestimable extent. Partly it was based on my pangs of conscience that we, the black and white theologians opting for sanctions, were situated in comfortable positions with secure incomes, while sanctions would cause further misery among millions of fellow South Africans. In the end, of course, Desmond Tutu and others were right: growing financial constraints decisively contributed to the change in direction of the regime.

That the worst fears at the time did not materialise gives me hope that the severe impasses the country faces today can again be resolved without burdening the poverty-stricken, who still form the majority, beyond the absolutely unavoidable.

48. DIVESTMENT, BOYCOTT AND TAX: THE CRUCIAL ROLE OF ECONOMIC JUSTICE IN THE KINGDOM OF GOD

David Haslam[1]

In March 1981 I was invited to give evidence to the United Nations Special Committee Against Apartheid in New York, about the international campaign to end bank loans to the South African government and its agencies. On arrival I was delighted to discover that giving evidence at that same session was then still Bishop Desmond Tutu, who was also the general secretary of the South African Council of Churches (SACC). I was able to sit in to observe his evidence to the committee, at the end of which, to everyone's surprise, he stood, raised his right arm and began to sing "Nkosi Sikelel' iAfrika". Fortunately as an active Anti Apartheid Movement member I was familiar with the words, so two churchmen led a rather embarrassed committee in the South African national anthem. I imagine they lost little time afterwards in learning the words, ready for the next time an irrepressible bishop was called to offer testimony.

I had become involved in the Banks Campaign in 1973 when visiting among other organisations the Interfaith Center on Corporate Responsibility (ICCR) in New York, and learning there that what was then the UK's Midland Bank was involved with five other European banks in the Europe American Banking Corporation (EABC). The EABC was engaged in lending to South African government agencies such as Eskom;[2] this had been discovered by a remarkable coincidence when South African exile and Methodist minister Don Morton had spoken on a New York winter night about apartheid to a small church audience. He was afterwards approached by an audience member who said he might have information to interest Don, and a few days later secretly provided him with a set of papers which detailed the EABC loans. This led to some of us in the UK setting up ELTSA, the End Loans to South Africa campaign, which then operated as part of an international network for nearly twenty years, challenging first the EABC banks and then when they agreed to cease the loans, many other banks – nicknamed the "Dirty Thirty" – who were engaged in lending in one form or another.

Archbishop Desmond's willingness to support, albeit with care, the various campaigns for divestment and boycott was a powerful symbol within the churches and beyond. The engagement of the SACC under his leadership meant the churches in Western countries found it increasingly uncomfortable not to back groups like ELTSA and Workgroup Kairos in the Netherlands. It also chimed well with the growing influence of the World Council of Churches' Programme to Combat Racism (PCR), set up in 1969, following the 1968 Uppsala Assembly. The PCR became best known for its grants to groups fighting racism worldwide but it was the grants to the liberation movements of Southern Africa, for their humanitarian work, which caused the most controversy. However, the PCR's work in the economic field was arguably even more important, as it became clear that apartheid was kept afloat by finance and trade, the oil and money which flowed in and the metals, manufactured goods and agricultural products which flowed out. Much of the latter were produced by segregated workforces, with black workers paid less and operating under far inferior and sometimes dangerous conditions.

For many Christians the wider anti-apartheid movement was a period when we realised how important economic factors are in seeking a more just and fair world. Churches could pass

---

[1] I am a Methodist minister who has entered the age of choice from the age of necessity (i.e. retired), but who continues to campaign for tax justice, a free Palestine and Dalit rights, along with local work on the environment, refugee support, anti-racism and justice issues in the local churches. I continue to be inspired by "Justice Heroes" such as Pope Francis, Nelson Mandela, Dorothy Day, Bhimrao Ambedkar and Desmond Tutu.

[2] Eskom is a South African electricity public utility, established in 1923 as the Electricity Supply Commission (ESCOM). In South Africa it is referred to as Eskom.

resolutions of concern, but it was when as investors they were urged to take action, challenging banks and companies in which they invested either to urge real change in Southern Africa or withdraw. As it became increasingly clear that companies could not or would not challenge the system from which they profited, churches were forced to face their complicity in an evil system. In the UK the churches supported the ELTSA campaign, and Midland backed down. However, Barclays continued as the largest bank in South Africa, and it was also revealed that Shell and BP were supplying both South Africa and what was then Rhodesia, and therefore breaking UN sanctions. The WCC PCR gave continuing support to the campaigners, the issues came up again at the 1983 Assembly in Vancouver, which Bishop Desmond also attended and at which he spoke. It was here the World Council's Programme on Transnational Corporations reported, and brought to wider attention the increasingly important role of the TNCs in shaping the global economy. Sadly the programme was discontinued but it left a legacy of awareness which has contributed to an ongoing theological suspicion of the priorities and influence of the largest companies.

One area where parallels to the economic dimension of the anti-apartheid movement have emerged is the situation in Israel/Palestine, with its ever-increasing oppression of the Palestinian people by the government of Israel. There was in the past considerable cooperation between Israel and the apartheid government, surprising in that some in that government had a record of collaboration with Nazi Germany in the 1930s and 1940s. Tutu himself drew attention to this and by 2014 the situation had deteriorated to the extent that, when Archbishop Desmond visited, he spoke of the "deeply distressing" parallels with apartheid in South Africa. He called for the setting up of a Palestinian state, and his support has given much encouragement to the activists in the Sabeel-Kairos movement for justice in Palestine, in its turn, to put pressure on the State of Israel to cease its occupation of territories which are Palestinian under international law.

The pressure has been growing on certain banks and companies which support, directly or indirectly, the occupation, and on church bodies which invest in them. A particular example has been Caterpillar, the US-based company which manufactures much of the equipment used to build the Separation Wall and to destroy Palestinian homes, fields and olive groves which are the lifeblood of the Palestinian people. Caterpillar distances itself from blame by selling via the US military or using local agents to deal with the Israeli security services. However, the Church of England and the Presbyterian Church of the USA both withdrew from Caterpillar some years ago, and in April this year the UK Methodist Church agreed to do the same. As in the days of apartheid this kind of non-violent economic pressure gives hope to people under oppressive systems that there are those supporting their struggle through such means.

Unsurprisingly there have been a number of delegations of black American and/or South African church leaders to Israel/Palestine who have expressed their horror at the situation. As long ago as 2006 a delegation from the US Historic Black Churches said that conditions for Palestinians in the West Bank painfully echo the injustices suffered by people of colour during South Africa's apartheid era and during the pre-civil rights era in America. They were sad to observe the fear of Palestinians felt by Israelis, similar to that apparently felt by whites of blacks in the US, and to realise that the Separation Barrier was being built "by US tax dollars". In 2019 a delegation of senior leaders visiting from both communities issued a searing statement, recalling among other things that there were many Christians that were silent and "closed their ears against the sound of the deadly apartheid jackboot in the lives of South African blacks". They wanted to retain "the option of utilizing economic pressure as a means of bringing recalcitrant dominant forces to the negotiating table", building on the experience of what brought hope to those suffering under apartheid, and finally undermined that destructive system. The Palestinians themselves are keen to promote resistance through non-violent means, see the "Cry for Hope" issued by Kairos Palestine in July 2020. In his book on Palestinian liberation theology Revd Naim Ateek says he believes it is a requirement for people of faith to resist injustice and that such resistance must continue "until justice is done according to international law, and the Palestinian people are free". Ateek also promotes the theme of "Sumud", Arabic for the "steadfastness" shown by the Palestinian people as they face Israel's oppression and continuing efforts to force them from their land.[3]

Learning of the importance of the economic sphere in the campaign against apartheid pointed me towards a greater interest in the global financial system, and how crucial it is in issues of racism and inequality in our world. In 2012 I came across the book *Treasure Islands* by Nick Shaxson,[4] which inspired me to set up first the Methodist Tax Justice Network, which has now expanded ecumenically into Church Action for Tax Justice (CATJ). The aim is again to inform and engage the churches in the economic dimension, in an area in which there are major moral questions alongside the financial ones. How can it be, in the case of the UK in particular, that so many of our "overseas territories", tiny geographically but very large in tax-dodging terms, are deeply engaged in this kind of economic subterfuge? In the latest listing by the international Tax Justice Network, which has been working on this issue for the last twenty-five years, the top three countries in their Corporate Tax Haven Index are the British Virgin Islands, the Cayman Islands and Bermuda, and five more other Overseas Territories or Crown Dependencies appear in the top twenty. The Netherlands, Switzerland and Luxembourg are all in the top ten, Ireland is at eleven and the UK at thirteen.

Campaigning by CATJ in the UK and with international partners has focused on raising awareness of the importance of tax, putting pressure on government to work for a much fairer global system and urging church investors to tackle companies in which they invest to declare their tax policies, and sign up to the Fair Tax Mark. It has been disappointingly difficult sometimes to convince churchgoers that tax is an issue in which they should not only be interested but that they should be actively promoting a fair tax system as a key aspect of the Christian calling. Churchgoers seem to think of "tax collectors" in a negative way, from the gospel stories, but they were collecting for a deeply unfair and exploitative system which milked the poor to pay for the upkeep of the Temple, Herod's Court and the occupying Roman army. It gave them nothing, while taxes today provide the public services which are so important and offer the social cohesion which binds us as a national (and international) community. Hence Christians should be willing and happy to pay their taxes – while continuing to campaign for them to be wisely spent. The fact that fairly small numbers of large corporations and wealthy individuals do all they can to avoid, evade and dodge their taxes – to the tune of hundreds of billions of dollars – is to be deplored, and persistently challenged.

Fortunately, over the past twenty years of campaigning, as with apartheid, the rest of the world has gradually realised this issue must be addressed, and the OECD (Organisation for Economic Co-operation and Development) – the West's economic "think-tank" – has got hold of the fact that the way to development, justice and peace is through a fairer economic system, which means global standards for tax. The arrival of Joe Biden as US president has strengthened this greatly and his proposal, for example, of a global corporation tax level of 21% is an enormous step forward. It is also the case that there are some of the very wealthy who are also committed to fair tax, including billionaires such as Warren Buffett. The UK government still seems resistant to this movement, possibly because one thing it is going to have to do is find alternative economic structures for its overseas territories which have become so reliant on harbouring the large amounts of money washing round the global tax system. These could be spent so much more productively, especially in the context of the pandemic and the climate crisis, as they do so much harm to the world's poorer countries. The witness of Archbishop Desmond Tutu in terms of the crucial importance of the economic sphere in seeking a just and peaceful world has been inspiring, alongside those of other Christian leaders such as Dr Martin Luther King, Archbishop Óscar Romero and US Catholic Dorothy Day.

Every Sunday, if not more often, Christians of all denominations around the world pray "Thy Kingdom come", presumably wanting to experience something of the meaning of the kingdom of

---

[3] Naim Stifan Ateek, *A Palestinian Theology of Liberation: The Bible, Justice and the Palestine–Israel Conflict* (Orbis 2017).

[4] Nicholas Shaxson, *Treasure Islands: Tax Havens and the Men Who Stole the World* (Bodley Head 2011).

which Jesus spoke here on earth. What seems to be far less thought about is what that means in practical terms and in the field of mission about which there is much Christian preaching and song. What theologians like Ched Myers and John Dominic Crossan have done is to point up the underlying essence of much of Jesus' teaching.[5] This has been too often hidden because of the depth of challenge it represents, especially to the Western way of life, founded on capitalism, which is ultimately about private profit. It is difficult if not impossible to contemplate how any thinking Christian can espouse capitalism, certainly in the kind of raw state which led to the growth of Empire and colonialism of the nations of Western Europe, and – alongside some of the positives produced – the damage which they did, the aftermath of which continues in today's unequal world.

The urgency of addressing economic structures in the context of Christian mission was drawn attention to by Pope Francis in *Laudato Si'*. In the context of focusing on the needs of the environment he said "the principle of the maximisation of profits, frequently isolated from other considerations, reflects a misunderstanding of the very concept of the economy".[6] This is such an important comment. Economies should be built on the basic questions "What do we want to do?", "What kind of society do we want?" and so "How do we organise it?" Not how we can make the most money for as few a number as possible. Tutu described himself as a socialist; in 1986 he said his experiences with capitalism had indicated that "it encourages some of the worst features in people. Eat or be eaten. It is underlined by the survival of the fittest. I can't buy that. I mean, maybe it's the awful face of capitalism, but I haven't seen the other face". Hence the economic face of mission should be inclined towards socialism, a collective approach to an economy whose ultimate value is "the common good", defined by a participative democracy.

Tutu promoted the idea of "*Ubuntu*"; he described it as referring "to gentleness, to compassion, to hospitality, to openness to others, to vulnerability, to be available to others and to know that you are bound up with them in the bundle of life".[7] Again the implication here is for Christian mission to promote vigorously a fairness in society, and an attention to the needs of the poorest, which implies in turn the churches should engage actively in the use of our investments to challenge injustice and exploitation in which corporations may be involved, whether in specific situations like Israel/Palestine or in more general areas like access to water, advertising of baby foods, excessive use of plastics, fossil fuel exploration, or mining – especially in remote areas or on the ancestral lands of indigenous people.

The tool of boycott is also important. The anti-apartheid struggle demonstrated that refusing to buy products from a context where there is discrimination and exploitation can be a powerful weapon. In today's world there are increasing calls for boycotts of clothing, footwear or electronic goods produced in "sweat-shops" of East Asia, of Esso petrol, as Exxon is one of the worst climate change deniers, of goods wrapped in single-use plastic, and of agricultural products from the Occupied Territories in Israel/Palestine. A kingdom of fairness also implies a just taxation system, at international level, and campaigners have long urged the involvement of the United Nations, as otherwise the voices of the poorer countries are marginalised or ignored. Authentic Christian mission, aiming to help create the kingdom of God, must include working for economic justice, using as and when appropriate the means of divestment, boycott and a fair tax system. The aim must be to ensure the kind of distribution of global riches in which Pope Francis, Archbishop Desmond Tutu and Jesus of Nazareth would jointly rejoice.

---

[5] Ched Myers, *Binding the Strong Man: A Political Reading of Mark's Story of Jesus* (Orbis 1997).
[6] Pope Francis, *Laudato Si'* (Catholic Truth Society 2015), 93.
[7] Desmond Tutu, *No Future Without Forgiveness,* Rider 1999, 34.

Gerhard Küsel[1]

It began at Jomo Kenyatta Airport in Nairobi, in 1986. About forty South African refugees had gathered at the airport. We waited in front of the arrivals lounge. When he came out of the door, the group Himosha started singing and all of them joined in, singing and dancing. With a typical smile on his face, Desmond Tutu spread his arms and joined in the dance. Every other person at the airport stood still and marvelled at the scene. The group with Tutu in the lead moved singing and dancing right through the airport towards the waiting car. It took just a short question to the Bishop and a meeting with him for the following day at midnight was arranged. His tight schedule left no other chance for an appointment.

Tutu had come to Nairobi to address the World Methodist Council. He was to stay only two nights.

On Saturday morning Bishop Tutu delivered a lecture at the World Methodist Council, and in the afternoon he had a meeting with the state president of Kenya, Daniel arap Moi, in which he confronted him with the question: "Why do my children in Kenya not get some sort of residence permit?" In the evening Bishop Tutu first met with some friends at the house of Rev. Maxime Rafransoa, the then secretary general of the All Africa Conference of Churches. At midnight he came to the church hall of the German-speaking Evangelical Lutheran Church of Kenya. There he was welcomed by about sixty South African refugees, who eagerly awaited him.

About thirty to forty of this group were students. They had fled from South Africa to Botswana after the Soweto uprising in 1976 and were brought to Kenya by the United Nations' High Commissioner for Refugees (UNHCR) to study. The remainder of the group were members who had fled in the sixties before and after the Rivonia Trial. The main group consisted of younger and older refugees, who had no refugee status in Kenya. Many of them had fled from a refugee camp of the ANC in Tanzania to Kenya. None of the African countries were able to offer refugee status to them, since at that time the Organisation of African Unity (OAU) had the policy of only supporting African National Congress (ANC) or Pan-Africanist Congress (PAC) refugees.

This group was supported by three former South African citizens who lived in Nairobi at that time: Rev. Sipho Mzimela, who was lecturer at St Paul's Theological College in Limuru, Sharon Manfred and myself, pastor of the German-speaking congregation in Nairobi. Together we had gathered funds from various organisations in the USA and in Germany to support this group that could not secure refugee status. The tension in the church hall was high until Bishop Tutu arrived. When he entered half an hour after midnight, everybody was eager to talk to him. Tutu, in his own charismatic way, soon took charge of the situation.

First there was a prayer for guidance. Then he started talking about the situation in South Africa, of what was going on within the churches and how the apartheid system was building up tensions. Afterwards he spoke about his own experiences within the system and the rivalry between followers of various groups like the South African Student Organisation (SASO), Congress of South African Trade Unions (COSATU) and the Black Consciousness Movement (BCM). He related a story about a funeral he had recently conducted: a black police officer had been killed in action and two of his white colleagues attended his funeral. Everything was all right until the sorrow and anger of the crowd was directed against the two white policemen. It soon became clear that their lives were in

---

[1] Gerhard Küsel was born in 1946 in Northern Natal; he studied first at the University of Natal in Pietermaritzburg, then in Oberursel, Göttingen and Berlin before taking up a ministry in the Swazi Diocese of the Evangelical Lutheran Church of South Africa (1975 to 1978). From there he went to Germany, Schortens, after which he was pastor of the German-speaking Evangelical Lutheran Church in Kenya from 1983 to 1988 before returning to Schortens. Today he lives as a retired pastor in Aurich.

danger. Then Bishop Tutu went to stand in front of the two men and said: "You will first have to kill me!" Slowly the crowd withdrew, and the situation calmed down.

Then one of the students in the church hall asked Bishop Tutu: "Father, why is it, that in South Africa we Blacks carry on fighting each other, whereas we should be united in fighting apartheid?" Tutu looked at them with great concern and answered slowly: "I think, we have not suffered enough yet!" Dead silence filled the hall for at least one minute and was disrupted only by the occasional sobs of the gathering. Tutu meant what he said and continued to elaborate the idea of suffering as a basis of unifying a society.

Then one young man stood up, opened his shirt, and showed his chest to Bishop Tutu. There were two awful scars on his skin. "This wasn't a bullet from the police or armed forces of South Africa. These wounds were inflicted by the guards of the ANC camp in which we were held like prisoners." Suddenly all those present exchanged their experiences and one could virtually feel the sense of hopelessness spreading over the meeting. But Desmond Tutu continued with his comforting talk to the gathering and slowly his great compassion for his "children" came to bear and the strength of his faith managed to comfort the young people without a country home.

Later, another young man asked him whether he had ever felt fear for his own life. To this question Bishop Tutu answered in his typical way, smiling: "No. You see, I am a small man, and nobody feels threatened by a small man. Small men don't get assassinated." And then he referred to Julius Nyerere and similar "small" men who might have been in danger of being assassinated. After that he remained in the church hall and listened to the sad stories of some of the group and comforted them where it was possible. At approximately half past two he finally left because he had to be at the airport at half past five in the morning to catch his flight back to South Africa.

At least he had managed to convince President Moi to provide residence permits for these refugees and allow them to stay legally in the country. I was privileged to be witness to this unique incident and grateful for having personally experienced the power of love and compassion of Bishop Tutu.

50. "Prisoner of Hope": Solidarity and Social Justice

Musimbi Kanyoro[1]

The privilege of knowing Bishop Tutu

For the twenty years that we lived in Geneva and worked at the Ecumenical Centre, Bishop Tutu was a welcome and frequent visitor who was known and valued both for his priestly work and for having been himself at one time a staff member of the World Council of Churches. Some of his contemporaries were still on the staff of the WCC in the 90s. Our children are proud to have a signed photo with Bishop Tutu. Our son was only thirteen years old and our daughter eleven when their dad took them along to an event in Geneva where the Bishop was a guest. In their thirties now, they still treasure that memory and we too as their parents celebrate those shared moments of a lifetime gift because this encounter has created for our family many pleasant conversations.

Three decades of immersion in ecumenical and theological work through the United Bible Societies, Lutheran World Federation, World Council of Churches and the World YWCA privileged me to cross paths with Bishop Tutu in forums across the world. Being in the presence of Bishop Tutu is transformational. His words invite reflection. He calls people to repentance, forgiveness and to commit to do right and live wholesome lives. This call is not only a spiritual call but also a call that is deeply rooted in our day-to-day earthly lives. It is about justice, fairness and care for one another. It is a Godly human call to become human together. Everybody has a part to play and no one is exempt from taking responsibility. Bishop Tutu stands in solidarity with the Jesus that I know – that one who dined with outcasts but also invited the rich and famous to the same conversation.

The impact of Tutu on my own journey

Over four decades, my professional work has been with women and girls, many of whom have no say in major decisions at home or in their community, and who, in their hundreds of millions, live with violence and violations of their very basic human dignity. Violence against women and girls in the world is so pervasive that it is a shame to society. Forty years of hearing women and girls tell their stories of gender-based violence have turned me inside out and tossed me upside down. It is a spiritual warfare to hear day in and day out about the terrible things that are done to women and girls in the name of culture, religion and politics. Hearing, seeing and knowing women's afflictions and oppression forced me to look for hope and inspiration far and wide from those who were speaking out against injustice.

It was during one of those restless moments that I heard a radio interview with Bishop Tutu. The journalist wanted to know what sustains the Bishop? The Bishop broke into his usual laughter and said "we are *prisoners of hope*". That registered for me and I do not remember much else in that

[1] Dr Musimbi Kanyoro is an accomplished leader with extensive experience in international non-governmental organisations, global multilateral organisations and ecumenical agencies. She is currently a member of the council of the London School of Economics and a board member of CARE International, UN Global Compact. She also serves as the senior advisor to Together Gender Equality, a program of UN Global Compact and a consultant on Faith and Gender for UN Women. Dr Kanyoro is the immediate past president and CEO of the Global Fund for Women. She holds a PhD in linguistics from the University of Texas in Austin and a Doctor of Ministry from San Francisco Theological Seminary. She was a visiting scholar of Hebrew and Old Testament studies at Harvard Divinity School. Dr Kanyoro has received numerous awards and recognitions internationally. She has served in an advisory role on gender issues with World Bank, UN Women, UNAIDS and various other organisations and initiatives. She currently chairs two international boards: the Women's Learning Partnerships and the United World Colleges.

interview but later I read that phrase from the Bishop Tutu's writings and then it stuck with me. I found myself quoting him in my writings and providing the same answer when asked the same question. I still do.

I became a human rights activist through students' movements that organised to advocate against apartheid in Southern Africa. Since then, I have a natural affinity towards those who fight racism and advocate for racial equality and I have used the same arguments to become a gender and women and girl's rights activist. I learned in my late teens that rebelling against injustice is a holy action and therefore I joined youth groups and church groups to organise local "Free Nelson Mandela" campaigns in my country, Kenya. We are a country which obtained political freedom by the force of organised movements. We continue to resist injustice and to speak up for justice. Working with affinity groups is a powerful thing but sometimes the group only serves some of the purposes. Over time, I developed my own agency to refuse to join the chorus of religious people focused on demonising women and girls under the pretext of abortion, sexuality rights and their asking for a seat at the leadership and decision-making tables.

Tutu as a respected follower of Jesus

More recently, I have been following Bishop Tutu's participation in the Elders Forum. His voice is recognised and respected as a follower of Jesus even in that secular forum. I am convinced that in all that he does, Bishop Tutu subscribes fully to the ultimate mandate of Jesus as recorded in Luke 4: 16-19. Some have called it "the Jesus Manifesto":

> He went to Nazareth, where he had been brought up, and on the Sabbath day he went into the synagogue, as was his custom. He stood up to read, and the scroll of the prophet Isaiah was handed to him. Unrolling it, he found the place where it is written: "The Spirit of the Lord is on me, because he has anointed me to proclaim good news to the poor. He has sent me to proclaim freedom for the prisoners and recovery of sight for the blind, to set the oppressed free, to proclaim the year of the Lord's favour.

In keeping with this manifesto, Jesus took actions to give hope to the poor, to victims of cruelty and systemic injustices; to women and children; to prisoners, to the sick – bleeding, blind, deaf, disabled and those locked out of any meaningful participation in society by bars of culture and religion. Jesus taught that God's purpose is to set the oppressed free to realise their potential, to be fully human and fully alive, to live abundant lives and to experience what it means to be under the protection of a loving God. The concern of Jesus was particularly for people in whom all hope had been crushed – who felt consigned to long days and even longer nights of desperation and despair! According to Jesus, the concern of the spirit is to motivate his followers to share the good news with these forgotten ones. The commitment of the spirit is to motivate us to have a passionate compassion – to be prepared to struggle in solidarity with those at the margins; to commit and work for their release from all personal, social and political forces that will debilitate them if left and abandoned on their own. The goal for justice in the manifesto is not just about rights – it is about compassion and love.

Similarly, Bishop Tutu always speaks on issues of public concern as part of his responsibility of love, inspired by the Jesus Manifesto. The message of truth-telling, reconciliation and forgiveness that Bishop Tutu preaches resonates with this Jesus Manifesto and urges activists like myself to listen, hear and do.

As I write the COVID-19 pandemic is ravaging the world. Gender-based violence has increased. Women are being killed, losing jobs, suffering from intimate partner's inflicted pain. Yet at this very moment, faith leaders are more concerned with other things. On this day, 1 June 2021, the Vatican has just announced a new law that will excommunicate anyone who ordains a woman. Even if the Catholic Church does not ordain women, Catholic women, especially nuns, are leading in the care of God's people. Ministry is about caring for people. Once again, the old story of the immense gender injustice is visibly undeniable and the sidelining and marginalisation of women continue.

My work as an advocate for gender justice

My faith is grounded in the courage that I have seen in women during my forty years of professional engagement. Before retirement in 2019, I was president and CEO of the largest public foundation devoted to women's human rights, namely, the Global Fund for Women (GFW). I heard directly from women representing more than 175 countries. The Global Fund for Women (GFW) began as an idea aimed at addressing women's's issues differently. The founders of the fund sought to shift the approach of international development by providing direct core funding to women for initiatives that improve their lives and communities. The pioneers of the fund prioritised populations that are hard to reach, such as widows, rural women, single mothers, women living with HIV, women's rights activists, peace activists, women advocating for sexual health and rights, environmental activists, sex workers, women in slums, women in conflict and post-conflict countries, women farmers, indigenous women and women working for political, religious and cultural inclusion. These are populations that usually cannot get a meeting with donors and are often sidelined or objectivised by governments, religious institutions and development agencies. At best, they are merely treated as "the problems" to be solved by other people through trickle-down funding after the middle class has been taken care of.

Until this day, Global Fund for Women supports women challenging the status quo in communities that tell "her" that because she's born female, she shouldn't pursue education, she shouldn't sit in on community meetings, her opinion is not important, she should focus on domestic chores, she shouldn't speak out if she's a victim of violence, her presence is not needed in parliament or to broker peace accords. She cannot be a spiritual or religious leader because God only accepts male leadership. This gender bias is exacerbated by race.

The fund supported women and girls organising to break the silence on their oppression and violence, to access education and ensure that their daughters and sons have equal opportunities for education and are safe and loved. Attention is given to those communities struggling to get better access to health care, more especially reproductive health care. The fund's logic is not to dish out money to solve "issues" but rather to support locally initiated efforts that ensure women's leadership that drives access to economic opportunities, environmental security and human rights for themselves and their communities and families. Women have been working to these ends with limited resources, while continuing to hold society together as mothers, grandmothers, aunts, daughters, career women, public servants, educators, volunteers etc. We often refer to these leaders as "empowered women." The immediate indicator of empowerment is the move from despair to hope. In other words, to join Bishop Tutu and become "a prisoner of hope".

Hope is the refusal to accept one form of reality. Hope is built on the premise that perceived reality can be changed for the better. Hope therefore is resistance. It actively resists the void of hopelessness by working for alternatives. Thus, hope is not merely an intellectual frame of mind. Hope is to be lived out. To hope for justice and peace is to work for elimination of injustice and to be a peacemaker. To hope for democracy means to practise being democratic in our personal relationships. To hope for wholeness means to face our own lack of wholeness with courage and to be prepared to go through the pain of self-examination, which leads to change. That change involves truth telling, accepting the responsibility and seeking forgiveness and reconciliation.

Efforts to achieve transformation are often hindered by self-defeating convictions that change is impossible or constant advice that tells the oppressed to be patient and not to alienate the liberals. As women and racialised people, we are told that change will only come slowly and will only happen if the oppressed are humble and respectful. Surely it is not a secret that delayed justice enhances distrust, hatred, fear and damages souls and bodies. As the saying goes: "Justice delayed is justice denied".

Looking back with gratitude, looking forward with hope

As I look back, I want to conclude with one historical moment where I indeed used Bishop Tutu's lenses to interpret the events of the time. The one central lesson I have learned from my ecumenical and human rights journey is that transformative change is possible and those who believe that "another world is possible" will not be silenced. The phrase "another world is possible" galvanised the World Social Forum in 2005 in Porto Alegre, Brazil.

I remember it as if it was just yesterday. The forum took place between 26 and 30 January 2005. Actually, two world forums took place in parallel. The World Economic Forum was held in Davos, Switzerland, the country where I was resident then. On the other side of the globe, the World Social Forum was happening in Porto Alegre, Brazil, a country which I frequented for my social activism and human rights work. Both of these forums claimed to address the world's problems, but their approaches to solving the problems were fundamentally different, underscoring the significance of being aware that what we do is as important as how we do it. The World Economic Forum attracted more than 2,000 participants, most of whom were representatives of multinational corporations and ministers of trade, chiefs of state, representatives of the World Trade Organisation and international financial institutions and a handful of invited representatives of civil society. On the other hand, the World Social Forum was open to anyone who wanted to attend and brought together tens of thousands of people, from non-governmental organisations, civil society and social movements, left-leaning political parties, sectoral groups, trade unions, women's organisations, churches and a few representatives of government, the United Nations and its agencies. All were invited. While the Davos meeting saw the solution to poverty as mostly financial investments, participants at the World Social Forum believed that poverty cannot be solved by focusing on the condition but rather you must give poverty a face. We must see who is poor and ask why. The Social Forum adapted the phrase "Another world is possible!" to guide them in the focus on people. I have used this phrase over the years and its presence in this reflection is also obvious. Here is why.

We know that poverty is an outrage against humanity. It robs people of dignity, of freedom and hope. It makes people powerless over their own lives. Women make up an estimated 70% of people living in extreme poverty worldwide. At the root of poverty lies lack of agency to access your rights, let alone demand them. Lack of power to live and thrive and not just survive. Lack of power to have your say and be heard!

Yet, most efforts in the fight against poverty focus on delivering services such as bed nets to prevent malaria and fertilisers to boost crop yield. These investments have documented impressive results and should be expanded because they have a "band-aid effect". What seems to be lacking is the moral voice that focuses on people's lack of agency, voice and equality. In his call for justice, Bishop Tutu, like the prophets of the Old Testament, epitomises that moral voice that demands that we see people behind the issues of concern.

We know that poverty does not come randomly. You are more likely to be poor if you are an ethnic minority, lack education and experience violence and discrimination. Poor people lack opportunities to realise their potential. They lack power and voice to influence the change they wish for and can sustain. They are extremely vulnerable to sickness, effects of disasters, climate change, conflicts and wars. People who are poor live in environments that are prone to toxic poisoning, crime, low-quality education and lack of opportunities for upward mobility. Poor people are often branded as dishonest, lazy, addicted to welfare, capable of fraud, corruption, bribes, vice, drug addiction, alcoholism and substance abuse, criminality, youth hooliganism, theft, mugging, robbery, pick-pocketing.

They are feared by others. They stand accused of claiming rights to benefits they have not worked for and flaunting the values by which decent people live. The life of the poor is painted as the hotbed of moral laxity, prostitution, sexual abuse, loose marital ties and neglect of parental duties.

This makes the realities of poverty less visible to better-off persons who may see these effects as crimes of the poor and advocate for policies that victimise them and punish them. One cannot advocate for the poor without being a prisoner of hope – you must believe another world is possible to remain active for the poor! This is the truth.

I learned from years of student activism that the struggle for life, dignity and freedom of a people is larger than any economic considerations. The story of the persistent woman in Luke 18: 1-8 is one of the Bible stories that motivates me to remain a prisoner of hope by believing that another world is possible for women and for poor people. This story has been used to illustrate Jesus teaching about persistent prayer to his disciples. I am absolutely in tune with persistent prayer but that story does more for me. It illustrates very clearly that, more often than not, justice has to be demanded. Justice does not become obsolete in time. The way to correct injustice is to provide justice. Persistence in search for justice is rooted in the belief that God is just and wants us to be the same. Women of the Bible, women of the church, women of the world and Bishop Tutu inspire me to believe that another world is possible because God is merciful and God is just.

51. DESMOND TUTU'S ROLE IN ESTABLISHING ECUMENICAL RELATIONSHIPS OF THE EVANGELICAL CHURCH IN GERMANY WITH CHURCHES IN SOUTHERN AFRICA

Werner von Hoerschelmann[1]

I learned to highly value Desmond Tutu during my time as head of the Evangelical Church in Germany's (EKD) Africa desk in the Church Foreign Office – and I still do today. A truly devout man: bishop, theologian, preacher, freedom fighter, politician – reconciler! All of this will be honoured on the occasion of his 90th birthday. My own memories of him are very personal. I remember his captivating charm, and the way he helped us, that is, the EKD, find a way out of our exclusive one-way-street relationship with the staunchly apartheid, "white" Lutheran churches of South Africa.

To grasp the full scope of his personality is no easy thing. Not long after he had taken over from the white Methodist layperson, John Rees, as general secretary of the South African Council of Churches (SACC), he visited the (then) Church Office of the EKD in Hanover. The issue under discussion was financial support granted by the Church Development Service (KED) to the SACC. The person responsible at the KED and the EKD's financial officer wanted to conduct audits of the SACC's accounts in Johannesburg to see whether the KED's funds were being spent properly, that is, in compliance with EKD financial rules; and under no circumstances on militant liberation movements.

I knew Desmond Tutu before. But I had never seen him as enraged as he was that day. The EKD's request to vet the SACC's finances, in total disregard of all conventions and subtleties of ecumenical partnership, and of the trust already built up and of the autonomy of the SACC, made his blood boil. With curt and harsh words, he dismissed this imposition.

Nevertheless, once the initial atmosphere of the meeting had calmed down, we experienced an exceedingly sociable and humorous Desmond Tutu. The heated confrontation ended with everyone laughing at Tutu's jokes. But on the matter at hand, he remained as tough as nails.

He was then asked to join the EKD Council which met in the conference room. I escorted him. On the very short walk there, I sensed his metamorphosis from, to begin with, a tough negotiator, to a humorous entertainer, and then to a bishop with spiritual authority and dignity. Moreover, in conversation with the council, he proved to be an extremely skilful diplomat. The gratitude he expressed to the EKD for the support it was providing through the KED came from the heart – along with his thanks for the partnership and trust shown in the way the funds were being spent. The row beforehand in the meeting room next door no longer mattered. Up to this point, the EKD's relationship with the SACC had in fact existed solely through the bank accounts of the KED.

As head of the Africa desk of the Church Foreign Office, I was at that time, if truth be told, no more than the official responsible for the agreements sealed between the EKD and the churches of German origin in Southern Africa. But the EKD's relationship with the UELCSA (the "white" United Evangelical Lutheran Church in Southern Africa) churches in South Africa and Namibia had long since lost its innocence – as a result of the synod of the EKD held in Bremen in 1973. From this point on, unreserved cooperation with pro-apartheid churches, whether Lutheran or Reformed, was

---

[1] Dr. theol. Werner Konstantin von Hoerschelmann 1967–1969, assistant to the Department of Theological Education in the Lutheran Church of Schleswig-Holstein, Germany. 1969–1974, chaplain for German-speaking protestants in South India and lecturer at United Theological College (UTC), Bangalore. 1974–1982, head of Africa Department in EKD Office for Foreign Relations, Frankfurt/Main. 1982–1997, Dean of St Peter's Cathedral and provost of Hamburg's city circuit Lutheran church. Lecturer at Hamburg University. Member of EKD Synod. Chairman of the Association of Christian Churches in Hamburg (ACK-H). 1994 election observer in South Africa. 1997–2003, chairman of "Kindernothilfe" (KNH), Duisburg (caring for c. 2 million children in need in thirty-six countries).

no longer possible. My colleagues Kremkau (EKD) and Benckert (Evangelische Arbeitsgemeinschaft für Weltmission (EAGWM)), and EKD office related to ecumenical mission activities, had set the course for an apartheid-critical position on the part of the EKD.

Tutu knew this because the theological master-brain at the SACC, Dr Wolfram Kistner, had tutored him on the EKD and its rather confusing organisational structures. He also knew that when Wolfram Kistner, as a professor from the "all-white" University of Natal, Pietermaritzburg, had struggled to switch his allegiance to the majority "black" SACC, I myself had supported him both on a personal and an official church level. The EKD took on the native South African Kistner as a "seconded pastor" and covered the associated costs.

The reserved, modest Wolfram Kistner was the bright mind in their struggle against apartheid. Tutu brought him to the SACC. Tutu knew that by winning over Kistner, the South African-born son of a German missionary couple, he would not only increase the strength of the SACC's argument, but also strengthen its relationship with the EKD. And Tutu also knew that we in the Foreign Office of the EKD had increasing qualms about sending pastors to UELCSA churches.

Kistner had also explained to Tutu, the Anglican bishop, the complicated systems of operation inside the Lutheran churches. The EKD was connected with the Lutheran churches in South Africa through treaties and the mission agencies – irrespective of whether "black" or "white".

In February 1975, the Conference of the Federation of Evangelical Lutheran Churches in Southern Africa (FELCSA) to which all Lutheran churches – black and white – belonged took place in Swakopmund, Namibia. For the EKD's own understanding of and positioning on Southern Africa, the result of the conference, the "Appeal to Lutheran Christians in Southern Africa concerning the Unity and Witness of Lutheran Church Members in Southern Africa" adopted by FELCSA was crucial. It aimed at a "new spiritual unity" to be witnessed in communion services held jointly by ELCSA (black Lutheran churches) and UELCSA (white Lutheran churches). This spiritual unity of the Lutheran confession was also to be expressed in terms of the churches' structures. Accordingly, an "Appeal to Lutheran ... Unity" was formulated. At the core of the wording of this appeal was the demand "to withstand ... alien principles". The alien principles the appeal's authors had in mind were apartheid policies in force in the churches.

Not just "spiritual unity" but conviviality across racial lines in worship and in practical church structures would have been a powerful witness to the Christian faith back then in 1975. It would have given credence to the "*status confessionis*" of the Lutheran churches in Southern Africa. The fact that this did not happen, that the "white" Lutherans withdrew from the thin ice of "spiritual unity" and refused to openly embrace it, then made them the "*casus confessionis*" of the Lutheran World Federation (LWF) Sixth Assembly in Dar es Salaam, Tanzania, in 1977. The Assembly suspended the membership of the UELCSA churches in the LWF.

The disputes between the "racially" different churches present in Swakopmund were fierce. The ELCSA's Bishop Rapoo and the provost of the GELCSWA (German Evangelical Lutheran Church in South West Africa), Kirschnereit, had become totally entrenched in their arguments. Rapoo, in a fit of anger, said: "It's no use! Lutheran unity is utopian in the face of political reality. The child will not grow. Let it die!"

Despite these heated exchanges, they did sign the appeal after all – all of them, including the white church leaders. I drove home from that conference knowing exactly what to say to the pastors who were to be sent by the Church Foreign Office to the associated UELCSA churches: "Read the Swakopmund Appeal, internalise it and try to bring it to life in your new place of work."

Even if the Council of the EKD considered this appeal to be good and proper, it was not made a precondition of its pastor-secondment scheme. In the end, their pro-white (in no way pro-apartheid!) sympathies were too strong to allow this to happen. But we in the Church Foreign Office told the pastors going to Southern Africa that they should make it the focus and (without doubt still distant) goal of their work there. We told them to be wise as serpents and not to rush things, so that they will prove to be doves of reconciliation between the racially divided churches.

PART III
PEACE

3.1. Prayer and Politics

52. THE CENTRALITY OF PRAYER

Thabo Makgoba[1]

As I think back on the ways in which I have saluted our church's oldest living archbishop emeritus over the course of my life, my mind's journey returns time and again to prayer.

Desmond Mpilo Tutu is for me synonymous with prayer and a reckless belief in the God who answers and must answer prayer – and in particular, prayer for the marginalised and the destitute. His prayer life is above all the thin but strong thread that characterises him in all his varied ministries, be it his advocacy for peace with justice, for the integrity of the environment, for sanctions against the perpetrators of injustice or for the ordination of women.

I have known and called him by various salutations: Father Desmond, Dean Desmond, Bishop Tutu, Arch, Archbishop Desmond, Arch Emeritus and now Tata. Each of these have reflected different milestones in the way his prayer and public lives have impacted mine.

As priest and pastor to his flock in Johannesburg and Lesotho, he had the strong sense of vocation he needed to carry his parishioners, whether as an eagle, metaphorically taking their faith to greater heights, or literally reaching out to them on horseback in the remotest mountains and valleys. Such ministry requires you to be steeped in prayer, with a deep connection with God, if you are not to drop your parishioners from your grasp.

As pastor, priest, bishop and ecumenist at the SA Council of Churches, Bishop Tutu was on his knees in the chapel daily, praying for the end of apartheid, for those in exile and for peace in the world. It was at a turbulent time in our country, but he had the gift of leading the staff into a deep silence, leaving no one in any doubt that they were hearing their God in the stillness. I had the privilege of working there as a student in my holidays and, although I was not there for long, his prayer life was contagious; once it grips you it never lets you go. Outside the chapel, you were intensely aware that when he spoke or wrote it reflected this intangible yet vividly real prayer life.

In my memoir, *Faith & Courage,* I recount his appearance in Jabulani Stadium in Soweto early in 1985, and my admiration for his courage in confronting publicly, without fear or favour, what he regarded as evil. At that time he was Father Desmond and Bishop Tutu, a combination of a priest with a pastoral heart steeped in a total belief in the God who triumphs over evil – the evil represented by the apartheid system which drove him to public prophesy, despite the risks he faced at a time when death squads roamed the land.

As archbishop and chair of the Truth and Reconciliation Commission, the tears that flowed when he broke down in sorrow would heal many. And the gift of tears were not only for the survivors and victims, they were also for perpetrators and wrongdoers, tears that join us with Jesus who wept, and still weeps for Palestine and Israel today. The staff at Bishopscourt testify to moments when only prayer could explain events, and even those at the TRC who were people of no faith were at a loss to explain significant moments.

As Archbishop and then as Arch Emeritus, he celebrated the Mass at St George's Cathedral on Friday mornings for nearly forty years, going home afterwards to continue his prayers at home,

---

[1] The Most Revd Thabo Makgoba, the Anglican Archbishop of Cape Town, was accepted for ordination training by Desmond Tutu when the latter was Bishop of Johannesburg. Dr Makgoba was elected Bishop Suffragan of Grahamstown in 2002, Bishop of Grahamstown in 2004 and Archbishop in 2008. He holds a BSc degree, a BA (Honours) in applied psychology and an MEd in educational psychology from the University of the Witwatersrand and a PhD from the University of Cape Town. He has honorary degrees from Canada, South Africa and the United States. He serves as chancellor of the University of the Western Cape.

where I would sometimes join him. Throughout his ministry and beyond, he has insisted on receiving prayer sheets issued by dioceses and parishes, and can be seen buried every morning in lists and lists of people and places, quietly praying for each person or intention individually. He never missed an opportunity to drop a note or send flowers on significant milestones.

When you visit him in hospital, the first things you see alongside him are his prayer book, Bible and intercessory folder. When you pray with him, he will pray in turn, reminding you of what you might have left out (on one recent occasion, my sister who had just died), lifting to God all of creation as it groans, and asking for hope and peace, light and love to be shared among all.

Archbishop Desmond Tutu used to say that an effective prayer life would never allow you to remain on your knees. No, it would compel you to get up and go out into the world to bring good news to the oppressed, to bind up the broken-hearted, to proclaim liberty to the captives, release to the prisoners and to proclaim the year of the Lord's favour.

Perhaps his most important but least recognised legacy as Archbishop is that he taught us the real, life-changing, world-changing power of prayer to empower us to carry the gospel to the world. The fruits of his prayer were encapsulated in an epitaph by which Tata could be remembered in future:

He laughed
He cried
He loved

53. Protest and Prayer

Konrad Raiser[1]

With pleasure I join those friends and colleagues who greet Archbishop Emeritus Desmond Tutu on the occasion of his 90ᵗʰ birthday. I have to admit though, that I cannot count myself among those who have been close to the Archbishop and have accompanied him on his extraordinary life-journey. My relationship with him has been mediated through my work with the World Council of Churches (WCC).

We both came into the energy-field of the ecumenical movement at about the same time: he in 1972 as associate director of the Theological Education Fund (TEF) in London, which was linked with the WCC through the Commission on World Mission and Evangelism; I – on the other hand – in 1969 as study secretary in the secretariat of the Commission on Faith and Order. In a way, we were both involved in the process of rethinking the role of theology in the ecumenical movement and shared in the first steps towards the shaping of contextual theology. But while he, following the mandate of the TEF on "contextualisation", spent much of his time in the years 1972–1975 visiting and working with theological schools and churches in Africa, I was involved in the challenging process of opening the concern for the unity of the church for the issues related to the emerging unity of the worldwide human community.

In the WCC it was the time when the Programme to Combat Racism (PCR) began to take shape. I had not been part of the processes which had led to the establishment of the PCR programme and it was only after 1973, when I had been appointed as one of two deputy general secretaries of the WCC, that I became involved in the intensive discussions about shaping WCC policy in the struggle against racism. I now realise that Desmond Tutu also had not been part of the earlier phase of ecumenical discussions with and among the churches in South Africa after the Sharpeville incidents followed by the Cottesloe Consultation in 1960, which led to the withdrawal of three white Reformed member churches of the WCC and the establishment of the Christian Institute under the leadership of Christiaan Beyers Naudé in 1963. One of his first direct contacts with, and involvement within the ecumenical programme against racism, especially in Southern Africa, was probably the special meeting with representatives of WCC member churches from South Africa in connection with the Central Committee meeting in Geneva in 1973 in which he participated as a WCC staff member. I was not involved in this meeting and therefore did not meet him there.

The first time I came across his name and his unmistakable voice was when I heard about and read his letter of 6 May 1976 to the then South African Prime Minister John Vorster. He had by then left the TEF and returned to South Africa in 1975 after his election as Dean of Johannesburg, thus becoming the first black African in this position in the largest diocese in the country and the highest-ranking black African clergy in the Anglican Church of the Province of Southern Africa. In this capacity he was invited to participate as an advisor in the Nairobi Assembly of the WCC. South African presence at the assembly had been hampered for political reasons. Apparently, he did not play a prominent role in the discussions before and at the assembly about nuclear collaboration between Western countries and South Africa.

As dean of the diocese of Johannesburg he decided to live in the black township of Soweto and thus became quite directly aware of the growing unrest and anger particularly among Soweto youth. On 6 May 1976 he wrote his afterwards famous letter to Prime Minister John Vorster which to my

[1] Konrad Raiser is a German protestant theologian, born 1938 in Magdeburg. He was executive staff in the World Council of Churches from 1969 to 1983, general secretary of the World Council of Churches from 1993 until 2002 and professor of theology and ecumenics at the Ruhr University of Bochum (1983–1993). Recent publications: *Religion-Macht-Politik*, Frankfurt 2010; *Ökumene unterwegs zwischen Kirche und Welt*, Münster 2013; *50 Jahre Reformation – weltweit*, Bielefeld 2016.

knowledge was his first public act in the struggle against apartheid.[2] He expressed to the prime minister his "nightmarish fear that unless something drastic is done very soon then bloodshed and violence are going to happen in South Africa almost inevitably". Reminding the prime minister of the experience of oppression and the struggles for liberation of his own people, the Boers, he stated that "nothing will stop a people from attaining their freedom to be a people, who can hold their heads high, whose dignity to be human persons is respected ...". He appealed to the prime minister to show that "your government and all whites really mean business when you say that you want peaceful change". This should be demonstrated through the following "meaningful signs": 1. granting to urban blacks citizenship rights in South Africa; 2. repealing the pass laws; and 3. holding a national assembly open to all South African leaders to discuss the evolution of South Africa into a more just society. In closing his letter, he referred to the fact that he had sought to discern God's will and to seek the illumination of the Holy Spirit during a prayerful retreat and that he had felt moved by God to write this letter. Already this first public utterance showed his characteristic approach linking prayerful concern with prophetic protest. Vorster wrote back accusing Tutu of engaging in political propaganda. He refused to take any of the steps recommended by Tutu.

Only six weeks after this letter, the situation in Soweto exploded on 16 June 1976 with more than 20,000 students protesting against the imposition of Afrikaans as the language of instruction in public schools. Their protest met with brutal violence on the part of the police leaving up to 700 people dead. The WCC Central Committee meeting in August 1976 issued a statement condemning the Bantustan policy of the South African government, which was about to be inaugurated by the declaration of "independence" of the Transkei. The forced removals of people into the so-called "homelands" later became one of the primary targets of Tutu's public protests as general secretary of the SACC.

The Soweto uprising inaugurated a process of continuously mounting tension with the killing of Steve Biko, the leader of the Black Consciousness Movement, in September 1977 followed by the banning of eighteen organisations involved in the struggle against apartheid, among them also the Christian Institute, in October 1977 and the uncovering of the information scandal (Muldergate) which ultimately led to the stepping down of John Vorster as prime minister. After the death of Steve Biko and the banning of the various organisations the WCC, through the Programme to Combat Racism, issued a background and reflection paper under the title: "South Africa's Hope – What Price Now?" It addressed the searching question of what form active solidarity with the struggle in South Africa could take, in a situation where the hope for peaceful change had been thoroughly disillusioned.

The events in South Africa between May 1976 and the end of 1977 had a strong impact on our agenda in the WCC, but Desmond Tutu to my recollection was not directly involved. Even before he wrote to Prime Minister Vorster he had been elected as Anglican Bishop of Lesotho, Botswana and Swaziland. On 11 July 1976 he was consecrated in this new position. In this capacity he was somewhat removed from the South African struggle. Only later did I take note of his significant role in leading the funeral service of Steve Biko in September 1977 in King William's Town where he pleaded with the authorities to listen to the appeals as long as there was still a chance of a "reasonably peaceful" change.

I became aware of Bishop Tutu again after he had been called back from Lesotho and was installed as the first black general secretary of the SACC in March 1978. Under his leadership, and after most of the other organisations had been banned, the SACC became a decisive instrument in the struggle against apartheid during the final years of the nationalist government under P.W. Botha who had taken over as prime minister from John Vorster in September 1978. There is no need here to recount the extraordinary way in which Bishop Tutu led and represented the South African churches in the struggle against apartheid and for peaceful change of the social order. For many of the activists

---

[2] Published in: Desmond Tutu, *The Rainbow People of God*. London, 1995, 7. The following quotations are from there.

in the struggle he was too moderate, but for the government he became a dangerous counterpart, particularly due to his international reputation. In particular, his call for international economic sanctions against the apartheid regime drew the anger of the government.

In November 1981 the government decided to take decisive action against the SACC and its general secretary by appointing a commission of inquiry under the chairmanship of C.F. Eloff, a Transvaal judge. The all-white commission was asked to investigate the council's activities, finances and personnel policy with the intention to undermine and silence the council and its leader. We followed the proceedings of the Eloff Commission with deep concern. Bishop Tutu gave evidence to the commission at its first hearing in September 1982. For me, his long and determined presentation to the Eloff Commission became a prime example of his way of speaking truth to power and witnessing to his faith in obedience to God's calling. He declared: "I want the government to know now and always that I do not fear them. They are trying to defend the utterly indefensible. Apartheid is an evil and as vicious as Nazism and Communism and the government will fail completely because it is ranging itself on the side of evil, injustice and oppression. The government is not God, they are just ordinary human beings who very soon, like other tyrants before them, will bite the dust."[3] And he continued later: "There is nothing the government can do to me that will stop me to be involved in what I believe is what God wants me to do … When I see injustice, I cannot keep quiet, for as Jeremiah says, when I try to keep quiet God's word burns like a fire in my breast. But what is it that they can ultimately do? The most awful thing they can do is to kill me, and death is not the worst thing that can happen to a Christian."[4]

While the commission was continuing to hear witnesses, in particular also from international partners of the SACC, the WCC was preparing its general assembly which took place in August 1993 at Vancouver, Canada. Bishop Tutu was among the invited guests, but the South African government once again had confiscated his passport. After lengthy negotiation he was eventually allowed to travel but arrived only midway through the programme of the assembly. It was on 6 August 1983: the assembly participants had returned from a peace rally on the day of transfiguration in commemoration of the nuclear bombing of Hiroshima. They were about to begin an all-night vigil praying for peace and reconciliation when Bishop Tutu suddenly appeared and was greeted enthusiastically. I do not recall the details of his spontaneous address that evening, but it could not have been more appropriate coming as it did out of his ongoing struggle for reconciliation and peace with justice in South Africa.

When the Eloff Commission presented its report in February 1984 it had to admit that it had failed to find any instances of financial or administrative mishandling. More importantly, the commission refuted the government's accusation that the SACC was being used by foreign powers to undermine the political order in South Africa. The government was therefore prevented from declaring the SACC as an "affected organisation" and thus silencing it. The most significant public support for Bishop Tutu and his mission in South Africa came shortly afterwards when on 10 December 1984 he received the Nobel Peace Prize in Oslo.

I had by then left the staff of the WCC and returned to Germany to take up a teaching position at the University of Bochum concentrating on systematic theology and ecumenics. I therefore witnessed, only from a distance, the rapid succession of further developments in Bishop Tutu's life-journey: first, his installation as Bishop of Johannesburg in February 1985; then in September 1986, he was elected and installed as Archbishop of Cape Town and Southern Africa followed by his election as president of the All Africa Conference of Churches in September 1987.

At the time, the discussion about solidarity with the struggle in South Africa in my context in Germany was largely focused on the Kairos document under the title "Challenge to the Church: A Theological Comment on the Political crisis in South Africa" (1985). To my initial surprise Bishop Tutu was not among the signatories. In hindsight I can understand the reasons: the sharp distinction

---

[3] "The Divine Imperative", in: Tutu, *The Rainbow People of God*, 58.
[4] Tutu, *The Rainbow People*, 76.

between church theology and prophetic theology could not really be applied in his case. As Bishop and later Archbishop and with his plea for non-violence and reconciliation he appeared as a representative of "church theology". However, his way of acting in public provided in fact a clear example of a "prophetic" vocation. When in 1985 during the state of emergency he was challenged because of his readiness to continue talking with the government he responded (in an interview with *Time* magazine): "I am not a politician. My paradigm comes from the Scriptures. I say to the government that it cannot prescribe to me what I preach. Equally, no one in the black community can prescribe to me what I should do … I have to follow biblical paradigms; prophets go on talking to kings, Moses goes to the Pharaoh, even when he is told that Pharaoh is going to harden his heart. But he goes."[5] And I was deeply impressed with what I learned later about his decisive role in negotiating with Prime Minister de Klerk as well as with Nelson Mandela to achieve the final transition towards the post-apartheid order in South Africa.

When in August 1992 I was elected as general secretary of the WCC, it had already been decided that the next meeting of the Central Committee in February 1994 should take place in Johannesburg. To prepare for this meeting I visited South Africa for the first time in the summer of 1993; in my earlier time on the staff of the WCC travelling to South Africa had not been possible. The visit this time was very exciting, not least because of my first personal encounter with the "Arch" in his residence Bishop'scourt in Cape Town. Much of our conversation turned around the forthcoming first non-racial, democratic election.

I cannot conclude these recollections of encounters with Archbishop Tutu without mentioning his impressive witness for justice and reconciliation as chairperson of the "Truth and Reconciliation Commission". He had originally decided to retire as Archbishop in 1996 and to follow an invitation for an honorary lectureship at Emory University in the USA. When the new commission was formed in 1995, he first hesitated to accept the invitation to become a member, because it would have interfered with his own plans. However, when President Mandela urged him to take charge of the commission as chairperson he could not refuse. In his way of leading the work of the commission, particularly in the sub-group on hearing accounts of the crimes and violations of human rights during the apartheid period from 1960 till 1994, he invested his public authority in the unceasing effort to give credence to the understanding and praxis of justice as rooted in the African vision of "*Ubuntu*". Where the human networks sustaining the life of the community have been violated, the purpose of establishing justice is to restore these vital networks of relationships and to reintegrate the perpetrator of the incriminated acts. This notion of "restorative justice" which resonates with the biblical understanding of justice has become one of the lasting legacies of Archbishop Tutu in his leadership role of preparing the ground for the process of reconciliation in post-apartheid South Africa.

---

[5] *Time Magazine*, 19 August 1985, 26.

A nice thought! But it didn't work. The first pastor sent out on this basis, my friend Christian Matthes, was soon dismissed. The leaders of the UELCSA churches said that was not what they had meant when they added their signatures to the Swakopmund Appeal.

And we in the Church Foreign Office were basically faced with a shambles. Should we take heed of the Mainz Research Group for Southern Africa (Mainzer Arbeitskreis für das Südliche Afrika, MAKSA), which had been trying for years to persuade us (the EKD) to pull out of the agreements with the pro-apartheid UELCSA?

In the meantime, a different line of ecumenical partnership between the EKD and South Africa had existed for some time. The KED had established a position for itself – purely via finances – and that was to the South African Council of Churches (SACC); the secretary general of the SACC at that time was Bishop Desmond Tutu.

This purely pecuniary connection to the EKD wasn't enough for Tutu. Wolfram Kistner, as head of the SACC's "Justice and Reconciliation" department, explained to him that the path by which the affiliation to the EKD could find intellectual and spiritual fulfilment was via the Church Foreign Office. This Church Foreign Office was after all established in 1945 after the end of World War II with its main tasks to re-establish ecumenical relations and the care for protestants in foreign countries – in exactly this order.

This led to countless meetings and discussions with representatives of the SACC, its president, the Methodist Bishop Peter Storey, and in particular Desmond Tutu and Wolfram Kistner, about the burning problems of South Africa and how to bring about a sea of change in the way they were perceived in Germany and throughout Europe. The questions raised by the World Council of Churches (WCC) in cooperation with the SACC with regard to economic relations with South Africa, foreign (German, European) investments in the apartheid state and the use of violence in the resistance movement kept us in the Church Foreign Office very busy. These discussions were also prevalent within the South Africa Commission (that is, all offices, ministries and works within the scope of the EKD concerned with South Africa) and a European "South Africa Dialogue Group" newly founded by the SACC and the Church Foreign Office. The row in Hanover, when Tutu had refused to even contemplate the SACC being treated as a mere policed recipient of alms from the EKD but had demanded they be treated as equals – that row proved to be productive!

The result was that the EKD shifted its primary partnership from the UELCSA churches to the SACC. But this still required some clarification. In 1977, Council vice-president Hild, vice-president of the EKD Church Office Wilkens and I attended the annual SACC national conference. Hild explained the EKD's position regarding church partners in South Africa based on the recent discussions held within the council. His clear anti-apartheid stance and desire for a close partnership with the SACC met with thanks and joy in a reply given by Tutu.

A little later, in 1978, council president Bishop Claß was himself in South Africa. He confirmed all the agreements between the EKD and the SACC that had come about through the talks with the EKD's Foreign Office and as a result of the trip conducted by Hild, Wilkens and myself.

The Council decision of 11 March 1982 entitled the "Declaration on the Partnership between the South African Council of Churches and the Evangelical Church in Germany" sealed the close relationship between the EKD and the SACC.

The actual ecumenical reality in South Africa was being played out in the South African Council of Churches, despite the Reformed and Lutheran white churches keeping themselves separate. But this again in reality still didn't resolve the problem for our Church Foreign Office. We now had to operate on two levels: fulfil the ongoing agreements with the (white) UELCSA churches and cultivate the substantive, close ties with the multi-racial, majority-black SACC.

I asked Tutu at that time how the EKD – meaning myself – should conduct itself in this balancing act. He told me, "As Africans, we always stand loyal to our people, our tribesmen. You (the EKD) should remain faithful to your churches of German origin and abide by your agreements. But tell them if they continue to play the pro-apartheid card, they will end up in a deadly dead end."

I received exactly the same advice from Bishop Auala in Namibia (Bishop of the Evangelical Lutheran Ovambo-Kavango Church (ELOK)) and his successor Bishop Dumeni who advised that a mindful person abides by their own kind, but they take care to ensure their kind don't destroy their own future.

The discussions between the SACC and the EKD's Foreign Office intensified. The aforementioned issues of foreign investment in South Africa and the call for economic boycott became ever more relevant and the subject of fierce debate. The issue of violent resistance also increasingly found its way into the dialogue.

In June 1978, the EKD Council issued a statement covering all of these points. The SACC wasn't really assured by it. There was a faction in the council that was interested in maintaining the status quo in South Africa. They were people who, either in their naive innocence or led by a clear pro-apartheid bias, took part in a "propaganda trip" to South Africa paid for by the South African state and arranged by the travel agent Hennenhofer in Germany. The agenda of this trip also included a "token" visit to the SACC in Johannesburg.

I received a call from Desmond Tutu in which he read me the riot act: what is actually gospel with you people in the EKD? The speech given by Hild? The supportive words of Claß? The partnership agreement between the EKD and SACC signed in 1982? Our umpteen conversations?

This propaganda trip by EKD Council members sponsored by the South African government means the end of the road for our partnership! Never had I received such a verbal slap in the face over the phone. But Tutu was right! For my part, I agreed with him, and I did so in no uncertain words, berating the council members who were on the apartheid propaganda trip. And I almost lost my job over this.

But the majority of the EKD Council were well aware of the reality of South Africa – both politically and ecumenically. I was allowed to stay. And the connection between the EKD and the SACC lived on. "Reconciliation" – that was the buzzword on the lips of all church people at that time. A woolly word in the escalating conflict between black and white. But Tutu said not so. Reconciliation is more than just love, peace and harmony. Forget it! There'll be no reconciliation without justice! And no reconciliation without sacrifice! God reconciled with us for the sake of his righteousness through the sacrifice of his son, Jesus Christ, on the cross. He was the strong one, and he gave! Reconciliation in South Africa is only possible if today's strong ones, the whites, are capable of giving [in the sense of political and economic power]. It may be the other way around tomorrow. But we are not yet there today. Justice, sacrifice and forgiveness – it's this trinity that constitutes reconciliation in the Christian sense.

Our well-intentioned attempts from the outside to seek reconciliation were often little more than an appeal to "be nice to one another!" Tutu stripped me of my illusions that these appeals would have any impact whatsoever – and at the same time gave me the courage to remain faithful to the Lutherans of German origin as a "thorn in the flesh". He was fully aware of the fact we were having to manage a balancing act between our intensive dialogue with the SACC on the one hand, while being loyal to the UELCSWA churches on the other – and that we found ourselves questioning whether there was any light at the end of the tunnel at all. It was his words of wisdom that put the EKD on the right track at that time.

On a personal and anecdotal note: while travelling to a meeting with German Foreign Minister Hans-Dietrich Genscher, Tutu and I found ourselves standing on a draughty platform at Frankfurt Central Railway Station. He took my "Elbseglermütze" (a type of peaked cap peculiar to Hamburg mariners) off my head with the words, "My South African head needs protection!" It fitted. I never got it back. For years, he continued to wear this type of cap, with me sending him a new one whenever necessary. When you look at the photos of Desmond Tutu on the internet you will find a lot of photos with Tutu's sailors' cap. He wore it also when he met President Botha!

It goes without saying that the many conversations I had with Tutu were not restricted solely to theologically profound discussions or high-stakes political issues. He also visited me at my home.

And my children still remember how he tried to teach them the click sounds used in many southern African languages.

I knew what a rhetorical genius he was – especially the clarity of his Christian preaching – and experienced it first-hand. As the senior pastor of Hamburg's St Peter's Church, I asked him once to conduct a service for us. The church was packed out – more so than on Christmas Eve. In his sermon, he radiated reconciliation. We celebrated communion. He baptised a group of Hamburg children. It took forever. But everyone was happy.

When I was an election observer in South Africa in 1994, we hoped to meet up in Cape Town. But I ended up staying in the Johannesburg area. I'm afraid we didn't see each other – never again in South Africa.

Seeking kindred spirits in the Struggle
Breathing the faith of Infinity
In each moment
You walk on water

dancing through life
with JOY
living out the destiny for which you are called
preaching Grace
and liberty to the captives
lifting the chains off the prisoners
WE ARE CREATED FOR FREEDOM!
You proclaim
Your lips touched with coals of fire

You counter the violence of hate
With the
VIOLENCE OF LOVE
until the day breaks
And though the shadows linger
You prophesy
A NEW TESTAMENT for all creatures

Deliverance from slavery
the vineyards restored
To the poor
Mothers and fathers may soar to the heavens
Children may know their names
The long night of bondage will be ended
All shall know the Truth
That sets the nations free
The Rainbow across mountain and valley
A new earth and
A new heaven

Captive for Freedom (For your 80th birthday on 7 October 2011)

From the shadows of Klerksdorp
You stride out,
Captive of your calling
Unfolding in sacrifice,
And the sacrament of service.

Remembering a time when
Fishing with your father
You dreamt of mothers'
Hands, weathered and calloused,
Being softened and caressed in solace.

Your ear is attuned to the laments of
Suffering people wounding your frail flesh,
Kindling your anger and indignation;
Tongues of fire, your mitre aflame,
The incense of your cries rising to the heavens:

"I am because we are!"
You shout across forest and mountain.

43. "CALLED TO SERVE" AND "CAPTIVE FOR FREEDOM": TWO BIRTHDAY POEMS

Betty Govinden[1]

My participation in the wider Anglican Communion, and in ecumenical structures in South Africa, was during the episcopacy of Archbishop Desmond Tutu. One of the highlights, during my attendance at the 1988 Lambeth Conference, was when I joined a small group of South Africans, led by Archbishop Tutu, to attend the celebration of Nelson Mandela's 70th birthday, held at Wembley Stadium, London, on 11 June 1988. Over 70,000 people attended this grand anti-apartheid concert, which was broadcast to sixty-seven countries, and an audience of 600 million. Special guests included Miriam Makeba, Hugh Masekela, Harry Belafonte, Stevie Wonder, Sir Richard Attenborough, Fr Trevor Huddleston and Archbishop Tutu, who addressed the gathering, to a rousing ovation. Mandela was on Robben Island for twenty-five years at the time. The Archbishop's brave and fearless witness over the decades for truth and justice has been inspiring and exemplary. It is in this spirit of inspiration and celebration that I offer these two birthday poems, written a decade apart from each other, in honour of Archbishop Tutu.

Called to Serve (For your 90th birthday on 7 October 2021)

In the beginning is the Word
the Word is with God
and the Word
Comes to dwell amongst us
The Word of TRUTH, JUSTICE, LOVE and PEACE
Stirring brave and spirited souls to
RISE
Rouse hearts
Raise voices
Heal a broken world

And the WORD finds a dwelling place
in your heart
You become the lodestar
Leading with your staff
In the long dry white season
A people bereft
wandering in the wilderness of
tyranny
longing for the Promised Land of
Freedom

Apostle of Peace
dreaming of wholeness and humanity for
oppressed
and oppressor
you are fearless in your quest

---

[1] Devarakshanam [Betty] Govinden [PhD] has published in literature and literary criticism, education, history, feminist theology, Gandhi and peace activism, among other disciplinary fields. She was a founder member of the Circle of Concerned African Women Theologians. She was a lay representative from the Anglican Church in South Africa [ACSA] to the Anglican Consultative Council [ACC], the ACC Standing Committee, and the 1988 Lambeth Conference, held in Canterbury, England, as well as the South African Council of Churches [SACC]. Betty is a lay minister at St Aidan's Anglican Church, in Durban.

54. WHEN PRAYER MEETS POLITICS: REFLECTIONS ON DESMOND TUTU IN DENMARK

Peter Lodberg[1]

In September 2004 Desmond Mpilo Tutu was in Copenhagen, Denmark, invited by the Centre for African Studies at the University of Copenhagen and DanChurchAid. It was ten years after the first democratic election in South Africa, and Tutu wanted to thank the Danish people and the churches in Denmark for their support of the struggle against apartheid during the critical years in the 1980s and 1990s leading up to the South African Election Day on 27 April 1994.

Tutu especially wanted to meet with a representative of Danish government. On a bright Friday morning the meeting took place at the Ministry of Foreign Affairs with the minister for development, Mr Bertel Haarder.

When we arrived at the Ministry of Foreign Affairs we were told that the minister was a little late because he was dealing with a number of urgent issues in his capacity of being not only minister for development, but also minister of immigration. We were invited to take our seats in the conference room and enjoyed the impressive view of Copenhagen and its harbour from the sixth floor in the building.

While we were waiting and enjoying the view of the city and the rising sun above the harbour, the minister burst into the room excusing his delay and began to offer coffee, cakes and fruits to everybody in the room.

I can still see from my inner eye the reaction of the minister when he was taken by surprise with a cup of coffee in his right hand and an apple in his left hand, because Tutu suddenly asked him: "Minister, could we start with a prayer?" The minister froze for a moment, and then he answered: "Yes, of course, yes of course". The tense and odd situation was redeemed, and we all came together in prayer around the conference table over coffee, cakes and fruits.

In his prayer Tutu prayed for the meeting and gave thanks for the support of the Danish people to the democratic struggle in South Africa, for the duty of the minister and his family. Tutu concluded his prayer by praying for the Danish soldiers involved in the war in Iraq and hoped for their quick and safe return to Denmark.

Tutu's reference to the situation in Iraq and the presence of Danish soldiers with the American and British forces in fighting Saddam Hussein and his government became the subject of a lengthy discussion afterwards between the minister and Tutu. It continued during the evening dinner given by the South African ambassador to Denmark in his private home.

The minister defended the decision of the Danish Parliament and government to join the multilateral international campaign in Iraq, and he compared the situation to South Africa. In both cases Denmark wanted to support the development of democracy. In South Africa the support was given financially and morally to the churches and other agents of democracy, while in Iraq the struggle for democracy was basically the actual fight against Saddam Hussein and his regime.

The minister was quite confident in his case and argument, but he seemed unprepared when Tutu replied: "Democracy is established democratically. You must never stop talking and negotiating." Tutu could say it with confidence and legitimacy, because he had fought democratically against the apartheid regime and insisted in democracy against all odds. His weapons had been the spoken and written word, not arms or appeals for violence.

It was exactly because of the non-violent struggle waged by Tutu and other church leaders that Denmark had supported their democratic cause. This was the very reason why Tutu was in Denmark ten years after the first democratic election in South Africa to thank the Danish people and churches for their support.

---

[1] Peter Lodberg, Dr Dr, professor of systematic theology, Aarhus University. Former general secretary of DanChurchAid and member of the Central Committee of the World Council of Churches.

For me as general secretary of DanChurchAid, this was the most important lesson in democracy I could get. It became clear to me how important it is to understand and use history in the right way when we are making historical references and arguments to serve our political positions as citizens and voters. The Danish government and the majority in the Danish Parliament had forgotten the lessons learned from South Africa about establishing democracy in countries ruled by dictatorship or according to racist principles.

The historical reference was not South Africa but World War II and the eradication of Nazi Germany. The year before – on 29 August 2003 – the prime minister of Mr Haarder's government, Mr Anders Fogh Rasmussen, had accused the Danish politicians of the 1940s of failing morally when they did not fight the German occupation of Denmark during World War II, but collaborated with the Nazis. The prime minister used his argument to defend Denmark's participation in the war on Iraq from 20 March 2003. He saw a direct parallel between fighting Adolf Hitler and Saddam Hussein in order to establish democracy.

I also recalled my old professor of church history at Aarhus University, Denmark, P.G. Lindhardt, who once told us as students that we can't learn anything from history. Historical moments and movements differ from time to time, because the material context differs constantly. Long before contextual theology became popular, P.G. Lindhardt taught his young students that context matters, and the only thing we can learn from history is that we can't learn anything. Each context and situation is unique because they involve people who too often behave irrationally and unpredictably. We can gather experience and knowledge about political and religious dynamics in society and churches, but previous historical occasions can never become an alibi or blueprint for how we act today or in the future. Each situation, conflict or crisis calls on their own interpretation, action and understanding.

Today, we see the devastating consequences of the wrong decisions taken by heads of governments in Washington, London, Copenhagen and other places, because they blindly followed the idea that war is more efficient in establishing democracy than talking and negotiating. Almost twenty years later Iraq is still in chaos, and we will never know if Tutu's approach to democracy in Iraq would have succeeded, but there are some important theological lessons learned from the meeting between Tutu and the Danish minister for development, Mr. Haarder.

Prayer matters

As general secretary of DanChurchAid I have participated in several meetings in the Danish Foreign Ministry, but when Tutu opened our meeting with Mr Haarder by praying it was the first and only time I have heard a public prayer being said in a government's conference room. Despite the differences of opinion between the minister for development and Tutu, prayer was natural and set the tone of the meeting. We were together in this meeting, and it was important how we would find common ground to discuss the issues on the agenda. The language of prayer is different to the language of politics even though some of the words are the same. The main difference is the perspective. By praying to God in a political setting, politics opens to a wider horizon that brings an eschatological dimension to what politicians are doing.

If eschatology is about bringing the future possibilities into the present reality, prayer as an eschatological event in time gives politics a dimension of hope and change. Politics in the perspective of prayer is not a human exercise that is concerned about how the privileged can keep their privileges at the expense of the unprivileged, but politics becomes a common human endeavour about achieving common aims that involve a change of power structures.

An eschatological understanding of history changes the perspective. We are no longer bound to our past and our many mistakes and shortcomings. This is what Christianity calls sin, but the sequences of time have changed, so the future becomes more important than the past. It is what we can be, and not who we were that is important. Christian theology uses several different words to describe the importance of the eschatological possibility for our understanding of our present situation. They all involve a dimension of change and hope such as re-conciliation, re-demption, re-surrection, and re-creation.

Prayer also helps us to maintain the right perspective between what belongs to God and to human beings like us. It is fascinating to remember that the first Christians when they were persecuted by the Roman imperial power elaborated a very important and sophisticated understanding of prayer. They distinguished between praying *to* the emperor and *for* the emperor. The persecuted Christians would not pray *to* the emperor, because the emperor is not God, but a human being with responsibilities, obligations and duties. Instead, they prayed *for* the emperor, because the emperor is also one of God's creatures and able to do God's will even though he doesn't believe in Jesus Christ as the Son of God.

When Tutu prayed for the minister and his responsibilities as a person with political power, Tutu stayed within this old Christian tradition of reminding a person with political power to use the political power to maintain peace in the world. It was made very concrete by Tutu's reference to the Danish soldiers in Iraq.

At the same time by praying, Tutu respected the line of different responsibilities between the two kinds of ministers present in the conference room. Mr Haarder as minister for development represented the political power, while Tutu represented the spiritual power as the minister of the Word. Both served as ministers in different capacities but with the same goal: to help to establish a society that maintains peace and respects human dignity as the will of God.

The conference room became the stage of the old relationship between secular and spiritual, faith and politics and church and state. Here, there were independent realms represented by two ministers in the same room with different obligations, and the realms belonged together without separation and without mixing, because together they shall fulfil God's will for this world from now on and always.

While praying my thoughts went back to my reading of Dietrich Bonhoeffer and his essay from April 1933, *Die Kirche vor der Judenfrage (The Church and the Jewish Question).*[2] In his essay Bonhoeffer states that the true church only lives from the gospel and does not play a direct political role. However, this does not mean that the church accepts uncritically what the state is doing. The role and responsibility of the church is to ask the state how it acts in a legitimate manner as state. Said differently, the church challenges the state to behave as a state which means to secure "law and order" in society.

According to Bonhoeffer, the state doesn't live up to its responsibility as a legitimate state if there is too little or too much law and order in society. Too little law and order is anarchy, and too much law and order is dictatorship, which places the church in *statu confessionis*, and the state in an act of self-denial. In *statu confessionis* it is the task of the church to remind the state of its responsibility as a state, but also about the limits of the state *vis-à-vis* the church.

Tutu could appeal to the minister and encourage him and his government to act as a responsible state to bring home the Danish soldiers to end a hopeless war in Iraq, because Tutu respects the different tasks between state and church but also the same responsibility: the well-being of people.

It may be a comparative imaging in an unguarded moment but I suddenly saw Tutu's prayer and what it represented in terms of theological content: as a necessary correction of a very common way of interpreting Martin Luther's understanding of the two regiments – worldly and spiritual – in Danish theology and within the Evangelical-Lutheran Church in Denmark.

It became clear to me that Luther's understanding of the secular and worldly regiments was not a doctrine that regulates a whole theology of society, church and state, and prayer and politics, but an important perspective on the different roles of theology and politics in the public square, in this case: a conference room in the Ministry of Development.

In Denmark, Luther's teaching on the two regiments is often used as an argument for the withdrawing of theology and the Evangelical-Lutheran Church from public debates and issues in the

---

[2] Dietrich Bonhoeffer, *Die Kirche vor der Judenfrage.* Dietrich Bonhoeffer Werke Bd. 12, München: Chr. Kaiser Verlag (1997), 349-358.

public square. The thinking has been that the public square should be free from religious interference and arguments, because it is framed according to its own religiously neutral rules of debate and decision-making.

But Tutu showed through his example and prayer what the real understanding of Luther´s social ethics is: engagement in public life for the benefit of people, who are suffering and longing for peace and justice. And I am grateful that the Danish minister for development, Mr Haarder, allowed Tutu to pray and showed that he himself was challenged by the words of the prayer. I guess that not all ministers in a government will behave in that way.

Final remarks

I first heard Tutu talk at a meeting organised by the Danish Mission Society in Aarhus, Denmark, as a young student of theology in 1979. Tutu has been an important theological inspiration, because he makes theology simple, relevant and funny in the best positive way. This inspires a deep theology of life and for life, that liberates and redeems new energy through a deep personal spirituality and courage in troubled times. It makes Tutu´s theology a Trinitarian theology that is informed and inspired by his faith in the power of the Triune God as a liberating God who surprises us today and always, because God is different from what we think and want God to be. This is my lesson learned from Desmond Tutu when he, one sunny morning, took not only a minister for development by surprise, but all those present around a conference table with coffee, cake and fruit. We shared a prayer and our life together for a short, but very important moment.

55. OPENING THE HEARTS OF THOUSANDS FOR THE SPIRIT OF GOD – TOGETHER WITH ARCHBISHOP DESMOND TUTU ADDRESSING THE EXPO 2000 IN HANOVER

Rolf Koppe[1]

The background of the story which this essay focuses on is the Expo 2000, which took place in Germany. This is the largest world exhibition sanctioned and decided upon (since 1928) by the intergovernmental organisation of Bureau International des Expositions (BIE), which in 1990 had decided to hold this massive exhibition in Hanover, Northern Germany (beating out Toronto). The Expo 2000 ran for a period of five months from June 2020 onwards and attracted some 25 million people as visitors. It focused thematically on technological, ecological and social solutions for the future of this world.

The responsible authorities from the secular as well from the church's side asked themselves some weeks before the opening of the Expo who could be the main speaker at the opening of the biggest cultural exposition the city of Hanover has ever seen.

In the planning process of the Expo the idea to use the big industrial exhibition ground, which normally gives enormous space for showing machines outside and inside the different exhibition halls, came from chancellor Gerhard Schröder, former prime minister of the regional state "Lower-Saxony" in which Hanover is located. The Expo was already planned as a world's fair for all nations

[1] Rolf Koppe was born 1941 in Mahlum, a village in Lower Saxony, Germany. After the study of protestant theology in Heidelberg, Vienna and Göttingen he was a research assistant of the Lutheran World Federation in Geneva, ordained as a pastor of the Lutheran Church of Hanover, and worked as a press and information officer of the EKD. After five years as regional bishop of the district of Göttingen he became the bishop for ecumenical and foreign relations of the EKD. Up to 2006 – the year of his retirement – he was a member of the Central and the Executive Committee of the WCC and from 1999 to 2002 the protestant co-moderator of the "special commission" of the WCC. In 1996 he was awarded an honorary doctorate of the University of Klausenburg, Romania. He is father of two girls and lives with his wife Ilse in Göttingen. Photos in this article are from the author's private collection.

with all the big halls of the nations and free spaces outside, but still the opening ceremony was not yet planned. From the side of the German churches, we were aware that the Protestant churches in Germany through the Evangelical Church of Germany (EKD) financed and built a huge church – like a monastery – in the midst of the world's exhibition grounds, which afterwards was to be used as a regional pilgrim church in Thuringia in the eastern part of Germany.

Many women and men of high standing had already been asked to serve as keynote speakers for the opening ceremony, but either they had no time or they declined. Mrs Birgit Breuel, the former minister for economics in the cabinet of the prime minister of Ernst Albrecht and responsible for the Expo from the secular side, asked us if we have any idea for a person to be asked from outside Germany, but still well known in Germany, whom we could ask for the opening sermon of "the day of churches" in the overall programme which was planned. We responded unanimously that the Anglican Archbishop Demond Tutu from South Africa should be asked to hold the sermon. We were certainly aware of the fact that Tutu got the Nobel Peace Prize for his struggle against the apartheid system in the year 1984.

"Arch" Tutu had become not only a symbol of fighting for a better world, but also known all over the world for his dynamic and humorous way to reach out to the hearts of the people. Thus, Rev. Volker Faigle, who had worked for eight years in Kenya with African churches and visited Archbishop Tutu and his family several times in South Africa, was asked to communicate the invitation to him personally. Volker Faigle, at that time secretary for Africa in the office of the EKD, then travelled to Cape Town, where the Archbishop lived. It took only some days that we got the message back that the "Arch" accepted the invitation. We all were very happy about the quick response – and about the fact that the Expo would cover all costs involved.

The weather was bad at Pentecost that year. It was rainy and windy. During the opening ceremony Bishop Margot Käßmann and myself took Archbishop Tutu into our midst so that we could watch his sheets of paper. But after the beginning of the music performed by a brass band and the singing nobody worried much about the bad weather but instead listened attentively to Tutu's sermon about the Holy Ghost, who refreshes the believers. Tutu raised up and waved with his manuscript so that we were anxious about what may follow. But the Archbishop suddenly lowered his voice and for some seconds it was amazingly quiet when he explained what was happening at Pentecost, namely that everybody could follow the sermon in his own language.

Desmond Tutu turned the attention of his listeners to the situation in South Africa where many people do not have enough to eat, not enough space in their houses and not enough jobs for many young men and women to earn their living. But still one could observe in South African churches: in worship services people are filled with joy, clapping their hands and listening to the word of God attentively. The same seemed to be happening right here in Hanover during this sermon at Pentecost, during the Expo.

The Archbishop reached out to the hearts in an emotional way, full of short stories. Tutu explained that Adam said "wow" when he saw Eve for the first time and how beautiful the Creator had made her. The people laughed and nobody thought about the nasty weather anymore.

Opposite we see Archbishop Tutu being accompanied by Volker Faigle, a Roman Catholic priest, and Bishop Rolf Koppe (second row, second from right) on the way from the Jesus Pavilion to the Pavilion of the Vatican crossing through the Expo grounds. The Vatican had brought the "Turin Shroud" to the Expo, in which according to ancient Roman Catholic tradition the contours of Jesus' face were shown as a dead young man after he was relieved from hanging on the cross. The Roman Catholic friends believe, like the Orthodox do, that the contours of this picture are historically true and showed a copy for public display. We do not know what Archbishop Tutu really thought about this, but the demonstration from Rome certainly made a lasting impression on him. The impression Desmond Tutu made on the huge gathering during the Expo was lively and left many deeply moved.

56. New Hope for South Africa – Desmond Tutu's Road to the Nobel Peace Prize

Raymond van Diemel[1]

"New hope has sprung in the breasts of many as the result of this Nobel Peace Prize." (Desmond Mpilo Tutu, Oslo, 12 December 1984)

South Africa is blessed with legendary individuals, who through their quest for justice have captured the admiration of fellow citizens and the outside world. Amongst this group we found Beyers Naudé, Allan Boesak, Ahmed Kathrada, Winnie Mandela, Helen Suzman, Fatima Meer and many more. Legendary individuals are always aware of their calling in life. These individuals are not driven by a desire for recognition or power, but instead by a duty to serve humanity whatever the personal cost to their life and safety. As persons with the highest degree of integrity, they do not harbour any trace of hate and revenge. Of course, Desmond Tutu (affectionately Tutu hereafter) must be added to this illustrious group of servanthood leaders.

Who is Tutu? How did he rise from teacher to Nobel Peace Prize winner? Why was he elected by the Norwegian Nobel Committee as an agent of peace-building? What were the tenets of Tutu's Nobel Peace acceptance speech? These are questions that are answered in this writing.

A warrior for peace, atonement and dignity

Religious people who ask why bishops talked of politics when it was their calling to speak of redemption reveal a false dichotomy. Those who know anything of Desmond Tutu realise he is not to be compartmented. The minister of religion who is at once pastor, preacher, theologian, historian, educationalist and active citizen, and who is proficient at each, is an apt description of Tutu. Tutu's religious philosophy, religious practice and the human rights values embraced by him are reflected in his sermons, public speeches and writings.[2]

One author claims that the late Father Trevor Huddleston's dignified activism inspired young Desmond Tutu to pursue justice in his homeland.[3] Huddleston was a British priest who became one of the first leaders of the resistance against South African apartheid. The 1960–1980 era represented an important period of the struggle of the South African people for human rights and democracy. During this vital time, Tutu held several important positions in the church and public life. In his position as secretary-general of the South African Council of Churches (appointed in 1978) Tutu criticised the National Party white minority government severely, both internally and externally. His condemnation of the government led to his passport being confiscated on two occasions. Despite this,

---

[1] Dr Raymond van Diemel is a military university educator at the South African Military Academy. He is the coordinator of telematic (online) education, Faculty of Military Science, Stellenbosch University. He holds degrees from the universities of the Western Cape (UWC) and South Africa (UNISA). He completed a PhD in historical studies from UWC in 1997. He is also an alumnus of the Haggai International having completed a course in Christian evangelism. My admiration for the former Archbishop Desmond Tutu as a "warrior for peace and justice" dates back to the late 1970s when I witnessed the protest marches to the parliament led by Desmond Tutu. Tutu's adage, "If you are neutral in situations of injustice, you have chosen the side of the oppressor" is engraved in my consciousness. I was privileged to be commissioned by the Cape Peninsula University of Technology (CPUT) to film the annual Desmond Tutu Peace Lecture held on 7 October 2008.

[2] Barney Pityana, "Foreword" in *Archbishop Desmond Tutu: Prophetic Witness in South Africa*, eds Leonard Hulley, Louise Kretzschmar and Luke Lungile Pato (Cape Town, South Africa: Human and Rousseau, 1996), 7-8.

[3] M. Haron, "Peace profile, Desmond Mpilo Tutu", *A Journal of Social Justice* 26, no. 4 (2014): 578-586.

during a visit to the United States and Europe in 1981, Tutu was allocated dignitary status, met the secretary-general of the United Nations (UN), Kurt Waldheim, and addressed the UN Special Committee Against Apartheid. In the UK, he met Robert Runcie, the Archbishop of Canterbury, who invited him to give a sermon in Westminster Abbey, while in Rome he spent a few minutes with Pope John Paul II. In 1983 he was appointed patron of the United Democratic Front (UDF). His unabated attacks upon the South African government in a time of "total strategy against total onslaught" brought him further national and international recognition as a leader of major importance.[4] The appointment of Tutu as Bishop of Johannesburg in 1984 created conflict in the Anglican Church with many elements of the white members becoming increasingly uncomfortable with his outspokenness.

Africa's peace bishop

5 October 1984 was a momentous day in the life of Tutu and South Africa. The world learned that the Norwegian Nobel Committee had chosen to award the Nobel Peace Prize for 1984 to Bishop Desmond Tutu.

The committee attached great importance to Tutu's role as a unifying leader figure in the campaign to resolve the problem of apartheid in South Africa. Through the award the committee wished to direct attention to the non-violent struggle for liberation to which Tutu belongs, a struggle in which black and white South Africans unite to bring their country out of conflict and crisis. Furthermore, the award should be seen as a renewed recognition of the courage and heroism shown by black South Africans in their use of peaceful methods in the struggle against apartheid. This recognition is also directed to all who, throughout the world, use such methods to stand in the vanguard of the campaign for racial equality as a human right. It is the committee's wish that the Peace Prize now awarded to Desmond Tutu should be regarded not only as a gesture of support to him and to the South African Council of Churches of which he is leader, but also to all individuals and groups in South Africa who, with their concern for human dignity, fraternity and democracy, incite the admiration of the world.[5]

A hope for the future

Tutu's Nobel Peace Prize ceremony on Monday, 10 December 1984 was interrupted for an hour and twenty minutes by a bomb threat. The bomb threat was telephoned by an anonymous caller to an Oslo newspaper and caused the police to evacuate the ceremonial hall and ask King Olav V, Bishop Tutu and hundreds of guests to stand outside while bomb-sniffing dogs and specialists checked the hall. Fortunately, no explosives were found. Standing outside Oslo University's Aula Hall with the dignitaries and guests in crisp, sunny weather, Tutu, clad in a purple cassock and clerical collar, said the bomb threat "show[ed] the desperation of those who are opposed to peace and justice."[6] "We simply had to take the bomb threat seriously", said Egil Aarvik, the Nobel Committee chairman. Hans Beukes, a Namibian exile living in Norway since the early 1960s, attended the event with his two sons and told me he had overheard the Norwegian King saying, "No prize is to be handed over until he returns to the ceremony".[7]

---

[4] M. Albeldas and A. Fischer, *A Question of Survival: Conversations with Key South Africans* (Johannesburg, South Africa: Jonathan Ball, 1987), 139-147.
[5] The Nobel Peace Prize 1984, "Press Release", https://www.nobelprize.org/prizes/peace/1984/press-release/ (accessed 20 May 2021).
[6] "Bishop Tutu given Nobel Prize in Oslo Ceremony", *New York Times*, 11 December 1984, https://www.nytimes.com/1984/12/11/world/bishop-tutu-given-nobel-prize-in-oslo-ceremony.html (accessed 20 May 2021).
[7] Hans Beukes's message to writer, May 2021.

His sense of prudence guided Tutu to recognise the value of rendering an inspirational message in African song as an apt introduction to his speech. After all, the association of singing with protest oppression and injustices continues to resonate deeply in African culture. With the well-known Christian hymn in isiXhosa entitled "Ma Sibulele kuYesu" (a hymn of thanksgiving to Jesus), Tutu, his family and entourage performed inside Oslo University's Aula Hall. Despite the strict conventionalism of the ceremony, the song was warmly applauded.

With the attention directed at him, Tutu seized the "power of the pulpit" with a glow in his eyes, and mental facilities developed to maturity by experience and spiritual strength. He referred to the "tremendous volume of greetings from heads of state, world leaders of the Christian church and of other faiths, as well as ordinary people, with the notable exception of the Soviet and South African governments." Highlighting the state of hopelessness prevalent in the world, he argued that his Nobel Prize has given fresh hope to many in a world that has sometimes had a pall of despondency cast over it by the experience of suffering, disease, poverty, famine, hunger, oppression, injustice, evil and war:

> A pall that has made many wonder whether God cares, whether He was omnipotent, whether He was loving and compassionate. The world is in such desperate straits, in such a horrible mess, that it all provides almost conclusive proof that a good and powerful and loving God such as Christians and people of other faiths say they believe in, could not exist. If he did, He really could not be a God who cared much about the fate of his creatures or the world they happened to inhabit. We seem to be so hostile to their aspirations to be fully human.

Never shy of cracking a joke, Tutu said that he once visited a friend in England. "I found a charming book of cartoons entitled 'My God'". One cartoon showed God with appeals and supplications, with people bombarding him from below, to which God responded, "I wish I could say, don't call me, I'll call you." Another cartoon declared, "Create in six days and have eternity to regret it." Tutu says that his favourite cartoon shows God somewhat disconsolate and saying, "Oh dear, I think I have lost my copy of the Divine Plan."

Returning to his prepared speech, Tutu proclaims:

> New hope has sprung in the breasts of many as the result of this prize. The mother – watching her child starve in a Bantustan homeland resettlement camp, or one whose flimsy, plastic covering was demolished by the authorities in the KTC squatter camp in Cape Town. The man – emasculated by the pass laws as he lived for 11 months in a single sex hostel. The student – receiving an inferior education. The activist – languishing in a consulate or a solitary confinement cell, being tortured, because he thought he was human and wanted that God-given right recognised. The exile – longing to kiss the soil of her much-loved motherland. The political prisoner – watching the days of her life sentence go by like the drip of a faulty tap – imprisoned because he knew he was created by God, not to have his human dignity or pride, trodden underfoot.[8]

Interweaving the struggle in South Africa with that in other countries, Tutu assured the audience that,

> a new hope has been kindled in the breasts of the millions who are voiceless, oppressed, dispossessed, tortured by the powerful tyrants, lacking elementary human rights – in Latin America, in South-East Asia, in the Far East, in many parts of Africa and behind the Iron Curtain, who have their noses rubbed in the dust. How wonderful, how appropriate, that this award is made today – December the 10th, Human Rights Day. It says more eloquently than anything else, that this is God's world, and He is in charge. That our cause is a just cause, that we will attain human rights in South Africa and everywhere in the world. We shall be free in South Africa and everywhere in the world.

Tutu concluded with a vote of thanks to the Nobel Committee.

[8] California Newsreel (2006) Have you heard from Johannesburg? *Apartheid and the Club of the West Transcript.* Available from: https://newsreel.org/ (accessed 21 September 2021).

I want to thank the churches in Norway and everywhere, for their support, their love, and their prayers. On behalf of all these, for whom you have given a new hope, a new cause for joy, I want to accept this award in a holy representative capacity. I accept this prestigious award on behalf of my family, on behalf of the South African Council of Churches, on behalf of all in my motherland, on behalf of those committed to the course of justice, of peace and reconciliation everywhere. If God be for us, who can be against us?

Conclusion

The Peace Prize undoubtedly affirmed Tutu's international standing as a peace builder. It captured the world's attention and gave South Africans a sense of hope. The broad media coverage made him a living symbol in the struggle for liberation, someone who articulated the suffering and expectations of South Africa's oppressed masses. There are many indications that Tutu's Peace Prize forced more countries to take note of the devastating effect of apartheid. His speech paved the way for a policy of stricter sanctions against South Africa in the 1980s. His Nobel acceptance speech unleashed the energy and force that merged with that of the people's struggle and that would eventually sweep the once mighty apartheid government out of office in 1990. In 1994, a decade after receiving the Nobel Prize, the first democratic government was elected in South Africa.

57. THE HUMILITY OF A PEACEMAKER:
NEGOTIATING THE NATIONAL PEACE ACCORD, 1991

Liz Carmichael[1]

My first encounter with Desmond was in London in 1971. With student friends, I was organising an all-night vigil in Southwark Cathedral for Christian Aid. The theme was "Reconciliation". Tutu was suggested as a speaker and I phoned him. He couldn't make the date but I remembered his enthusiastic endorsement of the topic, and his keenness to help.

In 1975 I was a young doctor just starting seven years at Baragwanath Hospital, Soweto. As a member of the cathedral congregation, I went to say hello to the new dean, and was struck by his friendly directness. Fifteen years later he was Archbishop, I had become a theologian, and he ensured I returned to Johannesburg as an ordinand.

South Africa in 1991 was extraordinarily different, but much remained unsettled. I had a diocesan job in spirituality and theological education, and I was spending a fair amount of time in townships but not taking much notice of politics. Suddenly, in March 1992 I found myself at a demonstration in Alexandra township, and a familiar scene re-played before me: a large crowd faces camouflage-clad riot police and it all ends in a chaos of teargas, stones and barricades. Fortunately the police did not shoot anyone, but apparently township residents were trying to kill the hostel-dwellers and vice versa. A few days later, I was parachuted into Alexandra as convener of an Interim Crisis Committee, a fledgling Local Peace Committee under something of which I had only just become aware: the National Peace Accord.

This was unbelievable. We were a mix of politicians, civil society and the security forces, working together for the first time in history to sort out this tangled, messy, deadly, highly emotional conflict. It was "ANC" versus "IFP", township versus men's hostels, both sides profoundly distrustful of the police and army. Thousands were displaced. Over the next year, we achieved peace in Alexandra. The 1994 election was exemplary, with nearly two hundred Alexandrans and fifty friends from the surrounding suburbs proudly serving together in the orange bibs of peace monitors.

But what was this National Peace Accord? It was South Africa's first consensus document, signed by twenty-nine parties and organisations including the government, ANC-Alliance, and IFP, on 14 September 1991. It set out rules for the behaviour of political organisations and security forces, and parameters for relief and reconstruction, and it created peace structures, that included civil society, to resolve conflicts and implement the agreements. The accord enabled CODESA to begin. Its structures grew throughout the transition period, to involve some 7,000 committee members and 20,000 peace monitors. It supported a massive National Peace Campaign, and played a large part in the success of the 1994 election.[2] The accord was the first of three consensus processes: the accord itself, the constitutional talks and finally the Truth and Reconciliation Commission (TRC).

---

[1] Revd Dr Liz Carmichael MBE is an emeritus research fellow at St John's College, Oxford. I got to know Desmond Tutu in 1975 when he became dean at St Mary's Cathedral, Johannesburg. I am British but had just started work as a doctor at Baragwanath Hospital. Desmond was strikingly friendly and direct: was I thinking of getting married? Would I like to be ordained? Soon afterwards I married Canon Michael Carmichael, whom Desmond admired (and it was mutual!). We hoped Desmond would not go to Lesotho. Desmond told me that after he accepted to go, he spent that night on a plane to London, jerking awake and thinking: "'What have I done?' I wanted to be a bishop – but not like that." But it was good he had that status when heading the SACC, where Michael was a colleague on the executive. As Archbishop, Desmond later made sure I returned, having studied theology, to be ordained in Johannesburg. His closeness to God is palpable.

[2] For the accord story see two books published by USIP, Washington DC: Peter Gastrow, *Bargaining for Peace* (1995) and Susan Collin Marks, *Watching the Wind: Conflict Resolution during South Africa's Transition to Democracy* (2000) and, forthcoming: Liz Carmichael, *Peacemaking and Peacebuilding in South Africa: The National Peace Accord 1991–1994* (James Currey, Boydell & Brewer, 2022).

While most people are aware of the Arch's chairing of the TRC, in 1996–98, it was only during recent research that I became aware of his much earlier role as a key facilitator of the National Peace Accord.

After Mandela's release in February 1990 it was widely expected that grassroots violence would abate and multiparty constitutional talks begin. Instead, the violence spread, bilateral talks proceeded slowly and an attempted peace agreement between ANC and IFP in January 1991 failed. By May 1991 an impasse had developed. The ANC was boycotting a summit on violence convened by F.W. de Klerk, and threatening to stop talking altogether.

Church and business leaders began to think of intervening. In 1988 the major businesses had formed a progressive coalition, the Consultative Business Movement (CBM), to play a pro-active role in the transition to democracy. In November 1990 at the ecumenical Rustenburg Conference the churches formed a similar united front, the Rustenburg Committee, of which Tutu was a member. It included the South African Council of Churches (SACC), the Dutch Reformed Church (DRC), the Catholics, evangelicals and charismatics. At the Rustenburg Conference, Professor Willie Jonker confessed, on behalf of the white DRC Synod, that apartheid had been a sin, and Tutu immediately accepted his confession and extended forgiveness. The conference called on the political leaders to meet urgently to negotiate a new order. It committed the churches to a democratic, non-racial and non-sexist South Africa, and to calling "a peace conference to bring together leaders who can help end violence."[3]

After days of intensive behind-the-scenes negotiations, F.W. de Klerk's Peace Summit took place on 24–25 May, without the ANC but with the agreement that the ANC and its allies would participate in a "second Peace Conference" to be convened by impartial facilitators. This represented a considerable climb-down by the government, which had been determined to be in sole charge of the transition and to resist any civil society mediation. As he closed the summit, F.W. de Klerk mandated Dr Louw Alberts, co-chair of the Rustenburg Conference, a government scientific advisor and prominent DRC layperson, to gather facilitators and convene a second, inclusive peace conference. The churches, de Klerk reluctantly admitted, did have a role to play in reconciliation.[4]

So it was that on Tuesday, 4 June 1991, a group of seven church and four business leaders met in the Town Room of the Carlton Hotel, with the awesome remit of initiating a national peace process. They had wide contacts and they agreed on a method: to get senior political representatives ("lieutenants") to negotiate agreements, reporting back to their principals; the principals would then sign the agreements, which would include an implementation mechanism.

The churchmen were the Rustenburg co-chairs Dr Louw Alberts and SACC general secretary Rev. Dr Frank Chikane (Apostolic Faith Mission); Archbishop Tutu; SACC president Rev. Dr Khoza Mgojo (Methodist); Pastor Ray McCauley (Rhema); Professor Johan Heyns (DRC); and Rev. Dr Gerrie Lubbe, a minister in the Indian "Reformed Church in Africa", lecturer in Islamic studies at UNISA and chair of the South African Chapter of the World Conference on Religion and Peace. With them was one woman: the Rustenburg Committee's indefatigable communications officer, ex-journalist Val Pauquet.[5]

The businessmen present were John Hall, a Barlow Rand director, president of the South African Chamber of Commerce (SACOC); his fellow director Sam Motsuenyane, president of the National African Federated Chamber of Commerce (NAFCOC); Bobby Godsell of Anglo American, the Chamber of Mines, and the employers' association the South African Consultative Committee on Labour Affairs (SACCOLA); and ex-diplomat Sean Cleary, now a mediator supported by business in KwaZulu-Natal. A fifth businessman, cheerful young Jabu Mabuza of the Foundation for African Business and Consumer Services (FABCOS), joined the team on 10 April, bringing the total to thirteen.

---

[3] Rustenburg Declaration, 4.3.3. Full text in Louw Alberts and Frank Chikane (eds), *The Road to Rustenburg* (Cape Town: Struik, 1991), pp.275-86. Val Pauquet is this book's un-sung compiler.
[4] SABC TV footage, 25/5/91, used in Val Pauquet's compilation "The Peacemakers".
[5] Minutes of these meetings, kept by Pauquet, currently in author's keeping.

The team had its mandate from the ANC-Alliance, and from the state president, to convene an inclusive peace process. Another main protagonist, Chief Buthelezi, was dragged along somewhat unwillingly in their wake; and to Mangosuthu Buthelezi, Tutu was a major stumbling-block.

Before the summit, McCauley was deputed to approach Buthelezi about the churches acting as peace facilitators. The Chief expressed his profound dislike of Chikane and even more of Tutu.[6] He differed with them politically, on sanctions and the "homeland" system, but in Tutu's case, unknown to McCauley, Buthelezi also nursed a deep personal antagonism. The two had first met in 1978, on the podium in a stadium in Graaff-Reinet at Pan Africanist Congress (PAC) leader Robert Sobukwe's funeral. When PAC youths noticed the Chief they menacingly surrounded the podium, chanting insults and calling for his death. Buthelezi, an Anglican, asked Tutu's advice; Tutu thought it safest if he left. To preserve the dignity of the occasion, Buthelezi reluctantly agreed to do so.

Perceptions differed on what happened next. Tutu's biographer writes that youths kicked the escorting clergy and Tutu turned to remonstrate with them.[7] Buthelezi recalls his aide firing in the air, people scattering, and "the Bishop who said he was going to protect me, I saw him run as fast as his short legs could carry him."[8] The Chief escaped to his car. A few days later Tutu told a journalist that the youths were a "new breed of blacks who have iron in their souls."[9] Ever after, Buthelezi believed that Tutu had abandoned him and then endorsed the youths' humiliation of him. Despite a reconciliatory meeting in 1985, which opened the way for later pastoral meetings, the relationship never really normalised.[10] In 2012 Chief Buthelezi told me they had talked it over "and, you know, brought about some reconciliation between us", but indignation, even then, still smouldered.

A Rustenburg delegation (Alberts, Chikane, Heyns, McCauley) had a lukewarm reception from Buthelezi on 3 June and could only cautiously report that he appeared willing to accept churchmen as conveners of the second peace conference.

The facilitators sent out "Strictly confidential" invitations asking all parties to send "senior leaders" to a consultative think-tank on Saturday 22 June, to gather ideas and start a process towards a second peace conference. John Hall arranged for Barlow Rand to host, in its 100-seat auditorium at Barlow Park in Sandton.

After a welcoming "finger lunch" and photo opportunity, some seventy delegates from around twenty-seven parties and organisations met, behind closed doors, from 2 pm to 10 pm. Hall, McCauley, Chikane and Godsell set the scene, then Tutu and Cleary co-chaired the brainstorming sessions.

Each party had five minutes to propose the issues to be negotiated. COSATU general secretary Jay (Jayaseelan) Naidoo spoke first. He said the issues were fourfold: a code of conduct for political parties to address the violence between them; a code of conduct for police and security forces to radically improve police–community relations; measures for socio-economic reconstruction; and dispute-resolving structures at local, regional and national levels, including a National Peace Secretariat. Naidoo's input became the template, to which other speakers added details.

Sean Cleary comments on Tutu's excellent chairing and "impish sense of humour which was capable of deflating any pomposity, and there was plenty of it from the floor".[11] The Democratic Party's Peter Gastrow noticed Tutu's undaunted command of the speakers: "There were attempts at brinkmanship, which Tutu quite powerfully dealt with. John Hall didn't have the clout to do it, he tried to handle it through, er, trying to be kind to everyone … whereas Tutu would use the stick, and say: 'No that's unacceptable, what you're saying!'"[12]

[6] Ron Steele, *Ray McCauley* (Cape Town: Struik, 1992), p.150.
[7] John Allen, *Rabble-Rouser for Peace* (London: Random House, 2006), p.318.
[8] Author's interview with Chief Buthelezi, 11/9/2012.
[9] Allen, *Rabble-Rouser for Peace*, p.318.
[10] Michael Nuttall, *Number Two to Tutu* (Pietermaritzburg: Cluster Publications, 2003), pp.62-3.
[11] Author's interview with Cleary, 20/7/2012.
[12] Author's interview with Gastrow, 13/9/2013.

Bobby Godsell rapidly collated the flipcharts under the four headings. At 4.15 pm the meeting broke for tea.

How to move forward? Tutu stayed on the podium, quietly praying. CBM Executive Director Theuns Eloff sat at the back, sketching a simple process diagram. It showed the meeting forming a preparatory committee which would set up working groups on the four issues. The groups would report to the committee and it would become the organising committee for the second peace conference, where the agreements would be signed. Eloff showed the diagram to Tutu, and after tea Tutu announced: "This young man has something to say to us".[13] The diagram was accepted, and now the question became: who would sit on the preparatory committee? After lengthy inconclusive jockeying, the meeting broke for supper. John Hall remarked to Tutu: "This thing looks as if it will be a real mess." Tutu said: "Wait, it will all work itself out."[14]

Supper was a stand-up buffet. Thabo Mbeki, leading the ANC-Alliance team, quietly worked the room, making agreements with Roelf Meyer, head of the NP/government delegation and Dr Frank Mdlalose of the IFP. After supper, with Sam Motsuenyane and Louw Alberts chairing, consensus was reached: the preparatory committee would consist of the twelve facilitators plus three representatives each from the three "main" parties: the NP/government, ANC-Alliance and IFP.

The preparatory committee convened on Monday 24 June. Tutu was absent but was assigned as a facilitator, with Jabu Mabuza, to Working Group 3 on "Socio-economic Reconstruction and Development". Chaired by Alec Erwin, it produced a succinct agreement to promote community-based development. Minutes are lacking, but Mabuza recalls discussing short-term relief and reconstruction needs with Tutu. Tutu attended three out of five preparatory committee meetings, on 14 and 29 August and 11 September.

On 14 August the date for the "National Peace Convention" was confirmed as Saturday 14 September. A draft convention agenda was tabled at the "Process Group", the secretariat which met just before the preparatory committee. Typed on it were the names of John Hall, who chaired the preparatory committee, and Archbishop Tutu, as co-chairs of the convention. Two hours later, a revised draft agenda appeared at the preparatory committee. Hall's name remained, but on this and all subsequent drafts his co-chair's name was left blank. This was certainly due to the IFP, whose combative representative Walter Felgate had attended the process group in a bad mood.

All parties were asked to consider all chairing options. A worried Gerrie Lubbe phoned Cyril Ramaphosa who responded: "'Don't you worry, we will stick to our guns and Tutu will go ahead, he will be there. We will not allow Buthelezi to get rid of him.'"[15] But there was little that the ANC could do.

Before the preparatory committee on 11 September, the facilitators agreed to propose Tutu. The signing would be a major symbolic occasion, and what better symbol than a Nobel Peace Prize laureate? But when the "chair" item was reached, the IFP suddenly proposed the Methodist Presiding Bishop Stanley Mogoba. He was Durban-based, a PAC, not ANC, supporter, and a quiet, consistent voice for peace. He could not, however, offer anything like Tutu's media appeal and international profile.

The church facilitators proposed Tutu. Felgate declared him unacceptable "because of his past statements – apparently meaning his support for liberation movements and sanctions."[16] Tutu recused himself and went to sit, and pray, in another room. Pam Saxby of the CBM, who had worked for him in Johannesburg, followed to ask if he was all right. "I just didn't like to see him being *hurt* like that. And he didn't want me to know that he was hurting".[17] He took no further part in the meetings that evening.

---

[13] Author's interview with Eloff, 8/2/2012.

[14] Val Pauquet's interview with Hall, 1994 (Pauquet's recording).

[15] Author's interview with Lubbe, 16/7/2013.

[16] Hennie Serfontein, *Vrye Weekblad* 20–26/9/91.

[17] Author's interview with Saxby, 16/9/2013.

The ANC delegation of Thabo Mbeki, Jayendra Naidoo and the Pahad brothers said little while the facilitators argued with the IFP contingent of Felgate, Frank Mdlalose and Suzanne Vos. Finally the meeting asked the facilitators to stay on afterwards and find a solution. They decided to seek a meeting with Buthelezi the next day. Early in the morning Hall, Cleary and McCauley secured an audience and flew down in a Barlow's jet, to meet Buthelezi in Mandeni.

He was adamant. He would refuse to attend if Tutu chaired. Ostensibly his reason was that churchmen should not chair "political" meetings, although businessmen might. Buthelezi expressed his lack of faith in the whole accord exercise: previous agreements had changed nothing and he doubted this one could be implemented. Finally he confirmed he would attend if Tutu did not chair, but conceded the Archbishop could close the convention in prayer.[18]

Tutu drew on deep contemplative wells. As he commented years later, "the cause is a great deal more important than personal pricks."[19] He agreed to pray, while realising this setback would prevent his serving as co-chair or vice-chair of the National Peace Committee which, otherwise, he admits, would have been "logical".[20]

The incident affected the profile of the churches at national level. The other church facilitators decided that, in solidarity with Tutu, neither they nor Stanley Mogoba should co-chair the convention. Instead, John Hall and Sam Motsuenyane chaired. The convention, in the Carlton Hotel, involved over 300 delegates and observers, and the world's press. Mandela, de Klerk, Buthelezi and twenty other signatories signed on behalf of twenty-nine parties and organisations.

Tutu inevitably made a memorable impact, prefacing his final prayer with a funny story about God creating human beings by baking them, the first batch overdone, the second underdone. He gave an ebullient lunchtime TV interview, and in a passionate follow-up article he wrote that the negotiations had,

> shown that even those who have been separated by the iniquity of apartheid make a major scientific discovery once they get down to talking; they realise they share a common humanity and long for the same things … Sceptics need to be urged to join the process. We are entering a new phase in the life of South Africa and this accord gives us the best chance we have ever had of bringing lasting peace to the country. We have no other option but to make it work. If we fail, I fear that we are for the birds.[21]

Church leaders were present in force, often chairing, in the 11 regional and 263 local peace committees, but their public profile at the convention and thereafter on the National Peace Committee (NPC) was lower than it might have been. Hall chaired the NPC, with Mogoba a faithful vice-chair. On 23 June 1993 Tutu and Mogoba managed to bring Mandela (Methodist) and Buthelezi (Anglican) together for their long-delayed ANC–IFP bilateral. The church facilitators including Tutu reunited with John Hall to visit King Zwelithini on 15 April 1994, in the tense days before the IFP entered the election, and elicited a powerful plea from him to cease the internecine killing.

In conclusion, as Susan Collin Marks writes, "In many ways, the Peace Accord was a tangible expression of the spirit of Ubuntu. It provided a mechanism for South Africans of all races, as individuals, to take responsibility for our collective reconciliation and healing."[22] Stanley Mogoba says simply: "My view is that without it there would have been no South Africa … no definitely, the Peace Accord was a major step in preparing South Africa, in moving it away from conflict and war to trying to get peace and people working together."[23]

Tutu's incisive, high-profile leadership was instrumental in creating the accord. Regrettably it could not carry through into the day-to-day work of the peace structures, and Tutu missed the insight

---

[18] Steele, *Ray McCauley*, p.173.
[19] Author's interview with Tutu, 7/9/2012.
[20] Author's interview with Tutu, 7/9/2012.
[21] Tutu, *Sunday Star,* 22/9/91.
[22] Marks, *Watching the Wind*, p.186.
[23] Mogoba interview, 21/8/2012.

into the complexities of violence and peacebuilding that continuing involvement would have given him; but the accord did work, and he had helped to bring about that miracle.

58. GROWING UP TO BE A CHILD: REFLECTIONS ON TUTU'S SPIRITUAL FRAMING

René August[1]

Several important titles have been bestowed on the revered Arch. He is a Nobel Peace laureate, he has dozens of honorary doctorates from all over the world, including his Archbishop Emeritus title. In this essay, however, I wish to reflect on the title I believe he treasures most: that of being a child. My reflections in this essay will be drawn from my remembered conversations with him on Friday mornings after the morning Eucharist, on a few hospital visits and occasional meals and teas at the Tutu's home and restaurants.

The focus of my essay is on how Tutu's spirituality shaped his identity. When I first entered the Tutu home, the image that greeted me was a sculpture on the floor of an embodied purple cassock, lying on the floor in a fetal position. I had heard the stories of how he made it through those dark days by beginning each day lying on the floor in a fetal position because he needed to remind himself that he was God's child. It was his simplest prayer. It fed, nurtured and sustained him. "It's the only thing that kept me going. Sometimes it was so bad that the only thing I could do was remember that we are all God's children."

These were words of confession, words of lament, words of humility, words of comfort and compassion, words of welcome, pain and holy anger; I can hear them now, it's only the tone that changes.

This simple prayer resonates in everything he says and does. "Our biggest problem is that we have forgotten that we belong to one another." These words have not only made him great, but affirm greatness in everyone.

I was driving home one day when I heard an interview with the late Debbie Ford. She asked the question, "What is it that you believe about your life that has created the world in which you now live?" This question frames my reflection on the life of Desmond Mpilo Tutu. What is it that he believes about himself that has created the person we celebrate today?

One of the first stories I heard about Tutu was, while he was the chaplain at the University of Fort Hare, a group of students were getting ready to "necklace" a young man who was found guilty of being an informer to the security police. They poured petrol over the boy's body and brought a tyre filled with petrol, to place over his head and neck before setting it alight. Everyone knew that if you tried to stop them, you would be guilty of being a traitor too. When Tutu saw what was going on, he ran into the crowd, fell on top of the boy, his cape covering him and the boy. When asked to step aside, Tutu refused. The students recognised him as their chaplain, the one who loved them and took care of them, which created a very difficult situation for everyone. Tutu clearly risked his life for this boy and helped him flee the scene. When asked why he did such a foolish thing, Tutu said, "he is also God's child".

---

[1] I am Revd René August, a self-supporting priest in the Cape Town diocese. I have been a distant disciple of Archbishop Tutu for most of my life. When I worked in the city 1993–1998, I used to attend the Friday morning Eucharist at St George's Cathedral. On Monday mornings, he would have breakfast with the then dean, Colin Jones, at the same coffee shop where we had our staff meeting and occasionally, they used to come over and greet us. In 2010, I was able to return to that Friday morning service and as the Arch got older, I used to help with taking photos after the service and sitting with him at the coffee shop, where we were sometimes joined by visitors from out of town. I got to eavesdrop on conversations with hundreds of people from all walks of life and almost every country in the world. I have had the joy of being invited to share meals with the family in their homes and restaurants over a number of years.

It was in the dark days of apartheid; under the state of emergency all mass gatherings (groups larger than four) were illegal and punishable by up to six months of detention without trial. We would gather in churches, at evening services and funerals. The Archbishop would walk up to the microphone, "Welcome! Welcome to this service of worship. Welcome if you have come from far away, welcome if you have come from Caledon Square (the police headquarters in the city). Welcome to those of you who have come to spy on us, welcome to the security police in plain clothing, welcome to all of you in the South African Defence Force. You are always welcome to join us. We are on God's side, we are on the winning side. All God's children are welcome here."

Another time I heard him invite us to see "others" as God's children was the day after our first democratic elections. The National Party (the architects of apartheid) had won the vote to rule the Western Cape. I was working at a church in the city. It felt like someone had died. Tutu came to address us in the city. "Are ... are we going to accept the results in Gauteng?" The crowd cheered, as the ANC had won in that province. "Are ... are we going to accept the results in the Eastern Cape?" The crowd cheered, as the ANC had won in that province too. He proceeded to ask the same question of every province where the ANC had won, seven out of nine in all. He then asked, "Are ... are we going to accept the results in the Western Cape?" "Booooooooo! No! Boo!" came the reply. Tutu leaned forward. "Now, you need to know that we never fought for the ANC to govern. We fought for equal rights! For the right to vote. For South Africa to be governed by a democratically elected government. We will accept the results, because this is the will of the people in the Western Cape, and the people have spoken, so we will celebrate with them." I felt like I had been reprimanded in public, in the most loving way. I walked away from that rally asking myself, "How does he even come to these conclusions? How can he be so generous?!" I now understand that he can only come to those conclusions because of what he believes about himself. He is a child of God. He is not an only child, we are all God's children, his siblings.

I attended the Eucharist services at St George's Cathedral on my day off on Friday mornings. The Arch would preside at the services and people came from all over the world to see him. They would bring gifts cards, write long speeches, render song items; mostly people just came to see him, to thank him, to take a photo with him or "have a photo orgy" as the Arch would call it. Whenever someone stood up to compliment or praise him, he always assumed the same posture; he took one step back, pressed his palms together, head bowed waiting until they were finished. He always concluded by thanking people and reminding them that he was able to do what he did because of the help of many others who in his words make him look good.

We would walk over to the coffee shop, where we all met together on Friday mornings. He stopped to pick up every bit of litter that he came across while he walked down St George's Mall. Obviously, I could not just carry on walking, and even today, I cannot walk past litter. Thanks to him, I have to stop and pick it up. It is so inconvenient!

At the coffee shop, we sat and had conversations with many visitors or groups who came to see him. There were many other things that he said, I noticed a consistent thread that punctuated every conversation. It was repeated more frequently than any other. "We are all God's children."

One Sunday afternoon after a late lunch, we were having tea and coffee. He suddenly jumped up from his seat, turned to his daughter and asked if he could use her bedroom please. It was as if he suddenly remembered something. Mthunzi Gxashe, his faithful son-in-law, simply said, "It must be 18:00." I looked at my watch and it was 18:00 exactly. "It's time for his prayers" they said. They showed him to the bedroom. He was so used to praying at 18:00 every evening that even his body could tell the time. His life and ministry were sustained by a life of prayer. The next time I was with him I asked him about his prayer life. "Ousie", as he affectionately calls me, "I don't think I pray, I just enjoy being in the presence of God. I need to pray, because I need to remember that I am God's child, that God cares about all the things that I can do nothing about. That God loves me, that God loves all God's children, that God cares about the whole world and all that God has created."

What is it that the Arch believes about his life that has created the world in which we now celebrate? I believe it is a simple, yet profound truth. His most prized identity is that he is God's child.

59. Let Us Pray

Gerhard Rein[1]

I first met Desmond Tutu in Stuttgart, in Angela Mai's small, crowded kitchen. Well, kind of. I was a young radio journalist and a nobody. In the crowd of all the well-known anti-apartheid activists in southern Germany, there was no chance for me to get a single sentence, a single word in edgeways with the Bishop. He was witty and tired, the star of a happy evening's party.

At around that time the respected *Frankfurter Allgemeine Zeitung (FAZ)* had launched another attack on Desmond Tutu. The paper called into question both his faith and his integrity. The *FAZ* objected to his critique of the German industry's collaboration with South Africa's ruling circles.

Decades later, in 1992, I was privileged to be made – for the next five years – the Southern Africa correspondent of the German public radio network (ARD).

These were the historic years of South Africa's transition. Mandela and Tutu were outstanding personalities. Foreign correspondents followed their every step. And they were eager to know how we felt about, and how we would report, their changing South African scene. We met with them in background talks and listened to them, when they appeared in public.

When I hosted visiting colleagues, a chance to meet "The Arch" was at the top of their agenda. I phoned Desmond Tutu's office or asked John Allen for help. No problem. I did not brief my colleagues. We arrived at Bishopscourt, a marvellous place. A guide took us to the library. The Bishop arrived in full episcopal attire. Before the first question could be asked, Tutu said: "Let us pray".

Secular journalists from around the world are not used to such a preface to an interview. However – as I know – they will never forget it. (In Germany, in forty years of interviewing, I had only one comparable Tutu-experience. It was with Kurt Scharf, Bishop of Berlin. He greeted me at his doorstep with "Brother Rein").

At the Truth and Reconciliation hearings, I was aware how the chair reacted to reports by victims of apartheid: he wept and he prayed.

Once, when we listened to a Truth and Reconciliation hearing in Zululand, we had with us good friends from East Germany, Almuth and Heino Falcke from Erfurt. One of the witnesses attacked capitalism as the real enemy of the people and praised socialism as the best freedom-loving alternative. The Archbishop replied laughingly: "Don't be so sure. There is an East German couple here in the back row. They have just seen out a socialist system. They could tell you of their experience of socialism and freedom". The Arch always answers in unexpected ways.

Ten and more years later, in Hamburg, at a conference in memory of Marion Gräfin Dönhoff, at a crowded press-conference, the Archbishop comes up to me and asks: "Is that you?"

Tears in my eyes.

---

[1] Gerhard Rein is a German journalist, now living in Berlin. He was a youth delegate at the World Council of Churches conference in New Delhi/ India in 1961. Since then the ecumenical movement became his place, his "Heimat". From 1992-1997 he was the foreign correspondent of the German public-radio network (ARD) in Southern Africa. During that time, he had close contact to Beyers-Naude, Wolfram Kistner and to the Archbishop.

3.2. Reconciliation and Resistance

60. WHAT ABOUT SISYPHUS AND THE ARCH?
ON RECONCILING MEANINGLESSNESS AND THE LABOURS OF LOVE

Demaine Solomons[1]

Reconciliation amid absurdity

We have seen and heard it all before. In fact, some of us have grown tired of debates over the promise of reconciliation, despite being reminded that it is fundamental to developing a just society. This makes it difficult to agree on what reconciliation means, how it works and why it is essential. If things go our way, we think of it as our most "prized idea", but in times of distress "cheap deception".[2] Behind such contestation is a longing for a South Africa that does not exist, a disparity between what is and what ought to be, in a country riddled with contradictions and obscurities. This is an absurd state of affairs arising from a system premised on the fundamental irreconcilability of people.

The quest for reconciliation emerges from the tension between our desire for order, meaning and contentment on the one hand, and an indifferent world unwilling to provide that on the other. In this sense, reconciliation and its connection with philosophical "absurdism" could not be more apt in the South African context. This is what the French philosopher Albert Camus wrestles with in his famous essay *The Myth of Sisyphus* (1942).[3] For Camus, the absurd encapsulates the human propensity to seek inherent value and meaning in the context of a chaotic, irrational, sometimes meaningless world. He compares the absurdity of life with the situation of Sisyphus, a figure of Greek mythology who is condemned to repeat the same arduous task of pushing a boulder up a mountain, only to see it roll back down again once the summit is reached. This sequence or metaphorical loop is repeated into the realms of eternity.

Driven by the desire for meaning amid meaninglessness, South Africans embarked on a journey of reconciliation, a romantic pursuit for a new way of being in the aftermath of the absurdity of apartheid. It was an audacious plan. Setting in motion a chain of events that culminated in what became the Truth and Reconciliation Commission (hereafter TRC), a process for better or worse, etched the dream of reconciliation in the hearts and minds of the people. At the centre of the TRC stood Archbishop Desmond Tutu, its charismatic chairperson. Affectionately known as the Arch, Tutu and his colleagues were tasked to breathe life into one of the most contested terms in the

---

[1] Demaine Solomons is a Mandela Rhodes Scholar, lecturer/researcher of systematic theology and social ethics in the Department of Religion and Theology at the University of the Western Cape. He is a recipient of numerous academic awards, including the Desmond Tutu Doctoral Fellowship, through which he was able to complete his doctoral studies at the Vrije Universiteit Amsterdam and the University of the Western Cape. Personal narrative: "I remember this quite vividly. My first encounter with Archbishop Tutu was when I was about five years old when he came to our church, St Joseph the Worker Anglican Church in Bishop Lavis. I was with my late grandmother, sitting in the front pew, her usual spot. It was a weekday morning so the church was not particularly full. At the start of the service procession, the Arch passed my grandmother and I. Looking at me, smiling, he stopped for a second, caressing my face and continued. Of course, like most kids at that age I did not think much of it. However, almost forty years later, I cannot help but appreciate the significance of my first encounter with the Arch. He probably does not remember, but I do!"
[2] Fanie Du Toit and Erik Doxtader (eds), *In the Balance: South Africans Debate Reconciliation,* Johannesburg: Jacana Media, 2010, ix.
[3] Albert Camus, *The Myth of Sisyphus*, trans. Justin O'Brien. Harmondsworth: Penguin Books, 2000.

struggle against apartheid. Not only was the notion and practice of reconciliation tied up with ideological conflict, but doubts concerning its potential to transform society were an ever-present reality.[4] That being the case, equating this endeavour to the taking of a poisoned chalice would not be an overstatement.

God is in the detail

Notably, reconciliation and its contestation cannot be separated from the influence of Christianity in South Africa. This should be understood in terms of the allegiance to Christianity in the country, moreover, the centrality of "reconciliation" in Christian soteriology and the significance of what is aptly described as the "church struggle" against apartheid.[5] Reconciliation was at the very centre of this struggle, challenging both the politics and theology of racial separation.[6] This is evident in the Message to the People of South Africa (1968), the South African Leadership Assembly (1979), the Belhar Confession (1982/1986), the National Initiative for Reconciliation (1985) and the Rustenburg Declaration (1990). However, the term elicited much controversy in the *Kairos Document* (1985), where the emphasis on reconciliation was severely criticised as a form of "church theology"; a theology of reconciliation considered "cheap" or "inauthentic".[7] Irrespective of its impact on the apartheid establishment, Archbishop Tutu declined to sign the *Kairos Document*. This is due to his displeasure in how "church theology" and reconciliation were caricatured and criticised, whether by those in defence of their supposed neutrality or those who rejected it as counter-productive to the liberation struggle.[8]

In retrospect, Archbishop Tutu's conception of reconciliation was bound to be at odds with popular ideas of the time, whether by those who supported or those who rejected apartheid – remembering that the need for reconciliation appears in the face of violence rendering its quest hostile to itself. In such instances, as with the *Kairos Document* and later the TRC, a pattern of binary thinking emerges where dilemmas are often oversimplified to arrive at convenient answers, rendering nuances less than obvious. The trouble with this form of binary thinking is that we tend to emphasise the things we agree with and avoid those things that contradict our position. Elsewhere I categorise such quandaries, including the quest for reconciliation, as a "wicked problem" since the many variables associated with the concept are often ignored for ideological alignment.[9] In this context, it might be worthwhile exploring the nuances of his position.

In recognising complexity, how does one augment Archbishop Tutu's theology of reconciliation? If the *Kairos Document* and the TRC are used as a reference, many seem to misinterpret or simply do not appreciate what is at stake. As someone who devoted much attention to the development of black theology in South Africa, his methodology is premised on an irreducible drive towards the liberation of oppressed people. This reveals an approach that is both uncompromising and humane – keeping in mind that this is much more than just a political quest.

Closer investigation reveals a theology of reconciliation that proceeds from a state of *kenosis*.[10] A word derived from the Greek word *kenao* found in Philippians 2: 5-11. The meaning of *kenosis* is "to empty", describing God's act of self-emptying through the incarnation. More broadly, the Christian doctrine of incarnation speaks to the very specific act of God's interaction with the world through

---

[4] Dirk J. Smit, "The Symbol of Reconciliation and Ideological Conflict", in: W.S. Vorster (ed.), *Reconciliation and Construction,* Pretoria: Unisa, 1986, 88.

[5] See John W. de Gruchy and Steve de Gruchy, *The Church Struggle in South Africa,* London: SCM, 2004.

[6] John W. de Gruchy, *Reconciliation: Restoring Justice*, London: SCM Press, 2002, 33.

[7] Demaine J. Solomons, "An Unlikely Conversation Partner: Gustaf Aulén's Connection to Reconciliation in South Africa", *Svensk Teologisk Kvartalsskrift*, 95 (2), 2019, 96.

[8] De Gruchy, *Reconciliation*, 36.

[9] See Demaine J. Solomons, "Overcoming Reconciliation as a Wicked Problem: A Theological Response to the Dominant Split between Heaven and Earth in South Africa", *Philosophia Reformata*, 85 (2), 2020, 198-211.

[10] Erik Doxtader, *With Faith in the Works of Words: The Beginnings of Reconciliation in South Africa, 1985-1995*, Cape Town: David Philip, 2009, 266.

Christ. With this at the forefront of our thinking, the *kenosis* of God in Christ becomes the ethical or philosophical mode through which Christian leadership is (or should be) expressed.

Adequately understood, *kenosis* requires one to transcend narrow self-interests to locate the other in the mutuality of love. This leads one to locate the other in their mutual humanity – a communal redefinition of what it means to be human founded on self-sacrificial love. Building on the doctrinal tenets of the incarnation, this understanding of *kenosis* becomes the foundation on which Archbishop Tutu's *Ubuntu* theology is based.[11] In turn, this *Ubuntu* theology became the lens through which he engages with the very notion of reconciliation.

The connection between *Ubuntu* and reconciliation is one of the hallmarks of his approach.[12] This was in sharp contrast to the logic of apartheid, turning the assumption of the fundamental irreconcilability of people on its head.[13] Instead, the restoration of friendship and the realisation of the need to make amends for wrongs committed took centre stage. Flowing from this, reconciliation becomes the pivot, a kenotic form of love that acknowledges the unity and diversity of peoples and their interdependence irrespective of the social markers that separate them. God's act of self-emptying, an undeserved act of love, becomes the basis on which the liberation and reconciliation of black and white compatriots are established.[14] In accepting the social and cultural locality, reconciliation's potential is given new meaning through *Ubuntu*, a philosophy of love that transcends individual autonomy and narrow self-interest.

The quest for reconciliation deferred

Unsurprisingly, the vision of the so-called "rainbow people of God" might be easier said than done.[15] Some argue that Archbishop Tutu simply set the bar too high by ascribing a theological as opposed to a political understanding of reconciliation's potential. Along with this, cautionary remarks were issued not to misrepresent the South African project as a search for spiritual reconciliation but instead appreciate it as a secular pact or a political agreement. For example, Jakes Gerwel argued that the spiritualisation of reconciliation poses the risk of "pathologising" a nation in relatively good health by insisting on the perpetual quest for the "Holy Grail" of reconciliation; further maintaining that the framing of reconciliation in the context of "love" and "forgiveness" takes us back to "primitive" notions not suitable for modern societies; and that the "mechanisms of solidarity" of contemporary South Africa are no longer "love for neighbour" but rather "commitment to consensus-seeking, cultivation of conventions of civility and respect for contracts".[16] In this context, some very prominent South Africans were quite adamant, in their terms, not to confuse politics with theology, especially as far as determining the contours for reconciliation in the country was concerned.[17]

Nearing three decades after the TRC first started its work, the quest for reconciliation remains as elusive as ever. Along with apartheid, the democratic dispensation has brought many new challenges. Today, discourses on reconciliation have become rather esoteric, a symptom of more pressing concerns plaguing the country coming to terms with a history of injustice. If reconciliation took

---

[11] See Michael Battle, *Reconciliation: The Ubuntu Theology of Desmond Tutu*, Cleveland Pilgrim Press, 1997.

[12] Philippe-Joseph Salazar, *An African Athens: Rhetoric and the Shaping of Democracy in South Africa*, London: Lawrence Erlbaum Associates, 2002, 1-17.

[13] Demond M. Tutu, "Apartheid is Heresy" in John W. de Gruchy and Charles Villa-Vicencio (eds), *Apartheid is a Heresy*, Cape Town: David Philip, 1983, 39-47.

[14] Desmond M. Tutu, *Crying in the Wilderness: The Struggle for Justice in South Africa*, Grand Rapids: Eerdmans, 1982, 43.

[15] Desmond M. Tutu, *The Rainbow People of God: The Making of a Peaceful Revolution* (ed.) John Allen. New York: Doubleday, 1994.

[16] Jakes Gerwel, "National Reconciliation: Holy Grail or Secular Pact?", in Charles Villa-Vicencio and Wilhelm Verwoerd (eds), *Looking Back, Reaching Forward: Reflections on the Truth and Reconciliation Commission of South Africa*, Cape Town: Cape Town University Press, 2000, 277-286.

[17] Allan A. Boesak and Curtiss. P. DeYoung, *Radical Reconciliation: Beyond Political Pietism and Christian Quietism*, Maryknoll: Orbis Books, 2012, 152.

centre stage during our transition phase, today, the notion has lost its premier status as a guiding vision for social transformation in the country. Along with this, the legacy of Archbishop Tutu (along with Nelson Mandela) is being contested more than ever before. This is prompted by views that under their leadership, the (over)emphasis on reconciliation did very little to disrupt the socio-economic vestiges of apartheid. Here reconciliation without addressing the root causes of injustice is often cited as a concern. This scepticism is best expressed in the tension between the work of the TRC and the reality of South Africa having one of the highest persistent income inequality rates in the world. This is hardly surprising given the social divisions, marked especially by race, class, gender and ethnicity, among other things.

Under these circumstances, one would have to once again (re)consider whether indeed reconciliation has the potential to transform society.[18] Since it is something that needs constant clarification, it often loses its power as a symbol. Properly understood, a symbol is self-evident and needs no explanation – it grips the imagination, prompting the need for some to invoke an expression of reconciliation that is considered "true" or "authentic". If anything, the question of whether reconciliation has a role to play in addressing some of our most difficult challenges would undoubtedly have to be addressed. The view that under current circumstances, it lacks the gravity to do just that might very well be contingent on a political as opposed to a theological understanding of its potential.[19]

Overcoming meaninglessness

The arduousness of the pursuit of the reconciliation ideal continues to baffle those looking for quick answers to a complex (wicked) problem. In this sense, I maintain that the quest for reconciliation has in some ways become an exercise in the absurd since there is no rational or succinct way of capturing what exactly is at stake.[20] While there may well be consensus on what reconciliation entails, controversies over how this ideal is to be realised suggest conflicting interpretations of its value and meaning. It is something that transcends our ability (or urge) for mastery and is, therefore, best described as an elusive mystery, a dream that cannot be fathomed or achieved. This is amid our propensity to forever search for meaning irrespective of the incongruity of the ideal and the absurdity that defines our chaotic, irrational and sometimes meaningless existence.

The TRC, as flawed as it might have been, is the audacity to dream of something beyond the meaninglessness that sometimes defines our existence; moreover, invoking a theology of reconciliation to achieve something extraordinary, resisting the temptation of utter hopelessness. In this context, Camus' conception of the absurd provides a glimmer of hope. It is a stark reminder that our efforts may very well be futile but that we should endure nevertheless. The Arch, like Sisyphus, was charged to roll a boulder up a mountain, only to see it roll down again, over and over again. As we celebrate this great South African, we are reminded that this task is not his alone. Like him, we should cope as best we can with whatever challenges come our way, embracing the absurd background of our existence. In the words of Camus, "each atom of that stone, each mineral flake of that night-filled mountain, in itself forms a world. The struggle itself towards the heights is enough to fill a man's [sic] heart. *One must imagine Sisyphus happy*".[21] This is a constant reminder of why some difficulties are worth enduring in a world that is as precarious and unsettling as ours. This diagnosis is not a fatality. The absurdity of the situation is our reality, but love saves us from it. The paradoxical presence of meaning amid meaninglessness. Perhaps this is the one thing we should learn from the life and work of our beloved Arch.

---

[18] Smit, "The Symbol of Reconciliation and Ideological Conflict", 88.
[19] Boesak and DeYoung, *Radical Reconciliation*, 154.
[20] Demaine J. Solomons, "The Absurdity of Reconciliation: What We (Should) Learn from Rustenburg and the Implications for South Africa", *Stellenbosch Theological Journal,* 6 (2), 2020, 393-412.
[21] Camus, *The Myth of Sisyphus*, 119. Emphasis mine.

61. EMBODYING RESTITUTIVE FORGIVENESS: THE LASTING LEGACY OF DESMOND MPILO TUTU

Nico Koopman[1]

In 1986 the newly elected Archbishop of the Anglican Church in Southern Africa, Archbishop Desmond Mpilo Tutu, addressed the synod of the former Dutch Reformed Mission Church. The church had just adopted the Confession of Belhar in 1986. In three articles, the Confession of Belhar articulates an understanding of God as the one who let God's children live in unity, reconciliation and justice. A few years later I was tasked to welcome Archbishop Tutu at an ecumenical service that the minister's organisation of Atlantis had organised. As a very young pastor I then described him as a symbol of our joint quest for one, united, undivided, non-racial, non-classist, non-sexist, democratic South Africa, where peace and justice reign supreme. Decades later, at the commemoration of his 90th birthday, I would like to describe Archbishop Emeritus Desmond Tutu as not only a symbol but an incarnation and embodiment of restituting forgiveness.

In this contribution I discuss Tutu's understanding of forgiveness as a forgiveness that calls forth unity, reconciliation and justice, specifically restitutive justice. I will argue that it is not without reason that he titles one of his greatest publications, *No Future Without Forgiveness*.[2] This contribution attempts to demonstrate how forgiveness paves the way for unity in solidarity, embracing reconciliation and restitutive justice. In a conclusive section I will infer some lessons for us today.

1. Forgiveness for unity in solidarity

Desmond Tutu's understanding of forgiveness is based on the heart of the Christian gospel. Forgiveness is not dependent upon and does not wait for the confession of guilt and contrition of the perpetrator. Jesus forgave them while they were busy nailing him on the Cross.[3] Forgiveness paves the way for contrition and confession of guilt; forgiveness paves the way for, calls forth and invites remorse, repentance, reconciliation, reparation, redress, restoration and restitution. In reflecting upon the Truth and Reconciliation Commission that he chaired, Tutu portrays forgiveness as the pathway to a new future. He reckons that the work of the TRC does give hope to people in South Africa as well as in other parts of the world where conflicts exist. The growing culture of forgiveness and reparation, to which the TRC contributed, can convince people in conflict that a new future of life in peace and friendship is possible. Tutu attributed the achievements of the TRC to the work of the Triune God, and does not view it as a human achievement:

> We were destined for perdition and were plucked out of total annihilation. We were a hopeless case if ever there was one. God intends that others might look at us and take courage. God wants to point to us as a possible beacon of hope, a possible paradigm ... Our experiment is going to succeed because God wants

---

[1] Nico Koopman is professor of systematic theology (public theology and ethics), and deputy vice-chancellor for social impact, transformation and personnel at Stellenbosch University. He has been engaging with the person and work of Archbishop Emeritus Desmond Tutu since his student days at the University of the Western Cape during the 1980s. As pastor and university chaplain, and later as vice-rector of Huguenot College, director of the Beyers Naudé Centre for Public Theology and dean of the Faculty of Theology at Stellenbosch University, and in his current position in executive university leadership, he cooperated with Archbishop Tutu in church and academic contexts.

[2] D. Tutu, *No Future Without Forgiveness* (London: Rider, 1999).

[3] D. Tutu, *No Future*, p.220.

us to succeed, not for our glory and aggrandizement but for the sake of God's world. God wants to show that there is life after conflict and repression – that because of forgiveness there is a future.[4]

Emeritus Archbishop Tutu strongly believes in the possibility and reality of forgiveness, and its potential to bring transformation for both the perpetrator and victim:

> The point is that if perpetrators were to be despaired of as monsters and demons then we were thereby letting accountability go out the window by declaring that they were not moral agents to be held responsible for their deeds ... Theology says they still, despite the awfulness of their deeds, remain children of God with the capacity to repent, to be able to change.[5]

Unity is not unity from a distance, but unity in nearness, unity in proximity. There is interaction, exposure, growing knowledge of each other, sharing in each other's experiences. This proximity paves the way for developing sympathy, when one member suffers, all suffer with. When one member is honoured, all rejoice (2 Cor. 12). This sympathy flows from empathy, from living in each other's skins and looking at the world through each other's lenses. And in contexts where people have been alienated from each other, or where they are from different ethnic, cultural and national backgrounds, they develop interpathy.[6] They feel with each other over all types of divisions. Unity in proximity enables us to develop oneness in thinking, feeling, willing and acting, true solidarity and cohesion. People from a diversity of backgrounds and socio-economic positions get to know, love and serve each other, and carry each other's burdens.

Archbishop Tutu's successor as secretary-general of the South African Council of Churches, Dr Beyers Naudé,[7] pleaded that people from different ethnic backgrounds be brought into contact on congregational level. They need to learn to communicate constructively with each other, in order to prevent conflict and to build peace and justice amongst them. Apartheid has deliberately estranged people from different language, cultural and ethnic groups. In the quest for unity deliberate efforts should be made to bring these estranged ones closer. Structural church unity and in other institutions of society should serve as a vehicle for unity in nearness, unity in proximity. Another South African theologian, Jaap Durand,[8] pleads that structural unity should open the doors to these quality encounters of formerly estranged Christians. The structural unity of churches should not be the end, but the start of the process to grow ever closer together. After structural unity can the problems of practical and attitudinal nature be addressed jointly.

2. Forgiveness for embracing reconciliation

Forgiveness paves the way for a life of farewell to alienation and rejection, and for a life of reconciliation and embracing each other across all boundaries. Paulinic thought reconciliation has two dimensions. Reconciliation as *hilasmos* has to do with the expiation of wrongs and stumbling blocks to atonement (at-one-ment). Reconciliation as *katalassoo* refers to harmony in the relationship

---

[4] D. Tutu, *No Future*, pp.229-230.

[5] D. Tutu, *No Future*, pp.74-75.

[6] David Augsberger makes a helpful distinction between sympathy, empathy and interpathy. "Sympathy is a spontaneous affective reaction to another's feelings experienced on the basis of perceived similarity between observer and observed. Empathy is an intentional affective response to another's feelings experienced on the basis of perceived differences between the observer and observed. Interpathy is an intentional cognitive and affective envisioning of another's thoughts and feelings from another culture, worldview and epistemology". See D. Augsberger, *Pastoral Counseling Across Cultures* (Louisville: Westminster/John Knox Press, 1989), p.31.

[7] See C.F.B. Naudé, "Support in Word and Deed" in: P. Réamonn (ed.), *Farewell to Apartheid? Church Relations in South Africa* (Geneva: World Alliance of Reformed Churches, 1994), p.71.

[8] See J. Durand, "Church Unity and the Reformed Churches in Southern Africa", in: P. Réamonn (ed.), *Farewell to Apartheid?*, p.66.

with the other. Reconciliation as in the embrace that Miroslav Volf[9] refers to: the embrace of different races, tribes, nationalities, socio-economic groups, genders, sexual orientations, age groups, people with different levels of ability and differently-abledness. Reconciliation pleads that stumbling blocks for peaceful living, for the embrace, be removed. Reconciliation therefore implies opposing injustices like racism, tribalism, xenophobia, classism, misogyny, homophobia, ageism and ableism.

And to this list we can add ecocide. The work of reconciliation of the Triune God, according to Michael Welker,[10] includes reconciliation with the environment. He specifically discusses the outpouring of the Spirit. The outpouring of the Spirit shows the universal breath and inexhaustibility of God, as well as his powerful concreteness and presence. This outpouring affects new communities in various structural patterns of life that are apparently foreign to each other. In this new community nature (environment) and culture (humans) become open to each other. The Spirit lays hold of, transforms and unifies apparently incompatible domains of life that obey different laws.

Reconciliation discourse is informed by the teaching of the long Christian tradition about reconciliation. Reconciliation, therefore, is viewed as the work of redemption of the Triune God which is done for us in Jesus Christ (cf. Anselm's objective theory of atonement); reconciliation refers to the transformation that the love of the Triune God brings about in our lives (cf. Abelard's subjective theory of atonement); and reconciliation refers to the victory of Christ over the cosmic powers of evil and our consequent liberation from them (cf. Irenaeus' theory of atonement). South African theologian, John de Gruchy,[11] is of the opinion that the aforementioned theory helps us to understand the social and cosmic dimensions of reconciliation.

Reconciliation has both vertical and horizontal dimensions. Donald Shriver aptly describes the horizontal (personal and even political) dimension of reconciliation. According to him reconciliation and forgiveness imply the honest and truthful facing of past evils, opposition to revenge, empathy for victims and perpetrators of evil and the commitment of victims to resume life alongside evildoers.[12] Forgiveness, unity in solidarity and embracing reconciliation are all building blocks for restitutive justice.

3. Forgiveness for restitutive justice

Justice can be described as compassionate justice. In line with the biblical use of these concepts, both the sacrificial (justice as *tzedakah* and *dike*) and forensic (justice as *mishpat* and *dike*) dimensions of justice are being referred to.

Through the work of redemption of Jesus Christ God declares us just. People who are justified by the grace of God and are participating in the quest for justice in the world. Justified people, people who are made right by the Triune God, i.e. right humans, seek human rights in our broken world. For Christopher Marshall[13] justification by faith is an expression of restorative justice.

The notion of sacrifice has a second dimension. It also indicates that justice cannot be reached in this world when the willingness to sacrifice for the sake of the other is not present. A third aspect of the sacrificial dimension of justice is the fact that justice does not seek revenge, but it is merciful. It seeks the healing and restoration of both perpetrators and victims. In fact, it seeks the healing of all broken relationships. Therefore, this justice is called restorative justice. Marshall's analysis of the use

---

[9] See M. Volf, *Exclusion and Embrace: A Theological Exploration of Identity, Otherness and Reconciliation* (Nashville: Abingdon Press, 1996), p.171.

[10] M. Welker, *God the Spirit* (Minneapolis: Fortress Press, 1994), pp.145-147.

[11] See J. de Gruchy, *Reconciliation: Restoring Justice* (London: SCM Press, 2002), p.58.

[12] See D. Shriver, *An Ethic for Enemies: Forgiveness in Politics* (Oxford/New York: Oxford University Press, 1995), p. 67. This book of Shriver's gives an informative church historical analysis of the public character of forgiveness, specifically on pp. 45-62. Another insightful and inspiring book of Shriver's on reconciliation in the public sphere is: D. Shriver, *Honest Patriots: Loving a Country Enough to Remember its Misdeeds* (Oxford: Oxford University Press, 2005).

[13] See C. Marshall, *Beyond Retribution: A New Testament Vision for Justice, Crime and Punishment* (Grand Rapids: Eerdmans, 2001), p.59.

of justice in the New Testament enables him to refer to justice as restorative or covenantal justice. This covenantal justice goes beyond retribution and punishment and seeks, like reconciliation, the healing of relationships. Like reconciliation, restorative and covenantal justice seeks embrace. It seeks the renewal of the covenant of God and humans, of humans amongst each other and of humans and the rest of creation.[14]

The notion of sacrifice should be used in a qualified manner in theological discourse. It can easily be interpreted as a notion that silences oppressed people, and encourages them to keep on sacrificing and tolerating oppression, and not resist it. Sacrifice also carries the resistance in some circles of a God who can only bring forth justice through the violence of sacrifice, blood and death on Calvary. The notion of sacrifice can only be used where it guards against these objections.[15]

US theologian Bernard Brady supports the notion of compassionate justice. He identifies five types of justice; namely, interpersonal justice (adherence to the standards and expectations of families and friends),[16] commutative justice (in the sphere of promises and contracts between individuals in private relationships),[17] distributive justice (the fair distribution and allocation of social benefits and social burdens to individuals through structures of government),[18] communal justice (the contribution to the common good of every member of society together with government)[19] and social justice (where the focus is not upon particular relationships but upon general patterns of social relationships and social interaction, and on the reviewing and evaluation of social policies, institutions and structures so as to defend, reject or amend them).[20] He is specifically describing social justice as compassionate justice. With an appeal to the 8th-century prophets, Brady pleads for the twofold understanding of justice as legal justice in the social structures and institutions, and justice as concern and compassion for the most vulnerable people in society.[21]

Miroslav Volf supports the notion of compassionate justice. He appeals to the ethics of care of Carol Gilligan. She describes the identity of humans as that of relationality and interdependency. Volf argues that justice should be redefined in terms of this anthropology of interdependency. Such a view of justice implies that we cannot think about justice in a rationalistic, detached way. Interdependency implies compassion and care of the other. And where the participants in such a justice, i.e. caring and compassionate justice, which is focused upon the quest for communion between interdependent humans, are called into communion with the Triune God, we are on the way to a life of embrace.

This rich and diversified understanding of justice finds its climax and even its acid test in the notion of restitutive justice. In a very helpful discussion of restitution, Dirkie Smit[22] mentions that the origin of restitution is in legal discourse, and indicates how it had become a central theme in moral discourse. In legal discourse about restitution Aristotle developed the notion of corrective justice that laid the basis of civil and criminal law. Thomas Aquinas developed restitution thinking in the context of commutative justice that focused on wider social relations. Restitution for the breach of commutative justice implied the restoration of conjugal rights by husbands and wives returning to

---

[14] See C. Marshall, *Beyond Retribution*, pp.35-95.

[15] Mark Heim discusses the objections against the classic Christian view that a sacrifice, cross, broken body and bloodshed are indispensable for our salvation. He, however, argues against doing away altogether with this doctrine, which constitutes the heart of the Christian gospel, and proposes constructive ways of keeping on using the notion of sacrifice. See M. Heim, *Saved from Sacrifice: A Theology of the Cross* (Grand Rapids, Michigan: Wm. B. Eerdmans Publishing Co., 2006).

[16] B.V. Brady, *The Moral Bond of Community: Justice and Discourse in Christian Morality* (Washington D.C.: Georgetown University Press, 1998), pp.95-97.

[17] B.V. Brady, *The Moral Bond*, pp.108-109.

[18] B.V. Brady, *The Moral Bond*, pp.113-117.

[19] B.V. Brady, *The Moral Bond*, pp.117-120.

[20] B.V. Brady, *The Moral Bond*, pp.120-122.

[21] M. Volf, *Exclusion and Embrace*, p.225.

[22] D. Smit, "Restitution", in R. Brawley (ed), *The Oxford Encyclopedia of the Bible and Ethics* Vol.2 (Oxford: Oxford University Press), pp.204-207.

cohabitation, as well as the return of goods unjustly acquired, and the reparation of harm done. In legal traditions in England, restitution implied contractual remedy. In the United States the contractual nature of restitution is aimed at fairness, the prevention of unjust enrichment and the benefit of victims of crime.

The moral intuitions behind these legal positions broaden restitution discourse to go broader than contractual and criminal violations and to include personal and social injustices, and historical harm and injury. This broader area of restitution refers to restitution for slavery, colonisation and racism in apartheid South Africa. It refers to discrimination and dehumanisation in the forms of sexism, patriarchy, classism, violation of dignity and human rights. Examples of violation of human rights include expropriation and dispossession of land, occupation and forced removals. One should add ecocide to this list of injustices, injuries and harms that call out for restitution.

Emeritus Archbishop Tutu spells out the concrete contours along which restitution should take place:

> ... the whole process of reconciliation has been placed in considerable jeopardy by the enormous disparities between the rich, mainly the whites, and the poor, mainly the blacks. The huge gap between the haves and the have-nots, which was created and maintained by apartheid, poses the greatest threat to reconciliation and stability in our country. The rich provided the class from which the perpetrators and the beneficiaries of apartheid came and the poor produced the bulk of the victims. That is why I have exhorted whites to be keen to see transformation taking place in the lot of blacks. For unless houses replace the hovels and shacks in which most blacks live; unless blacks gain access to clean water, electricity, affordable health care, decent education, good jobs and a safe environment – all things which the vast majority of whites have taken for granted for so long – we can kiss goodbye to reconciliation.[23]

In a speech that he made on 11 August 2011 at Stellenbosch University that was reported in in the *Cape Argus* of 12 August 2011,[24] Tutu spelled out the agenda of restitutive forgiveness. He pleads for restitution as the rehumanisation of wounded and dehumanised people. He called for economic restitution and called on senior government officials to share their personal resources. He called on white resourceful people to consider paying a form of wealth tax. He called for psychological restitution. Oppressed people should overcome the erosion of their self-esteem and the advent of self-hate in their midst. This dehumanisation, self-hate and low self-esteem pave the way for crime and violence, road anger and reckless driving, and even tolerance for littering.

Tinyiko Maluleke[25] indicated twenty-five years ago how big the need is for restitution in South Africa. Various hurts and harms, injuries and injustices need to be addressed. It is worth quoting his portrayal of these wrongs at length:

> The modern world is in a large measure the fruit of centuries of colonial exploitation and dispossession. Behind the grandeur of the modern world lies centuries of slavery and imperialist dispossession. It was the toil of peoples of colour in White peoples' plantations and colonies that paved the way for the modern world. South Africa is a microcosm of this experience. Although the sweat, blood and losses of the colonised are seldom acknowledged as foundational "contributions" to the much-vaunted modern economies and their revered "market" forces," the colonised have paid the ultimate price for the modern world.[26]

Smit explains that in various restitution discussions, restitution focuses on the past and on the future. In some cases, restitution seeks symbolic reparation and in other contexts material reparation. He explains further that for theological traditions that view justification by grace that calls forth good

---

[23] D. Tutu, *No Future*, p.221.

[24] D. Tutu, "Tutu calls for wealth tax on white", *Cape Argus*, 12 August 2011 (journalist Murray Williams).

[25] T. Maluleke, "Do I, With My Excellent PhD, Still Need Affirmative Action? The Contribution of Black Theology to the Debate", in *Missionalia* 24:3 (1996), pp.303-321.

[26] T. Maluleke, "Do I, With My Excellent PhD, Still Need Affirmative Action?", pp.307-308.

works, it is easier to adopt restitution language than for traditions that only emphasise grace, and that even those that view gratitude as a response to grace reduce the absolute and unconditional gift-character of grace. Desmond Tutu is indeed in a theological tradition that adheres to a grace that is not cheap, but that is seeking repentance and restitution. Tutu puts it clearly: "Confession, forgiveness, and reparation, wherever feasible, form part of a continuum."[27]

In her discussion of the transformative nature of grace, American womanist theologian Katie Cannon[28] explicates the socio-political consequences of forgiveness and grace:

> Divine grace that comes to us, exposing us as individuals directly to God's loving-kindness, must also be discussed from a critical perspective that is informed by our experiences in sociopolitical history ... First and foremost, grace is a divine gift of redeeming love that empowers African Americans to confront shocking, absurd, death-dealing disjunctions in life, so that when we look at our outer struggles and inner strength we see interpretive possibilities for creative change. Second, grace is the indwelling of God's spirit that enables Christians of African descent to live conscious lives of thanksgiving, by deepening our knowledge of forgiveness given in Christ, so that even in situations of oppression we celebrate our status as beloved creatures made in God's image. This double definition indicates the complex role that the doctrine of grace plays in the lives of black church folk.

Conclusion

Tutu's notion of no future without forgiveness and Nelson Mandela's reconciling approach are questioned by many, amongst others by a younger generation of public thinkers. In their ranks is Rekgotsofetse Chikane, son of church leader, struggle hero and director-general in the presidential office of former president Thabo Mbeki, Frank Chikane.[29] The fact that forgiveness is not accompanied by restitution is the reason for this suspicion of mainly black youngsters against Tutu and against his emphasis on forgiveness and reconciliation. Allan Boesak[30] rightly warns against this development where white people embrace Tutu just like white Americans cherished Martin Luther King Jr. Their emphasis on forgiveness and reconciliation was misused to only focus on forgiveness, rainbow unity and reconciliation, and to neglect restitution. In the process Tutu is domesticated by white people and used as a buffer between restitution and the perpetuation of white privilege and intergenerational racism and inequality. Boesak rightly pleads for the re-radicalisation of Desmond Tutu. This essay with its emphasis on restitutive forgiveness attempts to contribute to honouring Tutu by resisting a reduction of his subversive and transformative piety and radical Christian proclamation of forgiveness that brings forth contrition and confession, remorse, repentance, reconciliation, redress, reparation, restoration and restitution.

---

[27] D. Tutu, *No Future Without Forgiveness*, p.221.

[28] K. Cannon, "Transformative Grace" in A. Plantinga Pauw and S. Jones, *Feminist and Womanist Essays in Reformed Dogmatics* (Louisville/London: Westminster John Knox Press, 2005), p.151.

[29] See amongst others Rekgotsofetse Chikane, *Breaking a Rainbow, Building a Nation: The Politics Behind #MustFall Movements* (Johannesburg: Picador Africa, 2018).

[30] See the chapter of Boesak's, titled "Subversive Piety: The Reradicalisation of Desmond Tutu", in his book written with Curtiss Paul DeYoung, *Radical Reconciliation: Beyond Political Pietism and Christian Quietism* (Maryknoll, New York: Orbis Books, 2012).

62. THE FUNERAL AT BOIPATONG – BETWEEN ANGER AND RECONCILIATION

Heike Spiegelberg[1]

After Nelson Mandela's release from prison in February 1990 negotiations between the liberation movement and the white minority regime on a transition process from apartheid to a democratic South Africa became possible. However, the period up until the first democratic elections in April 1994 was a period of severe violence between different forces trying to secure their power for after the period of transition. There were events of violence between different political and interest groups within the black majority and targeted killings of political and peace activists, but also fierce attacks on civilians by the battle-experienced army of the apartheid regime. Some of the increasingly brutal attacks against the civilian population in the then so-called townships were committed by death squads. Since the beginning of the nineties the question about who instigated, organised and armed this violence in the townships became an urgent one. The Goldstone Commission, and later the Truth and Reconciliation Commission, uncovered involvement from within state security and secret service structures. It was found that the command structure was certainly linked to the government of the old regime, but the involvement of President de Klerk remained uncertain.

In this period of uncertainty and suffering before the first democratic elections, the South African Council of Churches accompanied the negotiation process, analysed the situation, supported local and national peace actions and stood with the victims and the suffering.

In the region around Johannesburg, in the year 1992, this violence seemed to move around: at the beginning of March it was rife in the township of Alexandra north of Johannesburg, where some areas developed into so-called no-go zones. By the beginning of April it increased in the informal settlement of Phola Park south-east of Johannesburg, where violence reached its peak with the nightly attack on the residents by the infamous 32 Battalion of the SADF (South African Defence Force). Violence also arrived in Boipatong, a small township community in the Vaal area south of Johannesburg. Many of these areas were placed under state of emergency regulations, which many people residing in the quiet so-called suburbs of Johannesburg only a few kilometers away were not even aware of. On the night of 17 to 18 June 1992 forty-seven people lost their lives in a massacre in Boipatong. Here also there were indications of an external support for these events, albeit that these facts are contested even until today. The newspaper the *Weekly Mail* reported: "The Weekly Mail has had access to statements of eye witnesses in Boipatong who claim that at about 10 pm groups of police in armed vehicles started to deposit armed men at various places around the township. Thereafter the massacre started."[2]

Parts of the events in Boipatong could even be watched on national South African TV, and we saw, as one will see in any war zone anywhere in the world: burning houses, people crying, dead children and members of the military clinging nervously to their armoured vehicles. In those same videos one also saw images of attackers, a group of some hundred men, equipped with traditional weapons such as pangas and axes, as they slowly proceeded up the street in formation. These images were not commented on. The attack on the residents lasted several hours without any authorities interfering in spite of alerts, and left forty-seven people dead, people randomly killed: a pregnant woman and children among them.

---

[1] Rev. Heike Spiegelberg is a recently retired minister of the Evangelical Lutheran Church in Germany. At the beginning of the nineties she served as an assistant to Dr Kistner and Dr Beyers Naudé at the Ecumenical Advice Office (EAB) in Johannesburg, and later at the Methodist Church of Southern Africa. The EAB and its staff assisted peace activists and survivors in violence-afflicted communities. Heike Spiegelberg is married to Samson Mhlambi of Thokoza. For the couple, Archbishop Desmond Tutu is one of the icons of the struggle who even today safeguards the ideas of the Freedom Charter.

[2] 26 June 1992. Quotation re-translated from German by the author.

I had the privilege and the burden to attend the pre-funeral rally on 27 June, together with Dr Wolfram Kistner and a church visitor from overseas. It was a typical winter day in one of the industrial areas near Johannesburg. Nearing the township we entered a zone under a stinking, yellow-dark cloud covering houses and shacks, giving the feeling of impending night in spite of the early afternoon time. Residents in these areas were constantly exposed to the pollution of the adjoining industries and household fires due to a lack of access to electricity. Even from a distance we could hear that the stadium must be packed with thousands of people, with more coming in, many running in formation. On arrival marshals accompanied us to our seats in a part of the stadium where most of the white participants were placed.

In an attempt to convey some of the horror the victims had to face and give survivors a voice, the first speaker was a resident of Boipatong. He gave witness to the events of the night of 17 June. He and his wife were just getting ready to go to bed when they heard a noise from the street. When he opened the door to check he saw how some men were in the process of killing one of his neighbours. Startled by the noise his wife also appeared behind him in the door. As they were standing there frozen in shock at what they witnessed, they suddenly became aware that they had also caught the attackers' attention. Scarcely dressed, they started running in the opposite direction. The resident reported how his wife, being heavily pregnant, soon became exhausted. They had to crawl under fences, which he was holding up for her, and after a short while his wife could not carry on. She fell and pleaded with him not to leave her there as the attackers were nearing, but he would also not have been able to defend his wife. As a result he had to leave her at the corner of a house and ran on to get help. When he reached the house of friends and they opened for him, he collapsed and passed out. Together they ventured out to find his wife, but already from a distance they saw someone lying at that corner, covered by a blanket. When they opened the blanket they saw the body of his wife, stabbed to death.

The funeral rally in Boipatong, in a packed stadium, became a culmination point for developments and discourses of the transition process. The scene in the stadium was radical; there was not much leeway for hopes, which were still in the process of inception. At a podium in front the eminent persons were seated, protected by marshals of the ANC: South African and international politicians and church leaders. This rally which, according to the tradition that had established itself in these days of many funeral rallies, provided an opportunity for political organisations to publish their positions, to redefine the relationship between each other and to rally for support of the black community. It was also used to draw in the support of international actors, as delegates of important international bodies participated, such as of the OAU, the UN and several ambassadors.

Yet at the centre of the stadium the thirty-seven coffins were placed, surrounded by the relatives of the victims, whose wailing in anger and mourning intermittently drowned out the audibility of the speeches. On this day, the speeches expressed even those positions which up to now were perhaps left unsaid due to tactical considerations, demands were made and resolutions announced. Whatever was publicly declared in this stadium could not be ignored in the future negotiation process. And in the tense atmosphere of speaking, singing and mourning, which seemed to last much longer than those six hours, every word sounded like an oath: we will force this regime to surrender – down with de Klerk. Then ANC general secretary Cyril Ramaphosa called for him to step down immediately, referring to a conversation between Mandela and de Klerk: "De Klerk actually said: 'Mr. Mandela, I have no power. I have no power over the police force.' We say De Klerk must go because he has proven to be either incompetent or totally useless as a State President."

The South African Council of Churches (SACC) had undertaken to function as the host of this event, and it was most likely because of this that it became possible to bring together such different political factions and organisations and this diversity of high-ranking guests. Rev. Frank Chikane, general secretary of the SACC, was the master of ceremony, Archbishop Desmond Tutu delivered the sermon and led in prayers. It was also most likely because of them that this highly emotional and tense event remained peaceful and disciplined. Had emotions spiralled out of control, there could have been further violence, as happened at the same time outside the stadium, where a young man was stabbed to death. All those who were part of this funeral event had to be grateful to Bishop Tutu and Rev. Chikane for their courage and faith to take this responsibility upon themselves. It was them who again and again during the course of these six hours, and amid many political ambitions being voiced, insisted on the first priority of the needs of the survivors and the relatives of the victims. The atmosphere was tense and speeches fiery and fierce, but listening closely one knew that the demands were nothing but legitimate: for a life without the fear of being killed at night, for a fast transition to democracy based on the principle of free and fair elections.

It was not as much the content of the speeches by church leaders as rather the achievement to convey a message of reconciliation amidst the tensions and the political demands and strategies. Archbishop Napier of the South African Catholic Bishops' Conference started the proceedings with a prayer of confession of guilt by all involved and a plea to God to grant reconciliation. Some of the church contributions were clearly political, as was the call of the president of the Anti-Apartheid Movement, Rev. Trevor Huddleston to the United Nations and the European Community: "Stop talking – and isolate the Apartheid regime."

Towards the end, as tensions in and around the stadium were rising, Archbishop Tutu delivered his sermon on Exodus 3: 1-12, the account of Moses' appointment as the leader of the oppressed people of Israel and the announcement of the exodus from Egypt. He recalled at length how he often had had the impression that God did not respond to the suffering of the oppressed people of South Africa. But then it did become visible that God had not forgotten about his people. When the political leaders were released from prison, even God himself danced. Freedom seemed to have arrived. In the meantime many obstacles were placed on the road to freedom. But the oppressed can rely on this truth: whoever opposes the liberation of God's people, will meet the resistance of the living God. Archbishop Tutu's description of his understanding of reconciliation was received with visible and audible consent and loud laughter: if you stole somebody's pen, a very nice and useful pen, it will not be enough to apologise and to say, when it comes out, that you are sorry. Of course you also have to give back the pen! Archbishop Tutu's way to preach is hard to describe on paper. At this sad, tense and potentially explosive event he did not only preach, but capture his audience with his spirit. The sermon was not only a speech, but also a theatre performance and an act of poetry. The mood in the fully packed stadium, among those many hurt and angry people, changed into a liberating laughter. Amid the mourning and wailing, the harsh realities of politics and the gloomy atmosphere, reconciliation became a tangible vision.

The press statement of the SACC from 24 June 1992, however, gave an impression of the long road that was still ahead and that would still cost many lives up until the first democratic elections in April 1994: "The massacre of Boipatong has confirmed our worst fears. Boipatong could happen because the government had decided not to listen to our suggestions and proposals and to act accordingly. Also it could happen, as can be seen now, because the government is not willing to hand over this power which it gained through the evil political process of Apartheid."[3]

---

[3] Quotation re-translated from German by the author.

63. EMBRACE: A SHORT STORY OF EMBODYING RECONCILIATION

Anne Jaborg[1]

During my 2014 sabbatical, I had an opportunity to meet Desmond Tutu. He had invited South African faith communities to Stellenbosch to attend a meeting called "Revisiting the Truth and Reconciliation's Faith Community Hearing". The purpose of the meeting was to ask questions about how churches and communities had fared in addressing some of the recommendations from the Truth and Reconciliation Commission (TRC), seventeen years after the first hearing of the TRC. As in 1997, Bishop Desmond Tutu presided over this hearing as well. Podium commissioners were the same as in 1997. So was the seating order. Two by two the delegates of individual faith communities took their seats at a table facing the commissioners. They quoted from their 1997 "Confessions". They delivered their reports. They spoke of small positive developments, of their efforts to engage in various social and charity projects as some sort of "reparation". And above all, they complained about the sluggish progress or even failure of new steps. They referred to Konrad Raiser's remark that "truth also creates new victims".[2] The general feeling was that truth rather than reconciliation had been followed up since 1997.

We as listeners were greatly moved by all this, especially by the report from a reverend of the Dutch Reformed Church in Africa. He came alone. He had not been delegated by his community. He told the audience that in the last few years his faith community had broken apart over theological contentions regarding apartheid, over strife and tribulation on truth and reconciliation. 5,000 members had left his church. After he had finished his report with: "We are a church with special needs of forgiveness, understanding and support", the tall, sturdy white man collapsed and broke into tears. Silence in the assembly room. Then we quietly rose from our seats – one after the other – and finally Desmond Tutu went over to the man and embraced him. There was applause in relief.

This incident with Bishop Tutu left a deep and lasting impression on my mind. It seems that almost everything is possible when people get up and walk over towards each other …

---

[1] Anne Jaborg, pastor from the Evangelical Lutheran Church of Oldenburg, Germany. For thirty years I have been working as a parish pastor and prison chaplain. At Deutscher Evangelischer Kirchentag in Köln, 2007, I met the Nobel Peace Prize laureate for the first time. Since then, I have been fascinated by his charisma and, in particular, by his statements on the subject of reconciliation. This little experience report is based on my personal diary entry during my sabbatical in Stellenbosch in 2014.

[2] Orally transmitted and noted in the personal diary from Anne Jaborg on 10 September 2014.

64. "WHERE DID THE RAINBOW GO?":
NARRATIVES OF PURSUING AN IDEAL OF RACIAL RECONCILIATION

John Allen[1]

Soon after Madiba was inaugurated as president in 1994, he invited Desmond Tutu to breakfast in Cape Town one morning. The chaplain at Bishopscourt wasn't available for some reason, so I was asked to drive the Archbishop the short distance to Westbrooke, the presidential residence – later renamed Genadendal, after the mission station where Moravians from Germany first worked among South Africa's indigenous people.

We arrived a few minutes before 7 am, and I prepared to wait. No, said Archbishop Desmond, you're coming in too. This was typical – he insisted on living out African inclusiveness even when visiting different people of different cultures, and many were the hostesses in London, Washington and the Upper East Side of New York who quickly had to rearrange their seating plans when he and Mama Leah arrived for dinner with members of staff in tow.

Typically for Madiba, he received the Arch promptly, and we sat down around a small breakfast table in an upstairs lounge. Jakes Gerwel, director-general in the presidency, arrived to join us as Madiba watched the 7 am SABC2 news bulletin.

What transpired at that breakfast later turned into a widely covered spat between the Arch and Madiba: over the new government's decision to retain the apartheid arms industry; over large pay increases for members of parliament; and – of less moment – whether a president should be attending funerals wearing his colourful Italian-style shirts (which the Arch said "looked like pyjamas") instead of a suit and tie.

Never publicised was an intervention that came from Madiba's side. Archbishop Desmond was at the time chancellor of the University of the Western Cape. Professor Gerwel had just stepped down as vice-chancellor. It was addressing the Arch and Jakes in these capacities that Madiba raised his worries. He was concerned, he said, that those whom he identified as coloured students were being swamped by too many "black" students entering UWC. He felt the coloured community needed a university they could see as largely their own.

To use a Tutu-ism, you could have knocked me down with a feather. Where had this old man been all these years? Yes, in the 1950s the racial groups identified in ANC debates over the "national question" were organised in different congresses. Yes, I had been influenced by my reporting as a journalist on the importance of black consciousness in the rise to office of black church leaders in the 1970s. But surely the post-June 16 generation of arrivals on Robben Island must have brought to that university an awareness of how the word "black" had come to include all the oppressed?

Later, upon reflection, I moderated my instinctive reaction and came to a better understanding of where Madiba was coming from. I recalled his reported advocacy of Allan Boesak as the first post-1990 elected leader of the ANC in Western Cape. I recalled the early warning signals from black clergy in Cape Town that F.W. de Klerk had a great deal of support in coloured communities. And I recalled travelling around polling stations with Archbishop Desmond on 27 April 1994, for him to be welcomed enthusiastically by long lines of voters in Gugulethu, but to be received in silence by all but small pockets of voters in some of the poorer communities of the Cape Flats.

Looking back now, I also recall how the Arch addressed a crowd on the Grand Parade outside the Cape Town City Hall on 13 September 1989, at the end of the watershed march which helped to clear

---

[1] John Allen is the author of *Rabble-Rouser for Peace*, a biography of Desmond Tutu, and the editor of three collections of Tutu sermons, speeches, writings and sayings. He has served as executive editor of the African news website, allAfrica.com, as communications director of Trinity Church Wall Street in New York and of the South African Truth and Reconciliation Commission, and as media secretary to Desmond Tutu while he was Archbishop of Cape Town.

the way for Madiba's release five months later. (A senior cabinet minister told a journalist that F.W. de Klerk's decision to overrule his generals and not to attempt to stop the march was "a more fearful leap into the dark" than the decision to release Madiba.) Looking out over 30 to 40,000 people of all races, the Arch was struck by the racial inclusiveness of the crowd. Addressing de Klerk rhetorically, he ad-libbed: "This country is a rainbow country! This country is technicolour. You can come and see the new South Africa!"

Later, wrapping up his remarks, he called on the crowd to hold hands and wave, the result being a vivid demonstration of how many whites had joined black South Africans on the march. Referring to the "purple rain" march ten days earlier, at which police had used a water cannon loaded with purple dye to break up a multi-racial protest march, he concluded: "They tried to make us one colour: purple. We say we are the rainbow people! We are the new people of the new South Africa!"

He went on to use the metaphor of a rainbow in sermons and speeches in the years to come, perhaps explaining it best in a sermon in Tromsø, north of the Arctic Circle, in 1991:

> At home in South Africa I have sometimes said in big meetings where you have black and white together: "Raise your hands!" Then I've said, "Move your hands," and I've said: "Look at your hands – different colours representing different people. You are the rainbow people of God."

> And you remember the rainbow in the Bible is the sign of peace. The rainbow is the sign of prosperity. We want peace, prosperity and justice and we can have it when all the people of God, the rainbow people of God, work together.[2]

In 1994, President Mandela adopted the metaphor in his inaugural address:

> We enter into a covenant that we shall build the society [my underlining] in which all South Africans, both black and white, will be able to walk tall, without any fear in their hearts, assured of their inalienable right to human dignity – a rainbow nation at peace with itself and the world.[3]

But in the 21st century, the "rainbow-ism" which Mandela and Tutu are purported to have advocated has fallen on hard times. In the media and public debate, Madiba's rainbow nation is supposed by its critics to have been something he declared as already in existence, brought into being by the magic wand of the 1994 vote. Just as the churches affiliated to the South African Council of Churches repudiated the idea of "cheap reconciliation" in the 1970s and 1980s, the people of South Africa justifiably reject any suggestion that inequality has been overcome, that we have liberated our economy and that people's dignity is adequately respected.

The current portrayal of the vision which our elders held out is a caricature which distorts what they were saying. In Madiba's case, he presented the idea of a rainbow nation as an ideal to which to aspire, as a society which still needed – and still needs – to be built. Any South African who tries to sell us the idea that what we have now already constitutes the ideal that he held out is, as the biblical expression has it, trying to sell us a mess of pottage.

We have a long way to go, and white South Africans particularly so. The Arch has often been disappointed with the commitment of whites to the building of a united nation, from such local experiences as their low attendance at diocesan family days to the indifference of many to the Truth and Reconciliation Commission. Within a few months of beginning to work for the Arch in the 1980s, I accompanied him on an "archiepiscopal visitation" to the Diocese of Swaziland. At the end of the visit, he was diverted at short notice to visit a rural school. We were already on our way to the airport, I wanted to get home and I had just eaten breakfast. At the school we were presented with a

[2] Desmond Tutu, *The Rainbow People of God: The Making of a Peaceful Revolution,* ed. John Allen. New York: Doubleday (1994), v.

[3] SAnews.gov.za, South African Government News Agency, https://www.sanews.gov.za/south-africa/read-nelson-mandelas-inauguration-speech-president-sa (accessed 7 June 2021).

feast. I declined the food, politely, or so I thought. The Arch came up, and said under his breath but in a voice of steel: "This is Africa. You. Will. Eat."

After decades of reporting on and working with people of all races in the churches, and accompanying the Arch in an extraordinarily wide array of cultures and communities, both urban and rural, in many corners of our country, I can't say I have more than scratched the surface when it comes to understanding our society – especially because I follow only two of our national languages.

When as a journalist in the 1970s I was covering the courageous decision of Catholic bishops, in defiance of apartheid law, to open their schools to all races, I asked Neil McGurk, the Marist brother who led the process, how much white resistance there was. Not much, he said. But black pupils still constituted a minority, he added. It might be different when they became a majority. Nearly fifty years ago, he pin-pointed the problem we still face too often today: the lack of understanding of whites that the norms and customs by which we live are not the norms and customs necessarily aspired to by most of the country's people.

It is hard to overstate how far we as white South Africans still need to go to understand the degree to which we have to set aside our unconscious assumptions of cultural superiority if we are truly to belong in the South Africa of the 21st century. Too many of my colleagues and friends are frustrated at the way in which their children at formerly all-white schools are still expected to assimilate into the prevailing culture at those schools, instead of being able to have their norms and values accepted and respected.

The problem is that many white South Africans have not yet accepted that, culturally, we are a minority, a privileged minority but a minority – just as those of Asian and Lebanese origin are in East and West Africa respectively. And although our constitution gives us exactly the same rights as those formerly oppressed, no more and no fewer, it does not give us the right to assume that "the way we do things" will continue to dominate our society.

We are not yet, and will take a long time to become, the nation to which Nelson Mandela aspired in his inaugural address. But whether we are the Arch's "Rainbow People of God" is another matter. Explaining the concept in 2006, he described the rainbow as a phenomenon in which each of the colours is "distinct but related". Each is different, the differences are important, and we "ought to be glorying in them."[4] At the same time, the whole cannot exist without each of its component parts. Each is necessary to the beauty of the whole, which exceeds the sum of those parts.

In this way of thinking, we celebrate the revival of life-giving indigenous customs all across the country, recognising in the churches that valuable cultural practices were destroyed by missionaries who assumed the superiority of European ways and believed that bringing the gospel was consonant with introducing Western culture. We celebrate the revival of a neglected Khoisan heritage that we are now seeing among the descendants of those communities. We affirm the celebration by families of Indian descent of the glories of the advanced civilisations which go back for millennia in that sub-continent. And those who claim Scottish heritage can celebrate the thrill of hearing a rendition of "Amazing Grace" by a massed band of pipers – as long as they don't inflict their bagpipes on others.

Since it appears unlikely that our governing party will be dislodged from power any time soon, it is worth quoting how one of its intellectuals, Z. Pallo Jordan, explained its approach in 2019: "Rather than bringing together the disparate elements of a potential nation into a homogeneous entity, our movement's approach is to embrace heterogeneity as a strength rather than as a source of tension."[5]

The Arch's language is more colourful. He used to tell charming, if apocryphal, stories about the answers children gave in response to exam questions on the Bible. One of the questions went something like this: "What did Moses say to the people of Israel?" The answer: "You are the children

---

[4] John Allen, *Rabble-Rouser for Peace: The Authorised Biography of Desmond Tutu.* New York: Free Press (2006), 392.

[5] Z. Pallo Jordan, "ABCs Of the National Question", in *Umrabulo,* Number 46 (2019): 9, https://www.ortamboschool.org.za/wp-content/uploads/2019/07/Umrabulo-46th-edition.pdf (accessed 7 June 2021).

of God. Now behave like them!" In like spirit, he might say today: "You are *already* the Rainbow People of God. Now behave like them!"

65. SOUTH AFRICA, 27 APRIL 1994: RECOLLECTIONS OF TENSION AND JOY

Rudolf Hinz[1]

When we arrived at the hotel in Johannesburg, we were informed that there was an explosion in the airport from where we just came. We were a small group of election observers sent by the organisation "European Parliamentarians with Africa" (AWEPA), Amsterdam. We were well informed about the tense situation in South Africa. We knew that radical political groups from all sides were fighting each other, not content with the results of the years-long negotiations between the ANC and the white government. There were still tensions between the Inkatha movement and the ANC, there were massacres in the early nineties, there was an attack on St James Church in Cape Town, July 1993 – just nine months ago! Members of the armed wing of the Pan Africanist Congress (PAC) burst into a Sunday service and fired with machine guns killing eleven worshippers and injuring fifty-six. And the white Afrikaner Weerstandsbeweging (AWB) had attempted an "invasion" with civil cars into Bophuthatswana, just a few weeks prior. Would the election on 27 April be calm and peaceful?

In the late evening of our arrival we were instructed to vacate our rooms in the hotel and to sit around the elevator shaft right in the middle of the hotel building. The reason was that the police had discovered a bomb very close to the hotel and prepared a controlled demolition of the bomb since the demolition engineer could not defuse the bomb. We heard a dull explosion outside, still worried what would happen next.

On my flight from Frankfurt to Johannesburg I had read an article written by Bartholomäus Grill in the weekly paper *Die Zeit* about the situation before the election in South Africa. He described the tense situation but also argued that there was a good chance for a peaceful election day because – after all conflicts – the vast majority of the total population – more than 70 percent – were committed Christians. If all of them would go to vote for change it would be clear that the majority of the people longed for a peaceful day. Would he be right?

After a short instruction about the key rules of an election observation we were informed about the places to where we were dispatched. Our area was Stellenbosch and surroundings in the Western Cape. My immediate thought was: close to Archbishop Tutu in Cape Town! Would we have a chance to meet with him? After all he was at that time chairperson of the Eminent Advisory Board of AWEPA!

When we arrived at Stellenbosch, a place I had visited before several times, I walked through the streets near the university. On a tall building I saw the old flag of South Africa flying over the university. Was that a sign of defiance and potential conflict?

The next day was election day, 27 April 1994. Since the early years of the 1970s I was engaged in the World Council of Churches' Programme to Combat Racism (PCR) with a focus on Southern Africa. In the 1980s I became Secretary for Africa in the Foreign Office of the Evangelical Church in Germany (EKD). At that time – not far from 1994 – I was not so confident that the struggle to overcome apartheid would be successful soon. But now I was in Stellenbosch to observe the first nation-wide election!

It was a wonderful day! It was a Wednesday, but it looked like a bright Sunday. People were standing in long queues waiting for the opening of the election centre. There were old and young, women and men in their best Sunday clothing, women in beautiful garments. When they saw us with our election caps on, everybody smiled and welcomed us. I discovered friends whom I knew,

---

[1] Pastor Dr h.c. Rudolf Hinz served as secretary for Africa in the Foreign Office of the Evangelical Church in Germany (EKD), director of the Department for World Service of the Lutheran World Federation (LWF), Geneva and lecturer for intercultural theology and ecumenism at the Theological Faculty of the University of Kiel.

members of the German-speaking Lutheran congregation in Stellenbosch and professors of the University of Stellenbosch amongst all of those who lived in and near Stellenbosch. All were waiting patiently, looking forward to vote. Most of the people were voting for the first time in their lives. It was a colourful procession to the voting centre and a celebration of democracy. One by one entered the centre when the door opened. The procedure was easy and clear for all. Everything went well. And after the ballot was cast the voters proudly showed their inked thumbs as proof of having voted.

Oh, what a wonderful day!

There were so many observers that we could work in several shifts of two hours only. Later I heard that there were more than 30,000 election observers, national and international, in the country. That was certainly exceptional and also a sign of solidarity with all South Africans who yearned for years to have an election for all people in this country.

When we came back to our hotel in Stellenbosch we received an invitation to meet with Desmond Tutu in Cape Town the next morning, just before we departed from the airport.

We met with him in the Archbishop's Chapel in St George's Cathedral in Cape Town. It was not a celebration of victory but a morning prayer. The Archbishop led us in prayer, silence and reflection. Desmond Tutu was relieved and happy that the election was so peaceful and festive. No jokes, no loud laughter, but a mood of thankfulness and gratitude. There was not a discussion after the prayer, just words of thanks for the long journey of working for justice and peace. We hugged each other and greeted the new day.

I had expected an exchange of our experiences and impressions during election day, but there was obviously something more important. It was like a meeting on the summit of a high mountain. I assume that mountain climbers are also silent and thankful when they look back at the difficult journey climbing upwards and look at the breath-taking view of the blue mountain range, the beautiful earth.

Six years later Desmond Tutu published his book *No Future Without Forgiveness* in 1999.[2] I bought and read it only this year in 2021 when we worked together in a wonderful team of editors on this book for the Arch's 90th birthday. Reading his book I discovered his memoirs and reflections on the election day in 1994. It is the first chapter of his book which mainly deals with the Truth and Reconciliation Commission (TRC) he chaired. The title of the first chapter is "The Turning Point".

I was surprised that he chose this chapter as an opening of his reflections of the process of the TRC. But I understood soon that this chapter was the key for what he had to go through during the process of the TRC.

In hindsight Desmond Tutu described the election day IN 1994 as "the fullness of time",[3] the Kairos. He placed this moment of grace as part of the great changes in the whole world in the late eighties and early nineties of the outgoing 20th century. Election day was part of it.

I am writing this essay in the days before and after Pentecost this year. Looking back at the great change in South Africa, especially the election day, I cannot but state that this day was an expression of a new and surprising spirit which encompassed a whole nation. It was an overwhelming experience and a powerful change. But this change was also a necessary beginning for a much longer process of healing the nation. How would South Africa deal with the legacy of violence and oppression?

Desmond Tutu began the first chapter of his book with the description of his memories of election day with his feelings of apprehension in the morning of this day: "The air was electric with excitement, anticipation and anxiety … Anything could happen … There was a tight knot of anxiety in the pit of my stomach".[4] But when he set out for Gugulethu, where he wanted to vote, he found all people "in good spirits". When he cast his vote he felt relieved. He shouted: "Wow and Yippee!" His

---

[2] Desmond Tutu, *No Future Without Forgiveness.* London, Sydney, Auckland, Johannesburg: Rider, 1999.

[3] Tutu, "Forgiveness", 37.

[4] Tutu, "Forgiveness", 1-2.

concern and worry changed with the weather: "The sky looked more blue and beautiful. I saw the people in a new light. They were transfigured. I too was transfigured. It was dream-like."

When he left the election centre he met happy people. They "cheered and sang and danced. It was like a festival."⁵ And then he decided to drive around to other election centres. Still there this dark shadow: "It would have taken just a few crazy extremists with AK-47 rifles to create havoc. It did not happen."⁶

Instead he observed: "It was also an amazing spectacle. People of all races were standing in the same queues, perhaps for the first time in their lives. Professionals, domestic workers, cleaners and their madams … South Africans found fellow South Africans – they realized what we had been at such pains to tell them, that they shared a common humanity … They discovered not a Coloured, a black, an Indian, a white. No, they found a fellow human being."⁷

It was, for Desmond Tutu, not just a secular political event. He observed that it was far more for everybody: "It was a veritable spiritual experience, a mountain-top experience. The black person entered the booth as one person and emerged on the other side as a new, transfigured one. She entered, weighed down by anguish and burden of oppression, with the memory of being treated like rubbish gnawing away at her like some corrosive acid. She reappeared knowing she was free, walking with her head held high, shoulders set straighter and an elastic spring in her steps."⁸

Looking at white persons in the queue he noted with emotion: "The white persons in the voting booth burdened by the load of guilt at having enjoyed the fruits of oppression and injustice. He too emerged as somebody new, somebody transfigured, from whom a burden had been lifted, and who was now free."⁹

Desmond Tutu stated with relief that what he feared in the morning did not happen. The election was declared to be free and fair.

But still on the top of the mountain there remained one question: how can we altogether translate the joy of the day into the work for establishing a lasting peace and a just society? The new constitution for South Africa had been negotiated; it was one of the best in the whole world. But how can we heal the deep wounds of the past?

Those questions moved Tutu on the same day: "… we South Africans will survive and prevail only together, black and white bound together by circumstance and history as we strive to claw our way out of the abyss of apartheid, racism, up and out, black and white together. Neither group on its own could make it. God had bound us together. In a way we are living out what Martin Luther King Jr said: 'Unless we learn to live together as brothers, we will die together as fools'."¹⁰

How could the experiences of the election day help to form a nation with equal rights and chances? The prerequisite was certainly that the wounds of apartheid were to be healed, justice and peace be established and forgiveness practised for those who repented. Desmond Tutu was on his way out into retirement, but he was needed to implement what he envisaged as chairperson of the Truth and Reconciliation Commission. He could do it with the spirit of election day. For him this was the power from above.

---

⁵ Tutu, "Forgiveness", 3.
⁶ Tutu, "Forgiveness", 4.
⁷ Tutu, "Forgiveness", 4.
⁸ Tutu, "Forgiveness", 5.
⁹ Tutu, "Forgiveness", 5.
¹⁰ Tutu, "Forgiveness", 6.

3.3. Religious Diversity and Plural Spirituality

66. DRINKING FROM OUR OWN WELLS OF RELIGIOUS AND THEOLOGICAL PLURALITY

Charles Villa-Vicencio[1]

Eileen and I had tea and "Christmas cake" with the Arch and Mama Leah (plus the ever-faithful Mthunzi) this past week. Both broaching their ninetieth birthdays, I silently pondered the source of the graciousness and demeanour of two remarkable people in the evening of their lives, frail of body and mentally alert. They spoke of their early days and of other people, asking about our families, and reflected on the sad state of the South African and global situation with selfless empathy. Looking for a single word to describe them, I resorted to "love". The Arch's prayer personalised a spirituality intertwined in the universe: everyone and everything within it. Inspired by this encounter, I offer what follows, drawing on over fifty years of working together and friendship – nuances and all.

30 April 2021

Archbishop Desmond Tutu is recognised as a prophetic voice around the world. This much is clear. Publications and the media provide a record that will ensure his name continues to be entrenched in history. His lasting struggle for democracy gave hope to the victims of apartheid and other forms of genocide around the world. He challenged the complacency of white society in the apartheid years and is today the conscience of the new South African elite, both black and white, suggesting "the gravy train stopped briefly to pick up new passengers, leaving the majority of expectant passengers on the platform". Aware of the unfulfilled promises of democracy, he is a source of irritation to the South African government.

His integrity and ability to relate to members of different faiths and secular beliefs, as well as political adversaries moulded by generations of social influence, has made him a formidable force in the rough and tumble of South African and global politics. Refusing to restrain the church from political engagement, he resisted ecclesial alignment with any particular political ideology or group. This, on occasions, earned him the reproach of leaders and cadres at the forefront of anti-apartheid movements at home and abroad. He has simultaneously been unequivocal in his opposition to racism, tribalism, gender injustice and the exploitation of the poor. This earned him the respect, if not the support, of people across the divisions of South African society who became appreciative of his willingness to embrace people of different identities in the quest for a new and different South Africa. Despite the criticism of the sectors within the African National Congress (ANC), the Archbishop is located alongside President Nelson Mandela as a founding father of the birth of South African democracy.

Committed to multi-cultural and religious inclusivity that resulted in the inauguration of a secular state in 1994, the Archbishop observed: "For me Jesus Christ is the revelation of God, but I am opposed to proselytism. Our task as Christians is simply to live lives that are consistent with the gospel. We take ourselves far too seriously when we think that God is relying on our evangelical campaigns to make everyone Christians, in order for them to enter into communion with God ... For goodness sake, God was able to look after God before we were around. It is not for us to decide who

---

[1] Charles Villa-Vicencio is emeritus professor at the University of Cape Town; visiting professor at Georgetown University, Washington DC; and former national research director of the SA Truth and Reconciliation Commission.

God is and where this God is to be found."[2] He affirmed Abrahamic theology as an apophatic theology, often called a negative theology, which affirms the unknowability of God, in resistance to any form of implied or explicit forms of theocracy.

Tutu vehemently laments the deviation from this truth as manifest in historic inter-religious conflicts, rooted in the European Crusades, the Medieval and Spanish Inquisitions, and subsequent atrocities that continue to haunt contemporary global conflicts. Within the midst of 11th-century chaos, St Bernard of Clairvaux resisted the religious wars of his time, counselling opponents to "drink from their own wells" in coexistence and healing. Gustavo Gutierrez, reflecting on the spiritual journey of Latin American Christians, asked "from what well can the poor of Latin America drink?"[3]

Spirituality, culture and identity

Tutu stood side by side with Jews and Muslims in his opposition to the apartheid state and endorsed the dawn of a religiously inclusive democracy. He, at the same time, condemned the increasing gap between values enshrined in the globally celebrated 1996 South African Constitution and the deviation from these values by the newly elected government. He was at the forefront of the fight against murder, rape, sexism, homophobia, LGBTIQ+ crimes and state capture.

Insisting on good governance and principled policing, he stressed the importance of the internalisation of respect for difference and moral values which, he argued, needed to be generated through open-ended, self-critical debate and shared human identity. This could prove to be among the greatest contributions that religious leadership can make to a future South Africa. An inclusive spirituality that could contribute to the elimination of religious narrow-mindedness that pits zealous theistic faiths against one another, as seen in zealous Jews, Christians and Muslims in the Middle East, Afghanistan and elsewhere.

Karen Armstrong poignantly warns that the understanding of a "personalized deity" as portrayed in monotheism, can slide into a notion of a protector-God of a particular group of people, shaped by race, gender, class or culture. Her "stern warning" is that the use of religious clichés and misspoken sacred or religious metaphors and symbols are often more than a manifestation of religious piety. In a volatile world they frequently contribute to lethal forms of militarism.[4]

A man for all seasons

Robert Bolt's play in 1960, *A Man for All Seasons*, captures the essence of religious partisanship in the events leading to the execution of Sir Thomas More, the 16th-century Lord Chancellor of England, whose ethical principles resulted in his confrontation with King Henry VIII. Fortunately, these practices are today censored on the public stage, while similar brutalities continue to prevail. In places this is nuanced. Elsewhere it is overtly brutal.

Tutu exercised leadership in church and society with passion and integrity through the turbulent 1980s, making the church a significant player in the run-up to the first democratic elections in 1994. Supported by the victims of apartheid, he faced intensified hostility from state authorities while the majority of white South Africans were ambivalent, if not suspicious, of Tutu, whom they viewed as a troublesome priest. At times authoritarian in a traditional Episcopalian mode, his pronouncements led to opposition from anti-apartheid leaders abroad and increasing impatience among militant groups at home.

Ready to work with adversaries and forgive his enemies, Tutu often acted against the counsel of his closest confidants and political associates. He demonstrated a single-minded commitment to a set

---

[2] In Charles Villa-Vicencio, *The Spirit of Freedom* (Berkeley: University of California Press, 1996), xxix, 283.

[3] Quoted in Gustavo Gutierrez, *We Drink from Our Own Wells: The Spiritual Journey of a People* (Maryknoll: Orbis Books, 1984).

[4] Karen Armstrong, *The Case for God* (New York: Alfred Knopf, 2009), 321.

of basic (sometimes unchangeable) ethical values. These at times contradicted individuals and sectors in the liberation movements, committed to ending apartheid "by any means necessary". He simultaneously became a leading figure in the campaign for international sanctions and disinvestment in South Africa that brought the apartheid regime to its knees. His relentless criticism of military violence by the South African state, as well as armed guerrilla activities by liberation forces, seized on by the liberal media, persuaded the broader public that Tutu could be a voice in the impasse between an increasingly desperate white government and black liberation forces in exile and the United Democratic Front (UDF) at home that were committed to "making the country ungovernable". This allowed him to provide leadership in a negotiated political transition that resulted in the election of Nelson Mandela as the first democratically elected president in the history of South Africa. This involvement by Tutu was shaped as much by the escalating conflict as it was by his life-long theological beliefs and practices.

He rejected populist religious beliefs in a partisan God who favoured all-conquering Hebrew tribes to the detriment of the Canaanites, interpreting these texts in relation to the social contexts within which they were written. Using the same critique, he rejected the sexist prescriptions of Scripture. He affirmed the feminine motifs in the Judeo-Christian tradition, acknowledging the tradition of Our Lady of Guadalupe, and affirmed the history of saints Monica, Catherine of Sienna, Theresa of Calcutta and others central to Roman Catholic and Orthodox churches.

An unequivocal and outspoken believer, Tutu, at the same time, embraces the language of the Judeo-Christian scriptures, while avidly rejecting the infallibility of deviously selected texts used by right-wing Christians and other reactionary fundamentalists to promote homophobic patriotism, narrow forms of nationalism, gender prejudice, classism and Zionism used to undermine the struggle for the liberation of Palestinians from Israeli occupation. His most candid response to these assertions is that the Bible is "written by man", reflecting time-bound prejudices that contradict the totality of biblical truth.

At the root of the Abrahamic faiths is the belief in the sacred *Tetragrammaton* (the Being of God) as captured in four sacred consonants (YHWH), which indicates that the name of God is too holy to be spoken. Central to this sacred teaching is the submission that the eternal mystery of the divine presence in history is ultimately beyond human understanding. Above all, this presence cannot be reduced to politics, ideology, or dogmatic theology. To Moses the divine was made known as an eternal "I am who I am" (Exod. 3:14). Central to Christianity, the Christ is the revelation of God the Father, not the same person, and the Holy Spirit, like the wind, "blows wherever it chooses, you hear the sound of it, but you do not know where it comes from or where it is going (John 3:8). In Islam God is *far* (transcendent) and yet *near* (immanent). The Qur'an has ninety-nine different names for Allah that include "… the Creator, the Originator, the Fashioner, to Him belong the most beautiful names: whatever is in the heaven and on earth …" (Qur'an 59:24). The Prophet Muhammad is the Seal of the Prophets but not divine, the Qur'an is the pure word of God but not God.

The more we delve into the quest for ultimate truth, the more the responses of the wise, the foolish, the young, the old, the rich and the poor, the more are we confronted with the mystery of life that we dare not diminish with easy answers. Naturalists understand the complexity of life as composed of interlocking particles, chemical reactions and the impact of energy, matter, heat and gravity on the universe. Theists with scientific awareness merge the biblical sense of creation into a biological account of evolution. God is present in all that exists rather than a celestial engineer or a skilled geneticist isolated from the natural order![5]

Open to the wonders of modern science, there are both people of faith and non-believers who prefer not to face the intricacies of debate between science and belief. There are also denizens of modernity who revel in this debate, to the point where it becomes a source of engagement with the mystery of life, if not a means of grace. Tutu, arguably, has the best of both worlds, rejoicing in the assurance of his faith, while being open to those who deviate beyond the margins of faith in

---

[5] Catherine Wallace, *Confronting Religious Denial of Science* (Eugene OR: Cascade Books), 35-36.

exploring the unknown. Embracing the maxim *credo ut intelligam*, "I believe so that I may understand", like St Anselm of Canterbury, Tutu embraces the mysteries of life in meditation, while engaging in intellectual debate with others. He has on occasions withdrawn from fractious debate to pray, after which he re-engaged in debate, sometimes with added conviction! To those intimidated or uninitiated in the clash of belief, Tutu is a "Christian *sangoma*" offering mental, emotional and spiritual support. Differently stated, Tutu is a pastor. An exponent of *Ubuntu*, he practises the importance of realising one's humanity in relation to the humanity of others. The common denominator between Judaism, Christianity and Islam is a single ethical feature, which is an ineffable belief that God is beyond human capacity to describe, define or understand. This age-old theological principle, often forgotten in popular religion, constitutes an insight that deserves renewed prominence in the dialogue between science and religion, as well as in the politics of regional, national and global conflict. Apophatic theology suggests a humility that undermines both implied and explicit forms of theocracy. Captured in Dag Hammarskjöld's "This It Was", it is about an unknown future that draws us forward:

> I am being driven forward.
> Into an unknown land.
> The pass grows steeper,
> The air colder and sharper.
> The wind from my unknown goal
> Stirs the strings of expectation.[6]

Far and near

Life is more than the future. It is about embracing the present. In the midst of the spiritual intimacy of God is a God who is a transcendent God, never reducible to the powers of this world, nor secluded from the universe and the affairs of humankind. In the engaging words of Anne Lamott, "You can safely assume that you've created God in your own image when it turns out that God hates all the same people and things you do."[7] The dialectic of theism is captured in the interface between transcendence and immanence. This is a concept of the divine that connects us to others. It is a concept that makes us aware of climate change and its impact on social and economic justice and the inequalities of global health care.

This level of theology links us to the insights of neuroscience that explores the connection between the physical brain, the mind, emotion and behaviour of humans. It further suggests that when isolated from others and the world around us we find ourselves cognitively and emotionally deprived, leading to anxiety and depression. We need physical and material contact with the greater universe and our neighbours, as well as the birds and bees around us. The sacred texts on theism witness to the place of the wilderness and the desert as sources of spiritual renewal. We encounter divine reality in gardens, the great outdoors, mountains, oceans and rivers, as well as in shrines and holy places that invite mindfulness and silence. A man of meditation and withdrawal during religious festivals, Tutu never neglected the centrality of *Ubuntu*. He reminds us of the importance of people-centred places: the marketplace, shantytowns and squatter camps where the essence of a broad and inclusive quest for meaning and purpose in life is to be found. A poor woman in a desperate situation mouthed a truth that an achievement and get-rich-driven culture can never understand. "To survive is to win", she observed. It gives us an insight into life that some of us (contributing to this book) can never understand. This is what makes prophets – old and new – and the record of the poor man of Nazareth, the desert mystics, Muhammad and *awliyā* different. There are people in our world who seek to emulate, if not approximate, this ideal. The Arch is among them.

---

[6] In Dag Hammarskjöld, *Markings* (London: Faber and Faber, 1966), 31.

[7] Anne Lamott, *Bird by Bird: Some Instructions on Writing and Life* (New York: Anchor Books, 1995), 22.

The question is whether the psychosomatic quest for fulfilment, meaning and wholeness is an inherent ingredient of what it means to be human. Saint Augustine's words take on new meaning within the context of scientific and neurological debate: "Thou hast made us for Thyself, O Lord, and our heart is restless until it finds its rest in Thee." Roughly stated, if science seeks to define the empirical evidence of what happened in the creation of the Planet Earth, the emergence of humanity and the future destiny of our universe, theology seeks to answer similar questions at a metaphysical level.

This quest for meaning, both within and beyond the institutions of Judaism, Christianity and Islam is often neglected in contemporary theological debate. A cursory read of philosophical and theological texts, however, reminds us of the roots of the human quest for truth. It is present in early theistic debate, through the Medieval period into the European Enlightenment. Notable is the dual focus or coexistence of rationalism and religious piety in Judaism, Christianity and Islam. This is witnessed in the (controversial) debate between the "three wise men" of the theistic faiths in the 12th century, Ibn Rushd (or Averroes), Moses Maimonides and Thomas Aquinas.[8] All three were either expelled or marginalised by the establishment in their respective faiths. Today they are remembered as formative scholars and theologians, reminding us of the conflicting and evolving journey of theological belief.

A tentative conclusion

Amidst the tyranny of Christian theocracy, Galileo (1564–1642) observed that it is impossible to understand the origins of the Planet Earth without being familiar with the mathematical language of triangles, circles and other geometrical figures. Affording most of us a little comfort, Stephen Hawking (1942–2018), the celebrated theoretical physicist, said that science has become too technical for "philosophers, scientists and just ordinary people" to participate in the discussion. And he added, if we find the answer to the complexity of the universe, "it would be the ultimate triumph of human reason – for then we would know the mind of God."[9] Observing that "science without religion is lame [and] religion without science is blind", Einstein argued that there are "only two things that are infinite, the universe and human stupidity, and I'm not too sure about the universe."[10] A reverent silence might be the most appropriate answer to the ultimate questions concerning the beginning and end of life as we know it. Sipping his tea, Tutu observed: "These days I prefer silence to words!"

A closing anecdote

Where does Tutu's persona fit within the philosophical/theological/identity continuum? Who is this man? He wears purple clerical dress to formal public events. This included public sessions of the Truth and Reconciliation Commission, opening each session with a Christian (Anglican) prayer and concluded these events with the Benediction. Wanting to appease his critics who reminded him of the secular nature of the Commission, he occasionally wore a business suit and a tie, while complaining that he felt half-dressed. He agreed to initiate proceedings with a period of silence, while frequently lapsing into prayer, making the sign of the Cross.

Inherently a Christian archbishop (*never to be forgotten!*) and unapologetically religious, it became clear that if the nation wanted Tutu to chair the commission (and it did), it would get an archbishop! Max Weber, the 19[th]century sociologist, once suggested that identity is more than a light

---

[8] Chris Lowney, *A Vanished World: Muslims, Christians and Jews in Medieval Spain* (New York: Oxford University Press, 2005). For a more succinct overview see Charles Villa-Vicencio, *Living Between Science and Belief: The Modern Dilemma* (Eugene OR: Cascade Books, 2021), 38-4, 135-39.

[9] Stephen Hawking, *A Brief History of Time* (New York: Bantam Books, 2017), 191.

[10] Albert Einstein, "Science and Religion." In *Science, Philosophy, and Religion: A Symposium*, New York: The Conference on Science, Philosophy, and Religion, 1941.

cloak thrown over one's shoulders and removed when needed. Tutu used his accustomed episcopal esteem to get the TRC through several internal tensions and to defend the political conflict the commission hearings often generated. A respected journalist observed at the time: "It's intriguing to note the impact a priest can still have in a broken secular society".

67. RELIGIOUS PRIVILEGE AND INTOLERANCE: UNVEILING THE RAINBOW NATION

Lee-Shae Salma Scharnick-Udemans[1]

"The rainbow nation moniker as a symbol of peaceful and inclusive religious co-existence, lovingly coined by Tutu, during a time of great socio-political upheaval and hope obscures the uneven ways that religious freedom as the constitutional commitment to promote and protect religions and religious diversity, is experienced by individuals and communities."[2] While the latest French legislation that further augments already ignominious restrictions on the hijab for Muslim women has left feminists and human rights activists reeling, this essay illustrates that in South Africa where religious freedom is protected constitutionally and promoted discursively, there is a record of Muslim women's sartorial choices being surveilled and scrutinised. Through exploring the notion of religious privilege and by drawing on two examples of institutional and individual attempted unveiling, this essay highlights the limited utility of rainbowism and constitutional religious freedom at the rock face of intolerance and exclusion.

I have previously argued that, despite the deeply theological origins of the rainbow nation sobriquet and the religious status of its principal articulator Emeritus Archbishop Desmond Tutu, the discourse of rainbowism that it generates has historically been deployed primarily in reference to issues of race, racism and racialisation.[3] As a result, religion as both a source site of privilege and discrimination, especially in the context of the multi-religious, semi-secular democratic state of South Africa is often overlooked and neglected. Despite its congenial overtone, the rainbow nation narrative has played a role in the universalising of Christianity as the unofficial public religious character of the new and democratic South Africa. However, even this unsanctioned status is powerful and has generated a culture of Christian political and public pre-eminence that disadvantages non-Christian religious groups.

Clearly, this condition is not only the result of rainbowism, which hardly has the political clout of a slogan. The enduring influence of colonialist and apartheid rule on the contemporary politics, policies and practices that regulate and police religious expression in public should not be under-estimated, nor should the impact of global trends including migration, secularisation, religionisation and the rise of transnational religious circulations. It may seem counter-intuitive to launch a strong critique in the context of a celebratory text; however, I think Tutu's profoundly expansive theology, political erudition and overall sassiness makes space for my claims as not merely contrarian intellectual articulations but, more significantly, as grounded in a yearning for a deeper and more comprehensive understanding and experience of justice and freedom for all of humanity.

The 1996 Constitution guarantees religious freedom with very few but specific limitations and, while we cannot compare the current measure of religious freedom to the brutalities of both the

[1] I am a senior researcher in the Desmond Tutu Centre for Religion and Social Justice at the University of the Western Cape. I have never met the Arch but his rainbow nation formulation has been a source of inspiration and frustration in both my life and my work! As a South African woman of colour, various renditions of violence and exclusion have conditioned my epistemological orientation and it is sometimes challenging to hold out hope for a truly free and equal South Africa. But, when my adorable, half-naked four-year-old son Khalil Hani sings "if you're happy and you know it, Allahu Akbar", with the random abandon of a being that has only ever known radical acceptance and appreciation, I know that Tutu's vision of the rainbow nation is always worth striving for. This work is based on research supported by the National Research Foundation of South Africa under the auspices of the Desmond Tutu Chair in Religion and Social Justice [Grant Number: 118854]. The opinions, findings and conclusions or recommendations expressed in the research are those of the author alone; the NRF accepts no liability in this regard.
[2] Lee-Shae Salma Scharnick-Udemans, "Religion: The Final Frontier of the Rainbow Nation", *Religion & Theology* 27, no. 3/4 (2020): 250-274.
[3] Scharnick-Udemans, "Religion: The Final Frontier", 251.

imperialist venture of Christianity and the Christian nationalism that produced and sustained the colonial and apartheid states respectively, we cannot be misled by the idea that the democratic and constitutional reform of the relationship between religion and the state, which took place after 1994, has offered a firm resolution. Despite constitutional promises and legal precepts, religious freedom in its broadest sense is not guaranteed to everyone in equal measure. Like gender, race and socio-economic status, religion is a category of power and privilege and religious freedom is perpetually both contextual and intersectional.

Religious privilege

Like any form of privilege, religious privilege, especially in multi-religious contexts where religious freedom is constitutionalised, is a slippery concept. The notion of religious privilege is always situated, it is produced and experienced in context, individually and institutionally.[4] Religious privilege is not synonymous with state-sanctioned theocracy since the latter is usually formalised through policy, whereas the former is a result of the production and circulation of both formal and informal discourses and practices, from politics to popular culture, that uphold and preserve the hegemony of the historical or numerical religious majority. Therefore, in theocracies religious privilege, while still problematic for liberal democrats, is declared and solemnised as such. As a result, what may be considered infringements on democratic freedoms are easier to identify than in contexts that claim all-encompassing freedom and equality.[5]

An example of violent religious privilege at play can be seen in India where religious freedom is constitutionally promised but has been eroded through the prominence of the political ideology of Hindutva, which has privileged Hinduism and Hindus.[6] Like male or white privilege, religious privilege, in any manifestation, is axiomatically linked to the exclusion, limitation, suppression and oppression of "the other". In the case of South Africa, the character of religious privilege is Christian. For some it may be difficult to accept this assertion especially since recent memory reminds us of the particular sensibilities and sensitivities related to the role that religion played both during apartheid and in the liberation of this country. As protest actions from various sectors of society including the mining industry, education, environmental conservation, public safety, and activism against gender-based violence continue to highlight issues of inequality, marginalisation and exclusion, demanding the justice that democracy promises to bring but fails to uphold, we are reminded that liberation is never complete.[7]

The nature of privilege is convoluted and complex. Anti-racist educator Peggy McIntosh's "White Privilege: Unpacking the Invisible Knapsack" is iconic for its cogent discussion of white privilege, for which she offers an enchanting definition. According to McIntosh: "White privilege is like an invisible weightless knapsack of special provisions, maps, passports, codebooks, visas, clothes, tools and blank checks".[8] McIntosh posits that we all carry many knapsacks of privilege associated with the various identity categories that we simultaneously hold. Social justice comedian Sam Killermann has adapted McIntosh's list of everyday privileges that white people enjoy, to produce a list of over

---

[4] See Abby Ferber, "The Culture of Privilege: Color-blindness, Postfeminism, and Christonormativity", *Journal of Social Issues* 68, no. 1 (2011): 63-77, https://doi.org/10.1111/j.1540-4560.2011.01736.x; see also Khyati Joshi, *White Christian Privilege: The Illusion of Religion Equality in America* (New York: NYU Press, 2021).

[5] Armin Langer, "Christonormativity As Religious Neutrality: A Critique of the Concept of State Religious Neutrality in Germany" in *Religious Freedom and the Law: Emerging Contexts for Freedom for and from Religion*, eds Brett G. Scharffs, Asher Maoz and Ashley Isaacson Woolley (London: Routledge, 2018).

[6] Pashaura Singh, "How Avoiding the Religion-Politics Divide Plays out in Sikh Politics", *Religions* 10, no. 5, http://doi.org/10.3390/rel10050296.

[7] Tom Lodge and Shuana Mottiar, "Protests in South Africa; Motives and Meanings", *Democratization* 23, no. 5 (2016): 819-837. doi: 10.1080/13510347.2015.1030397.

[8] Peggy McIntosh, "White Privilege: Unpacking the Invisible Knapsack", *Peace and Freedom Magazine*, July/August 1989, 10.

thirty examples of Christian privilege in the United States.[9] In tribute to the engaged and energetic, priestly and pedagogical performativity of Tutu, I would like to invite you, dear reader, to check your own religious privilege by considering the following prompts adapted from Killermann and expanded upon by a few South African vignettes.

Are you allowed time off to celebrate religious holidays, without asking for the permission of any authority figure? Moreover, is there widespread support of your religious holidays in public and commercial spaces? Labour law in South Africa does not regulate leave for religious holidays. Therefore, unless the religious holiday falls on an official public holiday, an employee would need to take annual or unpaid leave in order to observe their religious holidays. The official South African public holiday calendar supports the major Christian holidays and while it sometimes mentions non-Christian religious holidays it does not make allowance for these days as national public holidays.

Can you worship freely, without fear of violence or threats? While South Africa is not generally considered a hotspot for religiously sanctioned violence or violence directed at religious groups, in recent years there has been an increase in reports of threats against religious communities, particularly minority groups. These acts of tension, aggression and violence occur on a spectrum that ranges from covert microaggressions with no prospect for physical violence or lasting harm, to acts of terrorism aimed at intimidating, maiming, or killing. In one case of aggression directed at Muslims, a 120-year-old mosque was vandalised with anti-Islamic slurs. The Imam of the mosque explains: "I initially thought nothing of it. But after speaking to my wife and sister I realised the incident made parts of our congregation feel uncomfortable and not safe at the masjid. Then I realised that this act of vandalism was planned with the purpose of creating fear within us. It was intended to make us think twice before bringing our children and wives to a sacred space".[10] In another incident which took place in 2017, three men were attacked while praying: they were stabbed, and one man had his throat slit. These attacks have been linked to xenophobia and religious violence and contribute to a pattern of discrimination and violence directed at Muslim migrants from south Asia and east Africa.[11]

Are the politicians and lawmakers responsible for governance and the administration of justice most likely members of your faith? There is no shortage of openly Christian politicians and lawmakers in South Africa. While I am by no means implying that politicians or public figures should hide their religious affiliation, the displays of religiosity that have been made by powerful office bearers have blurred the lines between personal conviction and proselytisation. Despite being found guilty of breaching the code of conduct by becoming involved in political controversy or activity by the Judicial Conduct Committee for his religiously inspired, pro-Israel comments, Mogoeng Mogoeng, chief justice of the Constitutional Court, refused to apologise. He declared: "I stand by my refusal to retract or apologise for any part of what I said during the webinar. Even if 50 million people were to march every day for 10 years for me to do so, I would not apologise. If I perish, I perish". In the initial comments Mogoeng had cited Scripture and declared his love for Jerusalem and by extension Israel.[12]

Is it easy for you to find your faith accurately depicted in television, movies, books and other media? A complaint submitted to the Broadcasting Complaints Commission of South Africa alleged

---

[9] Sam Killerman, "30+ Examples of Christian Privileges", *It's Pronounced Metrosexual,* https://www.itspronouncedmetrosexual.com/2012/05/list-of-examples-of-christian-privileg/ (accessed 25 May 2021).

[10] Charlene Somduth, "PE Heritage Mosque Vandalized with Anti-Islamic Words on Walls", *The Post*, 7 May 2021, https://www.iol.co.za/thepost/news/pe-heritage-mosque-vandalised-with-anti-islamic-words-on-the-walls-d17b373a-f5b2-4f17-9404-759bc6de8dd0 (accessed 25 May 2021).

[11] Azad Essa, "Outrage After Deadly South Africa Mosque Attack", *Al-Jazeera*, 12 May 2018, https://www.aljazeera.com/news/2018/5/12/outrage-after-deadly-south-africa-mosque-attack (accessed 25 May 2021).

[12] Andisiwe Makinana, "Apologise For Your Pro-Israel Comments, Mogoeng Ordered", *Sunday Times Daily*, 5 March 2021, https://select.timeslive.co.za/news/2021-03-04-apologise-for-your-pro-israel-comments-mogoeng-ordered/ (accessed 25 May 2021).

religious offence based on a number of observations made by the complainant when viewing the Indian lifestyle programme on national television. The complaint was extensive but the first issue under discussion in the complaint was that a presenter in the programme said that Hindus worship "cows, bulls and other animals". Together with a disdain for the above comment, the complainant took particular issue with the fact that the presenter was allegedly non-Hindu. The complainant expressed the following opinion in that regard: "However such a comment is unacceptable even if it had been made by some hillbilly Hindu ignorant of his or her religion. The onus is on the public broadcaster to uphold the South African constitution, the Bill of Rights and its own code of ethics by ensuring that only bona fide Hindu scholars are allowed to make comments on the religion and cultural practices of the Hindu's [sic] in South Africa, and not disrespectful Muslim and Christian Indians who masquerade as our keepers".[13] The complainant felt that the offending broadcast perpetuated a historical pattern of misrepresentation of Hindus by non-Hindus. According to the complainant: "The nuances and subtleties of concepts, symbols and metaphors elude those who report from an alien perspective, especially from the prejudiced perspective of the colonising, conquering religions and cultures of the world".[14] The complainant then goes on to explain the significance of the cow and the animal world in the Hindu tradition and continues to lament the ill-informed and callous way in which Hinduism is presented in the media in general.

Can you reasonably assume that anyone you encounter will have a decent understanding of your beliefs? The following story was shared on Facebook and then picked up by mainstream media. Megan Furniss was walking her dog and came upon a scene that disturbed her. She posted the following message on Facebook: "Help! "There is a goat tied to a pole in the children's park in Queens Park. Huge crowd of people. Goat is screaming. Help".[15] Furniss' Facebook friend Jennifer Bradley agreed that a goat was slain in the park: "I am sure that goat was slaughtered", she posted. "Just been up there, no sign of goat, but strong smell of braai." She went on to infer that the crowd of Muslims had either slaughtered the animal or had sex with it. Later on it would be revealed that what was witnessed was a birthday party for a little boy who loves animals. All the correct permits had been attained in order to host the party and professional animal handlers were on site to assist. Seraaj Waggie, the father of the child, made the following statement in response to Furniss': "No one approached us to ask or find out about the goat and other animals. Yet they all found it fair and their right as saviours of humanity to accuse us of many ills".[16]

The examples above do not violate constitutional religious freedom nor are they presented as the decisive picture of the experiences of all non-Christians. These examples may contest the hundred daily expressions of inter-religious solidarity, interfaith engagement, celebration and accommodation that constitute non-events. However, these stories can also be seen as social barometers that record ongoing shifts in how religious freedom and diversity are understood and experienced in contemporary South Africa.

When considering Christian privilege within a broader matrix of popular discourse, politics and power, an intersectional lens reminds us that the contours of social inequalities are shaped within overlapping and intersecting oppressions. This extends to thinking through how categories of identity and social belonging converge and highlights how these categories are in fact fundamentally heterogeneous. Christianity is not a homogenous category of religious affiliation or belonging. Beyond denominational differentials; language, location, race, gender, sexual orientation, proximity to power (whether political or economic) and a range of other factors overlap and intersect to produce

---

[13] BCCSA, *Broadcasting Complaints Commission of South Africa: Eastern Mosaic*. Case Number: 16/2008 – SINGH VS SABC2 – RELIGION, South Africa, 2008, http://bccsa.co.za/2014/12/19/case-number-162008-singh-vs-sabc2-religion/ (accessed 31 May 2020).

[14] BCCSA, *Broadcasting Complaints Commission*, 4.

[15] *The Times* Editorial, "The Curious Case of the Misunderstood Goat", *Times Live*, 17 October 2017, https://www.timeslive.co.za/ideas/2017-10-17-the-curious-case-of-the-misunderstood-goat/ (accessed 25 May 2021).

[16] *The Times* Editorial, "The Curious Case", 2017.

an ever-changing hierarchy of preferential public and political consideration and treatment. Therefore, Christian privilege and the normativity that it produces and circulates does not fully extend to all Christians and all forms of Christianity are not regarded equally and afforded the same level of social and political privilege.

In the following section I offer a deeper reflection on religious privilege by exploring two cases of religious regulation which highlight the intersectional nature of religious privilege and bring into focus the multi-layered nature thereof.

Unveiling the rainbow nation

In March 2021, French senators approved an amendment to its so-called anti-separatism bill which declared the "prohibition in the public space of any conspicuous religious sign by minors and of any dress or clothing which would signify inferiority of women over men".[17] Despite the vagary of politico-legal language the outcome of this bill would directly affect young Muslim girls, stripping them of their agency and forcing them to unveil in public. In response, thousands of women of diverse religious orientations, some *hijabi*, some not, from all over the world gathered in protest, both on and offline. The hashtag #handsoffmyhijab went viral as thousands admonished this clearly Islamophobic and draconian application of *laïcité*.

While the management of Muslim women's religious agency by the French government has recently come to the attention of the media, this is not only a French issue. Globally Muslim women are inordinately affected by laws that regulate the sartorial expression of religious devotion and identity. Intersectional feminist scholars have agreed that, when it comes to the hijab, Muslim women are predominantly faced with two prospects.[18] The first is forced unveiling, as is the case in secularist states, and the second is forced veiling as is the case of Islamist states. Certainly, veiling and unveiling are not only or always enforced by the state and are subjected to the powerful effects of familial, community and other contextual conditions that play a role in determining the extent to which women are able to express their agency and are supported in their choices. Psychotherapists Noorjehan Joosub and Sumayya Ebrahim assert that: "The inclusion of the voices of Muslim women, whether they wear the hijab or not, is necessary to redress the constraints on the agency of Muslim women that has emanated both from those in the West, and from within the Muslim community itself".[19]

As a multi-religious democratic context, South Africa's politics around the hijab are different. The binary between religion and state for understanding the relationship between state authority and religious influence collapses under the auspices of the constitutionally underwritten cooperative relationship between religion and state which can be described as "inclusive secularism".[20] According to Amien: "The Constitutional Court also advocates the view that protecting religious freedom is intricately linked to appreciating religious diversity and that religious freedom should therefore be afforded maximum protection".[21] The constitution does not measure social realities and, despite this liberal approach to religious freedom, there are still reports of Muslim women experiencing discrimination in public institutions for wearing the hijab.

---

[17] Al-Jazeera, "'Law against Islam': French vote in Favor of Hijab Ban Condemned", *Al-Jazeera*, 9 April 2021, https://www.aljazeera.com/news/2021/4/9/a-law-against-islam (accessed 25 May 2021).

[18] Nina Hoel and Sa'diyya Shaikh, "Veiling, Secularism and Islamism: Gender Constructions in France and Iran", *Journal for the Study of Religion* 20, no. 1 (2017), pp.111-129 – see https://www.ajol.info/index.php/jsr/article/view/54415.

[19] Noorjehan Joosub and Sumayya Ebrahim, "Decolonizing the Hijab: An Interpretive Exploration by Two Muslim Psychotherapists", *Feminism & Psychology* 30, no. 3 (2020): 363.

[20] Waheeda Amien, "Postapartheid Treatment of Religious Freedom in South Africa", in *Politics of Religious Freedom*, ed. Winnifred Faller Sullivan, Elizabeth Shakman Hurd, Saba Mahmood and Peter G. Danchin (London: University of Chicago Press, 2015), 182.

[21] Amien, "Postapartheid Treatment of Religious Freedom", 182.

44444

Despite not being a *hijabi* I have been asked on many occasions to use my training as a scholar of religion to write letters to schools on behalf of parents advocating on behalf of their daughters who want to wear headscarves to school. In fact, at the beginning of the school year I get this request from at least three different parties in the Western Cape and maintain a template written in the first person that I give to parents to share, edit, sign and send to school principals. Below I share an excerpt from this letter:

> I write this letter in order to address the uncertainty, which has arisen around the issue of my daughter Laylaa*(pseudonym) observing the hijab. In this letter I would like to address three issues. The first is related to a misconception around the hijab. The second is related to the constitutional rights which can be potentially violated through prohibition regarding religious attire, and the third point is related to the practice of unity within diversity. Having established the basis of this letter, I will also state up front that I have not addressed the issue of Laylaa's hijab as a theological or even religious issue. I am placing it in the broader constitutional and democratic framework which is the context of South Africa.

The decision to base the request within a constitutional framework is strategic for two reasons. First, the Department of Education requires all uniform policies to conform to constitutional norms regarding religious expression. Second, within Islam there are various schools of thought and interpretations on the meaning and nature of the requirement for women to cover their heads and observe modesty in their sartorial choices. The prescriptive nature of some of these interpretations undermine the agency of women and, as a feminist, my main concern when it comes to debates about veiling or unveiling as a woman's right to choose is always paramount. While the constitutional approach is by no means beyond the scope of critique, the language of constitutionalism imbibes a level of inclusion that should ostensibly render the issue moot. Over and above the request for a headscarf I include a section that will allow the young women to further adapt the uniforms in order to both fully participate in school life while observing what they consider their part of their religious obligations.

The letter usually runs to three pages and is as comprehensive as possible to avoid argumentation and long-winded debate. In every case, the student has been allowed to wear her hijab and no school principal has ever taken the matter further. Although I must admit this might have something to do with the seriousness of my tone more than the content of the letter! The point here is not that the concessions are made, but that permission had to be sought in the first place.

Muslim model Rawdah Mohamed, who started the #handsoffmyhijab campaign, said the following in an Instagram post: "When I was 8 years old I was called into a meeting with my teachers. They were discussing ways to end the bullying I was subjected to by my classmates. Their solution was that I shouldn't wear the hijab to school. Sitting in a room full of adults discussing my body and what I could and couldn't wear as a young girl left more scarring than the bullying itself".[22] Her statement underscores the importance of how dignity and bodily integrity are intrinsically linked to issues about religious freedom and the absence of blanket reformation of uniform policy in public schools. Perhaps this could also be added to our test of religious privilege. *Have you ever had to write a letter or ask a scholar of religion to write a letter asking the school principal for permission for your child to sartorially express their religiosity while in school*? I hope that the letters which I write are able to preserve the dignity and support the agency of the young girls for whom they are written. The following example shows the limited utility of letter writing for the reformation of school uniform policy.

---

[22] Kathleen Farmilo, "VOGUE Scandinavia names Rawdah Mohamed, who went viral for 'Hands Off My Hijab' Campaign, as Editor", *B&T*, 28 May 2021, https://www.bandt.com.au/vogue-scandinavia-names-rawdah-mohamed-who-went-viral-for-hands-off-my-hijab-campaign-as-editor/ (accessed 31 May 2021).

In 2017 a thirteen-year-old girl was forbidden from wearing a headscarf during Ramadan by her school principal.[23] Despite constitutional reforms, schools maintain independent uniform policies and are encouraged by authorities to change these to reflect national policy; however, transformation has been slow. In this case it was further delayed by the ignorance and arrogance of one school principal who took it upon himself to offer a detailed exposition on why the hijab was not a compulsory practice and would not be allowed to be worn. The mother of the learner reports that the student would generally wear the headscarf on her shoulders and hide it under her jacket but that during the fasting period she wanted to wear it on her head.[24] Ramadan is generally considered a time of introspection, and increased devotional and charitable activities. For some women this includes wearing what can be considered more modest clothing, including the head scarf, especially in public.

The mother reports that she wrote the principal a letter where she requested permission for her daughter to wear the scarf during Ramadan. A day later the principal replied and, in a wanton display of hubris, not only declined to allow Zaakiyah permission to wear the scarf but also included a poorly worded explanation. The letter was based on internet research derived from the website of a Canadian Islamic legal body and the principal declared that since he could find no evidence to suggest that the hijab was compulsory for the fasting person to wear, he would not allow for it to be worn at school.[25] The education departmental authorities immediately responded that the uniform policy should be changed and that the learner be allowed to wear a headscarf to school. Cases of hijabophobia in South Africa are not only limited to schools and take place in various other public institutions.

In 2018, Major Fatima Isaacs, a clinical forensic pathologist working for the South African National Defence Force, was criminally charged with "willful defiance and failing to obey lawful instruction".[26] Her crime was her refusal to remove her headscarf, at the request of a senior officer, while in uniform and on duty. According to Isaacs and the multiple visual entries submitted to the court, the headscarf worn underneath her beret did not occlude any of the military insignia on her uniform. In the ten years prior to the charges and subsequent trial of Isaacs, she had been granted verbal permission provided that she complied with conditions that the headscarf be made of black net material, fitted to the head and that it not cover the ranks of her uniform or shoulders. Between 2009 and 2017, there were periods where the permission was rescinded, and Isaacs was compelled to remove her uniform and wear civilian clothing. After years of back and forth in 2018, when the military hospital where she was employed came under new management, the case was taken to court. Her council argued that the dress code was unconstitutional. She was granted permission to wear the headscarf but Isaacs and her council were unsatisfied with this outcome since it only made an exception for Isaacs. Her lawyers then prepared a case arguing for a change in uniform policy that would apply to all Muslim women in the army to take before the Equality Court. The military amended the policy before it could be taken to court. While Isaacs was not allowed to speak to the media during the legal proceedings she is reported to have told a newspaper that this was an important victory, not only for her, but for all those who were silently victimised because of their religion.[27]

---

[23] Justin Deffenbacher, "Cape Town Principal Vetoed After Claiming Wearing a Hijab During Ramadan is Not Compulsory", *Times Live*, 6 June 2017, https://www.timeslive.co.za/news/south-africa/2017-06-06-cape-town-principal-vetoed-after-claiming-wearing-a-hijab-during-ramadan-is-not-compulsory/ (accessed 31 May 2021).

[24] Deffenbacher, "Cape Town Principal Vetoed", 2017.

[25] Saaafia February, "'Teacher Ripped My Doekie Off'", *Daily Voice*, 7 June 2017, https://www.dailyvoice.co.za/news/teacher-ripped-my-doekie-off-9595396 (accessed 31 May 2021).

[26] Nicola Daniels and Siphokazi Vuso, "Groundbreaking Headscarf Victory for Muslim Women in SANDF", *Cape Times*, 28 January, 2021, https://www.iol.co.za/capetimes/news/groundbreaking-headscarf-victory-for-muslim-women-in-sandf-1e7e7840-1c0c-40ef-84c6-5184a5f5ebd2 (accessed 31 May 2021).

[27] Daniels and Vuso, "Groundbreaking Headscarf Victory", 2021.

Conclusion

It is easier to map how religious rights and personal choices are infringed upon when we only explore the far ends of the spectrum. Between violent religious persecution and harmonious peaceful co-existence there is an in-between space that is far more opaque. When we discern this in-between space more closely we are able to bring to light the microaggressions that are experienced regularly by those who enjoy less substantial religious privilege than others. We are also able to discern the micro-histories of religious oppression that do not constitute violent persecution but nonetheless erode the meaning and fulfillment of the democratic promises of freedom and equality. The notion that religious privilege and the social inequality that it generates is an ongoing issue in the context of a multi-religious democratic state is difficult to comprehend, especially when comparing places and times where religious privilege generates overt and violent religious persecution. However, given South Africa's relatively peaceful status, we cannot be falsely secure in our reliance on religious freedom as a constitutional right, lest these seemingly innocuous violations are left unchecked and flourish into more sinister contraventions. I am sure the Arch will agree that, between the storm and the rainbow, there is still much work to be done in the pursuit of justice and freedom and that this is indeed the kind of work that is worth doing!

68. Nothing is "Untransfigurable": Tutu and the Transfiguration of Politics

John W. de Gruchy[1]

One day, early in the 1970s, while we sat together in the garden at St Benedict's House in Rosettenville, Johannesburg, Archbishop Tutu told me that he would like to write a book on the "transfiguration". We briefly discussed the project several times over the following years, and even returned to the subject after the Tutus moved to Hermanus. To my knowledge, the Arch never found an opportunity to pursue it, but the intention remained, as did his conviction that the Transfiguration of Christ is fundamental for the Christian understanding of both personal and social transformation.

If transformation is understood, as it is by most people, as a secular or political term to describe fundamental change in society, something akin to revolution without violence, or similar change in an individual's personality, transfiguration is a theological understanding of transformation. For that reason, Tutu's desire and work for fundamental change, whether social or personal, were always pitched at a higher level and were more hopeful than for the average person who thinks about such things. Moreover, for him, nothing was "untransfigurable" because everything was not only created but also redeemed by God. This conviction was the source of his faith and hope which others inadequately called his idealism and optimism, and sometimes disparaged as unrealistic. But for Tutu, no person is a "nobody" because everyone is "made in the image of God" and has the God-given potential to change, and no society is beyond redemption because God's purpose is to create a new humanity.

All three synoptic gospels recount the story of the Transfiguration of Jesus.[2] In all of them this event is a turning point in the narrative, demarcating the transition from Jesus' ministry in Galilee to his journey to Jerusalem and his crucifixion. As such it is a revelation of the glory of God validating Jesus' life and anticipating the validation of his death in his resurrection. The story is not told in the Fourth Gospel probably because for John, the whole gospel is about the revelation of "the glory ... of a father's son full of grace and truth."[3] The Incarnation as a whole is, for John, the transfiguring mystery of God's glory manifest in the "the flesh" for the sake of the world. What is revealed on the Mount of Transfiguration is implicit in the Incarnation in anticipation of the Cross and Resurrection. This explains why, for Tutu, the reconciliation of the world, and therefore political reconciliation in South Africa, was a gift to be grasped, not only a mission to be achieved or an onerous task to be undertaken.

It is little wonder, then, that Tutu's critics, especially of his understanding of and leadership of the Truth and Reconciliation Commission, misunderstood what, why and how he was doing what he did. But, in opening each session of the TRC in prayer Tutu was declaring his hand. He was tapping into a source of transformation beyond the political or psychological mundane. He could do no other, for that was who he was, and who he was was inseparable from his faith-convictions. If President Mandela and his cabinet had wanted a forensic TRC they should have appointed a judge as chair, not a priest whose credentials were qualitatively different and more profound than his reputation as a struggle hero.

---

[1] John de Gruchy is emeritus professor of Christian studies at the University of Cape Town, and an extraordinary professor of theology at Stellenbosch University. Since his retirement in 2003 he and Isobel have lived at the Volmoed Christian Retreat Centre near Hermanus. I first met Desmond Tutu during 1965 when he was teaching at the Federal Theological Seminary in Alice. In one way or other that relationship has developed over subsequent years when our paths have crossed and our involvements have brought us together.
[2] Matthew 17:1-8; Mark 9:2-8; Luke 9: 28-36.
[3] John 1:14.

In his sermon during his enthronement as Archbishop of Cape Town in September 1986, Tutu had already made this explicit when he spoke about the "principle of transfiguration", that is, the process by which mundane things become a channel for divine life. This principle informed the Arch's life and ministry, convincing him, as he said in his sermon, that "no one and no situation is 'untransfigurable'." For this reason, he was (almost?) as committed to changing the heart and mind of P.W. Botha as he was to transforming the social reality of the poor and the oppressed. Despite being labelled a "political priest" he was not a priest playing politics nor was he a member of a political party. His political engagement was an expression of his witness to the gospel of God's love and justice, and therefore his hope for the transfiguration of people and the world despite every contradiction, all opposition and rejection. He was engaged in what Paul Lehmann once called the "transfiguration of politics".[4]

Lehmann's *The Transfiguration of Politics* is an examination of narratives of revolutionary change and a response to the fact that too often revolutions turn on themselves, "devouring their children", thereby destroying the humanity and hopes of the masses who put their trust in them. The fourth narrative he examines, the messianic story of Jesus, is the story that has shaped Tutu's life and informed his ministry. "The Christ story", Lehmann writes, "is the story of the presence and power of Jesus in and over the ambiguity of power in human affairs. It tells in word and deed of the liberating limits and renewing possibilities within which revolutionary promises and passions make room for the freedom to be and to stay human in the world."[5] For Lehmann, Jesus is as much a revolutionary as any other worthy of the name, but his purpose is humanisation not power, the birthing of a "new humanity", not the perpetuation of the old in new dress. So, he writes further: "The divisive, healing, transfigured, and transfiguring Christ is not to be despoiled as the model of a new humanity because of what has been made of him." On the contrary, as "he involves us in the struggle for a new and human future", we are led "from a politics of confrontation to a politics of transfiguration and the transfiguration of politics."[6]

It is no secret that Tutu is a profoundly spiritual person, and that his spirituality is shaped and sustained by his remarkable discipline. For him, saying the daily offices, celebrating the Eucharist every morning no matter where he was, and going on retreat, are sacrosanct. Likewise, every conversation he had with visitors, and even appointments with politicians and secular academics, or before leading a protest march, invariably began with prayer. This was not a matter of required ritual or piety; it is, for Tutu, a necessity. He well knew that it was not any self-developed gifts, his warm personality or astute insight, and certainly not his physical stature, that enabled him to provide wise counsel and take a courageous stand against state power and its instruments of control. The source of his ministry was the Spirit just as the gospel was his guide.

Much of the Arch's early formation as a Christian was influenced by the fathers of the Community of the Resurrection and more specifically by the example and friendship of Trevor Huddleston who, from 1944–1956, served the people of Sophiatown, the Johannesburg township where Tutu grew up. It was under Huddleston's influence that the young Desmond first experienced the relationship between pastoral care of the oppressed and prophetic denunciation of the oppressor; between spirituality and the struggle for justice and peace; between contemplation and action; and, therefore, between transformation and transfiguration.

For him, these are not polarized opposites, contradictions, or philosophical paradoxes – they are theologically connected and practically inseparable. They are united in God's love for the world which desires restorative justice, and wills reconciliation and peace. It was an understanding deeply rooted in the witness of the Old Testament prophets, and the testimony of many through the centuries – not least, among Tutu's heroes: Julian of Norwich, Francis of Assisi, Dietrich Bonhoeffer and Thomas Merton. And, of course, among the monks of the Community of the Resurrection at Mirfield

---

[4] Paul Lehmann, *The Transfiguration of Politics* (London: SCM, 1975).

[5] Lehmann, *The Transfiguration of Politics*, 20.

[6] Lehmann, *The Transfiguration of Politics*, 20.

in Yorkshire where Huddleston had trained and where Tutu the aspiring ordinand learnt both the disciplines of Christian spirituality and how these connect to the political struggle for justice.

Such convictions, theologically rooted in the Incarnation, whereby God and humanity are reconciled in one body on the Cross, and anticipated in the Transfiguration, when the glory of God is revealed as Jesus embarked on his final journey to Jerusalem, his suffering and execution, are far more than theological dogma or a series of events in salvation history; they are an expression of the relationship of God to the world and human life from the beginning of time which the Arch daily celebrated in the Eucharist as a prelude to his daily ministry. For as Tutu told the vast congregation gathered in St George's Cathedral for his enthronement "the principle of transfiguration is at work when mundane everyday fare, bread and wine, apparently recalcitrant matter ... becomes the channel for the divine life."[7]

Tutu's profoundly Incarnational spirituality in which he affirmed the material and rejected the triumphalist, stood in stark contrast to the Christianity of the dominant white religion of British colonialism and that of Afrikaner nationalism which gave birth to apartheid. Both forms of Christianity were inescapably political, but neither of them was truly Incarnational. For them piety and politics were either strange bedfellows ("keep religion out of politics"), or else their relationship was self-serving as religion kept the oppressed in their place and gave legitimation to the policies of domination which served the interests of the politically powerful. So, the question, for Tutu, was not whether Christianity was political, but what kind of politics did it represent: the politics of resistance and justice, or complicity and oppression? The question was never "can Christians be involved in politics?" but how they should be involved, what is their motivation, and what resources do they bring to the struggle for justice? And, therefore, how does the politics of transformation become the politics of transfiguration?

Towards the end of the 1970s Archbishop Tutu visited the Taizé Community in France. While worshipping in its Church of Reconciliation, he had a transfiguring vision of 144 young South Africans going there on a Pilgrimage of Hope.[8] This vision was fulfilled during 1980 when a racially diverse group visited Jerusalem, Rome, and then spent a week at Taizé to reflect on their lives, their country and the gospel. Tutu could not lead them because he was prevented from doing so by the apartheid government, but for those who went it was a life-changing experience, one that opened new horizons and provided signposts for life back in South Africa. Taizé had a special attraction for Tutu because it was such a powerful example of the need to connect spirituality and social activism. He was convinced that young Christian social activists such as those who went on the pilgrimage needed to discover the spiritual resources necessary both for the struggle and to remain hopeful.

But Tutu knew that it was not he alone, or those younger pilgrims, who needed such empowerment and guidance; so too did the priests and ministers of the church, whether of his own diocese, or all those engaged with him on the ecumenical front. During his tenure as general secretary of the South African Council of Churches he insisted that all members of staff irrespective of rank should attend daily morning prayer. They could not engage in the church struggle against apartheid unless they were daily renewed for the task. Indeed, some visiting public dignitaries and media correspondents who only knew of Tutu as a social critic and political activist were surprised about how much emphasis he placed in his enthronement sermon as archbishop on the need for his clergy to be people of prayer, just as many were later perplexed when he told his clergy not to be members of political parties. In pursuing this agenda, in 1987, soon after he became archbishop, Tutu established the Centre for Christian Spirituality in Cape Town,[9] and then he also invited the Order of the Holy Cross, with its mother house in West Park, New York, to send monks to South Africa,

---

[7] Desmond Tutu, *The Rainbow People of God: The Making of a Peaceful Revolution* (New York, NY: Doubleday, 1994), 121.

[8] See Tutu's review of Rex Brico, *Taizé: Brother Roger and his Community* (London: Collins, 1978) in the *Journal of Theology for Southern Africa*, no. 36, September 1981, 80.

[9] *Silence and Solidarity: Celebrating 30 Years of the Centre for Christian Spirituality*, edited by Laurie Gaum and Sallie Argent (Wellington, RSA: Centre for Christian Spirituality, 2017).

believing that the establishment of a monastery would help foster a deeper spiritual life within the church.

In telling the gospel story of the Transfiguration, in which the glory of God is revealed as Jesus begins his journey to the Cross, the New Testament evangelists tell us that what happened on the mountain top was not understood, even by Jesus' close disciples who witnessed the event. They were so dazzled by what they observed that they did not want to go back down the mountain and continue their journey. Peter even suggested building a sanctuary on the top where they could reside, maybe not forever, but at least until the dangers awaiting them below had passed. But not Jesus – and not Tutu. For him there was no gap between the sanctuary mountain top and the protest march or participating in the tense and often dangerous activities on the ground.

The tempting desire to remain on the mountain top was, of course, the danger facing all of us who were involved in the struggle against apartheid once the changes heralded in 1994 occurred. We all wanted to remain basking in the celebrations of transition where the glory of God was revealed as celebrities from across the globe joined us to witness the Mandela-led miracle. And no one more so than Archbishop Tutu. The victory was won, the rainbow nation had been born, the resurrection had occurred. We were all wrong. We had to go down from the mountain top of transfiguration and face reality once more; the struggle had to continue. And no one was more saddened than Desmond Tutu when it seemed that the "glory had departed". Was the "rainbow nation" simply a figment of pious imagination, as many began to say? Was the revolution once again "devouring its own children" as has happened too often in history. Was the Transfiguration the awakening of false hopes, as the disciples must have thought as they witnessed the Crucifixion? Can the world really change for the good, or must power inevitably corrupt, and corrupt so ruthlessly as time passes and triumphalist greed supplants the commitment to serve? These questions perennially perplex people of faith and hope, as they did and do Archbishop Tutu. Indeed, at the first Steve de Gruchy Memorial Lecture which he gave in March 2012, he boldly asserted: "God is God's worst enemy!" If only God had better public relations people, he would disallow bad news to disturb our peace, and in a moment of divine power would uproot racism and corruption at the flick of a switch, not just give us glimpses of glory along the way. But there is no short-cut in the struggle for justice, reconciliation and peace, because human injustice, division and violence are buried deeply in the human psyche. That is why the struggle must continue in every generation.

Archbishop Tutu's legacy is not just that of an anti-apartheid struggle icon or even an agent of reconciliation; it is that, of course, but a genuine icon is more than a photograph – it portrays its subject with a halo, that is, from the perspective of transfiguration. For that is the Arch's story, for how else do we portray a sickly young boy nurtured in the soil of Africa amid the poverty of an apartheid township, a golf caddy who became not just an archbishop of note but such a remarkably compassionate, joyful human being, and a global symbol of hope for so many? Indeed, his life is a witness to the conviction that the world is not a lost cause, that South Africa can fulfil its promise, that forgiveness of enemies is possible, that love can conquer hatred, and that while weeping may last during the night joy comes in the morning. In sum, a witness to the belief that nothing – not even our scepticism and doubt, our fear and lack of political will – is "untransfigurable".

69. "WITHOUT THE EUCHARIST, I COULD NOT SURVIVE"[1]: ON SACRAMENTS AND SOCIAL ACTION INSPIRED BY ARCHBISHOP DESMOND TUTU

Atle Sommerfeldt[2]

A different foundation for churches' involvement in society

It was an early morning in Grand Hotel in Oslo some years after Desmond Tutu had received the Nobel Peace Prize and had become the leading moral voice against the apartheid regime. He was visiting Norway together with his wife Leah. I was the facilitator for their programme that day. When I called from the reception, Desmond asked me to come to their room. Well into the room he invited me to participate in the morning Eucharist with the two of them. Celebrating Eucharist with three people in a hotel room was very different from my Lutheran tradition. With astonishment I realised that the liturgy was the ordinary liturgy and not an adjusted liturgy with language from the political struggle. Tutu`s foundation for involvement in social actions was revealed, different from the socio-ethical paradigm I was raised in.

I was raised in the theology of resistance developed in the Church of Norway during the Nazi occupation from 1940 to 1945. This tradition was further developed after the war and lead to a statement of the bishops' conference in 1968 on "The Universal Declaration of Human Rights". This statement became a platform for a broad involvement of the church in society and served and serves the church well. It includes spirituality in the form of thematic prayer services and new interpretations of the Scriptures, not least the Hebrew Bible. But it did not include a strong link to a sacramental life.

The support for the churches in South Africa and their participation in the political struggle against the apartheid state was theologically aligned with the resistance of the churches in Norway against the Nazi state and the commitment to the Universal Declaration of Human Rights. Desmond Tutu in his different capacities was seen and supported as an organiser, preacher and campaigner for justice and human rights in society, upholding basic Christian values.

However, that morning Eucharist with the Tutus opened the door for me to a different spirituality, rooting social action in the core worshipping tradition of the church with the sacraments as base and icon. It expressed a holistic spirituality where the encounter with God in the Eucharist and the encounter with people in society were integrated in one life. As the invisible God becomes visible in the elements of bread and wine, the invisible life of the sacred is intimately linked with ordinary life, including the struggle to change injustice and oppression.

Michael Battle has convincingly linked this eucharistic and holistic spirituality to the African reality of *Ubuntu*.[3] *Ubuntu* creates space for the mysteries of the sacraments. *Ubuntu* implies that a person is a person through other persons creating a community in mutual interdependence. This community reflects the community between the persons in the Holy Trinity and makes the communion with Christ in the sacraments part of a universal *Ubuntu* of all people and generations, in heaven and on earth.

---

[1] Desmond Tutu: "My Search for God". St Mary's Jubilee Lenten Talks, St. Alban's, Ferreira town, 5 April 1979. Quote from Michael Battle: *Desmond Tutu: A Spiritual Biography*. Westminster: John Knox Press, 2021, 28.

[2] Atle Sommerfeldt is a Norwegian prelate currently serving as the Bishop of Borg. Prior to becoming a bishop, he was assistant general secretary of the Botswana Christian Council from 1998 to 1993 and secretary general of the Norwegian Church Aid from 1994 to 2012.

[3] Michael Battle: *Desmond Tutu*, 46-50.

It is well known that the Community of the Resurrection in Sophiatown and their leader Trevor Huddleston were key to the formation of Tutu and many others, including his spiritual brother Archbishop Khotso Makhulu. The Community of the Resurrection lives a classical monastic life in the Benedictine tradition with four daily prayers and a daily Mass. While Protestant social actions put less weight on traditional eucharistic life and more on ethical values, the Community of Resurrection stated: "The summit of our worship is the Eucharist offered with the Church on earth and in heaven, for the sake of all creation".[4] This linkage between classical liturgy, spiritual discipline and radical social action in society was the core of the ministry of the Community of the Resurrection from its inception in industrial mining communities in England.

Archbishop Tutu and Archbishop Makhulu brought this spirituality to us in the Church of Norway. They stimulated us to discover the mysteries of the sacraments as a sustainable foundation for the struggle for justice, peace and integrity of creation. The liturgy with the Eucharist as the core became the bridge between the political struggle for transformation of society and the mysteries of the transcendental reality of God.

The prayer book

I'm not sure which Prayer Book Tutu used that morning in the hotel room, but it could have been the prayer book of the Anglican Church in the Province of Southern Africa issued by the Synod of Bishops under his leadership in 1989.[5] The prayer book is deeply rooted in the traditional Anglican Prayerbooks from the 16th and 17th century and aims to "express itself in a language and form which meets the needs of contemporary people" and thus "In its essential features it is true to the long history of our liturgical heritage. In its traits it aims to be true to contemporary language and insights".[6]

In the following I will honour Desmond Tutu by sharing reflections on how the liturgical language in the Order of the Holy Eucharist in the prayer book gives the church and the participant content and direction for life in society.

The source

Is there a link between our life in history and the almighty God?

The foundation of Christian liturgy is the confession by the people to the Triune God as expressed in the Nicene Creed. The creed itself links the invisible "maker of all that is, seen and unseen" with human history in the story of Jesus Christ and the continuous presence in the world through the Holy Spirit in visible events. The confession of the Nicene Creed is the common response to the readings from the Bible and the interpretation of the gospel in the sermon, leading into prayers expressing the needs of the people. The celebration of the Eucharist follows intercessions and is the encounter and mystical unity between the Triune God and the people, creating the fountain of life in the world and in all eternity.

Created

The reality of segregation and unequal distribution of resources between humans was extreme under apartheid as it still is in many societies. The liturgy states:

[4] John Allen: *Rabble-Rouser for Peace: The Authorised Biography of Desmond Tutu*. Random House, 2006, 27.
[5] *An Anglican Prayer Book, Church of the Province of Southern Africa 1989.* Collins Liturgical Productions, London 1989, authorised by the synod of bishops when Tutu was archbishop. This prayer book was also used in the Province of Central Africa where Khotso Makhulu was archbishop at the time.
[6] *Prayer Book*, General Preface, 9-10.

For he is your living Word; through him you have created all things from the beginning and formed us in your own image.[7]

If there is one prime message from Bishop Tutu it must be the proclamation that all humans are given the same dignity and equal rights by God. Confronted with apartheid ideology and regime, that statement was a political statement threatening the legitimacy of the whole apartheid project. Segregation and barriers between people are contrary to the most basic reality of creation.

The equal dignity of all is lived in the eucharistic fellowship. The whole procedure during the celebration bears witness to this equal dignity. Everybody is given the same and equal piece of bread and portion of wine from the same cup. A segregated eucharistic table is a denial of God the Creator. The "table" in society, outside the church, cannot be organised differently.

The creation of all people and persons giving us equal dignity implies that the struggle for dignity and equal human rights for all makes it necessary for the church to include all people in its struggle. The involvement cannot be limited to only members and believers. God is greater than the church, and the mission of the church is greater than caring for the congregation of Christians in a local community.

Incarnation

Is there any place in our existence where we can experience that God identifies with us and is near to us in the middle of existential loneliness? The liturgy offers us such a place: "We give you thanks and praise, almighty God, through your beloved Son Jesus Christ … by the power of the holy Spirit he took flesh of the Virgin Mary and shared our human nature"[8] and is present in bread and wine: "this is my body … this is my blood … do this in remembrance of me".

The Christian proclamation of God putting up a tent among humans, the unthinkable mystery of Incarnation, happens as often as we celebrate the Eucharist. In that mystery lies a deep confirmation of the created world and humanity. When God embraces humanity by being born as a human in a stable, all humans regardless of the situation have been given the icon of true humanity. The words "do this in remembrance of me" communicate the continuous confirmation of God's Incarnation into our world in the physical elements of bread and wine. The experience of the mystery of Incarnation in the Eucharist shows the divine model of embracing humanity and humans. That inspires a commitment to struggle for the realisation of our humanity.

A new community

The experience of divisive and segregated communities needs a model that a different community is possible:

> We ask you to send your Holy Spirit upon the offering of your holy Church. Gather into one all who share in these sacred mysteries[9]… Gracious Lord, accept us in him (Jesus Christ), unworthy though we are, so that we who share in the body and blood of your Son may be one with all your people of this and every age.[10]

The eucharistic encounter with God in Jesus Christ creates a new community beyond the barriers raised by ethnicity, social class, gender, sexual orientation and generations. The creation by God of a new community in the Eucharist makes it a necessity to struggle for the unity of people gathered in the Eucharist also outside the liturgy, in everyday life and in local and national communities. The

---

[7] The numbering is first the number in the Liturgy of the Holy Eucharist, then the page number P 61/120.

[8] *Prayer Book*, 74/125.

[9] *Prayer Book*, 76/126.

[10] *Prayer Book*, 58/119.

eucharistic community must be seen in the world. Any barriers raised in the society by the state or other actors preventing the building of this community, must be challenged and broken because they prevent the fulfilment of the unity of all people.

Social action

The sacramental experience in the church and the experience of a different community there – does it mean anything for our lives outside the sanctuary?

"Help us to persevere as living members of that holy fellowship, and to grow in love and obedience according to your will",[11] therefore this eucharistic fellowship prays:

> Give wisdom to those in authority, direct this and every nation in the way of justice and peace, that all may honour another and seek the common good … We pray for the use in trouble, sorrow, need, sickness or any other adversity – to all who suffer give courage, healing and a steadfast trust in your love …[12]

Integrated in the mystery of the Eucharist is the liturgy after the liturgy, outside the church, social actions to transform the incredible mercy, grace and compassion of Christ into creating the mystical union with him in the sharing of his body and blood to a lived reality. The prayers in the liturgy send the fellowship out in God's reality to be light and salt in society. The monastic principle from the ancient church, marked by the dialectic relationship between "Prayer and Labour" – "Ora et Labora" – lived by the Community of the Resurrection in Sophiatown, is an icon of that link.

Unity in political diversity

Can I have anything in common with my political opponents?

> "Inspire us with love, your love, and unite us in the body of your Son, Jesus Christ our Lord."[13]

The unity in the new community is a diverse community. The community is inclusive with different opinions about how justice and peace should be achieved. The unity is not rooted in common opinions or interests as in many other movements in civil society and in politics. This unity is different, based on the unity with God in Christ, not on political opinions. In times of intense discussions and struggles in society, it may be hard to keep that awareness, but unity in diversity is the essential nature of the church and gives witness to another reality outside human control.

Ecological wholeness

In grief over the lost future because of climate injustice and destruction of forests and biodiversity, the need for a sustainable connectedness between humanity and the whole of creation is pressing:

> Yours, Lord, is the greatness, the power, the glory, the splendour, and the majesty; for everything in heaven and on earth is yours. All things come from you.[14] Through your goodness we have this bread to offer, which earth has given, and human hands have made … this wine, fruit of the wine and work of human hands.[15]

The sacramental mystery is tied with nature. The water of baptism links us to all living, bread and wine link us to the fruits of nature. God chooses to meet humanity in the gifts of creation. The

---

[11] *Prayer Book*, 87/129.
[12] *Prayer Book*, 32/110+34/11.
[13] *Prayer Book*, 66/121.
[14] *Prayer Book*, 48/116.
[15] *Prayer Book*, 50.

Eucharist opens up therefore to understand the human family as part of the greater creation, even depending on the gifts of nature in the unique union between humans and the Creator in the sacraments. Destruction of the ecological space, the *oikumene* of the whole of creation, is therefore a destruction of the gifts of God.

Liberation from slavery

Too many people carry the burden of the slavery their ancestors were locked into, and too many people still live in modern forms of slavery. Is there hope?

"Through him (Jesus Christ) you freed us from the slavery of sin."[16]

The eucharistic unity with the body of Christ is a liberating reality. When liberation from slavery is part of the eucharistic liturgy it transforms an exclusive interpretation of Exodus – to a universal exodus for all people from the domain of oppression and slavery. God hears and sees the suffering of all creation and all humankind. In the South African context liberation from slavery was intrinsically linked to the apartheid ideology and its use of the Exodus event as their liberation story. It was therefore of enormous significance when the struggling church under apartheid proclaimed the Exodus event as a universal event for all people living in slavery, reflecting the liberation in the Eucharist.

Confession and repentance

The knowledge of one's own contribution to evil may lead to apathy, cynicism or indifference. There is a need for a space for confession: "Almighty God, to whom all hearts are open, all desires known, and from whom no secrets are hid: cleanse the thoughts of our hearts by the inspiration of your Holy Spirit",[17] leading to the confession of sins: "Almighty God, in penitence we confess that we have sinned against you through our own fault in thought, word and deed and in what we have left undone."[18]

The liturgy enables persons, movements and communities involved in society to avoid the hubris of infallibility. The human capacity for greatness is immense, but so is the capacity of involvement in destructive actions against others. History is full of movements and persons claiming that everybody else is the root cause of all that is wrong, and forgetting their own ability to do harm to other people. Positions of power, be it in a patriarchal family, in business, in church, in civil society or in politics, still give a multitude of possibilities to the misuse of power to the benefit of oneself at the expense of others, including not using the possibilities of power for change.

Being created by God gives everybody greatness. Intrinsic in that greatness is the ability and responsibility to contribute to the struggle against death and destruction as it unfolds in every society and context. The liturgical formula helps us to set language even on what we might not be able to confess on our own. The formula offers us words we may enter, including also the silent sinner.

Forgiveness

Carrying the burden of our shortcomings may lead to shame and paralyse the ability to act in love. Forgiveness is needed!

---

[16] *Prayer Book*, 61/120.
[17] *Prayer Book*, 7/105.
[18] *Prayer Book*, 13/106.

For the sake of your Son, Christ our Lord, forgive us all that is past … Almighty God who forgives all who truly repent, have mercy on you; pardon your sins and set you free from them; confirm and strengthen you in all goodness and keep you in eternal life.[19]

The great reality of the Christian gospel is the unlimited access of all kinds of people to be recipients of the love of God in the forgiveness of all kinds of sins as confessed. The gap between the reality of the kingdom of God with the community of perfect and continuous love, and on the other hand the reality of human society, was and is too large to be bridged by good intentions and efforts by people. God had to act to create a possibility for forgiveness. It was not cheap for God. Jesus Christ had to carry all the wounds of victims of sins and all the sinners on his own body and accompany the suffering even into death.

The word of forgiveness makes the confession and penitence a liberating event. Forgiveness frees each and everyone and the community to live out the experience of the love of God in the community and in the encounter with others. The process of confession, penitence and forgiveness breaks the cycle of revenge and retaliation. Nobody can force anyone to forgive as nobody can force God to forgive. Forgiveness opens the possibility for another future between humans, where the circle of revenge is buried.

The joy of celebrations in heaven and earth

Is there a future with hope which is accessible here and now?

He (Jesus Christ) chose to bear our griefs and sorrows, and to give life on the cross, that he might shatter the chains of the evil one and banish the darkness of sin and death. By his resurrection he brings us into the light of your presence.[20] … Grant that we await the coming of Christ our Saviour in the glory and triumph of his kingdom … It is indeed right, it is our duty and our joy, at all times and in all places, to give you thanks and praise … by the power of the Holy Spirit, all glory and honour be given to you, almighty father, by the whole company of earth and heaven, throughout all ages, now and forever.[21]

The future is coming to us with images of heaven and manifest itself in glimpses here and now. The victim will come and is already coming to us as a victor. The eucharistic mystery forms the foretaste of the reality of the kingdom of heaven and gives space to joy and songs of praise. An eucharistic community which lives the eucharistic liturgy is constantly reminded of the greatness of our Lord and the reality of the love of God for us and in us and with us. Overwhelmed by fear and suffering, the broken body of Jesus Christ handed to humans in love and grace becomes the fountain of life in society. Desmond Tutu's ability to communicate that joy with humour and laughter is one of the many gifts he has given to us.

Conclusion

The liturgy of the Holy Eucharist is a fountain of life in society, enabling the eucharistic community to uphold a sustained struggle for justice, peace and integrity of all people and the whole creation. The visible expression of the love of God in the eucharistic act and the possibility it offers to drink from this fountain without conditions and regardless of human prejudices, gives content and direction for our involvement in society.

---

[19] *Prayer Book*, 14/106.
[20] *Prayer Book*, 74/125.
[21] *Prayer Book*, 58/119.

70. "WHAT WE WILL BE HAS NOT YET BEEN REVEALED": EXPLORING THE VALUE OF THEOLOGICAL PLURALITY FOR CHRISTIAN UNITY

Christine Lienemann-Perrin[1]

1 See what love the Father has given us, that we should be called children of God; and that is what we are. The reason the world does not know us is that it did not know him. 2 Beloved, we are God's children now; what we will be has not yet been revealed. What we do know is this: when he is revealed, we will be like him, for we will see him as he is. 3 And all who have this hope in him purify themselves, just as he is pure. (1 John 3:1-3, NRSV)

1. The biblical text

There is little certainty about the authorship, addressees and circumstances of the origins of the Johannine text quoted above. It probably goes back to an author from the Johannine school related to the Gospel of John. The letter is likely addressed to communities in Asia Minor or Syria around 100 AD. They live as Christian minorities in the midst of a religiously mixed population and go their own way in questions of faith and behaviour. The world meets them with incomprehension, perhaps even rejection. But more threatening than the world around them are the divisions by which the believers in Christ are torn apart and which cause deep insecurities in the communities. There are those who cannot see the Messiah in Jesus and deny that God became man in Jesus. Furthermore, there are those who agree with the addressees in the apostle's teaching, but do not act accordingly. The rift through the church has led to a good part of it leaving: "They went out from us, but they did not belong to us; for if they had belonged to us they would have remained with us. But by going out they made it plain that none of them belongs to us." (1 John 2:19). The uncertainty among the church members is great: which doctrine should they follow? Have those who have left done right? What is the point of continuing as a small remnant and holding on to the previous way of believing?

Into these uncertainties and self-doubts, the author addresses the congregations and gives them criteria so that they can distinguish in teaching and behaviour between what is true and good and what is untrue and sinful. The admonition not to let oneself be guided by hatred of those "others" and by feelings of revenge towards those who have turned away runs through his letter: "Those who say, 'I love God,' and hate their brothers or sisters, are liars; for those who do not love a brother or sister whom they have seen, cannot love God whom they have not seen." (1 John 4:20).

The first three verses of Chapter 3 are first of all a statement, and it records how the Christians of the first and second generation can understand themselves. Behind them lies the transition from ignorance to knowledge and from unbelief to faith. The present is blessed by the confidence that they are children of God: "See what love the Father has given us, that we should be called children of God; and that is what we are." At the same time, they are in hope of a future way of being that is still hidden from them: "what we will be has not yet been revealed." The congregation lives in the expectation that the new way of being will soon dawn at the end of time. Although the future is hidden from the congregations, there is nevertheless something that they know now and that shapes

[1] Christine Lienemann-Perrin is prof. em. of missiology and ecumenical studies at the Faculty of Theology, University of Basel. Born in Switzerland, 1946, she studied theology in Bern, Montpellier (F) and Heidelberg (G). From 1977 to 1985 she was an academic staff member of the Protestant Institute for Interdisciplinary Research, Heidelberg. Research work and lectures brought her to Kinhasa, Congo, South Africa, South Korea, Brazil, Japan and USA. Her publications are focused on mission and inter-religious dialogue, feminist missiology, ecumenical political ethics, religious conversion in diverse contexts and world Christianity. For her publications see http://lienemann-perrin.ch/lienemann_christine.html.

their presence: "What we do know is this: when he is revealed, we will be like him, for we will see him as he is." The final section of the text deals with the remaining period of existence as a church in the world in the face of the dawning kingdom: "And all who have this hope in him purify themselves, just as he is pure." The verb *hagnō heautón* (to sanctify oneself) is in harmony with later statements of the Epistle, which speak of doing the faith. Just a few verses later it reads: "Everyone who does what is right is righteous, just as he is righteous." (1 John 3:7); and in the last chapter of the letter it is stated: "By this we know that we love the children of God, when we love God and obey his commandments. For the love of God is this, that we obey his commandments." (1 John 5:2f). Conclusions are drawn for the existence of God's children in this world: *hagnō heautón* signifies making faith and action coherent.

It is striking that there is a close connection between identity and recognition: "we should be called children of God; and that is what we are." This self-understanding is possible once Jesus is recognised as the Son of God. Those who know are distinguished from the "world" which does not recognise Christ and therefore also fails to recognise the identity of the church.

The break between the Now and the Then places the identity of the children of God under the condition of life in earthly time, i.e. the status of being God's children is and remains imperfect in relation to what is to come, just as cognition will always remain imperfect in view of cognition in the hereafter. We live by faith, not by sight (2 Cor. 5:7). Without the immediate sight of God, there is no likeness or similarity to Him. Here, too, knowledge and being are closely related. Paul expresses this thought with a metaphor: "For now we see in a mirror, dimly, but then we will see face to face. Now I know only in part; then I will know fully, even as I have been fully known" (1 Cor. 13:12). Being aware of this condition and in the hope of this promise, people in the present time may attain new knowledge of faith and orient their lives accordingly.

2. What will I be? A teenage memory

In what situations does this biblical text meet us today? When I heard it for the first time, I was fifteen years old. My father, whose confirmation classes I had attended, chose 1 John 3:1-3 as my confirmation verse. "What we will be has not yet been revealed": these words sounded to my ears at the time like a reserve (Latin: *reservatio*; German: *Vorbehalt*) vis-à-vis everything I had heard in confirmation classes and discussed in numerous conversations with my father. Until then, I had regarded what my father had taught me about faith as his assured knowledge. Now, with his choice of the confirmation verse, he emphasised the not-knowing, which at the same time enables openness to new insights that put a caveat on my previous knowledge. I was happily surprised by these enigmatic words, because I recognised that they opened up the space for new insights and other forms of faith on the path of life ahead of me. At the same time, I also felt the risks that always accompany freedom to new insights.

Five years later, I started my studies of theology, in which the caveat echoed in 1 John 3:2 was foremost in my mind. Increasingly, however, I now related this passage to theology and Christianity in different contexts of the world. How is theology expressed outside Europe? How is it practised there? A research project that followed my postgraduate training gave me the opportunity to explore this question in depth.[2]

---

[2] Christine Lienemann-Perrin, *Training for a Relevant Ministry: A Study of the Work of the Theological Education Fund* (Madras: CLS, 1981).

3. Fifty years ago: what will become of Christianity and theology?
Meeting Desmond Tutu in Bromley

In 1973 I stayed in Bromley, a suburb of London, with the purpose to do archival studies at the headquarters of the Theological Education Fund (TEF).[3] It was fortuitous for me that my various study visits to Bromley occurred at the very time when Desmond Tutu was associate director of the TEF (1972–1975). For him, the early 1970s were a time of theological reorientation based on insights gained during his extensive travels through virtually all the countries of sub-Saharan Africa.[4] He gave several unforgettable accounts of his travels at Bromley. I could not have found a better place to broaden my horizon than the spacious old house in which the TEF was accommodated at the time. It was not only the archival materials that opened up new horizons for me. The TEF's staff, which embodied global perspectives on theological teaching and thinking, made sure of that. In addition to Desmond Tutu, the staff included four other people: Shoki Coe (Taiwan), Ivy Chou (Malaysia), Aharon Sapsezian (Brazil) and Herbert Zorn (USA). They all travelled various times a year for weeks or months in the continents assigned to them, in order to sound out in theological colleges, seminaries and faculties what the burning issues were – politically, economically, culturally, as well as theologically. In the early 1970s, the TEF provided the decisive impulse for the development of theology "in context". Its funding programmes can be described as the birth of contextual theology, which has since spread worldwide.[5] Selected theological training institutions were supported by it to the effect that theological thinking was carried out in awareness of and critical engagement with the socio-political challenges on the ground. I see this as an intermediate step on the way to what sometimes is called today "decolonising" theological education and theology. I experienced the house in Bromley with its stimulating atmosphere, but especially the meetings with the TEF team, as a place where developments in world Christianity became visible as a focal point. The conversations were filled with poignant accounts of life in the aftermath of the colonial era, in military dictatorships, poverty – and Christians asking about the tasks of theology under these conditions.

On the one hand, the contextualisation of theology has experimented with new possibilities of "doing theology". However, this has also been associated with risky developments that have brought new challenges. Multiple theological models resulted in a lack of common orientation. Occasionally, a growing indifference could be observed related to the mood that everyone is already satisfied with his or her own peculiar theology. Critical questions were raised: have the many contextual theologies not diverged too much, so that they have become more like strangers to each other? Can the new contextual theologies still question each other critically and struggle for common knowledge? Can all these theological concepts be translated from one context to another? "[A]re there any theological frameworks that can facilitate the many tongues and languages into a cohesive yet faithful proclamation of the wondrous words of God for the globalizing world of the twenty-first century?"[6]

---

[3] Founded at the World Missionary Conference in Ghana in 1958, the TEF contributed significantly to the improvement of theological education in the Global South through its three mandates until 1977, while promoting the overcoming of a purely Western concept of theology. With the support of the TEF, over 20 associations of 1200 theological education centres were founded in Asia, Africa and Latin America. These developments strengthened ecumenical cooperation and at the same time the autonomy of theological education in the Global South.

[4] John Allen, *Rabble-Rouser for Peace: The Authorised Biography of Desmond Tutu* (London et al: Random House 2006), 123-139.

[5] Contextualisation of theology was understood by the TEF as follows: "It [contextualisation] means all that is implied in the familiar term 'indigenization' and yet seeks to press beyond. Contextualization has to do with how we assess the peculiarity of third world contexts. Indigenization tends to be used in the sense of responding to the Gospel in terms of traditional culture. Contextualization, while not ignoring this, takes into account the process of secularity, technology, and the struggle for human justice, which characterize the historical moment of nations in the Third World." TEF Staff, *Ministry in Context: The Third Mandate Programme of the Theological Education Fund (1970–1977)* (Bromley: TEF, October 1972), 20.

[6] Amos Yong, *Renewing Christian Theology: Systematics for a Global Christianity* (with artistic images and commentary by Jonathan A.) (Waco, Texas: Baylor University Press, 2014), 11.

It is not clear what the appropriate path would be in dealing with theological plurality and current developments in global Christianity. As children of God, we see dimly and know only in part indeed, but at the same time our hope in the Son of God inspires us to live and act in faith. In an interview, Desmond Tutu once said: "We will never reach the point where any of us could say, 'Now I understand God completely!'" But he went on to say that he himself would one day like to have the assurance "of having done everything to make the world a better place for all God's children."[7] Tutu's tireless commitment to the oppressed, the despised and the outcast has never been accompanied by hatred for those who have pursued contrary goals; for, according to his confidence in God's reconciliation with humankind, God is also for them. In the midst of contradictory problems, liberation, justice and reconciliation have always been the guidelines of his thoughts and actions.

4. Switzerland, 2021

Edward W. Said (1935–2003), a Palestinian literary critic with Christian roots, suffered throughout his life from the fact that his ethnic and cultural background did not fit into the society in which he lived.[8] First, he and his family were expelled from Jerusalem. In Egypt, the family found refuge and built a new existence until they became unwanted there as well. Another stop was Lebanon, but the civil war again made emigration necessary. Finally, the family found a place to stay in the USA. But even there Said always remained a stranger. In his biography, he hints that under the constant compulsion to reorient and adapt, his Christian identity also suffered greatly. Said expresses what many migrants and asylum seekers experience. Some of them have left their country of origin where they lived "out of place" religiously, culturally, economically or politically. In the region where 2,000 years ago communities like those addressed in the 1st Letter of John lived, today only tiny remnant communities can be found. Perhaps even more than by the hostile environment, they are unsettled or irritated by fellow believers who have moved to Europe in the hope of living their faith unchallenged and safely in "Christian lands".

But in Switzerland Christian migrants often end up in another situation of dispersion – this time in the midst of secularised societies. This again confronts migrants with a problem of identity, which is already evident when they have to give information about their identity to an authority as asylum seekers. A Syrian Christian from Tur Abdin in Eastern Anatolia once told that he was taught in his home country that he and his family were Christians. But that was not the answer to the question put to him by the Swiss authorities. When they inquired further, he said he was a Syrian Orthodox. But that was not the expected answer either. He had to look for new answers to the question of his identity. Asylum seekers are required to provide information about their language, culture, nationality, ethnic roots, and above all their identity papers.

Wherever they live, wherever they move, they seem always to be in the wrong place – a place where they don't really want to live.[9] And yet, it is precisely those people who live in wrong places or have no place where they can live in dignity that the words "We are children of God" can strengthen their self-confidence. This is testified in their worships and prayers: from their knowledge of being children of God there emanates an identity-forming power. Of course, many questions remain unanswered: should they separate themselves from the society of the host country and preserve the identity they have brought with them? Or has the time come for integration? How far can they get closer towards the established churches without betraying their own church tradition? Should the children be given freedom to other forms of worship and even to turn away from religious life?

---

[7] Interview by Björn Eenboom with Desmond Tutu, 27 July 2015, https://www.cicero.de/desmond-tutu (7.4.2021).
[8] Edward W. Said, *Out of Place: A Memoir* (New York: Knopf, 1999).
[9] Katutura – "place where we don't want to live" – is how the Herero called the township near Windhoek (Namibia) that was built for blacks in the 1950s.

"What we will be has not yet been revealed." This also applies to the future of faith in the established churches in Switzerland. Do they aim at an identity in isolation or at a shared identity together with migration churches and in dialogue with people of other faiths? Because what we will be has not yet appeared, the established forms of being the church must not be indisputable. And just as new challenges call for new forms, new insights and practices also create new identities. This involves an openness that does not lead to arbitrariness; for it is through hope that renewal remains oriented towards that great future in which there will be an immediate and full knowing of God.

What makes people of foreign origin feel they are in the wrong place in Switzerland? They feel the hostility of those Swiss people who want to protect their identity against the influences of foreign elements – whether these are people, languages, cultures or religions. In fact, those who think this way have an identity problem without realising it. This is also what happens to established parishes and churches when they want to be a church for themselves alone. This is, of course, self-deception. Could it not be just the other way around? "Being in the wrong place" probably characterises a church which thinks that it can preserve its ecclesial identity in self-selected isolation from other churches and without open, respectful encounters with people of other religions and cultures. I hope that we will succeed in transforming Switzerland into a country that is the right place for all those who live in it; for in such an inclusive vision our hope as children of God becomes visible, a hope that owes its existence to God's coming into the world.

71. SPIRITUAL FRAGRANCES, SOCIAL HORIZONS: A MUSLIM TRIBUTE TO ARCHBISHOP DESMOND TUTU

Sa'diyya Shaikh[1]

There are many doors to the Divine Presence.

Each has its own unique architecture, qualities, and aesthetics – particular slants and textures here, variable shapes and solidity there, shifting timbres and tones, distinctive cadences and scents … drawing some of us to one path, and beckoning others to another.

Sometimes these doors are religions and spiritual paths, and sometimes they are human beings …

Every now and then, a rare soul provides a portal of such magnificent beauty and spiritual fragrance that the neighbours look out of their windows and marvel, and might even dance ecstatically at such loveliness. Some might sing in admiration and awe, "*Al-hamdu lilah, dhul jalali wal ikram,* All Praise is due to God, the Possessor of Sublime Majesty and Breathtaking Generosity."

I am such a Muslim neighbour, or perhaps a kindred traveller wandering through the shared gardens and valleys of our world. When the terrain is particularly bleak and treacherous, turning my existential gaze to such resplendent souls is a source of renewal and hope. Archbishop Desmond Tutu has been one such glimmering beacon, embodying the best of religion, showing how people of spiritual fortitude are able to transform the world. Keenly observing Desmond Tutu for many decades, I recognise a living, loving "Arch-way", exemplifying some of the most capacious ways to be human. I celebrate him as a universal teacher, a holy friend and a discerning guide, who, drinking from the sacred centre, quenches the thirst of others, serving humanity as we yearn and work for a world of love, justice and dignity of all living beings.

I lovingly offer this Muslim prayer of thanksgiving for him on his 90th birthday.

Bismillah Al- Rahman Al-Rahim

In the name of God, the All-Compassionate, Most Gracious
"God is the light of the heavens and the earth" (Quran 24:35)
"Our Sustainer, perfect our Light for us …" (Quran 66:8)

Ya Nur,[2] Oh Luminous One, *Ya Latif,* Oh Subtle One

Thank you, Compassionate God, for Archbishop Tutu, whose life journey illuminates the powerful contours of human struggle, courage, resilience and enduring hope.

Thank you for one who is a shimmering testimony that divine love can only be fully manifest when it embraces justice.

Thank you for blessing us with one who is a fountain of radiant wisdom, playful joy and delicious laughter.

Thank you for a role model that integrates the delicate inner life with engaged outer action so that we might be born anew in each moment through the Breath of the Merciful.

Thank you for one whose strong dedicated spirit, through active surrender to your Divine light and guidance, becomes a conduit of Your grace and generosity in the world.

*   *   *

"Put your trust in God, and God is enough as your Trustee" (Quran 33:3)

---

[1] Sa'diyya is associate professor in the Department for the Study of Religions at the University of Cape Town.
[2] There are ninety-nine different attributes/names/qualities of God in the Islamic tradition, and the author has selected a few of these to focus her prayer.

"God is intimately close and ever-responsive" (Quran 11:61)

Ya Wakil, Oh Trustee, *Ya Wadud*, Oh All-Loving

Thank you for gifting us with this embodiment of Your loving guardianship, and Your trustworthy refuge.

Thank you for a guide whose melting heart and intimate worship, whose prayer and retreat, nourish a deep love and service of the lives of others.

Thank you for one who extends Your gaze of protection and care to the oppressed, marginalised and desolate, who embraces those on the margins and peripheries of our communities and our worlds.

Thank you for his brave heart, that does not cower from speaking uncomfortable truths to power, all the while never losing sight of the full humanity of "the other".

Thank you for a model of leadership who receives the Divine trust as a sacred responsibility to treat each life as one's own.

Ameen Ya Rabb Al-Alameen

Amin, Oh Sustainer of all the worlds.

*　　*　　*

Happy Birthday, beloved Arch, and thank you.

May Divine grace and blessings shower unceasingly on you.

May your heart be pleased and well-pleasing in each moment of Returning.

May you remain amongst the intimate friends of The Friend.